SOURCES OF THE CHRISTIAN SELF

Sources of the Christian Self

A Cultural History of Christian Identity

Edited by

James M. Houston *&* Jens Zimmermann

WILLIAM B. EERDMANS PUBLISHING COMPANY
GRAND RAPIDS, MICHIGAN

Wm. B. Eerdmans Publishing Co.
2140 Oak Industrial Drive N.E., Grand Rapids, Michigan 49505
www.eerdmans.com

Published 2018
Printed in the United States of America

27 26 25 24 23 22 21 20 19 18   1 2 3 4 5 6 7 8 9 10

ISBN 978-0-8028-7627-0

Library of Congress Cataloging-in-Publication Data

Names: Houston, J. M. (James Macintosh), 1922– editor.
Title: Sources of the Christian self : a cultural history of Christian identity /
    edited by James M. Houston & Jens Zimmermann.
Description: Grand Rapids : Eerdmans Publishing Co., 2018. |
    Includes bibliographical references and index.
Identifiers: LCCN 2017056971 | ISBN 9780802876270 (hardcover : alk. paper)
Subjects: LCSH: Identity (Psychology)—Religious aspects—Christianity.
Classification: LCC BV4509.5 .S68 2018 | DDC 270.092/2 [B]—dc23
    LC record available at https://lccn.loc.gov/2017056971

Contents

Abbreviations

Acta	*Acta Canonizationis S. Dominici.* Edited by Angelus Walz. Monumenta Ordinis Fratrum Praedicatorum Historica 16, 89–194. Rome, 1935
AFP	*Archivum Fratrum Praedicatorum*
ANET	*Ancient Near Eastern Texts Relating to the Old Testament.* Edited by James B. Pritchard. 3rd ed. Princeton: Princeton University Press, 1969
BCP	Book of Common Prayer
Beat	Gregory of Nyssa. *De beatitudinibus.* In *Gregorii Nysseni Opera.* Edited by Johannes F. Callahan, Vol. 7/2: 75–170. Leiden: Brill, 1992
BEATAJ	Beiträge zur Erforschung des Alten Testaments und des Antiken Judentum
BECNT	Baker Exegetical Commentary on the New Testament
BETL	Bibliotheca ephemeridum theologicarum lovaniensium
CANE	*Civilizations of the Ancient Near East.* Edited by Jack M. Sasson. 4 vols. New York, 1995. Repr. in 2 vols. Peabody, MA: Hendrickson, 2006
CBC	Cambridge Bible Commentary
CBQ	*Catholic Biblical Quarterly*
CD	Karl Barth. *Church Dogmatics.* Edited by G. W. Bromiley and T. F. Torrance. 2nd ed. Translated by G. W. Bromiley. Edinburgh: T & T Clark, 1956–1975
CIL	*Corpus inscriptionum latinarum*
CP	*Classical Philology*
CSEL	Corpus scriptorum ecclesiasticorum latinorum

DBW	*Dietrich Bonhoeffer Werke.* Edited by Eberhard Bethge et al. 17 vols. Munich and Gütersloh: Chr. Kaiser-Gütersloher Verlagshaus, 1986–1999
DBWE	*Dietrich Bonhoeffer Works.* Edited by Wayne Whitson Floyd. Minneapolis: Fortress, 1996–2015
ESV	English Standard Version
FC	Fathers of the Church
GNB	Good News Bible
HALOT	Ludwig Koehler, Walter Baumgartner, and Johann J. Stamm. *The Hebrew and Aramaic Lexicon of the Old Testament.* Translated and edited under the supervision of Mervyn E. J. Richardson. 4 vols. Leiden, Brill: 1994–1999
JSOTSup	Journal for the Study of the Old Testament: Supplement Series
KD	Karl Barth. *Die Kirkliche Dogmatik.* Zurich: TVZ Verlag, 1932–1967
KJV	King James Version
LHBOTS	The Library of Hebrew Bible/Old Testament Studies
Life	Teresa of Avila. *The Book of Her Life.* In *The Collected Works of St. Teresa of Avila*, edited by Kieran Kavanaugh. Washington, DC: ICS Publications, 1976
LW	*Luther's Works.* American ed. (Libronix Digital Library). 55 vols. Edited by Jaroslav Pelikan and Helmut T. Lehman. Minneapolis: Fortress, 2002
LXX	Septuagint
MOPH	Monumenta Ordinis Fratrum Praedicatorum Historica
NCBC	New Century Bible Commentary
NIDOTTE	*New International Dictionary of Old Testament Theology and Exegesis.* Edited by Willem A. VanGemeren. 5 vols. Grand Rapids: Zondervan, 1997
NIGTC	New International Greek Testament Commentary
NIV	New International Version
NIVAC	The NIV Application Commentary
NLT	New Living Translation
NTL	New Testament Library
NPNF[1]	*A Select Library of the Nicene and Post-Nicene Fathers of the Christian Church.* First Series. Edited by Philip Schaff. 14 vols. Edinburgh, 1886–1880
OTL	Old Testament Library
PC	Primitive Constitutions. In *Constitutiones antiquae ordinis*

	Fratrum Praedicatorum. Edited by A. H. Thomas. In *De oudste Constituties van der Dominicanen: Voorgescheidensis, Tekst, Bronnen, Onstaan en Ontwikkeling, 1215–1237,* 304–69. Leuven, 1965
PG	Patrologia graeca [= *Patrologiae cursus completus*: Series graeca]. Edited by Jacques-Paul Migne. 162 vols. Paris, 1857–1886
PL	Patrologia Latina [= *Patrologiae cursus completus*: Series Latina]. Edited by Jacques-Paul Migne. 217 vols. Paris, 1844–1864
SS	Bernard of Clairvaux. *On the Song of Songs.* 4 vols. Kalamazoo: Cistercian Publications, 1971–1980.
ST	St. Thomas Aquinas. *Summa Theologiae.* Latin Text and English Translation, Introduction, Notes, Appendices, and Glossaries. Cambridge, UK: Blackfriars, 1964–1975.
StA	*Martin Luther Studienausgabe.* 6 vols. Edited by Hans Ulrich Delius. Berlin: Evangelische Verlangsanstalt, 1979–c. 1999
TWOT	*Theological Wordbook of the Old Testament.* Edited by R. Laird Harris, Gleason L. Archer Jr., and Bruce Waltke. 2 vols. Chicago: Moody Press, 1980
WA	Weimarer Ausgabe (The Weimar edition of Luther's works) *D. Martin Luthers Werke, Kritische Gesamtausgabe, Schriften.* 73 vols. Weimar: Böhlau, 1883–
WBC	Word Biblical Commentary
WUNT	Wissenschaftliche Untersuchungen zum Neuen Testament
ZAW	Zeitschrift für die alttestamentliche Wissenschaft

Editors' Introduction

What does it mean to identify oneself as a Christian? According to the biblical record, it was in Antioch that followers of the growing Christian movement were first called "Christians" or Christ-people (Acts 11:26).[1] These were a people wholly identified with Jesus the Christ, and the appellation "Christian" probably coincided with using the title *Christos* (Messiah/anointed one) as a proper name for Jesus. Contemporary scholarship is still trying to determine Jesus's identity but often misses the crucial link between the understanding of who Jesus is and a lifelong process of identification with him through discipleship by the early Christians on whose testimony scholarship relies. Christians had, of course, many other names for themselves—disciples, called-out ones, apostles, believers, saints, brothers, people of the way, and so on—but it seems that outsiders in Antioch recognized how radically these people were to be identified simply and wholly with Jesus Christ, wherefore they coined the nickname *Christianos*.

The name stuck. If anything, the identification with the name of Christ became something more simple and radical under the threat of persecution, the very force that had first dispersed the disciples and sent them in the direction of Antioch. In a letter to the Christian diaspora suffering a "fiery ordeal" and living under hostile social conditions, the apostle Peter calls believers to a more radical identification with Christ's own martyrdom, and here again the label "Christian" appears: "If you suffer as a Christian, do not be ashamed, but praise God that you bear that name" (1 Pet 4:16). One further use of the term "Christian" in the New Testament, besides those we have considered in Acts 11:26 and 1 Peter 4:16, comes from the mouth of King Agrippa in response to Paul's testimony before him in Acts 26:28. Agrippa asks Paul, no doubt with

---

1. *chrēmatisai te prōtōs en Antiocheia tous mathētas Christianous.*

some irony, "Are you so quickly persuading me to become a Christian?" The term is used again by an outsider, and the context is again charged with the intensity of trial and persecution, where an entire identification with the person of Jesus Christ is a matter of one's life and one's death.

When the infant church in Bithynia was under persecution, the believers radically challenged the cult of Caesarism. In order to garner the attention of governor Pliny and the emperor Trajan, Christians insisted publically, as Luke emphasizes, that Jesus Christ is "Lord of all." Their correspondence demonstrates again how the question of identity at the most basic level had to do with simple confession of the name: I am a Christian. The role of the martyrs had opened. In martyrdom we see the entire union of word and deed, for one's identification with Christ is inscribed bodily in the holocaust offering of the martyr. This is the theology of martyrdom expressed most clearly and passionately in Ignatius of Antioch's letter to the Romans. Thus Christian identity begins at its most basic level with a simple and entire identification of the whole of one's life with Christ. Moreover, as Ignatius's letter makes clear, identification with Christ entailed more than an inner or moral transformation but extended to one's human identity as a whole. Ignatius finishes his letter by pleading with this congregation not to hinder his martyrdom because by following Christ into death, he would become "a human being." Ignatius wants to be "an imitator of the passion of God," for in this way he will *begin* to be a disciple. "Allow me to receive the pure light," he writes, "for then I will be truly human."[2] This remarkable phrase indicates that from early on, Christian identity was both a deeply personal and also a universal or global matter, because sharing in Christ's identity also meant sharing in the future promise of god-likeness to which he had restored humanity through his life, death, and resurrection.

From this time forward it would be by the name "Christian" that the followers of Jesus would be identified. But what did this term denote for believers down through the centuries? What did it mean to identify oneself as a Christian in different times and places? This is the question posed by this book. The basic calling of a Christian is to identify with "the name" wholly and simply, in a way that one's confession of Christ becomes the most essential fact of one's life. But this calling upon every generation of believers takes place under cultural conditions and, indeed, under *changing* cultural conditions, wherefore it should be possible to write a history of Christian self-identity from the early church to the present. This book is a beginning and a modest contribution to the construction

2. The Greek simply has "when I arrive there, I will be a human being." See *Ignatius of Antioch: The Letters*, Popular Patristics Series (Yonkers, NY: St. Vladimir's Seminary Press, 2013), 70–71.

of such a cultural and social history, exploring what it has meant for women and men to identify with Christ in very different contexts—under the state persecution of Diocletian, under the Constantinian privileges of the Nicene era, on the oriental borders of the Byzantine Empire, during the collapse of Romanitas in the late antique period, and so on, through the various episodes in the history of culture, East and West, during which the Holy Spirit has been at work gathering a people who confess that Christ is Lord under their unique conditions, each one saying, "I am *Christianos.*"

Perhaps even more than any other kind of historical work, biographical narratives of identity require hermeneutic awareness, and the following essays were written with a fairly clear (if not exactly detailed) theoretical framework in mind. The title of this essay collection, *Sources of the Christian Self*, alludes to the now classic study of Charles Taylor, *Sources of the Self: The Making of the Modern Identity* (Cambridge, 1989). Taylor's work has shown the importance of identity for shaping the horizons of meaning in our modern age; he has also indicated the significance of religion for modern ideals of selfhood. Our volume is both an adoption and adaptation of his path-breaking work. We adopt Taylor's historicizing and narrative example by setting the discussion of Christian identity in the context of an exposition of the cultural conditions, including both the intellectual conditions (from above) and the social conditions (from below) under which believers identify with Christ. We also recognize, however, that Taylor's broad sweep of intellectual history is too general, and takes too little account of the concrete social and ecclesial contexts of seminal Christian thinkers. A properly *cultural* history of Christian identity ought to be *prosopographical*, that is, to be based on studies of the individual lives of believers in their concrete, particular social and historical contexts, viewed comparatively across time and space. In short, this volume seeks to tell the story of Christian identity in terms of lived reality. Just as martyrdom made visible the union of word and deed in the offering of the body of the martyr as his or her final confession of the name of Christ, so also a cultural history of Christian self-identity is best explored not in terms of discarnate ideas but in the particular embodied narratives of those men and women who have identified with Christ. Extant autobiographical material from seminal Christian thinkers suggests a number of key aspects that inform the construction of a Christian identity. The essays in this volume endeavor to include such cultural sources and practices of identity formation that are often neglected: name changes, distinctive practices of prayer, forms and uses of Scripture, the role of the Psalms, the identification with Bible characters, forms of confession, letters, memoirs and diaries, forms of music (for example, hymnody), liturgical practices, and the like.

The contributions to this volume thus take into account the complex interweaving of common Christian assumptions, practices, and doctrines with their individual embodiment. One crucial aspect of identity formation, for example, is *metanoia*—experiencing a radical and countercultural paradigm shift of identity—as the subject discovers what it means to be "in Christ." Once again, however, we must consider that this universal aspect is realized within different social contexts, thus crystallizing different facets of Christian identity. For the apostle Peter *metanoia* meant to become "a fisher of men." For Stephen, it was to identify with the cross of Christ at his martyrdom, saying, "Father, forgive them, for they know not what they do." For Paul, it was no longer to be "a Pharisee of the Pharisees." For Justin Martyr, it was to break with both Jewish and Roman culture, with a new consciousness of a new society now being called "Christianity." For Tertullian, it was a further severance from classical culture in pursuit of Christian holiness. For Augustine it was to embrace a confessional life that began in the garden at Cassiciacum when "he took up and read." For Bernard of Clairvaux, turning to Christ meant engaging in "a new knighthood." *Metanoia* also initiated a new beginning for Teresa of Avila when she began to experience mystical visions of Jesus that transcended anything known to the Inquisition. In identity narratives that move within the same religious tradition, a moment of radical change may be more difficult to identify, and yet new turnings were occurring within established Christian institutions, as we see with Bede, Anselm, Aquinas, Luther, Calvin, and especially in the conversion narratives of the Protestant, evangelical traditions that follow them such as Wesley, Bonhoeffer, and others.

The order and coherence of this essay collection is both organic and theoretical. A natural order imposes itself through the chronological sequence of narratives, beginning with the Old and New Testaments, moving through patristic, medieval, and early modern periods through the enlightenment into the modern age. Coherence, however, is also provided by a number of guiding theoretical assumptions. All authors are keenly aware of the hermeneutic axiom that the writing of history is a theory-dependent interpretation of the historical material. Understanding of the past, as the German hermeneutic philosopher Hans-Georg Gadamer has taught us, occurs through a "fusion of horizons," that is, the past only speaks to us through our present concerns. Put differently, every appropriation of the past contains a dimension of application to our present cultural situation. Just as the history of legal precedents only really speaks to a judge when he interprets them with a specific case in mind, so also the case studies in Christian narratives are mediated through our own cultural horizon, which they in turn have shaped and continue to shape. The social and intellectual historian thus has the task to make explicit, as much as possible, the theoretical assumptions that tacitly guide the interpretation of our sources. Our authors have written their essays with the following theoretical assumptions in mind.

First, the authors write in light of the fundamental shift in epistemology from a reductive model of truth advanced by scientific rationalism in modernity to a richer, more complex concept of human knowing developed by "postmodern" paradigms of knowing. Philosophers such as Edmund Husserl, Martin Heidegger, Gabriel Marcel, Hans-Georg Gadamer, Alasdair MacIntyre, and Paul Ricoeur, among many others, have recovered a fuller spectrum of human reasoning that includes transcendent, religious sources as legitimate modes of perception. Understanding sympathetically the Christian faith of each selected character in this volume covers a historical sequence that contemporary scientific methodology cannot capture. Rather, as Jean Ladrière has explored in *Discours scientifique et parole de foi*, the term "explanation" encompasses much more than mere description based on detached observation.[3] According to Ladrière, explanation can be expanded to encompass four differing modes of accounting for phenomena. First, applied to religious identities, their explanation should account for the dynamic process of conscious subsumption of one's life under a guiding principle that shapes an individual identity. In addition, explanation of Christian identity must take into account the reciprocal shaping relation between Christian identity and doctrine. Indeed, one important aspect of our essay collection is to show the reader how previously established Christian identities inform and shape subsequent ones, on the one hand, and how unique, or countercultural Christian identities arise from within accepted narrative tradition, on the other hand. Such broader forms of "explanation" and depiction widen our angle of vision, allowing us to appreciate the "rationality of faith" that operates in the unique source of identity that believers have identified as being "in Christ."

Second, the essays are written with a clear sense of the cultural changes in terms of personhood and identity that have developed from premodern to modern culture. Wolfhart Pannenberg has helpfully sketched the negative and positive aspects of these changes: patristic theology with its focus on God's incarnation laid the groundwork for increased Christian anthropological interests, which "in the Augustinian tradition of western Christianity became preoccupied with the salvation of the individual."[4] According to Pannenberg, the stress of medieval piety on penance further intensified this individualist tendency, which also determined especially Lutheran spirituality in the Refor-

3. Jean Ladrière, *Discours scientifique et parole de foi* (Paris: Le Cerf, 1970).
4. Wolfhart Pannenberg, *Anthropologie in theologischer Perspektive* (Göttingen: Vandenhoeck & Ruprecht, 1983), 12.

mation with its subsequent emphasis on individual conscience.[5] Theology itself thus contributed to a general tendency of the modern era, equally reflected in philosophy and social history, to become concerned with personal identity. No doubt, the very idea of individual personhood owes much to the influence of the Hebraic tradition with its personal creator God.[6] Yet especially Romantic philosophers—from Herder to Fichte, Schelling, and Schlegel—to modern psychologists such as Sigmund Freud and, particularly, Erik Erikson have introduced the notions of "the self" and "identity" into our modern vocabulary.[7] Of particular relevance to our topic of Christian identity is the question already debated by Kant, Fichte, G. H. Mead, and other modern thinkers: namely, the relation between the ego as a stable, core identity and the self as a constantly developing entity or subject. Paul Ricoeur has provided the philosophically most nuanced and profound contribution to this debate, beginning with his studies on narrative identity, *Time and Narrative*,[8] and culminating in *Oneself as Another*.[9]

Ricoeur has contributed greatly to our understanding of personal identity by suggesting a hermeneutics of selfhood. Ricoeur describes self-identity (*ipseity*) as a dialectic between changing historical-cultural factors, including that of character formation (*idem*), by which we identify ourselves and the ultimate *ipse* self, determined by our address in ethical responsibility through another. This emphasis on ethical responsibility makes evident Levinas's influence on Ricoeur, whose hermeneutics of selfhood, however successfully, avoids the two extremes presented by Levinas and Heidegger, both of whom abolish the subjectivistic, ego-centric framework of Cartesian and Idealist philosophies. Ricoeur objects to Levinas's radical stress on the other as the ethical demand that determines human identity as too one-sided. Ricoeur rejects Levinas's opposition of self and other for two reasons: First, because this asymmetry cannot account for the self to receive the word of the other. Reception, Ricoeur argues,

---

5. Ibid., 13.

6. For a philosophical discussion of this influence, see Robert Spaemann, *Personen: Versuche über den Unterschied zwischen "etwas" und "jemand"* (Stuttgart: Klett-Cotta, 1996). For theological (Protestant) accounts, see Helmut Thielicke, *Being Human—Becoming Human: An Essay in Christian Anthropology* (Garden City, NY: Doubleday, 1984), and especially Emil Brunner's Gifford lectures, *Christianity and Civilization*, 2 vols. (New York: C. Scribner's Sons, 1948-49). A more general historical assessment of Judeo-Christian influence on anthropological values from a Catholic perspective is offered by Christopher Dawson, *Religion and the Rise of Western Culture* (New York: Doubleday, 1991).

7. See Pannenberg, *Anthropologie*, 194–217.

8. Paul Ricoeur, *Time and Narrative*, 3 vols. (Chicago: University of Chicago Press, 1984).

9. Paul Ricoeur, *Oneself as Another*, trans. Kathleen Blamey (Chicago: University of Chicago Press, 1992).

requires a capacity of reception based on common reflexive structures. He also worries, secondly, that Levinas only knows of one "other," namely the master who teaches; what if the other turns out to be "the master who requires a slave," or the "executioner"? Levinas, in short, leaves no room for critical discernment in the formation of identity through another.[10]

While Heidegger avoids Levinas's traumatic imposition of identity through the other's ethical demand, Ricoeur adopts Levinas's criticism that Heidegger's philosophy depersonalizes the self. Heidegger indeed manages to liberate reflection on selfhood from a false starting point in the subject's consciousness by focusing on one's being-in-the-world. At the same time, however, Heidegger "too hastily ontologizes" the voice of conscience as a call to authentic selfhood, which he later defines as one's defining relation to being. Heidegger thus loses the crucial personal-ethical dimension in identity formation.[11] For Heidegger, self-attestation is no longer linked to an ethical injunction.[12] Ricoeur's point is that selfhood, to remain relational (and thus to remain *human*), requires this ethical dimension, which ultimately points to a personal dimension that transcends both myself and the other, a dimension that directs us toward theology. In keeping with the limits of philosophical thinking, Ricoeur himself refuses to comment on this dimension: "Perhaps the philosopher as philosopher has to admit that one does not know and cannot say whether this Other, the source of the injunction, is another person whom I can look in the face or who can stare at me, or my ancestors for whom there is no representation, . . . or God—living God, absent God—or an empty place. With this aporia of the Other, philosophical discourse comes to an end."[13] Theological discourse, to be sure, cannot be silent on this issue, nor are the representatives and narrators of Christian identity in this volume. Especially the essays by Ryan Olson and Jens Zimmermann show, however, how pertinent Ricoeur's hermeneutics of selfhood proves to be for understanding Christian identity.

We end our introduction with a few thoughts on the timeliness of a cultural history of Christian sources of selfhood through comparative narrative accounts from the ancient world to modern times. We who live and think within a Western and North American context currently experience the decline of secularism and therefore a renewed sense of religion's importance for the meaning and purpose of human existence. Cultural philosophers like Taylor, but also sociologists such as Peter Berger, Hans Joas, and José Casanova have

---

10. Ibid., 339–49.
11. Ibid., 351.
12. Ibid., 355.
13. Ibid., 355.

shown that the "subtraction narrative" at the heart of secularism—human progress entails the demise of religion—is no longer credible and has ceased to be common sense. Jürgen Habermas has articulated the sense of a missing moral dimension within secular reasoning and argued that communicative ethics in secular, pluralist societies need the input of religious sources. Religious concepts of human nature, as reflected, for example, in the Judeo-Christian idea of the *imago Dei*, are needed to uphold human dignity and counter the potentially dehumanizing influences of bio-genetic advancements together with the threat of naturalistic reductions of human nature that deny any spiritual dimension. These developments renew the importance of religious identity narratives such as we offer in this book. It is no longer easy, or even plausible, to belittle as "irrational" the transcendent source of identity that provides hope and direction to the lives discussed in these contributions.

Postmodern theory, while recovering the crucial importance of narrative for truth statements, has generally been too reticent about transcendence, confining identity to local narratives and reducing individual identity to cultural roles or habits. Yet the very logic of identity formation points to the necessity for transcendence because identity formation requires a certain polarity between social roles and individual identity. To return one last time to Pannenberg: "the moment of an individual's identification of his own existence as either agreeing with or differing from a social identity by means of *self-identification cannot be reduced* to social influences." Unless, of course, one no longer desires the notion of individual selfhood at all and thus is prepared to give up personhood as such and along with it one of Western culture's great achievements that found human dignity and human rights. As Dostoyevsky has memorably expressed in his *Notes from the Underground*, the struggle for individual identity (which is not the same as endorsing individualism) is the essentially human trait of refusing any reduction to biology and thus to quasi-mechanical predictability.[14]

Moreover, belief in a transcendent source of identity and trust in a basic, meaningful transcendent order of reality (even if this order is not simply posited in nature) is crucial for the human ability to master adversity and thus to grow in wisdom and maturity. The psychologist Erik Erikson was right to argue for a "basic trust" required for a proper mediation between individual and world that is first effected by parents and family and has to be maintained after the detachment from the shelter of familial life without which the process of personal maturing would be impossible.[15] In the case of Christians,

---

14. Fyodor Dostoyevsky, *Notes from the Underground*, trans. Richard Pevear and Larissa Volohkonsky (New York: Vintage Classics, 1994), 27–28.

15. Erik H. Erikson, *Identity and the Life Cycle* (New York: Norton, 1980), 71–73.

belief in the providential care of a sovereign creator God allows the maintenance of this basic trust in the face of adversity and suffering. This trust does not mean that senseless sufferings are transformed into a higher meaning and thus transcended by a necessary "higher divine harmony" of all things. Once again, Dostoyevsky has brilliantly refuted such a non-Christian vision of reality in Ivan Karamazov's refusal to accept such a denial of evil's concrete reality.[16] Retaining one's basic trust in a meaningful world is the very opposite of such intellectual escapism, and thus the exact opposite of infantile regression into some religious fantasy. Retaining one's basic trust in God's providence, justice, and love for humanity enables a critical realism by which one may face reality as it truly is rather than escape into fantasy worlds, but to do so with realistic hope and confidence rather than fear. It is our hope that the portrayal of the Christian identities in these pages will inspire this kind of engagement with reality in our readers, both Christian and non-Christian.

Fundamentally, the question of Christian identity should interest any Christ-follower, and also those curious about identity-formation through religion through concrete historical and biographical circumstances. The essays in this volume should attract anyone—from the interested layperson to the cultural historian, who wonders what it has meant throughout history for someone to say "*I am Christianos.*" We also realize, however, that our interdisciplinary study on Christian identity was conceived for the kind of audience represented best by the ethos of Regent College: theologically interested, broadly educated readers with interdisciplinary affinities, eager to understand their own Christian tradition and to engage the wider intellectual and often secular world. Therefore, the present book, or selections thereof, should be of use for Christianity and culture classes, or any courses that embark on an interdisciplinary foray into identity and culture.

---

16. In his conversation with Alyosha, leading up to his sharing of the Grand Inquisitor parable, Ivan renounces "all higher harmony. . . . And if the suffering of children goes to make up the sum of suffering needed to buy that truth, then I assert beforehand that the whole of truth is not worth such a price." Fyodor Dostoyevsky, *The Brothers Karamazov: A Novel in Four Parts with Epilogue*, trans. Richard Pevear and Larissa Volokhonsky (New York: Farrar, Straus & Giroux, 2002), 245.

Acknowledgments

Originating from James Houston's ever fertile, creative mind, the present book embodies his original vision for Regent College and expresses his gratitude for the faculty, board, and staff in their tireless labor to clarify and sustain what it means to be Christian and therefore a fully human being. In particular, this book is intended as acknowledgment to Regent alumni, who have continued to live out and clarify their Christian identity in every conceivable academic and nonacademic place in the world. It is only with the alumni's continued support—financially, intellectually, and spiritually—that we can keep Regent's vision alive. In a spirit of encouragement and gratitude, this book is meant to draw together the Regent Community. We therefore dedicate the book to them, and to those friends of Regent who continue to support the college with their donations, prayers, and time.

As editors, we owe particular thanks to the contributors, and also to Alex Fogleman for editing the manuscript. We are also grateful for Bill Reimer's (Regent Bookstore) and Michael Thomson's (Eerdmans acquisition editor) help in getting this book published, along with the efforts of Eerdmans's editorial staff (senior project manager Linda Bieze). Finally, a special thanks to Mary Ellen Bork, wife of Judge Robert H. Bork, for granting us permission to reprint her husband's piece on law and identity.

PART ONE

Identity in the Old Testament

Chapter 1

Abraham: Friend of God, Father of the Faithful

V. Phillips Long

> "In short, the deeper you go into understanding the *Old Testament,* the closer you come to the heart of Jesus."
>
> —Chris Wright[1]

If at first blush it seems odd to launch a collection of essays on "Christian" identity with several entries on the Old Testament, one need only recall, first, that to be a Christian is to be a Christ-follower and, second, that Christ's own sense of his identity and mission was formed by his own careful study of his Bible (what we now call the Old Testament). As Chris Wright observes,

> the Old Testament tells the story which Jesus completed. It declares the promise which he fulfilled. It provides the pictures and models which shaped his identity. It programmes a mission which he accepted and passed on. It teaches a moral orientation to God and the world which he endorsed, sharpened and laid as the foundation for obedient discipleship.[2]

It makes perfect sense, then, to begin the present volume on sources of the "Christian" self with a focus on the key source of Jesus's own sense of self: the Old Testament Scriptures. And it makes sense to start with Abraham, famously regarded, as our title suggests, as "friend of God" and "father of the faithful." Of all the humans featuring in the Genesis narratives, none is mentioned in the remainder of the Old Testament as often as Abraham (44x) nor, for that matter, in the New Testament (73x). For the sake of convenience, I shall generally use the

---

1. *Knowing Jesus through the Old Testament* (London: HarperCollins, 1992), ix.
2. Ibid., 252.

name Abraham throughout this essay, while recognizing that Abram ("exalted father") was not renamed Abraham ("father of a multitude") until Genesis 17:5.[3]

The goal of the present essay is to consider this Abraham, his place in Genesis and in the sweep of redemptive history, and quintessentially the character of his engagement with God—or, more properly, God's engagement with him. It will be impossible, of course, to do full justice in a short essay to the depth and breadth of the Abraham narratives, to say nothing of doing justice to the constant stream of secondary literature surrounding his story.[4] Our goal, then, as we move quickly through the biblical portrait of Abraham's life, will be to reflect on key moments in his experience that have formed, encouraged, and challenged all those through the centuries who have sought to follow after him in faithfulness to the call of God and to experience something of what it means to be a friend of God.

Before launching into the story proper, with the famous "call of Abraham" in Genesis 12, we should note that "Abram" is mentioned already in genealogical notices near the end of the so-called Primeval History (Gen 1–11).[5] The placement of these notices is significant. As Gerhard van Rad observed some decades ago,[6] each of the Primeval History's episodes exhibits a pattern of sin, judgment, and *grace* (e.g., in respect of Adam and Eve, Cain, Noah)—each, that is, except the last. Of the last episode, von Rad writes:

> The story about the Tower of Babel concludes with God's judgment on mankind; there is no word of grace. The whole primeval history, therefore, seems to break off in shrill dissonance, and the question . . . now arises even more urgently: Is God's relationship to the nations now finally broken; is God's gracious forbearance now exhausted; has God rejected the nations in wrath forever?[7]

---

3. On the significance of this and other (re)namings, see the discussion below of Genesis 17.

4. The following is but a tiny sampling of recent literature, which may be consulted for further bibliography: T. E. Fretheim, *Abraham: Trials of Family and Faith* (Columbia: University of South Carolina Press, 2007); S. A. Hunt, ed., *Perspectives on Our Father Abraham: Essays in Honor of Marvin R. Wilson* (Grand Rapids: Eerdmans, 2010); J. D. Levenson, *Inheriting Abraham: The Legacy of the Patriarch in Judaism, Christianity, and Islam* (Princeton: Princeton University Press, 2012); N. MacDonald, "Did God Choose the Patriarchs? Reading Election in the Book of Genesis," in *Genesis and Christian Theology*, ed. N. MacDonald, M. W. Elliott, and G. Macaskill (Grand Rapids: Eerdmans, 2012), 245–66; R. W. L. Moberly, "Abraham and Aeneas: Genesis as Israel's Foundation Story," in *Genesis and Christian Theology*, 287–305; R. W. L. Moberly, *The Bible, Theology, and Faith: A Study of Abraham and Jesus* (Cambridge: Cambridge University Press, 2000).

5. See especially 11:26–32.

6. *Genesis*, trans. J. H. Marks, rev. ed., OTL (Louisville: Westminster John Knox, 1973), 152–54.

7. Ibid., 153.

The seemingly pedestrian genealogical notices that follow the Babel debacle offer a first glimpse of the answer to these questions. This answer, as von Rad notes, is nothing other than the "election and blessing of Abraham."[8] The call of Abraham, and the whole history of redemption that flows from it, is God's word of grace.

The (Co)mission of Abraham (Genesis 12:1–3)

Leaving home is never easy. Parting from friends, family, and all that is familiar can be difficult. And yet many have done so—some for fortune, some for fame, some for adventure, some to escape a hard situation. But most challenging of all is to strike out from home not knowing where one is going but simply because God has called. This is precisely Abraham's situation when his story opens in Genesis 12. The LORD (Yahweh) speaks, and Abraham listens. (In the present essay, I shall render the Hebrew divine appellation *'elōhîm* as "God" and follow the convention of many English translations by rendering the more personal, covenantal name *yhwh* as "the LORD.")

The LORD instructs Abraham to leave behind kin and country (v. 1), and Abraham obeys, taking with him his wife Sarah (or Sarai, as she was known until her name change in 17:15) and his nephew Lot (12:4–5). Lacking in specificity—"Leave . . . and go to the land I will show you" (12:1)—the LORD's words are nevertheless rich with promise. In some of the most famous lines in Scripture, he promises Abraham blessing upon blessing:

> I will make you into a great nation,
> and I will bless you;
> I will make your name great,
>   and you will be a blessing.
> I will bless those who bless you,
> and whoever curses you I will curse;
>   and all peoples on earth
>   will be blessed through you. (Gen 12:2–3)[9]

Five "I wills" mark the divine commitment to Abraham: to make him a "great nation," to "bless" him and make his "name great," to bless those who bless him

---

8. Ibid.

9. Citations of biblical passages in English will in this essay follow the 2011 version of the New International Version.

and to curse those who curse him. The one instance of "you will" reveals that the divine plan is to bless more than just the family of Abraham. The Hebrew syntax of the last line of v. 2 carries an injunctive sense, namely, "and you *shall* be a blessing." Abraham's calling is not for his own benefit only but *so that he may bring blessing to* "all peoples on earth" (v. 3). Thus, what Abraham receives at the beginning of Genesis 12 is not just a divine vocation but a "(co)mission," involving a "mission" in which he is to *co*operate in God's plan to bless the world.

Father of the Faithful: Part I (Genesis 12:4–14:24)

The initial episodes following Abraham's call and commission reveal a great deal about him. He steps out in faith in obedience to the LORD's instructions. But soon his faith begins to falter, as he fears that his wife's beauty may prove costly to him in a foreign land where others hold power and privilege. And so he passes her off as his sister, bringing harm to his host. Abraham again shows faith in allowing his nephew Lot to choose the seemingly more favorable land in which to settle, and he even comes to Lot's rescue when his choice proves to be more dangerous than anticipated. Through it all, the LORD keeps faith with Abraham and blesses him.

Abraham Goes (12:4–9)

As the text unfolds, Abraham accepts his *commission* and leaves home, though none of the promised blessings are yet realized, nor will they be for a very, very long time (cf. Rom 4:19; Heb 11:8–12). He follows the call of God because he trusts him. In so doing, Abraham proves indeed to be the "father of the faithful," including those spiritual children of Abraham (Rom 4:16; Gal 3:29) who through the last twenty centuries have sought to trust and follow Jesus, the greater son of Abraham. At a very deep level, Christian identity is anchored in trust—and not just a passive trust, but trust that issues in obedience to God's promptings. It is worth noting as well that the Christian pilgrimage begins, as Abraham's began, with God's taking the initiative.

From a historical perspective, one may wonder what, in fact, Abraham was asked to leave behind. The answer is, possibly quite a lot.[10] Scholarly debate continues regarding the proper identification of Abraham's home city of "Ur"

---

10. Cf. D. Rosenberg, *Abraham: The First Historical Biography* (New York: Basic Books, 2006), esp. 33–64.

(Gen 11:28, 31), whether at Tell el-Muqayyar, a major ancient city situated on the bank of the lower Euphrates River and excavated by Leonard Woolley between 1922 and 1934, or possibly, as Cyrus Gordon argued, a more northerly "Ur" in what is today southern Turkey.[11] Uncertainty of the site identification makes it difficult to be dogmatic about the cultural context in which Abraham grew up,[12] but at least this much seems clear, both the Ur of Abraham's birth and the upper Mesopotamian city of Haran, where Abraham settled for some decades before setting out for Canaan (Gen 11:31–32), were developed urban environments boasting material prosperity and advanced law codes (as well as other literature) and worshipping a plurality of gods, chief among them the moon god. To leave behind material comfort and high culture in order to follow the call of God must have been challenging for Abraham, and such is the case also for many of Abraham's spiritual descendants.

And yet Abraham sets out, with both divine blessing and the mandate to *be a blessing* ringing in his ears. He arrives in Canaan and is told by the LORD that "this land" will one day be given to his descendants (12:7). As he moves through the land from north to south, he builds altars "to the LORD," as if staking claim to the LORD's divine right to the land (12:7, 8; 13:18). Ironically, however, when famine forces Abraham to seek refuge in Egypt, Abraham proves to be anything but a blessing to his host (12:10–20).

Abraham in Egypt (12:10–20)

Fearing that the beauty (and thus desirability) of his wife could cost him his life, Abraham instructs Sarah to say she is his sister. Predictably, the Egyptian king takes the beautiful newcomer into his palace (whether into his harem is not stated), and he treats Abraham well on account of her. To alert the king to his inappropriate, if unwitting, action, the LORD visits "great plagues" on the king and his house on account of "Abraham's wife" (12:17). The king protests his innocence and sends Abraham away, but only after enriching him (vv. 16, 20).

Confronted with such a sad first performance, can we still regard Abraham as father of the faithful? Yes, though not of faithful*ness* per se. Rather, we must

11. The Septuagint's Greek translation of the four occurrences of "Ur of the Chaldeans" in the Hebrew text (i.e., Gen 11:28, 31; 15:7; and Neh 9:7) attests in each instance not "Ur" but, rather, "land" or "country" of the Chaldeans, the difference being explicable if the final letter of the Hebrew "land" (*'rṣ*) somehow was lost, leaving the name "Ur" (*'r*).

12. For a cautious defense of the traditional view that Abraham's Ur was in what would later become the land of the Chaldeans, see A. R. Millard, "Where Was Abraham's Ur? The Case for the Babylonian City," *Biblical Archaeology Review* 27, no. 3 (2001): 52–53, 57.

understand "the faithful" to be those who, positionally, count as God's people. Such "faithful" are often far from perfect (cf. the often not-so-saintly "saints" in New Testament parlance). In this episode of faltering trust, as in other episodes, Abraham is indeed the archetype of "the faithful." Throughout the centuries, the faithful have been marked by similar episodes of faltering and failure. Nevertheless, to "faithless Israel," the LORD declared himself "faithful" (Jer 3:12). And the New Testament people of God receive similar assurances: "if we are faithless, he remains faithful, for he cannot deny himself" (2 Tim 2:13).

Abraham Making Peace and War (13:1–14:24)

Returning from Egypt to Canaan, both Abraham and his nephew Lot have become "very wealthy in livestock and in silver and gold" (13:1–2), so much so that they are crowding one another and mutually agree to split up. Abraham gives Lot first choice of location, and he chooses the lush grass and stable climate of the Jordan valley. It seemed to Lot "like the garden of the LORD" (13:10). But greener pastures are no guarantee of a place in which to thrive spiritually. Indeed, as the narrator is quick to remind the reader with his parenthetical comment—viz., "this was before the LORD destroyed Sodom and Gomorrah" (v. 10)—Lot's choice is home to the infamous cities to be wiped out in Genesis 19. Abraham's hill country location poses greater physical challenges but, evidently, fewer direct temptations to evil (see 13:13). In this more challenging environment, Abraham receives, yet again, the divine promise of blessing for himself and his descendants (13:14–17).

It is not long before Lot finds himself in need of physical rescue, as he is taken captive by a coalition of four enemy kings (Gen 14:11–12). Abraham, armed with allies (v. 13), "318 trained men born in his household" (v. 14) and astute military strategy (v. 15), manages to rescue Lot, "the other people," and even "all the goods as well" (v. 16). Returning from battle, Abraham is met by the king of Sodom in "the King's Valley" (v. 17) and also by the mysterious "Melchizedek, king of Salem," who blesses Abraham in the name of "God Most High, Creator of heaven and earth" (vv. 18–19). To Melchizedek Abraham gives a "tenth of everything" (v. 20). Abraham's actions suggest that he views Melchizedek as speaking of the one true God whom he himself also worships (a perspective confirmed in the appellations of v. 22). Melchizedek, whose name sounds like "king of righteousness," not only finds a place in Israel's messianic expectation as it later develops (Ps 110:4) but ultimately provides the model of a priest-king that the writer of the book of Hebrews applies to Jesus himself (Heb 5–7).

While Abraham readily accepts bread and wine from Melchizedek (14:18), he refuses to accept anything from the king of Sodom, explaining that he has sworn an oath to "the LORD, God Most High, Creator of heaven and earth" not to accept anything from the king of Sodom, lest the latter should claim credit for Abraham's material success (vv. 21–24). The text does not say so explicitly, but we may assume that Abraham understands it is the LORD who deserves credit for his successes. Throughout the centuries, Abraham's spiritual heirs have understood the same, namely, that God himself is the one to whom every victory is to be credited and the one who is the believer's true reward and supply. The next episode opens with this very point.

The Faithful God (Genesis 15–19)

This part of the story foregrounds God's faithfulness. Reassuring Abraham in the light of Sarah's ongoing childlessness, the LORD makes a covenant with Abraham. Remarkably, he shows faithfulness also to the castaways from Abraham's household, the concubine Hagar and Abraham's son, Ishmael. For his part, Abraham is called to respond in the LORD's covenant by embracing the covenant sign of circumcision. God's faithfulness is further evidenced when he takes Abraham into his confidence regarding the imminent destruction of Sodom and Gomorrah.

God's Promise to Make Good (15:1–21)

No sooner—in narrative time at least—has Abraham refused the reward proffered by the king of Sodom than the LORD comes to him in a vision with the reassurance that "I am your shield, your very great reward" (15:1). But Abraham is apparently not reassured. Promises are one thing, tangible evidence another, and childless Abraham feels a lack of the latter: "what can you give me since I remain childless" (v. 2). When the LORD does not immediately respond, Abraham reiterates his point, adding that "a servant in my household will be my heir" (v. 3). Not so, is the LORD's response, "but a son who is your own flesh and blood will be your heir" (v. 4). Then taking Abraham out under the night sky, the LORD promises Abraham that his descendants will be numerous like the stars in the sky (v. 5).

At this point, the biblical narrator interrupts the flow to insert one of the most famous statements in the whole of the Abraham story: "He [Abraham] believed the LORD, and he credited it to him as righteousness" (v. 6). The Hebrew syntax of the first clause may suggest that Abraham's believing/trusting of the LORD was not a one-time event but, rather, was his regular habit.[13] This posture of faith and trust in respect of the LORD is a key marker—perhaps *the* key marker—of Abraham's relationship to God, as indeed it must be of all his spiritual descendants (Rom 4:23–24). While such faith should lead to faithful action and often does in Abraham's experience—though with some notable exceptions!—the striking truth of the present declaration is that Abraham is credited with righteousness simply because he placed his faith/trust in God. Not just the apostle Paul (see the entirety of Rom 4 and Gal 3) but Christians in every generation have recognized in the belief/trust/faith exhibited by father Abraham the sine qua non of Christian identity.

But trust does not silence all questions. So when the LORD adds to his promise of descendants that Abraham will also receive a homeland (v. 7), Abraham asks how he can know that he will "gain possession of it" (v. 8). There then follows one of the most remarkable episodes in the Bible. The LORD instructs Abraham to prepare for a covenant ceremony that will involve the sacrifice and dividing in half of several specific animals (v. 9). Such ceremonies are designed to signify that if the covenant is broken, death will be the result. *Usually* it is the lesser party in the relationship who is required to pass between the severed carcasses in a form of self-malediction. Such ratification ceremonies are mentioned not only in the Bible (Jer 34:18–19) but also in several ancient Near Eastern texts.[14] The astonishing feature of the present episode is that, contrary to expectation, it is not the lesser but the greater party, God himself (symbolized by a "smoking firepot and a blazing torch," v. 17), who passes between the pieces. In this act of *divine self-malediction*, the LORD signals that, should the covenant be broken, the penalty will be paid by God himself! As Fretheim observes, "God in effect puts the divine life on the line, 'writing' the promise in blood," and thus "indicating the unilateral character of the promise."[15] While Abraham could never have guessed the full extent of this remarkable promise, those living in the Christian period cannot but marvel at this early adumbration of the heart of the gospel, namely, that God himself, in the person of the Son, takes the curse of a broken covenant on himself, dying that his people might live (Eph 5:2; Heb 9:11–28; 1 Pet 3:18).

---

13. See, e.g., G. J. Wenham, *Genesis 1–15*, WBC (Waco, TX: Word, 1987), 330.

14. Cf. W. W. Hallo and K. L. Younger Jr., eds., *The Context of Scripture* (Leiden: Brill, 1997), 1:61; 2:82; 2:137.

15. Fretheim, *Abraham*, 37.

God's Promise to Castaways (16:1–16)

Divine promises, though sure, do not always come immediately to fruition. And waiting for God to act can be hard. The text does not indicate how long after the events of Genesis 15 the episode of Genesis 16 takes place. Whatever the time lag, childless Sarah apparently begins to despair of ever having a son of her own. Or perhaps she is uncertain about how the divine promise of a son for Abraham is to be effected. In any case, at this point in the narrative she does what many in her time would have done: she offers to Abraham her maidservant, Hagar, as a kind of surrogate wife. Abraham, perhaps equally weary of waiting or similarly uncertain of the means by which the promise is to be fulfilled, agrees to Sarah's suggestion, and the Egyptian handmaid Hagar is soon carrying Abraham's child (16:1–4a). Unsurprisingly, things do not go well. Hagar disrespects Sarah, Sarah oppresses Hagar and blames Abraham, and soon Hagar simply flees (vv. 4b–6). There the story of this ill-advised human attempt to hasten an outcome promised by God might have ended. But it doesn't.

The "angel of the LORD" seeks out Hagar in the wilderness, addresses her as "Hagar, servant of Sarai," thus reminding her of her duties, and enjoins her to return and fulfill them (vv. 7–9). Then comes something remarkable. Though Hagar is not carrying the child of promise, the LORD pronounces a blessing upon her that mirrors in some ways the promise to Abraham—"descendants . . . too numerous to count" (v. 10). For Hagar's child the LORD has a name, "Ishmael" ("God has heard") (v. 11), and a promise that he will be a "wild donkey of a man" (v. 12). Modern readers of this promise tend to understand the description of Ishmael as saying something negative, but Hagar apparently doesn't. It is worth considering, therefore, that the LORD may simply be saying that Ishmael's descendants will be dwellers of the steppe, independent of oppressive structures such as Hagar herself must endure. Be that as it may, God's concern for Hagar underscores his intent not just that the chosen line be blessed but, as had been clearly stated in the call of Abraham, that "all peoples on earth" be included in what God is doing (12:3).

The Name-Changing, Game-Changing God (17:1–27)

After the ill-advised initiatives of Sarah and Abraham in Genesis 16, the divine initiative in chapter 17 marks a reorienting correction and something of a new beginning. Thirteen years have passed since the birth of Ishmael,[16] and

16. Cf. 16:16 and 17:1; 17:25.

11

Abraham is ninety-nine years old when the LORD appears to him again, this time to confirm and to "order," or "establish" (Gen 17:2),[17] the covenant already made in Genesis 15. Confirmation includes the LORD's reiteration of earlier promises—descendants, land, and blessed relationship with God (vv. 2–8)—and also the institution of the covenant sign of circumcision (vv. 9–14). As the LORD had "cut a covenant" (the Hebrew expression for making a covenant) with Abraham in Genesis 15:18, so in this ordering of the covenant, cutting (circumcision) is involved, and any of Abraham's male descendants who refuse to be so cut "will be cut off from his people" (17:14). If this covenant "cutting" sign may be associated with the "cutting" rite of Genesis 15, then Abraham and his seed may be seen as in some sense bearing in their bodies a reminder of the divine commitment to make good on his promise, even should it require a divine "passage between the pieces."

The new beginning of Genesis 17 is marked by the appearance of four names for the first time in the Bible. The first is the divine appellation 'ēl šadday (v. 1), which is sometimes simply transliterated in English translations as "El Shaddai" and sometimes translated as "God Almighty" or the like. No definitive answer to the question of what El Shaddai means has yet been given,[18] but it is worth noting that in the Pentateuch the name most frequently appears in contexts where the patriarchs are being enjoined to trust and obey the God of the covenant.

Just as the name El Shaddai does not introduce a new deity into the story but, rather, underscores the character of the God of Abraham as a powerful provider who can be trusted, so it is also with the next two (re)namings. The first involves Abraham himself, who to this point in the narrative has been called Abram, "exalted father." In Genesis 17:5, God changes his name to "Abraham," underscoring the divine promise that he will become the father of a "multitude" (Hebrew *hāmôn*) of peoples. Name changes in the Old Testament often involve literary wordplay, and the name "Abraham" may have arisen from the combination of the first parts of both Abram and *hāmôn*, yielding Abra-ham, "father of a multitude."[19] Sarah, too, receives a divine name change,

17. While most English translations speak of God "making" a covenant here, the normal Hebrew expression for making a covenant (lit. "cutting a covenant") is not used.

18. An older rabbinic view took the name to mean "God who is enough," while more recent theories link the word Shaddai either to a verb (*šdd*) meaning to "destroy or overpower" or, as in Arabic, to be "strong," or to an Akkadian word *šadu*, meaning "mountain," or even to the Hebrew word *šad*, meaning "breast" (yielding something like the God who provides, nourishes). On these various theories, see the major Hebrew lexica, especially *HALOT*, *NIDOTTE*, and *TWOT*, ad loc.

19. Cf. M. Garsiel, *Biblical Names: A Literary Study of Midrashic Derivations and Puns*, trans. P. Hackett (Ramat Gan, Israel: Bar-Ilan University, 1991), 18.

though the text does not explain its significance. Since Sarai and Sarah both suggest the meaning "princess," it may be that the name change is meant simply to reinvigorate the name. When she is first introduced as Abram's wife in Genesis 11:29–30, Sarai's childlessness is foregrounded. But now, that is to change. She is no longer to be Sarai the (childless) "princess" of Abraham but shall be Sarah the "Princess" from whom "nations" and "kings of peoples" descend (17:16).

The fourth name introduced for the first time in Genesis 17 is the name "Isaac" (17:19), the child of promise to be born to Abraham and Sarah. His name means "laughter" (or more accurately, "he laughs"), and laughter will indeed surround his birth. Both Abraham (17:17) and Sarah (18:12) will laugh (in amazement? in disbelief? in bitterness?) when they first hear the promise. The improbability of the scenario, humanly speaking, is obvious, and it is not beyond imagining that God himself laughs with pleasure at the opportunity to demonstrate that nothing is "too hard for the LORD" (18:14).

Abraham's first thought is for Ishmael (17:18), and God, though insistent that Isaac is to be the child of the covenant promise (vv. 19, 21), pronounces abundant blessings also upon Ishmael, who himself will become the father of rulers and of a great nation (v. 20). As the episode and the chapter draw to a close, the reader is reminded of the broad reach of the blessing of Abraham. Included in the circumcision ceremony are not only Abraham and "his son Ishmael"—the epithet is repeated three times!—but all in Abraham's household, including foreigners (vv. 23–27).

Genesis 17 anticipates much that would later become central to the Christian understanding of self: God is presented as El Shaddai, a God of power and provision, and with a specific plan for his people; God is a name-changer, one who transforms and expands the mission of his chosen to become fruitful and in that fruitfulness to bring blessing to the world; and God marks his people with a sign of his covenant commitment to them and, in response, of their covenant commitment to trust and obey him. This same God calls, changes, and commissions the New Testament children of Abraham and marks them with the covenant sign of baptism. At the heart of both the Old Testament and New Testament covenant signs is a divine "passage between the pieces," a "baptism" unto death (Rom 6:3–4; Col 2:12). Jesus referred to his coming passion and death on behalf of sinners as his "baptism" (Luke 12:50) and likened his being baptized with his "drink(ing) the cup" of suffering and death (Mark 10:38). Just as Abraham's "righteousness" was a matter of his trust/faith in a self-giving God, so it is also with his spiritual heirs: "So in Christ Jesus you are all children of God through faith, for all of you who were baptized into Christ have clothed yourselves with Christ" (Gal 3:26–27).

V. PHILLIPS LONG

The God Who Involves His People in What He Is Doing (18:1–33)

The mysterious visitation recounted in Genesis 18 highlights further key aspects of the character of God and signals his desire to involve his people in what he is doing. The reader is told immediately that it is the LORD who appears to Abraham "near the great tree of Mamre" (18:1), but all Abraham sees is "three men standing nearby" (v. 2). In the course of Abraham's showing the strangers generous Middle Eastern hospitality, they inquire after his wife, Sarah, and, learning that she is in the tent, proclaim that within the year she will have a son (v. 10). Overhearing, Sarah, who knows her body and her husband's, laughs at the thought (v. 12). Whether the visitors hear the laugh or simply have privy knowledge, the LORD queries Abraham regarding Sarah's skepticism—does Abraham suspect by this point that the three men are more than everyday travellers? Referencing Sarah's laugh, the LORD asks "Is anything too hard for the LORD?" (vv. 13–14). The consistent answer of both Old and New Testaments to this rhetorical question is, of course not! Nothing is too hard for God.[20] Nor is anything hidden from God, as this episode demonstrates. When Sarah lies about having laughed, the LORD responds, "Yes, you did laugh" (v. 15). This seemingly abrupt ending to the LORD's exchange with Sarah may contain a hint of mercy, inasmuch as the LORD speaks the truth but does not belabor it—a mode of rebuke that bears emulation.

As the three visitors prepare to continue their journey, they turn their attention from Abraham and Sarah to the cities of the plain, particularly Sodom (v. 16). Before taking their leave, the LORD says (in Abraham's hearing?), "Shall I hide from Abraham what I am about to do?" (v. 17). He then rehearses Abraham's special status as recipient and conduit of divine blessing (vv. 18–19), and discloses his intent to visit Sodom and Gomorrah to see if the outcry against them and the grievousness of their sin are as great as has been reported (vv. 21–22). This exploratory visit raises a question. If nothing can be hidden from the LORD, then why the need of a visit? Perhaps part of the point is to pursue "due process." The behavior is, in any case, commensurate with the human form in which the LORD appears to Abraham. More importantly, though, the investigation provides an opportunity for the LORD to draw Abraham into his confidence and to involve him in the divine plan. Abraham does become involved, famously pleading that Sodom—where his nephew Lot has taken up residence—be spared if fifty righteous can be found, and pointedly asking, "Will not the judge of all the earth do right?" (v. 25).

20. To cite but a few representative examples, see Job 42:2; Jer 32:17; Matt 19:26; Luke 1:37; Rom 4:19–22.

14

Deeply engrained in the Christian sense of self is the belief that God is all powerful ("Is anything too hard for the LORD?") and all knowing (recall the visitors' privy knowledge). Should this limitlessly powerful, comprehensively knowledgeable "judge of all the earth" *not* do right, then all is lost and humanity faces nothing but dread. But Abraham's question and the LORD's patient accommodations (vv. 26–32) confirm that the judge will indeed do right. Even if the number of righteous in Sodom be not fifty, or forty-five, or forty, or thirty, or twenty, but only ten, "for the sake of ten," says the LORD, "I will not destroy it" (v. 32). But not even ten can be found, and Sodom is destroyed. Why didn't Abraham bargain for even fewer than ten? We are not told, but perhaps Abraham has reached a point in the negotiation where he is utterly convinced that God can be trusted; God's concern for the righteous in the city is at least as deep as Abraham's. But still, why stop at ten? One suggestion is that this (round) number may represent the minimum "critical mass" (or social unit) that might hope to have a curative effect in a corrupt city; fewer than ten would simply represent individuals, who could be led out of the city.[21] As the story continues into Genesis 19, Lot, his wife, and his two daughters are taken by the hand and led out by the two men.[22] Worth underscoring, before leaving Genesis 18, is the picture of a God who takes his people into his confidence and draws them into conversation (prayer), and for whom their input makes a real difference.

The God Who Does Right (19:1–38)

The picture of God that emerges in Genesis 18 is very much in line with his later declaration of his character to Moses (and with the consistent testimony of the Old Testament): "The LORD, the LORD, the compassionate and gracious God, slow to anger, abounding in love and faithfulness" (Exod 34:6).[23] Boundless in love, the LORD is willing to forgive "wickedness, rebellion and sin" (Exod 34:7a). Were the LORD's self-declaration to end there, one might be tempted to assume a rather impotent and ineffective "judge of all the earth" and to despair of ever seeing the world made right again. But the divine self-declaration to Moses continues: "Yet he does not leave the guilty unpunished" (Exod 34:7b). Genesis 19's account of the destruction of Sodom and Gomorrah confirms the

21. Cf. Fretheim, *Abraham*, 84.
22. Called *hā'anāšîm*, "the men," in 19:12, 16, but *hammal'ākîm*, "the angels, messengers," in 19:1.
23. For this combination of divine attributes, see also Num 14:18; Joel 2:13; Jonah 4:2; Ps 86:15; 103:8; and Neh 9:17.

point. When Abraham returns near the end of Genesis 19 to the spot where he had conversed with the LORD in chapter 18 and looks down "toward Sodom and Gomorrah," all he sees is "dense smoke rising from the land, like smoke from a furnace" (19:28). The God of the Bible takes no delight in the death of the wicked (Ezek 18:23; 33:11) and is patient, "not wanting any to perish, but all to come to repentance" (2 Pet 3:9), but in the face of unrelenting, intractable evil, judgment must fall. And what was the evil of Sodom and Gomorrah? As Provan succinctly notes, their "sins are variously remembered in both the Bible and in the later reading tradition as including a lack of justice (e.g., Isa 1.9–10; 3.9), idolatry (e.g., Deut 32:15–43), arrogant disregard for the poor (e.g., Ezek 16.49–50) and sexual perversity (e.g., Jude 7, Philo)."[24]

Not to be overlooked in this account of multi-city destructions is the fact that much of the chapter is focused on rescue, particularly the rescue of Lot and his family. The angelic visitors not only pull Lot out of immediate danger (19:10) but plan and effect his escape from Sodom before it is destroyed. He is to take all his family with him: wife, two daughters, and the two "sons-in-law" engaged to be married to his daughters (vv. 12–13). Unfortunately, the latter two take Lot's words as "joking" (yet another play on the Hebrew root ṣḥq, "laugh"), ignore his warning (v. 14), and are destroyed. Lot's wife, too, perishes when she ignores the visitors' instruction to leave and *not look back* (vv. 17 and 26). When the dust settles, only Lot and his daughters have survived, and they find themselves in a cave. Despairing of finding husbands, the daughters conspire to ply their father with drink and become pregnant by him (vv. 30–36). A sad commentary on the effects of growing up in a city like Sodom and a rather sordid end to a terrible episode. As the focus returns to Abraham himself in Genesis 20, misguided behaviors continue.

Father of the Faithful: Part II (Genesis 20–21)

The next two chapters reveal that even though the father of the faithful sometimes falters, the LORD remains ever true to his promises, a truth quintessentially demonstrated in the birth of the long-awaited Isaac.

---

24. I. W. Provan, *Discovering Genesis: Content, Interpretation, Reception* (London: SPCK, 2015), 141. On the nature of the sexual perversion in view in Jude 7, see R. J. Bauckham, *Jude, 2 Peter*, WBC 50 (Waco, TX: Word, 1983), 53–55.

When Faith Falters (20:1–18)

As noted earlier, Abraham, though rightly called the father of the faithful, is not always a paragon of faithful*ness*. As he had done once already at the end of Genesis 12, so now in Genesis 20 Abraham passes off Sarah as his sister, and she is again taken by another man, in this instance not an Egyptian king but Abimelech, king of Gerar (20:2). The LORD's reaction is swift, providential, and decisive, not only alerting Abimelech in a dream that Sarah is a "married woman" (v. 3) but also preventing him from touching her (v. 6). Heeding Abimelech's protestations of his own innocence (vv. 4–5), the LORD instructs him, under threat of death, to return Sarah to Abraham, whom he describes as a "prophet" whose prayer will contribute to the survival of Abimelech and his kin (v. 7).

This is the first use of the term "prophet" (*nābî*') in the whole of Scripture, and Abraham's experience offers the first insights into what the title means. Abraham, like later prophets, is one to whom God speaks, is one privileged to stand before God, and is one whose prayers and petitions God hears. Given these privileges, it is ironic that Abraham, when confronted by Abimelech for his deception (vv. 8–10), seeks to justify himself in a couple of ways: first, he cites what he perceived to be a lack of "fear of God in this place" and claims that this caused him to fear for his own life; and, second, he cites the more purely technical point that Sarah is in fact his (half-)sister (vv. 11–12). One might even hear a slight blaming of God in his linking his behavior to God's causing him to "wander from my father's household" (v. 13). So Abraham is not a fearless paragon of faithfulness in every circumstance, but yet he remains a friend of God, a prophet whose prayer God heeds (vv. 17–18), and one whom God blesses despite his failings (vv. 14–16). In all these respects, father Abraham truly is an archetype of God's people.

Laughing and Crying: Isaac Is Born and Things Get Complicated (21:1–34)

If Abraham's actions are "mixed," the actions of the God of Abraham are not. As Genesis 21 opens, the long-standing promise of a son for Abraham and Sarah is fulfilled: "the LORD did for Sarah what he had promised . . . at the very time he had promised" (vv. 1–2), and Abraham responds, as instructed (see 17:19), by naming the child "Isaac," meaning "laughter" (v. 3), for much joy and laughter accompany the birth (v. 6). Sarah's wonderment—"who would have said to Abraham that Sarah would nurse children?" (v. 7)—makes perfect sense from a human perspective, but the reader of Abraham's story cannot but respond that this is *precisely* what God had said would happen. The God of Abraham is a promise-making and a promise-keeping God. Confidence in this fact is fundamental to those who later would be called children of Abraham by faith (cf. Gal 3:7; Heb 11:11). "Without (such) faith it is impossible to please God" (Heb 11:6).

It is not all laughter in Genesis 21, however. Or, it might be better to say that all the laughing is not of the same sort. Earlier impatience with the timing of God has led to a complication; Abraham has another son, Ishmael. One day, after Isaac is weaned (at about age three, according to ancient custom), Sarah sees Ishmael (probably about seventeen at the time) "mocking," or "laughing (at)," her son—the root of Isaac's name and all the other "laughing" references is used here as well. Incensed, Sarah insists that Abraham send the boy and his mother, Hagar, away (v. 10). Abraham is distressed, but God reassures him of two things: "it is through Isaac that your offspring will be reckoned" and "I will make the son of the maidservant into a nation also" (vv. 11–13). The remaining verses of the episode recount Abraham's compliance and God's provision for Hagar and her son Ishmael (vv. 14–21). God's concern is expansive, including not just the well-being of Isaac, the one through whom Abraham's "offspring will be reckoned" (v. 12), but also the well-being of Ishmael: "God was with the boy as he grew up" (v. 20).

The concluding episode in Genesis 21 shifts from Abraham's family relations to his relationship to outsiders and, indeed, to the Abimelech whom he had duped and endangered in Genesis 20. Here he reaches an understanding with Abimelech over a disputed well and "the two men [swear] an oath there" at Beersheba. To seal the oath, Abraham presents seven lambs. As elsewhere in the Abraham narrative, key words mark the episode; the name Beersheba sounds like both "well of an oath" and "well of seven."[25] At Beersheba Abraham plants a memorial tree and "calls upon the name of the LORD, the Eternal God" (v. 33), and there he lives "in the land of the Philistines for a long time" (v. 34). Noteworthy in terms of Abraham's calling to be a blessing to the nations is Abraham's sojourning among "others" and Abimelech's recognition that "God is with you in everything you do" (v. 22).

The Trial of Abraham (Genesis 22)

If Genesis 15:6—"Abram believed the LORD, and he credited it to him as righteousness"—is one of the most famous and *reassuring* verses in the entirety of the Old Testament, Genesis 22 is one of the most famous and *troubling* chapters in the entire Bible. It raises the question of what kind of God could test his ser-

---

25. "Oath" and "seven" employ the same consonants in Hebrew, *šbʿ*.

vant by instructing him to sacrifice his "only son" (v. 2). It raises the question of what kind of man Abraham is, that he sets out to do just that (v. 3). And it raises the question of what effect the whole event will have on Isaac; will he ever after suffer the psychological trauma of a victim of child abuse? Such questions, and many more besides, have plagued readers of the "Akedah" (the "binding" of Isaac) throughout the centuries. In one of his best-known treatises, Søren Kierkegaard wrestles at length with the fact that "while Abraham arouses my admiration, he also appals me."[26]

And who doesn't find the present chapter appalling? Having determined to "test" Abraham (v. 1), God issues a command that seems to transgress every boundary ethical and familial: kill your son (v. 2). And what is it about Abraham that God wishes to test? The answer comes in v. 12, after Abraham has stood the test: "Now I know that you fear God, because you have not withheld from me your son, your only son." The Hebrew text reads more literally: "Now I know that you are a God-fearer." To be a God-fearer is to be one who trusts God implicitly and absolutely. Abraham's checkered history to this point in the narrative—recall his lapses with respect to Sarah, Hagar, and foreign kings— gives point to the test. In the face of the most severe of trials, will Abraham's belief (his faith and trust) in God fail? Or will he emerge as a God-fearer? Will he remain the Abraham of Genesis 15:6, one who trusts God?

Kierkegaard insists that if one removes the question of faith from the narrative as "a nix and naught,"[27] the true sense of the narrative is lost. The fact is—and here we may draw Genesis 15:6 and the Akedah into relation—that "Abraham had faith. His faith was not that he should be happy sometime in the hereafter, but that he should find blessed happiness here in this world. God could give him a new Isaac, bring the sacrificial offer back to life."[28] This line of thinking is confirmed by Hebrews 11:19: "Abraham reasoned that God could even raise the dead, and so in a manner of speaking he did receive Isaac back from death." Thus, we see that the test of Abraham is a true test, though Abraham is not told that it is a test. His unquestioning and immediate obedience is "a sign that he has *understood* that God is God, and that in this whole matter of life and destiny, he and his beloved son are entirely in God's hands."[29]

Once we grasp the nature and maturity of Abraham's faith by this point in the narrative, we read various elements in the account differently. His response to Isaac's question—"where is the lamb" (v. 7)—is no longer read as a coy eva-

26. Søren Kierkegaard, *Fear and Trembling*, trans. A. Hannay (1843 [Danish original]; London: Penguin, 1985), 89.
27. Ibid., 60.
28. Ibid., 65.
29. Provan, *Discovering Genesis*, 147.

sion, but as a sincere expression of trust: "God himself will provide the lamb" (v. 8). Similarly, his earlier remark to the servants can be taken at face value: "I and the boy (will) go over there. We will worship and then we (not just I!) will come back to you" (v. 5; my parentheticals). And what of Isaac? We read nothing of struggle as he is bound and laid on the altar by Abraham (v. 9). Are we to understand, as Fretheim suggests, that "Abraham's trust in God has become Isaac's trust: God will provide"?[30] As the story continues, God does provide "a ram caught by its horns" in a thicket (v. 13), leading Abraham to name that place "The LORD Will Provide" (v. 14).

In numerous ways, Genesis 22 foreshadows God's climactic provision in the suffering, death, and resurrection of Jesus, the "only son" of God, in the line of Abraham and the head of the new humanity in Christ. It is in Jesus, ultimately, that all nations on earth are blessed (Acts 3:25; Gal 3:7), and it is he who undergoes a baptism unto death (cf. Luke 12:50; Mark 10:38), who "passes between the pieces" as it were, to bring reconciliation between God and the spiritual descendants of Abraham.

The story of Abraham in Genesis continues for a few more chapters, gradually becoming the story of Isaac and Rebekah, but the climax of his story is reached already here in chapter 22.

The Gospel according to Abraham

Among the sources of the Christian self, the story of Abraham deserves a prominent place. Standing at the head of the long history of redemption that finds its climax in Jesus, it lays the groundwork for understanding who God is, what human beings are, and how the two can become faithful friends. The story begins with God taking the initiative. It begins with God's invitation to trusting response. It establishes a relationship that survives human failings. And it witnesses an expansiveness in the graciousness and universal intent of God to bring blessing to all peoples on earth. The story sees God turn ill-conceived human initiatives into opportunities for restoration and even blessing. It presents a God whose commitment to his people is unconditional, whose desire to enter into joyful relationship with his people is such that he is willing even to sacrifice himself to make the relationship work. From call, to covenant, to correction, to culmination, it is a remarkable story, a story that gets to the heart of what it means to be a God-fearer and, ultimately, a Christ follower.

---

30. Fretheim, *Abraham*, 131.

Chapter 2

Moses: Man of God

Iain Provan

With the fall of the Old Kingdom in Egypt near the end of the third millennium BC (ca. 2190 BC)—the kingdom that produced, near its first capital city of Memphis (just south of modern Cairo), the pyramids that are so closely associated with Egyptian history in the modern mind—Egypt entered a lengthy period of internal conflict. During this period the rulers of Lower (northern) Egypt, based in Herakleopolis, exercised only minimal control over the fertile Nile Delta, so attractive throughout Egyptian history to the pastoral peoples of Sinai and Canaan, who routinely suffered from shortages of both food and water. These "Asiatics" now settled in the eastern Delta in significant numbers, and their numbers swelled during the Middle Kingdom that followed (2106–1786 BC) with the arrival of significant numbers of prisoners of war and others sent as tribute by vassals of Egypt, as well as many people involved in commercial ventures. As centralized Egyptian power began once again to break down during the eighteenth century BC, these Semitic immigrants increasingly gained sovereignty over the eastern Delta and then (by the middle of the seventeenth century BC) over the entirety of Lower Egypt and some of the territory even further to the south. Only with the accession of the Eighteenth Dynasty of Pharaoh Ahmose I in Thebes in 1550 BC were the rulers of southern Egypt able to drive these "Hyksos" rulers out of the land and establish the unified New Kingdom (1550–1069 BC), with its famous pharaohs such as Amenhotep III (1390–1352 BC), Akhenaten (1352–1336 BC), Tutankhamun (1336–1327 BC), and Ramesses II (1279–1213 BC).

This is the general background against which we must understand the arrival of the biblical Jacob's family in Egypt at some point between the latter years of the Middle Kingdom and the beginning of the New Kingdom,[1] and

---

1. The imperative arises, of course, only for those who are prepared to take seriously the

21

their settlement in the region of "Goshen" (Gen 45:10; 47:27) or "Ramesses" (Gen 47:11) in the northeastern Delta.[2] It is also the background against which we must understand the later story of Moses, set by the book of Exodus in a time when Jacob's descendants had "multiplied greatly" and had become "exceedingly numerous, so that the land was filled with them," and "a new king, who did not know about Joseph," had come to power in Egypt (Exod 1:7–8). Although this pharaoh is not named in the book of Exodus, possibly out of an intention to mimic the normal practice in New Kingdom Egyptian texts of not naming the pharaoh's enemies, the strongest contenders remain Horemheb, last king of the Eighteenth Dynasty (1323–1295 BC), and Seti I, the second king of the Nineteenth Dynasty (1294–1279 BC)—two of the three immediate predecessors of Ramesses II ("the Great"). It was during Horemheb's reign that the New Kingdom pharaohs renewed their interest in the northeastern Delta in the aftermath of the Hyksos expulsion. Horemheb renovated the temple of Seth in the old Hyksos capital of Avaris, and Seti I (who like his briefly reigning father Ramesses I [1295–1294 BC] was born in Avaris) is known to have built a palace close by in what is now Qantir. It was around this palace that Ramesses II, the likely pharaoh of the Exodus (after the previous "king of Egypt died," Exod 2:23), later built his great city of Pi-Ramesses, whose construction is then alluded to in Exodus 5.[3]

The Cultural Conditions

What was the nature of the culture into which Moses was born? From ancient times, Egyptians invested supreme power in a single ruler who was regarded as the very embodiment of divinity and as the ultimate owner of the entire land. The stone pyramids of the earliest pharaohs self-consciously proclaim not only

---

evident intent of the book of Genesis, in telling the story of Jacob and his family, to describe real people inhabiting a real world (whatever else the book is also intent on accomplishing). Those more inclined to try to reconstruct ancient Israelite reality out of the surviving rubble of the civilizations with which the Israelites had contact will recognize no such imperative, and will indeed (in this case) have even less than usual with which to work—since for various reasons even the rubble of ancient Egypt lies thin on the ground in the Nile Delta. See K. A. Kitchen, *On the Reliability of the Old Testament* (Grand Rapids: Eerdmans, 2003), 245–46.

2. For a discussion of the names, both of which appear to derive from the period of the text's composition post-Ramesses II rather than that of the events described, see Kitchen, *Reliability*, 255–56, 61; and J. K. Hoffmeier, *Israel in Egypt: The Evidence for the Authenticity of the Exodus Tradition* (New York: Oxford University Press, 1997), 121–22. In other words, Jacob's family was settled in the region *later known as* "Goshen" or "Ramesses."

3. Hoffmeier, *Israel in Egypt*, 109–12, 122–26.

their wealth and power, but also this divine kingship, and official dogma about the institution remained fundamentally unchanged throughout the centuries that followed. The divine king was

> an absolute monarch, the chief executive officer of the state. As chief justice, he was thought to be the fount of all laws and thus the foundation of moral righteousness. As the supreme priest, he was the main link between gods and men, and thus guaranteed the triumph of order over chaos on earth. He was a strong and noble sovereign, against whom no enemy could stand: a defender of the nation. He was believed to be omniscient, one who could divine the innermost thoughts of all men. Thus, he was the wise ruler in whom the population could put its trust. He was also said to be a shepherd to his people, who ensured the well-being of his subjects and protected all, rich or poor.[4]

As this "link between gods and men," the king had certain responsibilities toward the gods; he had to build and look after their temples, and ensure the performance of the prescribed religious rituals, which in turn would encourage the gods to extend their visits to the earth and thus bring blessing to it. He did all this, however, as a participant in the divine life himself—the embodiment of the god Horus, first of all, and later of the sun-god Re. Still later, in the New Kingdom, the kings are typically said to be the sons of Amun-Re, king of the gods and creator of the universe. As this divine figure, the pharaoh of Egypt was responsible for maintaining the primordial order of the universe on earth, which involved (centrally) the oversight of the annual flooding of the Nile that was so important to the fertility of the whole land. After his death, he was equated with Osiris, the ruler of the underworld.

Beneath the divine ruler, all officials of the state were, at least in theory, completely dependent on the royal will—although the periods of unrest between the Old, Middle, and New Kingdoms put this theory to the test. Nevertheless, the theory suggests a resolutely hierarchical society, with the divine king at the top, followed by his vizier (the person in charge of the central government) and other top officials like the Overseer of the Granary. Then there were all the provincial and more local officials throughout the land of Egypt who answered to the vizier, and last of all the ordinary people who supported the entire edifice at the base of the social pyramid: "Most of Egypt's people were cultivators of free or unfree status. 'Unfree' includes the possibility of a serflike

---

4. R. J. Leprohon, "Royal Ideology and State Administration in Pharaonic Egypt," in *Civilizations of the Ancient Near East* [hereafter *CANE*], ed. J. M. Sasson (Peabody, MA: Hendrickson, 1995), 1:273–87 (273).

attachment to the land as well as slavery."[5] Just this kind of structure is clearly evidenced in historical records from Egypt throughout the periods in which societal disorder gave way to strong, centralized government, and most especially during "the period of the New Kingdom, which was probably the apex of royal prestige, a time when the king managed to successfully wield supreme authority over the whole country."[6] Everyone thus found their rightful place in the eternal order of things, from the king down to the slaves—there was little possibility for social mobility in Egypt during the stable periods of its history—in a universe whose divinity was manifested through all sorts of channels apart from the pharaoh. The gods could appear in the guise of animals, for example (like Anubis, the god [or jackal] of the dead), or by way of the sky, personified as the goddess Nut, or the moon, personified as the god Thoth. The gods were everywhere in this resolutely polytheistic society; indeed, the cosmos existed primarily for them, its order reflected in the cities and temples and monuments that were everywhere to be seen.

It was this culture into which Moses was born and was soon to challenge in every respect, from its beliefs about the gods and the nature of the world, through its convictions about the nature, vocation, and destiny of human beings, and on to its understanding of individual righteousness and of the good society.

The Historical Moment

The book of Exodus identifies the moment of Moses's birth as occurring in the midst of a crisis for the Hebrew immigrants to Egypt settled since the time of Joseph in the Nile Delta. A new king comes to power who knows nothing about Joseph—as, indeed, no pharaoh of the late Eighteenth or early Nineteenth Dynasty of the New Kingdom *would*. The Eighteenth Dynasty (1550–1295 BC) separated these pharaohs by over two hundred and fifty years from the time when the now-expelled Hyksos elites had governed Lower Egypt from Avaris, and the rest of the land had looked on from a distance. This new king of a long-reunified Egypt now looks to the far north of his country, a region that had perennially caused trouble for Egyptian central government, and he sees more trouble coming. There is a large immigrant Semitic population still living there in the aftermath of the Hyksos expulsion and subsequent developments, of some economic value to Egypt, but nevertheless a potentially destabilizing

---

5. D. Lorton, "Legal and Social Institutions of Pharaonic Egypt," *CANE* 1:345–62 (351).
6. Leprohon, "Royal Ideology," 283.

political entity—natural allies for Egypt's "enemies" to the north and east (Exod 1:10). This concern makes perfect sense against the background of the events of the preceding centuries. The Egyptian solution is, first of all, to restrict the freedoms of these foreigners in their midst, and at the same time to make them useful to the Egyptian state. They are forced to work on two building projects at "Ramesses" (the site of the later Pi-Ramesses, center of pharaonic rule in the eastern Delta from Ramesses II through to Ramesses III) and "Pithom" (probably the nearby Tell er-Retaba, Exod 1:11).[7] When these oppressive arrangements do not curtail Hebrew flourishing, the Egyptians develop a policy of infanticide with respect to male Hebrew babies (Exod 1:15–22). It is this policy that ultimately results in Moses's growing up in the Egyptian court, adopted by Pharaoh's daughter (Exod 2:1–10). There he would have joined many other foreign children known as "children of the nursery"—often hostages of the pharaoh being educated in Egyptian ways with a view to replacing their fathers upon their deaths as Egyptian vassals. These children could also rise to become court officials in Egypt itself, with a few attaining high office.[8] As the adopted son of an Egyptian princess, however, Moses would have been in an even more privileged position, as "a member of the ruling body of courtiers, officials, and attendants that served the pharaoh as his government leaders under the viziers, treasury chiefs, etc."[9]

It is worth considering what it would have meant for Moses to have been "educated in all the wisdom of the Egyptians" under these circumstances (Acts 7:22). He would have become fluent in Egyptian, learning both the hieratic (everyday) and hieroglyphic (much more specialized) scripts. He would thus have been inducted into an Egyptian literary tradition that went back hundreds of years, and included narratives, autobiographies and biographies, "instructions" on various topics, and literature of both protest and despair. Libraries of literature were to be found both in the royal court and in temples, their earliest mention occurring already in texts from the Old Kingdom; from the very founding of the Egyptian state, evidently, "a marked archival tendency informed the scribal mind."[10] A significant number of such texts would have been explicitly religious in nature—part of the way in which Moses would have been inducted into the Egyptian worldview described above, with its particular understanding of the gods and their relationship to the pharaoh and to

7. For a discussion of the location, see Kitchen, *Reliability*, 256–59.
8. Hoffmeier, *Israel in Egypt*, 142–43.
9. Kitchen, *Reliability*, 297.
10. D. B. Redford, "Ancient Egyptian Literature: An Overview," *CANE* 4:2223–41 (2224–25). See also J. A. Black and W. J. Tait, "Archives and Libraries in the Ancient Near East," *CANE* 4:2197–209.

everything else. By the time that he had completed his formal education and had entered government service, he would likely also have been "exposed to such disciplines as mathematics, accounting, geometry, surveying, and simple engineering."[11] He may also have come across literature that in form or content owed something to external influence, like the surviving treaty of Ramesses II with the Hittites, or even mythological texts from other parts of the ancient world.[12] There were also opportunities in the educational curriculum to learn something about medicine, astronomy, and magic, as well as the geography of the Near East (including Syro-Palestine) and foreign languages (such as Akkadian, Hittite, and Minoan).[13]

The Prince of Egypt

It is such a "prince of Egypt" (as the movie has it) that we must reckon with meeting in the closing verses of Exodus 2, as we encounter a Moses who has now "grown up" (Exod 2:11). And now for the first time we can say something about his character, for we have some words and actions to consider. Who is Moses at this point in his story? He is certainly "an Egyptian" (as Reuel's daughters will shortly describe him to their father, v. 19)—one who watches the Hebrews in their hard labor rather than participating in it (v. 11). He is at the very least, however, a compassionate Egyptian, who cannot bear to watch excessive violence being perpetrated by the powerful against the weaker, even if the latter are slaves. This is clear in his reaction both to the Egyptian overseer in verses 11–12 and to the Hebrew in verse 13. He is also an active rescuer of the weak from trouble, as we find not only in these two examples, but also in the case of Reuel's daughters in verses 16–17. This "rescuing" aspect of his character leads him in the case of the Egyptian to murder (v. 12). It is not clear from the story whether he regards this killing as problematic in itself, or as problematic simply if he is caught. Certainly from the point of view of later Israelite (Mosaic!) law it is problematic in itself, since it represents a disproportionate response (rather than "life for life, eye for eye, tooth for tooth, hand for hand, foot for foot, burn for burn, wound for wound, bruise for bruise," Exod 21:23–25). The biblical story itself suggests that proportionality in such matters was already an ethical and

11. E. F. Wente, "The Scribes of Ancient Egypt," *CANE* 4:2211–21 (2216).

12. On the treaty, see Kitchen, *Reliability*, 297–98. On the myths, we certainly know that the Mesopotamian *Gilgamesh Epic* was available at least in nearby Palestine by the fourteenth century BC, for excerpts from it have been found at Megiddo. B. B. Schmidt, "Flood Narratives of Ancient Western Asia," *CANE* 4:2337–51 (2343).

13. Wente, "Scribes," 2216–17.

legal norm long before we get to the book of Exodus (e.g., Gen 4:23–24; 9:5–6), and the angry words of the fighting Hebrew in Exodus 2:14 also imply as much.

How are we to think of Moses in this story, then? Is he in any meaningful sense a Hebrew as well as an Egyptian? Even at the level of ethnicity, this is not entirely clear in Exodus 2. He does go out to watch "his brothers" (NIV's "his own people) as they labor (v. 11), and he does intervene on behalf of such a "brother"; but does the author, in telling us this, mean to tell us also about Moses's own sense of solidarity with the Hebrews, or only about the facts of the matter? Again, the words of the Hebrew in verse 14 do not imply any recognition of solidarity, at least from Moses's point of view. Leaving ethnicity aside, there is certainly no hint in the story that Moses yet has any awareness of the *faith* of his Hebrew forefathers, which is alluded to in verse 24. We are justified in reading Moses in Exodus 2, then, as already an empathetic man of his time and culture, and already as someone who, at least in certain circumstances, will stand up for the oppressed over against the oppressor. He is yet very far short of the man of God who will later be the means by which the justice of God is visited on the Egyptians and by which the Israelites will be permanently released from all, and not just temporarily relieved from a tiny amount, of oppression. He is, at present, much more an Egyptian than a Hebrew. It will take an enforced exile in Midian in northern Arabia, on the run from an angry pharaoh (who may *well* have interpreted Moses's actions in terms of solidarity with the Hebrews), and an extraordinary vision of God in that land, before any of this changes.

At the Burning Bush

Time passes; the wrathful pharaoh dies (Exod 2:23). This does not mean any change for the better in the circumstances of the Israelites in Egypt, for the building program continues, and slave labor still drives it. Meanwhile, Moses has settled down in Midian with a new wife (v. 21), and is working as a shepherd for his father-in-law Reuel (also known as Jethro, Exod 3:1). One ordinary day in his new life leads him onto the slopes of Mount Horeb (elsewhere known as Sinai), which the author reminds his readers is "the mountain of God" (although this description, too, is only retrospectively provided, because God has not yet appeared there). It is on the slopes of Horeb that Moses catches sight of the famous burning bush, and is drawn thereby into an encounter with God that ultimately changes everything for him. It is the beginning perhaps of the most fundamental *metanoia* of the entire biblical story, since it ultimately *generates* the fundamentals of the biblical story, whose radical and countercultural nature (not only in respect of Egypt, but also in respect of the entire ancient world) stands as a direct reflection of the radical and countercultural paradigm shift of identity that begins in Moses in these moments.

We arrive at the heart of the matter by paying careful attention to the course of the conversation between Moses and God in Exodus 3–4. The opening words of God immediately seek to reconnect Moses with the story of his originating people, and to detach him from his adoptive family and culture: "I am the God of your father, the God of Abraham, the God of Isaac and the God of Jacob" (Exod 3:6). He is the son of a particular father, from a particular people-group, and God is the God of that Hebrew father. He is also the God of other "fathers," stretching back in Israel's story as far as Abraham. This, then, is the story in which Moses must now relocate himself and find his identity, leaving Egypt behind—the story of his ancestors; and in doing so, he must identify himself with the oppressed over against the oppressor, as God himself has identified with the former and intends "to rescue them from the hand of the Egyptians and to bring them up out of that land into a good and spacious land, a land flowing with milk and honey" (Exod 3:8). Indeed, Moses is to play a crucial role in this venture: "go, I am sending you to Pharaoh to bring my people the Israelites out of Egypt" (v. 10). Moses must cease being an Egyptian, and become once again a Hebrew.

For his own part, Moses is somewhat resistant to this change of identity and all that it entails in action: as George Rawlinson once put it, "the diffidence of Moses is deep seated, invincible."[14] Thirteen times God addresses Moses in these chapters; Moses's typical responses are "questioning or demurral."[15] Invited to read himself into God's story and thus to discover his true identity, he persists in asking, "Who am I?" (v. 11). "Who am I, that I should go to Pharaoh and bring the Israelites out of Egypt?" He may have grown up as a prince of Egypt, but faced with the enormity of this task, he quails before it. Pharaoh is, after all a god-king, and Egypt a mighty kingdom. Moses does not possess the resources for the task—as indeed those called to the prophetic office in the Old Testament never did: "Neither previous faith nor any other personal endowment had the slightest part to play in preparing a man who was called to stand before Jahweh for his vocation."[16] God's response to Moses's question is, significantly, not to reassure him about either his faith or his personal endowment, but simply to assure him of the divine presence with him (v. 12).

14. G. Rawlinson, *Moses: His Life and Times* (New York: Revell, 1887), 77.

15. T. E. Fretheim, *Exodus*, Interpretation (Louisville: John Knox, 1991), 58.

16. G. von Rad, *Old Testament Theology*, trans. D. M. G. Stalker (Edinburgh: Oliver & Boyd, 1965), 2:57.

Moses's next question concerns the Israelites rather than the Egyptians: he is worried that they might ask for God's "name" (v. 13). Perhaps his words express a real fear, but the question is just as likely one that occurs to Moses from his Egyptian perspective as it is a question that the Israelites might actually have asked. In the ancient Near East in general, "naming" was simply part of the process by which something came into existence and was assigned a function.[17] Thus, the Egyptian *Ritual of Amun* tells us that prior to creation "no god had come into being and no name had been invented for anything." The Mesopotamian text *Enuma elish* likewise speaks of the period when "no gods whatever had been brought into being, uncalled by name, their destinies undetermined."[18] In this ancient worldview, the birth of the gods, in particular, was intrinsically bound up with the assigning of their functions and roles in the cosmos. As to the names of Egyptian gods in particular, Jan Assman says this: "'Name' refers not only to proper names such as Osiris and Amun but denotes everything that may be said and told about a deity in epithets, titles, pedigrees, genealogies, myths—in short, its entire linguistic representation."[19] To know the name of a god, then, was to know where that god "fitted" in the cosmos—where, on the map of divinity (and indeed of divinely ordained society), it might be found. It was also thereby to know of what use the divinity might be to the worshipper—which benefits might accrue from its worship. This is, it seems, what Moses is asking: where, in the whole religious scheme of things, does *this* God fit—a God hitherto unknown in Egypt, as Pharaoh will later confirm: "Who is the LORD, that I should obey him and let Israel go? I do not know the LORD and I will not let Israel go" (Exod 5:2). The answer that Moses receives to his question is extraordinarily important, for it amounts to a refusal to *be* named, even as a name is apparently provided: "I AM WHO I AM [or, 'I will be who I will be']. This is what you are to say to the Israelites: 'I AM has sent me to you' . . . The LORD . . . has sent me to you.' This is my name forever" (Exod 3:14–15). There *is* a name; but it is the name of a God who first and foremost refuses to fit the normal categories of ancient Near Eastern thought and to be available to worshippers in normal ways. "I AM WHO I AM"; I am not like the many gods of whom you, Moses, already know. It is for the same reason that, when the Israelites eventually arrive back at Mount Horeb after the Exodus, the first three of the ten opening "words" (commandments) that they receive from God not only forbid them from having "other gods before me" but also from making

17. J. H. Walton, *Ancient Near Eastern Thought and the Old Testament: Introducing the Conceptual World of the Hebrew Bible* (Grand Rapids: Baker Academic, 2006), 87–92, 188–90.
18. *ANET*, 61.
19. J. Assman, *Of God and Gods: Egypt, Israel, and the Rise of Monotheism* (Madison: University of Wisconsin Press, 2008), 10.

standard ancient Near Eastern cult-images for use in worship. Walter Brueg-gemann nicely sums up the significance of these first three commandments, and what he says about them casts light also on the way in which "naming" is addressed in Exodus 3:

> The first three commands . . . assert the oddity of Yahweh, who has no util-itarian value and who cannot be recruited or used for any social or human agenda. The God who commands Israel is an end to be honored and obeyed, and not a means to be used and exploited. If it is correct . . . that an imageless quality is Yahweh's distinctive characteristic, then we may see in the prohibi-tion of images an assertion of the unfettered character of Yahweh, who will not be captured, contained, assigned or managed by anyone or anything, for any purpose.[20]

This is now the second lesson that Moses has received at the burning bush. He should not rest on his own resources, but depend upon the God who is speaking to him; and (now) he must be under no illusion that this is any kind of "normal" god. In due course he will begin more fully to understand what this means, not just for the human relationship with God, but for relationships within human society itself, as the first three commandments are joined with the remaining seven, and it becomes more clear at the level of detail how God, who will not be treated as an object to be exploited, also demands that we do not treat our neighbor as such.

A third objection follows, after God has revealed his entire plan for the Exodus to his reluctant servant and has assured him of success (Exod 3:16–22): "What if they [the Israelites] do not believe me or listen to me and say, 'The LORD did not appear to you'?" (Exod 4:1). And here, after the uncompromising insistence that Moses must repent of his Egyptian ways, we find a divine conces-sion: he will be permitted to demonstrate that he has met God by way of signs and wonders that would have been familiar to those accustomed to the Egyp-tian magical arts (cf. Exod 7:8–12). The fourth objection concerns, apparently, a speech impediment: "O Lord, I have never been eloquent, neither in the past nor since you have spoken to your servant. I am slow of speech and tongue" (Exod 4:10). This objection is met with an explicit claim by Yahweh that he is the creator God, well able to "help you speak and . . . teach you what to say" (vv. 11–12). With this, Moses has run out of excuses, which is not to say that he is ready to concede. His final plea is simply that God should send someone else (v. 13)—a request to

20. W. Brueggemann, *Theology of the Old Testament: Testimony, Dispute, Advocacy* (Minne-apolis: Fortress, 1997), 184–85.

which God is disinclined to acquiesce. With this final plea rejected, we soon find Moses (and his brother Aaron) back in Egypt and addressing Pharaoh in his royal court (Exod 5:1). Moses has adjusted himself to reality—the reality of the one true and living God, allegiance to whom requires the rejection of much that Egypt has taught him about the gods, the world, human beings, and the nature of the good society. Before he dies, he will have laid down at least the outlines of a great story that builds on this new understanding of reality, reshaping the myths of the ancient world, adding the stories of his ancestors, and recounting the story of the Israelites from the Exodus to the borders of the promised land, so as to produce the beginnings of what will later become known as the Pentateuch (in Christian circles) or Torah (in Jewish ones). Pharaoh Akhenaten had flirted with a form of monotheism in Egypt, earlier in the New Kingdom period, but it was nothing like this. *This* was something quite different, and over the course of time it made a great difference to the way people perceived and acted in the world, not just in the Near East but also across the planet.[21]

From Egypt to the Promised Land

What happens next in the story directly confirms the truth of what Yahweh has said to Moses, and thereby inducts him ever more deeply into the narrative that ultimately entirely shapes his identity. A contest develops between Yahweh (through Moses and Aaron) and the god-king Pharaoh (with his magicians), the point of which is to persuade the Egyptian ruler to let the Israelites go, by way of demonstrating who is really God. Ten plagues fall on Egypt, comprising three groups of three and then a final one. The first three plagues concern the waters and their creatures (Exod 7:14–8:19), the second three, the land and its creatures (Exod 8:20–9:12); and the third three, the air and its creatures (Exod 9:13–10:29).[22] To a very great extent these first nine plagues are best understood as having their proximate cause in an unusually high annual flooding of the Nile, whose normal activity was essential to the fertility of Egypt that was a primary responsibility of the pharaoh.[23] This is implied in the Exodus story in

---

21. Readers interested in pursuing the manifold ways in which this is so might refer to I. W. Provan, *Seriously Dangerous Religion: What the Old Testament Really Says and Why It Matters* (Waco, TX: Baylor University Press, 2014).

22. For interesting discussions, see Hoffmeier, *Israel in Egypt*, 146–49; and Kitchen, *Reliability*, 249–54.

23. See K. W. Butzer, "Environmental Change in the Near East and Human Impact on the Land," *CANE* 1:123–51 (135–36); and C. J. Eyre, "The Agricultural Cycle, Farming, and Water Management in the Ancient Near East," *CANE* 1:175–89.

the nature of the first plague (blood): "The first water of [each] inundation is red because of the ferruginous earth that it carries from the Ethiopian mountains."[24] The point about a normal Nile inundation, however, is that it was viewed with relief by the Egyptians, bringing to an end an often disease-ridden dry season and promising prosperity ahead. The inundation in the book of Exodus brings with it only death and pestilence (plagues one through six), and it is followed in turn by a devastating hailstorm, a plague of locusts, and a sandstorm that brings "darkness."[25] It is in these events that the reader comes to understand that Yahweh is indeed God, and that Pharaoh is not, although Pharaoh himself refuses to accept this (albeit that at times in the story he is seemingly close to doing so). Indeed, an ancient reader familiar with Egyptian culture would have understood the extent to which all the plagues, and not just the final one, represent "judgment on *all* the gods of Egypt" (Exod 12:12)—from Hapy, the "personification of the fecundity of the Nile,"[26] whose capacity to bring new life through its waters is obviously questioned in the narrative, through to Amun-Re, the creator god and king of the gods, who as the sun is obscured in the darkness of the ninth plague, and whose creatorship and kingship is radically questioned in the tenth (the death of the firstborn)—the very event that at last persuades the god-king Pharaoh himself to relent (Exod 12:31). As Hoffmeier succinctly puts it, all "the gods of Egypt and their power are shown to be impotent in the plagues narrative."[27]

The Moses who emerges from this contest is one who has learned to trust Yahweh more fully than before, when asked for obedience (e.g., Exod 7:10, 20, 8:17; 9:10; cf. Exod 3–4), and who has also learned the vocation of intercessory prayer, even on behalf of his enemies (e.g., Exod 8:12–13, 30–31; 9:33). This same trust is on display at various later points in the story, as when the Israelites are trapped by an Egyptian military force in Exodus 14, and Moses is commanded to "raise your staff and stretch out your hand over the sea to divide the water so that the Israelites can go through the sea on dry ground" (Exod 14:16); or when use of the same staff is called for in Exodus 17, so that "water will come out of

---

24. J. van Dijk, "Myth and Mythmaking in Ancient Egypt," *CANE* 3:1697–1709 (1707).

25. Note here the *Encyclopedia Britannica* entry on *khamsin*: a "hot, dry, dusty wind in North Africa and the Arabian Peninsula that blows from the south or southeast in late winter and early spring. It often reaches temperatures above 40° C (104° F), and it may blow continuously for three or four days at a time. . . . On its forward side, the centre brings warm, dry air northward out of the desert, carrying large amounts of dust and sand." *The New Encyclopaedia Britannica* (15th ed., ed. Philip W. Goetz [Chicago: Chicago University Press, 1991]), 6:830.

26. H. te Velde, "Theology, Priests, and Worship in Ancient Egypt," *CANE* 3:1731–49 (quotation from 1737).

27. Hoffmeier, *Israel in Egypt*, 149–55 (quotation on 155).

[the rock] for the people to drink" (Exod 17:6). Both his trust and his commitment to intercession are astonishingly on display, in particular, in Exodus 32. Here he is atop Mount Sinai, receiving God's law on behalf of the people. Down below, the people have decided to dispense with the alarmingly uncontrollable, un-imaged God who led them out of Egypt, and to return to the kind of normal, ancient Near Eastern religion that they have only a short time beforehand left behind. With the surprising connivance of Aaron—a man "who did not share Moses' lonely visions and did not possess his brother's absolute sense of mission"[28]—they produce "an idol cast in the shape of a calf," proclaiming to themselves, "These are your gods, O Israel, who brought you up out of Egypt" (Exod 32:4).

Faced with this spectacular apostasy, Yahweh announces his intention to do away with this "stiff-necked" people and to continue dealing only with Moses. And now we recognize for the first time just how deeply shaped Moses has become by the new story into which he has been inducted, and by his convictions about the character of the God who is authoring it. For at this crucial moment in his life his trust in God issues, not in obedience to God's expressed will, but in argumentative prayer, in which he "reminds" God of who he is and what he has been intent on doing in the world—the very God of whose existence and character Moses had earlier possessed no grasp at all! And so, to the God who tells Moses that the Israelites are "*your* people" (Exod 32:7), Moses asks, "why should your anger burn against *your* people?" (Exod 32:11). Why should the Egyptians, who have just learned something of the truth about who God really is, now have the opportunity to slander Yahweh's name (Exod 32:12)? Surely God will remember his relationship with, and his commitment to Abraham, Isaac, and Jacob, of which God himself first reminded Moses in Midian (Exod 3:6, 15–17; 32:13)? Thus we discover that Moses, like Abraham before him, when faced with the wickedness of Sodom and Gomorrah (Gen 18:16–33), is able to penetrate to the heart of God and of the story that God is telling, even beyond some of God's own words. Or perhaps he is actually exceedingly attentive to the true implication of God's words, recognizing that "leave me alone" (Exod 32:10) in fact "leaves the door open for intercession."[29] One way or another, Moses has learned well with whom he is dealing, and what is this person's fundamental posture toward the world; his confidence in that person is found to be amply justified in Exodus 34, after still more prayer (Exod 33:12–23). For here it is explicitly affirmed that although Yahweh "does not leave the guilty unpunished," he is nevertheless "the compassionate and

---

28. D. Daiches, *Moses: The Man and His Vision* (New York: Praeger, 1975), 134.
29. B. S. Childs, *The Book of Exodus*, OTL (Louisville: Westminster, 1974), 567.

gracious God, slow to anger, abounding in love and faithfulness, maintaining love to thousands, and forgiving wickedness, rebellion and sin." It is this fact that leads him to his renewed promise that, even though the Israelites have not changed at all in *their* character, and are still "a stiff-necked people" (Exod 34:9), he will nevertheless go before them and lead them into the promised land. Walter Moberly, commenting on the close connection between what happens here in Exodus 32–34, and what happens earlier in the flood story of Genesis 6–9 (where God *also* maintains his relationship with people whose character has not fundamentally changed even after judgment has befallen them, Gen 6:5 and 8:21), says this:

> This narrative analogy suggests a deep theological vision. God deals with the world in general in the same way as with Israel in particular. If both Israel and the world show themselves to be faithless at the outset and to be continuingly faithless . . . then their continued existence is similarly to be understood in terms of the merciful forbearance of God toward those who do not deserve it. Life for both Israel and for the world is a gift of grace.[30]

It is this that Moses understands, even before God explicitly confirms it.

A Scripted Life

As Alasdair MacIntyre puts it in *After Virtue*,

> I can only answer the question "What am I to do?" if I can answer the prior question "Of what story or stories do I find myself a part?" We enter human society, that is, with one or more imputed characters—roles into which we have been drafted—and we have to learn what they are in order to be able to understand how others respond to us and how our responses to them are apt to be construed. It is through hearing stories about wicked stepmothers, lost children, good but misguided kings, wolves that suckle twin boys, youngest sons who receive no inheritance but must make their own way in the world . . . that children learn or mis-learn both what a child and what a parent is, what the cast of characters may be in the drama in which they have been born and what the ways of the world are. Deprive

30. R. W. L. Moberly, *The Theology of the Book of Genesis* (Cambridge: Cambridge University Press, 2009), 120.

children of stories and you leave them unscripted, anxious stutterers in their actions as in their words.[31]

I would put the matter slightly differently: I can only answer the question "Who *am* I, and what am I to do?" if I can answer the prior question "Of what story or stories do I find myself a part?" Moses is not presented in the Bible as by any means a perfect man,[32] and he certainly does not understand himself as such; indeed, as far as his physical capacities are concerned, he may well have been an "anxious stutterer" (Exod 3:10). "Unscripted," however, he was not. Confronted by the living God on Mount Horeb, he entered however falteringly into a relationship with that God that changed the course of his life, impressing upon him an idea of who he was and what he was to do that was entirely different than the idea he had possessed before. He spent the rest of his life "leaving Egypt," and encouraging his fellow travellers (with limited success) to do the same. The biblical writings that tell the story of this "man of God" (Deut 33:1 and five other occasions in the Old Testament) have in turn encouraged generations of readers to attempt the same journey—the journey of a hero of biblical faith who is much celebrated in the rest of Scripture.[33] If "the story of the Bible is nothing less than God's initial intimacy with his creation, the severing of that intimacy, and the steps he takes to restore that intimacy,"[34] then Moses remains for us a powerful model of the person who comes to understand who he or she might be in intimacy with "I AM WHO I AM"—the one who reveals his glory to Moses and to us, and invites us into "radiance" as we speak with him (Exod 34:29).[35]

31. A. MacIntyre, *After Virtue: A Study in Moral Theory* (Notre Dame: University of Notre Dame Press, 1981), 216.

32. This is especially clear in Deut 32:48-52, where he is denied entry into the Promised Land because he "broke faith with [Yahweh] in the presence of the Israelites at the waters of Meribah Kadesh in the Desert of Zin and . . . did not uphold my holiness among the Israelites" (cf. also Ps 106:33).

33. Note, e.g., the constant reference back (or allusion) to "the law of Moses" (e.g., Josh 8:34-35; 23:6; 1 Kgs 8:9), and other references to the man himself (e.g., 1 Sam 12:6-8; Ps 77:20; 99:6; 103:7; 106:23; Isa 63:11; Jer 15:1; Mic 6:4; Matt 17:1-13; Mark 12:26; Acts 7:20-44.

34. P. Enns, *Exodus*, NIVAC (Grand Rapids: Zondervan, 2000), 561.

35. I am grateful to Professor James Hoffmeier for reading this essay in its draft form and offering good advice.

Chapter 3

David: The Anointed Israelite

KEITH BODNER

King David is the most extensive representation of a human character in the historiographical literature of the Bible.[1] The reader variously witnesses his early life and anointing in 1 Samuel 16 followed in turn by his long fugitive period in the wilderness, his enthronement as king of all Israel in the newly-conquered city of Jerusalem, the disastrous rebellion of Absalom that fractures the nation, and finally David's death in 1 Kings 2. Erich Auerbach famously argued that biblical narrative—in contrast to Homeric epic—is "fraught with background"—and nowhere is this more evident than in the long and complicated story of David's reign with its multiple layers of irony, double-voiced discourse, strategic deployment of motifs, shades of ambiguity, multiple shifts in temporal and spatial settings, intertextuality, and thematic complications that abound from start to finish.[2] But by no means is the attention on David restricted to Samuel–Kings, for there is copious mention of Israel's most famous king elsewhere in the biblical material. In addition to the prophetic oracles that speak of a scion of the Davidic house and the forthcoming Branch of Jesse, David is the most prominent figure in both the book of Psalms and 1–2 Chronicles, the last book of the Hebrew canon.

In this essay I would like to briefly remark on three particular dimensions of David's presentation in the Hebrew Bible. First, the profile of David's kingship in Samuel–Kings is discussed, with some comparisons drawn between the vicissitudes of the king's career and the larger journey of the nation of Israel. If

---

1. Note the wide-ranging collection of essays in Raymond-Jean Frontain and Jan Wojcik, eds., *The David Myth in Western Literature* (West Lafayette, IN: Purdue University Press, 1980).

2. Erich Auerbach, *Mimesis: The Representation of Reality in Western Literature* (Princeton: Princeton University Press, 1953), 11–12.

we assume that the final version of Samuel–Kings is of exilic provenance, such comparisons become especially compelling. Second, David's configuration in the oft-neglected book of Chronicles is surveyed, since the picture of the king is radically different from that of the Former Prophets. Most scholars agree that Chronicles is composed during the postexilic period when God's people are rebuilding their broken world, and it could be that David is presented as an archetype of the repentant sinner with special relevance for the community in the shadow of the empire. Third, why is David so closely associated with the book of Psalms? In the third section of the essay several different theories are mentioned, including the organization of the Psalter and those specific super-scriptions that refer to an event in David's career. What are the best options for interpreting these Psalms (e.g., Psalm 34 and David's encounter in Gath), and what difference does it make for the reader? Altogether, these three por-traits—David as the Israelite whom God chastens through exile in the Former Prophets, the penitent sinner in Chronicles, and the leader of Israel's praise in Psalms—make an important contribution to the identity of God's people then and now.

David in the Deuteronomistic History:
The Travails of the Lord's Anointed

"The story of David," says Robert Alter in a recent commentary that illumi-nates David's complex portrait from a predominantly literary perspective, "is probably the greatest single narrative representation in antiquity of a human life evolving by slow stages through time, shaped and altered by the pressures of political life, public institutions, family, the impulses of body and spirit, the eventual sad decay of the flesh. It also provides the most unflinching insight into the cruel processes of history and into human behavior warped by the pursuit of power."[3] Indeed, when surveying the lineaments of David's career in the extraordinary narrative of Samuel–Kings, one may be hard-pressed to disagree with such an assessment in light of the narrative's radical highs and lows. From the moment of his formal introduction David becomes the dominant figure in the narrative, quickly eclipsing Saul and even the prophet Samuel himself as the central point of reference. It is vital for the reader to recognize, however, that David's anointing in 1 Samuel 16 follows a pattern familiar from Genesis: a preference for a younger son and the reversal of primogeniture. It would also

---

3. Robert Alter, *The David Story: A Translation with Commentary of 1 & 2 Samuel* (New York: Norton, 1999), ix.

37

appear that David's appointment as Israel's next king is a clandestine affair, making his arrival at Saul's court thick with irony in the second half of 1 Samuel 16: only he can soothe the king's heightening madness with his music. No doubt this is one of many reasons why David is labeled "the sweet psalmist" of Israel (2 Sam 23:1 KJV), and akin to Saul, the songs and lyrics of David are seen as a balm for those afflicted by the maddening world.

The famous victory over Goliath in 1 Samuel 17 can also be interpreted as a throwback to the era of the conquest, and a reminder to the nation of what the conquest *could have been* with audacious trust in God. It is no accident that Goliath himself is a hybrid figure: he hails from the traditional Anakite city of Gath—the old race of giants—and is also a Philistine of Greek ancestry. In light of the threat that Hellenism poses for emerging Judaism in the postexilic era, David's conquest over this ancient Achilles has multiple applications for the people of God. During David's long period as a fugitive in the wilderness (1 Sam 19–31) there are plethora of tests and challenges not unlike the Israelites in the desert between Sinai and the promised land. While there are ample instances of God's faithfulness during this prolonged era, when David is finally ensconced in Jerusalem his kingship appears secure. Perhaps the most astonishing moment occurs in 2 Samuel 7, when God articulates a promise about a lasting dynasty announced through Nathan the prophet: "When your days are fulfilled and you lie down with your ancestors, I will raise up your offspring after you, who shall come forth from your body, and I will establish his kingdom. . . . Your house and your kingdom shall be made sure forever before me; your throne shall be established forever" (vv. 12, 16). The only comparison for this promise is the earlier assurance to Abraham that through his offspring all the families of the earth would be blessed (Gen 12:1–3; 18:18), and to be sure, the promise to David must represent a corollary to or extension of that earlier articulation. David's reaction to God's startling word is to sit in obeisance in the second half of 2 Samuel 7, but this promise will appear to be sorely tested before his career comes to an end.

While there are some questionable moments earlier in David's life, countless interpreters nonetheless have observed that a drastic turning point for David occurs in 2 Samuel 11–12. In an intense and densely packed sequence, the king's adulterous liaison with Bathsheba rapidly spirals out of control, first with an attempted cover-up and later with the murder-by-proxy of Uriah the Hittite.[4] The arrival of Nathan the prophet—the same prophet who earlier announced the promise of a lasting dynastic house—marks the day of judgment for the king: the promise is not abrogated, but there is an addendum, for out of David's

---

4. Note the classic treatment of this text by Meir Sternberg, *The Poetics of Biblical Narrative: Ideological Literature and the Drama of Reading* (Bloomington: Indiana University Press, 1985).

own house "evil" will arise against him (2 Sam 12:11), and from his house the sword will never depart (v. 10). Almost immediately the fulfillment of this grim utterance is set in motion, as the attack of his firstborn son Amnon on his sister Tamar is followed by Absalom's rebellion, and David's calamity reaches a dour climax as he vacates Jerusalem and marches into exile by preparing to cross the Jordan River. A poignant scene takes place in 2 Samuel 15:30 as David reaches the Mount of Olives: it is here that he learns of the treachery of Ahithophel—a leading member of his inner circle—and David prays that God would frustrate Ahithophel's counsel. Readers of Matthew's gospel will recognize some similarities, as in the vicinity of the Mount of Olives a later descendant of David is betrayed by an insider, and the treachery of Ahithophel has eerie parallels to Judas in that both hang themselves afterwards (2 Sam 17:23; Matt 27:5). Meanwhile, when Hushai the Arkite arrives it would seem that David's prayer is answered, as Hushai succeeds in frustrating the counsel of Ahithophel and the rebellion is doomed. Even though David survives the ordeal, he is deeply chastened and arguably never recovers; the promise of a lasting dynasty has been severely taxed, but it survives intact despite the king's catastrophes.

At this point a word is in order about the composition of the work, as the story of David is embedded within a larger corpus: the six-book collection of the Former Prophets or what is frequently referred to by scholars as the Deuteronomistic History. This coherent narrative in Joshua–2 Kings recounts Israel's story from entrance to exile, that is, from the conquest of Canaan in Joshua to the collapse of the nation at the end of 2 Kings: "It is called the Deuteronomistic History because scholars have recognized how much it has in common—theologically and linguistically—with the unique and last of the Five Books of Moses, the book of Deuteronomy."[5] The voice of Moses in Deuteronomy, one recalls, exhorts the people of Israel to live faithfully in the land of their inheritance or risk expulsion and displacement. Compiled at some point during the exilic period, the long narrative of Joshua–2 Kings diagnoses the problem—the unfaithfulness of Israel—but also adumbrates that God has not given up. The great promise to David about a lasting dynasty increasingly is interpreted in terms of messianic rather institutional kingship during the exile and beyond.[6] For those members of the community who are acquainted with the crisis of Jerusalem's destruction, they surely would recognize that the long story of David's journey has many resonances with their own: in other words,

5. Israel Finkelstein and Neil Asher Silberman, *David and Solomon: In Search of the Bible's Sacred Kings and the Roots of the Western Tradition* (New York: Free Press, 2006), 13. Cf. Martin Noth, *The Deuteronomistic History*, JSOTSup 15 (1943; Sheffield: JSOT Press, 1981).

6. Note the study of William M. Schniedewind, *Society and the Promise to David: The Reception History of 2 Samuel 7:1-17* (New York: Oxford University Press, 1999).

the election of David, his "conquest" of Goliath, kingship over Israel, exile due to his own covenant unfaithfulness, and chastened return *resemble Israel's national journey.* The very name "David," after all, means *beloved*, and in the context of the Deuteronomistic History the name is typologically configured to illustrate that God is faithful to the ancestral promise and will be faithful to Israel notwithstanding their self-inflicted disaster.

David and the Chronicler: The King as the Repentant Sinner

One of the reasons that 1–2 Chronicles has not fared well among Christian readers is because of the canonical location. Since the Christian Bible follows the ordering of the Septuagint tradition, Chronicles immediately follows 1–2 Kings, to which it has been compared as a "poorer cousin" because of the seeming avoidance of any scandalous material and a fondness for long lists and interminable genealogies. Such antipathy is perhaps best epitomized by Julius Wellhausen in his influential *Prolegomena*: "See what Chronicles has made out of David! The founder of the kingdom has become the founder of the temple and the public worship, the king and hero at the head of his companions in arms has become the singer and master of ceremonies at the head of a swarm of priests and Levites; his clear cut figure has become a feeble holy picture, seen through a cloud of incense."[7] Despite the dismissive posture of Wellhausen and those who followed in his wake, in recent days Chronicles has been reevaluated much more positively for its literary, historical, and theological richness. Appreciating its place in the Hebrew canon—where in fact Chronicles is located at the very end, constituting the last words of the Masoretic Text—and its position in the Writings of the Hebrew Bible, a different approach is increasingly advocated by leading scholars. To be sure, strange things happen in the world of Chronicles that standard modes of interpretation are ill equipped to handle. For instance, the height of the temple vestibule in 2 Chronicles 3:4 is four times higher than in 1 Kings 6:2, and despite the NIV's efforts to reduce the structure ("twenty cubits high"), the point remains that the temple is the architectural focal point of the Chronicler's narrative.[8] Furthermore, in 2 Chronicles 21:12–15 there is a

---

7. Julius Wellhausen, *Prolegomena to the History of Israel*, trans. J. S. Black and A. Menzies (Edinburgh: Black, 1885), 182, cited in Mark J. Boda, "Gazing through the Cloud of Incense: Davidic Dynasty and Temple Community in the Chronicler's Perspective," in *Chronicling the Chronicler: The Book of Chronicles and Early Second Temple Historiography*, ed. Tyler F. Williams and Paul S. Evans (Winona Lake, IN: Eisenbrauns, 2013), 215–45, at 215.

8. See John Jarick, "The Temple of David in the Book of Chronicles," in *Temple and Worship in Ancient Israel*, ed. John Day, LHBOTS 422 (London and New York: T&T Clark, 2005), 365–81.

remarkable letter from the prophet Elijah perhaps twenty or more years *after* his fiery departure in a heavenly chariot, a letter that surprises the reader as it must have surprised King Jehoram who receives it. Even more unexpected is the repentance of Manasseh—arguably the vilest of Judah's kings—in 2 Chronicles 33, who turns aside from his idolatrous enterprises and repairs the temple in Jerusalem.[9]

Along the same lines, David himself is uniquely profiled in 1 Chronicles, and despite the more positive characterization, the king is configured as the archetypal repentant sinner. Readers have long noticed some startling omissions in the story when compared with the Deuteronomistic History: there is no protracted civil war with the house of Saul, the debacle with Bathsheba and Uriah's murder is essentially elided, and instead of the deadly succession struggle between Adonijah and Solomon there is a smooth and bloodless transition set in motion as early as 1 Chronicles 22:5. If David is essentially an absent father in 2 Samuel, he is a sage guide and mentor in Chronicles. Rather than extensive attention on the sphere of human machination, other aspects of David's reign and legacy are highlighted, and there is a concentrated focus on matters relating to the temple or Israel's worship in keeping with the theme of Chronicles as essentially a biography of the temple. David emerges from the text as the leader of the nation's chorus of praise and founding father of the temple's schematics. Most commentators assume that Chronicles is composed during the postexilic period, suggesting that "the Chronicler was at work somewhere between 425 and 250 BC, writing to a community of Jews who needed to return to Jerusalem to the reconstructed Temple and to participate in its worship as they awaited the full realization of the restoration of the kingdom of David."[10] Exactly how this kingdom was anticipated as taking shape has been the subject of vigorous debate, but need not overly detain us here; the more pressing point is that the Chronicler consistently portrays the people of God as "successful" when they rally round the Davidic king and are united in worship, in keeping with the expansive vision of the community as heirs of great promise.

As one comparative example, consider the Chronicler's treatment of the conquest of Jerusalem. The parallel text in 2 Samuel 5:6 reads, "The king and his men marched to Jerusalem against the Jebusites, the inhabitants of the land," whereas in 1 Chronicles 11:4 we read, "David and all Israel marched to Jerusa-

9. Note the studies of John C. Endres, "The Spiritual Vision of Chronicles: Wholehearted, Joy-filled Worship of God," *CBQ* 69 (2007): 1–21; Philippe Abadie, "From the Impious Manasseh (2 Kings 21) to the Convert Manasseh (2 Chronicles 33): Theological Rewriting by the Chronicler," in *The Chronicler as Theologian: Essays in Honor of Ralph W. Klein*, ed. M. P. Graham, S. L. McKenzie, and G. N. Knoppers, JSOTSup 371 (London: T&T Clark, 2003), 89–104.

10. Mark J. Boda, *1–2 Chronicles*, CBC 5a (Carol Stream, IL: Tyndale House, 2010), 8.

lem, that is Jebus, where the Jebusites were, the inhabitants of the land." The reader straightaway observes that the capturing of Jerusalem—the urban center of the story for the rest of the Chronicler's narrative—is a corporate undertaking of considerable proportion. In 2 Samuel 5:6 it is the king *and his men* who march against the city, meaning David and his personal militia (a group of figures presumably from Judah who are distressed and in debt, according to 1 Sam 22:2). By contrast, in Chronicles it is a unified and national effort involving all the tribes, and not only Judah. Moreover, this collective takeover of Jerusalem is David's first action as king in Chronicles, and it is much less the acquisition of a personal throne and more the procurement of a national capital.[11] The value of this kind of comparison is that the major emphases of the Chronicler can be discerned, not least the expansive vision of the identity of God's people. In addition to the conquest of Jerusalem, one could also compare the Chronicler's "ark narrative" in 1 Chronicles 13–16, much longer than its parallel text in 2 Samuel 6, with a heightened emphasis on the king's involvement highlighting his personal energy and empowerment of the Levites during the installation of the ark of the covenant in the newly conquered capital city of Jerusalem.[12] It should be stressed that in 1 Chronicles 13–16 the king is not pictured as usurping a priestly role, but rather as taking the lead in laying the foundations for national worship, and as we will see, the king also takes the lead in repentance when events take a disastrous turn.

While it is true that David's catastrophic failings of 2 Samuel 11 are not given much detail in Chronicles, the "census narrative" certainly appears to be afforded a central position in 1 Chronicles 21 with a number of variations from its parallel in 2 Samuel 24. Indeed, in the context of David's career in Samuel–Kings the census narrative is attached as part of an appendix to David's reign, whereas the Chronicler includes it as a central episode in the story. A striking feature in the opening verse of 1 Chronicles 21 is the presence of "Satan" (שָׂטָן)—variously interpreted as a human or spiritual adversary—as David is incited to "count" Israel, and this military census brings great wrath on the na-

---

11. Steven L. McKenzie, *1–2 Chronicles*, Abingdon Old Testament Commentaries (Nashville: Abingdon, 2004), 124. There may also be a further contrast with Saul's aborted kingship in this episode: in 1 Chr 10:7 the Philistines (first mentioned in 1 Chr 1:12 as a potentially dangerous group) occupy Israelite cities vacated in the wake of Saul's death, but now David occupies the city of the dislodged Jebusites, also mentioned among the nations of 1 Chr 1:14 (see John Jarick, *1 Chronicles*, Readings [London: Sheffield Academic Press, 2002], 86). Consequently, David's kingship is presented as the paradigm in the Chronicler's narrative.

12. For a comprehensive study, see Robert Rezetko, *Source and Revision in the Narratives of David's Transfer of the Ark: Text, Language, and Story in 2 Samuel 6 and 1 Chronicles 13, 15–16*, LHBOTS 470 (New York/London: T&T Clark, 2007).

tion. Throughout Chronicles, as in Samuel–Kings, the conduct of the monarch is not regarded as isolated or personal, but has national implications, and here David's focus on Israel's military strength rather than God's power results in the punitive measure of a divine striking.[13] As the lesser of three evils, David chooses a plague as punishment, yet the plague is dramatically stopped in 1 Chr 21:15–17), eliciting a radical confession from the king:

> God sent his angel to Jerusalem in order to destroy it. When he was destroying, the LORD saw, and repented concerning the evil, and said to the agent, "Enough! Now, relax your hand!" The angel of the LORD was standing at the threshing floor of Ornan the Jebusite. Then David lifted up his eyes, and saw the angel of the LORD standing between heaven and earth, with his drawn sword in his hand, stretched out toward Jerusalem. David and the elders fell—covered with sackcloth—upon their faces. David said to God, "Didn't *I* order that the people be counted? *I* am the one who sinned, and acted with exceeding evil—but these ones are sheep! What have they done? O LORD my God, please let your hand be against me and my father's house, but against your people may there not be a plague!"

The remainder of 1 Chronicles 21 is about the purchase and establishment of the threshing floor as an altar, culminating (v. 26) in divine fire sent as a sign of acceptance, prompting David to exclaim: "This is the house of the LORD God, and this is the altar of burnt offering for Israel" (22:1). It would therefore be misleading to suggest that Chronicles presents merely a whitewash of David's character; rather, there are an extended study of what repentance looks like and a focus on the experience of *metanoia* in this narrative. As one leading scholar summarizes, "The stress on Davidic responsibility may be understood in the context of a larger movement characterized by wrongdoing, confession, intercession, renewed obedience, and divine blessing. The story of the census, plague, and establishment of a permanent altar underscores the highly positive consequences of David's ability to confront and manage his own failure."[14]

---

13. Of course, the same theology is poetically articulated in the Psalms; see J. Clinton McCann Jr., "The Shape and Shaping of the Psalter: Psalms in Their Literary Context," in *The Oxford Handbook of the Psalms*, ed. William P. Brown (New York: Oxford University Press, 2014), 350–62, at 352: "At first sight, Psalms 1 and 2 seem completely unrelated. But because the earthly king was the human figure entrusted with the enactment of God's justice in the world (see Psalm 72), it makes sense that the king becomes the focus of attention in Psalm 2, a royal psalm. In any case, the effect of the juxtaposition of Psalms 1 and 2 is to highlight and hold together the two key concepts of *tôrâ* and kingship."

14. Gary N. Knoppers, "Images of David in Early Judaism: David as Repentant Sinner in

David's career in Chronicles, it could be argued, is typologically configured to provide a portrait of the king as exemplar of a repentant sinner, because in "the context of a national disaster of his own making, David is able to turn that catastrophe into the occasion for a permanent divine blessing upon Israel."[15] Not only is David sorry in 1 Chronicles 21, but proves his sorrow with his deeds, and pays *twelve times more with gold instead of silver* for the threshing-floor than in the Deuteronomistic History: 50 shekels of silver in 2 Samuel 24:24 compared to 600 shekels of gold in 1 Chronicles 21:25. The payment in gold anticipates the extensive use of gold in the temple and its ubiquity in Jerusalem (see 2 Chr 1:15) during the reign of Solomon, and commentators often point to Rashi's interpretation of six hundred as "twelve times fifty," stressing the inclusive ideology of the temple for each member of every tribe of Israel.[16] David himself later underwrites the construction of the temple with perhaps the largest individual donation in Israelite history (1 Chr 29:1–5), further drawing attention to the centrality of the place of atonement. Again in contrast to 1 Kings, Solomon is well-equipped and mentored for the task of building the temple, and this is probably why there is no record of his apostasy in Chronicles, further adding to the profile of David as a repentant sinner who invests in the next generation rather than obsessing about his own comfort and self-interest. Consequently, there are grounds for suggesting that 1–2 Chronicles provides a template for the postexilic community—a story from the past that unfolds their identity in the present—and likewise speaks into our own cultural context today:

> Chronicles is more than just a record of the past. It is filled with theological potential for the church today, a church living in what is often described as a post-Christendom era in which the church has been pushed from its place of cultural privilege to the private margins of society. In this way the church today resonates with a community struggling to cope with life at these margins and can leverage not only the theology of the early church who saw themselves as aliens and strangers but also that of a book like Chronicles. Through this book the Chronicler speaks to those searching for identity as the people of God in an age when the surrounding culture (empire) dominated their lives so profoundly. Chronicles identifies key spiritual rhythms for individual and community living in this context, whether the call to revival and renewal through repentance, the invitation to make prayer a pri-

---

Chronicles," *Biblica* 76 (1995): 454. Knoppers further notes: "David's unequivocal admission of guilt, his mediation on behalf of Israel, his diligent observance of divine instructions, and his securing a site for the future temple contribute positively to his legacy" (ibid.).

15. Knoppers, "Images of David in Early Judaism," 469.

16. H. G. M. Williamson, *1 and 2 Chronicles*, NCBC (Grand Rapids: Eerdmans, 1982), 150.

ority in their lives and communities, or the provision of a robust theology of worship—outlining David's innovations in verbal worship alongside the enduring Mosaic tradition of sacrifice.[17]

Overall, the Chronicler's subtle and sophisticated portrait of David as *the representative of God's people and a figure of their identity* draws attention to the reality of continuing divine faithfulness in accordance with the great ancestral promises. In fact, it is later disclosed that the threshing-floor purchased by David is actually located on Mount Moriah (2 Chr 3:1), where Abraham's daring obedience—when "the sacrifice of Isaac was to have taken place and was averted only at the last moment by the substitutionary offering of a ram"—results in a reaffirmation of God's commitment to multiply his descendants and a reiteration that through his offspring all nations of the earth will be blessed (Gen 22:18).[18] Only in Chronicles is this connection between the threshing-floor and Mount Moriah recorded, and it merges the experience of Abraham with David's recognition of the need for atonement for himself and all Israel: "Thus, here on the mountain of Moriah when Abraham's latest descendent, David, was about to bring the angel of destruction on his people, God himself interposed to save the remnant (1 Chr 21:14–15). The Temple marks the spot where the new substitutionary rites of atonement take place and will continue to take place."[19] The Chronicler's extended portrait of David's repentance and the legacy of atonement for God's people accords with the larger profile of the king in the book of Psalms, to which we will now turn in the third section of this essay.

King David in the Psalms: The Representative of Israel

The longest and arguably most complex book of the Bible, the compositional history of the book of Psalms perhaps extends over a one-thousand-year period with potentially dozens of contributors along the way. The Hebrew collection includes 150 prayers and poems for a host of public occasions and private exigencies, and altogether exhibits a stunning diversity of historical memories and theological probing. The first two psalms in the collection ostensibly serve to introduce the Psalter as a whole and acquaint the reader with central ideas such as walking in the way of the Torah and the kingship of God over and against the

17. Boda, *1–2 Chronicles*, 19.

18. William Johnstone, *1 and 2 Chronicles*, vol. 1, *1 Chronicles 1–2 Chronicles 9: Israel's Place among the Nations*, JSOTSup 253 (Sheffield: Sheffield Academic Press, 1997), 316.

19. Johnstone, *1 and 2 Chronicles*, 1:316.

nations.[20] The final two psalms likewise bring a sense of crescendo to the entire collection with a reminder of ultimate futility of overconfidence of foreign nations and an invitation to corporate praise.[21] Among other things, in between are a host of prayers and meditations on the character of God and the formation of human identity. In his magisterial study of the modern identity *Sources of the Self*, Charles Taylor poignantly diagnoses "the unique combination of greatness and danger, of *grandeur et misère*, which characterizes the modern age."[22] During his appraisal of rationalized Christian belief represented by a thinker such as John Locke, Taylor remarks: "if one starts from a vision of humans as potentially rational but with an inherent penchant for irrationality and evil, doomed on their own resources even to frustrate their own best potentiality, one can see that their condition cried out for a God who would pull them beyond it."[23] This sentence embedded within Taylor's lengthy argument captures an experience that can be perceived in many of the Psalms, as the tension between human possibility and orientation towards God's grandeur is countered by the frequent laments of failure and suffering. In the third section of this essay I would like to offer a few remarks on the configuration of human identity in the book of Psalms through the lens of the figure of David, and suggest that it unfolds some powerful and creative resources for reflecting on human personhood in our contemporary era. By way of summary, consider William Brown's reflection on the complex matter of human identity in the Psalms:

> Because most of the Psalter is cast as human speech embedded within a variety of settings, the question "What does it mean to be human?" is an appropriate one to pose. Or, put more generally, how is the self constructed in the Psalms? Invariably, the psalmist casts the question theologically: "What are human beings that you are mindful of them, mortals that you care for

---

20. Patrick D. Miller, "The Beginning of the Psalter," in *The Shape and Shaping of the Psalter*, ed. J. Clinton McCann, JSOTSup 159 (Sheffield: JSOT Press, 1993), 83–92; note also Robert Cole, "An Integrated Reading of Psalms 1 and 2," *Journal for the Study of the Old Testament* 98 (2002): 75–88.

21. Derek E. Wittman, "Let Us Cast Off Their Ropes from Us: The Editorial Significance of the Portrayal of Foreign Nations in Psalms 2 and 149," in *The Shape and Shaping of the Book of Psalms: The Current State of Scholarship*, ed. Nancy L. deClaissé-Walford, Ancient Israel and Its Literature 20 (Atlanta: SBL Press, 2014), 53–70.

22. Charles Taylor, *Sources of the Self: The Making of the Modern Identity* (Cambridge: Harvard University Press, 1989), 241.

23. Taylor, *Sources of the Self*, 241. As one contemporary writer puts it, "The world we inhabit today also teeters between becoming either the lovely garden or the barren desert that our contrary impulses strive to bring about" (David Zweig, *Invisibles: The Power of Anonymous Work in an Age of Relentless Self-Promotion* [New York: Penguin, 2014]).

them?" (8:5[4]). The answer in Psalm 8 lies in God's creating humankind "a little lower" than the divine realm, "crowned with glory and honor" (v. 6[5]). Profiled in royal terminology, human beings are invested with God-given dignity and power, with the earth as their charge (cf. 115:16; Gen 1:27–28). . . . The question of human identity in Psalm 8, however, is repeated in variant form in Ps 144:3, and the answer given could not be more different: human beings "are like a breath; their days are like a passing shadow" (v. 4). Psalmic testimony of the human condition, thus, covers the extremes: human beings are both powerful and fragile, filled with dignity and fraught with affliction. They are at once endowed with nearly divine capacities and beset with profound debilitations.[24]

A number of theories have been proffered as to the organization of the book of Psalms, which in its final form has a five-book structure that says something about how the collection was *viewed* and *used* in Israel's life of worship. There is certainly no consensus among scholars, but Nancy deClaissé-Walford contends that a guiding metanarrative in the book of Psalms can be discerned: "An overview of the story of the Psalter is as follows: It begins in Book I with the story of the reign of King David. Solomon's reign is recounted in Book II. Book III tells the story of the divided kingdoms and their eventual destructions by the Assyrians and the Babylonians. Book IV relates the struggle of the exiles in Babylon to find identity and meaning in a world of changed circumstances. Book V celebrates the return to Jerusalem and the establishment of a new Israel with God as sovereign."[25] If one allows that the basic shape of the Psalter is akin to the story of Israel from land and promise to exile and restoration, then by extension it might be possible to suggest that the metanarrative of the book of Psalms also bears a resemblance to the lineaments of David's own career from a position of security and settlement to the uncertainty of warfare and displacement. Even apart from the Psalms David is by far the most prominent poet amongst Israel's royal personages, as

---

24. William P. Brown, "The Psalms: An Overview," *Oxford Handbook of The Psalms*, 1–23, at 19. Brown also notes, "In the Psalms, Calvin saw quite vividly the struggle between 'flesh manifesting its infirmity' and 'faith putting forth its power'" (11).

25. Nancy L. deClaissé-Walford, "The Meta-Narrative of the Psalter," in *Oxford Handbook of The Psalms*, 363–76, at 368. Book I of the Psalter includes Psalms 1–41, and deClaissé-Walford's later summary includes the book divisions: "Books I and II (1–72) chronicle the reigns of Kings David and Solomon. Book III (73–89) tells of the dark days of the divided kingdoms and their eventual destructions. Book IV (90–106) recalls the Babylonian exile during which the Israelites had to rethink their identity as the people of God. Finally, Book V (107–50) celebrates the community's restoration to the land and the sovereignty of God over them" (374).

his sonorous eulogy for Saul and Jonathan (2 Sam 1:17–27) and purported last words in 2 Samuel 23:1–7 variously testify.

Moreover, his prayer in 2 Samuel 7:18–29 is the longest by a sitting king, and as we have already discussed, David is prominently associated with the Jerusalem temple from its inception. So, there are a host of compelling reasons why David should be closely identified with the Psalms, but for our purposes another reason is that the life of David mirrors the life of Israel: as the representative of God's people, through David's life the community is invited to corporate repentance and is provided with a template for viewing themselves in a host of different circumstances. I would like to briefly explore this notion by means of a psalm with a superscription relating to an episode in David's career, although as we will see, it has been considered problematic by many.

Psalm 34

Several categories of superscriptions can be found in the psalms, ranging from liturgical instructions that seem to indicate a musical notation, to the identification of a psalm with a historical figure such as Moses or Solomon, to the association of a particular psalm with some event in the life of David. Scholars generally conclude that such annotations are later additions—and there is ample scribal evidence to support such a contention—but there nevertheless is considerable value in appreciating how the psalm may have been used or interpreted according to the superscription. In the latter category—those psalms that are linked to an event in David's life—it can be tricky to connect the setting in the Deuteronomistic History with the words of the poetry.

Take Psalm 3 as an example, the first to occur with such a superscription: "A Psalm of David, when he fled from Absalom his son." To be sure, there are some linguistic affinities between the Psalm and the material of 2 Samuel 15–19 where David flees from Absalom and his troops, but otherwise the linkage is not obvious. Clinton McCann offers a helpful overview: "The superscription assigns the psalm to David and specifies a setting (see 2 Sam 15–18). This should not be taken as a historically accurate remembrance, but some scholars do conclude from the superscription that the person praying was a king and that Psalm 3 is a royal psalm. The juxtaposition with Psalm 2 and the shared phrase 'holy hill' (2:6; 3:4) may provide support for this conclusion; however, it is by no means necessary, nor is it the majority view."[26] So what is the purpose of the

---

26. J. Clinton McCann Jr., "The Book of Psalms: Introduction, Commentary, and Reflections," in *The New Interpreter's Bible* (Nashville: Abingdon, 1996), 4:639–1280, at 694.

superscription? In this horrendous episode in David's life the worshipping community is invited to pray the text from the king's perspective, and even though the disaster is primarily of David's own making, to believe that God remains actively involved in the lives of his anointed ones. McCann reviews the central events of Absalom's rebellion, including the rape of Tamar and the engulfing of the nation in civil war, and concludes: "The whole sorry situation is illustrative of the messy situations we regularly experience—violence, turmoil, rebellion, threats to job and even to life itself. Following Psalms 1–2, Psalm 3 proclaims that 'happiness'/'blessedness' consists of the good news that God's help (v. 8) is forthcoming precisely in the midst of such threats in order to make life possible (vv. 3–4) and to offer us a peace (v. 5) that the world says is not possible (v. 2)."[27] The superscription provides a new perspective on both the life of David and the context of the community as they are invited to recognize their own lives in terms of David's travails.

Consider now the acrostic Psalm 34 in the NRSV rendering:

Of David, when he feigned madness before Abimelech,
so that he drove him out, and he went away.

1 I will bless the LORD at all times; his praise shall continually be in my mouth.
2 My soul makes its boast in the LORD; let the humble hear and be glad.
3 O magnify the LORD with me, and let us exalt his name together.
4 I sought the LORD, and he answered me, and delivered me from all my fears.
5 Look to him, and be radiant; so your faces shall never be ashamed.
6 This poor soul cried, and was heard by the LORD, and was saved from every trouble.
7 The angel of the LORD encamps around those who fear him, and delivers them.
8 O taste and see that the LORD is good; happy are those who take refuge in him.
9 O fear the LORD, you his holy ones, for those who fear him have no want.
10 The young lions suffer want and hunger, but those who seek the LORD lack no good thing.
11 Come, O children, listen to me; I will teach you the fear of the LORD.
12 Which of you desires life, and covets many days to enjoy good?
13 Keep your tongue from evil, and your lips from speaking deceit.

27. McCann, "The Book of Psalms," 4:694.

14 Depart from evil, and do good; seek peace, and pursue it.

15 The eyes of the LORD are on the righteous, and his ears are open to their cry.

16 The face of the LORD is against evildoers, to cut off the remembrance of them from the earth.

17 When the righteous cry for help, the LORD hears, and rescues them from all their troubles.

18 The LORD is near to the brokenhearted, and saves the crushed in spirit.

19 Many are the afflictions of the righteous, but the LORD rescues them from them all.

20 He keeps all their bones; not one of them will be broken.

21 Evil brings death to the wicked, and those who hate the righteous will be condemned.

22 The LORD redeems the life of his servants; none of those who take refuge in him will be condemned.

There are long-standing difficulties with the superscription of Psalm 34 because of the Philistine king who is identified. The context of David's predicament, one recalls, is at the outset of his lengthy period as a fugitive from the court of the rather manic Saul, introducing an immediate irony, as David feigns madness to survive in a foreign land while Saul is incrementally descending into genuine madness:

> David arose and on that day he fled from the presence of Saul, and came to Achish king of Gath. Achish's servants said to him, "Isn't this David, king of the land? Isn't he the one they sing to each other about in their dances, saying, 'Saul has struck his thousands, David his ten thousands?' So David took these words to heart, and he was very afraid in the presence of Achish king of Gath. And he altered his behavior [lit. "changed his taste"] before their eyes, and while he was in their hand he acted like a lunatic. He began scratching the doors of the gate, and spittle ran down his beard. (1 Sam 21:10–13)

The problem with the superscription, as any sensible undergraduate student could readily observe, is that *Achish* is the king that one expects to be mentioned, not Abimelech. The latter is a Philistine king, but prominent in the stories of Abraham and Isaac in the book of Genesis, centuries before the flight of David in 1 Samuel. There is no shortage among commentators of identifying the problem nor of offering possible solutions. Willem Prinsloo remarks, "This is probably a reference to the incident described in 1 Sam 21:10–15 where David feigned madness before Achish—not Abimelech, as in Psalm 34—the Philistine king. The difference between 1 Samuel 21 and Psalm 34 can be due to a scribal error or it can be that Abimelech is a general name for Philistine kings just as Pharaoh is for Egyptian kings."[28] Prinsloo goes on to suggest that the title is a later addition, and even though he says that the psalm bears little relation to David's adventure, an editor noticed an association between some miraculous escapes and this psalm where God is portrayed as responding and rescuing those who cry for help. C. S. Rodd similarly comments, "The heading presents problems. If the reference to the incident in David's life recorded in 1 Sam 21:10–15 was added by a later editor it is odd that the name of the Philistine king is given as Abimelech and not Achish. Attempts at an explanation include the unlikely suggestions that Abimelech was the dynastic name, a royal title, or the Semitic name for Achish. The error is surely too blatant to be a simple scribal error, though it is surprising that it was not corrected later."[29] Rodd further remarks that the psalm's content has only an oblique connection with the 1 Samuel incident, the most notable being the strange verb "taste" used in two quite different ways: David changes his taste—that is, feigns madness—whereas the psalmist invites the hearers to "taste" and see that the LORD is good.

Despite these verdicts, there are alternative ways of interpreting the superscription. For instance, rather than a scribal blunder, Vivian Johnson believes that an editor intentionally substituted the name of an earlier Philistine potentate: "That the author of the superscriptions proffers the name of a Philistine Abimelech instead of Achish prompts associations with stories in which Abimelech appears. Patriarchal encounters with Abimelech found in the stories of Genesis make the aspect of 'fear' more prominent in all of the stories. The psalm too places emphasis on the idea of fear, but proclaims that the only thing one has to do is fear God."[30] On this level, the psalm takes on a striking immediacy with its stress on fear, the ubiquity of deceit, trust in God evidently away from the land, and imparting wisdom to the next generation. Along parallel lines, John Goldingay reflects on the superscription as a much more integral component for the interpreter:

> The heading links the psalm with an occasion when David had fled from Saul and taken refuge with a Philistine king, but then came to be afraid of that king. . . . Fear is a rare experience for David, who normally is surrounded

28. Willem S. Prinsloo, "The Psalms," in *Eerdmans Commentary on the Bible*, ed. James D. G. Dunn and John W. Rogerson (Grand Rapids: Eerdmans, 2003), 364–436, at 386.
29. C. S. Rodd, "Psalms," in *The Oxford Bible Commentary*, ed. John Barton and John Muddiman (Oxford: Oxford University Press, 2001), 355–405, at 377.
30. Vivian L. Johnson, *David in Distress: His Portrait through the Historical Psalms*, LHBOTS 505 (London: T&T Clark, 2009), 76.

by others' fear and is a cause of it. In 1 Samuel the king is Achish of Gath, but introducing the name of Abimelech, king of Gerar, in the psalm reinforces the point, since he was an earlier Philistine king whom Abraham and Isaac attempted to deceive because of their fear (the fear is more explicit in the Isaac story) (Gen 20; 26). Readers are thus encouraged to imagine how Abraham, Isaac, or David might have conquered fear by learning the lesson of this psalm, and/or how they might do something different with their fear. The psalm puts great emphasis on fear/reverence in relation to Yhwh, and sees this as the key to deliverance in the kind of danger Abraham, Isaac, or David were in.[31]

As noted in our discussion of Chronicles above, the postexilic community was threatened by Greek culture arguably as much as David's generation was threatened by the (Greek) Philistines, so there is a vast amount of material in this psalm that would be of immediate relevance, not least the fear of God in the midst of worldly power struggles and the contest for communal identity. As Peter Craigie comments, "The fear of the Lord establishes joy and fulfillment in all of life's experiences. It may mend the broken heart, but it does not prevent the heart from being broken; it may restore the spiritually crushed, but it does not crush the forces that may create oppression. The psalm, if fully grasped, dispels the naiveté of that faith which does not contain within it the strength to stand against the onslaught of evil."[32] In Christian tradition Psalm 34 has also been used in the context of celebrating the Eucharist, and verses such as "taste and see" along with "The LORD redeems the life of his servants" take on a certain urgency.[33] These are just a few thoughts on a very rich psalm, but they

31. John Goldingay, *Psalms*, vol. 1, *Psalms 1–41*, Baker Commentary on the Old Testament Wisdom Psalms (Grand Rapids: Baker, 2006), 477–78. When this interpretative approach is considered, even the enigmatic term *taste* can be revisited, since it forms an intriguing wordplay. Goldingay further notes, "A more precise parallel with the David story, which apparently suggested the link, lies in the expression 'disguised his good sense' (*ṭaʿam*), which comes in 1 Sam 21:13 [14] in connection with David's acting crazy. The psalm uses this unusual word in urging people to use their good sense (v. 8). It also commends praise (*tithallel*, v. 2) as an alternative to acting crazy (*wayyitholel*, 1 Sam 21:13 [14])" (478). Cf. Johnson, *David in Distress*, 75: "This word occurs in v. 3 of Ps 34 and in 1 Sam 21:14, albeit with different meanings. The Hitpael form of the word in the psalm means 'to rejoice proudly,' while in the Polel form in 1 Sam 21:14 it means 'to make into a fool.' Remarkably, this word directs the reader to the same verse in the narrative as does the psalm title. In 1 Sam 21:14 the text states that David pretended to be mad and then further explicates that 'he made himself as a fool.'" In light of the Eucharistic overtones stressed by later interpreters, the notion of foolishness in the eyes of the world takes on a new angle.

32. Cited in McCann, "The Book of Psalms," 4:815.

33. On the use in *The Orthodox Study Bible*, see Susan Gillingham, *Psalms through the Centu-*

do illustrate how the superscription's relating this psalm to David's experience provides an additional texture to the poem and provides a sense of how it has been used by the worshipping community.

Such thoughts could naturally be extended to other superscriptions, perhaps most famously to Psalm 51, "*A Psalm of David, when the prophet Nathan came to him, after he had gone in to Bathsheba.*"[34] In my view the configuration of David in the Psalms is a most fertile area for future research, and has much to contribute to our understanding of theological anthropology in the Psalter. Combined with David's portrait in the Deuteronomistic History and the books of Chronicles, David ("beloved") is the prototypical Israelite who represents the identity of God's people then and now.

ries, vol. 1, Blackwell Bible Commentary Series (Oxford: Blackwell, 2008), 252–53. Note also McCann, "The Book of Psalms," 815–16: "Psalm 34 is traditionally associated with the Lord's supper, primarily because of the word 'taste' in v. 8. In a sense, this connection is superficial; however, as a whole, Psalm 34 is appropriately associated with the Lord's Supper. The Lord's Supper celebrates God's gracious provision for life, which is the good news proclaimed by Psalm 34. The proper response is gratitude (vv. 1–3)—eucharist!"

34. Note the discussions of Gerald H. Wilson, *Psalms*, NIV Application Commentary (Grand Rapids: Zondervan, 2002); Bruce K. Waltke and James M. Houston, with Erika Moore, *The Psalms as Christian Worship: A Historical Commentary* (Grand Rapids: Eerdmans, 2010), 446–83.

Chapter 4

Jeremiah: How the Prophet Self-Identified

Bruce K. Waltke

Jeremiah was regarded as so great that some thought Jesus was Jeremiah redivivus (Matt 16:14). Hopefully, this essay on Jeremiah's self-identification as a particular kind of person will add substance to faith, ardor to virtue, confidence to confession, and will aid fidelity to the Lord in testing. The essay is organized according to the primary source material in the book of Jeremiah: its editorial superscript (1:1–3); Jeremiah's autobiographical accounts of his call to be a prophet (1:4–12) and of his commission to uproot or to plant nations (1:13–19); and other autobiography, especially his personal "confessions," in which he struggles with his difficult calling (11:18–12:6; 15:10–21; 17:14–18; 18:18–23; 20:7–18). The essay is drawn to conclusion with reflections on Jeremiah's self-understanding and the church.

The Superscript

The superscript alludes to three influences on Jeremiah's self-understanding: his origins, his historical context, and the word of the Lord that "came" to him. We will piggy-back on reflections on his origins with reflections on his friendship with scribes, and we will reflect on the word of the Lord in connection with Jeremiah's call and commission.

Jeremiah's Origins

Jeremiah was the "son of Hilkiah, one of the priests at Anathoth in the territory of Benjamin" (1:1), indicating that Jeremiah knew himself to be an Israelite and, more specifically, a priest.

Jeremiah identified himself with true Israel's faith in the LORD, Israel's covenant-keeping God. He boasted that he knows the LORD (9:23–24); his hope was in the LORD (17:13), not in man (17:5). Correlatively, he identified himself with the LORD's chosen people. He is known as the "weeping prophet" in part because he prophesied judgment on nominal Israel[1] for its covenant infidelity, through a veil of tears:

> Oh, my anguish, my anguish! I writhe in pain.
> For I have heard the sound of the trumpet; I have heard the battle cry. (4:19)

Together with the LORD he identified with his people's sufferings:

> Since my people are crushed, I am crushed. (8:21)

He prayed that God would avenge the wrong done to his people:

> Pour out your wrath on the nations that do not acknowledge you. . . ,
> for they have devoured Jacob . . . and destroyed his homeland. (10:25)

Paradoxically, he combined complaining of unjust treatment by friend and foe with interceding for them (cf. 7:16; 11:14; 14:11).

Finally, he identified himself with his people's sin:

> Our backsliding is great; we have sinned against you. (14:7)

Jeremiah also understood himself as belonging to a generation of Israelites under divine wrath. The LORD commanded him not to marry and have children, for the mothers and fathers of his times "will die of deadly diseases . . . ; they will perish by sword and famine, and their dead bodies will become food for the birds and the wild animals" (16:1–4).

As for his origins, Jeremiah also understood himself to be a priest. Anathoth, Jeremiah's hometown, was one of the cities given to the Levites. As a priest, Jeremiah had more opportunity than most to learn Israel's sacred history, and, since the LORD sanctified him in his mother's womb to be a prophet, we may assume that he confessed that history from his earliest awareness of it. Moreover, as an Anathite, our priest had ready access to the temple, its liturgies, and its psalms.

---

1. In this essay "Israel" may refer to both the Northern and Southern Kingdoms, or to either of them.

Let us reflect first upon his identification with Israel's sacred history. Memories of our past inform who we are, shape our self-understanding, and give us a vision of our destiny, and that vision or hope moves us forward, forging our will and determination. Jeremiah believed in the LORD as the Creator of heaven and earth. He described the ruin of the whole land in language with unmistakable echoes of the creation account in Genesis 1.

> I looked at the earth, and it was formless and empty; and at the heavens, and their light was gone. (4:23)

He echoed the Abrahamic covenant when he prophesied that all the nations will bless themselves in Israel, Abraham's offspring:

> If you, Israel, will . . . return to me, . . . and if in a truthful, just and righteous way . . . swear, "As surely as the LORD lives," then the nations will invoke blessings by him and in him they will boast. (4:1–2; cf. Gen 12:3; 28:14)

Our prophet said "Amen" to Israel's *magnalia Dei* in the forming of her into a nation:

> They did not ask, 'Where is the LORD, who brought us up out of Egypt
>   and led us through the barren wilderness . . . ?'
> I brought you into a fertile land to eat its fruit and rich produce. (2:6–7)

As for Jeremiah's hoped-for destiny, he linked the promises of the Noahic covenant with those of the Davidic and Abrahamic covenants:

> This is what the LORD says: "If you can break my covenant with the day and my covenant with the night, so that day and night no longer come at their appointed time, then my covenant with David my servant . . . can be broken. . . . I will make the descendants of David my servant . . . as countless as the stars in the sky and as measureless as the sand on the seashore." (33:20–22; cf. Gen 8:22; 2 Sam 7:28–29; Gen 22:17)

Jeremiah knew from the LORD's covenants with Abraham and David that ultimately God's people, when born again, would triumph over their enemies. The LORD would fulfill his purpose through those who survived the seventy years of exile that Jeremiah foretold (Jer 29:10). In days to come, he prophesied, the LORD will enact with Israel a new covenant, one based on forgiveness of sin and with the provision of giving her a new heart to keep God's covenant, and so assure her final victory (31:27–34).

Our priest by birth also had ready access to the temple inasmuch as Anathoth was only three miles north by east of Jerusalem. And so Jeremiah participated in Israel's liturgies: he petitioned, thanked, and praised God in the hymns that David, Asaph, and other inspired poets had composed, and these songs won their way into his spiritually sensitive heart and he embodied them.[2] His so-called confessions have the form of lament psalms in the Psalter.

Reflections on his origins also entail his friendship with scribes. Although seemingly cursed by everyone, he was befriended by some scribes. Scribes were an elite class in Israelite society. As a leisured class, they were well educated in reading and writing literature and in rhetoric.[3] Jeremiah also seems to have wealth—he owned property in Anathoth and was able to redeem his uncle's property (chap. 32). He was well educated: he wrote letters to the exiles in Babylon (chap. 29) and composed a Book of Consolation (30:1–3). His rhetoric is rarely matched. Indeed, he understood himself to be a poet and composed dirges for Josiah's death (2 Chr 35:25).

The scribal school of Shaphan befriended him. Ahikam son of Shaphan delivered him from enemies who were intent on killing him (Jer 26:24). Gemariah son of Shaphan and Micaiah son of Gemariah played important roles in Baruch's reading an early edition of Jeremiah's collected sermons to the people at the temple and to Jerusalem's officers (36:1–19). After the fall of Jerusalem, Nebuchadnezzar appointed Gedaliah son of Ahikam as governor over the remaining Judeans, and Jeremiah lived with him (40:1–6). The scribes Baruch and Seraiah, who were probably responsible, respectively, for the shorter Egyptian version of the book of Jeremiah and for its longer Babylonian version, were Jeremiah's disciples (36:32; 51:59–64). Also, it says something of Jeremiah's importance that he could enlist the cooperation of senior priests to witness his symbolic action (19:1) and that Zedekiah asked Jeremiah to pray for the nation (37:3).

Jeremiah, however, condemned scribes who falsified the written law and thereby misled the deluded wise into thinking they had the Law of the LORD, when in fact they were rejecting the Law of the LORD (8:8–10).

2. William L. Holladay, "The Background of Jeremiah's Self-Understanding: Moses, Samuel and Psalm 22," *Journal of Biblical Literature* 83 (1964): 153–64.

3. Karel van der Toorn, *Scribal Culture and the Making of the Bible* (Cambridge: Harvard University Press, 2007), 104–8.

Jeremiah's Historical Context

Jeremiah knew he was genetically shaped to be a prophet; his historical context, spanning forty years (627 BC–587 BC), refined that self-understanding. He prophesied during a tumultuous time of political upheaval. Assyria's vassal states were declaring their independence, and Babylon was ascending to supremacy.

In 628 BC Josiah (640–609) asserted his independence from Assyria by reestablishing King David's religion, which was based on the Mosaic covenant (2 Chr 34:3–7). In 627 BC the word of the LORD first came to Jeremiah while he was still a youth (1:6, Hb. *na'ar*[4]). (In that same year Ashurbanipal, the last great king of Assyria, died, and in the following year Nabopolassar of Babylon defeated the Assyrian army outside the city of Babylon.) The LORD declared through his newly minted prophet that Josiah's reform was superficial:

Judah did not turn to me with all her heart, but only in pretense. (Jer 3:10)

Jeremiah prophesied that, unless Israel turned wholeheartedly to the LORD, the ascending kings of the northern kingdoms, which were led by Babylon, would "set their thrones in the entrance of the gates of Jerusalem" (1:13–16). From 627 to 605, "return" was the defining cause of Jeremiah's career. He prophesied:

This is what the LORD says: "Stand at the crossroads and look; ask for the ancient paths, ask where the good way is, and walk in it, and you will find rest for your souls." (6:16)

In 622, Hilkiah the high priest, while repairing the temple, found Moses's Book of the Law, which had been lost in the temple during the fifty-five years of Manasseh's apostate religion.[5] The discovery so profoundly affected Jeremiah that one could say that he spiritually devoured it. It can be heard in Jeremiah's cadence, his subjects and vocabulary,[6] and in his understanding that God

---

4. Describes infancy (Exod 2:6) and advanced adolescence (1 Sam 30:17).

5. For the credibility that the book of the Law of the LORD was found and not fraudulently composed, see Bruce K. Waltke, with Charles Yu, *An Old Testament Theology* (Grand Rapids: Zondervan, 2008), 736.

6. E.g., of love (2:25; Deut 6:5); of rain (3:3; Deut 11:11); of certificate of divorce (3:8; Deut 24:1–4); "evil you have done" (4:4; Deut 28:20); "eagle" (4:13; Deut 28:49); "whose language you

blesses his nominal people according to their obedience or disobedience to the covenant stipulations:

> The God of Israel says: "Cursed is the one who does not obey the terms of this covenant—the terms I commanded your ancestors when I brought them out of Egypt. . . ." I said, "Obey me and do everything I command you. . . . Then I will fulfill the oath I swore to your ancestors, to give them a land flowing with milk and honey—the land you possess today." I answered, "Amen, LORD." (11:2–5)

Holladay and Lundbom document that Jeremiah's oracles resonate with the Song of Moses (Deut 32). They also argue, albeit questionably, that Jeremiah referred to the Book of the Law when he said:

> When your words were found, I ate them; they were my joy and my heart's delight. (Jer 15:16)[7]

In 605, the fourth year of Jehoiakim (609–598 BC), the Babylonians decisively defeated the Egyptians at Carchemish, establishing Babylon as the new superpower of Jeremiah's world. In that same year the word of the LORD came to Jeremiah:

> Take a scroll and write on it all the words I have spoken to you concerning Israel, Judah and all the other nations from the time I began speaking to you in the reign of Josiah till now. Perhaps when the people of Judah hear about every disaster I plan to inflict on them, they will each turn from their wicked ways; then I will forgive their wickedness and their sin. (Jer 36:2–3)

But Jehoiakim, Nebuchadnezzar's puppet king, as he heard the word of God being read to him, cut up the scroll strip by strip and threw the pieces into the fire of the brazier burning before him (chap. 36).

The fate of Judah was now sealed, and Jeremiah's self-understanding changed from being a prophet of reform to a prophet of doom. Now Jeremiah prophesied that Nebuchadnezzar king of Babylon would triumphantly invade the holy land and that Israel's only hope to spare Jerusalem from being burned

---

do not know" (5:15; Deut 28:49); "fortified cities in which you trust" (5:17; Deut 28:52); "eyes that do not see" (5:21; Deut 29:4).

7. Jack R. Lundbom, *The Early Career of the Prophet Jeremiah* (Eugene, OR: Wipf & Stock, 2012), 59–64.

to the ground and to save their lives from death or exile was to surrender to the Babylonians. Some listened to him, but the spiritually deaf leaders of Jerusalem regarded him as a traitor and a collaborator with Babylon. They imprisoned Jeremiah in a dungeon for many days, and later put him in a cistern where Jeremiah sank in its muddy bottom. Ebed-Melek, an Ethiopian eunuch and high official, let down ropes and rescued him (chap. 38). Jeremiah's prophecy was fulfilled in the eleventh year of Zedekiah (598–587), "when the people went into exile" (1:2).

Jeremiah's Call and Commission

Jeremiah understood his ministry in the same way as political orators of ancient Greece understood theirs. Demosthenes (384–322 BC) says: "But for what is he [an orator] responsible? For discovering the trend of events at the outset, for forecasting results, and for warning others."[8] Is this not what Jeremiah did?

The Word of the LORD and the Words of Jeremiah

The superscript identifies the contents of the book of Jeremiah both as "the words of Jeremiah" (1:1)[9] and as "the word of the LORD" (v. 2). The word of the LORD (usually singular) refers to the supersensory message that came to him in visions and/or auditions. "Jeremiah's words" (usually plural) verbalized the message.[10] He did so under divine inspiration:

> Then the LORD reached out his hand and touched my mouth and said to me, "I have put my words in your mouth." (1:9)

These two notions—the message revealed to him and that he accepts, and the inspired words he speaks and that people usually reject—made him a "prophet," the mark that truly distinguished him from most people, and the reason the book of Jeremiah bears his name. Moreover, he understood himself as predestined to this calling, for the LORD said to him:

---

8. Charles S. Shaw, *The Speeches of Micah: A Rhetorical Historical Analysis*, JSOTSup 145 (Sheffield: Sheffield Academic Press, 1993), 21.

9. This identification forms a frame around the book: "the words of Jeremiah end here" (51:64).

10. So Andrew G. Shead, *A Mouth Full of Fire: The Word of God in the Words of Jeremiah*, New Studies in Biblical Theology 29 (Downers Grove, IL: InterVarsity Press, 2012), 41–64.

Before I formed you in the womb I knew you, before you were born I set you apart. (1:5)

The word of the LORD is the book of Jeremiah's active subject. It jettisoned Jeremiah from a rural priestly family in Anathoth into the political chaos of Jerusalem and determined where he went and what he did. The LORD declared to him:

"You must go to everyone I send you to and say whatever I command you." (1:7)

He was mute unless God spoke to him. Upon a time, Jeremiah had put a wooden yoke on his neck to symbolize the subjugation of Israel and the nations to the Babylonian king. But the false prophet Hananiah took the yoke off Jeremiah's neck and broke it. Amazingly, Jeremiah said nothing to defend himself; rather, presumably humiliated, "he went on his way." Then, at some later time, "the word of the LORD came to Jeremiah," and then, and only then, he prophesied that the yoke of wood would be replaced with a yoke of iron and that Hananiah would die that same year; as in fact he did (chaps. 27–28; cf. also 42:1–7).

He says he devoured the word of the LORD, "for I bear the name of the LORD Sabaoth"—that is to say, he identified himself as the LORD's property (15:16); he did not live doing his own will but doing only the will of God.

A mark that distinguished Jeremiah as a true, not false, prophet was that his prophecies came to pass (Deut 18:22). Upon a time, the LORD revealed to Jeremiah that his uncle Hanamel would come to him with the ridiculous request that Jeremiah redeem his property on which the Babylonian army was encamped![11] When it happened just as the LORD had said, Jeremiah "knew it was the word of the LORD" (32:8). Jeremiah did not think his words had magical power. Rather, he was confident that they would come to pass because the LORD watches over them to fulfill them (1:11–12).

The Vocabulary for the Word of the LORD

Andrew Shead documents that far more often than any other prophet Jeremiah punctuates his oracles with "declares the LORD" (*ne'um yhwh*)[12]—that is to say,

11. Jack R. Lundbom, *Jeremiah 21–36*, Anchor Bible (New York: Doubleday, 2004), 505.
12. Shead, *A Mouth Full of Fire*, 46.

he speaks in the divine spirit. Often Jeremiah introduces his prophecies with the messenger formula: "This is what the Lord says." That is to say, Jeremiah understood himself as having stood in the heavenly council with the Lord and his angels and was then sent to communicate what he had seen and heard to his earthly audience (cf. Isa 6:1–8). The Lord asks of the false prophets:

> But which of them has stood in the council of the Lord to see or to hear his word . . . ? If they had, they would have proclaimed my words to my people and would have turned them from their evil ways. (23:18, 22)

A Prophet to the Nations

The Lord predestined Jeremiah to be a prophet to the nations (1:5). When the Lord touched his mouth, he also said:

> See, today I appoint you over nations and kingdoms to uproot and tear down, to destroy and overthrow, to build and to plant. (1:10)

Since the word of the Lord is the active agent, Jeremiah rightly understood that his prophecies determined the destiny of nations; their destiny depended on their acceptance or rejection of the Lord and his covenant people.

The book of Jeremiah mentions "Lord Sabaoth" (i.e., the Lord of the armies of the nations) eighty-two times, more than any other Old Testament book.

A Prophet like Moses

More specifically, Jeremiah understood himself as a fulfillment of the Lord's promise to Israel that he would raise up a prophet like Moses (Deut 18:18a). Concerning that prophet the Lord promised:

> I will put my words in his mouth. He will tell them everything I command him. (18:18b)

Jeremiah's call narrative reprised this promise: the Lord said to Jeremiah: "I have put my words in your mouth" (Jer 1:9), and commanded him: "You must say whatever I command you" (1:7). Moreover, both Moses and Jeremiah instructed the people "on the way they should go," and "the thing/deeds they should do" (Exod 18:20; Jer 42:3).[13] As early as the time of the Qumran scrolls, Jeremiah was seen as a Mosaic figure.[14]

Jeremiah's Confessions

Jeremiah's laments, which protest his innocence, are called "confessions" because they are, like Augustine's *Confessions*, honest autobiography. When the Lord commissioned Jeremiah, he promised him:

> Today I have made you a fortified city . . . against the kings of Judah, its officials, its priests and the people of the land. They will fight against you but will not overcome you, for I am with you and will rescue you. (1:18–19)

His confessions wove that promise into the fabric of his character. We reflect only on the first and last confessions.

Jeremiah's first confession (11:18–12:4) occurs after Jeremiah learned from the Lord that his own relatives in Anathoth were plotting to kill him; he questioned God's justice, which is a basic tenet of Israel's faith: "Why," he asked, "does the way of the wicked prosper?" The Lord's answer: your suffering will only get worse!

> If you have raced with men on foot and they have worn you out, how can you compete with horses? (12:5)

Jeremiah identified himself as a prophet who must suffer for being faithful to his predestined calling.

Jeremiah's fifth confession (20:7–18) consists of a lament psalm (vv. 7–13)[15] and a cursing poem (vv. 14–18). His lament gives insight into his psyche. After

13. Wolfgang Oswald, "Jeremiah and Moses, A Comparison of Their Public Offices in Exod. 18:13–27 and Jer. 42:1–6," in *My Spirit at Rest in the North Country (Zechariah 6.8)*, ed. Matthias Augustin and Hermann Michael Niemann, BEATAJ 57 (Frankfurt/Main, 2011), 265–72.

14. G. J. Brooke, "The Book of Jeremiah and Its Reception in the Qumran Scrolls," in *The Book of Jeremiah and Its Reception*, ed. Curtis and Roemer, BETL 128 (Leuven: Leuven Press, 1997), 191. The similarity has been noticed by many since then: William L. Holladay, "Jeremiah and Moses: Further Observations," *Journal of Biblical Literature* 85 (1966): 17–27; Christopher R. Seitz, "The Prophet Moses and the Canonical Shape of Jeremiah," *ZAW* 110 (1989): 3–27; Lundbom, *Early Career of the Prophet Jeremiah*, 47.

15. Bruce K. Waltke and James M. Houston, *Psalms as Christian Lament* (Grand Rapids: Eerdmans, 2014), 187.

complaining that "the word of the Lord has brought me insults . . . all day long," he added:

> But if I say, "I will not mention his word or speak anymore in his name,"
> his word is in my heart like a fire, a fire shut up in my bones.
> I am weary of holding it in; indeed I cannot.

Nevertheless, he remained confident that he would be vindicated:

> But the Lord is with me like a mighty warrior; so my persecutors will stumble and not prevail.

Like the imprecatory psalms, and like his second, third, and fourth confessions (cf. 15:15; 17:18; 18:21–23), he prayed to be avenged:

> Let me see your vengeance on them, for to you I have committed my cause.

And so he called for praise:

> Sing to the Lord! . . .
> He rescues the life of the needy from the hands of the wicked.

The cursing poem returns him from the transcendent realm of faith to the grim reality of earth:

> "Cursed be the day I was born!
> Why did I ever come out of the womb to see trouble and sorrow and to
>   end my days in shame?"

Though Jeremiah never received an explanation for his battle-scars of being a prophet, he broke through the trouble and sorrow that accompanied his call into the transcendent reality of God's salvific presence. Kathleen O'Connor adds: "Such is the testimony of Augustine in his *Confessions*, Theresa of Avila, John of the Cross, Martin Luther, Thomas Merton."[16]

---

16. Kathleen M. O'Connor, *The Confessions of Jeremiah: Their Interpretation and Role in Chapters 1–25*, SBL Dissertation Series 94 (Atlanta: Society of Biblical Literature, 1988), 159–60.

Jeremiah's Self-Understanding and the Church

In many ways the church shares Jeremiah's self-understanding. She believes in and trusts the same Lord, not in human power; identifies herself with his same covenant people; confesses the same sacred history and sings the same psalms. She understands that she was predestined to suffer on behalf of God's word. She accepts God's word, albeit that word now comes to her in sacred Scripture, including the book of Jeremiah; she is commissioned and gifted to preach it; and she embodies it. She too understands she is the Lord's property; she lives to do her Lord's will, not her own. She seeks reform, confessing her sins. She too regards herself as God's medium of death or life to the nations according to their response to curse or bless her. She understands herself as living in the age of Jeremiah's hoped-for New Covenant. Although perplexed, she knows that the gates of Hades will not prevail over her, and she longs for the consummation of God's kingdom.

PART TWO

Identity in the New Testament

Chapter 5

Simon Peter: The Transformation of the Apostle

Markus Bockmuehl

What does it mean to be a Christian? What has made, and what makes today, the distinctive reality of those who discover and establish who they are in following Jesus Christ? The simple reality of being and belonging with this person and his people, rather than with oneself, one's tribe or community of shared interests—this constitutes for all its complexities and discontinuities a distinctively grace-filled, elusive, mysterious, life-sustaining stream of identity down the ages.[1]

Near the fountainhead of that DNA of spiritual tradition stands the apostle Simon Peter, who is for the Gospels of Matthew, Mark, and Luke the first to be called to leave what he was to become a follower, to find his purpose and being no longer in what he did or whom he was with, but in leaving his past to follow Jesus. (Peter is perhaps in this respect second only to Mary the Mother of Jesus, who precedes him in the response of discipleship invited in the Annunciation, and who finds the deepest joy in belonging to the Lord—"Behold, I am the servant of the Lord. . . . My soul magnifies the Lord" [Luke 1:38, 46].)

Why did Peter, this mysterious apostle, about whom so little is known from the New Testament, nevertheless take on such enormous significance in the later life of the church? Part of the answer to that complex question undoubtedly lies in the extent to which, ever since the earliest years of the church, he has seemed to exemplify something of the essence and meaning of Christian discipleship. The figure of Peter somehow embodies both its frail complexity and its dynamic grace of personal transformation, from heights

---

1. This essay is revised and adapted for the present volume from a version first published as "From Unlikely Birthplace to a Global Mission" in Marcus Bockmuehl, *Simon Peter in Scripture and Memory* (Grand Rapids: Baker Academic, 2012), 165–77.

of buoyant success into the abyss of abject failure, and yet onward to a joyful peace and a purified hope.

I propose here to illuminate this exemplary, identity-constituting aspect of Peter's discipleship by gradually closing in from its general appearance to its twin foci of testing and faithfulness. To that end we will begin with half a dozen "big questions" about Peter before zeroing in on one particular text from the passion narrative and pairing it with a fascinating second-century tradition about the apostle's martyrdom.

The Call of Simon to Be Peter: The Big Questions

Simon Peter's story is more complex than a surface reading will reveal. More can be discerned than the rapid rise of a Jewish fisherman to the missionary apostle of Jesus whose story is preserved in the New Testament with several traditions about him that survive as well.

Who Was Peter?

The answer to this question is less self-evident than might appear at first sight. Simon Peter was a Jewish fisherman from the village of Bethsaida on the northeastern shore of the Sea of Galilee, who at some stage moved a few miles west to Capernaum in the Galilean heartland—quite plausibly in conjunction with his marriage. Having perhaps been first introduced to Jesus by his brother Andrew, an adherent of John the Baptist, Peter in due course became one of the Twelve close disciples of Jesus, indeed the one singled out as their leader and spokesman. A character of enthusiasms more than of caution or discretion, Peter became keenly invested in identifying Jesus as Messiah. But as for all Jews of his day, including Jesus's closest disciples and for that matter Saul of Tarsus, this affirmation was for him incompatible with the idea of the Messiah's violent death, certainly not by crucifixion. After denying Jesus on the night of his arrest and abandoning him to an ignominious criminal's fate as his ship was evidently sinking, Peter was stunned and transformed by an encounter with the risen Jesus in the days that followed. He found himself commissioned as the leading missionary of the newly minted Jerusalem church to Jewish believers—from Judea to Antioch, Northern Asia Minor, Greece and Rome, where he died as a martyr under Nero. The New Testament shows this transformed Peter exercising a decisive pioneering role in the mission of Jesus to the world. And the early church credits him not only with two letters preserved in the New Testament, but with a large number of traditions and legends associated with his name.

It is a worthwhile and rewarding exercise to engage and to probe this rapid sketch more fully.[2] In grappling with the question of his identity in what follows, we begin with several evocative and less familiar aspects of both his formation and his death before reflecting on the powerfully pastoral and exemplary hold that his story of discipleship exercised on the imagination of a Christian identity.

Peter's Names as Clues to His Identity

The New Testament, confusingly, knows Peter by four different names, one Greek and three Hebrew or Aramaic: Simon or Simeon, Peter (*Petros*), Bar Yona or Son of Jonah, and Cephas (*Kefa*).

Simeon was the name of an Israelite patriarch and one of the twelve tribes. What is not widely understood is that this tribe struggled from the start to get established: it is the only one to decline in size between the first and second census in Numbers 1 and 26; its assigned territory in the promised land was soon subsumed under that of Judah, and little more is heard of it after that. Indeed the very name Simeon disappeared for many centuries and returned to popularity only about two hundred years before the birth of Christ, apparently in connection with a rise in Jewish hopes for national restoration (a similar revivalist naming custom was also widespread among Zionist settlers in the twentieth century). This resonance of hope and renewal was potentially still in the air around the time of Peter's birth in the late first century BC, when Simeon had become one of the most popular boys' names—and the choice of name might hint at parents who shared in such Jewish aspiration.

Yonah, the name of Peter's father, is shared with the Old Testament prophet Jonah but otherwise appears only rarely; the prophet himself was a Northerner, and rabbinic use also suggests that it may have been a particularly Galilean name. Its connection with the name John is affirmed in the Fourth Gospel (cf. John 1:42; 21:15) but otherwise not straightforward to substantiate.

Cephas means "rock." Significantly, however, it was not in fact used as a name by Jews or even Christians in late antiquity. This means, conversely, that the Aramaic-speaking churches of first-century Judea seized on *this* unique

2. Readers may be interested in my two books on the subject: *The Remembered Peter in Ancient Reception and Modern Debate*, WUNT 262 (Tübingen: Mohr Siebeck, 2010); and *Simon Peter in Scripture and Memory*.

name as the one that most clearly distinguished Peter. And it may in turn explain why Paul, too, almost always calls Peter Cephas—quite possibly ever since he first made his acquaintance in Jerusalem (Gal 1:18, 22; the only exception is Gal 2:9–11).

So what about the Greek name Peter? Although relatively rare, this does in fact occur as a name in ancient Jewish sources, both Greek and Semitic. My own view is that the apostle's unusual background in Bethsaida, with a brother and a close friend known only by their strongly Hellenized names (Andrew, Philip), means that he probably spoke tolerable Greek from childhood and may well have carried the *Greek* nickname *Petros* ("stone" or "pebble") from quite early in life, perhaps to avoid any embarrassment associated in a Greek-speaking environment with the Hebrew name Simeon (even as Hellenized to Simon). If so, then it was Jesus who applied to him the *Aramaic* translation *Kefa* as a name, interpreting his Greek name in Jewish terms of "the Rock": your name is *Petros*, you will in fact be *Kefa*, the Rock on which I will build my church (Matt 16:16–19). Wordplay on the Greek word *petra* ("rock") is also found in Jewish sources to identify a faithful person like Abraham on whom God builds the foundation of his people. Cephas the name was to shape the identity of Peter the man.

Bethsaida as the Place of Peter's Cultural Formation

John 1:44 is the only place in the New Testament that tells us that Peter and his brother Andrew came from the village of Bethsaida on the Sea of Galilee. Excavations since the late twentieth century have shown it to be a small town of humble architecture and modest material culture. Surprisingly, archaeologists have found no indication of any substantial Jewish presence or religious observance. Its culture in the first century was under strongly Hellenistic and Greek-speaking influence. If there were any Jews there, then, unlike in other towns in the area, they seem to have left no material signs of an identity or way of life that distinguished them culturally or linguistically from their Gentile neighbors.[3]

That milieu of relative accommodation or assimilation is perhaps also reflected in the Greek names of Jesus's disciples Peter, Andrew, and Philip,

---

3. Jewish settlers in the Transjordan tetrarchy of Philip (today's Golan Heights) appear to have increased considerably under his rule (Josephus, *Ant.* 17.2.2, §28); indeed Philip's father, Herod the Great, had already offered hospitality to wealthy Babylonian Jewish immigrants (e.g., *Ant.* 17.2.1, §24). Nearby towns showing much clearer signs of Jewish settlement than Bethsaida include Gamla and Yehudieh.

all of whom the Fourth Gospel identifies as coming from the same village of Bethsaida (John 1:44; 12:21), and whose Hellenizing heritage is apparent in several Gospel stories. These three are the only ones among the Twelve whose primary names are Greek. In John 12:20–22, Philip and Andrew are the contact point for the Greeks who want to see Jesus, and in John 6:5 Jesus turns unhesitatingly to Philip for local knowledge of the area before the feeding of the multitude.

This realistically defined identity need not of course entail any abandonment of Jewish religious praxis or observance. But it is true that particularly east of the Jordan Jewish culture and religion were generally more marginal here in the lands of the former Northern tribes, long since settled predominantly by Gentiles. Even in Galilee, west of the Jordan, the majority Jewish population were descendants not of those lost Northern tribes of Zebulun and Naphtali romanticized in Matthew 4:13, but overwhelmingly of settlers since the second century BC in the wake of a deliberate recolonization policy implemented by the temporarily independent Maccabean state. To the Judean establishment, Galilean Jews appeared just as uncouth and unwashed as "colonials" of any other age might seem to those in the perceived center: culturally boorish, religiously suspect, and mocked for their accent—a prejudice Peter encounters when he is challenged at the trial of Jesus "the Galilean" in the house of Caiaphas (Matt 26:73; cf. v. 69). Peter thus probably grew up fully bilingual in a Jewish minority setting. That his family and their friends were at ease with their Greek-speaking environment seems in any case reflected in the names they gave to their children—interestingly Peter is the only one of the Bethsaida trio whose *Hebrew* name (Simon, i.e., Simeon) we know. Philip the Tetrarch, the local potentate, liked the place and visited periodically until a couple of years after Jesus's ministry he decreed that the village should be turned into a proper Hellenistic city called Julias—though he died before the work progressed very far. It is certainly interesting that Luke and John refer to Bethsaida as a city (Luke 9:10; John 1:44), while Mark reflects the earlier usage during Jesus's ministry in describing it as a village (8:23, 26). Understandably given Philip's pro-Roman politics, there were considerable sympathies for the pagan imperial cult, including apparently even a small temple to Julia Livia.

Bethsaida's rejection of Jesus is a famously puzzling sore point in the Gospels. Given its association with no fewer than three of the leading followers of Jesus, why is it quite so strikingly sidelined in the Gospel tradition? Matthew, Mark, and Luke mention the village only five times, but nowhere do they give us the slightest hint that Peter came from there or had any dealings with it. Based only on the Synoptic Gospels, we would have guessed that Peter had always lived in Capernaum. It is there that we find "the house of Simon and Andrew";

and there he lives together with his wife and her mother.[4] Only John tells us about Bethsaida's connection with any of Jesus's disciples. According to Matthew and Luke it was certainly (like Chorazin) a place where Jesus performed "mighty deeds" (Luke 10:13, par. Matt 11:21). But both villages had spectacularly failed to respond to Jesus's ministry, and he dramatically condemns them:

> Woe to you, Chorazin! Woe to you, Bethsaida! For if the deeds of power done in you had been done in Tyre and Sidon, they would have repented long ago, sitting in sackcloth and ashes. But at the judgment it will be more tolerable for Tyre and Sidon than for you. (Luke 10:13–14)

Given the claims here, it is striking that the evangelists tell us virtually nothing about these supposed "deeds of power" at Bethsaida. Matthew in particular, despite his keen interest in Peter, virtually eliminates Bethsaida: his one reference to it comes in this harsh word of judgment. It is possible that even in the evangelist's day it continued to prove particularly resistant to the gospel mission.[5] A similar disappointment may speak in a Jewish Christian annotation preserved in the church fathers, which claims that Jesus performed no less than fifty-three miracles at Bethsaida and Chorazin![6]

So it seems reasonable to suppose that the New Testament Gospel tradition engages in something of a conspiracy of silence against Peter's birthplace. We find that the canonical Gospels locate only *two* miracles near Bethsaida, neither of them based in the village itself: the feeding of the multitude somewhere in the vicinity of Bethsaida in Luke 9[7] and the unusual two-stage healing in Mark 8 of the blind man who first sees "people walking like trees" (8:22–26).

Whatever their Bethsaida background may have been, at some stage Peter and his brother moved to the more clearly Jewish environment of Capernaum and made contact with the national renewal movements of John the Baptist and Jesus. There is a remarkably twenty-first-century ring about the idea that growing up in an embattled minority context can force you either to translate and sublimate or else to intensify and radicalize your tribal convictions.

What did this mean for Peter's formation and identity? His background

---

4. Mark 1:29–31; cf. Matt 8:14–15 par. Luke 4:38: "Peter's house." Peter's wife is also mentioned in 1 Cor 9:5.

5. Judgment on Bethsaida is clearly expressed in the Spanish recension of 5 Ezra 1:11, an early-second-century Christian addition to a Jewish apocalypse preserved in Latin: "Did I not destroy Bethsaida because of you?"

6. Gospel of the Nazarenes, frg. 27.

7. Note that while 9:10 implies the narrative may be entering the "city," by 9:12 it has clearly moved to the wilderness.

in Bethsaida certainly taught him how to survive in a minority situation. Like Saul of Tarsus, he might become either a militant Jewish nationalist concerned with the ethnic restoration of Israel or alternatively fully engaged in articulate converse with the Gentile world. There may certainly be hints of nationalist zeal not least in narratives of Caesarea Philippi or of the conflict at Gethsemane. Yet one way or another, we also know that Peter did come to be persuaded of the gospel's outreach to both Jews and Gentiles. His upbringing outside the Galilean heartland left him culturally better equipped than many of his fellow disciples to integrate that vision of the gospel in his future ministry from Jerusalem to Antioch and Rome.

The Identity of Peter the Fisherman

Does Peter's background yield anything more for our understanding of the man he became, the reasons for his move to Capernaum, or how his fishing career in Galilee relates to his second career as a fisher of people? The church fathers consistently assumed that Peter came from exceedingly humble circumstances, that in his youth he was very poor and perhaps even orphaned.[8] By the time we encounter him in the Gospel call narrative, it is true that as a fisherman near Capernaum he enjoyed somewhat greater socioeconomic security than Galilean day laborers or tenant farmers for absentee landlords, who suffered the constant threat of unemployment and typically struggled along at a precarious subsistence level. That said, Peter was evidently not as well off as certain other disciples—notably the family of Zebedee who had their own boat and hired staff (Mark 1:19–20). In terms of his education, the Jerusalem authorities in Acts 4:13 evidently regard Peter as an uneducated, common man. We cannot assume he had anything more than a basic Jewish family upbringing.

More specifically, the Gospels articulate a number of intriguing insights into Peter's connection with the northern coastline of the Sea of Galilee near Bethsaida. Only one single passage in Luke implies that Peter may have owned or even had the use of a boat (Luke 5:3). Mark and Matthew, by contrast, give the impression that Jesus walks along the shore and finds Simon and Andrew standing and casting their nets "into the sea" (Mark 1:16) from there. Until the beginning of the twentieth century, indeed, the deployment of such circular cast-nets still continued with Palestinian fishermen standing on the shore or in the shallows of the lake. Whether on the shore or from boats, they would

---

8. So Chrysostom, *Hom.* 4 on Acts 2:1–2: "he of Bethsaida, the uncouth rustic"; cf. *Hom.* 2 on John 1:1; Ps.-Clem., *Hom.* 12.6.

take advantage of the large shoals of indigenous fish (*musht*, sold to today's tourists as "St. Peter fish") that in the winter months congregate in the rich feeding grounds near the northern end of the lake. Favorite locations were Capernaum's fishing outpost of Tabgha with its warm springs on the lakebed, and also the mouth of the Jordan near Bethsaida. It is there that fish entered or left the lake, and so they were often sufficiently plentiful to catch without using a boat.

All this does not of course limit Peter's call story to a particular time and location; in fact Luke has quite a different version, in which, moreover, Jesus seems already to have a prior relationship with Peter (cf. 4:38–39). But the distinctive use of the cast-net does make excellent sense on the shoreline around Capernaum and Bethsaida and lends a particular vibrancy to the fishing metaphors used in connection with Jesus's teaching on discipleship.

The name of Peter's hometown of Bethsaida itself means "place of fishing." Even after its decline in the third century, the rabbis long remembered the locale precisely for the rich variety of its fish.[9] The Gospels of course deploy plenty of stories, miracles, and teachings about different kinds of fish, fishermen,[10] fishing nets,[11] the fishing "catch,"[12] and so on. Mary Magdalene comes from Magdala, home to a successful fish drying and pickling industry (it was known to Josephus simply by its Greek name Taricheae, "of the fish salters").

Most famously, perhaps, Jesus calls Peter and Andrew to become men who "fish for people."[13] This is an eschatologically charged assignment that evokes Jeremiah's prophecy about the final ingathering of Israel: "I will bring them back to their own land that I gave to their ancestors. I am now sending for many fishermen, says the LORD, and they shall catch them" (Jer 16:15–16 NRSV).

Such fishing images turn out to be not just incidental but integral to the very fabric of Peter's apostolic role. The book of Acts offers tantalizing hints of the extent to which these metaphors continue to evoke Peter's past as a fisherman in understanding the future missionary. In a kind of flashback to Bethsaida, Peter in Acts 10 had an eye-opening vision at Jaffa in which he saw lowered from heaven in a fishing boat's sail,[14] the sort of indiscriminate com-

---

9. Simeon ben Gamaliel, the son of St. Paul's teacher, was reputedly offered at Bethsaida a dish made of 300 fish (Jerusalem Talmud, *Šeqalim* 6.2, 50a). Some scholars suspect here a catch of sardines.

10. Matt 4:18; Mark 1:16–17; Luke 5:2.

11. Matt 4:18, 20, 21; 13:47; Mark 1:16, 18, 19; Luke 5:2, 4, 5, 6; John 21:6, 8, 11.

12. Luke 5:4, 9.

13. Mark 1:16, 17.

14. Acts 10:11; 11:5: an *othonē* with "four points." The meaning "sail" is well attested in Jewish and Greek sources. Fishing boats with "four-pointed" rectangular sails appear on mosaics and

mingling of clean and unclean fish and animals that was indeed the diet of his neighbors at Bethsaida. In light of this, he understands God's gospel as reaching out to all nations, and thus he is encouraged to set out into the deep unknown and put down his net for a catch.

The End of Peter

Given how consistently important Peter seems to be among the disciples and in the Gospel narrative, it is certainly striking how silent the rest of the New Testament is about what happened to him. The book of Acts presents itself in its opening verses as the Acts of the risen and ascended Jesus; and the two chief human protagonists within it are clearly Peter in chapters 1–12 and Paul in 13–28, who engage in parallel missions involving preaching to Jews and to Gentiles, miracles as well as persecution. So it seems an extraordinary fact that Acts makes no reference to the deaths of either Peter or Paul, and does not even place Peter anywhere near Rome—despite the fact that its narrative ends in Rome and it may even have been written there in the last couple of decades of the first century.

The last we hear of Peter is that he is imprisoned by an opportunistic Herod Agrippa I at Passover in the year 41 or 42 and then miraculously escapes—after which Luke simply adds, perhaps with a nod and a wink, "he went to another place"—leaving us to wonder, rather like his prison guards, "what had become of Peter" (12:17–18). Peter does resurface for a brief cameo appearance at the apostolic council held in Jerusalem seven years later (Acts 15), but that is the last we hear of him in Acts.

Aside from Acts relating Peter's stay in places like Lydda, Joppa, and Caesarea on the coast, the letters of Paul and Peter suggest he also went further afield to Antioch, Corinth, and perhaps even as far as the Black Sea. Nowhere does the New Testament unambiguously mention his presence in Rome, although there may well be an allusion to this at the end of 1 Peter (5:13). Although 1 Corinthians knows about Peter as a missionary traveling with his wife, it is intriguing that Romans, written by Paul to Rome around the year 57, makes no mention of Peter (though some detect a diplomatic allusion in 15:20).

For these and other reasons, a number of recent scholars in Germany and elsewhere have argued quite seriously that Peter never left Palestine but must have died in his bed in Jerusalem, perhaps around the year 55. But in

coins of the period. Contemporary visitors are shown an example in a first-century Magdala floor mosaic on display at Capernaum.

fact the evidence for Peter's ministry and martyrdom in Rome, although limited, is notably diverse and widespread. It includes well over a dozen Christian literary sources from the first and second centuries, and the dramatic twentieth-century archaeological discoveries of a mid-second-century memorial on the Vatican hill. There are even occasional corroborating hints in pagan sources like Phlegon of Tralles, Tacitus, and others. No Jewish or pagan critic of Christianity ever disputes the claim that Peter was crucified in Rome under Nero. Just as significantly, no other Christian site was ever claimed to be Peter's tomb.

Simon Peter and the Formation of Christian Identity

And why should any of this matter? After all, it seems to make no difference to any major Christian beliefs in Scripture or the Creeds.

In spite of that, I want to suggest that Peter's life and death actually matter a great deal for the meaning of Christian discipleship, even if the contemporary language and terminology of "identity" is undoubtedly somewhat anachronistic in relation to the first-century Jesus movement. This is because it is arguably the memory of Peter's faithfulness in discipleship that underwrites and shapes the integrity of subsequent Christian faith and life. If the twin apostolic pillars Peter and Paul were indeed martyred in Rome within a relatively short time of each other, then their uncontradicted adoption as exemplary twin witnesses by the Christian community of that place inevitably weakens the explanatory power of theories that try to explain the New Testament church as irreconcilably divided from the start between Peter and Paul, between communities of Jewish and others of Gentile believers in Jesus.

Such dichotomous views, persistently popular among some New Testament scholars for two centuries or more, certainly also have an ancient and venerable pedigree. They were famously advocated as early as the second century by Marcion of Sinope (d. ca. 160), a powerful interpreter of Paul and temporary resident of Rome. And they may help to shine a probing critical searchlight on some interesting silences and puzzles of the New Testament sources about Peter. But the idea that Peter ended his life literally and metaphorically two thousand kilometers from Rome, or indeed from Paul, finds no known support, whether friendly or hostile, during the period when Christian writers could still legitimately appeal to the memory of the apostolic generation or of their students.

Throughout the later first and second centuries there is in fact a continuity of living memory that attests Peter's death in Rome, both in the East and in the West. He was remembered as the leading apostolic witness of Jesus, who, like Paul, came to Rome to advance the gospel and gave his ultimate testimony there. In that sense he went on to live out his unique ministry of responsible under-shepherd for the Good Shepherd who entrusts him with the care of his sheep (John 21:15–17). On that history hangs not perhaps the truth of Jesus and his gospel, but certainly the truth of his church as the bearer of that gospel. It is this that grounds its link with the apostolic witness—and thus with what the New Testament claims is "the faith once for all delivered to the saints" (Jude 3).

Simon Peter as the Second-Chance Disciple

Peter's story is not an uninterrupted arc from humble beginning to world missionary. His is the story of a failure in crisis and faithfulness in the wake of that failure.

Talking the Talk at Gethsemane

Peter's transformation from backwoods fisherman to global fisher for people certainly makes for an engaging story. But there is one additional human element of the story that has persistently intrigued readers of the Gospels, and which accounts for this apostle's peculiar and lasting power to exemplify and inspire Christian discipleship since antiquity. It is the profoundly transformative sense of a fallible and imperfect character given grace to make good on his failings: the work of Christ in his life is seen to empower this well-intentioned but rough-hewn and flawed disciple to do the right thing at the second time of asking.

The argument famously takes its point of departure immediately following the Last Supper.

> When they had sung a hymn, they went out to the Mount of Olives. Then Jesus said to them, "You will all become deserters because of me this night; for it is written, 'I will strike the shepherd, and the sheep of the flock will be scattered.' But after I am raised up, I will go ahead of you to Galilee." Peter said to him, "Though all become deserters because of you, I will never desert you." Jesus said to him, "Truly I tell you, this very night, before the cock crows, you will deny me three times." Peter said to him, "Even though I must die with you, I will not deny you." And so said all the disciples. (Matt 26:30–35 NRSV)

All four Gospels depict Peter as the first among disciples, time and again singled out as the spokesman and leader among the Twelve. Although quick and enthusiastic to follow Jesus and affirm him as God's chosen Messiah, he is at the same time slow and strongly resistant to the idea that this Messiah might be called to die sacrificially for Israel by surrendering his life into the hand of God's enemies. The Peter of the Gospels is committed but lacks discretion and staying power. He is courageous but easily thrown by things he cannot accept, and may then resist them forcefully.

This already happens to him at Caesarea Philippi: When Jesus asks his disciples in Matthew 16, "Who do you say that I am?" Peter makes the first clear confession of Jesus as Messiah and Son of the living God (16:16). Jesus praises him for voicing this insight revealed to him by God, and in Matthew identifies Peter the Rock as the one on whom he will build his church. But as soon as Jesus goes on to elaborate that God has sent him as a Messiah who will lay down his life for God's people, Peter immediately objects strongly and rejects Jesus's interpretation out of hand. That is not what he meant at all! As a result Jesus rebukes him as harshly and forcefully as if he were the mouthpiece of Satan.

Clearly that story paints a picture of mixed emotions for Peter, as within the space of two or three sentences Jesus follows an affirmation of the highest praise with a volley of ferocious condemnation.

In Gethsemane, at the point where Jesus is about to give up his life, Peter resists once again. He refuses out of hand the idea that Jesus might die without resistance and alone, that the disciples will simply abandon him in his hour of need. He speaks for the disciples in this respect, but is determined to outdo them all: "Though all become deserters because of you, I will never desert you. . . . Even though I must die with you, I will not deny you."

Dying with Jesus as such appears not to trouble Peter. What he cannot accept is the Messiah who dies without a fight, and the prediction of his own failure. And indeed he is depicted in all the Gospels as sticking with Jesus longer than any of the Twelve—though it is unclear whether he is more foolhardy in pulling his sword at Jesus's arrest, or in then having the *chutzpah* of following him all the way into the high priest's compound. Yet when it comes to the crunch at the house of Caiaphas, where Peter is challenged to identify with Jesus, he crumbles just as Jesus predicted: three times he flatly denies knowing Jesus, and when the cock crows as predicted he turns and runs away. Narratively and morally, it is the point of abject failure and darkest despair, and it was understood to be such by ancient Christian artists and hymnodists who developed this scene into a powerful parable of sin, repentance, and redemption.

Walking the Walk, the Second Time

It is a well-known commonplace, heard from Protestant pulpits as much as from Catholic propagandists, that the New Testament Peter appears as a forgiven sinner, denying his Lord but rehabilitated and charged with a new mission. After three denials of Jesus, in John three times he answers Jesus's question "Do you love me?" and three times his "Yes" receives Jesus's response that he is to tend the flock of Jesus.

But did Peter in fact take that second chance? Do we know if he did get it right the second time around and stood by the promise he made at Gethsemane? The New Testament only hints at an answer to that question, as we saw earlier: Acts is eloquently silent about what happened to Peter. Even the quasi-testamentary letter known as 2 Peter only hints at the apostle's impending martyrdom, recalling the importance of Petrine eyewitness testimony of Jesus's transfiguration but making very little of any element of "second-chance" faithfulness.

Precisely that element, however, surfaces with a poignant explicitness in second-century Christian memory of Peter's death in Rome. The apostle here has become the flawed but forgiven and restored disciple whose life is an encouragement to other believers. Some time around the middle decades of the second century there emerged an account of Peter's final contest with the church's enemies in Rome, culminating in his death at the hands of Nero. Anticipated around AD 100 in texts like *1 Clement*, the *Ascension of Isaiah*, and the letter of Ignatius *To the Romans*, this theme comes to narrative development in a complex of stories later known as the *Acts of Peter* (which date back to the second century but did not achieve final form until the fourth century or later). Parts of that narrative complex are clearly fanciful and legendary, though not everything necessarily falls into that category. Comparison with other sources highlights some touchingly human reflections on the ways in which Peter's martyrdom was remembered by the church.

In chapter 7 of that document, Peter encourages the church in Rome by confessing that he denied Jesus three times, but that Jesus had compassion on him. He encourages his fellow Christians to be loyal in the face of opposition, to stand fast, and not to doubt.

By the time we reach chapter 35, it has become clear that Peter's life is in danger, and the Christians of Rome entreat Peter to leave the city in order to be able to continue the Lord's work. There follows a famous description of what happens to him on his escape through the city gates onto the Appian Way:

But Peter said to them, "Shall we act like deserters, brothers and sisters?" But they said to him, "No, it is so that you can go on serving the Lord." So he was persuaded; he departed alone and said, "Let none of you leave with me, but I will leave alone in disguise." And as he went out of the gate he saw the Lord entering Rome; and when he saw him he said, "Lord, where are you going?" And the Lord said to him, "I am going to Rome to be crucified." And Peter said to him, "Lord, are you being crucified again?" He said to him, "Yes, Peter, I am being crucified again." And when Peter came to himself and saw the Lord ascending into heaven, he turned back to Rome, rejoicing and praising the Lord because he had said, "I am being crucified." For this was about to happen to Peter. (Acts of Peter 35)

When the church persuades Peter to flee from Rome in disguise, he balks at this and objects that this would be to act like a deserter—a role he evidently does not want to play again. But in the end he listens to the community and takes their advice, until his visionary encounter with Jesus on his way to crucifixion tells him dramatically where he is meant to be: with Jesus, who suffers with and through his people. So Peter turns back—a change of course that represents a spiritual conversion as much as it is a physical U-turn. The denial of the night in which Jesus died has now become the good confession. Third-century Christian artists liked to capture this point by depicting Peter together with an oversized crowing rooster on a pillar: as the rooster heralds the dawn of a new day just when the night is at its darkest, so this image of Peter juxtaposes the moment of his greatest failure with the foreshadowing of the resurrection and the powerful grace of his restoration.

The third-century church father Clement of Alexandria cites a tradition from a different but possibly related story cycle: as Peter was being taken out for crucifixion he saw his wife being led out to her death and called out to her, "My dear, remember the Lord!"[15]

According to the Acts of Peter, the apostle is then crucified, like Jesus, but upside down, in the gardens of Nero. It is a matter of historical record that since at least the mid–second century the church marked the memory of his burial on the adjacent Vatican hill—a spot that was excavated in the twentieth century and which can be visited today.

What follows from all this for the exemplary role of Peter in early Christian memory? Peter may be the disciple who most strikingly and encouragingly exemplifies Christian discipleship for those who may not always get things right the first time around. Peter tragically fails to keep his promise at the arrest and

---

15. *Strom.* 7.11.63; cf. Eusebius, *Eccl. hist.* 3.30.2.

trial of Jesus, but he goes on to embody the dramatic gospel grace of second chances. Within the period of living memory, when there were still Christians in Rome who remembered the apostle or his pupils, the accounts of his martyr-dom recalled that when the crunch came a second time he did not again deny or desert Jesus, but like his Lord bore testimony with his life on a Roman cross.

Peter, then, became in life and in early Christian memory a powerfully for-mative paradigm of the transformative grace that is at the heart of the Christian identity. This is a grace that, like the rooster anticipating the dawn, embraces the undaunted hope of a second-chance discipleship, activating the ever-fresh invitation to turn again from the darkness of the old self, to be forgiven and made new, and to be reidentified in following the Lord.

Chapter 6

James and Jude: Brothers of Jesus

Mariam Kamell Kovalishyn

The brothers of Jesus often receive an undeservedly negative reputation if their letters are examined closely. Given the significantly greater focus on the Pauline corpus and the figure of Paul himself, at least in the last four hundred years and likely well before then as well, the smaller epistles toward the back of the New Testament have endured significant neglect. Never quite secure in the early canon lists, the epistles of James and Jude (which faced a significantly harder journey) have struggled to make their voices heard amidst the bulkier presence of the Pauline corpus and the Gospels. But despite, or perhaps because of, their size, and even more because of their relation to the central figure of the New Testament, Jesus, these books—and their authors—deserve a hearing.

The epistles of James and of Jude bear witness to the earliest form of Christianity, the one most closely related to that which we read about in the Gospels and the first half of Acts, a Jewish Christianity still rooted in Judea and tied to the family of Jesus. They reveal something of core teachings of the early church, not to just Gentiles and unbelievers, but to the community of believers scattered from Jerusalem who had been raised as Jews. They see Jesus as the promised Messiah, but are now struggling to live faithfully in difficulties. In this we catch a brilliant glimpse of what the preaching of the *church* (not evangelism) might have looked like. Moreover, we can draw the veil back a small bit into the very family of Jesus and we can gain insight into how the teaching of Jesus both reflected and shaped his family's kerygma.

To understand the characters of James and Jude as they appear in their epistles, it is worth looking at how the family of Jesus is depicted in the Gospels, particularly at Mary's role in shaping the family dynamic, and then see how the brothers of Jesus were portrayed outside the New Testament. At this point, then, we will turn to the epistles themselves to see how they reveal their own emphases of their family's teachings, looking both to the commonalities between the epistles but also to their distinctive elements that reveal something of the identity of these two brothers. Through this, we discover both the nature of these two particular brothers of Jesus, as well as what they have to teach us about our own identities as Christians.

It must be acknowledged at the start, of course, that there is significant debate over whether these letters can be traced back to the actual brothers of Jesus. Regarding the Epistle of James, heavy hitters like Dale Allison[1] and John Kloppenborg[2] both argue strongly against Jacobean authorship.[3] On the other hand, Richard Bauckham[4] and Peter Davids,[5] among others, defend the authorship of James as per cited in the epistle and the identity of this James as extrapolated to be the brother of Jesus described by Paul in Galatians. Jude has a smaller discussion, largely due to its general scholarly neglect, but even so, the relation of the text of the epistle to the brother of Jesus mentioned in the Gospels is in dispute. That said, this article assumes a relation between the epistles and their claimed authors, whereby we can learn about the brothers of Jesus themselves from these letters. And what we learn, of course, is how the teachings of Jesus shaped the leaders and teaching of the earliest church.

Brothers/Family Evidenced in the Gospels

We may begin, however, with a brief note regarding how opinions of the brothers of Jesus are often shaped not by their epistles but by their brief appearances in the Gospels. From this, unfortunately, they have gained an unnecessarily

---

1. Dale C. Allison, *A Critical and Exegetical Commentary on the Epistle of James* (London: Bloomsbury, 2013), 28.

2. John Kloppenborg, *James*, Hermeneia (Minneapolis: Augsburg Fortress, forthcoming); as seen in John S. Kloppenborg, "Diaspora Discourse: The Construction of Ethos in James," *New Testament Studies* 53, no. 2 (April 2007): 242–70.

3. See also David R. Nienhuis, *Not by Paul Alone: The Formation of the Catholic Epistle Collection and the Christian Canon* (Waco, TX: Baylor University Press, 2007), 106–21.

4. Richard Bauckham, *James: Wisdom of James, Disciple of Jesus the Sage* (London: Routledge, 1999), 16–25.

5. Peter H. Davids, *The Epistle of James*, NIGTC (Grand Rapids: Eerdmans, 1982), 21–22; Peter H. Davids, *A Theology of James, Peter, and Jude: Biblical Theology of the New Testament* (Grand Rapids: Zondervan, 2014), 41, where he concludes: "It is therefore our conclusion that the best explanation of the data is that the letter of James was written shortly after the death of James, the brother of Jesus, making use of sermons and sayings stemming from James." Thus he represents the hybrid view of authorship with the basis being James's own words.

negative reputation. The most prominent account of the family of Jesus is in Matthew 12:46–50 (par. Mark 3:31–35[6]; Luke 8:19–21).

> While he was still speaking to the crowds, his mother and his brothers were standing outside, wanting to speak to him. Someone told him, "Look, your mother and your brothers are standing outside, wanting to speak to you." But to the one who had told him this, Jesus replied, "Who is my mother, and who are my brothers?" And pointing to his disciples, he said, "Here are my mother and my brothers! For whoever does the will of my Father in heaven is my brother and sister and mother." (NRSV)

In this confrontation scene, Jesus rejects locating one's identity in one's family of origin. Instead, he locates each person's identity in their obedience to the will of his heavenly Father; this relationship supersedes any other markers of identity. This is not, however, necessarily a rejection of his biological family, it is simply that Jesus understands each person's identity to spring primarily from their relationship with the Father (cf. Heb 2:11).

In another scene where the brothers are mentioned, the Nazarenes fail to grasp the question of Jesus's identity, instead, focusing again on his familial relations and therefore failing to understand Jesus's mission. In this particular scene, Jesus is identified by his work and his relatives, an identification that, according to his fellow townspeople, should limit his options. Intriguingly for us, Matthew and Mark invert the ordering of the brothers' names, Matthew placing Jude last, and Mark placing him third:

> *Matt 13:55:* Is not this the carpenter's son? Is not his mother called Mary? And are not his brothers **James** and Joseph and Simon and **Judas**?

> *Mark 6:3:* Is not this the carpenter, the son of Mary and brother of **James** and Joses and **Judas** and Simon, and are not his sisters here with us?" And they took offense at him.

---

6. John Painter ("Who Was James? Footprints as a Means of Identification," in *The Brother of Jesus: James the Just and His Mission*, ed. Bruce Chilton and Jacob Neusner [Louisville: Westminster John Knox, 2001], 25) argues that the statement in Mark 3:20–21 that his family was setting out to restrain Jesus "is found only in Mark and these verses appear to be a Markan composition characterized by Markan vocabulary. We may doubt the historicity of the incident." Moreover, he is convinced that the better reading of *hoi par' autou* in 3:21 is better translated as "his friends" or "'associates,' that is, his disciples. Indeed, this seems to be the most natural reading. Given that those described by this phrase are not identified, it is most natural to think it refers to the group which has just been chosen to be with Jesus (3:13–19)." This would mean it is the *disciples* who seek to restrain Jesus, not his brothers.

In each list, James is listed first, but Jude and Simon are inverted. Richard Bauckham calls this change "less easy to understand. It may mean that Matthew thought he knew better than Mark the actual order of the brothers in seniority and so corrected Mark."[7] If Matthew is correct, then the epistles we have are from the eldest and youngest of the brothers of Jesus, but of greater importance for our purposes is Bauckham's comment that "the preservation of all four names of the brothers of Jesus in Matthew and Mark indicates that all four brothers were well-known figures in the early church."[8] If Bauckham's reasoning is correct, then all of the family came to understand what Jesus taught earlier in Matthew 12: their identification stems primarily from their relationship with the Father, which makes them all family in a much truer sense.

Finally, it is worth noting that while many do not see the brothers of Jesus necessarily following him during his life, after the resurrection, the brothers are mentioned in Acts 1 among the core disciples awaiting the coming of the Spirit: "All these were constantly devoting themselves to prayer, together with certain women, including Mary the mother of Jesus, as well as his brothers" (Acts 1:14).[9] While we cannot be certain at what point they started to follow, we know from Paul's first letter to Corinth that James was given his own personal resurrection sighting (1 Cor 15:7).[10] Though the other brothers of Jesus are not

---

7. Richard Bauckham, *Jude and the Relatives of Jesus in the Early Church* (Edinburgh: T&T Clark, 1990), 7. He continues, "Whether the tradition on which he relied was actually more accurate than Mark's at this point we cannot tell. But if Matthew was correcting Mark from the list of the brothers he knew in his own tradition, then at least this tradition confirms Mark as far as the seniority of James and Joses goes."

8. Bauckham, *Jude and the Relatives*, 9. Regarding what "kind" of brothers these are to Jesus, see ibid., 19–32, for an extended introduction to the debates.

9. Craig S. Keener (*Acts: An Exegetical Commentary* [Grand Rapids: Baker Academic, 2012]) writes that Mary fills a special role in Luke; her role in both Luke and Acts is qualified, but ultimately she is a disciple of Jesus. James, too, had a major role in the early church; however, he is not considered one of the Twelve Apostles in Acts 1:15–26 because he was not a present witness of Jesus's ministry (1:21–22). This all changes in Acts 1, "Jesus taught that the disciples must be prepared to risk alienating and losing the support of their families for the sake of the kingdom (Luke 14:26; 18:29; 21:16). . . . Jesus had treated his own family accordingly, ranking discipleship above family ties (8:19–21; cf. 18:22–30); that his family now followed him (Acts 1:14) might encourage others who had to make similar sacrifices (cf. 16:31–32). Luke's contemporaries probably would have found perfectly credible the portrait of a great sage not being believed by his brother (cf. John 7:3–5) but the brother's being won over by the sage."

10. The early-second-century document, *Gospel according to the Hebrews*, describes the encounter: the Lord "went to James and appeared to him. For James had sworn that he would not eat bread from that hour in which he had drunk of the cup of the Lord until he should see him risen from among those that sleep. And shortly thereafter the Lord said: Bring a table and bread! And immediately it is added: he took bread, blessed it and broke it and gave it to James the Just

mentioned in Paul's resurrection liturgy, he had earlier held them up as one model of missionary activity (1 Cor 9:5). Thus, the lives of the brothers had been transformed by the resurrection of Jesus, and they all changed directions from following their father's carpenter path to evangelizing and leading in the early church.

Mary's Influence on Family Teaching

It is important to note that Jesus does not repudiate his family; he merely redefines it in terms of obedience to God. This redefinition of family the early church took seriously. As we approach the epistles of James and Jude, there is one more aspect that we should look at, namely, the shape of this extended family. Luke gives us the most information on the family in Luke 1, where we see both Mary and her aunt Elizabeth acting in ways indicative of families actively looking for the Messiah's arrival. Elizabeth celebrates her Lord's arrival when Mary visits her (foreshadowing Elizabeth's son John's role in pointing to the Messiah), and Mary herself submits willingly to a shocking angelic pronouncement. One can see why this family was chosen to raise the Messiah.

Most telling, however, is Mary's celebrated Magnificat. This poem is nothing short of a prophetic announcement of the kingdom of God, in line with the best of Isaiah or the Psalter.[11] She is a woman trained in the Scriptures, who sings in celebration of the justice that God will bring in his reign. The upside-down kingdom, or perhaps better the right-side-up kingdom of which she sings is nearly exactly duplicated in James, while Jude also highlights God's justice and mercy. The woman who praised God's faithfulness in acting to restore his reign through her unborn son, raised sons who trusted in God's faithfulness to act on behalf of his people and to right the wrongs done by the powerful. This does not, however, elevate Mary herself to a particularly lofty spiritual state.

---

and said to him: My brother, eat your bread, for the Son of Man is risen from among those that sleep." Quoted in Ralph P. Martin, *James*, WBC 48 (Waco, TX: Word, 1988), xliv. This early tradition clearly ascribes to James faith *before* the crucifixion, and not merely a faith created by the resurrection appearance.

11. Joel B. Green (*The Gospel of Luke* [Grand Rapids: Eerdmans, 1997], 100–101) writes that in Mary's Magnificat, God "is the 'Mighty One' who accomplished 'great things,' who shows 'strength' and scatters the proud. . . . This is the God who engages battle on behalf of his people (cf. Ps 24:7–10; Isa 42:13; Zeph 3:17)." God is also the Mighty One who is merciful and demonstrates loving-kindness (*hesed*) to Israel. This is all in anticipation of the Messiah, as Darrell L. Bock (*Luke 1:1–9:50*, BECNT [Grand Rapids: Baker Books, 1994], 157) writes: "[Mary] trusts God's just vindication in the approaching messianic reign. . . . Mary is looking to the future, not the past. She is anticipating in the child she bears, total vindication."

Rather, it helps to show the shape of the whole family together in faithfulness, with Mary fulfilling the proper role of a mother raising faithful children (cf. Prov 1:8; 6:10; 31:1).

Much like Elijah, who could see the reality of God's kingdom even when others could not, this family looks for and sees God at work all around them in and for those who love God. If one takes Luke seriously as a historian, "the inference is that Jesus' family—both spiritual and natural—are in Luke's sights [in 8:19–21]; and that the Nazareth family are 'examples of the seed that has fallen on good soil'. . . , to be brought to fruition in the scene after the resurrection in Acts 1."[12] Roland Deines has argued that the extended family was likely all Messianically oriented, eagerly awaiting the redemption of God, and that even possibly Nazareth had a reputation for being so focused on the coming of the Messiah that it was a common joke (cf. John 1:46).[13] The significance of Luke's account in particular is that it highlights how the family played a significant role in how these brothers grew up, embedding them in Scriptures that speak of God's faithfulness, God's justice, and God's mercy. This family from Nazareth raised children—Jesus and his siblings—who found their primary identity as God's servants, willing to be used for whatever God sought from them.

Commonalities between Their Epistles

Turning to the epistles of James and Jude, the attentive reader is struck by several significant parallels. First, both authors reveal a heavy dependence upon the Jewish literary tradition, particularly the wisdom and apocalyptic literature such as 1 Enoch and Sirach.[14] Their dependence, however, is not a simple copying mechanism; rather, each reveals a creative integration of the prior literature and exemplars with their current pastoral needs. James, like Ben Sira before him and Jude after him, "re-expresses and develops the insights of the wisdom he has learned from the tradition and made his own."[15] Unlike Paul, who willingly uses

---

12. R. E. Brown, K. P. Donfried, J. A. Fitzmyer, and J. Reumann, *Mary in the New Testament* (Philadelphia, Fortress; New York: Paulist Press, 1978), 170; quoted in Martin, *James*, xli.

13. Roland Deines, "Can the Historical James Help Us to 'Understand the Historical Jesus'?" (paper presented at Tyndale Fellowship, Cambridge, July 8, 2015).

14. Jude's interest in *1 Enoch* is obvious (Jude 14–15), but there is reason for seeing James as influenced by *1 Enoch*, particularly the Epistle of Enoch (91–108), but also by other sections (cf. 42:1–3 and the description of wisdom coming down). See Mariam J. Kamell, "James and Apocalyptic Wisdom," in *A Companion to Jewish Apocalyptic Thought and the New Testament*, ed. Benjamin Reynolds and Loren Stuckenbruck (Philadelphia: Fortress, 2016).

15. Bauckham, *James*, 81.

quotations from Greco-Roman philosophers and playwrights, James and Jude depend solely on biblical exemplars (and, in Jude's case, some extra-canonical Jewish stories). This may tell us something about their intended audiences, but more importantly, it speaks of authors who were steeped in their Scripture and whose identities were fully shaped by those Scriptures through the emulation of the heroes who preceded them.

Second, both brothers describe themselves as "servants of the Lord" (Jas 1:1, *theou kai kyriou Iēsou Christou **doulos***; Jude 1, *Iēsou Christou **doulos***). While this is, it must be highlighted, "an honorific title of authority," it also "is recognition that natural relationship to Jesus is not a basis for authority in the church."[16] Neither brother grasps for authority based on relation to Jesus; rather, their service is what sets them into places of authority. Their identity, by which they introduced themselves, was wrapped up in being servants of the one who called his followers to be "servants of all" (Mark 9:35). Since they knew their Hebrew Scriptures, they knew that the "servants of the Lord," like Abraham or Moses, were significant characters.[17] This title is not necessarily one of self-denigration as we may be prone to think, but with this self-designation, they reveal that they understand Jesus's contrast in Matthew 12 discussed above. They do not take their biological identity as significant; instead, their obedience to the work of the Father is their core self-identification.

Third, it is worth noting that both authors show a deep concern with a person's choices. They portray people as responsible for wrongful choices, and also having volition in righteous choices. Both epistles have a great deal of concern for the choices that their audiences are making, the reality and deadly dangers of temptation and thus the necessity of endurance, and the concern that God's people reflect God's merciful character to one another. The exemplars they use point the audience to look at the ideal role models for hospitality, endurance, and mercy,[18] or the exemplars provide warnings concerning the dangers of giving in to temptation for lust, wealth, or power. Both epistles use graphic nature imagery as well, to encourage faithfulness and highlight the sheer illogic of sinful living as believers.

---

16. Bauckham, *Jude and the Relatives*, 129. He continues: "This relativizing of family relationship to Jesus may well have its roots in the Gospel tradition. . . . They reflect Jesus' own teaching that what counts in the kingdom of God is not natural relationship to himself, but doing the will of God."

17. Cf. Gen 26:24; Exod 32:13; Num 12:8; Deut 9:27; 1 Kgs 18:36; 1 Chr 6:49; 2 Chr 24:9; Neh 10:29; Jer 33:26; Dan 9:11; etc. These references all culminate in Acts 3:13: "The God of Abraham, the God of Isaac, and the God of Jacob, the God of our ancestors has glorified his servant Jesus."

18. Cf. Robert J. Foster, *The Significance of Exemplars for the Interpretation of the Letter of James*, WUNT 2.376 (Tübingen: Mohr Siebeck, 2014).

Finally, although this does not exhaust the similarities between the texts, this concern with choices springs from their sense that every person in their audience has a new identity formed by God's faithfulness, not the individual's choices or work. This is the key to both of their discussions about endurance and faithfulness: all of life is to be a response to the work of a changed identity that already happened in believers by the grace of God. James 1:18 proclaims, "In fulfillment of his own purpose he gave us birth by the word of truth, so that we would become a kind of first fruits of his creatures," while Jude writes, "To those who are called, who are beloved in God the Father and kept safe for Jesus Christ" (v. 1). For both of these brothers, every believer's identity is wrapped up in the work of God's calling and rebirthing them, and this work has been done solely by the will of God. Believers can trust in God's faithfulness and mercy to sustain them through the final judgment—provided, of course, that they choose to grow in their mimicry of God's character.

These two brothers write from a knowledge that their identity is firmly in God's gracious hands and that this is the reality for all believers. This transformed identity is a gift, not a work—one that calls for a totally transformed way of life that mirrors God's gracious character. They teach through their letters that the only ones who are truly of the family of God will "[do] the will of [the] Father" in all aspects of their lives.

Uniqueness of James from His Epistle

When we read the Epistle of James, we learn a few further details about the character of James. For one, although he begins by declaring himself the "servant of God and the Lord Jesus Christ," his authority is unmistakable. He feels no need to add further qualifications to explain who "James" is; rather, he assumes his audience will immediately know who he is—despite its being one of the most common names of the time. Also, there are more imperatives concentrated within this letter than anywhere else in the New Testament; in this short letter of 107 verses, there are 54 imperatives.[19] This is a letter by a man who has no doubts about his place to interpret the teaching of Jesus for the church. Interestingly, the apocryphal Gospel of Thomas confirms this leadership. In Logion 12, the disciples ask Jesus who should lead them after he departs, and the response is, "Wherever you have come from, you are to go to James the

---

19. By comparison, Galatians has 21 imperatives in 149 verses; Hebrews has a mere 29 in 303 verses, and Romans has 62 in 432 verses. First Peter comes the closest with 35 in 105 verses, but that is still 20 less in an almost identical verse count.

Just, for the sake of whom heaven and earth came into being."[20] Whether the Gospel of Thomas accurately records Jesus's words is a matter for speculation; we can, however, affirm the early witness to James's leadership and this at least provides one early explanation for whence his authority derived. Suffice it to say, however, that the James whom we meet in this epistle, as we see him in Acts, does not hide from divinely given authority.

James's epistle is perhaps the closest echo of Mary's Magnificat outside of Jesus's own teaching in the New Testament.[21] James, more so than Jude, focuses on the intersection between the rich and the poor, between wealth and poverty. As with Mary's song, James highlights the topsy-turvy nature of God's reign (1:9–11) and warns any who oppress their workers or presume on their business freedom that God's judgment looms. James does not want any in his care to find their identity in their wealth (or lack thereof). Rather, each one is to remember that "you are a mist that appears for a little while and then vanishes" (4:14), and so, submit everything they undertake to the Lord's will (4:15). Echoing his brother, James teaches that one's identity cannot be formed from wealth or from work, but from doing the Lord's will. Presuming on one's wealth and ability to make further money, however, James declares a sin, but he promises that the Lord will raise up the humble (4:10). The contrast James seeks to make, it is worth noting, is not necessarily between the rich and poor, but rather between those who find their identity in being rich and those who find their identity in God alone, those who have humbled themselves before the Lord and receive from him their identity.[22]

Another emphasis of the Epistle of James is a complete trust in God's justice, although it comes with a warning and a promise. Warnings of God's judgment sit behind several of James's discussions such as favoritism at the start of chapter 2 (see also the warning against grumbling in 5:9). Arguably, 2:12–13 is

20. Simon Gathercole, *The Gospel of Thomas: Introduction and Commentary* (Leiden/Boston: Brill, 2014), 249. Gathercole concludes that James is meant as "a 'serious' symbolic figure," who might have functioned to "undercut the authority of the twelve (with the possible exception of Thomas)" (252–53). He also notes that it is a common Jewish argument to have seen the world as created on behalf of the "righteous" (255–56).

21. Cf. Scot McKnight, *The Letter of James* (Grand Rapids: Eerdmans, 2011), 25–26, for a listing of similarities between the teachings of Jesus and James. Patrick Hartin, "The Religious Context of the Letter of James," in *Jewish Christianity Reconsidered: Rethinking Ancient Groups and Texts*, ed. Matt A. Jackson-McCabe (Minneapolis: Fortress, 2007), 229, concludes: "There is nothing in the Letter of James that does not conform to the vision, teaching, and mission of Jesus."

22. Mariam J. Kamell, "The Economics of Humility: The Rich and the Humble in James," in *Economic Dimensions of Early Christianity*, ed. Bruce W. Longenecker and Kelly Liebengood (Grand Rapids: Eerdmans, 2009), 157–75.

the hinge of chapter two, holding together both the discussion on favoritism (toward those with money and against the poor) and a faith that works (wherein the prime example is ignoring a person in need). James 2:12–13 warns that we must be merciful in our dealings with one another and that, if we fail to practice mercy, judgment that is mercilessly just will be passed on us (cf. Matt 5:7; 7:2; 18:23–35).[23] For those who do take on God's character, however, as part of their identity, speaking and acting in accordance with God's implanted law of freedom, James promises that "mercy triumphs over judgment." Thus the promise is tied integrally to the transformed identity of the believer who has received (by grace) the implanted word and acts accordingly (1:21–25). One's identity *must* be transformed by having received the mercy of God and acting in accordance with it.

While the believer *must* take on God's character of mercy as integral to their identity, they *cannot* take on his role as judge. In his strongest statement about the imminence of judgment in 4:11–12, James warns his audience that God is the sole judge and to encroach on his right is presumption. This pithy yet profound statement again calls for humility on the part of the audience:

> Do not speak evil against one another, brothers and sisters. Whoever speaks evil against another or judges another, speaks evil against the law and judges the law; but if you judge the law, you are not a doer of the law but a judge. There is one lawgiver and judge who is able to save and to destroy. So who, then, are you to judge your neighbor?

Obviously, the concern here is with unjust judgments, but James has already flagged that their favoritism for the rich reveals that they are "judges with evil thoughts" (2:4).[24] Ultimately, only the one who has given the "perfect law of liberty" (1:25) can judge whether people have fulfilled the law according to its intent. In light of this, it is worth noting that James was called "the Just" in the early Christian literature, such as in the Gospel of Thomas quote above and in Eusebius's narration:

> He has been called the Just by all from the time of our Savior to the present day. . . . Because of his exceeding great justice he was called the Just, and

---

23. Dan McCartney (*James*, BECNT [Grand Rapids: Baker Academic, 2009], 146), like myself (Mariam J. Kamell, "The Soteriology of James in Light of Earlier Jewish Wisdom Literature and the Gospel of Matthew" [PhD diss., University of St. Andrews, 2010], 164), takes this saying as an echo of Jesus's warning parable of the unmerciful servant in Matthew 18.

24. Martin, *James*, 75, warns, in showing partiality, "one is failing to see the Lord himself who laid his glory aside and chose to identify with the least of 'these his brothers' (Matt 25:31–46)."

Oblias, which signifies in Greek, "Bulwark of the people" and "Justice," in accordance with what the prophets declare concerning him.[25]

Even as James cautions his audience against wrongful judgment of one another, he became known universally for his righteousness and justice.[26] Bauckham notes, "As a singular feature of the new Temple, James as the rampart compares only with Peter as the rock."[27] Having so completely received his identity as a new creation (1:18), shaped to live out the implanted word (which is the law of freedom), his whole life reflected the righteous character of God.

One final key to James's identity that we can discern through the shape of his epistle is the importance of prayer. Much like Jesus, who throughout the Gospels is constantly seen to be in prayer, James's whole epistle hangs on prayer. It is in all the key locations of ancient writing: beginning (1:5–8), middle (4:1–10, concluding the second main discourse), and end (5:13–18). James longs for his audience to understand how important prayer is to a thriving life: it is how you know the will of God and also how you are able to fulfill it. Early Christian tradition supports this focus. Along with the titles described above, James is consistently described as a man of prayer: "And he was in the habit of entering alone into the temple, and was frequently found upon his knees begging forgiveness for the people, so that his knees became hard like those of a camel, in consequence of his constantly bending them in his worship of God, and asking forgiveness for the people."[28] Unlike the selfish and competitive pray-ers of 4:1–4, James was known for seeking mercy for his people, so much so that it

25. Eusebius, *Hist. eccl.* 2.23.4–7, quoting Hegesippus, ca. AD 165–75. Jerome, *De Viris Illustribus* 2, also cites that James was called "the Just."

26. This reputation may call for some reevaluation of the scholarly opinion that James and Paul did not get along and so James (mis)used his leadership role to cause problems for Paul at the end of Acts. There is nothing in the literature of the early church to suggest such an abuse.

27. Richard Bauckham, "James and the Jerusalem Church," in *The Book of Acts in Its Palestinian Setting*, ed. Richard Bauckham (Grand Rapids: Eerdmans, 1995), 449–50. Bauckham argues, "A reference to James as 'the righteous one' was found in Isaiah 3:10 (*cf.* Hegesippus, *ap.* Eusebius, *Hist. Eccl.* 2.23.15; 2 Apoc; Jas 61:14–19) and probably other texts. A reference to James as 'righteousness' was probably found in Isaiah 54:14, which would make James the means by which God builds the eschatological Zion, and/or Isaiah 28:17 (which continues the favorite early Christian text about Christ as the cornerstone of the messianic Temple), which would make James the plumbline which God uses to build the new temple. . . . But the most important aspect of the use of this term for James may be that, of the various architectural features mentioned in Isaiah 54:11–12, it is the only one which occurs in the singular. It was therefore appropriate to describe the unique position James came to hold at the head of the mother-church in Jerusalem. . . . [James was not a] merely local leader, but the personal embodiment of the Jerusalem church's constitutional and eschatological centrality in relation to the whole developing Christian movement, Jewish and Gentile" (450).

28. Eusebius, *Hist. eccl.* 2.23.4–7, still quoting Hegesippus.

shaped his physical body. This is the key to understand how James rose to the prominence he did: his whole life was spent so closely communing with the Father in prayer that his whole character came to reflect his brother's.[29] This was done through conscious action on James's part to submit himself in prayer and humble himself to the Father; hence he cannot imagine that a person could claim to have faith and not live according to the Father's ways. New birth entails entire transformation, which James himself modeled.

Uniqueness of Jude from His Epistle

With Jude, we have less to go on (25 in contrast to 107 verses), but we can still gain a glimpse of this brother's character. Jude immediately conveys less certainty about his authority, only insofar as he introduces himself not simply as "a servant of Jesus Christ," but adds "and brother of James."[30] Functionally, therefore, this brother announces himself by two of his siblings, rather than simply pointing to Jesus and assuming everyone knows who he is.[31] Again, this kind of introduction adds to the sense of James as the prominent leader in the church, but this does not diminish Jude's authority. While he may need further identifying marks in his introduction, his letter reveals no insecurity about his right and ability to tackle a very difficult situation.

The Epistle of Jude evinces a stronger concern about the problem of false teaching and its subsequent descent into immoral behavior. When one misses the gospel, he proclaims, it does not simply affect one's head knowledge, it shows in that person's actions. To combat this, Jude uses illustration after illustration, both from history and from nature, to show how the false teaching has consequences on both an individual's identity and actions, and also on one's fate. A failure to trust the gospel of Jesus Christ leads one into a useless pride (cf. vv. 12–13: "they are waterless clouds carried along by the winds; autumn trees

29. It is also worth noting that James's first discussion about prayer is in the context of the believer's need for wisdom, for understanding from God to know how to live into the new creation life they have been given.

30. For an assessment of how Jude locates himself within his family in this verse, see David DeSilva, *James and Jude*, ed. John Painter and David DeSilva, Paideia Commentaries on the New Testament (Grand Rapids: Baker Academic, 2012), 191.

31. Richard Bauckham (*Jude, 2 Peter*, WBC 50 [Nashville: Thomas Nelson, 1983], 21) observes, "Palestinian Jewish-Christian circles in the early church used the title 'brother of the Lord' not simply to identify the brothers, but as ascribing to them an authoritative status, and therefore the brothers themselves, not wishing to claim an authority based on mere blood-relationship to Jesus, avoided the term."

without fruit, twice dead, uprooted; wild waves of the sea, casting up the foam of their own shame; wandering stars, for whom the deepest darkness has been reserved forever"[32]). Jude's concern, of course, is that if one finds her identity in anything other than Christ, then she has put herself outside of the salvation that is in Christ. It is that simple—and that dangerous. Hence Jude writes strongly and with great passion to recall his audience to their true identity.

With that, Jude emphasizes, more obviously than James, the profound grace that drives this new reality. Starting from verse 1, wherein his audience are those who are "called, who are beloved in God the Father and kept safe for Jesus Christ," to his glorious benediction in verse 24, "Now to him who is able to keep you from falling, and to make you stand without blemish in the presence of his glory with rejoicing," the whole work of their transformed identity is in God's hands. They have merely to "keep" within it and not trade their God-given identity for their own pride or desires.[33] He also emphasizes their need to mirror God's mercy in their interactions with each other, seeking always to help one another stay within God's way, even though that may also entail being careful not to get pulled astray in the process. Jude's whole letter demonstrates how this can work: remind people of the truth of God's grace and their place within his story, and do not give up on them. Jude's letter itself is an act of grace from a man who knows his own place as kept within God's grace by the work of Christ. He does not write from a place of arrogance, but from the humility that comes from knowing each one is also vulnerable to falling.[34] That reality,

32. Lewis R. Donelson, *I & II Peter and Jude*, NTL (Louisville: Westminster John Knox, 2010), 188: "Waterless clouds are useless to others. People that are driven by the wind are unreliable, unanchored to orthodoxy, and thus unfit for leadership. . . . The accusation of being disconnected from tradition and lacking in righteousness is reinforced in the description of waves that are wild, foaming up their shame, and in the final image of wandering stars. Stars should stay in their assigned position. Wandering stars are rebelling against cosmic order."

33. Bauckham, *Jude, 2 Peter*, 27: "Jude knows that the divine action in calling, loving, and keeping safe must be met by a faithful human response, and when he takes up the themes of v. 1 in v. 21, it is to put the other side of the matter: his readers must *keep themselves* in the love of God and faithfully *await* the salvation which will be theirs at the Parousia. The divine action does not annul this human responsibility. But in his final doxology Jude will return to the note on which he began: his confidence that the God who is their Savior through Jesus Christ can keep them safe until they come to their eschatological destiny (v. 24)."

34. See David R. Nienhuis and Robert W. Wall, *Reading the Epistles of James, Peter, John and Jude as Scripture: The Shaping and Shape of a Canonical Collection* (Grand Rapids: Eerdmans, 2013), 242, who note, "Of course, while expressing loving concern for the wayward they must carefully avoid being led astray by their ungodly practices (vv. 22–23)—but even in the face of this danger they can act in confident faith, knowing that their ongoing faithfulness to God is not simply a matter of their own strenuous efforts (vv. 24–25). They must prove their love to God, of

however, does not stop him from acting to save those who are going astray (thereby fulfilling Jas 5:19–20).

Jude's imagination is shaped by the Jewish literature of his time. He ranges through Israel's history to find appropriate illustrations, revealing the link between wrongful thinking and sinful actions. As Donelson observes, "this passage connects the impious to well-known stories and persons in Jewish texts, characters who are always on the wrong side of the story. . . . The ancient texts describe them perfectly. This passage uses the language of those sacred texts to identify, unmask, and condemn these impious people."[35] It is likely that Jude's audience would be Jewish Christians like himself, so they would also be familiar with these illustrations, but Jude's letter reveals the proper response to history. Instead of persisting in sinful behaviors, as his audience seems to be doing, he takes these examples as teaching graphics to help God's people know how to behave. He trusts that the God he knew in Jesus Christ and that he learned about from his mother Mary is indeed the same God yesterday, today, and tomorrow, and can therefore be trusted.[36] Jude may not have been as well known a leader as his brother James, but he is confident in his brother Jesus and writes from that confidence and sure hope.

---

course, but in the end it is God who will prove God's love for them by keeping them safe in the salvation they seek."

35. Donelson, *I & II Peter and Jude*, 188–89. He states, "they are portrayed as people who aspire to leadership but lack all the qualities needed. Unlike the readers of the letter, who are admonished in verse 20 to build each other up, these people shepherd themselves, have no loyalty to tradition or order, practice shameful deeds, and endanger the community. In doing this, they join a long line of unrighteous and rebellious people."

36. Scott J. Hafemann, "Salvation in Jude 5 and the Argument of 2 Peter 1:3–11," in *The Catholic Epistles and Apostolic Tradition: A New Perspective on James to Jude*, ed. Karl-Wilhelm Niebuhr and Robert W. Wall (Waco, TX: Baylor University Press, 2009), 337–38: "Against the backdrop of Exodus 32–34 and Numbers 14, the force of Jude 5 within the argument of the letter as a whole becomes evident. Rather than merely restating that the readers have known all things 'once for all,' Jude 5 reminds them of the lesson to be learned from Israel's experience in the wilderness: the Lord destroyed those among Israel who did not believe because he had earlier saved them 'once for all' by extending mercy to them in spite of their hardened condition. The use of *hapax* to modify *sōsas* indicates that the salvation in view is God's final and decisive act of patient mercy on behalf of those who have experienced God's provision and deliverance (Exod 34:6; Num 14:18–19), which we have seen refer to his earlier acts of covenant renewal after Israel's sin with the golden calf. Though they deserved to be judged because of their hard-hearted breaking of the covenant with their idolatry, God nevertheless acted mercifully to save them. . . . Hence, their eventual judgment in Numbers 14 is brought about because their subsequent unbelief *to deuteron* (cf. Num 14:11) dishonors God's earlier definitive bestowal of mercy and grace on their behalf."

Half-Brothers and Servants of the Lord

What can be said about these brothers of Jesus? First, despite being half-brothers to Jesus, they did not view family relationship to be as important as obedience to God's will. Their identity came not from what most would focus on as the ideal claim to fame, but they show that they have understood Jesus's definition of family. Second, they are deeply aware that what one *does* with grace is of vital importance. Believers need to live merciful lives that mimic the grace shown to them, recognizing always that God is the just judge.[37] In God's mercy, their leadership roles in the church do not come from their status as family of Jesus, but, rather, because they live their lives according to the "kingdom law" (Jas 2:8) and teach others to do the same: "to do justice, and to love kindness, and to walk humbly with your God" (Mic 6:8). This quote pushes us to recognize that these brothers *knew* their Scripture, and knew God through his Scriptures. Their imaginations and identity were shaped by stories of the faithful before them and of God's faithfulness and mercy despite Israel's unfaithfulness. Finally, David DeSilva summarizes:

> The distinctiveness of James's and Jude's teaching lies principally in their commitment to their half brother as God's eschatological agent, who taught the way of God accurately, whose teaching they are committed to handing on, who continues to exercise lordship over the people of God gathered in his name, and who will yet appear to fulfill all that was expected of the Son of Man.[38]

Both James and Jude saw their identity as the firstfruits of the newly restored people of God in Christ, and all of their work was dedicated to calling others into this reality.

And what can we learn from these brothers? First, if we take them seriously, the debates over faith versus works should vanish. As the restored people of God, our calling is to be the servants of God, a possibility that grace alone has opened to us. Servants, however, are the ones who do the work of their master, representing him in all they do. Instead of a faith/works (or a works/grace)

---

37. Darian Lockett, "Objects of Mercy in Jude: The Prophetic Background of Jude 22–23," *Catholic Biblical Quarterly* 77 (2015): 336. He states, "Jude's message, then, suggests that readers— both ancient and modern—should heed the command to show mercy in the context of God's judgment. Calling attention to this feature of Jude furthermore suggests a common concern shared between Jude and his brother James, namely, that 'mercy triumphs over judgment' (Jas 2:13b)."

38. David DeSilva, *The Jewish Teachers of Jesus, James, and Jude: What Earliest Christianity Learned from the Apocrypha and Pseudepigrapha* (Oxford: Oxford University Press, 2012), 258.

dichotomy, these brothers teach it is grace that allows and enables us to be the new creation we are made to be. Second, they both encourage us now to have Scripture-shaped imaginations.[39] These brothers knew their texts and understood how the Scriptures pointed toward Jesus and what that meant for them to be the people of God. We need to gain more than a passing familiarity with the Old Testament, realizing that to be the people of God, we need to know God through his revealed word. We cannot know who he is or who we are supposed to be if we hamstring ourselves by failing to read the Scriptures. One of the first things Jesus did upon his resurrection was to unpack Scripture for his disciples. The whole family of Jesus was clearly immersed in God's word and formed their own identities through reflection on Scripture. This formation of identity is still the calling for God's people today.

39. Cf. Luke Timothy Johnson, "The Use of Leviticus 19 in the Letter of James," *Journal of Biblical Literature* 101 (1982): 391–401; also deSilva, *The Jewish Teachers*.

Chapter 7

Paul: The Christian as an "In-Christ" Person

Sven Soderlund

If the apostle Paul were asked today, "What is a Christian?" I imagine him saying something like, "A Christian is a person 'in Christ.'" But that simple answer would inevitably provoke another question, "Pray tell, brother Paul, what does it mean for a person to be 'in Christ'?" At which point I visualize Paul sitting down to tell the story of redemption beginning with Abraham, Moses, and David, then the prophets, both "major" and "minor," before ending with an account of Jesus's life, death, resurrection, and ascension. Woven into the narrative would be an account of how he himself came to be a person "in Christ," what that meant for his own sense of identity and what it should mean for all persons who call themselves "Christians."

The scene is admittedly speculative, yet not totally without warrant. Paul's most frequently repeated phrase of substance in his letters is the phrase "in Christ" (or a variant thereof such as "in the Lord," "in him," "in whom") occurring as many as 166 times.[1] With the exception of the letter to Titus, the phrase is found in all writings attributed to Paul, while used elsewhere only in 1 Peter (3:16; 5:10, 14). In light of these observations, we would not be far wrong in calling this phrase Paul's signature expression. In fact, Kevin Vanhoozer puts it even more strikingly when he says: "*To be or not to be in Christ* was, for Paul, the only question—new, urgent, and ever relevant."[2] For us the phrase will

---

1. See the section "Basic Literary Data" and n. 5 below.

2. Kevin J. Vanhoozer, "From 'Blessed in Christ' to 'Being in Christ'": The State of Union and the Place of Participation in Paul's Discourse, New Testament Exegesis, and Systematic Theology Today," in *"In Christ" in Paul*, ed. M. J. Thate, K. J. Vanhoozer, and C. R. Campbell, WUNT (Tübingen: Mohr Siebeck, 2014), 3, emphasis original. Albert Schweitzer expressed the same sentiment famously when he said, "This 'being-in-Christ' is the prime enigma of the Pauline teaching: once grasped it gives the clue to the whole" (*The Mysticism of Paul the Apostle*, trans. William Montgomery [New York: Henry Holt, 1931], 3).

serve as our point of entry into the larger question of Paul's understanding of Christian identity. As it happens, it will also take us very close to some of the core issues in the contemporary debate surrounding Paul's theology, especially his soteriology or doctrine of salvation.

Basic Literary Data Related to the "In Christ" Phrases

The following list summarizes the basic data for the occurrences of the "in Christ" phrase (and variants) in Paul's writings.[3]

"in Christ" (*en Christō*)	32
"in Christ Jesus" (*en Christō Iēsou*)	45
"in Christ Jesus our Lord" (*en Christō Iēsou kyriō hēmōn*)	4
"in the Lord" (*en kyriō*)	43
"in the Lord Jesus" (*en kyriō Iēsou*)	4
"in the Lord Jesus Christ" (*en kyriō Iēsou Christō*)	3
"in him" (*en autō*)	21
"in whom" (*en hō*)	11
"in Jesus" (*en Iēsou*)	1
"in the beloved" (*en tō ēgapēmenō*)	1
"in the one strengthening me"(*en tō endynamounti me*)	1
	166[4]

---

3. That is, all those letters attributed to Paul, without indulging the question of ultimate authorship.

4. Although it is difficult to come up with an exact number because of different criteria on what to include, the most comprehensive total of relevant phrases with the preposition *en* is 166. Sang-Won (Aaron) Son, *Corporate Elements in Pauline Anthropology: A Study of Selected Terms, Idioms, and Concepts in the Light of Paul's Usage and Background*, Analecta Biblica 148 (Rome: Editrice Pontificio Istituto Biblico, 2001), excludes *en autō* in Col 2:15, which he takes to refer to the cross rather than to Christ (8 n. 5), and hence counts 165 occurrences (cf. "Appendix, Table 1, 187–88). Constantine R. Campbell (*Paul and Union with Christ: An Exegetical Theological Study* [Grand Rapids: Zondervan, 2012]) includes Col 2:15 (190) but excludes "in Jesus" in Eph 4:21b, and the phrases "in the one strengthening me" (Phil 4:13) and "in God the Father and the Lord Jesus Christ" (1 and 2 Thess 1:1). Adolf Deissman, *Paul: A Study in Social and Religious History*, trans. William E. Wilson (1st German ed., 1912; 2nd ed., 1926), counted 164 occurrences (140), a number frequently cited in the literature. Schweitzer included Gal 6:15, which however has weak textual support (cf. Son, *Corporate Elements*, 8 n. 5).

Common to all the above phrases is the Greek preposition *en* with the dative case, *en* being the most frequently used of all Greek prepositions in antiquity, but also the one with the greatest degree of elasticity of meaning. Thus, grammarians of New Testament Greek typically identify several categories of usage with which the preposition *en* + dative case may be associated according to context. But this kind of grammatical classification of the preposition can easily become complex and subjective as seen in the various grammatical groupings documented in modern lexicons and grammars of New Testament Greek.[5]

When these classifications are applied to the phrase *en Christō* (and variants), the range of usage proposed by scholars remains quite diverse. See for instance the six categories of usage proposed by Murray Harris: incorporative union, agency, mode, cause, location, and sphere of reference.[6] Alternatively, some scholars have proposed thematic classifications of the phrase. Thus Ernest Best, in his 1955 book, *One Body in Christ*, proposed nine classifications, and Constantine Campbell, in his 2012 study *Paul and Union with Christ*, proposed the following eight subthemes for analyzing the "in Christ" phrases in Paul: (1) Things Achieved for/Given to People *in Christ*, (2) Believers' Action *in Christ*, (3) Characteristics of those *in Christ*, (4) Faith *in Christ*, (5) Justification *in Christ*, (6) New Status *in Christ*, (7) *In Christ* as a Periphrasis for Believers, and (8) Trinity *in Christ*.[7]

For detailed and extended exegetical work, these types of analyses can be very helpful, but for our immediate purposes we need a more basic and accessible system of classification. One such scheme revolves around the *objective* and *subjective* uses of the "in Christ" formula, according to which the phrase points either to a redemptive act done on behalf of believers "in" or "by" or "through"

---

5. Compare the twelve uses of the preposition *en* (with subcategories) proposed in the third edition of the standard *Greek-English Lexicon of the New Testament and Other Early Christian Literature*, ed. F. W. Danker et al., 3rd ed. (Chicago: University of Chicago Press, 2000), 326–30, with the ten uses identified by Daniel B. Wallace in *Greek Grammar Beyond the Basics* (Grand Rapids: Zondervan, 1997), 372–75, the nine uses listed by Murray Harris in his book *Prepositions and Theology in the Greek New Testament: An Essential Reference Resource for Exegesis* (Grand Rapids: Zondervan, 2012), 118–20, and the eight uses summarized by A. J. M. Wedderburn in his article "Some Observations on Paul's Use of the Phrases 'in Christ' and 'with Christ,'" *Journal for the Study of the New Testament* 25 (1985): 84–86. According to Wedderburn, the eight uses are the instrumental, temporal, local, "sociative" or "modal," relation or respect, descriptive, "in the power of," and "in the presence of."

6. Murray Harris, *Prepositions and Theology*, 122–25.

7. Ernest Best, *One Body in Christ: A Study in the Relationship of the Church to Christ in the Epistles of the Apostle Paul* (London: SPCK, 1955), 1–8; C. Campbell, *Paul and Union with Christ*, 73–199.

Christ (the objective usage) or to a state of being "in Christ" experienced by believers (the subjective usage).[8] To this may be added yet a third set of contexts in which the apostle has in view his own activity or passages in which he exhorts believers to live out their calling both in relation to those outside of Christ as well as to those "in Christ." For convenience we may speak of the latter type of "in Christ" phrases as having to do with applied or *hortatory* contexts.[9] These three categories of usage will therefore provide a convenient structure for the rest of this article, followed by a final section on how Paul himself was able to exhibit the characteristics of an "in Christ" person.

The "In Christ" Phrases in "Objective" Contexts in Paul's Letters

What we are looking for here are passages that speak of redemptive acts brought about on behalf of believers in or by Christ, or are anticipated yet to be accomplished through Christ. A few passages illustrating this "objective" use of the "in Christ" formula are the following:

Rom 3:24—Believers "are justified freely by [God's] grace through the redemption that came *in Christ Jesus*" (or *by Christ Jesus,* NIV; or *through Christ Jesus,* GNB, NLT)

Rom 6:23—"the gift of God is eternal life *in Christ Jesus our Lord*" (or *through Christ Jesus our Lord,* NIVmg, NLT)

1 Cor 1:4–5—"I always thank God for you because of his grace given you *in Christ Jesus* [or *through Christ Jesus,* GNB], that *in him* [or *by him,* C. Campbell, 176] you have been enriched in everything"

8. Such objective/subjective schema have been proposed previously by Michael Parsons in his article "'In Christ' in Paul," *Vox Evangelica* 18 (1988): 25–44; by James Dunn, *The Theology of Paul the Apostle* (Grand Rapids: Eerdmans, 1998), 397–98; and most recently by Kevin Vanhoozer, "From 'Blessed in Christ' to 'Being in Christ.'" Vanhoozer expresses the distinction between the "objective" and "subjective" uses of the phrase nicely: on the one hand "God has acted in Christ to bring about an objective state of affairs (i.e., a new humanity)"; on the other hand, "believers subjectively realize this union by experiencing one or more of its blessings (e.g., sanctification)" (24).

9. Each of the authors mentioned in the previous note (Parsons, Dunn, and Vanhoozer) also acknowledges the existence of a third category. For his part, Parsons refers to this as Paul's *ethical* usages. Dunn leaves the category unnamed but describes it as containing phrases "where Paul has in view his own activity or is exhorting his readers to adopt a particular attitude or course of action" (398). Vanhoozer focuses on the several instances where the community dimension of the experienced reality "in Christ" comes to the fore and calls this Paul's *intersubjective* use of the phrase (24).

1 Cor 15:22—"*in Christ* [or *through Christ*, C. Campbell, 142] all will be made alive"

2 Cor 5:19—"God was reconciling the world to himself *in Christ*" (or *through Christ*, Campbell, 79–80; Harris, 125–26)

2 Cor 5:21—"so that we might become the righteousness of God *in [Christ]*," cf. NLT, "so that we could be made right with God *through Christ*"

Gal 2:17—"in seeking to be justified *in Christ Jesus* . . ." (or *by Christ*, Harris, 123; or through *faith in Christ*, NLT)

Gal 3:14—"that the blessing of Abraham might come to the Gentiles *in Christ Jesus*" (or *through Christ Jesus*, NIV; or *through the work of Christ Jesus*, NLT; or *by means of Christ Jesus*, GNB)

Eph 4:32—"forgive each other just as God *in Christ* [or *through Christ*, Harris, 123] forgave you"

Col 1:14 "*in* [or *through*] him [i.e., Christ] we have redemption, the forgiveness of sins"

Summarizing the above, we can say that for a person to be "in Christ" means to have had something done by or through Christ on their behalf. Specifically, it means for persons to be recipients of God's grace through Christ (Rom 3:24, 6:23) resulting in a status of having been "justified" by God (Rom 3:24; 2 Cor 5:21; Gal 2:17), reconciled with God (2 Cor 5:19), and forgiven (Eph 4:32, Col 1:14). Moreover, it means to have received "the gift of God [which is] eternal life" (Rom 6:23), to be enriched in everything by virtue of having received God's grace (1 Cor 1:4–5), and to have inherited the "blessing of Abraham" (Gal 3:14).

In yet other passages the apostle writes of additional blessings associated with being "in Christ" such as freedom from the law of sin and death (Rom 8:2) as well as freedom from the fear of separation from the love of God (Rom 8:39). Also, it means to have been sanctified through Christ (1 Cor 1:2) and to have a clear understanding of God's covenant (2 Cor 3:14). In one way or another, all of these passages make reference to the objective saving work of Christ on behalf of believers. Vanhoozer summarizes this instrumental use of the preposition *en* in these contexts thus: "God forgives us 'in Christ' by making Christ and his cross the instrument of the action by which God deals with sin."[10]

The point made in the above review of the benefits obtained in or through Christ on behalf of the believer is reinforced by several passages that employ not only the preposition *en* with the dative but also the preposition *dia* with the genitive case, the standard translation of which is "by" or "through." Five passages in Romans chapter 5 will illustrate the point nicely.

10. "From 'Blessed in Christ' to 'Being in Christ,'" 14.

Rom 5:1—"Since we have been justified by faith, we have peace with God *through our Lord Jesus Christ.*"

Rom 5:8-9—"Since we have been justified by his blood, how much more shall we be saved from God's wrath *through him!*"

Rom 5:11—"We also rejoice in God through our Lord Jesus Christ, *through whom* we have now received reconciliation.*"

Rom 5:17—"how much more will those who receive God's abundant provision of grace and of the gift of righteousness reign in life *through the one man, Jesus Christ.*"

Rom 5:21—"as sin reigned in death, so also may grace reign through righteousness to bring eternal life *through Jesus Christ our Lord.*"

As in the case of the preposition *en* with the dative, so in the above passages the benefits that accrue to believers "through Christ" (*dia Christou*) are those of salvation (Rom 5:9), reconciliation (5:11; cf. 2 Cor 5:18), eternal life (5:17, 21), and peace with God (5:1). Yet other passages refer to the victory (1 Cor 15:57) and comfort (2 Cor 1:5) obtained through Christ, or even to the special gift of apostleship received by Paul (Rom 1:5; Gal 1:1, 12).

If we now inquire into the role of faith in this process, the two key passages are those of Romans 3:22 ("God's righteousness [has come] through faith *Iēsou Christou*") and Galatians 2:16 ("no one is justified by the works of the law but by faith *Iēsou Christou*"). But thereby hangs a controversy of major proportions in contemporary Pauline scholarship, the question being how to translate the underlying Greek genitive construction *Iēsou Christou,* namely, as a subjective genitive ("the faith/faithfulness *of* Jesus Christ") or as an objective genitive ("faith *in* Jesus Christ"). Grammatically either is possible, meaning that we are left with context as the only arbitrator. Persuasive arguments are proposed on both sides (cf. Richard Hays, who argues for the subjective genitive contra James Dunn, who argues for the objective genitive).[11] But even if the subjective genitive construction were deemed more probable, the point about faith being deposited *in* Christ is not compromised by these passages since the critical passage of Galatians 2:16 has embedded within it also the statement "we have believed in [*eis*] Christ Jesus," with which may be compared Galatians 3:26, "you are all children of God through faith in [*en*] Christ Jesus."[12]

If this sounds too much like a case of Protestant proof texting, it is nonethe-

---

11. Richard B. Hays, *The Faith of Jesus Christ: The Narrative Substructure of Galatians 3:1–4:11,* 2nd ed. (Grand Rapids: Eerdmans, 2002), 119–62 and 272–97; Dunn, *Theology of Paul,* 379–85.

12. See also the phrase "your faith in Christ Jesus" with both *eis Christon* (Col 2:5; cf. Acts 20:21; 24:24) and *en Christō / en tō Kyriō* (Eph 1:1, 15; Col 1:4; 1 Tim 1:14; 3:13; 2 Tim 1:13; 3:15).

less where a basic review of the "in Christ" language seems at least initially to lead us. Contemporary Pauline scholarship has examined from every angle the doctrine of "justification by faith" as traditionally formulated and found it wanting in many respects. It is said to be a grossly inadequate construct by which to describe Paul's soteriology.[13] But even if it is an inadequate formulation by which to represent an exhaustive articulation of Paul's doctrine of salvation, yet when looking for a basic identity marker of an "in Christ" person (that is, a "Christian"), the exercise of personal faith in the person and completed work of Christ was surely one of the foundational components of Paul's soteriology (Rom 10:9–11).

But it is not only faith that is critical to the appropriation of the benefits of Christ's death, so is the role of the Spirit. This is clear from the several times Paul uses the phrase *en pneumati*, literally "in the Spirit," a phrase that, like the phrase *en Christō*, often needs to be understood instrumentally, hence "by the Spirit." Thus, heart "circumcision" is effected "by the Spirit" (Rom 2:29); Gentile converts are "sanctified by the Spirit" (Rom 15:16); former sinners are "washed," "sanctified," and "justified" "in the name of the Lord Jesus Christ and by the Spirit" (1 Cor 6:11); believers "live by the Spirit" (Gal 6:1; cf. 2 Cor 3:6; Rom 8:4, 5) and have access to the Father through Christ and "by the Spirit" (Eph 2:18).[14]

In short, according to the apostle, a person "in Christ" is someone who by faith in Christ has been "justified" (declared/made "just") by God (Rom 3:24; Gal 2:17), has received the gift of eternal life (Rom 6:23), as well as having been made alive and sanctified by the Spirit (Gal 6:1; 1 Cor 6:11). Paul, it seems, identified these "objective" facts as some the sine qua non identity markers of the Christian.

The "In Christ" Phrases in "Subjective" Contexts in Paul's Letters

As important as the expression of faith in the completed work of Christ was for Paul, resulting in the creation of a person newly justified by God and made alive by the Spirit, this was by no means the totality of what the apostle considered integral to Christian identity. For although Paul often used the "in Christ" phrase

13. Cf. among others, Douglas A. Campbell's radical reinterpretation of Paul's letter to the Romans in his study, *The Deliverance of God: An Apocalyptic Rereading of Justification in Paul* (Grand Rapids: Eerdmans, 2009), esp. 36–95.

14. Adolf Deissmann, in his enthusiasm to explain the "in Christ" theme in Paul, argued for the identification of the phrases *en Christō* and *en pneumati* (*Paul*, 138, 142–43), but this was clearly an oversimplification and misinterpretation of the relationship between the Spirit and Christ (cf. Son, *Corporate Elements*, 18–20).

in contexts requiring an instrumental or agency reading as seen in the previous section, grammarians are agreed that the root meaning of the preposition *en* was in fact spatial or locative, referring to a space or sphere in which something or someone was found. Hence one should not be surprised to find that the "in Christ" phrases sometimes also carry such a locative or incorporative/participatory sense, that is, contexts that assume a level of personal participation in Christ that goes beyond the expression of faith-as-trust.

The following are some of the most common passages associated with this more subjective or "incorporative/participatory" usage of the "in Christ"/*en Christō* constellation of phrases:

Rom 8:1—"There is now no condemnation for those who are *in Christ Jesus*"
Rom 12:5—"we all are one body *in Christ*"
1 Cor 1:30—"It is because of [God] that you are *in Christ Jesus*"
1 Cor 15:17–18—"If Christ has not been raised . . . then those who have fallen asleep *in Christ* are lost"
2 Cor 5:17—"if anyone is *in Christ* [they are] a new creation [or, a new creation has come]"
Gal 1:22—"I was personally unknown to the churches of Judea which are *in Christ*"
Gal 3:28—"you are all one *in Christ Jesus*"
Eph 1:13—"you also were included *in Christ* when you heard the message of truth"
Phil 1:1—"To all God's holy people *in Christ*"
1 Thess 4:16—"The dead *in Christ* will rise first"

Similar "incorporation" passages can be found with the "in the Lord"/*en (tō) kyriō* phrases. Thus Paul regularly sends greetings to individuals "in the Lord" (Rom 16:8–13; 1 Cor 4:17), or he calls the Corinthians his "workmanship in the Lord" (1 Cor 9:1), as he also calls Onesimus a beloved brother "both in the flesh and in the Lord" (Phlm 16). With these should be compared the several occasions on which the apostle uses the preposition *syn*, "with," referring to believers' close personal association with Christ.[15]

But what are the implications of this locative use of the "in Christ" phrases? What does it mean for the believer to be placed or to be dwelling "in Christ"?

---

15. Paul uses the phrases *syn [tō] Christō, syn kyriō, syn Iēsou, syn autō* a total of 12 times, but uses even more frequently the preposition *syn* compounded with both nouns and verbs (14 different words in 20 different contexts; see Son, *Corporate Elements*, 20 n. 74; cf. Dunn, *Theology of Paul*, 402–3 nn. 62, 63; also chap. 5 in C. Campbell, *Paul and Union with Christ*, 217–36).

In the history of the investigations of the "in Christ" motif beginning at the end of the nineteenth and early twentieth centuries, especially in the studies by Adolf Deissmann, Wilhelm Bousset, and Albert Schweitzer,[16] it was generally assumed that most if not all of Paul's "in Christ" passages were those of the locative or incorporative type, prompting the assumption that Paul practiced a mystical relationship of one sort or another with Christ. But even if the assumption of a mystical relationship of whatever kind was reading too much into the phrase, the challenge remains to understand what Paul could have meant by those passages where a participatory sense seems to be required by the context. The challenge has been engaged and continues to be pressed home in a number of probing works.

For instance, Professor C. F. D. Moule of Cambridge, writing in his 1977 book, *The Origin of Christology*, cited three scholars of his day (Lady Helen Oppenheimer, Prof. Cunliffe-Jones, and Dr. A. R. Peacock) who had expressed their puzzlement at trying to come to terms with the meaning of the "in Christ" motif in Paul. Professor Cunliffe-Jones spoke for them all when he asked, "What does [the phrase] mean in the context of the 20th century? Apart from the direct biological connection, it is hard to see what sort of solidarity we might have with Christ." Since "direct biological union" was obviously not an option, Professor Moule confessed that he himself was puzzled at the meaning of the phrase, especially since no one prior to Paul had written like this before.[17]

Writing in the same year that Professor Moule's book was published (1977), E. P. Sanders also concluded that although Paul's language of participation "in Christ" was highly significant for understanding the apostle's theology, he was still left asking at the end of the book, "But what does this [participation in Christ] mean? How are we to understand it? We seem to lack a category of 'reality'—real participation in Christ, real participation in the Spirit by which to understand Paul on this point." Generously, however, Sanders acknowledged that his own bewilderment did not mean that Paul himself did not have an appropriate category for comprehending the notion of "real participation" or union with Christ.[18]

Different attempts have been made to address these concerns. In fact, Moule himself proposed the notion of the "corporate Christ" as the best way

16. Adolf Deissmann, *Die Neutestamenliche Formel "in Christo Jesu"* (Marburg: N.G. Elwert, 1892), followed by *Paul: A Study in Social and Religious History*, trans. William E. Wilson (1st German ed., 1912; 2nd ed., 1926; esp. 135–57); Wilhelm Bousset, *Kyrios Christos*, trans. John E. Steely (1st German ed., 1913; English translation of 5th edition, Abingdon, 1970), 153–72; and Albert Schweitzer, *Mysticism of Paul*.

17. C. F. D. Moule, *The Origin of Christology* (Cambridge: Cambridge University Press, 1977), 47–51.

18. E. P. Sanders, *Paul and Palestinian Judaism* (Minneapolis: Fortress, 1977), 522–23.

to explain the use of the "in Christ" phrase, according to which Christ serves as the representative head of the new humanity, as Adam served as representative head of humanity apart from Christ (cf. 1 Cor 15:22),[19] a point of view later associated with the writings of James Dunn and others.[20]

More recently Richard Hays has proposed four helpful categories by which to understand Paul's concept of "participation in Christ."[21] The first has to do with the notion of participation as "Belonging to a Family," according to which "believers are said to be part of the household of which Christ is the head" and as such *participate in* the privileges and benefits of that family." Other categories are those of "Political or Military Solidarity with Christ," "Participation in the *Ekklēsia*," and "Living within the Christ Story."

Hays's third category, "Participation in the *Ekklēsia*," looks on the surface to be similar to N. T. Wright's concept of believers belonging to the new covenant community. Thus, for Paul to be "in the anointed one" (that is, "in Christ" or, as Wright prefers, "in the Messiah"), "is to be part of the people over which he rules." It means to come "'into Messiah' in baptism (*eis Christon*, Rom 6:23)" and then to stand, to exist "in Messiah," which in the end amounts to "a basic statement of Christian identity."[22]

As exciting as it is to see contemporary New Testament scholars engaging the question of what it means for believers to participate in the life of Christ, it would be wrong to think that this is an exclusively modern discussion. As has recently been pointed out, even Luther and (especially) Calvin had much to say on the subject. Although both reformers have been interpreted to emphasize primarily the objective results of Christ's work through the doctrine of justification by faith, it is now recognized that even they placed much weight

19. The view was first articulated in C. F. D. Moule's *The Phenomenon of the New Testament: An Inquiry into the Implications of Certain Features of the New Testament*, Studies in Biblical Theology (Naperville, IL: Alec R. Allenson, 1967), chap. 2, "The Corporate Christ," 21–42, esp. 22–29; later again in *The Origin of Christology* (Cambridge: Cambridge University Press, 1977), chap. 2, "The Corporate Christ," 47–96, esp. 47–62. The same notion was later elaborated by Michael Parsons in his 1988 article "'In Christ' in Paul," 25–44, and further defended by Son, *Corporate Elements*, esp. 27–28.

20. Dunn, *Theology of Paul*, 408–10. Related to this is Stanley Porter's proposal for a "spherical" use of the "in Christ" formula, "according to which it is said that one is in the sphere of Christ's control," for which Porter (like Dunn) cites the Adam/Christ contrast in 1 Cor 15:22. See Stanley E. Porter, *Idioms of the Greek New Testament*, 2nd ed. (London: Sheffield Academic Press, 1994), 159.

21. Richard B. Hays, "What Is 'Real Participation in Christ'? A Dialogue with E. P. Sanders on Pauline Soteriology," in *Redefining First-Century Jewish and Christian Identities: Essays in Honor of Ed Parish Sanders*, ed. Fabian E. Udoh et al. (Notre Dame: University of Notre Dame Press, 2008), 336–51.

22. N. T. Wright, *Paul and the Faithfulness of God* (Minneapolis: Fortress, 2013), 830–33.

SVEN SODERLUND

on the importance of being related to Christ in more than juridical ways. In the case of Luther, this dimension of his teaching has been brought to light in the so-called Finnish School of interpretation, which highlights several passages in Luther's writings that give expression to his concern for something more than juridical justification.[23] In the case of Calvin various scholars point to the high degree of importance that Calvin attached to the believer being closely related to Christ in personal ways.[24] In the twentieth century it is impressive to note how a Reformed theologian such as Karl Barth emphasized this subjective or experiential dimension of a Christian's personal identity.[25]

In the Eastern Orthodox tradition there is a longstanding interest in the believer's close union with Christ, and there are those scholars today who are mining this tradition for what it can contribute to our understanding of what it means to live in and be united to Christ. In fact, Richard Hays himself closed his article referred to above by cautiously pointing in the direction of the "thought and spirituality of Eastern Orthodoxy" as a possible source for understanding what is entailed in Paul's participatory language. Hays illustrated the potential for helpful insights along these lines by focusing briefly on Gregory of Nyssa's treatise *On Perfection*, in which Gregory proposes, among other things, that conformity to Christ occurs through contemplative prayer.[26] The question is even asked whether we can appropriate in any way the Eastern concept of *theosis*, according to which the believer also participates in a process of divinization or deification.[27] Two Protestant writers who unapologetically feel free to use

23. See Carl E. Braaten and Robert W. Jenson, eds., *Union with Christ: The New Finnish Interpretation of Luther* (Grand Rapids: Eerdmans, 1998), featuring the writings of Tuomo Mannermaa. Also, Stephen Chester, "Apocalyptic Union: Martin Luther's Account of Faith in Christ," in *"In Christ" in Paul*, ed. M. J. Thate, K. J. Vanhoozer, and C. R. Campbell, WUNT (Tübingen: Mohr Siebeck, 2014), 375–98.

24. Often quoted in this regard is *Institutes* III.1.1: "First, we must understand that as long as Christ remains outside of us, and we are separated from him, all that he has suffered and done for the salvation of the human race remains useless and of no value to us . . . for, as I have said, all that he possesses is nothing to us until we grow into one body with him" (here quoted from Marcus Peter Johnson, *One with Christ: An Evangelical Theology of Salvation* [Wheaton, IL: Crossway, 2013], 16). See also J. Todd Billings, "John Calvin: United to God through Christ," in *Partakers of the Divine Nature: The History and Development of Deification in the Christian Traditions*, ed. Michael J. Christensen and Jeffrey A. Wittung (Grand Rapids: Baker Academic, 2007), 200–18, and Julie Canlis, "The Fatherhood of God and Union with Christ in Calvin," in *"In Christ" in Paul*, ed. M. J. Thate, K. J. Vanhoozer, and C. R. Campbell, WUNT (Tübingen: Mohr Siebeck, 2014), 399–425.

25. Adam Neder, *Participation in Christ: An Entry into Karl Barth's Church Dogmatics* (Louisville: Westminster John Knox, 2009).

26. In the section "Insights from Eastern Orthodoxy," 347–49.

27. See Michael J. Christensen and Jeffrey A. Wittung, eds., *Partakers of the Divine Nature:*

the term in explaining the process of justification, sanctification, and transformation are Veli-Matti Kärkkäinen and Michael Gorman. According to Gorman, the degree of participation in the life of Christ should be so personal and intimate as to constitute a kind of coexistence and co-crucifixion with Christ, language borrowed from Paul himself (cf. Gal 2:19–20).[28]

Having briefly reviewed two important dimensions of the Christian identity as portrayed in the writings of the apostle Paul—what we have called the objective and subjective dimensions of the life "in Christ"—the question now emerges whether the apostle himself privileged the objective work of Christ on the believer's behalf over the believer's subjective experience of participation in the life of Christ, or vice versa. In other words, does the Christian's identity consist more in being justified by faith or in experiencing intimate union with Christ? The consensus of classic Protestant theology has been strongly in favor of the former, declaring the doctrine of justification of faith as articulated especially in the Lutheran tradition central to Paul's theology. It was the early-twentieth-century work of Adolf Deissmann and Albert Schweitzer that initially challenged this consensus. In Schweitzer's famous analogy, the doctrine of righteousness by faith was but "a subsidiary crater . . . within the rim of the main crater," namely "the doctrine of redemption through the being-in-Christ."[29]

But are we really compelled to opt for one being more important than the other? Would that not be like choosing between which wing of the airplane is more important, the right or the left? The question is absurd, of course, as much in application to airplanes as in relation to Paul's theology. Therefore we can agree with N. T. Wright when he says that the division between "juristic" and "participationist" analysis of Paul's soteriology is a false dichotomy because it seeks to drive a wedge between ways of thinking about Paul alien to his theology. Thus Wright can paraphrase Romans 8:1 tongue-in-cheek as follows: "There is therefore now no contradiction between 'justification' and 'being in Christ,' between law court language and incorporative language." Why? Because

---

The History and Development of Deification in the Christian Traditions (Grand Rapids: Baker Academic, 2007).

28. Veli-Matti Kärkkäinen, *One with God: Salvation as Deification and Justification* (Collegeville, MN: Liturgical Press, 2004); also his chapter "Deification View," in *Justification: Five Views*, ed. James K. Beilby and Paul Rhodes Eddy (Downers Grove, IL: IVP Academic, 2011), 219–43, in which he seeks to apply the new interpretation of Luther by Finnish scholars to the relationship between justification and participation in the writings of Luther. For Michael J. Gorman, see especially his book *Inhabiting the Cruciform God: Kenosis, Justification, and Theosis in Paul's Narrative Soteriology* (Grand Rapids: Eerdmans, 2009), as well as his article "Paul's Corporate, Cruciform, Missional *Theosis* in 2 Corinthians," in *"In Christ" in Paul*, ed. M. J. Thate, K. J. Vanhoozer, and C. R. Campbell, WUNT (Tübingen: Mohr Siebeck, 2014), 181–208.

29. *Mysticism of Paul the Apostle*, 225.

a full-orbed understanding of Paul's theology will show that they, like mercy and truth, have met together and kissed each other.[30]

In short, a Christian's identity consists as much in being justified by faith "in/through Christ" as in being united to him and participating in his life in the closest possible way.

The "In Christ" Phrases in "Hortatory" Contexts in Paul's Letters

On the basis of what has been observed so far, it seems clear from Paul's use of the "in Christ" phrases that the apostle understood the Christian life to consist both in faith and fellowship, justification and participation. But is there more? Indeed there is, for Paul also uses this phrase in contexts that describe the kind of interpersonal conduct expected of believers.

One of the notable things about the apostle Paul's ministry is the fact that he was at the same time missionary, theologian, and pastor. As a missionary he called people to faith in Christ; as a theologian he instructed them in the meaning of their standing in Christ; as a pastor he exhorted them to live in community in vital relationship to other believers since they were all "one in Christ Jesus" (Gal 3:28). It is for this reason that his "in Christ" expressions are often found in plural contexts. To the Roman Christians he writes that they are to "count [themselves] dead to sin but alive to God in Christ Jesus" (Rom 6:11). At the end of his letter to the Corinthians he sends his love to "all [who are] in Christ Jesus" (1 Cor 16:24), and he reminds the Colossians that "in Christ you [plural] have been brought to fullness" (Col 2:10).

On the basis of this communitarian identity of all believers, the apostle could appeal to his young converts to be "kind and compassionate to one another, forgiving each other, just as in Christ God [had forgiven them]" (Eph 4:32). Similarly, it was because of their relationships to "one another" that he could urge the Philippians to have the same disposition of mind to others as had been demonstrated to them "in Christ" (Phil 2:5). He urged the Thessalonian believers to excel in living "in the Lord Jesus" in accordance with his verbal instructions while present with them (1 Thess 4:1). And in spite of all the internal struggles and dysfunction that the Corinthian believers had experienced, he

---

30. Wright, *Faithfulness of God*, 900–902. Interestingly, even Sanders acknowledged that "righteousness by faith and participation in Christ ultimately amount to the same thing" (*Paul and Palestinian Judaism: A Comparison of Patterns of Religion* [Minneapolis: Fortress, 1977], 506), though it still is probably true, as Hays expressed it, that the idea that "righteousness can be *equated* with participation in Christ is a subsidiary crater in Sanders' thought" ("Real Participation," 337–38).

could nevertheless encourage them with the word that all their labor "in the Lord" was not in vain (1 Cor 15:58). Moreover, Paul expected his converts to apply the same standards of conduct in their dealings with those outside the Lord as with those "in the Lord." This meant that since the converts were now "light in the Lord," they needed to live as "children of light" in relation to those outside (Eph 5:8).

Paul's Own Experience as an "In Christ" Person

But by what authority, one wonders, could Paul claim the right to give commands and make exhortations such as those enumerated above? For Paul there was no doubting this authority. On several occasions he claimed that it was his status "in Christ" or "in the Lord" that authorized him to exhort others to conduct themselves in a manner consistent with their calling. After all, he said, it was "in Christ" he had become their father through the gospel (1 Cor 4:15), and it was as a result of his work "in the Lord" that they had become the seal of his apostleship (1 Cor 9:1–2). Hence, as someone sent from God "in Christ," he claimed the right to admonish the Corinthians to corrective action (2 Cor 2:17; cf. a similar claim in 12:19, "We have been speaking in the sight of God as those in Christ"). Similarly, it was because of his status "in the Lord" that he could insist that the Ephesians no longer live as Gentiles in the futility of their thinking (Eph 4:17). With the Galatians, it was his confidence "in the Lord" that led him to believe that they would ultimately see things from his point of view and act accordingly (Gal 5:10). Because he rejoiced "in the Lord" (Phil 4:10; cf. 1:18; 2:17) even in the midst of his own threatening circumstances, he had earned the right to exhort the Philippians to do the same (Phil 4:3, 4; cf. 2:17–18).

All this is admirable in its own way, but it also raises the question to what extent Paul was able to live out his own experience "in Christ" consistently. If an "in Christ" person was someone who had appropriated the objective work of Christ's death, who was subjectively pursuing a life of intimate fellowship with Christ, and who was living out all of this with integrity and sensitivity in one's social contexts, and commanded others to do the same, what evidence is there that Paul exemplified these identity markers in his own life? In other words, what evidence is there that Paul himself practiced the "in Christ" message that he preached?

As for understanding and accepting the finished work of Christ, can there be any doubt that if anyone had grasped and appropriated the significance of Christ's death it was the former persecutor of the church, Saul of Tarsus? Was anyone so radically transformed in their thinking from one worldview to another? For Christ's sake he considered himself to have lost everything of worth in his former life. Not that he regretted it, for what he had considered of value in his earlier life he now regarded as less than worthless in comparison with the privilege of being found "in Christ," accepted by God not on the basis of fulfilling the law but on the basis of relating to Christ through faith (Phil 3:7–9). Conscious of the enormous privilege of having been given special insight into the meaning of Christ's life and death, he also felt keenly the responsibility of sharing these insights with his contemporaries (Eph 3:7–10).

Now it was one thing for Paul to fully grasp the new theological insight inherent in the gospel and to celebrate his standing in Christ, but how would this affect his own life of discipleship? As a learned person with a razor-sharp mind, how would the "in Christ" encounter affect not only his new worldview but also his own "habits of the heart"? The intellectual life could be intoxicating in itself; nonetheless, far from his "in Christ" experience ending up as a mere intellectual engagement, it meant instead the beginning of a lifelong pursuit of fellowship with Christ at the deepest levels, a pursuit that can best be described as a passion to be united to Christ in his life, death, and resurrection (Phil 3:10). As a new creation "in Christ" (2 Cor 5:17) Paul was consumed by love for this one who had become not only his heavenly Redeemer but also his personal and intimate friend, so much so that he regarded departing to be with Christ preferable to continued life on earth (Phil 1:21–23; 2 Cor 5:8).

Given this special relationship between Paul and Christ, it was as though the apostle felt himself co-crucified with Christ, even to the point not only of dwelling in Christ but also of Christ dwelling in him (Gal 2:20). Conscious of this special relationship with Christ and his unique calling, it became Paul's ambition always to live in a way that would please his Lord (2 Cor 5:9). But that also meant living in relation to others "with integrity and godly sincerity" (2 Cor 1:12), not being double minded but always speaking the truth, saying what he meant and meaning what he said (2 Cor 1:15–17; 7:4). Similarly, it meant rejecting any thought of being engaged in his ministry for monetary gain (2 Cor 2:17; cf. 8:20), just as it meant renouncing secret and deceitful devices in pursuit of his apostolic ministry (2 Cor 4:2). He would disown any attempt to distort the word of God, his goal being instead to teach the truth of the gospel plainly (2 Cor 4:2b; cf. Col 4:4). As a servant of the gospel, it also meant living the exemplary life in dealing with hardships and practicing purity, patience, and kindness in all his dealings with those inside and outside the church (2 Cor 6:4–10), doing what was right not only in the eyes of the Lord but also in the eyes of others (2 Cor 8:21).

Thus, Paul both taught and modeled the "in Christ" life, a life characterized by objective, subjective, and practical realities. Of some things he was sure they pertained to the essence of Christian identity, for example, having been freely justified by God's grace through the redemption that came in/through Jesus Christ (Rom 3:24), as well as participating in the life of Christ and being united to him in bonds of intimate fellowship (Phil 3:10–11). At the same time, he was keenly aware that such a life "in Christ" was intended not for private enjoyment but was to be lived out in community relationships. Moreover, such a community life "in Christ" would inevitably entail sacrificial service, even to the point of being misunderstood and rejected by the very communities for whom he had endured so much of "troubles, hardships and distresses" (2 Cor 6:4).

Do these marks of Christian identity and lived experience still apply today? Certainly there is no indication in Paul's writings that he thought they were limited to his time and place in history. On the basis of the testimony and experience of this remarkable man, we are invited to test and see for ourselves whether his description of the "in Christ" life still has relevance for today.

PART THREE

Identity in the Early Church

Chapter 8

Justin Martyr: Christian Identity-Formation in the Second Century CE

MIKAEL TELLBE

Justin Martyr (ca. 100–167 CE) is one of our most important sources for the formation of Christian identity in the second century. Justin was born into a non-Jewish family in Samaria (in Flavia Neapolis, formerly Shechem) at the turn of the century.[1] Early on he desired to study philosophy and turned to a certain Stoic philosopher. After some time Justin left him in disappointment from not getting enough answers to his theological and metaphysical questions. He continued his search and turned to a Peripatetic (a follower of Aristotle's philosophy), then to "a famous Pythagorean" and after some time to a Platonist, to whom he also became a disciple (*Dial.* 2.2–6).[2] The philosophy of Plato seemed to be the end of his search for truth, until he met "a certain old man, by no means contemptible in appearance, exhibiting meek and venerable manners," who encouraged him to rethink the platonic understanding of the human soul and its immortality (*Dial.* 3.1). Justin was heavily impacted by the old man's Jewish-Christian teaching: "a flame was kindled in my soul; and a love of the prophets, and of those men who are friends of Christ, possessed me; and whilst revolving his words in my mind, I found this philosophy alone to be safe and profitable" (*Dial.* 8.1). He was also challenged by the ascetic lives of the early Christians and their courage in face of death: "For I myself, too, when I was delighting in the doctrines of Plato, and heard the Christians slandered, and saw them fearless of death, and of all other things which are counted fearful,

---

1. Cf. *1 Apol.* 1.1. For an introduction to Justin's life, see L. W. Barnard, *Justin Martyr: His Life and Thought* (Cambridge: Cambridge University Press, 1967), 1–13; E. F. Osborn, *Justin Martyr*, Beiträge zur historischen Theologie 47 (Tübingen: Mohr Siebeck, 1973), 6–10. Cf. also Eusebius's account of the life of Justin, *Hist. eccl.* 4.8.3–5; 4.11.8–11; 4.16.1–4.18.10.

2. Quotations from *1–2 Apology* (*Apol.*) and *Dialogue* (*Dial.*) follow the translation of A. Roberts and J. Donaldson, in vol. 1 of *The Ante-Nicene Fathers* (Grand Rapids: Eerdmans, 1950).

perceived that it was impossible that they could be living in wickedness and pleasure" (2 *Apol.* 12.1).

Sometime before 135 CE, Justin decided to convert to the Christian faith, and now spread the knowledge of Christianity as the "true philosophy" (*Dial.* 8.1). During the reign of the Roman emperor Antoninus Pius (138–161 CE), he arrived in Rome and started his own school. After some years, Justin became one of the great second-century Christian apologists and philosophers, defending and explicating the Christian faith towards non-Christians as well as Jews. At the end of his life, Justin was tried, together with six of his students, by Junius Rusticus, a Roman urban prefect. According to *The Martyrdom of Justin*, Justin was scourged and beheaded in ca. 167 CE, during the principate of Marcus Aurelius.

Justin was a prolific author writing in Greek, by some regarded as "one of the original thinkers Christianity produced."[3] Although Eusebius mentions numerous works by Justin, few of them have survived and only three works bearing his name have generally been considered authentic: *1–2 Apology* and *Dialogue with Trypho*. The first text-corpus, *1–2 Apology*, was written in order to defend the Christian faith and urge the emperor and the senate to abandon the persecution of the Christians and to treat them fairly in the imperial courts.[4] The second text, *Dialogue with Trypho*, captures the conversation between Justin and an unknown, distinguished Jewish teacher called Trypho. Justin's texts demonstrate that he was a man "who learned to move between cultures": between the Greco-Roman paganism in which he grew up, the Greek-speaking diaspora Judaism, and the emerging Christian movement.[5] His texts are set within a conflict context: *1–2 Apology* articulate Justin's understanding of the Christian belief in the external conflict setting between the secular Roman society and the Christians, and *Dialogue with Trypho* articulates Justin's understanding of the Christian belief in the context of an internal conflict between non-Christian Jews and Christians (whether of Jewish or Gentile origin). Since both personal and social identities, whether ancient or modern ones, are primarily formed and expressed in relation to other individuals or groups and become particularly salient in conflict settings, Justin's texts are especially useful in order to capture the articulation of Christian identity in the mid–second century CE.

Before the analysis of Justin's articulation of Christian identity, a short

3. Osborne, *Justin Martyr*, 201.

4. I do not intend to discuss the complex relation between the *1 Apology* and *2 Apology*. For this, see D. Minns and P. Parvis, *Justin, Philosopher and Martyr: Apologies* (Oxford: Oxford University Press, 2009).

5. So S. Parvis and P. Fosters, eds., *Justin Martyr and His Worlds* (Minneapolis: Fortress, 2007), 126–27.

word on the notion of identity employed in this chapter is appropriate. As the individual thinks of oneself and others as belonging to the group, he or she stereotypes both him or herself and other ingroup members. The interest of the group becomes the interest of the individual, and the norms of the group become the norms of the individual. A fundamental notion in this process of self-definition and social identity formation implies differentiation from one or more "others" by the drawing of boundary lines, what is called "othering." The "other," or the enemy, becomes an intrinsic part of a group's self-definition; the authors understand themselves and their readers in terms of what one is not. Difference and similarity reflect each other across a shared boundary; as expressed by the sociologist Richard Jenkins, "at the boundary we discover what we are in what we are not."[6] Hence, the definition of deviants, antitypes, and outsiders becomes significant as a way of defining the prototypical member, the normative insider, and the social identity of the group. This process may be referred to as a form of categorization, a process that is based on stereotyping, whether positively (of group members) or negatively (of nonmembers).[7]

Based on this understanding of identity, the following analysis of Christian identity as expressed by Justin Martyr will be explored; first, from Justin's defense of Christian identity in conflict with the Roman state and the pagan world in *1–2 Apology*, and then from his defense of Christian identity in conflict with non-Christian Jewish faith in *Dialogue with Trypho*. Hence, in *1–2 Apology*, Christian identity is primarily articulated versus pagan (Gentile) identity, and in *Dialogue with Trypho*, Christian identity is primarily articulated versus Jewish identity.[8]

6. R. Jenkins, *Social Identity* (London: Routledge, 2004), 79.

7. For a further discussion of this definition of social identity, see H. Tajfel, "Social Categorization, Social Identity and Social Comparison," in *Differentiation Between Social Groups*, ed. H. Tajfel (London: Academic Press, 1978), 61–76; H. Tajfel, *Human Groups and Social Categories: Studies in Social Psychology* (Cambridge: Cambridge University Press, 1981); H. Tajfel, *Social Identity and Intergroup Relations* (Cambridge: Cambridge University Press, 1982); J. C. Turner, "Towards a Cognitive Redefinition of the Social Group," in *Social Identity and Intergroup Relations*, ed. H. Tajfel (Cambridge: Cambridge University Press, 1982), 15–40.

8. Although T. L. Donaldson ("'We Gentiles': Ethnicity and Identity in Justin Martyr," *Early Christianity* 4 [2013]: 216–41, at 240) correctly points out that Justin frequently makes use of the term *ta ethnē* ("people," "nations") as a self-designation of Christians (i.e., as an insider-term) as a community drawn from "all the nations" (e.g., *1 Apol.* 53; *Dial.* 41.3; 130.2), this does not imply that Justin does not distance himself from the ungodly and immoral ways of *ta ethnē* (*Dial.* 95.1; cf. 10.3; 17.1–2).

1–2 *Apology*: Christian Identity versus Pagan Identity

Probably ca. 155 CE Justin gave his own written petition to the imperial council in Rome, hoping that his writing would be read by Emperor Antoninus Pius (138–161 CE). The petition, *1–2 Apology*, was written in order to defend the Christian faith and urge the emperor and the senate not to invoke death sentences on the Christians. However, this does not mean that it was written only for that purpose; several scholars argue that *1–2 Apology* also was written for Christians in general to encourage them in face of opposition.[9] In fact, such a purpose brought the issue of Christian identity all the more into focus: Justin not only wanted to defend Christian belief in face of the opposing authorities, he also wanted to form and reinforce the self-understanding of his Christian readers at a time when the new Christian movement and its system of belief was indeed something foreign and provoking to the ancient mind. How did the Christian faith distinguish itself from Greco-Roman religions and pagan philosophies? What was true Christianity and what was not? And who was a Christian and who was not? In *1–2 Apology* there are at least three traits in particular, I would argue, that shaped Justin's understanding of Christian identity.

First, the most explicit indication of someone becoming a Christian believer is the acknowledgment that the pagan gods are false gods. It is well known that conversion to Christian faith in the early centuries did not necessarily entail a radical break from paganism.[10] Having this in mind, Justin draws clear and distinct borderlines: Christian identity is expressed in the conversion from the pagan gods. Justin points out that these gods are "soulless and dead," made by craftsmen "carving and cutting, casting and hammering, fashioning the materials" (*1 Apol.* 9.1–2; cf. 24.1–3). Repeatedly he makes the point that the pagan cults, including the Greek philosophies, are not only human inventions but also in the end created and influenced by "the wicked demons, to deceive and lead astray the human race" (*1 Apol.* 54.1).[11] The concept of one sovereign God

---

9. E.g., M. J. Edwards, "Apologetics," in *The Oxford Handbook of Early Christian Studies*, ed. S. Ashbrook Harvey and D. C. Hunter (Oxford: Oxford University Press, 2008), 549–65; D. E. Nyström, "The *Apology* of Justin Martyr: Literary Strategies and the Defence of Christianity" (Doctoral thesis, University of Cambridge, 2012), 39–70. Commenting on the implied audience of *1–2 Apology*, Nyström concludes: "Justin would eventually have alienated any pagan audience, even a sophisticated one. The implied audience . . . are clearly people who stand outside the popular religious system altogether, which translated into social realities would equate to Jews and/ or Christians" (62).

10. See C. Markschies, *Between Two Worlds: Structures of Early Christianity* (London: SCM Press, 1999), 152–54.

11. Cf. *1 Apol.* 5.4; 9.1; 10.6; 12.5; 14.1; 23.3; 26.1, 4–5; 54.4; 56.1; 58.3; 62.1–2; 66.4; *2 Apol.* 12.3.

and creator—and therefore only one true cult—is with Justin an axiom. Hence, there is only one thing to do in turning to God: reject all the other so-called gods. Speaking of the Greek and Roman gods, he thus says, we "have now, through Jesus Christ, learned to despise these, though we be threatened with death for it, and have dedicated ourselves to the unbegotten and impossible God" (*1 Apol.* 25.1–2).

As a result of the rejection of the pagan gods, the Christians were charged with atheism, being called "atheists" (*atheoi*) and accused of "ungodliness" (*asebeia*) by outsiders. This Justin willingly admits: "And we confess that we are atheists, so far as gods of this sort are concerned, but not with respect to the most true God, the Father of righteousness and temperance and the other virtues, who is free from all impurity" (*1 Apol.* 6.1; cf. 13.1). Justin is conscious of the precarious position within which Christians were set, that people who refused to pay worship to and honor the gods failed to contribute to a society in peace with the gods (*pax deorum*). They were therefore a potential threat to the welfare of the Roman society (*pax romana*), causing aversion and hatred towards Christians (*1 Apol.* 20.3). Thus, in a word play with the words *Christianoi* ("Christians") and *chrēstos* ("good," "excellent," "useful"), Justin defends the Christians: "For we are accused of being Christians, and to hate what is excellent is unjust" (*1 Apol.* 4.5; cf. 24.1). The Christians should, however, not be surprised; the hatred of mankind towards Christians was even foretold in the Scriptures (*1 Apol.* 49.6–7). In the end, Justin explains, all hatred towards Christians is caused by demons (*2 Apol.* 8.2). But a true Christian does not fear death (*1 Apol.* 57.2–3; cf. *2 Apol.* 11; 12.1).

Justin is the first ancient writer to make an extended use of the name "Christian," and he does so with pride, confidence, and a specific self-understanding. However, he takes an ambiguous position concerning the designation "Christian" (*Christianos*). On the one hand, this is the true identity label of those belonging to Jesus Christ (*1 Apol.* 12.9), and to confess this is enough for punishment: "if any one acknowledge that he is a Christian, you punish him on account of this acknowledgment" (*1 Apol.* 4.6).[12] He is also well acquainted with those who are called "Christians" but do not live according to the moral standards of the Christian faith (*1 Apol.* 4.7–8),[13] and with those who are called

---

12. Cf. *Mart. Just.*, where the confession "I am a Christian" (e.g., the confession of Hierax, "I was and I shall be a Christian," 4.5), was enough for executing the Christians to death.

13. The texts do not say whether they were called "Christians" by themselves or by the Romans. Commenting on this issue, J. Lieu (*Christian Identity in the Jewish and Greco-Roman World* [Oxford: Oxford University Press, 2004], 258) says, "However we answer this, the texts strive to control possession or application of the label 'Christian,' even while admitting the impossibility of securing any ultimate means of control."

"Christians" but teach heresies, for example, Simon, Menander, and Marcion (*1 Apol.* 16.8–14; 26.1–8). One the other hand, he redefines and broadens the term, wanting to embrace all those in the past "who lived with the Logos" ("those who lived reasonably are Christians, even though they have been thought atheists," *1 Apol.* 46.3), including such as Socrates as well as Abraham.

Second, in the center of Justin's articulation of Christian identity stands Jesus Christ as the divine Logos. Justin argues that the Christian belief is the origin of all cults and philosophies (*1 Apol.* 20.4–5). In fact, the pagan cults are actually thefts from the one and only true cult, that is, the Christian belief with its Jewish roots. This is commonly called the "theft theory," an idea that Justin probably received from Jewish apologetic tradition in order to refute any potential charge of plagiarism from the Greeks and Romans. Hence, similar to authors such as Philo and Josephus, Justin argues the antiquity of the Jews relative to that of the Greeks. However, he takes one step further in arguing that the source of wisdom and prophecies of Moses and the other Hebrew prophets in fact was Christ, the Logos and the true origin of wisdom. Before the advent of Christ, men had possessed seeds of the Logos and so had been enabled to arrive at such fragments of truth as they could grasp (*1 Apol.* 32.8; 46.3; *2 Apol.* 8.1; 10.2; 13.3). Hence, Christian belief becomes for Justin the original ancient philosophy. Thus, when Plato and the other Greek and Roman philosophers plagiarized Moses and the prophets, they actually plagiarized the teachings of Christ.[14] Justin points out that Socrates was an instrument for the Logos (*1 Apol.* 5.4), even claiming that Socrates knew Christ partially (*2 Apol.* 10.7). After having repeatedly asserted that Plato borrowed vital ideas from Moses, Justin triumphantly concludes: "It is not, then, that we hold the same opinions as others, but that all speak in imitation of ours" (*1 Apol.* 60.10).

This argument from antiquity becomes an effective weapon in Justin's apology, justifying oneself in the face of the doubts of "the other" as well as building up the ingroup's sense of identity.[15] In arguing from antiquity, Justin effectively shapes the self-understanding of the Christians in a way similar to what the Jews in the Roman Empire had done before, appealing to the Romans' reverence for antiquity. Justin sets the Christian faith in traditions that ultimately go back to the beginning of all things. Thus, Christian belief must independently be established as an ancient religion, if not the most ancient one.

Justin's use of the Logos concept seems to stem from a general philosophic conception, especially as it was being used among the Stoics. In particular, it bears similarities to Philo's use of the term, the origin of the eternal source of

---

14. Nyström, "Literary Strategies," 86.
15. Cf. Lieu, *Christian Identity*, 86.

all goodness and all truth. The Logos was with God and "was begotten before the works, when at first He created and arranged all things by Him" (*2 Apol.* 6.3), now being incarnated in the historical Christ (*1 Apol.* 23.2). Justin spends a considerable time arguing with proofs from prophecy (*1 Apol.* 32–53; 63).[16] The coming of Christ was foretold in detail by the prophets (31.7–8), being inspired by the divine Logos, in other words, Christ himself spoke through the prophets (*1 Apol.* 36.1).

The particular identity marker that distinguishes Christianity from all other religions is the crucifixion of Christ. On the one hand, Justin argues for the commonality of the symbol of the cross—it could be seen almost anywhere: in the sail of a ship, the farmer's plough, in the tools of diggers and mechanics, and in the forehead of every living creature (*1 Apol.* 55.3–5). On the other hand, he is also aware of the uniqueness of the cross: "But in no instance, not even in any of those called sons of Jupiter, did they imitate the being crucified; for it was not understood by them" (*1 Apol.* 55.1). To believe in a God manifested in a crucified man was condemned by the outsiders as "madness" (*mania; 1 Apol.* 13.4), contributing to the ostracism of the Christians in society. The followers of the Logos are thus marked by the symbol of the complete "otherness" in Roman society.

Third, Justin's understanding of Christian identity is expressed in a godly behavior. Since common behavior norms and values normally are vital concepts in the articulation of social identity, it is of no surprise that Justin describes in detail how the honorable conduct of the Christians distinguishes them from the "others."[17] Christian belief is a "discipleship in the divine virtue" (*2 Apol.* 2.13). As a part of Justin's argument not to worship the pagan gods, he claims that God is not in need of the material offerings that men may give. God "accepts those only who imitate the excellences which reside in Him, [namely] temperance, and justice, and philanthropy, and as many virtues as are peculiar to a God who is called by no proper name" (*1 Apol.* 10.1). Only those are deemed worthy who "by their works show themselves worthy of this His design" (*1 Apol.* 10.2). Hence, Christian identity is articulated in a holy and honorable conduct.

Justin emphasizes the temporal distinction between "then" and "now" in the lives of the believers, clearly explicated in terms of new moral values and a change in lifestyle:

---

16. See especially O. Skarsaune, *The Proof from Prophecy: A Study in Justin Martyr's Proof-Text Tradition: Text-Type, Provenance, Theological Profile* (Leiden: Brill, 1987).

17. See R. Roitto, "Behaving as a Christ-Believer: A Cognitive Perspective on Identity and Behavior Norms in Ephesians" (Linköping University, 2009), 63–88. Title also published by Eisenbrauns, Warsaw Indiana, 2011.

we who *formerly* delighted in fornication, but *now* embrace chastity alone; we who *formerly* used magical arts, dedicate ourselves to the good and unbegotten God; we who valued above all things the acquisition of wealth and possessions, *now* bring what we have into a common stock, and communicate to everyone in need; we who hated and destroyed one another, and on account of their different manners would not live with men of a different tribe, *now*, since the coming of Christ, live familiarly with them, and pray for our enemies, and endeavour to persuade those who hate us unjustly to live conformably to the good precepts of Christ, to the end that they may become partakers with us of the same joyful hope of a reward from God the ruler of all. (*1 Apol.* 14.2–3; italics mine)

For Justin, there is a transforming effect on those who embrace the Christian faith in full that should be manifested in the abandonment of the old life with the evils of Greco-Roman paganism and the return to a more authentic way of life.

Another way of forming the identity of the Christian believer is contrasting the moral values of the insiders with those of the outsiders. This becomes a dualism of two people: those who live according to the Logos (Christians) and those who live without it (the rest). While the outsiders are characterized by ignorance, the insiders are characterized by a love for truth (*1 Apol.* 12.11); while the outsiders are living in immorality and promiscuity (*1 Apol.* 29.2; *2 Apol.* 12.5), the Christians are living in chastity (*1 Apol.* 15.1–8; *2 Apol.* 2.1–8), and so on. Hence, Justin creates clear borders and demarcations, constructing a Christian self-understanding as being wholly "other" to its pagan surroundings.[18] Justin repeatedly maintains that Christians have higher moral standards than non-Christians, for example, the Christians are against exposing infants (e.g., *1 Apol.* 27.1–5; 29.1) and are taking care of all those in need (*1 Apol.* 15.10–17). Defilement and depraved morality becomes firmly attached to the outsiders, directing charges of sexual licentiousness not only against the Greek and Romans (e.g., *2 Apol.* 2.1–8) but also against the heretics (e.g., Simon Magus was supposedly accompanied by a former prostitute, *1 Apol.* 26.3).

In front of his accusers, Justin urges that a person should not be judged by confessions alone but by true behavior or actions (*1 Apol.* 4.6; 16.8–14). As pointed out previously, Justin knows well that to confess "I am a Christian" could be enough to be sentenced to death by the Roman authorities. He therefore urges his addressees not only to judge according to a confession but also according to the lives of the Christians, being convinced that the conduct of

---

18. Nyström, "Literary Strategies," 161.

a true Christian believer also will demonstrate his or her innocence: "And let those who are not found living as He taught, be understood to be no Christians, even though they profess with the lip the precepts of Christ; for not those who make profession, but those who do the works, shall be saved" (*1 Apol.* 16.8). In the end, however, the ultimate mark of Christian identity for Justin is the willingness to serve and die for Christ.

Justin's articulation of Christian behavior is closely related to his understanding of Christian worship. Rituals are typical examples of identity-forming behavior; in fact, it can be said that rituals are embodied expressions of identity.[19] Accordingly, the Christians are expected to meet for worship weekly on Sundays, including Scripture reading, exposition, and prayers (*1 Apol.* 67.3, 8). For Justin, Christian worship is particularly expressed in three things: Christian baptism, the celebration of the Eucharist, and acts of charity. The baptism of the believer is an act of conversion and regeneration (*1 Apol.* 61.1–3). Justin calls the baptism an "illumination," demonstrating the illumination of the understanding of the one being baptized (*1 Apol.* 61.9–13): the convert has turned himself from the pagan gods and his ungodly behavior to the one living God manifested in the Logos, Christ. Baptism is described as the point of entry into the Christian community; after the baptism, the one baptized is brought to "the brethren," is prayed for and welcomed to the community by a holy kiss (*1 Apol.* 65.1–2). He or she is then offered bread and wine. Justin is careful to point out that the *eucharistia*, as an integrated part of the weekly worship service, is only for the baptized believer "who is so living as Christ has enjoined" (*1 Apol.* 66.1; cf. 67.5). Finally, Justin stresses the importance of giving charity to all who are in need; "the wealthy among us help the needy," whether these are orphans, widows, the sick, prisoners, strangers, or sojourners (*1 Apol.* 67.1, 6–7). Justin's stress of these acts of charity certainly gives the impression that this certainly marked true Christian identity. This also is confirmed by his repeated insistence on showing mercy to all in need (e.g., *1 Apol.* 15.10–17; 27.1–5; 29.1).

Dialogue with Trypho: Christian Identity versus Jewish Identity

According to Eusebius, Justin's *Dialogue with Trypho*, written ca. 160 CE, was "held in the city of Ephesus against Trypho, the most distinguished Jew of the day" (*Hist. eccl.* 4.18.6).[20] Although we cannot know definitely if this dialogue

---

19. See K.-P. Köpping, B. Leistle, and M. Rudolph, *Ritual and Identity: Performative Practices as Effective Transformations of Social Reality* (Berlin: Lit Verlag, 2006), 28.

20. The *Dialogue* was written after *1 Apol.*, any time between 155 and 167 CE. See C. D. Al-

was an original historical debate, Justin's discussion with Trypho "provides a window into second-century debates between Jews and Christians, whether or not he ever existed."[21] According to *Dialogue* 1.3, Trypho came to Asia Minor and Greece (Corinth) in connection with the Jewish War (132–135 CE). He was, however, not an actual Pharisaic Jew, nor a rabbi strictly trained in rabbinical methods of interpretation, but a Hellenistic layman with a philosophical training versed in Jewish lore.[22]

The *Dialogue with Trypho* gives an invaluable insight into Jewish-Christian relations and the articulation of Christian identity in the mid–second century CE. By the time of Justin, it is fairly clear that the relationship between Judaism and early Christian belief had developed into two more or less incompatible religious systems, Judaism and Christianity (albeit Justin never uses the latter term). Although Justin clearly acknowledges the continuity between Judaism and Christianity, it is the discontinuity that is stressed. For Justin, the Christian belief is something new and clearly distinguishable from Judaism.

In the debate with Trypho, we need to consider the vituperative character of this apologetic literature. Justin writes in a language marked by competition and uncompromising takeover.[23] Trypho, the opponent, becomes the intrinsic "other" in the process of forming Christian self-definition. Justin's audience was most likely composed primarily of Christians who were either drawn from the synagogues (Jews or God-fearing Gentiles) or who were potentially on their way to succumb to the Jewish faith.[24] Justin offers his readers a sharp either/or decision. The Jews are portrayed as the "others" or as the outsiders, and Justin describes Judaism as something that is clearly distinguishable from the Christian belief.

In the *Dialogue*, Justin forms Christian identity in three ways in particular. First, following in the steps of Paul, Justin is the first Christian writer to make a consistent reinterpretation of the main Jewish boundary markers, in particular

---

lert, *Revelation, Truth, Canon and Interpretation: Studies in Justin Martyr's* Dialogue with Trypho (Leiden: Brill, 2002), 33–34.

21. C. J. Setzer, *Jewish Responses to Early Christians: History and Polemics, 30–150 CE* (Minneapolis: Fortress, 1994), 135.

22. Cf. Barnard, *Justin Martyr*, 25.

23. Cf. J. Lieu, *Image and Reality: The Jews in the World of the Christians in the Second Century* (Edinburgh: T&T Clark, 1996), 136–37.

24. So, e.g., J. T. Sanders, *Schismatics, Sectarians, Dissidents, Deviants: The First One Hundred Years of Jewish-Christian Relations* (Valley Forge, PA: Trinity Press International, 1993), 52; S. G. Wilson, *Related Strangers: Jews and Christians, 70–170 CE* (Minneapolis: Fortress, 1995), 265. Lieu (*Image and Reality*, 106) suggests that the intended audience is a "'bridge-group', perhaps gentiles strongly attracted to Judaism, on the verge of becoming proselytes, yet who now provide fertile ground for Christian proselytising."

circumcision, the food regulations, and observance of the Sabbath and other Jewish feasts.[25] Since Jewishness for Trypho is demonstrated by the upholding of these boundary markers, these identity markers are repeatedly at the center of the debate. According to Justin, the major Jewish objection to Christians concerns their nonobservance of key Jewish boundary markers: "Is there any other matter, my friends, in which we are blamed, than this, that we live not after the law, and are not circumcised in the flesh as your forefathers were, and do not observe Sabbaths as you do?" (*Dial.* 10.1). Further, Trypho expresses his surprise that the Christians do not separate themselves from the pagans and that they eat things offered to idols (*Dial.* 8.4; 10.3; 19.1; 20.2; 35.1; 46.2). In a polemical mode, Justin counters that the commandments to observe food regulations, feasts and rituals, and to keep purity regulations were given to the Jewish people because of "your sins," i.e., "your unrighteousness" (*Dial.* 21) and "on account of the hardness of your people's heart" (43.1).

The circumcision, the principal—and most controversial—distinguishing mark that separated Jews and Christians, is a crucial theme for Justin.[26] Justin's main point is that, since there was apparently no need of the observance of circumcision before Abraham, nor "of the observance of Sabbaths, of feasts and sacrifices, before Moses," there is no longer any need of these identity markers (*Dial.* 23.2; cf. 46.3-5). He says, "Or why did He not teach those—who are called righteous and pleasing to Him, who lived before Moses and Abraham, who were not circumcised in their foreskin, and observed no Sabbaths—to keep these institutions?" (*Dial.* 27.5). Hence, Justin speaks of another, a second circumcision (*Dial.* 12.3; cf. 43.1; 114.4), that is, a spiritual circumcision, made by Jesus Christ: "Jesus Christ circumcises all who will . . . with knives of stone; that they may be a righteous nation, a people keeping faith, holding to the truth, and maintaining peace" (*Dial.* 24.2). In this way, standing in the legacy of Paul, Justin ultimately redefines the true people of God (cf. Rom 2:28-29; Phil 3:3).

Second, Justin forms Christian identity by his Christocentric interpretation of the Jewish Scriptures. The problem with the Jews, says Justin, is that they do not understand their own Scriptures.[27] For Justin, faith in Christ is the only key to understanding the Hebrew Scriptures; these writings are Christian and they should thus be understood only christologically, being interpreted by the Christian traditions (*Dial.* 29.2).

The bulk of *Dialogue* 32–110 is taken up by various christological disagree-

25. E.g., *Dial.* 8.4; 10.3; 18; 19.1; 20.2; 26–27, 35.1; 46–47, 67, 92, 114.

26. See N. L. Livesey, "Theological Identity Making: Justin's Use of Circumcision to Create Jews and Christians," *Journal of Early Christian Studies* 18, no. 1 (2010): 51–79.

27. Cf. *1 Apol.* 31.

ments, in particular the claim that Jesus is the Messiah and the threat to mono-theism implied by the divinity of Jesus. For, as Trypho argues, if Jesus is the Messiah, then he is human—not divine (*Dial.* 49.1; cf. 67–68). For this reason the prophecies are called to mind in order to prove the event of Jesus Christ. Justin's interpretation is clearly typological in its outworking, and he uses the Hebrew writings to demonstrate two main truths: Jesus as the end of the Law and the fulfillment of the prophecies (*Dial.* 14; 34; 43; 51; 67; 110; 118; 121; 122), and Jesus as the Logos of God (*Dial.* 61–62; 127; 129).[28] Justin repeatedly tries to prove to Trypho that God has a second person, distinct in number from himself. Throughout the *Dialogue*, Justin is very concerned to define the Jews as those who do not believe in the Logos. One of Justin's most original exe-getical contributions is probably the section on the theophanies (*Dial.* 56–62; 75; 126–129), where Justin draws on older testimonial material that proved the existence of a "second God" in the Old Testament and where he develops this into a general theory about Old Testament theophanies.

All this results in the idea that religion is separate and distinct from eth-nicity. Daniel Boyarin argues that Justin's establishment of a binary opposition between the Christ-believers and the Jews over the question of the Logos ac-complishes two purposes at once: it articulates the Christian identity as theolog-ical (as distinct from non-Christian Jews, the Christians believe in Jesus Christ as the Logos), and by founding this distinction between nonbelieving Jews and Christ-believers on theological grounds, the Jews are made into heretics, that is, they are those who do not believe in the Logos.[29] Thus, Justin works with two binary pairs, namely, Judaism/Christianity and heresy/orthodoxy. Boyarin concludes, "The double construction of Jews and heretics—or rather of Judaism and heresy—effected through Justin's *Dialogue* thus serves to produce a secure religious identity, a self-definition for Christians."[30]

Third, Justin forms Christian identity by redefining the notion of *verus Israel*, the true Israel. From the start, Justin makes it clear that "the true spiritual Israel, and descendants of Judah, Jacob, Isaac, and Abraham (who in uncircum-cision was approved of and blessed by God on account of his faith, and called the father of many nations), are we who have been led to God through this crucified Christ" (*Dial.* 11.5). The idea of the true Israel dominates particularly in the third section of the *Dialogue* (111–142), where the main point of Justin's argument is the salvation of the Gentiles and the universality of God's people.

---

28. See Allert, *Revelation*, 168–83, 223–53.

29. D. Boyarin, *The Partition of Judaeo-Christianity* (Philadelphia: University of Pennsylvania Press, 2004), 39 (cf. 43).

30. Boyarin, *Partition*, 39.

Justin repeatedly points to the universal promises given to the fathers and the prophets. The holy people promised to Abraham in Genesis 12:1–3 are now made up of Christians: by listening to God's voice through the apostles, they have been called, just like Abraham (*Dial.* 119).

In particular, Justin makes use of passages from the prophet Isaiah that contain some universal strain. For example, in interpreting Isaiah's commission to Israel to be "a light to the Gentiles" (Isa 42:6), he says, "These words, indeed, sirs, refer also to Christ, and concern the enlightened nations" (*Dial.* 122.3). When Justin emphasizes that the new Israel is a different Israel, Trypho reacts with surprise: "Are you Israel?" (*Dial.* 123.7). Justin then makes it clear that it is not enough to be a proselytizing Gentile in order to become a member of God's people, because the true sons of God are defined by Christ: "As therefore from the one man Jacob, who was surnamed Israel, all your nation has been called Jacob and Israel; so we from Christ, who begat us unto God, like Jacob, and Israel, and Judah, and Joseph, and David, are called and are the true sons of God, and keep the commandments of Christ" (*Dial.* 123.9; cf. Isa 42:1–4). In the closing sections, Justin points out that his account of the new Israel is quite simple; "there are two seeds of Judah, and two races, as there are two houses of Jacob: the one begotten by blood and flesh, the other by faith and the Spirit" (*Dial.* 135.6). Hence, the true people of God are no longer ethnically defined but defined by Christ alone. Triumphantly, Justin declares the universality of his belief in Christ: "For there is not one single race [*ethnos*] of men, whether barbarians, or Greeks, or whatever they may be called, nomads, or vagrants, or herdsmen living in tents, among whom prayers and giving of thanks are not offered through the name of the crucified Jesus" (*Dial.* 117.5).[31]

In his redefinition of Israel, Justin continually takes honorary titles and designations of ethnic Israel and applies them to the community of Christ-believers. Those who believe in Christ are called "the sons of Abraham" (*Dial.* 25.), "the sons of God" (*Dial.* 123–124), "Israel" / "Israelites" (*Dial.* 11.5; 117.2; cf. 119; 125; 130; 135), "a holy people" (*Dial.* 119.3), "those who are called" (*Dial.* 121.4), "the true high priestly race of God" (*Dial.* 116.3), "the pious and righteous" (*Dial.* 52.4),"the God-fearing and righteous" (*Dial.* 119.4–5), and so on. This use of Israel's honorary designations stresses both the continuity and the discontinuity between Israel and the new people of God. Above all, it underlines Justin's view of the Christ-believers as the true and honored members of

---

31. As Denise K. Buell (*Why This New Race: Ethnic Reasoning in Early Christianity* [New York: Columbia University Press, 2005], 95) points out, Justin's way of presenting the Christians as constituting the true Israel is to be seen as an example of "ethnic reasoning," attempting to identify Christians "as an ethnoracial group with an esteemed historical pedigree (despite their recent arrival on the historical scene)."

the people of God. As such, whether they are Jews or Gentiles, they should call one another "kinsmen and brethren" (*Dial.* 47.2). As previously pointed out, by the time of Justin, it is clear that this new community called themselves "Christians" (*Christianoi*).

In the end, we can see how Justin also favors a social separation between the Christian and the Jewish communities—at least in theory.[32] Justin knows of Jewish Christians who keep in touch with the synagogue and also of Gentile Christians who Judaize, but he sees no future for them while they continue to associate with the Jewish community and to promote the observance of the Torah. Somewhat reluctantly, Justin allows for both Christian Jews and Gentiles to practice Jewish customs and rites—as long as they do not promote this position among other Christians (*Dial.* 47). For Justin, however, it seems that the ideal Christian community is a community that is socially distinct from the Jewish community. In terms of the complex process of the so-called parting of the ways, we may say that Justin marked the end of the road.

Differentiating in the Eyes of the Others

By the mid–second century CE, we meet a distinct articulation of Christian identity in the writings of Justin Martyr. Towards the Roman authorities and the pagan world, Christian identity is, according to *1–2 Apology*, marked by conversion from the pagan, false gods to the one living God, manifested in the historical Christ, the Logos, and expressed in a new, godly way of living. Towards the non-Christian Jewish believers, Christian identity is, according to *Dialogue with Trypho*, marked by a rereading of the Scriptures resulting in a reinterpretation of Israel's identity markers such as circumcision, food regulations, and Sabbath observance, and the identity of the true Israel: through Christ, the Logos, the Christians are the *verus Israel*. Thus, the outsiders (the pagans and the non-Christian Jews) are used by Justin as "anti-types" in order to articulate and form the true insiders, the prototypical believers. For Justin, to confess and behave like a "Christian" was definitely to differentiate in the eyes of the others, something that certainly caused a clear break with the common Judaism of his day as well as with the surrounding pagan world.

---

32. Although Livesey ("Theological Identity Making," 57; cf. 74) probably is correct, concluding, "Justin's constructions are theological and do not correspond with contemporary social situation among Christians and Jews," Justin also prepares for the later social outcome.

Chapter 9

Origen: Exegete, Theologian, Disciple

CHRISTOPHER HALL

What are we to make of Origen's exegesis? What factors and influences shaped Origen's Christian identity? Is he to be applauded or condemned for his exegesis and the theological models he proposed? For hundreds of years, some in the church have taken the latter route. Origen's speculations concerning the preexistence of the soul and the final restoration of all things (*apokatastasis*) led to his condemnation by many Christians as an untrustworthy guide for the faithful, whether in terms of his biblical exegesis, his theological explorations, or the advice he frequently gave concerning key areas of spiritual formation, such as his thoughts on prayer.

Yet despite the distrust that remains among many regarding Origen's thinking and writing, others continue to read Origen with interest and delight. For some, Origen is considered among the greatest of biblical interpreters in the history of the church. Perhaps the best way to deal with the mixed reviews and reception that Origen's work has received in the Christian community is to take a close look at three key areas of Origen's thought and life: Origen's biblical exegesis, Origen's theology, and Origen's practices on central issues of spiritual formation. All three areas were deeply influenced by a number of factors: Origen's family background; Origen's rigorous education in Greek philosophical and religious thinking and practice, including the proper manner with which to interpret texts; Origen's immersion in the text of the Bible; and Origen's life as an educator and later as a priest within the church.

Origen's Family Background

Origen's family background is significant for comprehending the seriousness, fervor, and commitment with which Origen viewed and practiced Christian identity. Origen, for example, witnessed the martyrdom of his father during the Decian persecution in Egypt. Eusebius writes that Origen "sent his father a most encouraging letter on Martyrdom, in which he exhorted him with these very words: 'Persevere, do not change your mind on our account.'"[1]

He not only encouraged his father as his martyrdom approached, but strongly desired to die with him for the sake of Christ. Only the intervention of Origen's mother—she hid his clothes—prevented Origen from experiencing martyrdom at a very early age. His modesty overcame his determination to follow in his father's steps. Origen's eagerness for martyrdom, Eusebius comments, was "the first evidence of Origen's youthful readiness and of his genuine disposition toward godliness."[2]

Eusebius describes in some detail both Origen's personality and his personal spiritual disciplines, many taught him by his father. He writes that Origen had "been trained in the divine Scriptures even from his boyhood." Origen received a thorough education in both secular and sacred subjects, though his father "urged him to train himself at the sacred studies, requiring him each day to study and recite."[3]

From a very early age Origen demonstrated an interest in the depth of the Bible's meaning. He worked so diligently "at these that the simple and superficial readings of the sacred words did not satisfy him, but he sought for something more, and already at that age busied himself with deeper speculations, so that he even caused his father annoyance, as he inquired what the intent of the inspired Scripture really was."[4]

Behind his father's seeming annoyance was a deeper awe at the giftedness Origen demonstrated in both his intellect and his life: "privately by himself he rejoiced greatly, and gave most profound thanks to God, the author of all blessings, for having deemed him worthy to become the father of such a boy." Eusebius movingly describes a poignant scene as Origen's father stood "near his boy as he slept and uncovered his breast, as if the Holy Spirit were enshrined within it, and reverently kissed it, and counted himself blessed in his goodly offspring."[5]

---

1. Eusebius Pamphili, *Ecclesiastical History (Books 6–10)*, trans. Roy J. Deferrari, The Fathers of the Church 29 (Washington, DC: The Catholic University of America Press, 1955), VI.2.6.
2. Ibid.
3. Ibid.
4. Ibid.
5. Ibid., VI.6–7.

To have witnessed his father's death and to desire to imitate his father's martyrdom in faithfulness to Christ tells us much about Origen and much about his family, cultural, and ecclesial environment. Origen was a courageous, strong-willed, faith-filled man; at times in his fervency it seems as though his mind was on fire with his love for God, the church, and those whom the church had yet to reach. At the end of Origen's life his desire for martyrdom would be fulfilled. Eusebius relates "how many and of what nature were the sufferings which the man endured for the word of Christ, bonds and tortures of the body, and torments under iron and in the recesses of a prison, and how for a great many days, with his feet stretched four spaces in that instrument of torture, the stocks, he steadfastly bore threats of fire, and all the other things inflicted by his enemies."[6]

Though Origen suffered horrendous torture at the hands of the Roman government, he lived through it. Soon, though, he died of his sufferings, pains willingly endured for the sake of the God he loved. Henri Crouzel comments that the Roman judge in charge of Origen's case "was in no hurry to put him to death, hoping to obtain from this most celebrated of Christians an apostasy that would have had a widespread effect."[7] This Roman's wish was never fulfilled, for after his release Origen continued to write letters to the imprisoned and tortured, "words full of value for those who needed to be strengthened."[8]

A staggering intellect was joined to Origen's indefatigable faith. At a very young age, perhaps while still in his late teens, Origen was chosen to succeed Clement as leader of the well-known catechetical school in Alexandria. Already the depth of Origen's knowledge and his skills as a writer and teacher were recognized in the church.

Origen's Exegesis

In many ways, the methodology employed by Origen in interpreting the Bible would have raised few eyebrows in his own day. Yes, Origen's theological conclusions—based on both his exegesis and influences from Greek philosophy and Greek hermeneutics—were later to cause problems for his whole-hearted reception in the Church as an authoritative teacher, but during his lifetime neither his hermeneutics nor his theology was viewed as significantly problematic.

---

6. Ibid., VI.39, 66.

7. Henri Crouzel, *The Life and Thought of the First Great Theologian* (San Francisco: Harper & Row, 1989), 35.

8. Ibid.

As Origen read and interpreted the Bible, a key principle guided his exegesis, one that would have met with approval from almost all ancient Christian biblical interpreters during his time: *the Bible in its entirety is a Christian book and must be read as such.* Every book, every chapter, every sentence was imbedded with a christological core that the trustworthy and skilled biblical interpreter must discern and explain to the Christian reader.

How was one to discern and interpret Christ's presence on every page of Scripture? Origen proposed a fourfold hermeneutical strategy. First, many texts could be interpreted literally, a level of interpretation Origen believed was largely for people whose knowledge and interpretive skills were relatively undeveloped. Second, all readers should look for the moral teaching Origen expected to be present in almost all biblical passages. Origen surely believed God had provided the church with the Bible for more than intellectual comprehension. The Scripture was designed by God to change how believers lived their lives; its ethical import could be understood through a careful sifting of texts for their moral teaching. Third, the Bible contained an anagogical sense; biblical texts were meant to lead us upward, toward our final destination in the world to come. Hence, the Bible should be mined for its eschatological meaning, a meaning pointing to the future but possible to apprehend in the present. Finally, we have the fourth meaning of the Bible—its christological heart—a significance the interpreter comprehended and explained through the use of allegorical interpretation.

Christians in the Protestant tradition and surely most evangelicals view the use of allegory in biblical interpretation with great suspicion. Doesn't allegory pose the threat of an interpretive free-for-all in which every interpreter can find allegorical meaning wherever he wants and to the extent he desires? Scripture then becomes a wax nose that can be shaped in whatever way seems plausible to the exegete, with little if any hermeneutical control. Who is to say what a text actually means if through the use of allegory an exegete can posit hidden meaning wherever one wishes? It is this lack of hermeneutical control that most upsets Origen's opponents in our modern setting, and surely some in the ancient church.

Yet is this suspicion entirely justified? Is it true that allegorical interpretation necessarily leads to hermeneutical confusion? How might Origen himself respond? Origen and other ancient Christian interpreters readily turned to texts such as 1 Corinthians 9:7-11, 1 Corinthians 10:1-11, and Galatians 4:21-31 as clear apostolic teaching on how the Old Testament should be interpreted as Christian canonical Scripture. When Paul refers to a text from a Levitical context concerning the muzzling of farm animals while they are treading grain, he asks: "Is it about oxen that God is concerned? Surely he says this for us, doesn't he? Yes, this was written for us, because when the plowman plows and the thresher threshes, they ought to do so in the hope of sharing in the harvest" (1 Cor 9:8–10). Origen believed it is absolutely clear to Paul that God was not concerned about the muzzling of an animal, but rather the support of those serving in the church, as Paul himself says. Paul allegorizes a text from Deuteronomy because he is discerning—in the light of the gospel—that all biblical texts point to Christ and find their fulfillment in him, down to the smallest phrase or number.

We see the same Pauline hermeneutic at work in Galatians 4:21–31, where Paul readily allegorizes texts from Genesis concerning Hagar and Sarah as actually referring to two covenants. Abraham had "two sons, one by the slave woman and the other by the free woman" (Gal 4:22). Not only so, but in light of the coming of the incarnate Son, "These two things may be taken figuratively, for the women represent two covenants. One covenant is from Mount Sinai and bears children who are to be slaves: This is Hagar. Now Hagar stands for Mount Sinai in Arabia and corresponds to the present city of Jerusalem, because she is in slavery with her children" (Gal 4:24–25). In turn, Sarah has borne the child of the promise and represents "the Jerusalem that is above . . . she is our mother" (Gal 4:26).

Perhaps most clearly we see Paul's christological hermeneutic at work in 1 Corinthians 10:1–11, where Paul explicitly connects the experience of Israel in the wilderness with the coming of Christ. In fact, from Paul's perspective, Christ was with Israel in the wilderness. "They all ate the same spiritual food and drank the same spiritual drink; for they drank from the spiritual rock that accompanied them, and that rock was Christ" (1 Cor 10:3–4). What could possibly justify such an interpretation? Paul's affirmation that "the fulfillment of the ages has come" upon the Christian community (1 Cor 10:11). What happened to Israel were "examples and were written down as warnings for us" (1 Cor 10:11). If so, Origen reasons that the wise Christian interpreter of Scripture—one whose identity is being formed into Christ's image—will surely expect to find Christ throughout the Old Testament. Why? Because the Old Testament is a Christian book. In Origen's words: "These words were not written to instruct us in history, nor must we think that the divine books narrate the acts of the Egyptians. What has been written 'has been written for our instruction' and admonition."[9]

Ronald Heine illustrates this dynamic from Origen's homilies on Exodus. Heine notes that in Origen's view, Exodus 1:8–11, on the basis of Paul's teaching in 1 Corinthians 10:11,

---

9. Origen, *Hom. Exod.* 1.5; quoted in Mark Sheridan, *Language for God in Patristic Tradition* (Downers Grove, IL: InterVarsity Press, 2015), 226.

was not written merely to teach us history but to instruct us for living. . . . the purpose of these words, Origen claims, is to teach you that if you wish to return to the world after you have been baptized and God has become your king, you "may know that 'another king has arisen in you' . . . and that he is compelling you to his works." This new king who takes control over the Christian is none other than the devil, Origen says, and it is he who says "The race of Israel is stronger than us" (Exod. 1:9). The devil would say this of Christians if we were stronger than he is. This only happens, Origen continues, if "I . . . repel his 'fiery darts with the shield of faith'" when he "hurls evil thoughts at me." Only by such conscious and repeated rejection of Satan's approaches can we cause him to "say of us also, 'The race of Israel is great and is stronger than us.'" (*Hom. Exod.* 1:5)[10]

The fundamentals of Origen's thought on interpreting the Bible, then, contain the following salient points and are directly related to Origen's understanding of his identity as a Christian interpreter of the Bible.

The Bible is a book for people of varying skills and background. Some people are naturally gifted intellectually and have received a more thorough education than others. Happily, even for those who have only the most rudimentary education, the Bible possesses riches that can be mined through the literal method of interpretation.

The literal sense of Scripture is not only for those who cannot attain to its deeper meaning. An understanding of the literal meaning of Scripture is an essential building block for reaching its deeper meaning, senses hidden by the Holy Spirit beneath the literal meaning of the text. Origen never overlooks the importance of the literal meaning, but does argue that a deeper sense on the level of the ethical, anagogical, and allegorical should be sought by the insightful interpreter.

The apostolic pattern of interpretation as seen in Paul's interpretation in 1 Corinthians 9:7–11; 10:1–11, and Galatians 4:21–31 endorses the use of allegory as a fruitful tool in plumbing the depths of Scripture, depths revealing the wonder of the incarnation of the Son. Allegorical interpretation, then, is christologically controlled through the hermeneutical framework of the incarnation and all its implications; allegory should always illuminate who Christ is and what Christ has done in his redemptive work. Allegory's christological

---

10. Ronald Heine, *Reading the Old Testament with the Ancient Church* (Grand Rapids: Baker Academic, 2007), 86; Heine is quoting his translation in Origen, *Homilies on Genesis and Exodus,* trans. Ronald E. Heine, FC 71 (Washington, DC: Catholic University of America Press, 1982), 234, 236–37.

anchor, from Origen's perspective, effectively forecloses the danger of an exegetical free-for-all.

All of Scripture is inspired by God. An entailment of the Bible's inspiration is the Holy Spirit's work in bringing into existence ancient texts that the Spirit knew would be canonized as Christian Scripture. Thus, the Old Testament must be interpreted christologically and pneumatically, from Origen's perspective, in light of its identity as a Christian text.

Origen's Christian identity—and that of the Bible as a Christian text—naturally leads him to view the Old Testament as a christological treasure chest. Origen would insist that his use of allegory recognizes and preserves the Christian identity of the Bible from the first verse of Genesis to the last verse of Revelation. Origen never overlooks the literal, ethical, or eschatological nature of Scripture. He believes the teachings of the Bible are clearly given to us so that we can live ever more fruitfully and deeply into the wonder of the kingdom of God. And he believes the eschatological nature of the Scripture, that is, its christological fulfillment in Jesus Christ, provides the hermeneutical lodestar for making sense out of the entire biblical message. Origen's use of allegory doesn't fancifully and foolishly distort the meaning of the Bible. Instead, his use of allegory—with its christological and pneumatological foundation—actually helps us to make sense of the Bible *as Christian readers.* A comparison with modern exegetical practice may prove helpful at this point.

Evangelical exegetes such as Andrew Hill and John Walton begin their exegesis of Old Testament texts with detailed study of historical, cultural, and linguistic issues.[11] They are convinced, for instance, that ancient Near Eastern texts significantly illuminate our understanding of the biblical author's intentions in an Old Testament book such as Genesis or Leviticus. And Hill and Walton are right. Indeed, I think that Origen would find many of Hill and Walton's thoughts on Old Testament texts to be thoughtful and wise. As we have seen, Origen is very interested in the literal meaning of texts and would seek all the help he could get at comprehending the literal sense of a biblical passage.

After doing all their exegetical groundwork and discovering as best one can the original author's intent in an Old Testament passage—invariably an intent addressed to the nation of Israel—Hill and Walton will tend to derive a fairly general meaning for Christians who are reading these Jewish texts inspired by the Spirit of God. Prophetic texts, some Psalms, and occasionally historical texts may have a more specifically Christian meaning, but it is fair to say that Hill, Walton, and other evangelical scholars struggle to find significant Christian

11. Cf. Andrew E. Hill and John H. Walton, *A Survey of the Old Testament* (Grand Rapids: Zondervan, 2009).

nuggets in the detailed legal regulations of a book such as Leviticus. Christian exegetes who believe that all Scripture is inspired by God will surely insist that Leviticus is inspired and study it as an inspired text, but it is likely that verse by verse preaching through Leviticus is a fairly rare event in evangelical churches or within the wider church as a whole.

Origen would be surprised by this. Indeed, Origen preached an entire series of sermons on Leviticus, a series that fills an entire book in the "Fathers of the Church" volumes published by the Catholic University of America Press. Origen's surprise would be multifold and based on his extremely elevated understanding of the inspiration of the biblical writers and the manner in which the apostles read and interpreted the Old Testament.

Origen believed that the Holy Spirit inspired every author of the Bible. The Spirit who inspired these writers—including the author of Leviticus—understood many things of which these writers were unaware. The Holy Spirit, for instance, knew what was going to happen hundreds of years after the text of Leviticus was composed. The Spirit knew that the Father was going to send the Son to redeem the nation of Israel and the nations of the world. The Spirit knew that there would come a day when the death of the incarnate Son on a Roman cross would actually make salvation possible for all God's image-bearers. The Spirit knew that "water" would always be special in the pages of the Scripture, from the waters of the flood, to the waters of the Jordon, to the water in the stone jars at the wedding in Cana, to the water that flowed from Jesus's side with his life blood, to the water of baptism. The Spirit knew all these things, as did the Father and the Son.

So, Origen would argue, when the Spirit through the human authors of the Bible began to inspire the texts we now have in the canon of Scripture, all these texts were produced with the end of the story in mind. Though the writer of Leviticus did not know the end of the story, the Spirit did. And in light of this divine knowledge of the beginning and end of God's purposes for all of creation and the great events of salvation history, the Spirit engendered exegetical clues to these wonders in almost every line of Scripture. Surely this was to be expected, Origen would argue. Hence, when Origen comes to the text of Leviticus—or any other text of Scripture—*he expects that text to be a Christian text*, not simply a Jewish one. Both Origen's identity as a Christian exegete and the text's inspiration and identity as a Christian text influence what Origen expects to find there.

If so, for example, when we run across texts that mention "wood" in the Old Testament, it is entirely legitimate—indeed, deeply Christian, to expect these texts to have something to say about the cross of Christ.[12] In the same

12. Augustine, for instance, writes that Noah, his sons, and the wood of the ark prefigure the

way, when we encounter texts speaking of water—whether in blessing or in judgment—we should expect that there is a Christian meaning hidden in these texts, one often referring to baptism. And this meaning, Origen believes, can be discovered through reading these texts allegorically through the prism of the gospel, and particularly through the wonder of the incarnation.

After all, Origen would argue, this is how the apostles read them. Indeed, Origen would insist, if this is how the apostles read and interpreted the Old Testament, shouldn't the church follow their example? Again, the exegetical control modern commentators are seeking is found in the profundity of the gospel itself.

Origen's Theology

Origen possessed a lively, inquisitive mind, one immersed in the Scriptures and in the worldview of an educated Greco-Roman. He read the Bible through a specific lens, one honed in the gospel and in the leading Greek and Roman ideas of his time. These characteristics were both strengths and weaknesses. Positively, as we have seen in our discussion of Origen's exegetical method, Origen's reading of the Bible was a deeply Christian one. He thought the same of his theology. He had no desire to be innovative or to depart from the theological traditions passed on to him by the church. His thinking, his praying, and his worship are never divorced; occasionally spontaneous ejaculations break forth in the midst of his theological ponderings. At the close of a key chapter in *On First Principles*, one in which he has explored the creation of the world in time, free will, and Trinitarian relationships, he exclaims: "from what causes or on what occasions these things happen, or what the divine wisdom sees as it looks into these men or what movements of theirs will lead God to arrange all these things thus, is known to God alone and to his only-begotten Son, through whom all things were created and restored, and to the Holy Spirit, through whom all things are sanctified, who proceeds from the Father himself (cf. John 15:26), and to whom is the glory forever and ever, Amen."[13]

---

church and the cross. "And is not the church prefigured by Noah and his sons? They escape the flood, with wood (which symbolizes the cross) carrying them." Andrew Louth, ed., *Genesis 1–11*, Ancient Christian Commentary on Scripture: Old Testament, vol. 1 (Downers Grove, IL: InterVarsity Press, 2001), 136. Origen would applaud Augustine's insightful interpretation as deeply Christian.

13. Origen, *On First Principles*, trans. Butterworth (Notre Dame, IN: Christian Classics, 2013), 3.5 (319). I have slightly modified the translation.

Yet it must be admitted that at times Origen's speculations, particularly concerning the preexistence of human souls and the later restoration and reconciliation of all things to God—including the devil—strayed beyond the bounds of orthodoxy, especially as defined by later Christian generations. Origen, indeed, is generally not recognized as a father of the church because of his idea of *apokatastasis*—the teaching that God will ultimately reconcile all creation and created beings to himself, including Satan. How and why did Origen drift away from orthodox doctrine in his understanding of the extent and nature of reconciliation?

Origen firmly believed his ideas about *apokatastasis* were the natural implication of biblical texts such as Psalm 110:1 (Ps 109:1 LXX): "The LORD says to my Lord, 'Sit at my right hand until I make your enemies your footstool.'" "We think, indeed," Origen comments, "that the goodness of God, through His Christ, may recall all His creatures to one end, even his enemies being conquered and subdued."[14] Origen concludes that God's Word was "stronger than all evils in the soul," and that the healing, reconciliation, and renewal brought by the Word applied "to every man." The goodness of God and the power of the Word demanded "the destruction of all evil" in the final consummation with the ultimate reconciliation of all members of God's creation, whether in heaven, on earth, or in hell.

Origen appears to err by allowing his rational inferences from certain aspects of the biblical revelation to blind him to other equally important facets of the scriptural narrative. Yet there is a clear rhyme and reason to his argument. If sin, evil and death are to be finally and completely destroyed, Origen asks, how can they remain in existence as God's enemies in the age to come when all creation is reconciled to God? Through a slow and imperceptible process, one lasting "countless and unmeasured ages," even the last enemy—death—will be reconciled to God.

> "[A]nd thus God will be 'all,' for there will no longer be any distinction of good and evil, seeing evil nowhere exists. . . . [T]hat condition of things will be re-established in which rational nature was placed, when it had no need to eat of the tree of the knowledge of good and evil. . . .[When] all feeling of wickedness has been removed, and the individual has been purified and cleansed, he who alone is the one good God becomes to him 'all,' and that *not in the case of a few individuals, or of a considerable number, but He Himself is 'all in all'* [emphasis added]. And when death shall no longer

---

14. Origen, *On First Principles* 1.6.1; cited in Johannes Quasten, *Patrology* (Westminster: Christian Classics, 1986), 2:87.

anywhere exist, nor the sting of death, nor any evil at all, then verily God will be 'all in all.'"[15]

For evil, for the demonic, Satan, or hell to remain in existence, at least in the manner that Origen envisioned if they were left unreconciled to God, would prevent God from being "all in all." At this juncture, the church said "No" to Origen's conclusions. It judged Origen's deduction to be outside the bounds of orthodox thought. Yet Origen's thinking—in this matter and a host of others—continues to be studied and appreciated.[16]

Spiritual Formation

Mark Sheridan helpfully develops the devotional implications of Origen's hermeneutical methods.[17] The hidden christological meaning—always with pneumatological and soteriological implications—that is contained in Scripture can be mined for its spiritual riches.

Sheridan points to Origen's exegesis of 1 Thessalonians 5:23 to illustrate the intimate connection in Origen's thinking and practice between biblical exegesis and spiritual growth. Paul writes: "May God himself, the God of peace, sanctify you through and through. May your whole spirit, soul and body be kept blameless at the coming of our Lord Jesus Christ" (NIV). Sheridan explains that Paul's anthropology here, the distinction in God's image-bearer between spirit, soul, and body, becomes for Origen a template for describing "three different stages of initiation in the spiritual life of the Christian."[18] Origen writes: "For just as man consists of body, soul and spirit, so in the same way does the scripture, which has been prepared by God to be given for man's salvation."[19] The three senses of Scripture are in turn related by Origen "to three different stages of initiation in the spiritual life of the Christian: beginners, those who had progressed, and the advanced or 'perfect,' a distinction inspired by 1 Corinthians 2–3."[20]

Origen never denigrates the believer who may be a spiritual novice. In-

---

15. Ibid., 3.6.3; cited in Quasten, *Patrology*, 89.

16. I have been here drawing on my writing in Christopher A. Hall, *Reading Scripture with the Church Fathers* (Downers Grove, IL: IVP Academic, 1998), 52–53.

17. I am drawing on Sheridan's insights in Sheridan, *Language for God*, 218–19.

18. Ibid., 218.

19. Origen, *On First Principles*, trans. Butterworth (London: SPCK, 1936), 276; quoted in Sheridan, *Language for God*, 218.

20. Ibid., 219.

stead, he rejoices in the kindness and grace of God in providing an inspired text wide enough and deep enough to accommodate the work of the Holy Spirit in every Christian's life, whether a believer be young in the faith or much more developed and gifted. The goal for all is to continue to advance spiritually. Origen understands that God begins with where people are and generously, patiently, and powerfully moves them to a new place, growth always guided by the richness of the Bible as a Christian text. Origen is far from being a spiritual elitist and vigorously rejects the Gnostic attempt to reserve the truth of Scripture to a hidden interpretation only known to a select few.[21]

Eusebius was impressed with the congruence between Origen's words and the quality of his life. He writes that Origen's "everyday deeds included most marvelous right actions of a very genuine philosophy."[22] Like many of his contemporaries and future church fathers, Origen's understanding of "genuine philosophy" was identifiably Christian. For Origen, the philosophic life was not simply a matter of thinking—"philosophizing" as we might put it in modern terms. Instead, for the early Christian community, a philosophic life was a spiritually disciplined life, a truism for all the church fathers.

"Christian philosophy" for the ancient Christian is the art of learning to think and live like a disciple of Jesus Christ. In a word, Christian *philosophia* is *Christian* thinking and living as opposed to the life and thought of the pagan world. It is a way of life founded on the basic tenets of the Christian faith and nurtured through the practice of specific spiritual disciplines. Christian identity, then, demands both a distinct mindset and a willingness to adopt a corresponding style of living.[23]

21. Henri Crouzel argues that some interpreters of Origen have misunderstood Origen's advice about not casting pearls before swine as indicating Gnostic tendencies in Origen toward spiritual elitism and a hidden knowledge available to only a few. Crouzel believes this is a serious error. Rather, Origen is concerned that there are Christian mysteries that can only be grasped slowly and with the help of a mature guide. Crouzel comments: "Indeed, to anyone that is not ready, this revelation can do harm, like over-rich food given to one with fever; and, worse still, it has happened that a wrong understanding of these mysteries, spread abroad, has turned against the faith; reading the apologists of the second century is enough to show the calumnies spread among the pagans because of a mistaken understanding of the Eucharistic mystery and this explains the reluctance of the primitive Church to talk about it. But this advice of Origen's has often been wrongly interpreted as implying that there were in his teaching secret traditions like those to which the Gnostics appealed, traditions that were only passed on to the initiated. . . . Now there is no question in the work of Origen of secret traditions circulating in the Great Church: he knows of them among the Jews and the Gnostics, but not in orthodox Christianity." Henri Crouzel, *Life and Thought*, 104.

22. Eusebius, *Hist. eccl.* VI.3.10.

23. I am here drawing on my doctoral dissertation. Cf. Christopher A. Hall, *John Chrysostom's*

"As the saying goes," Euscbius writes, "'surely as was [Origen's] speech, so was the manner of life he displayed,' and 'as was his manner of life, so was his speech.'"[24] And the manner of life Origen adopted at a very early age was one of disciplined *ascesis* or spiritual discipline. Eusebius includes a detailed list of the spiritual disciplines Origen practiced on a regular basis, including fasting and simplicity. "He persevered as much as possible," Eusebius notes, "in a very philosophical life, sometimes by exercises in fasting, sometimes by limiting his time for sleep, which he zealously managed to take never on a couch but upon the ground."

Eusebius emphasizes that Origen not only studied the words of Jesus. He attempted to live the words of Jesus, sometimes in a remarkably literal fashion. "He thought that those words of the Savior in the Gospel should especially be observed which exhort us not to have two cloaks and not to use shoes, and not be exhaustively solicitous for tomorrow. He exhibited a zeal beyond his age, and by persevering in cold and nakedness, and proceeding to the limit of excessive poverty, he especially astounded his followers, causing grief to a great many who desired to share their professions with him because of the labors which they saw him bestow upon the teaching of divine subjects." Eusebius observes that "for many years" Origen walked barefoot and was sparing in his use of wine and food. Indeed, Origen, like John Chrysostom in his younger fervor for the ascetic life, sometimes upset and injured his health in his desire to follow Christ's example.[25]

Should we be surprised at Origen's fervency of faith and strength of character? Or his desire to imitate Christ's own life and teachings in such a detailed and strenuous fashion in his devotional life and practice? No. For whether it be in his biblical exegesis, his theological constructions, or his spiritual discipline, Origen longed to fuse his identity with that of the incarnate Son of God. And to a significant and surprising extent, he succeeded.

"*On Providence*": *A Translation and Theological Interpretation* (Ann Arbor, MI: University Microfilms International, 1991), 15–64.
    24. *Hist. eccl.* 6.3.10.
    25. *Hist. eccl.* 6.3.11.

Chapter 10

Gregory of Nyssa: Becoming Human in the Face of God

Hans Boersma

Patristic and medieval theologians regarded the beatific vision as the undisputed purpose of the Christian life.[1] This notion helped to maintain the unity of spiritual and dogmatic theology through many centuries of Christian thought, for doctrinal reflection on the beatific vision was, by default, deliberation on the spiritual telos of human existence.[2] The marginalization of the beatific vision as a dogmatic (and spiritual) locus may be traced to a variety of factors. The theology of the Reformation played some role,[3] as have a self-conscious marginalization

---

1. While doctrinal attention to the beatific vision has largely disappeared, the topic has continued to garner attention among historians of doctrine, no doubt as a result of the ubiquity of the doctrine in the history of Christian thought. See, most notably, Kenneth E. Kirk, *The Vision of God: The Christian Doctrine of the Summum Bonum: The Bampton Lectures for 1928* (London: Longmans, Green & Co., 1932); Vladimir Lossky, *The Vision of God*, trans. Asheleigh Moorhouse (Leighton Buzzard, UK: The Faith Press, 1973); Christian Trottmann, *La Vision béatifique des disputes scolastiques à sa définition par Benoît XII* (Rome: École française de Rome, 1995); Severin Valentinov Kitanov, *Beatific Enjoyment in Medieval Scholastic Debates* (Lanham, MD: Lexington, 2014).

2. Cf. the helpful discussion on the split between spirituality and theology in Hans Urs von Balthasar, "Theology and Sanctity," in *The Word Made Flesh*, vol. 1 of *Explorations in Theology* (San Francisco: Ignatius Press, 1989), 181–209.

3. See Suzanne McDonald, "Beholding the Glory of God in the Face of Jesus Christ: John Owen and the 'Reforming' of the Beatific Vision," in *The Ashgate Research Companion to John Owen's Theology*, ed. Kelly M. Kapic and Mark Jones (Burlington, VT: Ashgate, 2012), 141–58. Franciscus Junius, Amandus Polanus, Antonius Walaeus, and Francis Turretin are among the scholastic Reformed theologians who pay attention to the beatific vision. Puritan theologians (such as Lewis Bayly, Isaac

---

An earlier version of this essay was published as "Becoming Human in the Face of God: Gregory of Nyssa's Unending Search for the Beatific Vision," *International Journal of Systematic Theology* 17 (2015): 131–51.

of teleological notions in modern science[4] and a broader modern tendency to emphasize this-worldly goods as the ends of human life. The cumulative force of a series of factors is an unfortunate neglect of the doctrine of the beatific vision.[5]

There is good reason for a *ressourcement* of this aspect of classical theology. The decline of the beatific vision as a key element of eschatological reflection impoverishes Christian spirituality—in particular the Christian hope and, by implication, Christian identity—in serious ways. Its replacement in extra-theological reflection by the presumption that the pursuit of pleasure and material well-being represents the telos of human life renders impossible the proper flourishing of the human soul. This essay thus aims at an unapologetic *ressourcement* of the doctrine and spirituality of the beatific vision by means of a discussion of Gregory of Nyssa's understanding of the theme. A genuine and successful retrieval of this telos will prove to be ecclesially and culturally no less significant than its loss in the modern period.

The long tradition of reflection on the beatific vision is based primarily on the biblical promise that after death believers will see God face to face,[6] along with descriptions of theophanic experiences of Old as well as New Testament saints[7] (which occur despite repeated biblical claims that no one

---

Ambrose, Richard Baxter, John Owen, Thomas Watson, and later also Jonathan Edwards) picked up on the theme as part of their focus on matters of Christian spirituality and anagogy. The recent book by Anthony C. Thiselton also contains two chapters dealing with the beatific vision: *Life after Death: A New Approach to the Last Things* (Grand Rapids: Eerdmans, 2012), 185–215.

4. M. B. Foster's renowned essay, "The Christian Doctrine of Creation and the Rise of Modern Natural Science" (*Mind* 43 [1934]: 446–68) is revealing in this regard. Failing to recognize either the explicitly anti-Christian roots or the secularist outcomes of seventeenth-century philosophical developments, Foster erroneously attributes them to the Christian doctrine of creation. While he celebrates the occlusion of teleology and the separation between Creator and creature in the modern period, my starting point in this essay is that the materialist and immanentist focus of modernity is something to be lamented. Although I speak of the occlusion of teleology, empiricism does have its own presuppositions and aims; it simply hides them and is often unconscious of them. In modernity, the satisfaction of desires through ever-increasing material consumption has replaced the beatific vision as the telos of human existence.

5. This neglect includes, to some extent, Catholic theology. However, for an insightful contemporary Catholic treatment that draws on Thomas Aquinas, see Matthew Levering, *Jesus and the Demise of Death: Resurrection, Afterlife, and the Fate of the Christian* (Waco, TX: Baylor University Press, 2012), 109–25.

6. The most obvious passages we may think of here are Job 19:26–27; Matt 5:8; John 17:24; 1 Cor 13:12; 2 Cor 5:6; and 1 John 3:2.

7. The most-discussed theophanies are the Lord's appearing to Abraham (Gen 18), Jacob (Gen 28 and 32), Moses (Exod 33–34; Num 12:7–8; Heb 11:27), Micaiah (1 Kgs 22:19), Isaiah (Isa 6:1–5), Ezekiel (Ezek 1:4–28; 8:1–4), Peter, James, and John (Matt 17:1–8 and pars.), Paul (Acts 9:3–9; 2 Cor 12:1–4), and John (Rev 1:12–16; 4:5).

can see God),[8] and passages that speak more broadly about life before God in terms of vision and/or light.[9] In much of the Christian mystical tradition, particularly where the influence of Gregory of Nyssa and of Dionysius has been prominent, reflection on these passages is linked with attention to texts that speak of God's self-revelation in terms of darkness.[10] In this essay, I will reflect particularly on Nyssen's engagement with biblical passages that to his mind speak of the beatific vision itself, and so my focus will be on his homilies on Matthew 5:8, his commentary on Moses's ascent of Mount Sinai, and his sermons on the Song of Songs.

Engagement with the fourth-century Cappadocian mystical theologian Gregory of Nyssa is particularly germane in an attempt to retrieve the spiritual and dogmatic theme of the beatific vision. The theme was of great significance to the Bishop of Nyssa, as he repeatedly reflected on it, often in passing, and on three occasions at some length. His sixth homily on the Beatitudes (probably written in the mid to late 370s), as well as his commentary on *The Life of Moses* and his *Homilies on the Song of Songs* (both of which probably stem from the 390s),[11] deal extensively with the beatific vision. Furthermore, Gregory was a theologian for whom Christian doctrine, biblical interpretation, pastoral theology, and personal ascetical practices were closely linked together. In each of these areas, St. Gregory's anagogical (or upward-leading) approach to theology inspired in him a desire to move from this-worldly, earthly realities to otherworldly, heavenly ones. The doctrine of the beatific vision fits neatly with Nyssen's view of biblical interpretation as an upward move from history to spirit, with his desire to prepare his congregation for eternal life, and with his conviction that a life of almsgiving, care for the sick, and bodily renunciation are indispensable in reaching the aim of the Christian life.

For Gregory, therefore, the beatific vision is not a doctrine about which to speculate abstractly. Instead, he regards it as the very aim of the Christian

8. Exod 33:20; John 1:18; 1 Tim 6:16; 1 John 4:12.

9. Some of the passages most frequently referenced in the Christian tradition in this regard are Pss 27; 36:9; 80:19; Isa 26:10; 53:2; 64:4; 66:14; Matt 18:10; John 14:8–9; 1 Cor 2:9; 2 Cor 3:18; 4:6; and Rev 21:23–24.

10. Exod 20:21; 24:18; Ps 18:11; Song 2:3; 5:2; 5:5–6. For Gregory's use of the biblical theme of darkness, see Martin Laird, "Darkness," in *The Brill Dictionary of Gregory of Nyssa* (Leiden: Brill, 2010), 203–5. Laird, following the lead of Bernard McGinn, emphasizes that Gregory uses the apophatic theme of darkness only in exegetical contexts that demand such attention to it (*Gregory of Nyssa and the Grasp of Faith: Union, Knowledge, and Divine Presence* (Oxford: Oxford University Press, 2004), 174–203.

11. On internal grounds, it seems to me that *The Life of Moses* was written before the *Homilies on the Song of Songs*. See Hans Boersma, *Embodiment and Virtue in Gregory of Nyssa: An Anagogical Approach* (Oxford: Oxford University Press, 2013), 231 n. 95.

life—and hence also of his own, personal existence. Gregory looked forward concretely to experiencing the beatific vision at the point of death; this vision also constituted the aim for which he strove throughout his life, and as such it determined his overall outlook on life. Gregory, we could say, was someone who made it the purpose of his existence to seek the face of God. The aim of the spiritual journey here on earth was, for Gregory, identical to the telos of seeking God in the hereafter. This concord between the destiny of the heavenly future and the aim of everyday spirituality means that the quest to see God lies at the heart of Gregory's mystical-theological approach. For him, God makes himself visible to saintly believers in their spiritual lives by means of theophanies, in anticipation of the beatific vision in the hereafter. Gregory's reflections on the beatific vision draw, therefore, on the spiritual, theophanic visions that saints such as Moses, Paul, and John (as well as the bride of the Song of Songs) experienced during their earthly lives. St. Gregory worked on the assumption that we are to pursue the vision of God in this life, and that the resulting theophanies give us insight into the reality of the beatific vision in the hereafter.

In what follows, then, I will highlight some of the characteristics of Gregory's doctrine of the beatific vision, based as it is on his insights in the biblical text.[12] I will argue that, for St. Gregory, human souls find their telos when in union with Christ they become ever purer, in an ever-increasing growth in the beatific vision. Gregory was a theologian always in search of Christ, and though he was convinced he had indeed found him, Nyssen's desire to see Christ impelled him to seek still further. For Gregory this theological longing was grounded in his understanding of the beatific vision: the eschatological future of perpetual progress (*epektasis*) in the life of Christ meant that already in this life Gregory set his desire on seeking the face of God in Jesus Christ. For Gregory, then, the soul's true end—depicted under the biblical images of

---

12. To be sure, Gregory does not see biblical exegesis as being at odds with philosophical reflection. I do not have the space here to discuss in detail Gregory's reliance on Platonic philosophy and how this relates to the biblical character of his approach. Suffice it to say that I believe Gregory to be primarily a biblical theologian. Jaroslav Pelikan strikes the right balance when he comments that the Cappadocians "stood squarely in the tradition of Classical Greek culture, and each was at the same time intensely critical of that tradition" (*Christianity and Classical Culture: The Metamorphosis of Natural Theology in the Christian Encounter with Hellenism* [New Haven: Yale University Press, 1993], 9). To my mind, then, it is a gross exaggeration to state with Harold Fredrik Cherniss that, "but for some few orthodox dogmas which he could not circumvent, Gregory has merely applied Christian names to Plato's doctrine and called it Christian theology" (*The Platonism of Gregory of Nyssa* [Berkeley: University of California Press, 1930], 62). At the same time, Jean Daniélou may unduly minimize the importance to Gregory of a Platonic metaphysic. See *Platonisme et théologie mystique: Doctrine spirituelle de Saint Grégoire de Nysse* (Paris: Aubier, 1944), 8-9.

the pure in heart, Moses, and the bride—can be realized in the soul's mystical vision of God in Christ, prior to the eschatological beatific vision. At the same time, Gregory is convinced that human personhood will never be fully realized, since the soul will always remain in search of greater fulfillment of its desire. The reason for this is that seeing God implies at the same time a nonseeing, since the soul can never (not even in the hereafter) attain to the very nature or essence of the infinite God.

Homilies on the Beatitudes: Obstacles to Purity

Gregory first extensively discusses the beatific vision in his *Homilies on the Beatitudes*.[13] Anticipating the approach of many others in the later tradition, Gregory begins by positing the obvious paradox that the canonical witness presents: on the one hand, John, Paul, and Moses all rule out the possibility of seeing God (John 1:18; 1 Tim 6:16; Exod 33:20);[14] on the other hand, none of these three saints "failed to achieve that sublime blessedness which comes as a result of seeing God."[15] This paradox is closely linked to two obstacles that may prevent us from seeing God, both of which would appear to justify the belief that human beings cannot possibly do so. The first obstacle has to do with the nature of God. The promise held out by the sixth beatitude—that the pure in heart shall see God—is a promise that "exceeds the utmost limit [*horon*] of blessedness."[16] Gregory maintains that the divine nature "transcends all conceptual comprehension."[17] God's nature is beyond human limits, so that the only way to speak of the divine nature is by using apophatic negations: God is inaccessible, unapproachable, incomprehensible, and untraceable.[18] The second obstacle concerns the lack of purity on the part of human beings. Gregory is keenly aware of the passions that stand in the way of the purity required to see God. Worrying about the "intractable difficulty" that the passions pose,[19]

---

13. For the Greek text, I follow the critical edition of *De beatitudinibus* (hereafter referred to as *Beat*) in vol. 7/2 of *Gregorii Nysseni Opera*, ed. Johannes F. Callahan (Leiden: Brill, 1992), 75–170. I use the English translation by Stuart George Hall in Hubertus R. Drobner and Albert Viciano, eds., *Gregory of Nyssa: Homilies on the Beatitudes: An English Version with Supporting Studies* (Leiden: Brill, 2000).

14. *Beat* 6.137.13–22 (Hall, 66).

15. Gregory appeals to 2 Tim 4:8, John 13:25, and Exod 33:17.

16. *Beat* 6.138.9–10 (Hall, 67).

17. *Beat* 6.140.16–17 (Hall, 68).

18. *Beat* 6.140.17, 19, 20 (Hall, 68).

19. *Beat* 6.144.16 (Hall, 71).

St. Gregory exclaims, "What sort of Jacob's ladder (Gen 28:12) is to be found, what sort of fiery chariot like the one which carried up the prophet Elijah to heaven (2 Kgs 2:11), by which our heart might be lifted up to the marvels above, and shake off this earthly burden?"[20] Gregory makes clear to his readers that the Lord's promise faces tremendous hurdles.

Both the depth of the dominical saying and the intractable challenge that it poses to the spiritual quest make Gregory's mind "spin," "whirl," and "reel."[21] In fact, he begins his homily by speaking of the vertiginous experience of looking down from a mountaintop into a deep sea:

> People who look down from some high peak on a vast sea below, probably feel what my mind has felt, looking out from the sublime words of the Lord as from a mountain-top at the inexhaustible depth of their meaning. It is the same as in many seaside places, where you may see a mountain cut in half, sliced sheer on the seaward side from top to bottom, at whose upper end a projecting peak leans out towards the deep. As a person might feel who from such a view-point looked down from the great height on the sea at the bottom, so my mind spins now, sent reeling by this great saying of the Lord.[22]

By comparing the impact that the sixth beatitude has on him to an experience of vertigo, Nyssen indicates that the Lord's saying about the pure in heart is one that involves paradoxes and difficulties of such magnitude that they render us unable to explain the saying.[23] Gregory is alluding to an experience of rapture or ecstasy that takes him beyond the powers of sense and discursive reasoning.[24]

The paradox and obstacles surrounding the beatific vision do not render

---

20. *Beat* 6.144.22–26 (Hall, 71). Within the context of the struggle against the passions, it is hard to imagine that the mention of Elijah's chariot does not at the same time call to Gregory's mind Plato's allegory of the chariot, which he relates in *Phaedrus* 246a–254e.

21. *Beat* 6.137.10 (Hall, 66); 6.137.25 (Hall, 66); 6.138.26 (Hall, 67). In each case, Gregory uses forms of the verb *ilingiaō* or of the noun *ilingos*.

22. *Beat* 6.136.26–137.11 (Hall, 66).

23. Gregory uses the imagery of vertigo to describe the move beyond rational knowledge also in his seventh homily on Ecclesiastes. See *In Ecclesiasten homiliae*, in vol. 5 of *Gregorii Nysseni Opera*, ed. Paulus Alexander (Leiden: Brill, 1986), 7.413.5–414.9. The English translation is "Gregory, Bishop of Nyssa: Homilies on Ecclesiastes," trans. Stuart George Hall and Rachel Moriarty, in *Gregory of Nyssa: Homilies on Ecclesiastes: An English Version with Supporting Studies*, ed. Stuart George Hall (Berlin: de Gruyter, 1993), 125–26.

24. It does not seem to me that Gregory's rhetorical reference to his experience of vertigo implies that he actually has a mystical experience during the writing or preaching of his sermon. More likely, he playfully suits the rhetoric of the homily's opening paragraph to the theme of the sermon.

Gregory silent or agnostic on the topic. Both the paradox of seeing the invisible God and the obstacles that impede the vision can be subjected to rational analysis. Gregory takes several steps toward a resolution of the difficulties. With regard to the first difficulty, that of divine incomprehensibility, he notes that it is possible—even for the "wise of the world"—to move from God's energies or operations to the divine operator.[25] In particular, God's operations teach us about his transcendent wisdom, goodness, power, purity, and immutability.[26] Gregory here distinguishes between God's nature (*physis*) or being (*ousia*) and his energies (*energeiai*). This distinction—which through Gregory of Palamas's use during the fourteenth-century Hesychast controversy has taken on particular prominence in Orthodox theology—helps Gregory affirm both that God cannot be seen (in his being) and that he can be seen (in his operations). "He who is by nature invisible," affirms Gregory, "becomes visible in his operations, being seen in certain cases by the properties he possesses."[27] As a result of this distinction, the paradox becomes a little less intolerable: it is apparently possible for us to see God in creation, while he remains invisible inasmuch as he transcends the created order.

St. Gregory explains that the *visio Dei* also becomes a reality when we wash away the accumulated filth of sin "by scrupulous living"[28] or when, as a whetstone strips off rust from iron, our heart recovers its original likeness to its archetype.[29] This means that it is possible to see God's beauty in ourselves as in a mirror.[30] The result is that, "even though you are too feeble to understand the unapproachable light, yet if you go right back to the grace of the image which was built into you from the first, you possess in yourselves what you seek. Godhead is purity, absence of passion, and separation from every evil. If these are in you, God is certainly in you."[31] Gregory thus "resolves" the paradox of seeing the invisible God by limiting in two ways what it is that we see of God: we observe only his operations—not his nature—in creation (with the physical eyes), and we see merely a reflection of God's nature in the mirror of our lives

25. *Beat* 6.142.2–4 (Hall, 69).

26. *Beat* 6.141.8–142.4 (Hall, 69).

27. *Beat* 6.141.25–27 (Hall, 69).

28. *Beat* 6.143.11–12 (Hall, 70).

29. *Beat* 6.143.13–20 (Hall, 70).

30. Cf. the comment of Edwart Baert: "Ainsi la réapparition de l'image de Dieu qui est un retour à l'état originel est aussi une vision de Dieu dans le miroir de l'âme pure" ("Le Thème de la vision de Dieu chez S. Justin, Clément d'Alexandrie et S. Grégoire de Nysse," *Freiburger Zeitschrift für Philosophie und Theologie* 12 [1965]: 492). For discussion of Gregory's use of the "mirror" metaphor in his *Homilies on the Song of Songs*, see Boersma, *Embodiment and Virtue*, 99. Cf., more extensively, Daniélou, *Platonisme*, 210–22.

31. *Beat* 6.143.27–144.4 (Hall, 70).

(with the "eye of the soul").[32] Both of these limitations to the *visio Dei* imply that something remains inaccessible to human sight: in the first instance we do not see the nature or being of God, and in the second instance we see his light only inasmuch as the soul reflects it. To be sure, we should not conclude that this means human beings do not really see God: by witnessing the operations of God or the likeness of the archetype, we really do see God himself. After all, by drawing rational conclusions about God's operations we do get to see God in some way: "each sublime idea brings God into view," comments Gregory.[33] And he encourages his listeners to recover their likeness to the archetype, for, he says to them, the result will be that "you possess in yourself what you seek. . . . God is certainly in you."[34]

It should be clear from this that for Gregory everyday spirituality—seeing what God is like by looking at the world around us and observing with the "eye of the soul," "the luminous outpoured rays of the divine nature" in our hearts[35]—is intrinsically linked to the beatific vision. Seeing God is not just a matter of the eschaton. Already today we get to contemplate in some fashion the light of God's being. What is more, for Gregory, earthly anticipations of the beatific vision take the form not just of ecstatic, theophanic experiences—though, as will see, he does discuss them. Much more mundanely, however, we already experience the *visio Dei* in a real sense when we see traces of God in the ways in which he works in the world and in the reflection of his purity in our own lives.

Of course, in none of this exposition has Gregory "solved" the paradox of seeing the invisible God. What he *has* done is to delineate, as it were, certain aspects of God's presence in the world (in his operations and in human purity) that make him visible, while limiting the invisibility of God to those inner aspects of God's

---

32. At the same time, as we will see, for Gregory the "resolution" does not really remove the paradox, which remains as a result of his doctrine of perpetual progress (*epektasis*). For discussion on Gregory of Nyssa's approach to the spiritual senses, see Boersma, *Embodiment and Virtue*, 93–100; Sarah Coakley, "Gregory of Nyssa," in *The Spiritual Senses: Perceiving God in Western Christianity*, ed. Paul L. Gavrilyuk and Sarah Coakley (Cambridge: Cambridge University Press, 2012), 36–55. Arguing that the later Gregory turned against his own earlier Platonic body-soul dualism, Coakley wrongly claims that Gregory turns from a "disjunctive" to a "conjunctive" approach, according to which sense perception itself can become spiritual perception. This interpretation overlooks that when Gregory wants us to use the senses to arrive at the reality that surpasses them, this "use" of the senses typically takes the form of a renunciation of the senses. Coakley underestimates the (Platonist Christian) emphasis on ascent and anagogy throughout Gregory's writings, even in his later mystical commentaries (though it is true that these tend to be more thoroughly christological than some of his earlier works).

33. *Beat* 6.141.17–18 (Hall, 69).

34. *Beat* 6.144.2–4 (Hall, 70).

35. *Beat* 6.144.8–9; 6.144.12 (Hall, 71).

being that are beyond ordinary human observation. But while in some significant way Gregory has dealt with the paradox of seeing the invisible God, one of the two obstacles to the vision of God remains more or less intact: the requirement of "purity of heart" (and so our vision of God in ourselves as in a mirror) still hardly seems feasible. God's character is perfect purity, and a mere mirroring of this purity would hardly seem the kind of purity required for the vision of God. Regardless of Gregory's attempts thus far at securing the human vision of God, therefore, he has not yet fully addressed the gap separating the creature from the Creator. Nor would it be out of place for his audience still to have questions about their ability to attain to the "purity of heart" that allows for the vision of God.

As we will see shortly, Gregory is keenly aware of the difficulty of attaining genuine "purity of heart." Nevertheless, in this homily on the sixth beatitude he never fully resolves this second obstacle to the vision of God—the lack of human purity vis-à-vis the holiness of God. Nyssen simply insists that the dominical saying is not only a warning but also a promise, which as such is attainable.[36] Purity of heart cannot be out of reach, Gregory explains. He references the Lord's sharpening of the Old Testament Law in the remainder of the Sermon on the Mount (Matt 5:17–28), and he insists that we find in this teaching a "sharp-edged word like a plough digging out the roots of sins from the bottom of our heart," identifying Christ's words as "instruction which leads us to our goal."[37] Gregory merely reinforces the urgency of Christ's demand as he insists that purity of heart is within our reach. We cannot but wonder how Gregory's audience would have responded to their preacher's optimistic assessment of our ability to achieve the goal of purity. After all, the passage concludes with the demand to "be perfect, as your heavenly Father is perfect" (Matt 5:48). Christ's "instruction" regarding this perfection may not at all imply that people in fact have the ability to follow up on it. Purity may still be out of reach.

Gregory is quite aware of the exegetical and doctrinal difficulty that he faces at this point: if perfection is unattainable, this means that purity is out of reach. And if purity is wishful thinking, then we will never see the face of God. In this particular sermon, Gregory leaves the issue unresolved. He simply warns his congregation at the end about the choice of either a life of virtue taking on the shape of the Divinity or a life of vice taking on the form of the Adversary.[38] He even adds that it is up to us which one to choose, since "there is offered to us the power to go either way by our own freedom of choice."[39] This ending of

---

36. *Beat* 6.145.20–146.2 (Hall, 72).
37. *Beat* 6.147.15–16; 6.147.19–20 (Hall, 73).
38. *Beat* 6.148.3–8 (Hall, 73).
39. *Beat* 6.148.15–16 (Hall, 73–74). While it is tempting perhaps to accuse Gregory of Pela-

the sermon seems rather unsatisfying, as it leaves Nyssen's congregation with a demand for purity that appears for all intents and purposes impossible to fulfill. Quite likely, Gregory leaves the question of the attainability of purity unresolved for homiletical reasons—either so that he can end the sermon with a stern warning or so that he doesn't have to start up a lengthy new discussion of what it means to attain perfection or purity. Whatever his reason for ending the sermon the way that he does, Gregory clearly leaves the onus of purity resting firmly on the shoulders of his listeners.

The Life of Moses: Vision as Perpetual Desire

Both in his book *On Perfection* and in his two masterful mystical treatises on Moses and on the Song of Songs, Gregory does develop a carefully considered christological response to this issue.[40] Toward the end of his life, he resolves the issue of the apparent impossibility of perfection (and, by implication, also of purity) by redefining it in terms of infinite progress towards perfection as it exists in God himself. Thus, he writes in *On Perfection*: "For this is truly perfection: never to stop growing towards what is better and never placing any limit on perfection."[41] Gregory gives a similar definition in *The Life of Moses*, when he comments that "the perfection of human nature consists perhaps in its very growth in goodness."[42] Gregory here speaks of perfection as unending growth or progress in the life of God (*epektasis*), which is an important theme in the

gianism at this point, his overall theology (and particularly his christological understanding of participation) should caution us in this regard. See Boersma, *Embodiment and Virtue*, 211–50.

40. There is some difference of opinion as to the dating of *On Perfection*. Considering the less developed solution to the problem of perfection in this work (as compared to *The Life of Moses* and the *Homilies on the Song of Songs*), I am inclined to go with Gerhard May's dating of 370–378 for *On Perfection* (rather than accept Daniélou's suggestion of a later date). Cf. Jean Daniélou, "La Chronologie des œuvres de Grégoire de Nysse," *Studia Patristica* 7 (1966): 168; Gerhard May, "Die Chronologie des Lebens und der Werke des Gregor von Nyssa," in *Écriture et culture philosophique dans la pensée de Grégoire de Nysse: Actes du colloque de Chevetogne* (September 22–26, 1969), ed. Marguerite Harl (Leiden: Brill, 1971), 56.

41. *De perfectione* (hereafter referred to as *Perf*), in *Gregorii Nysseni Opera*, ed. Wernerus Jaeger, vol. 8/1 (Leiden: Brill, 1986), 214.4–6; the English translation is *On Perfection*, in *Saint Gregory of Nyssa: Ascetical Works*, trans. Virginia Woods Callahan (Washington, DC: Catholic University of America Press, 1999), 122.

42. *De vita Moysis* (hereafter referred to as *Vit Moys*), in vol. 7/1 of *Gregorii Nysseni Opera*, ed. Hubertus Musurillo (Leiden: Brill, 1964), 5.2–4; the English translation is *The Life of Moses*, ed. and trans. Abraham J. Malherbe and Everett Ferguson (New York: Paulist Press, 1978), 31. For detailed discussion of Gregory's unfolding of the notion of perfection, see Boersma, *Embodiment and Virtue*, 225, 227, 230–34, 237–38.

mystical works written toward the end of his life. Nyssen takes the concept from Philippians 3:13–14, where St. Paul states, "Brothers, I do not consider that I have made it my own. But one thing I do: forgetting what lies behind and straining forward [*epekteinomenos*] to what lies ahead, I press on toward the goal for the prize of the upward call of God in Christ Jesus" (ESV). For Gregory, ever-increasing growth in purity and perfection is possible, explains Lucas Mateo-Seco, "because one already participates in a real manner in this good; an infinite growth is possible because this good is inexhaustible."[43] It is the infinite goodness of God that secures for Gregory the notion of perpetual progress in the life of God.

Gregory closely links his notion of *epektasis* to that of participation (*metochē* or *metousia*), which is common in the Platonic tradition. Gregory holds that created beings (especially created intelligibles) participate in the being of God, particularly through the life of virtue. He regards this as participation in the energies of God (as opposed to his nature or essence).[44] Since God is infinite, human progress must likewise be infinite, believes Gregory. David L. Balás, in his excellent study on participation in St. Gregory, comments that "participation is, according to Gregory's conception, intimately connected with change, even continuous change."[45] Gregory's notion that participation allows for continuous (eternal) growth is an answer to the problem that a more static view of the beatific vision would seem to entail: if the vision of God fully satisfies human desire, would this satiety (*koros*) not lead to weariness with regard to the expe-

43. Lucas Francisco Mateo-Seco, "Epektasis – ἐπέκτασις," in *The Brill Dictionary of Gregory of Nyssa*, ed. Lucas Francisco Mateo-Seco and Giulio Maspero (Leiden: Brill, 2009), 265. For further discussion on the notion of *epektasis* in Gregory, see Daniélou, *Platonisme*, 291–307; Everett Ferguson, "God's Infinity and Man's Mutability: Perpetual Progress according to Gregory of Nyssa," *Greek Orthodox Theological Review* 18 (1973): 59–78; Ronald E. Heine, *Perfection in the Virtuous Life: A Study in the Relationship between Edification and Polemical Theology in Gregory of Nyssa's De Vita Moysis* (Cambridge, MA: Philadelphia Patristic Foundation, 1975), 63–114; E. Ferguson, "Progress in Perfection: Gregory of Nyssa's *Vita Moysis*," *Studia Patristica* 14 (1976): 307–14; Albert-Kees Geljon, "Divine Infinity in Gregory of Nyssa and Philo of Alexandria," *Vigiliae Christianae* 59 (2005): 152–77.

44. Cf. David L. Balás, *ΜΕΤΟΥΣΙΑ ΘΕΟΥ: Man's Participation in God's Perfections according to Saint Gregory of Nyssa* (Rome: Herder, 1966), 128; Paulos Mar Gregorios, *Cosmic Man: The Divine Presence: The Theology of St. Gregory of Nyssa, ca. 330 to 395 AD* (New York: Paragon, 1988), 110–23; Elie D. Moutsoulas, "'Essence' et 'énergies' de Dieu selon St. Grégoire de Nysse," *Studia Patristica* 18 (1989): 517–28; Verna E. F. Harrison, *Grace and Human Freedom according to St. Gregory of Nyssa* (Lewiston, NY: Edwin Mellen, 1992), 24–60, 88–131; Giulio Maspero, *Trinity and Man: Gregory of Nyssa's Ad Ablabium* (Leiden: Brill, 2007), 27–52; Alexis Torrance, "'Precedents for Palamas' Essence–Energies Theology in the Cappadocian Fathers," *Vigiliae Christianae* 63 (2009): 47–70.

45. Balás, *ΜΕΤΟΥΣΙΑ ΘΕΟΥ*, 136.

rience of God in the hereafter, and hence possibly to another fall, a recurring lapse from this beatific experience? That this was a genuine theological conundrum is clear from Origen's speculations on the topic of satiety, and it is likely in response to this Origenist problem that Gregory posits the notion of *epektasis*.[46]

Nyssen's combination of the themes of purity (or perfection), participation, and *epektasis* is of great significance for the way that he articulates the doctrine of the beatific vision, both in *The Life of Moses* and in the *Homilies on the Song of Songs*.[47] Following Jean Daniélou, scholars have tended to analyze *The Life of Moses* in terms of the three theophanies that Moses experiences: God appears to him in the burning bush (Exod 3), in the darkness of Mount Sinai (Exod 20:21), and by the cleft in the rock (Exod 33:21–22). The three stages have been characterized as a move from light, via the cloud, into darkness.[48] In actual fact, however, Nyssen's understanding of Moses's progress does not proceed quite this neatly by way of three distinct stages. Gregory does indeed trace Moses's ascent by following the three theophanies in the book of Exodus. But when we analyze what distinguishes them, it becomes clear that the notion of *epektasis* radically blurs the lines between the second and the third "stages" of the ascent. There is only one genuine marker in the ascent; it falls, as we will see, between the first and second theophanies. The result is that there are really only two major stages in the ascent of the soul.

At the burning bush—in its material form a witness to the incarnation[49]— Moses comes to recognize that neither sense perception nor understanding gives true access to Being: "It seems to me that at the time the great Moses was instructed in the theophany he came to know that none of those things which are apprehended by sense perception and contemplated by the understanding really subsists, but that the transcendent essence and cause of the universe, on which everything depends, alone subsists."[50] Nyssen then distinguishes between

---

46. Cf. Marguerite Harl, "Recherches sur l'originisme d'Origène: La 'satiété' (*koros*) de la contemplation comme motif de la chute des âmes," *Studia Patristica* 8 (1966): 373–405; Heine, *Perfection*, 71–97.

47. Lucas F. Mateo-Seco observes that Gregory refers to 1 Cor 13:12 (which speaks of the beatific vision) in *The Life of Moses* "precisely when he speaks of the infinity of God and, as a consequence, when he affirms the existence of progression towards infinity in the contemplation of God, that is, when he presents his thought on what scholars of Saint Gregory of Nyssa usually call *epektasis*" ("1 Cor 13, 12 in Gregory of Nyssa's Theological Thinking," *Studia Patristica* 32 [1997]: 153–62).

48. Cf. Daniélou, *Platonisme*, 17–23. I followed this approach in Hans Boersma, *Heavenly Participation: The Weaving of a Sacramental Tapestry* (Grand Rapids: Eerdmans, 2011), 160–61.

49. Nyssen mentions a number of ways in which he believes this passage of Exodus 3 speaks of the Incarnation. See Boersma, *Embodiment and Virtue*, 241.

50. *Vit Moys* 40.13–17 (Malherbe and Ferguson, 60).

created realities, which exist by way of participation in Being, and immutable Being itself, which is "participated in by all but not lessened by their participation—this is truly real Being."[51]

The second theophany leads Moses into the cloud on the mountain (Exod 20:21). This theophany is a vision of God in darkness, and the reason for this is that Moses comes to see that "knowledge of the divine essence is unattainable"[52] and that God is "beyond all knowledge and comprehension."[53] Here, Moses "slips into the inner sanctuary [*adyton*] of divine knowledge" and enters into the "tabernacle not made with hands" (Heb 9:11).[54] Gregory identifies this heavenly tabernacle with Christ, uncreated in his preexistence,[55] and he speaks of the incarnate Christ (as well as of his church) as the earthly tabernacle.[56]

Having arrived at the "inner sanctuary" already in the cloud (the second stage), Moses's further ascent cannot possibly involve advancing to a distinctly different stage. The first theophany taught him that created being exists only by way of participation, and the second theophany made clear that the Being of God is beyond knowledge. At this point, Moses (as well as Gregory himself) faces a dilemma. On the one hand, there can be no knowledge of God that reaches beyond the "inner sanctuary." On the other hand, however, Moses has not yet arrived at the destiny of his ascent: at the very apex of his journey—the inner sanctuary itself—he appears to realize that he will never come to know the Being of God. And so, even though he has already seen God "face to face" (Exod 33:11), Moses still asks God to show him his glory (Exod 33:18)[57]—which then leads to the third theophany, where Moses is allowed to see God's back from within a cleft of the rock—a divine manifestation that St. Gregory again explains christologically, with Christ being identified as the rock.[58] For Gregory, Christ is never left behind: the human person finds his identity always and only in him.

It is at this point that Gregory embarks on a detailed discussion of *epektasis*.[59] Even though Moses has already come to Christ as the tabernacle and

51. *Vit Moys* 40.24–25 (Malherbe and Ferguson, 60).
52. *Vit Moys* 87.12–13 (Malherbe and Ferguson, 95).
53. *Vit Moys* 87.16–17 (Malherbe and Ferguson, 95).
54. *Vit Moys* 88.13 (Malherbe and Ferguson, 96).
55. *Vit Moys* 91.19 (Malherbe and Ferguson, 98).
56. *Vit Moys* 91.16–20; 95.11–13 (Malherbe and Ferguson, 98, 101). I have emphasized the christological character of Moses's entry into the tabernacle in Boersma, *Embodiment and Virtue*, 240–45. For a similar analysis, see Nathan Eubank, "Ineffably Effable: The Pinnacle of Mystical Ascent in Gregory of Nyssa's *De vita Moysis*," *International Journal of Systematic Theology* 16 (2014): 25–41.
57. *Vit Moys* 110.6–11 (Malherbe and Ferguson, 111).
58. *Vit Moys* 118.20 (Malherbe and Ferguson, 117).
59. *Vit Moys* 110.3–122.3 (Malherbe and Ferguson, 111–20).

the inner sanctuary in the cloud, further progress still appears possible. But it is progress that takes place after the senses and the understanding have already long been left behind (in the first two theophanies). All that needs to be abandoned has already been let go by the time Moses experiences the third theophany. Already in the second theophany, he has achieved the experience of mystical ecstasy, the sense of vertigo, which comes from leaving behind every this-worldly apprehension of God. The reason why Moses can nonetheless ascend still higher is that his entrance into the "inner sanctuary" does not mean the arrival at a point of static rest. Moses recognizes that even his "face-to-face" encounter with God (Exod 33:11) beyond sense and understanding does not give him access to God's "true Being" (*hōs ekeinos estin*).[60] Moses still wants to see God "not in mirrors and reflections, but face to face."[61]

The reason for Moses's continued desire to see God face to face is that "the Divine is by its very nature infinite, enclosed by no boundary."[62] So, even though Moses has, in fact, had the rapturous experience of seeing God in the cloud, this does not satiate his desire: "The munificence of God assented to the fulfillment of his desire, but did not promise any cessation or satiety of the desire."[63] Therefore, just as "purity of heart" (human perfection) means "never to stop growing towards what is better and never placing any limit on perfection,"[64] so the beatific vision—which itself is true purity or perfection—always progresses. Nyssen comments, therefore, that "the true sight of God consists in this, that the one who looks up to God never ceases in that desire."[65] And he adds a little later: "This truly is the vision of God: never to be satisfied in the desire to see him."[66] Gregory's definition of the *visio Dei* is nearly identical to his definition of purity. The pursuit of both elements of the dominical saying— purity and the vision of God—is driven by never-ending desire.

At this point, Gregory has provided a theological as well pastoral response to the seemingly intolerable burden that the conclusion of his sixth homily on the Beatitudes imposed on his audience. Recognizing that the promise of the beatific vision seems out of reach as a result of a lack of purity, he ended that sermon simply by impressing on his hearers all the more strictly the demand for purity. In *The Life of Moses*, however, Gregory takes a different approach. He recognizes that our growth in purity—or, we could also say, our participation in

---

60. *Vit Moys* 115.9 (Malherbe and Ferguson, 114).
61. *Vit Moys* 114.13–14 (Malherbe and Ferguson, 114–15).
62. *Vit Moys* 115.114–16 (Malherbe and Ferguson, 115).
63. *Vit Moys* 114.17–19 (Malherbe and Ferguson, 115).
64. *Perf* 214.4–6 (Woods Callahan, 122).
65. *Vit Moys* 114.21–3 (Malherbe and Ferguson, 115).
66. *Vit Moys* 116.17–19 (Malherbe and Ferguson, 116).

Christ—leaves much to be desired. Regardless of how far we may have ascended in terms of purity, the Christian life is never one of absolute achievement; it always remains one of progress. That progress, in fact, is what defines the life of purity for Gregory. And he recognizes that even when Moses reaches the peak of his theophanic experiences, or when we ourselves reach our heavenly future and see God face to face, growth in God—in and through Christ—will still continue. For Gregory, seeing God kindles a desire to see ever more of him, so that the beatific vision implies a perpetual desire to see God—so much so, that Gregory even defines the vision itself as the never-ending desire to see the face of God.

Homilies on the Song of Songs: Seeing More and More of Christ

St. Gregory's *Homilies on the Song of Songs* similarly approach the vision of God by interweaving the themes of purity (often discussed as virtue), participation, and *epektasis*. Again, while much of the metaphysical structure is Platonic, Gregory refuses to separate the beatific vision from Christology. Christ is always the object of our vision. When the bride comments, "Behold, you are beautiful, my kinsman, and glorious, in the shadow by our bed" (Song 1:16),[67] Gregory takes this to mean that she praises Christ's nobility, compared to which everything else—human approval, glory, celebrity, and worldly power—pales:

> For these things are tinged with a show of nobility for those whose attention is focused on sense perception, but they are not what they are reckoned to be. For how should something be noble when it lacks entire reality? That which is honored in this world, after all, has its being only in the heads of the people who make the judgment, but you are truly beautiful—not only beautiful [*kalos*], but the very essence of the Beautiful [*autē tou kalou hē ousia*], existing forever as such, being at every moment what you are, neither blooming when the appropriate time comes, nor putting off your bloom at the right time, but stretching your springtime splendor out to match the everlastingness of your life—you whose name is love of humankind.[68]

---

67. Throughout, I quote the Song of Songs from the translation of Gregory's own use of the Greek text, as found in Gregory of Nyssa, *Gregory of Nyssa: Homilies on the Song of Songs* (hereafter referred to as *Cant*), ed. and trans. Richard A. Norris (Atlanta: Society of Biblical Literature, 2012). For the Greek text of the sermons, I use the same volume, which includes a critical edition of the text.

68. *Cant* 4.106.4–107.11.

For Gregory, Christ is not only "beautiful" (*kalos*) but also "the very essence of the Beautiful" (*autē tou kalou hē ousia*). In Nyssen's Christology, Christ is the very definition of beauty, which means that he always equates the vision of God's beauty with the vision of the beauty of Christ.

Much as in *The Life of Moses*, so also in these homilies, the incarnation is the central event through which God becomes visible to the human eye. After the bride has already accomplished a number of ascents, Gregory notes that none of this could yet be characterized as "contemplation," properly speaking. Commenting on Song of Songs 2:8—"The voice of my kinsman: Behold, he comes leaping over the mountains, bounding over the hills"—Nyssen remarks that "all these ascents are described not in terms of contemplation or clear grasp of the Truth, but by reference to the 'voice' of the One who is desired, and the characteristics of a voice are identified by hearing, not known and rejoiced in by understanding."[69] In the words "Behold, he comes," Gregory reads a reference to prophetic announcements of God's manifestation in the flesh, and he quotes from "the prophet: 'As we have heard, so also we have seen' (Ps 47:9 [48:8]). *The voice of my beloved*: this is what we have heard. *Behold, he is coming*: this is what the eyes see."[70] The prophets announce the coming of Christ; the incarnation makes him visible to the eye.

In line with this, when in the next verse the kinsman stands behind the wall, "leaning through the windows, peering through the lattices" (Song 2:9), Gregory sees this as a reference to the Law and the Prophets, which offer only marginal illumination.[71] The "anagogical sense of the words," he maintains, shows us that

> the Word follows a certain path and a certain sequence in adapting human nature to God. First of all he shines upon it by means of the prophets and the law's injunctions. (This is our interpretation: the windows are the prophets, who bring in the light, while the lattices are the network of the law's injunctions. Through both of them the beam of the true Light steals into the interior.) After that, however, comes the Light's perfect illumination, when, by its mingling with our nature, the true Light shows itself to those who are in darkness and the shadow of death.[72]

Although the Law and the Prophets do carry some borrowed light from the true Light, it really is the Light's perfect illumination in the incarnation that enables us to see. So, it is when the bride comes to "the shelter of the rock" and asks the

---

69. *Cant* 5.138.20–23.
70. *Cant* 5.140.19–20.
71. Cf. Boersma, *Embodiment and Virtue*, 83.
72. *Cant* 5.144.24–145.3.

Groom, "Show me your face" (Song 2:14), that she recognizes the presence of Christ. Gregory imagines the bride speaking as follows: "Speak to me no longer by way of the enigmas of the prophets and the law, but show me yourself clearly so that I may see. In that way I can leave the outworks of the law behind and come to be within the rock of the gospel."[73]

The encounter with Christ, therefore, fulfills the desire to see God face to face. The Law no longer separates the bride from "union with the one she desires."[74] When the bride comments, "My kinsman is mine and I am his; he feeds his flock among the lilies, until the day dawns and the shadows depart" (Song 2:16–17), Gregory offers the following paraphrase: "'I have seen,' she says, 'the One who is eternally what he is face to face. I have seen him rising up in human form on my account out of the synagogue my sister, and I am resting in him and am becoming a member of his household.'"[75]

Similarly, when much later, in Homily 15, Nyssen reflects at length on the mystery of the incarnation, he refers to the union between the Groom and the bride ("I am for my kinsman, and my kinsman is for me"—Song 6:3). Gregory insists that

> through these words we learn that the purified soul is to have nothing within her save God and is to look upon nothing else. Rather must she so cleanse herself of every material concern and thought that she is entirely, in her whole being, transposed into the intelligible and immaterial realm and make of herself a supremely vivid image of the prototypical Beauty.[76]

This transposition of the soul into the intelligible realm implies, St. Gregory explains, that "she is conformed to Christ, that she has recovered her very own beauty."[77] Just as a mirror shows the exact imprint of the face that it reflects, so the soul, argues Gregory, "has graven into herself the pure look of the inviolate beauty."[78] Accordingly, the mirror of the soul boasts of being shaped by the beauty of Christ: "Since I focus upon the face of my kinsman with my entire being, the entire beauty of his form is seen in me."[79]

Gregory adds to this christological *visio Dei* the notion that it is fueled by a never-ending, epektatic desire. The homilies on the Song of Songs do not de-

---

73. *Cant* 5.163.26–30.
74. *Cant* 5.168.34–35.
75. *Cant* 5.168.2–4.
76. *Cant* 15.439.12–16.
77. *Cant* 15.439.21–22.
78. *Cant* 15.440.28–29.
79. *Cant* 15.440.30–32.

velop this theme in the same programmatic way as *The Life of Moses*. My hunch is that the simple reason for this is that the Song lacks the textual scaffolding of the three theophanies of the book of Exodus from which to construct the increasing progression of epektatic growth in the life of God. But just because it is more difficult to trace the *epektasis* textually in the Song of Songs, this does not mean that St. Gregory fails to develop the theme. As in his first homily he reflects on the Song's opening words ("Let him kiss me with the kisses of his mouth"), Nyssen refers back to the "bride Moses" loving the Bridegroom in the same way as does the Song's virgin, and he explains:

> through the face-to-face converse accorded him by God (as the Scripture testifies [cf. Num 12:8]), he became more intensely desirous of such kisses after these theophanies, praying to see the Object of his yearning as if he had never glimpsed him. In the same way, none of the others in whom the divine yearning was deeply lodged ever came to a point of rest in their desire. And just as now the soul that is joined to God is not satiated by her enjoyment of him, so too the more abundantly she is filled up with his beauty, the more vehemently her longings abound.[80]

Rather than satisfying his desire for God, Moses's face-to-face contact with God intensifies his longings.

Gregory argues that the Song of Songs reflects this same pattern. The various segments of the Song replicate the soul's ordered ascent into the life of God. Thus, at the beginning of Homily 5, Nyssen explains that the Song evokes both desire (*epithymia*) and despair (*apognōsis*) at the same time: "For how is it possible to be without grief when one considers that the purified soul—even though through love she has been exalted toward participation in the Good by a whole series of ascents—does not yet seem, as the apostle says [Phil 3:13], to have laid hold on what she seeks?"[81] And so, as he reflects on "the ascents already accomplished," Gregory mentions that he had earlier thought he would be able to "pronounce the soul blessed on account of her progress toward the heights";[82] but he then makes the distinction between merely hearing the "voice" of the beloved and "contemplating" the Bridegroom himself, which I discussed above.[83] Contemplation of the Groom is the point in the epektatic ascent at which one moves beyond just hearing his voice.

80. *Cant* 1.31.26–32.32. Square brackets in original.
81. *Cant* 5.137.4–7. Textual reference in square brackets added.
82. *Cant* 5.137.9–10.
83. *Cant* 5.138.19–140.12.

In the next sermon the bride journeys toward even "better things," as she becomes "more clear-sighted and discerns the glory of the Word."[84] She reaches such perfection that she even instructs others about "eagerness for the same goal."[85] But this still does not imply the end of the journey: "Who, then, would not say that a soul exalted to such a degree had come to the highest peak of perfection? Nevertheless the limit that defines the things that have already been accomplished becomes the starting point of her being led to realities that transcend them."[86] Then—and here Gregory refers to the Groom appearing to the bride in the form of a gazelle and of a fawn (Song 2:9)—as an additional step, the bride begins "to see the One whom she desires when he appears to her in a form other than his own."[87] Coming ever closer to perfection, she "prays to see the very countenance of the One who addresses her, and she receives from him a word that no longer comes by way of intermediaries."[88]

When in Song of Songs 2:16, the bride exclaims, "My kinsman is mine and I am his," it is clear to Gregory that at this point "the two actors move into one another. God comes into the soul, and correspondingly the soul is brought into God."[89] Again, Gregory uses this new stage of the bride's ascent as an occasion to reflect on the perpetual character of her progress:

> [S]he seems to attain the hope of the very highest good. For what is higher than to be in the One who is the object of desire and to receive the object of desire within oneself? But in this situation too she bewails the fact that she is needy for the Good. As one who does not yet have what is present to her desire, she is perplexed and dissatisfied, and she broadcasts this perplexity of her soul in her story, describing in her account how she found the one she sought.[90]

Gregory concludes from the bride's "perplexity" that the limitless greatness of the divine nature (*physis*) means that "no measure of knowledge sets bounds to a seeker's looking."[91] In fact, concludes Nyssen, "the intelligence that makes its course upward by seeking into what lies beyond it is so constituted that every

84. *Cant* 6.176.11–12.
85. *Cant* 6.177.26–72.
86. *Cant* 6.177.29–178.31.
87. *Cant* 6.178.34–35.
88. *Cant* 6.178.8–9.
89. *Cant* 6.179.16–18.
90. *Cant* 6.179.22–28.
91. *Cant* 6.180.31. Gregory repeatedly denies that God is subject to "limit" (*peras*) and boundary (*horos*), thereby alluding to his strong insistence on the infinity of God.

fulfillment of knowledge that human nature can attain becomes the starting point of desire for things yet more exalted."[92]

It is only after the bride has departed from the watchmen making their rounds in the city, having asked them where the Groom might be (Song 3:3), that she finds her lover and brings him into her mother's chamber (Song 3:4). St. Gregory has the bride explain that, no sooner had I "departed from the whole created order and passed by everything in the creation that is intelligible and left behind every conceptual approach, than I found the Beloved by faith, and holding on by faith's grasp to the one I have found, I will not let go until he is within my chamber."[93] The chamber, explains Gregory, is the heart, where God comes to live so as to return it to its original condition at the time of creation.[94]

Nyssen perceives that the ascent has still not come to a halt when he reads the following words in Song of Songs 4:8: "Come away from frankincense, my bride, come away from frankincense. You shall come and pass through from the beginning of faith, from the peak of Sanir and Hermon, from the lions' dens, from the mountains of the leopards." The bride's ever-continuing movement makes Gregory think of the fact that St. Paul reflects on his own *epektasis* to a still higher ascent (Phil 3:13) *after* he has already been in the "third heaven" (2 Cor 12:2).[95] Our capacity to see God increases continuously, maintains St. Gregory. Yet, "the infinity and incomprehensibility of the Godhead remains beyond all direct apprehension."[96] Gregory again asserts that "the outer limit of what has been discovered becomes the starting point of a search after more exalted things,"[97] while "the desire of the soul that is ascending never rests content with what has been known."[98]

Nyssen then discusses the particularities of Song of Songs 4:8 by explaining that the bride has already accompanied the Bridegroom to the "mountain of myrrh"[99] —which is a reference to being buried with Christ by baptism into death (Rom 6:4)—and that she has come with him also to the "hill of frankincense"[100] (having risen with him to new life and to communion with the Godhead). Now, maintains Gregory, she is prepared through "unending growth" for yet greater heights.[101]

92. *Cant* 6.180.33–180.2.
93. *Cant* 6.183.20–24. For Gregory, faith allows one to move past the limits of the senses and of discursive knowledge to union with God in Christ (and so to the beatific vision). See Laird, *Gregory of Nyssa*, 100–107.
94. *Cant.* 6.183.24–26.
95. *Cant* 8.245.25–26.
96. *Cant* 8.246.14–15.
97. *Cant* 8.247.3–4.
98. *Cant* 8.247.6–7.
99. *Cant* 8.249.4.
100. *Cant* 8.249.4–5.
101. *Cant* 8.252.26–27.

Finally, in Homily 12, St. Gregory draws attention to the apparent incongruity between Song of Songs 5:3 ("I have removed my tunic. How shall I put it on?") and 5:7 ("the watchmen of the walls took my veil away from me"). How is it possible, Gregory asks, that the watchmen take the veil away from the bride when earlier she has already been "stripped of all covering"?[102] Nyssen sees here yet another reference to *epektasis*: the bride has so increased in purity, he explains, "that by comparison with the purity that now becomes hers she does not seem to have taken off that clothing but again, even after that former stripping, finds something on her to be taken off."[103] To Nyssen, the bride here faces the same situation in which Moses found himself when he asked God to show him his glory (Exod 33:18) even though he had already seen him face to face (Exod 33:11).[104] The ascent into the life of God—which both for Moses and for the bride means union with Christ—is never-ending or epektatic growth in the divine life, spurred on by a desire that never comes to a point of rest. Christ, for Nyssen, is a never-ending source of enjoyment; he therefore continuously increases our longing to be found in him.[105]

Becoming Human in the Beatific Vision

Gregory's search for the vision of God in Christ continues to have a great deal to commend itself. First, Gregory was someone for whom this-worldly realities—accessible to the senses and the intellect—were unable to fulfill his deepest desires. To be sure, his Sixth Homily on the Beatitudes makes clear that sensible and intellectual apprehension in this world already involves some incipient vision of God. But Gregory regards purity of heart as central to attaining the beatific vision, since it is through growth in purity that we come to participate in the purity of God himself. It is growth in purity, then, that allows us to participate in the energies of God and so in the beauty of Christ himself.

Second, Gregory recognizes that human desire is insatiable, so that a proper Christian spirituality holds out the hope of a vision that does not culminate in a static point but ever continues and increases in relation to the ultimate object

---

102. *Cant* 12.360.2.

103. *Cant* 12.360.6–8.

104. Cf. Boersma, *Embodiment and Virtue*, 91–92, 237.

105. In the three writings that I have analyzed, Gregory does not clarify explicitly how he sees the relationship between participating in the divine energies and participating in Christ. Since, in his other writings, he identifies Christ repeatedly with virtue, with perfection, with virginity, with wisdom, and so on, it seems to me that Gregory assumes a close link between Christ and the energies of God. For Gregory, to the degree we are united to Christ, we also participate in the life of God.

of this vision. When, in his two climactic mystical exegetical works, Nyssen reflects on what it is that makes one most genuinely a human person, he turns to Moses and to the bride of the Song of Songs. Through the purity of their lives, they arrive at astounding theophanies. United to Christ, they see God. For Gregory, the epektatic character of this journey into the "inner sanctuary" means that we should not think that this vision fully resolves the paradox of the dominical saying that the pure in heart shall see God. For Gregory, they both shall and shall not see God. If perfection or purity means "never to stop growing towards what is better and never placing any limit on perfection,"[106] and if "the true sight of God consists in this, that the one who looks up to God never ceases in that desire,"[107] then this implies that what makes the beatific vision glorious is that the soul revels with increasing intensity and intimacy in the infinite, ever-greater gift-giving of the invisible God who in Christ has made himself visible.

Third, and more than anything else, St. Gregory makes us aware that human beings cannot find their true identity, and therefore cannot flourish, when they exclude serious reflection on the transcendent purpose of the human person. Human personhood is defined by its telos. As human beings—both as individuals and in our common life together—we attain our identity (and so become fully human) only to the degree that we explicitly aim for the supernatural goal of the beatific vision, which God places before us as our true fulfillment. The reductionism inherent in the modern abandonment of the beatific vision is, therefore, much more serious than may at first appear. It means a turning away from the infinite God who gives all good things in the vision of Christ in favor of a reorientation of the human gaze toward this-worldly goods. The loss of the beatific vision as the purpose of human existence leads to a "spirituality" in which nothing any longer exceeds the ebb and flow of this-worldly human desires. Gregory knew human nature well enough to recognize that our desires are infinite. When such infinite desire is directed away from its proper telos of the vision of God in Christ, the objects of desire inevitably end up holding their immanent sway over human existence in frightening ways, holding us in a form of bondage that, ironically, we have willed into existence by our own misshapen desires. We are perhaps more than ever in need, therefore, of the witness of St. Gregory of Nyssa: only when with Gregory we redirect our gaze upon God in Christ can human persons find their true identity and aim.[108]

---

106. *Perf* 214.4–6 (Woods Callahan, 122).

107. *Vit Moys* 114.21–23 (Malherbe and Ferguson, 115).

108. I want to express my gratefulness to Tracy Russell and Matthew Thomas for their careful reading of an earlier draft of this essay.

Chapter 11

Ambrose: Baptismal Identity and Human Identity

Gerald P. Boersma

De Isaac is a notoriously challenging text.[1] It is a rhapsodic and seemingly haphazard commentary on two diverse texts: the title and opening gamut of the treatise relate the initial encounter of Isaac and Rebecca at the well in Genesis 24. However, Ambrose summarily abandons this course of exegesis (to which he never fully returns); what the reader expects will be a close textual analysis of Genesis evolves into a spiritual exposition of the Canticle (Song of Songs). Even if we are able to trace the unifying thread Ambrose intends between these two texts—that the relation between Isaac and Rebecca is a typological expression of the union of Christ and the soul given voice in the passionate idiom of the Canticle—the treatise still seems utterly bereft of structural cohesion.[2]

In this essay I propose that Ambrose's *De Isaac* provides an integrated, unified answer to the question the bishop poses at the outset of the treatise: "What is man?" I argue that Ambrose's treatise uses this initial question to articulate a baptismal anthropology. Baptism, for the Milanese bishop, profoundly reorients and fulfills human identity. My argument is predicated on the common (and I think plausible) assumption that—despite the challenges that *De Isaac* poses for the interpreter[3]—*De Isaac* was first delivered as a cat-

1. I initially published this essay as "Ambrose's *De Isaac* as a Baptismal Anthropology," *Pro Ecclesia* 26 (2017): 311–32. I am grateful to the editor of *Pro Ecclesia* for permission to reprint. I have used the translation of *De Isaac* by Michael P. McHugh in the Fathers of the Church series (65) and the Latin version in CSEL 32.

2. Jean-Rémy Palanque describes Ambrose's treatises on the patriarchs as "mal compris." Palanque, *Saint Ambroise et l'empire romain* (Paris: Boccard, 1933), 443.

3. Allan Fitzgerald rightly points to the difficulties in trying artificially to impose a unifying theme on *De Isaac*. "Ambrose at the Well: De Isaac et anima," *Revue des Études Augustiniennes* 48 (2002): 82. The apparent lack of structural cohesion has frequently been noted. For example, the

echetical oration[4] that Ambrose preached in (perhaps) 387[5] to his catechumens (including, possibly, Augustine), either preparing for or recently having received baptism. While scholarship is nearly unanimously agreed upon a baptismal context for the treatise, it has not treated a baptismally grounded anthropology as the overall focus.[6] If, however, a baptismal anthropology is indeed the cement that holds the treatise together, this gives a heretofore-unperceived coherence to the treatise as a whole. I will suggest that Ambrose begins outlining his baptismal anthropology by offering an account of the human person as a composite of body and soul. Building on this overall anthropology, Ambrose then explains to the catechumens how, through God's grace in baptism and growth in virtue, the human person comes to fulfill his baptismal identity in mystical union with God.

The Maurist editors (Migne, Patrologia Latina 14, 1845) maintain it is unclear whether *De Isaac* was preached before or after Easter.[7] However, the mystical character of the treatise would suggest it was intended for those who had already received the Easter mysteries.[8] Ambrose's reference to the Pasch and

---

seemingly random excursus on the "wells" that Isaac dug (*Isaac* 4.20–30) is described by Solange Sagot as "un bloc erratique." Sagot, "La triple sagesse dans le De Isaac uel anima," in *Ambroise de Milan: XVIe centenaire de son élection épiscopale*, ed. Yves-Marie Duval (Paris: Études Augustiniennes, 1974), 109. I deal with these apparent incongruities throughout the essay.

4. The Maurist editors describe it as unclear (*obscurrius est*) whether the patriarchal sermons were first preached to the people and subsequently transcribed (PL 14, c. 499–500, ed. 1845). More recently Moretti has convincingly argued that Ambrose's preached sermons were subsequently edited for publication. See P. Moretti, *Non harundo sed calamus: Aspetti letterari della "Explanatio psalmorum XII" di Ambrogio* (Milan: Edizioni Universitarie di Lettere Economia Diritto, 2000), 27–28. However, J.-R. Palanque maintains there is no evidence the treatises were ever orally delivered. See Jean-Rémy Palanque, *St. Ambroise et l'Empire Romain* (Paris: Boccard, 1933), 441.

5. Dating the composition of *De Isaac* is fraught with difficulties. It is unclear whether Ambrose preached *De Isaac* in 387 (or, even, if it was ever actually preached in its written form). Pierre Courcelle was intent to date *De Isaac* to 386 and thereby anchor Augustine's Neoplatonism to his time in Milan and, particularly, to the influence of Bishop Ambrose. See Pierre Courcelle, *Recherches sur les Confessions de saint Augustin* (Paris: Boccard, 1968), 93–138. Michaela Zelzer dates *De Isaac* to 389/390: "Zur Chronologie der Werke des Ambrosius," in *Nec Timeo Mori* (Milan: Vita e Pensiero, 1988), 92. Allan Fitzgerald offers the relatively late date of 395/396: "Isaac at the Well," 79–99. For a summary of this debate, see Marcia Colish, *Ambrose's Patriarchs: Ethics for the Common Man* (Notre Dame, IN: University of Notre Dame Press, 2005), 25–28.

6. For discussion of the bishop's anthropology most scholars point instead to Ambrose's moral treatises, and especially to *De officiis*, in which the bishop offers an anthropology constructed on what seems a fusion of scriptural teaching and Ciceronian Stoicism.

7. "at revocari in dubium potest utrum ante festa paschatis id evenerit, an postea." PL 14:525–26.

8. "Ipsius quidem scriptionis, in qua de spirituali conjugio quo nihil habet perfectissimorum Christianorum vita sublimius, materia videtur indicari ista non pertinere ad catechumenos,

the forgiveness of sins (*venit pascha, venit remissio peccatorum*) (4.35) led the
Maurist editors to suggest *De Isaac* was part of a post-baptismal catechumenate.
Ernst Dassmann and Mechthild Sanders agree with the conclusion of the Maurist editors and maintain that it is highly probable that *De Isaac* was preached
after the Easter baptism as part of a series of post-baptismal catechesis with a
spiritual and ethical emphasis focusing especially on the newly baptized.[9]

Others have argued *De Isaac* is part of Ambrose's prebaptismal catechumenate. In his introduction to the critical edition of *De Isaac*, Karl Schenkl
argues that Ambrose's original audience was the catechumens being prepared to
receive baptism at Easter.[10] Schenkl contends that the patriarchal treatises were
derived from sermons preached to the catechumens who, at this point, were
competentes—those preparing for baptism.[11] Marcia Colish and Warren Smith
likewise argue the patriarchal sermons were preached *before* Easter. During the
Lenten weeks leading up to Easter, Ambrose would preach twice daily to the
competentes.[12] The sustained theme of these Lenten homilies would be the ethical transformation required of the baptized.[13] Colish writes, "In the early weeks

---

utpote quibus certa mysteria tegebantur, ipsis postmodum jam baptismate initiatis revelanda."
PL 14:525–26.

9. Dassmann writes, "Es ist höchst wahrscheinlich, dass die schriftliche Fassung von De Isaac
uel anima der Niederschalg von Predigsten ist, die Ambrosius kurz nach Ostern seinen Gläubigen
mit besonderem Blick auf die Neugetauften gehalten hat." Ernst Dassmann, *Die Frömmigkeit des
Kirchenvaters Ambrosius von Mailand* (Münster: Aschendorff, 1965), 197. Cf. Mechthild Sanders,
*Fons vitae Christus: Der Heilsweg des Menschen nach der Schrift De Isaac et anima des Ambrosius
von Mailand* (Altenberge: Oros, 1996), 15.

10. Ambrose, *De Isaac*, ed. Karl Schenkl, CSEL 32/1 (Prague-Vienna-Leipzig, 1896).

11. Schenkl writes that the treatises stem "ex sermonibus ad catechumenos, qui iam nomen
ad baptismum dedissent et competentes essent" (CSEL 32.1.ii).

12. Cf. Colish, *Ambrose's Patriarchs*, 15, where Colish offers a substantial bibliography of the
Milanese catechumenate process. Also, see Warren Smith, *Christian Grace and Pagan Virtue:
The Theological Foundation of Ambrose's Ethics* (New York: Oxford, 2010), 11. The catechumenate
process in Milan during the time of Ambrose is described in detail by Bonaventura Parodi, *La
catechesi di sant'Ambrogio: Studio di pedagogia pastorale* (Genoa: Scuola Tipografia Opera SS.
Vergine di Pompei, 1957). See also Craig Satterlee, *Ambrose of Milan's Method of Mystagogical
Preaching* (Collegeville, MN: Liturgical Press, 2002). The catechumens in Milan were comprised
of two groups. The *aspirantes* had as yet made no formal commitment to the Church but were
interested in further instruction. The *competentes* were those who had enrolled their names with
the bishop on the Feast of the Epiphany for the reception of baptism the following Easter.

13. It was only during Holy Week that the theme of instruction shifted from a heavy ethical
focus to that of doctrine. During Holy Week the bishop would present the *traditio symboli*—the
handing over of the Creed to the *competentes* to be memorized and recited in front of the rest of the
assembly at Easter. The bishop would make sure that the Creed was understood in a theologically
orthodox manner. Cf. Colish, *Ambrose's Patriarchs*, 15–16; J. N. D. Kelly, *Early Christian Creeds*, 3rd
ed. (London: Longmans, 1972), 172–211. Finally, after Easter there was a period of post-baptismal

of Lent, the bishop placed his catechetical emphasis on ethics. This, precisely, was the context in which Ambrose made use of the lives of the patriarchs as sermon material."[14] If Colish is correct, *De Isaac* fits into the series of homilies on the patriarchs in which Ambrose holds up these Old Testament saints as models of heroic virtue worthy of imitation for the catechumens.

Whether preached before or after Easter, the sermon's focus on baptism is evident. Baptismal language and imagery suffuses the treatise. References to the mysteries, water, streams, fountains, wells, drawing, cleansing, washing, thirsting, and drinking are recurrent.[15] The three most conspicuous references to baptism include, first, the description of Isaac digging a well in order that "the water of his well might first wash and strengthen the reasoning faculty of the soul and her eye to make her sight clearer."[16] Water here serves as a source of purification for restored inner vision. This (as I will argue below) aligns with Ambrose's understanding of baptism as illumination. Second, commenting on Song of Songs 8:6—"Love is as strong as death"—Ambrose remarks that the death of sin is brought about both through love and through physical death. However, baptism is also as strong as death: "Strong, too, is that death through the bath through which every sin is buried and every fault forgiven."[17] Finally, Ambrose suggests that the "Gentiles are baptized" by the same fire that purified the mouth of Isaiah (6:6–7) and the sons of Levi (Mal 3:3). This is the baptism to which John bore witness: "He will baptize you with the Spirit and with fire" (Matt 3:11).[18]

A baptismal context for *De Isaac* best makes sense of the many indirect references to water and cleansing, the significance of "wells" in the treatise (with reference to Genesis 24 and John 4). Most significantly for my argument, a baptismal context is able to offer a coherent account of Ambrose's aims in

---

catechesis. Ambrose explains in *De Mysteriis* that his "mystagogical" catechesis would be better understood after receiving the grace of the Easter mysteries and the illumination of the Holy Spirit. Thus, three parts constitute the catechumenate preaching in Milan during Ambrose's time: pre-baptismal homilies with an ethical emphasis, the *traditio symboli* during Holy Week (with a doctrinal emphasis), and the "mystagogical" catechesis that further explained the spiritual realities of baptism, Eucharist, the Lord's Prayer, and the spiritual "reading" of Scripture.

14. Colish, *Ambrose's Patriarchs*, 15.

15. For example, forms of the word *mysterium* occur thirteen times, forms of *aqua* occur fourteen times, and forms of the word *fons* appear 22 times.

16. *Isaac* 4.22: "ut eius putei aqua primum rationabile animae oculumque eius dilueret et foueret, quo uisum eius faceret clariorem."

17. *Isaac* 8.76: "est et mors illa ualida per lauacrum, per quam peccatum omne sepelitur et culpa dimittitur."

18. *Isaac* 8.77: "harum alarum igni purgati sunt filii Leui et baptizantur populi nationum, sicut testificatur Iohannes dicens de domino Iesu: ipse uos baptizabit in spiritu et igni."

De Isaac, which I am suggesting is the articulation for the catechumens of a baptismal anthropology.

Baptismal Characters: Isaac and Rebecca

At the outset of *De Isaac* we are introduced to the characters of Isaac and Rebecca. At first glance it seems the typological identity of both is immediately secured. Isaac represents Christ, and Rebecca represents either the individual soul or the Church. Isaac's miraculous birth, which was the fulfillment of a divine promise, and the willingness of his father to offer him up as a sacrifice, make clear that "there were prefigured in him the birth and the passion of the Lord."[19] Isaac was born as the child of promise to an "incomparably great father" and thus anticipates the promised Christ born of the eternal Father.[20] Isaac's miraculous birth from an aged sterile woman foreshadows Christ's even more miraculous birth from a virgin. Isaac anticipates Christ, who was offered as a sacrifice while nonetheless not being lost to his father. The very name "Isaac" means laughter, explains Ambrose, which prefigures the grace to come in Christ.[21] For Ambrose there can be no doubt about the typological identity between Isaac and Christ: "The one is named and the other denoted, the one portrayed and the other foretold."[22] It does not take long before the historical Isaac gives way to the true Isaac (*verus Isaac*)[23]: *in figura per Isaac, in ueritate per Christum.*[24] It is the true Isaac (*verus Isaac*) and the soul (*anima*) who are soon revealed to be the real characters of *De Isaac*: "And so Isaac is good and true, for he is full of grace and a fountain of joy."[25]

19. *Isaac* 1.1. The typological reading of Isaac much predates Ambrose, who, in this case, seems to draw from Origen. Cf. Jean Daniélou, "La typologie d'Isaac dans le christianisme primitive," *Biblica* 28 (1947): 363–93. The significance of Origen's exegesis for Ambrose is highlighted in Solange Sagot, "La triple sagesse dans le De Isaac uel anima," in *Ambroise de Milan: XVIe centenaire de son élection épiscopale*, ed. Yves-Marie Duval (Paris: Études Augustiniennes, 1974), 109; Hervé Savon, *Saint Ambroise devant l'exégèse de Philon le Juif* (Paris: Études Augustiniennes, 1977), 71–81; Gérard Nauroy, "La Structure du De Isaac vel Anima et la cohérence de l'allégorèse d'Ambroise de Milan," *Revue des Études Latines* 63 (1985): 228; Sanders, *Fons vitae Christus*, 33–40.

20. *Isaac* 1.1.

21. Cf. Catherine Conybeare, *The Laughter of Sarah: Biblical Exegesis, Feminist Theory, and the Concept of Delight* (New York: Palgrave Macmillan, 2013).

22. *Isaac* 1.1: "itaque ille nominabatur et iste designabatur, ille exprimebatur et iste adnuntiabatur."

23. *Isaac* 3.7 and 4.17.

24. *Isaac* 4.22.

25. *Isaac* 1.2: "bonus igitur Isaac uerus utpote plenus gratiae et fons laetitiae." The typological

And what of Rebecca? Straightaway Ambrose clarifies also her typological identity. If Isaac represents Christ, the fountain of joy, Rebecca represents both the Church and the soul (*uel ecclesia uel anima*), as she comes to the fountain to fill her water jar.[26] To play this dual role of Church and soul Rebecca is given the bridal language of the Song of Songs. Ambrose links the scene of Jesus's encounter with the Samaritan woman at the well (John 4) with Rebecca's approach at the well (Gen 24).[27] In both cases the bride found at the well signifies the Church comprised of both Jew and Gentile. The Samaritan woman represents the Gentiles, grafted into the Church, and Rebecca figures both as a Gentile—she is obtained as an "alien wife"[28]—and as a relative of Abraham.[29] Both Rebecca and the Samaritan woman are described as representing "the beauty of the Church" (3.7; 4.26). Ambrose writes that the soul of the patriarch Isaac sees Rebecca coming "as if she were the Church with the people of the nations."[30]

Rebecca is also a representation of the individual soul that comes to the true Isaac. Ambrose explains that the appearance of Rebecca denotes not only the Church, since "this passage can be interpreted in reference to the soul."[31] However, the Isaac-Christ and Rebecca-Church/soul typology is not clear-cut. For Ambrose, Isaac functions not only as a type of Christ, but also (following Philo's exegesis) as a model sage perfected in wisdom. Twice the patriarch Isaac is described as going into the field to meditate to prepare for Rebecca's com-

---

reading that Ambrose models in *De Isaac* is a spiritual practice he intends the baptized to acquire as well. Much of the treatise is devoted to the soul's passionate search for the Word (given voice in the Canticle). Integral to this search is discovering Christ in all of Scripture: "Then, by reading the prophets and remembering their words, she sees him looking through their riddles, looking, but as if through a window, not yet as if present" (*Isaac* 4.32). Ambrose is likely making an indirect reference to 1 Cor 13:9–12.

26. *Isaac* 1.2.

27. Cf. *Isaac* 1.2; 4.20; 4.25; 8.78. Quoting John 4:5–6, Ambrose notes that the Samaritan woman is "a guardian of the heavenly precepts" and "manifests the beauty of the Church" (*Isaac* 4.26).

28. *Isaac* 1.1.

29. Likewise at *Isaac* 4.18, Rebecca is told that her twin boys are "two nations in your womb." As a figure of the Church "filled with peace and piety, she joins two nations together by her faith and by prophecy and encloses them in her womb, so to speak." Ambrose's casting of Rebecca as a type of the Church drawn from both Jews and Gentiles is likely derived from Origen, *Commentary on the Song of Song*, prologue I, 2.1; *Homily* 1.1. Cf. Daniélou, "La Typologie d'Isaac"; Sagot, "La triple sagesse"; Sagot, "Le 'Cantique des Cantiques' dans le 'De Isaac' d'Ambroise de Milan," *Recherches augustiniennes* 16 (1981): 3–57.

30. *Isaac* 3.7: "tamquam ecclesiam cum populo nationum."

31. *Isaac* 3.7. Fitzgerald sees the emphasis in *De Isaac* to be on the union of Christ with *anima*. Fitzgerald, "Ambrose at the Well," 79–99.

ing (1.1; 3.6).[32] As such, Isaac represents the good soul in ascetic preparation awaiting the infusion of wisdom. But Rebecca also represents this good soul engaged in contemplative preparation. It is Rebecca who prays in the words of the Canticle, "Let him kiss me with the kisses of his mouth."[33] In this case, *she* is the purified soul seeking union with wisdom. Thus, both Isaac and Rebecca symbolize the soul seeking union with wisdom.[34] The representation of Rebecca (and, to some degree, Isaac) as the catechumens (both as individuals as "the soul" and collectively as the Church) comports with the baptismal context of *De Isaac*. The emphasis underlying the fluidity between the representative roles of Isaac and Rebecca is the union between the soul and wisdom, which for the catechumens takes place in their baptisms.

A Theological Anthropology

Ambrose's understanding of baptismal identity is predicated on a developed theological anthropology. It explains why Ambrose abruptly abandons the scene of Rebecca at the well to pose an unexpected question: "What, then, is man?" (*quid est . . . homo*).[35] The dissonance of this unexpected question is mitigated if we interpret *De Isaac* as framing, for the catechumens, the nature of their baptismal identity. Ambrose asks, "What, then, is man? Soul, or body, or a union of both?"[36] This is a fundamental, but complex, question.[37] Like most

32. Philo of Alexandria describes the meeting between Isaac and Rebecca as the perfect sage coming into the fullness of wisdom. Cf. Daniélou, "La Typologie d'Isaac," 380.

33. *Isaac* 3.8.

34. Both Isaac and Rebecca are presented as detaching themselves from corporeal concerns and desiring to be in a contemplative posture towards the presence of divine wisdom. The stylization of Isaac is derived from Philo (1.1; 3.6) while that of Rebecca is taken from Origen (3.8). Cf. Nauroy, "La Structure du De Isaac," 222. Nauroy also underscores this ambiguity by pointing out that it is as if we are presented with a poorly stitched patchwork of two sermons, one inspired by Philo and the other by Origen.

35. *Isaac* 2.3.

36. *Isaac* 2.3: "quid est itaque homo? utrum anima an caro an utriusque copula?" Perhaps the question contains a reference to Psalm 8:4 and Hebrews 2:6. Plotinus asks a similar question: "So what is left which is 'we'? Surely, just that which we really are, we to whom nature gave power to master our passions" (*Ennead* II.3.9.14–16). For a fuller discussion of Ambrose's understanding of the relation between body and soul see chapter 3 of Gerald P. Boersma, *Augustine's Early Theology of Image* (New York: Oxford University Press, 2016), from which this section borrows.

37. One wonders whether the philosophical anthropology developed in *De Isaac* is, in fact, too complex for an audience of catechumens. Perhaps so. However, it is not, strictly speaking, necessary for Ambrose's audience to be familiar with the philosophical staging of his hortatory preaching. Colish suggests the catechumens were well-educated leaders of Roman society. The

classical and Christian thinkers, Ambrose regards the soul as definitive of the human person—but does he treat the body also as integral to being human?[38]

Part of the complexity of this question stems from the fact that in *De Isaac* Ambrose speaks of two different aspects of the word "body."[39] On the one hand, the body is a composite *with* the soul; that is to say, the body is an instrument that can be skillfully played to manifest the virtue of the soul. On the other hand, "body" also has a negative valuation as distinct from the soul, tempting the soul with material loves, dragging it down through concupiscence.[40] Am-

---

education of the upper class involved studying historical and literary *exempla uirtutis* as models of leadership. Ambrose intends the patriarchs, who are themselves heads of households with vast estates, to serve as new *maiores* for imitation. As such, Colish argues that Ambrose assumes his audience is comprised of "persons with domestic and public responsibilities, that they are literate in Greek as well as in Latin, familiar with literary classics in both languages, and familiar as well with Roman law and classical ethics." Colish, *Ambrose's Patriarchs*, 17.

38. The putative binary between Hellenic (i.e., "philosophical") disparagement of the body and Hebraic (i.e., "pre-corrupted Christian thought") celebration of embodiment leads some commentators to see in Ambrose a capitulation to Greek philosophy. John Moorhead writes, "Ambrose's identification of individuals with their souls and his understanding that these are released by death are views for which there is scarcely any support in Judeo-Christian Scriptures. . . . His views represent the triumph of Greek speculation over any dignity Christian thought vested in the body." John Moorhead, *Ambrose: Church and Society in the Late Roman World* (London: Longman, 1999), 172. However, Hebraic and Greek thought are not at all easily distinguished in the ante-Nicene world (a fact to which a figure such as Philo of Alexandria attests). Caricatures of Hebraic and Greek thought are, by and large, variations on Harnack's Hellenization thesis. Cf. Margaret Miles, *Plotinus on Body and Beauty* (Oxford: Blackwell, 1999). I agree with Warren Smith's assessment: "[Ambrose's] anthropology is both Platonist and biblical. Yet Ambrose's appropriation of Platonist language to speak of the soul and body is ultimately governed by biblical rather than philosophical commitments. Specifically, his appropriation and deployment of Platonic and Plotinian ideas rest upon a deep logic derived from his reading of the letters of Paul" (Smith, *Christian Grace*, 14).

39. One might wish Ambrose would use *caro* (flesh) for a negative evaluation of "body" and *corpus* (body) as a positive description of the body as it relates to the soul. However, Ambrose uses the terms interchangeably: "[G]o out from the body [*corpore*] and divest yourself of it wholly, for you cannot be with me, unless you are first absent from the body [*corpore*], because those who are in the flesh [*carne*] are absent from the kingdom of God" (*Isaac* 5.47). Warren Smith rightly notes that only the context can help us understand how Ambrose evaluates "body." Smith, *Christian Grace*, 22. Ambrose's valuation of *caro* stems, no doubt, from his reading of St. Paul. However, Ambrose is evidently also familiar with Origen's interpretation of Paul. In his *Commentary on the Song of Songs*, Origen suggests that the two creation narratives relate to Paul's "inner" and "outer" man. The human person fashioned according to the image and likeness of God (Gen 1:26) refers to the "inner man" and the human person formed from the dust of the earth (Gen 2:7) refers to the "outer man." Cf. Origen, "Prologue," *Commentary on the Song of Songs*, 220.

40. This distinction is also at play in Ambrose's other works. Cf. *Hex.* VI.7.42 (CSEL 32.1 233). The negative valuation of "body" is strikingly apparent when Ambrose states with remarkable

brose gives expression to this tension between two senses of "body" in his treatment of Romans 7. The apostle Paul writes, "I am carnal, sold into the power of sin. For I do not understand what I do, for it is not what I wish to do, but what I hate, that I do" (Cf. Rom 7:14–15).[41] It is almost as if there are two men wrestling inside the apostle, notes Ambrose, because Paul says, "I see a law of my flesh warring against the law of my mind and making me prisoner to the law of sin" (Rom 7:23).[42] The apostle's soul is warring against his body—not the body as it is part of the composite, but as it is "flesh," and desirous of material good.[43] This is why, explains Ambrose, Paul prefers to speak of the internal and the external man.[44] Both inner and outer man are "Paul," and yet the apostle identifies with the inner man; it is the true man, the soul, that cries out, "Who will deliver me from this body of death?" (Rom 7:24).[45] Here Paul expresses the desire to be liberated "from an external enemy, so to speak."[46] Once the battle against the external man is victorious, the soul will no longer be at war with the body:

> Now she is not aware of the remnants of the flesh [*carnis*]; now, like a spirit [*spiritus*], she has divested herself of the connection with the body [*corporis*]; now, as if she had forgotten and could not remember their union [*copulae*],

---

terseness, "God preferably seeks the soul when it is alone, thus dissociating Himself from the slime of the body and cupidity of the flesh." *Hex.* VI.8.46 (CSEL 32.1 237): "melius enim quaerit ista, si sola sit, abducens se a corporis caeno et a cupiditate carnali."

41. *Isaac* 2.3.

42. *Isaac* 2.3.

43. There is not only a complexity between *caro* and *corpus* in Ambrose, but also between *anima* and *spiritus*. Ambrose identifies Paul's soul [*anima*] warring with his body [*corpus*]: "Although Paul said that both men were at war in him, the internal and the external, yet he preferred to establish himself in the part that comprises the soul [*animae*] rather than in the body [*corporis*]" (*Isaac* 2.3). In fact, however, Paul describes the *flesh* (*sarx/caro*) lusting against the *spirit* (*pneumatos/spiritum*). See Gal 5:17; Rom 8:5. Ambrose's frequent use of *spiritus* is often indistinguishable from *anima*. However, "God is Spirit" (4.26), and the human spirit, for Ambrose, seems to share something of the divine spirit—something beyond materiality and temporality. In *De Isaac* the human *spiritus* is often set in opposition to the flesh (*caro*): "Go forth, not in the flesh [*carne*], but in the spirit [*spiritu*]" (4.16); "He who is in the flesh [*carne*] is not in the spirit [*spiritu*]" (5.47); "She could not be present with Christ in the flesh [*carne*] but could be with him then, if she were present in the spirit [*spiritu*]" (6.52).

44. Cf. Goulven Madec, "L'Homme intérieure selon saint Ambroise," in *Ambroise de Milan: XVIe centenaire de son élection épiscopale*, ed. Yves-Marie Duval (Paris: Études Augustiniennes, 1974), 283–308.

45. *Isaac* 2.3. The reception of Romans 7:24–25 in Augustine (especially via Origen and Ambrose) is carefully catalogued by Thomas Martin, *Rhetoric and Exegesis in Augustine's Interpretation of Romans 7:24–25a* (Lewiston, NY: Edwin Mellen, 2001).

46. *Isaac* 2.3.

even if she wished, she says, "I have taken off my robe, how shall I put it on?" [Song 5:3]. For she took off that robe of skins which Adam and Eve had received after their sin, the robe of corruption, the robe of the passions. "How shall I put it on?" She does not seek again to put it on, but by this she means that it has been thrown away, so that it cannot now be her covering. "I have washed my feet, how shall I defile them?"; that is, I have washed my steps while I move on and lift myself up from companionship with the body [*corporis*]; from the former connection and familiarity of fleshly [*carnalis*] embrace; "how shall I defile them?" to return to the enclose of the body and the gloomy prison of its passions?[47]

One might assume that here the body is wholly negative—it is identified with Paul's external man, the body of death, corruption, and the passions. Indeed, it seems as if the composite of body and soul here gives way to the well-known Platonic description of the body as the "prison house" from which the soul ought to escape.[48]

Ambrose, however, appears to be developing a baptismal anthropology, and in doing so he limits his negative evaluation of the body to its post-lapsarian state. The statement above appeals to a "washing" that has taken place [*laui*].[49] And Ambrose appropriates St. Paul's analogy of baptism as "taking off" one's old clothes and "putting on" or "clothing" oneself in Christ ("For as many of you as have been baptized into Christ have put on Christ" [Gal 3:27]).[50] Thus, Ambrose treats the body with suspicion only in its fallen state (after the fall and prior to baptism). The original, created constitution of body and soul was a harmonious one, and in baptism this created composite is set on the path of reintegration for eschatological perfection.[51]

---

47. *Isaac* 6.52: "iam non sentit carnis exuuias, iam quasi spiritus exuit se corporis coniunctione, iam quasi oblita et quae, si uelit, copulae illius meminisse non possit, ait: exui tunicam meam, quomodo induam eam? exuit enim tunicam illam pelliciam, quam acceperunt Adam et Eua post culpam, tunicam corruptelae, tunicam passionum. quomodo induam eam? non requirit ut induat, sed ita significat abiectam, ut iam indumento sibi esse non possit. laui pedes meos, quomodo inquinabo eos? hoc est: uestigia mea laui, dum egrederer ac me eleuarem de corporis contubernio, de illa conexione et familiaritate carnalis amplexus, quomodo inquinabo ea, ut in corporis claustrum et illum tenebrosum passionum eius carcerem reuertam?" I have corrected the translation by Michael P. Hughes in the Fathers of the Church series (65).

48. Cf. Pierre Courcelle, "Tradition platonicienne et chrétienne du corps-prison," *Revue des études latines* 43 (1965): 406–43. Courcelle is attentive to this motif in Ambrose (423–26).

49. The past tense (*lavi*) might indicate that baptism has already taken place.

50. Cf. Rom. 13:14; Col 2:11; 3:10; Eph 4:22–25.

51. The inner man (the soul) remains, for Ambrose, the true man. He is clear that the soul both rules and gives life to the body (cf. 1.2). The soul will either move "downward" and become "glued to the body" (2.5), or it will move in the opposite direction: "It is attentive to things divine but shuns

Baptism, maintains Ambrose, restores the proper integration of body and soul that is distorted by sin. While he differentiates between rational and irrational elements of the human person, neither is superfluous.[52] The soul is the ruling and animating principle of the body; this necessitates for Ambrose that they belong together.[53] The ideal composite unity of body and soul entails, for Ambrose, that sin and disordered desires affect both body and soul. On the one hand, misdirected loves originate in the soul. Concupiscence and ignorance are "to be ascribed more to form than to matter."[54] On the other hand, because form and matter coinhere, there is "culpability" also for the body: "The flesh is matter, ignorance and concupiscence form. Then why is the flesh blamed when there are such great blemishes in the form? Because the form can do nothing without the matter. . . . For what would concupiscence be if the flesh did not inflame it? [Cf. Jas 1:13–15]."[55] For Ambrose, body and soul (matter and form) act as a loop, each affecting the other, and baptism restores the proper integration of the two.

---

earthly matter" (3.6). In short, Ambrose's handling of the body-soul relationship is complex: on the one hand, Ambrose urges the catechumens to flee the prison house of the body, while, on the other hand, he also describes body and soul as a harmonious and integral unit. It is important to keep in mind that the "flight" is from the "body of death"—not the body in its created goodness or its eschatological restoration. An excellent study of Ambrose's understanding of body and spirit is offered by Wolfgang Seibel, *Fleisch und Geist beim heiligen Ambrosius* (Munich: Zink, 1958), 7–9, 16–69. See also Ragnar Holte, *Beatitude et sagesse* (Paris: Études Augustiniennes, 1962), 167–76; Madec, *Saint Ambroise et la philosophie*, 320–23; Donna M. Foley, "The Religious Significance of the Human Body in the Writings of Ambrose of Milan" (PhD diss., University of Saint Paul, 1996).

52. Colish, *Ambrose's Patriarchs*, 33. Colish suggests that Ambrose's evaluation of the unity of body and soul situates him squarely in the Aristotelian tradition: "Ambrose comes down vigorously in favour of a hylomorphic understanding of human nature." Colish, *Ambrose's Patriarchs*, 33. Likewise, see Smith, *Christian Grace*, 29–43. Smith notes the influence of both Aristotle and Plotinus on Ambrose's "hylomorphic" view of human nature.

53. Drawing on the broader Platonic tradition, Ambrose regards the soul as the form of the body. The soul gives the body its life and essence—what the Platonic tradition would call its "animating principle" and "formal cause." One of Ambrose's favorite analogies from the Platonic tradition is the soul "playing" the body as a musical instrument: "Like a highly skilled artisan the soul leads the body in its service where it will, fashions out of it the form it has chosen, and makes the virtues it has willed resound in it: now it composes the melodies of chastity, again those of temperance, the song of sobriety, the charm of uprightness, the sweetness of virginity, the seriousness of widowhood" (*Bon. mort.* 6.25). With rhetorical prowess, Ambrose exploits the analogy in the *Phaedo* of a musical instrument, which on its own is lifeless and dumb, but which in the hands of an accomplished musician becomes alive and sonorous. See *Phaedo* 85e–86c.

54. *Isaac* 7.60: "ignorantia et concupiscentia animae sunt aegritudines, sed ad speciem quam ad materiem magis referuntur."

55. *Isaac* 7.60: "materia est caro, species est ignorantia et concupiscentia. cur igitur caro accusatur, cum tantae sint in specie labes? quia nihil species potest sine material. . . . quid enim esset concupiscentia, nisi eam caro inflammaret?"

Baptismal Images

Ambrose never directly refers to the recent (or impending) baptism of the catechumens. Nevertheless, his handling of the motifs of kisses and wells suggests
essential elements of his theology of baptism. Rebecca expresses an intense
desire for the Word, even before her baptism, when she says, "Let him kiss me
with the kisses of his mouth" (Song 1:2).[56] Ambrose turns to the catechumens
and asks,

> What does it mean, then: "Let him kiss me with the kisses of the mouth"?
> Think upon the Church, in suspense over many ages at the coming of the
> Lord, long promised her through the prophets. And think upon the soul,
> lifting herself up from the body and rejecting indulgence and fleshly delights
> and pleasures, and laying aside as well her concern for worldly vanities. For
> a long time now she has desired to be infused with God's presence and has
> desired, too, the grace of the Word of salvation, and has wasted away, because
> he is coming late, and has been struck down, wounded with love as it were,
> since she cannot endure his delays.[57]

Rebecca's desire for the Word's kiss expresses the desire of both the soul and the
Church for spiritual union with Christ. Indeed, the longing of the catechumens
for the kiss of the Word in baptism—"to be infused with God's presence"—is
identified with the desire of the Church throughout the ages. This desire finds
expression in the amorous language of the Canticle.

---

56. *Isaac* 3.7. The reception of the Song of Songs in patristic writing is vast. The earliest
Christian commentary is from Hippolytus. Cf. J. A. Cerrato, *Hippolytus between East and West:
The Commentaries and the Provenance of the Corpus* (Oxford: Oxford University Press, 2002). The
most significant use of the Song of Songs is by Origen, who wrote a ten-volume commentary and
a series of homilies on the Canticle. Many of Origen's Greek manuscripts are no longer extant.
Cf. Elizabeth Clark, "Uses of the Song of Songs: Origen and the Later Latin Fathers," in *Ascetic
Piety and Women's Faith: Essays on Late Ancient Christianity*, Studies in Women and Religion 3
(Lewiston, NY: Edwin Mellen, 1986); Christopher King, *Origen on the Song of Songs as the Spirit
of Scripture: The Bridegroom's Perfect Marriage-Song* (Oxford: Oxford University Press, 2005);
Karl Shuve, *The Song of Songs and the Fashioning of Identity in Early Latin Christianity* (Oxford:
Oxford University Press, 2016).

57. *Isaac* 3.8: "quid est igitur: osculetur me ab osculis oris sui? considera uel ecclesiam iam diu
promisso sibi per prophetas dominico aduentu per tempora multa suspensam uel animam, quae
eleuans se a corpore abdicatis luxurie atque deliciis uoluptatibus que carnalibus, exuta quoque
sollicitudine saecularium uanitatum iam dudum infusionem sibi diuinae praesentiae et gratiam
uerbi salutaris exoptet, commacerari, quod sero ueniat, et adfligi et ideo quasi uulneratam caritatis,
cum moras eius ferre non possit."

Ambrose links the "kiss of the Word" (*osculum uerbi*) with "enlightenment" so that the "kiss" becomes a dominant metaphor for baptism.[58] The impatient and passionate desire for the kiss of the Word reveals an active agency on the part of Rebecca. Her longing for baptism is the longing to "fulfill her desire." She is a "lover," and she is "not satisfied with the meager offering of a single kiss, but demands many."[59] Rebecca is "enlightened" by "the kiss of the Word,"[60] and Ambrose continues, "For this is the kiss of the Word, I mean the light of holy knowledge. God the Word kisses us, when he enlightens our hearts and man's very governing faculty with the spirit of the knowledge of God."[61] Thus, Rebecca is discovered to have a latent desire for the presence of the Word and his kiss in baptism, while the Word has been seeking her out and drawing her to himself.

Ambrose develops the metaphor of the kiss so as to include a rich pneumatology. This becomes clear when he comments:

> For it is with the kiss that lovers cleave to each other and gain possession of the sweetness of grace that is within, so to speak. Through such a kiss the soul cleaves to God the Word, and through the kiss the spirit of him who kisses is poured [*transfunditur*] into the soul, just as those who kiss are not

---

58. Hippolytus referred to the impassioned plea of the bride for the Bridegroom's kisses as Israel's prayer for the coming Messiah. Cf. Hippolytus, *Commentary*, 2.2, in Yancy Smith, *The Mystery of Anointing: Hippolytus' Commentary on the Song of Songs in Social and Critical Contexts*, Gorgias Studies in Early Christianity and Patristics 62 (Piscataway, NJ: Gorgias, 2015), 443; Origen interprets the desire for kisses as the desire of the Church for union with Christ. This is a prayer that is answered in the Incarnation: "The kisses are Christ's, which He bestowed on His Church when at His coming, being present in the flesh, He in His own person spoke to her the words of faith and love and peace." Origen, *Commentary on the Song of Songs* 1.1, in *The Song of Songs: Commentary and Homilies*, trans. and ed. R. P. Lawson, Ancient Christian Writers 26 (New York: Newman, 1956), 60. Catechumens were often called *electi* in the Latin Church, and in the Greek Church they were called *phōtizomenoi* (illuminated or enlightened). Cf. Justin, *Apol.* 1.61.12; PG 6:421: "This bath is called *enlightenment*, because those who receive this [catechetical] instruction are enlightened in their understanding." Gregory of Nazianzus, *Oratio* 40.3–4; PG 36:361C: "Baptism is God's most beautiful and magnificent gift.... We call it gift, grace, anointing, enlightenment, garment of immortality, bath of rebirth, seal, and most precious gift. It is called *gift* because it is conferred on those who bring nothing of their own; *grace* since it is given even to the guilty; *Baptism* because sin is buried in the water; *anointing* for it is priestly and royal as are those who are anointed; *enlightenment* because it radiates light; *clothing* since it veils our shame; *bath* because it washes; and *seal* as it is our guard and the sign of God's Lordship."

59. *Isaac* 3.8.

60. *Isaac* 3.8.

61. *Isaac* 3.8: "hoc est enim osculum uerbi, lumen scilicet cognitionis sacrae; osculatur enim nos deus uerbum, quando cor nostrum et ipsum principale hominis spiritu diuinae cognitionis inluminat."

satisfied to touch lightly with the lips but appear to be pouring [*infundere*] their spirit into each other.[62]

Ambrose's repeated use of the language of "pouring" calls to mind the mode of the Spirit's presence described in Romans 5:5 ("The love of God has been poured out [*ekkechytai*] within our hearts through the Holy Spirit"). In his kiss, explains Ambrose, "God the Word poured [*infundit*] himself into her wholly."[63] By sharing his Spirit, the soul now "breathes [*adspirat*] in the Word"; in his baptismal kiss, the Word offers "the fragrance of grace and the forgiveness of sins."[64] "Poured out into all the world, this forgiveness has filled all things and the ointment has been emptied out, as it were, in wiping away the heavy dregs of vice among men."[65] Thus, the kiss of baptism is the privileged moment in which the Spirit is "poured into the soul" and Christ's Spirit is united with the human spirit. It seems the "kiss of the Word" is a plausible metaphor to describe baptism (drawn from the cadence of the Song of Songs), through which the soul is intimately united with the Word, who communicates (*infundit*) "the sweetness of grace" to the soul who is "forgiven" and "enlightened."

The Canticle gives expression to the mutuality between the Word and the soul as it is consummated in a baptismal kiss. The soul requests that "she be drawn to Him," explains Ambrose,[66] because she recognizes her own finite condition as unsuited to ascend on her own to the Word. Therefore, the soul prays, in the words of the Canticle, "Draw us" (*adtrahe nos*) (Song 1:4).[67] To a

62. *Isaac* 3.8: "osculum est enim, quo inuicem amantes sibi adhaerent et uelut gratiae interioris suauitate potiuntur. per hoc osculum adhaeret anima deo uerbo, per quod sibi spiritus transfunditur osculantis, sicut etiam ii qui se osculantur non sunt labiorum praelibatione contenti, sed spiritum suum inuicem sibi uidentur infundere." With reference to this passage of *De Isaac*, Matthias Scheeben writes, "This is the way, then, in which the Holy Spirit comes to our soul and becomes present in it formally in His own person, as the outpouring and pledge of the love of the Father and the Son, and hence also as the outpouring and pledge of the fatherly love with which the Father loves us, His adoptive children. He comes to us as the flower of the sweetness and loveliness of God; in a word, as the osculum or kiss of the Father and the Son which we receive in the innermost recess of our soul. And when we for our own part know and love the Holy Spirit thus dwelling within us in His own character, and rejoice at our possession of Him, we return God's kiss and taste His ineffable sweetness." Matthias Scheeben, *The Mysteries of Christianity* (New York: Herder & Herder, 2006), 160.

63. *Isaac* 3.9.

64. *Isaac* 3.9.

65. *Isaac* 3.9: "adspirat enim in uerbo odor gratiae et remissio peccatorum, quae in totum diffusa mundum omnia tamquam exinanito repleuit unguento, quia per uniuersos grauis conluuies detersa uitiorum est."

66. *Isaac* 3.10.

67. *Isaac* 3.10. Ambrose is likely fusing the request in the Canticle to be "drawn" with the Johannine language of Christ and the Father "drawing."

degree, then, Rebecca is passive and receptive to the power of the Word, who takes the initiative. Ambrose notes, "You see how gladly He draws us, so that we may not be left behind as we follow."[68] However, Rebecca is not only a passive recipient of the Word's drawing; rather, she herself is eagerly running to obtain the prize: "But let him who desires to be drawn so run as to obtain, and let him run forgetting the things that are past and seeking those that are better, for thus he will be able to obtain Christ."[69] Rebecca's baptismal identity is formed both by being "drawn" and by "running."

The combined themes of well (*puteus*) and fountain (*fons*) also figure prominently as the locus of the union between Christ and the soul (as well as the Church).[70] Three scriptural narratives are linked in Ambrose's imagination: Rebecca at the well in Genesis 24, the Samaritan woman at the well in John 4, and the garden containing a fountain and a well of living waters in the Canticle (4:15). The union between Rebecca and Isaac originates at a well, just as the union between Christ and the catechumens finds its origin in the baptismal font. It is fitting, then, that in Genesis 24 we initially discover Rebecca at the well, filling her water jar. Her search for water mirrors the search of the catechumens. Ambrose writes, "And so the Church or the soul went down to the fountain of wisdom to fill its own vessel and draw up the teachings of pure wisdom."[71] Thus, in the very opening of *De Isaac*, Ambrose endows the historical narrative of Genesis 24 with contemporary significance for the catechumens who are to recognize themselves in the narrative. Isaac is already identified as Christ—"that fountain" (*ad quem fontem*), to which Rebecca comes to fill her water jar; she comes to him who is "full of grace and a fountain of joy."[72] At the end of the treatise "that fountain" is unambiguously referred to as Christ: *quia fons est omnium vitae Christus*.[73] If Rebecca is a typological representation of the catechumens (as individual souls and as the Church—*uel ecclesia uel anima*), we are invited to give a "spiritual" (*spiritualia*) gloss to what precisely Rebecca "draws" from the baptismal well.[74] Ambrose lists five elements that Rebecca draws. She

---

68. *Isaac* 3.10.

69. *Isaac* 3.10. Cf. 1 Cor 9:24–25; Phil 3:13–14; 2 Tim 4:7; Heb 12:1.

70. Ambrose secures the linkage between *puteus* and *fons* with texts from Scripture that use both terms: "Drink water from your own vessels and from the fountains of your own wells [Prov 5:15]" (*Isaac* 4.22). "The fountain of gardens, the well of living water [Song 4:15]" (*Isaac* 4.26). Cf. Fitzgerald, "Ambrose at the Well," 91.

71. *Isaac* 1.2: "descendit itaque ad sapientiae fontem uel ecclesia uel anima, ut totum uas inpleret suum et hauriret purae sapientiae disciplinas."

72. *Isaac* 1.2. This is a likely reference to John 4.

73. *Isaac* 8.79.

74. Ambrose frequently reminds his readers/listeners anagogically to lift their minds up to more spiritual understandings of the scriptural letter. Cf. *Isaac* 4.21.

draws up (1) the teachings of pure wisdom;[75] (2) moral instruction;[76] (3) love;[77] (4) understanding of the divine mysteries;[78] and (5) virtue.[79] Thus, Rebecca can be understood as coming to a baptismal fountain to receive ethical, doctrinal, and sacramental instruction, but, most significantly, at the baptismal "well" she is united with Christ.[80] Rebecca's experience at the well typologically captures the experience of the catechumens; it also, however, proleptically leans toward the terminus of the treatise, namely, the soul's mystical union with Christ. Allan Fitzgerald rightly notes that the relationship between Isaac and Rebecca—which is to say, the relationship between Christ and the Christian—coming together here at the well "could easily be a summary of the whole work."[81]

De Isaac 4.20–30 is an extensive excursus on the wells that the patriarch Isaac dug. Its placement in the treatise may seem disorienting. Having ostensibly abandoned the discussion of the relationship between Isaac and Rebecca to comment on the Song of Songs, Ambrose abruptly and without explanation turns to consider the "wells" that Isaac dug.[82] These ought not to be understood in an "earthly" (*terrena*) manner, but require "spiritual" (*spiritualia*) interpretation, reminds Ambrose.[83] He proceeds to list examples of divine encounters by wells: Hagar, Jacob, and Moses. Perhaps the bishop intends the catechumens to expect a similar divine encounter by a "well." Isaac dug several (*plures*) wells "so that [*ut*] the water of his well might first wash [*dilueret*] and strengthen [*foueret*] the reasoning faculty of the soul and her eye, to make her sight clearer."[84] Ambrose continues, "The more [wells] there are, the richer is the overflow of graces" (*uberior redundantia gratiarum*).[85]

Ambrose delineates three wells that Isaac dug: the Well of Injustice or Enmity, the Well of Room-enough, and the Well of the Oath. Each well cor-

75. *Isaac* 1.2: "hauriret purae sapientiae disciplinas."
76. *Isaac* 4.22: "merito que postea pura aqua in eo puteo sit reperta tamquam doctrina moralis utilis ad hauriendum."
77. *Isaac* 4. 26: "si uero haurire uelis affluentiam caritatis."
78. *Isaac* 4.26: "hausit de puteo illo diuina mysteria cognoscens." Cf. *Isaac* 5.43: "ut cognoscam mysteria tua, ut hauriam sacramenta tua"; *Isaac* 6.50: "anima hausit mysteriorum ebrietatem caelestium."
79. *Isaac* 6.53: "praesentia enim uerbi hausit anima uirtutem."
80. Cf. Fitzgerald, "Ambrose at the Well," 83.
81. Fitzgerald, "Ambrose at the Well," 89.
82. Nauroy, "La Structure du De Isaac," 225.
83. *Isaac* 4.21.
84. *Isaac* 4.22: "ut eius putei aqua primum rationabile animae oculumque eius dilueret et foueret, quo uisum eius faceret clariorem."
85. *Isaac* 4.22: "fodit etiam alios puteos plures. . . . quanto plures fuerint, tanto est uberior redundantia gratiarum."

responds to a stage of growth in the Christian life—a greater realization of baptismal identity. The first well signifies moral teaching (*doctrina moralis*), for it was at this well that division was overcome. The second well contains natural teaching (*naturalibus disciplina*), for it teaches a person to desire true and eternal happiness. The third well offers mystical teaching (*doctrina mystica*). At this well God appeared to Isaac and said, "I am with you" (*tecum enim sum*). This well teaches the soul's mystical union with Christ. The wells are dug for the express purpose of cleansing and strengthening the spiritual vision of the soul. The excursus on wells (4.20–30) may seem like an abrupt, parenthetical deviation. In the context of baptism, however, the excursus turns out to support Ambrose's overall aim of showing how baptism restores the human person, uniting him to Christ. The wells "overflow with grace," in order to overcome discord (moral teaching), to detach the soul from worldly anxieties (natural teaching), and, finally, to effect a profound mystical union in love (mystical teaching).[86]

An Ecclesial Anthropology

Ambrose presents the clearest response to his anthropological question—"What, then, is man?"—at the outset of the treatise in his description of Isaac: he is "mild, humble, and gentle."[87] Isaac's character comports with the Gospel's description of Christ (Matt 11:29). It is particularly Isaac's perfect detachment from earthly goods that makes him a model for (the catechumen) Rebecca:

> [Isaac] went out [*exivit*] into the field to meditate, when there came Rebecca (or patience). For a wise man should remove himself [*segregare*] from fleshly pleasures, elevate [*eleuare*] his soul, and draw away [*abducere*] from the body; this is to know [*cognoscere*] oneself a man.[88]

86. The threefold distinction of philosophy stems from Xenocrates and is given Christian dress by Origen. Ambrose's exegesis of the wells that Isaac dug in relation to the books of Solomon and the threefold division of philosophy is considered in Madec, "Saint Ambroise et la philosophie," 193–94; Savon, *Saint Ambroise*, 71–77; Luigi Pizzolato, *La dottrina esegetica di sant' Ambrogio* (Milan: Vita e Pensiero, 1978), 168–73; Pierre Hadot, "Les Divisions des parties de la philosophie dans l'Antiquité," *Museum Helveticum* 36 (1979): 206; Gérard Nauroy writes, "La tripartition de la philosophie, attribuée à Xénocrate, est, pour Ambroise, un enseignement qui, comme toutes les autres vérités de la philosophie profane, représente, selon le thème topique de l'apologétique chrétienne et déjà juive, un larcin des sages antiques, qu'il convient de restituer à l'Écriture." "La Structure du De Isaac," 227.
87. *Isaac* 1.1: "ipse est, mitis humilis atque mansuetus."
88. *Isaac* 1.1.

It is this ideal of detachment and contemplation, which Isaac models at the outset of the treatise, that is the aim of Rebecca's catechesis.[89] This motif of detachment, self-denial, self-knowledge, and finally unitive contemplation (*exivit, segregare, eleuare, abducere, cognoscere*) is, for Ambrose, modeled in the incarnate Word (typologically witnessed in Isaac). This is also the perfection of the baptismal identity to be formed in Rebecca. The verbs that describe the movement of Isaac's ascent are repeated at key points in the soul's journey to contemplative union with Christ (*Isaac* 3.8; 5.44; 7.57).[90]

Ambrose's carefully developed anthropology regarding the relation of body and soul is foundational to the hortatory intentions of *De Isaac*; the bishop exhorts the catechumens to assume their baptismal identity. Baptism offers the *competentes* grace to work towards the reintegration of body and soul. Grace will assist the catechumens' desire to detach themselves from earthly attachments, so that the soul may govern and rule the body, skillfully playing the body like an instrument in order to give voice to virtue.

Rebecca is spiritually prepared for her union with Isaac, explains Ambrose. This preparation of course mirrors that of the catechumens. Ambrose underscores Rebecca's state of spiritual anticipation: "For she came already endowed with heavenly mysteries."[91] Rebecca comes to her new home wearing earrings, suggesting her attentive disposition, and bracelets, suggesting the good works of her hands. Just as Rebecca does not come empty-handed but arrives with vessels of gold and silver, so too, the catechumens come to Christ already having been made beautiful, having subdued the passions by ordering them to virtue. Isaac, seeing Rebecca approach with vessels of gold and silver, regards her "as if she were the Church with the people of the nations, and marveling at the beauty of the Word and of His sacraments."[92]

The catechumens are baptized into Christ's death and share in his resurrection. They are given a new baptismal identity. As participants in Christ they

89. Gérard Nauroy notes, "Isaac représente alors la perfection de la nature humaine, qui ne s'est parfaitement incarnée qu'en la personne du Christ." Nauroy, "La Structure du De Isaac," 224.

90. Nauroy notes that while Isaac is seen to be immediately perfect in detachment, self-knowledge, and contemplation, Rebecca's path to detachment (representing that of the soul and the Church) is arduous and involves many steps: "Pour l'âme humaine, au contraire, le chemin, de la perfection morale implique des étapes, des progrès, des efforts répétés." Nauroy, "La Structure du De Isaac," 223.

91. *Isaac* 3.7: "ueniebat enim caelestibus iam dotata mysteriis." The past tense may suggest that *De Isaac* was preached as a post-baptismal catechesis.

92. *Isaac* 3.7: "ergo uel anima patriarchae uidens mysterium Christi, uidens Rebeccam ueni-entem cum uasis aureis et argenteis tamquam ecclesiam cum populo nationum mirata pulchritudinem uerbi et sacramentorum eius." Again, we see the fluidity between the characters of Isaac and Rebecca, as it is Isaac who sees in Rebecca not only the Church, but also the Word.

cling to his feet and ascend with him. For Ambrose, a theology of ascent is inextricably linked to baptism:

> Go to the Father, but do not leave Eve behind; else she may fall again. Bring her with you, for now she is not wandering astray, but holding fast to the tree of life. Seize her as she clings to your feet, so that she may ascend with you [*ut tecum ascendat*]. Do not let me go; else the serpent may spread his poisons again and may seek again to bite at the woman's foot so that she may trip up Adam. Therefore let your soul say, "I take hold of you and I will lead you into my mother's house and into the chamber of her that conceived me" [Song 3:4] that I may know your mysteries and drink in your sacraments [*ut cognoscam mysteria tua, ut hauriam sacramenta tua*]. And so take Eve, not now covered with the leaves of the fig tree, but clad in the Holy Spirit and glorious with new grace. Now she does not hide as one who is naked, but she comes to meet you arrayed in a garment of shining splendor, because grace is her clothing.[93]

Baptism undoes the cataclysmic wounds of sin that mar the human condition; in baptism, explains Ambrose, Eve's primordial innocence is restored. In baptism the catechumens are to ascend, clinging to Christ's feet. Christ leads those given a new baptismal identity to the Church, to what the Canticle describes as "my mother's house" (*in domum matris*). It is in "my mother's house," where the soul was first conceived in baptism, that she is given life in the Holy Spirit and clothed in a white baptismal garment—clad in a "garment of shining splendor." There, in secret (*in secretum*), she is made intimate with the mysteries of the Word and nourished by his sacraments.[94]

Union with the Word through baptism cannot be separated from the ecclesial context in which this identity is conceived. Thus, in an intimate scene the Bridegroom is caressing the soul, reminding her where their "union of love" first originated. He tells her, "Under the apple tree I raised you up. There your

93. *Isaac* 5.43: "uade ad patrem, sed non relinquas Euam, ne iterum labatur. te cum eam ducito, iam non errantem, sed arborem uitae tenentem. rape tuis pedibus inhaerentem, ut te cum ascendat. noli me dimittere, ne iterum serpens uenena sua fundat, ne iterum quaerat femineum mordere uestigium, ut supplantet Adam. dicat ergo anima tua: teneo te et inducam te in domum matris meae et in secretum eius, quae concepit me, ut cognoscam mysteria tua, ut hauriam sacramenta tua. suscipe igitur Euam iam non ficulneae foliis adopertam, sed sancto amictam spiritu et noua gratia gloriosam, quia iam non tamquam nudata absconditur, sed tamquam circumdata uestimenti splendore fulgentis occurrit, quia uestit eam gratia." I have altered Michael P. McHugh's translation found in the Fathers of the Church series.

94. Variations of the word *mysterium* are found thirteen times in *De Isaac*.

mother brought you forth [*parturiuit*], there she brought you forth [*parturiuit*] who bore [*peperit*] you" (Song 8:5).[95] In the next paragraph Ambrose repeats this maternal birthing image, ensuring that his listeners catch the ecclesial and baptismal referent: "There your mother brought you forth, there she brought you forth who bore you. For we are born [*nascimur*] there, where we are born again [*renascimur*]."[96] The unmistakable reference to Jesus's discourse with Nicodemus (John 3:3–6) suggests Ambrose is speaking of baptism.

The language of ascent and mystical union that pervades the second half of *De Isaac* describes the culmination of a restored anthropology in baptism.[97] While Ambrose's ascent is constructed within a traditional Neoplatonic frame-

---

95. *Isaac* 8.73: "sub arbore mali eleuaui te. illic parturiuit te mater tua, illic parturiuit te quae peperit te."

96. *Isaac* 8.74.

97. The notion of "descending" and "ascending" has a rich legacy in patristic spirituality that draws from (and distinguishes itself from) (neo-)Platonic motifs of ascent. In Ambrose we find a particularly interesting instance of a theologian who draws profoundly (and subtly) from classical literature and pagan philosophy and at the same time an example of a strident voice that opposes the Christian faith to classical culture. For a detailed exposition of this theme in Ambrose see my "'Let Us Flee to the Fatherland': Plotinus in Ambrose's Theology of Ascent," *Nova et Vetera* 14 (2016): 375–89.

A Plotinian spirituality of ascent is particularly evident in the last two paragraphs of *De Isaac* (8.78–79), which Ambrose models after Plotinus's treatise *On Beauty* (*Ennead* I.6). Ambrose's call to purgation, ascent, and union is presented in a Plotinian register: His call to ascend—to "take up wings" (*alas*) and aim for the "higher regions" (*ad superiora*), to "flee to our real, true fatherland" (*fugiamus ergo in patriam uerissimam*) would certainly be familiar to readers of the *Enneads*. Also recognizable would be the call to "enter within" oneself (*ingrediatur intro*) and purify the inner sanctum like "gold cleaned by fire" (*sic enim purgatur anima ut aurum optimum*), and by cleansing "that inner eye" (*illum oculum mundet*) to see "true and great beauty"—to see "the good on which all things depend, but which itself depends on none" (*ut uideat illud bonum, ex quo pendent omnia, ipsum autem ex nullo*). And, finally, in seeing "to be joined to it" (*misceri*): "For what is seen ought not to be at variance with him who sees" (*quod enim uidetur non debet dissonare ab eo qui uidet*).

Nevertheless, Ambrose transposes this tradition so that its spiritual conclusions lie not in the *Enneads*, but in Scripture. For Ambrose, purifying internal vision allows one to see outside and above oneself; the "turn within" is precursory to the "turn above." So, for Ambrose, the psalmist best expresses the love and longing of the soul to be joined with the Good: "One thing I have asked of the Lord, this will I seek, that I may dwell in the house of the Lord all the days of my life and see the delight of the Lord and contemplate his temple" (Ps 26 [27]:4) (8.78).

One might look for parallels between the descent of the second hypostasis in Plotinus's cosmological schema and Ambrose's emphasis on the descent (*condescendat*) of the Word, who lowers himself so that all may be able to ascend with him (*Isaac* 7.57; 8.69). However, less strained parallels are found by considering the manner in which Ambrose draws from the Pauline theology of the "self-emptying" Word, whose descent to participate in humanity makes possible the ascent through participation in ("being in") Christ. Cf. Phil 2:6–11; Eph 4:8.

work and borrows the language and spiritual cadence of this tradition, the ecclesial character of the ascent also necessitates a sharp demurral from this tradition. Plotinus (particularly *Ennead* I.6, the treatise *On Beauty*) functions as the textual *Vorlage* to Ambrose's injunction to ascend; however, the baptismal context of *De Isaac* entails by necessity a number of substantive correctives to Plotinus. The most significant of these correctives is Ambrose's emphasis on the communal character of the ascent.[98] The baptismal ascent of *De Isaac* is constructed within the drama of the Canticle, in which the soul does not ascend alone, but is in the ecclesial company of the "daughters of Jerusalem." They look up with astonishment as they see the soul that loves the Word, clinging to him and ascending with him. In amazement they ask, "Who is she who goes up from the desert [*ascendit a deserto*]?" (Song 3:6).[99] The goal of the baptismal ascent, for Ambrose, is not the flight of the alone to the Alone, but union "with God" as a fellow "citizen with the saints."[100] The aim is not a turn within, but an ascent outside oneself to a *city* (*ciuis sanctorum*). For Ambrose, the life of the saints is social.[101] As the good soul ascends, she is joined (*admixta*) by the daughters of Jerusalem; she does not go it alone. A robust ecclesiology animates this ascent. The soul searches for the Word "among the prayers of his saints and remains close to them."[102] The catechumens must know that only among the prayers of the saints (*inter orationes sanctorum*) will they find Christ. It is in this commu-

---

98. The very last line of the *Enneads* is emblematic of the solitary flight that defines Plotinus's philosophy of ascent: "This is the life of gods and of godlike and blessed men, deliverance from the things of this world, a life which takes no delight in the things of this world, escape in solitude to the solitary." *Ennead* VI.9.11 (Loeb 468 344–45). Cf. *Ennead* I.6.7; VI.7.34. The call to ascend in solitude (or, as it is often translated, the "flight of the alone to the Alone") encapsulates the isolated and introspective nature of the Plotinian ascent. For Plotinus, the upward ascent is also the inward turn into the self; it is deep within the self that one discovers oneself already to be divine. How is the soul to ascend? asks Plotinus. "Turn within yourself and look!" The soul in its deepest nature retains something of its divine nature, which needs only to be discovered. Cf. *Ennead* IV.8.2–4: "[O]ur soul does not altogether come down, but there is always something of it in the intelligible." Pierre Hadot comments, "Here we come across Plotinus's central intuition: the human self is *not* irrevocably separated from its eternal model, as the latter exists within the divine Thought. The true self—the self in God—is within ourselves." Pierre Hadot, *Plotinus or the Simplicity of Vision* (Chicago: University of Chicago Press, 1993), 27. Andrew Louth writes, "As the soul ascends to the One, it enters more deeply into itself: to find the One is to find itself. Self-knowledge and knowledge of the ultimate are bound up together, if not identified. Ascent to the One is a process of withdrawal into oneself." Andrew Louth, *The Origins of the Christian Mystical Tradition: From Plato to Denys* (Oxford: Oxford University Press, 2007), 39.

99. *Isaac* 5.44.
100. *Isaac* 6.54. Cf. Eph 2:19; Phil 3:20.
101. *Isaac* 6.54.
102. *Isaac* 6.56.

nity that they will be nurtured, cared for, and instructed.[103] Drawing from the Canticle, Ambrose writes, "she understands that he feeds his Church and the souls of his just ones among the lilies."[104]

The communal and ecclesial dimension of the soul's union with the Word is manifest in the deep concern that the soul exhibits for the spiritual well-being of others. Despite the intimate union that the soul shares with the Word, she is told, "Turn your eyes from me" (Song 6:5). The Word tells the good soul that although she has been made perfect through her baptismal union with him, and on account of her great faith and devotion has advanced far beyond her natural state, the Word is still eager to unite others with himself. When we hear in the Canticle, "Turn your eyes from me," explains Ambrose, this means, "Although you have been perfected, I must still redeem other souls and strengthen them. For you exalt me by looking upon me, but I have descended that I may exalt all men."[105] The good soul does not begrudge the Word his universal mission. Her personal relation with the Word does not become private.[106] The good soul would not want the Word to "attain the higher regions" (*ad superiora*) while leaving other souls behind.[107] And the Word, like a good teacher, lowers himself (*condescendat*) so that all his pupils can understand, not only the bright ones.[108] The emphasis, for Ambrose, is that the whole body of Christ must ascend in unity.

Although the motif of ascent to contemplative union finds expression for Ambrose in the conjugal love of the bride and the Bridegroom in the Canticle, their love is hardly exclusive.[109] Ambrose writes, "It was as if she had been made perfect, not for herself, but for others."[110] She is seen interceding (*exeat*) that the

---

103. An unexpected passage is found at the outset of the most exuberant movement of *De Isaac*. Ambrose compares the soul to the Platonic charioteer who guides his horses up to the heavens. Quite surprisingly Ambrose interjects, "Now where is the Church, save where the bishop's staff flourishes and his charism? Often she [the good soul] is there, so that she may be put to the proof in bitterness and temptation" (*Isaac* 8.64). Ambrose's emphasis on the particularity of the episcopate to confer and ensure unity is striking. It is in the context of the Church gathered around her bishop, maintains Ambrose, that the ascending soul frequently (*frequenter*) finds the necessary nourishment and direction to overcome the challenges of ascent.

104. *Isaac* 6.56.

105. *Isaac* 7.57.

106. Colish, *Ambrose's Patriarchs*, 83.

107. *Isaac* 7.57.

108. Cf. *Isaac* 7.57.

109. For this reason, explains Ambrose, the Canticle frequently refers to the good soul as "sister" rather than "wife": "Not without reason is she called sister rather than wife, because her gentle and peaceable soul enjoys a reputation for affection common to all rather than for union with one individual, and because she thought that she was bound to all rather than to one" (*Isaac* 4.18).

110. *Isaac* 8.69: "ergo quasi perfecta non pro se, sed pro aliis interuenit."

Word might go forth and run his course, that he might descend and be present to those are weak. She intercedes so that the Word would not "linger on the distant throne of the Father and in that light," but come to the aid of his weaker members; that he might lead up those without strength to follow, that they also might, in turn, be led with her into the intimacy of the "dwelling of the bride and her chamber" (Song 8:2).[111] For Ambrose, the good soul identifies with the apostle Paul, who is in labor until Christ is formed in the Galatians (Gal 4:19): "Now she is in labor who receives the spirit of salvation in her womb and pours it out [*infundit*] to others."[112] A recurring motif, then, is that the good soul is a fecund soul: "The soul is praised for her fertility," notes Ambrose; it is filled with good things and, therefore, overflows.[113]

"Taking On" a Baptismal Identity

The question posed at the outset of the treatise, "What is man?" finds its fullest answer, for Ambrose, in his catechumens "taking on" a baptismal identity. As such, Ambrose considers this fundamental question within the horizon of their baptism. Ambrose draws on the cadence of the Platonic tradition, speaking of the body as extraneous to a person's true self—as "clothing" that can be stripped or even a "prison" to be escaped. Nevertheless, there is also a positive appraisal of embodiment in Ambrose: Baptism works towards the full reintegration of body and soul, so that the soul may direct and guide the body in virtue, playing it skillfully like an instrument, and setting it on course for perfect eschatological harmony.

The language of the Canticle allows Ambrose to express the intimate character of baptism, through which the soul is united to Christ. In baptism the Word kisses the soul, giving enlightenment through the Spirit, who has been poured into the heart. The exposition of Isaac's "wells" offers Ambrose the opportunity to relate the moral, natural, and mystical teaching given in baptism and also to express the union of the soul with Christ, the *fons* of all life.

Much of *De Isaac* concerns the eschatological fulfillment of the catechumen's baptismal identity: the soul's contemplative union with the Word, a union in which the soul has become perfect, has herself become a resting place for the

111. *Isaac* 8.69.

112. *Isaac* 8.74.

113. *Isaac* 7.60. In this respect, Fitzgerald notes that in *De Isaac* "the goal of perfection is set within a relational context. Perfection is defined as participation in *caritas*, of which Christ is the fullness. Rather than a merely individualistic ideal, it was to be lived in the midst of the Christian community." Fitzgerald, "Ambrose at the Well," 88.

Word. Despite framing this perfection of baptismal identity within the structure of Plotinus's ascent and union with the One, Ambrose's ecclesial emphasis continuously corrects the individualism of Plotinus. Baptismal identity is intimate and personal, but not private—the good soul is eager to invite others to ascend with her. For Ambrose, therefore, the union of the soul and the Word finds its origin in the Church's baptismal font; it is around the "bishop's staff" that the soul's baptismal identity is formed; it is in the Church that her intellectual and moral virtues are cultivated; and it is in the Church that she ascends—among the prayers of the saints—to a *city*, as a fellow "citizen with the saints."

De Isaac remains in many ways an enigmatic and multivocal text; a bricolage of subjects, sources, and themes vies for our attention. Nevertheless, consistent lines of interpretation and a unifying aim to the text as a whole emerge if we understand the work as articulating a theological anthropology within a baptismal context.

Chapter 12

John Chrysostom: Vision of the Angelic Life

PAK-WAH LAI

Among the many legends about John Chrysostom (ca. 349–407), one of the most insightful comes from the biography of George of Alexandria (ca. 620). One night, Chrysostom's secretary, Proklos, peered into his room and found the bishop working hard on his Pauline homilies. All of a sudden, the apostle himself appeared and began whispering "exegetical suggestions into his ear."[1] This, we are told, would occur not once but three times in a row! Notwithstanding its veracity, the tale well summarizes Chrysostom's esteem for Paul, and the formative role that the apostle played in his life and ministry. As the bishop puts it, "I love the saints, but I love most the blessed Paul!"[2]

Though he may have loved "blessed Paul" the most, it is nonetheless true that the saints occupy an important role in Chrysostom's thought. When one surveys Chrysostom's voluminous corpus, it becomes clear that their *vitae* are a prominent feature in his sermons and writings. This is by no means coincidental but rather a deliberate strategy on his part to construct "exemplar portraits" that will not only educate but persuade his listeners to embrace their new life in Christ—in short, to live an angelic, or indeed, deified life by the power of the Holy Spirit through the practice of asceticism.

To trace how Chrysostom achieves this, we will begin by looking at the bishop's life and ministry in the cities of Antioch and Constantinople, before examining his understanding of the angelic life in relation to his views on soteriology and asceticism, and how he reconceptualizes these ideals rhetorically for his audiences.

---

1. Margaret Mary Mitchell, *The Heavenly Trumpet: John Chrysostom and the Art of Pauline Interpretation*, Hermeneutische Untersuchungen zur Theologie (Tübingen: Mohr Siebeck, 2000), 489.

2. *Hom. 2 Cor.* 11:1.

From the Syrian Mountains to Constantinople

By the mid–fourth century, Christianity was no longer a religion of the minority or the persecuted. Rather, it was one favored by the imperial authorities, and thus also by the populace. As it so often happens, such conversion *en masse* often led to varied spiritual commitments among Christians. There were many, of course, who were attracted by the religion's tenets and fervent for their faith. Yet, there were also others who converted more for the social or political privileges that Christianity now conferred. Chrysostom's hometown, the cosmopolitan city of Syrian Antioch, was a good microcosm of this new religious climate. Since its apostolic inception, the church of Antioch had grown steadily, reaching a population of 100,000, or one-third of the city, by the fourth century. The same period also saw local Christians undergoing several persecutions and contributing not a few martyrs to its rich martyrological tradition and cult. Christian asceticism, it seems, also took root as early as the second century. Like the rest of the empire, it would flourish by the mid–fourth century, so much so that vibrant monastic communities would be found in both the city and Syrian mountains nearby.[3] This being said, it was not uncommon to find Christians in compromising stances. Not a few continued to participate in pagan customs and superstition. Some even engaged in Judaizing behavior. Chrysostom himself was painfully aware that whenever the chariot races were held, his church was visibly emptier, and he had to raise his voice just to overcome the cheers echoing from the stadium nearby.[4] Even among the faithful, not all was well. When the Council of Nicaea was held in 325, it was conceived as the means of resolving the christological crisis brewing in the empire. What transpired, however, was a host of ecclesiastical schisms, with pro-Nicene supporters pitched against the Arians and those uncomfortable with the Nicene formulation. The situation was particularly pronounced in Antioch. Not only was the church split between the Arian and pro-Nicene camps, but the latter themselves were further divided into those supportive of Bishop Meletius (d. 381) and those of Bishop Paulinus (d. 388).

3. R. M. Price, "Introduction," in *Theodoret of Cyrrhus, A History of the Monks of Syria*, Cistercian Studies Series (Kalamazoo, MI: Cistercian Publications, 1985), xxi–xxii; David G. Hunter, "Introduction," in *John Chrysostom: A Comparison between a King and a Monk against the Opponents of the Monastic Life*, Studies in the Bible and Early Christianity (New York: Edwin Mellen, 1988), 62–63.

4. Chrysostom, *Adv. Jud.* 1.3 (FC 68:10–14); Robert Louis Wilken, *John Chrysostom and the Jews: Rhetoric and Reality in the Late 4th Century*, Transformation of the Classical Heritage (Berkeley: University of California Press, 1983), 17–19; Ramsay MacMullen, *Christianity and Paganism in the Fourth to Eighth Centuries* (New Haven: Yale University Press, 1997), 150–54; Glanville Downey, *Antioch in the Age of Theodosius the Great* (Norman: University of Oklahoma Press, 1962), 115.

This was the spiritual context into which Chrysostom was born. The son of a pious widow, Chrysostom probably came from a family of means, and was thus able to enjoy a Greek education, or *paideia*, and a rhetorical training under the famous Libanius (314–392), the official orator of Antioch. If Sozomen is to be believed, Chrysostom was actually Libanius's star pupil, who, the orator lamented, would have been his successor "if the Christians had not taken him from us."[5] In any case, Chrysostom did not become a teacher of rhetoric or pursue the usual career path expected of an orator, that is, legal or civil service. At the age of nineteen (ca. 368), he was so drawn by the ascetic lifestyle that was becoming popular in Antioch that he abandoned any career aspirations that his family might have held for him and joined an *asketerion*, or urban ascetic community. Here, he came to know Theodore (350–428), the future bishop of Mopsuestia and was trained by Diodore of Tarsus (d. 390). For the next three years, the young man was also an assistant to Bishop Meletius. After the bishop was sent into exile, he decided to leave the city and retreat to the Syrian mountains to pursue a harsher asceticism in solitude, with only an elderly Syrian as a guide. According to his biographer, Palladius, it would be four more years before he returned to Antioch (ca. 375), motivated either by a breakdown in his health, the reinstatement of Bishop Meletius or, perhaps, both.[6]

Thereafter, Chrysostom served as a deacon for several years before being ordained as a priest in 386. The following decade also saw him becoming well known as a preacher and the author of many writings and homilies, including his famous *On the Priesthood*. Indeed, he was even listed by Jerome, if one may put it this way, as one of the up and coming Christian leaders in the empire.[7] In all likelihood, Chrysostom was probably the successor designate to the current bishop, Flavian. Unfortunately, things did not turn out as planned. In the autumn of 397, Chrysostom received an unexpected summons from Constantinople and was soon whisked off to the capital to become its new bishop. In his new office, Chrysostom initiated a series of reforms that would, as Palladius puts it, change "the very colour of the city . . . to piety" and make everyone look "bright and fresh with soberness and Psalm-singing." His same efforts, however, also won him not a few enemies among the local clergy and monks. The latter two, in fact, would conspire against him and ultimately had him exiled to the remote shores of the Black Sea, where he would perish en route to the city of Pityus.[8] It would be another three decades before

5. Sozomen, *Eccl. hist.* 8.10.

6. J. N. D. Kelly, *Golden Mouth: The Story of John Chrysostom: Ascetic, Preacher, Bishop* (London: Duckworth, 1995), 30–31.

7. *De viris illustribus* 129.

8. Kelly, *Golden Mouth*, 282–85.

Chrysostom was reinstated and his relics welcomed back into the Church of the Holy Apostles in Constantinople.[9]

The Angelic Life

Among the Eastern Fathers, Chrysostom is, without dispute, the most prolific author, whose writings amount to more than eight hundred homilies, treatises, and letters. In these writings, the motif he employs most frequently to discourse about Christian spirituality and identity is that of the angelic *politeia,* or the angelic way of life.[10] The characters to which he applies this motif are myriad and diverse. Of predominance are the Christian monks and virgins, whose lives he takes to be the closest approximation of the angelic hosts.[11] Biblical characters, such as David, Elijah, Abraham, and John the Baptist are also well regarded as exemplars of this lifestyle. Equally significant are the apostles, such as Paul and Peter, whose achievements, he believes, are even greater than the angels themselves.[12] Just in case his lay listeners assume that this epithet and its traits are applicable only to the "heroes of the faith," he counts them also as fellow participants of the angelic life, reminding them that they should neither "shame our Benefactor" nor "render in vain so great a grace," but "exemplify the life of the angels, the virtue of the angels, [and] the conversation of the angels."[13]

The angelic motif itself is not unique to Chrysostom. In fact, by the fourth century, it had become quite commonplace to portray Christian ascetics in this manner.[14] Neither did the concept originate from this period. Rather, its roots run deeper and can be traced back to the Second Temple period, when both the Hellenistic and Palestinian Jews began to teach that the telos of the faithful was to participate in the angelic life.[15] The first three centuries of the Common Era, however, saw the motif undergo two important transpositions. The first was how the martyrological traditions, from a very early stage, started to depict their protagonists in ways resembling the angels found in the Jewish

---

9. Socrates, *Eccl. hist.* 7.45.

10. *Hom. Eph.* 23; *Hom. Rom.* 11.

11. *Virginit.* 11.1.

12. *Laud. Paul.* 1.5, *Hom. Act.* 12 (*NPNF*[1] 11:78–79); PG 57:707.

13. *Hom. Eph.* 1 (*NPNF*[1] 13:55).

14. See, for example, *Historia Monachorum in Aegypto* (2.1; 7.5–6; 10.12–14) and *V. Ant.* 15, 58, 60–64, 82–89.

15. Cf. 2 Baruch 51:10; 1 Enoch 14:18–25; 4Q403; 1QS4:24, etc. Jesus certainly presumes this religious expectation when he proclaims that "in the resurrection [the faithful] neither marry nor are given in marriage, but are like angels in heaven" (Matt 22:30 NRSV).

Apocalyptic traditions. Namely, that the martyrs were also participants in God's cosmic battle against the demonic realms, recipients of heavenly visions, and workers of miracles.[16] The second was the fact that Christians from Clement of Alexandria onwards began to regard Christian contemplation of God as intrinsic to the angelic life. In the fourth century, these two traditions would converge in the flourishing ascetic movement, with the Christian monk and contemplative esteemed not only as successors of the martyrs, but also as the new exemplars of the angelic *politeia*.[17]

Chrysostom's formative years, as mentioned earlier, were spent first in an urban ascetic community and later with the monks in the Syrian mountains. In all likelihood, these were the original sources that inspired his views on the angelic life. His reception of this tradition was by no means passive, however. Neither was it theologically unreflective, as traditional scholarship has often presented him.[18] This being said, the manifold contexts and diverse ways by which he employed this motif mean that the elucidation of his views is no straightforward or, indeed, easy exercise. Due attention must be paid to the web of ideas that he developed throughout his writings, particularly his homilies, so that the dominant features of his thoughts may be clarified.[19]

Interestingly, his most comprehensive treatment of this subject is to be found not in his treatises and homilies on the monastic life, but in his exposition of the Edenic Adam, as given in his *Homilies on Genesis*. It is to these that we will first turn to establish the contours of Chrysostom's teachings on the angelic life.[20]

Edenic Adam: Prototype of the Angelic Life

The first man, as Chrysostom sees it, was created from dust, a substance "more lowly" than the earth, and was therefore no different from "the plants and irra-

---

16. Norman Russell, *The Doctrine of Deification in the Greek Patristic Tradition*, Oxford Early Christian Studies (Oxford: Oxford University Press, 2004), 77–78.

17. Gus George Christo, "The Notions of Martyrdom according to St. John Chrysostom" (MA thesis, University of Durham, 1984), 25–28.

18. Chrysostom was traditionally regarded as a "mere Christian moralist and pastor" who did not "take much interest in the academic [or theological] disputes of the day." Hans von Campenhausen, *The Fathers of the Church*, trans. L. A Garrard (Peabody, MA: Hendrickson, 1998), 140, 144.

19. For an extensive discussion of how to analyze Chrysostom's theology, as given in his homilies, see Raymond Laird, *Mindset, Moral Choice and Sin the Anthropology of John Chrysostom*, Early Christian Studies 15 (Strathfield: St Pauls, 2012), 7.

20. For the correlation between Chrysostom's portraits of Adam and the Christian ascetics, see Pak-Wah Lai, "John Chrysostom and the Hermeneutics of Exemplar Portraits" (PhD diss., Durham University, 2010), 173–234.

tional beings." Yet, out of his loving-kindness, God decreed that Adam would be "a rational being by reason of a soul, by means of which this living thing emerged complete and perfect."[21] Henceforth, the human body would be subordinated to the soul, like a lyre to a musician, so that

> because of the soul's being, we who are intertwined with a body can, if we wish and under the influence of God's grace, strive against disembodied powers, can walk on earth as though coursing across heaven, and pass our lives in this manner, suffering no inferiority.[22]

This spiritual life in the body is characterized also by the enjoyment of the pleasures and delights God provides for humanity.[23]

> Provision had been made for his [Adam's] spending life in the garden, for enjoying the beauty of visible things, for gladdening the eye from that experience, and gaining much *pleasure* from that enjoyment. Consider, after all, how great a thrill it was to see the trees groaning under the weight of their fruit, to see the variety of the flowers, the different kinds of plants, the leaves on the branches, and all the other things you would be likely to chance upon in a garden, especially a garden planted by God.[24]

Remarkably, it is within this hedonistic context, this life of pleasure, that Chrysostom envisages the idyllic angelic life. Humanity, as he sees it, was meant to "pass his days on earth like some terrestrial angel," to live the "angelic way of life in a human body." Like these heavenly beings, all the needs of the primal couple were provided for, and they, therefore, had no "need of shelter or habitation, clothing or anything of that kind." "Created incorruptible and immortal," they were also "clad in that glory from above."[25]

This being said, a life of "exceeding indulgence" that was relieved of work was a formula for disaster, since Adam "would immediately slip into careless negligence [*rathymia*]."[26] For this reason, God also decreed

> the task of tilling and guarding for Adam so that along with all those delights, relaxation and freedom from care he might have, by way of a

21. *Hom. Gen.* 12.15.
22. *Hom. Gen.* 12.17 (Hill, FC 74:167).
23. *Hom. Gen.* 13.14.
24. *Hom. Gen.* 14.12, emphasis mine.
25. *Hom. Gen.* 15.14–15; 16.2.
26. *Hom. Gen.* 14.8.

stabilizing influence, those two tasks to prevent him from overstepping the limit.[27]

Despite God's providential care, laments Chrysostom, the primal couple gave in to *rathymia*, disobeyed God, and fell from his grace. As a result, they were not only stripped of their garment of glory, but also lost control of their soul. Henceforth, "throngs of passion" arose in humanity so much so that the irrational aspects of the soul would always threaten to overcome their rational counterpart.[28]

When we compare Chrysostom's portraits of Adam and his depictions of the Christian ascetics, notable similarities emerge. In his *Homilies on Matthew*, for example, the Syrian monks are presented as leading carefree and tranquil lives—similar to that of Adam. Indeed, they spend all their time

> meditat[ing] upon the things of the kingdom, holding converse with groves, and mountains, and springs, and with great quietness, and solitude, and before all these, with God. And their cell is pure from all turmoil, and their soul is free from every passion and disease.[29]

Like Adam, the monks are also engaged constantly in "digging in the earth, and watering, and planting, or making baskets, or weaving sackcloth, or practising any other handy works." Such labor is aimed not only at helping the monks avoid the indulgence and *rathymia* that so plagued Adam, but also at cultivating the virtues of humility and moderation in them.[30] In short, for Chrysostom, the ascetic life is no less than the recapitulation of Adam's life in Eden, or the latter is essentially the life that every Christian should enjoy in the *eschaton*.

> Their work is what was Adam's also at the beginning and before his sin, when he was clothed with the glory, and conversed freely with God, and dwelt in that place that was full of great blessedness. For in what respect are they in a worse state than he, when before his disobedience he was set to till the garden? Had he no worldly care? But neither have these. Did he talk to God with a pure conscience? These also do these; or rather they have a greater confidence than he, inasmuch as they enjoy *even greater grace by the supply of the Spirit*.[31]

27. *Hom. Gen.* 14.10.
28. *Hom. Rom.* 13 (*NPNF*[1] 11:427).
29. *Hom. Matt.* 68.3 (*NPNF*[1] 10:417).
30. *Hom. Matt.* 72.3–4 (*NPNF*[1] 10:438–39).
31. Ibid, emphasis mine.

This being said, there is an important distinction between the Edenic Adam and the Christian ascetic. This is already suggested in Chrysostom's qualification above: that the monks "enjoy even greater grace by the supply of the Spirit." As he sees it, the lives of the ascetics exemplify not only the idyllic state of the Christian life but also the means by which this angelic life is achieved, that is, through the salvation work of Christ by the Holy Spirit. As to what all these entail exactly, we must now consider Chrysostom's soteriology and how he correlates this with his ascetic ideals.

Chrysostom's Soteriology

Up until recently, scholars have often regarded Chrysostom as a representative of the School of Antioch, whose theology is similar to those of his peers: Diodore of Tarsus and Theodore of Mopsuestia. In the case of his soteriology, this does seem to be the case, at least on first glance. When interpreting the *imago Dei* in his Genesis homilies, Chrysostom takes the "image" as referring exclusively to man's (*anēr*) rule and authority, and the woman's authority over creation as a derivative of this—a position similar to that of his fellow Antiochenes.[32] Yet there is also a clear difference between them. This is to be found in Chrysostom's distinction between humanity's "image" and "likeness" to God. As he sees it, while "image" delineates human similitude to God's authority, it is "likeness" that fully describes humanity's potential to become like God, "according to the ability of the human nature" (*kata dynamin anthrōpinēn*). Chrysostom's use of *kata dynamin anthrōpinēn* is instructive, as it strongly suggests to us that his theological sentiments may lie elsewhere, that is, with the Alexandrian-Cappadocian soteriological traditions.

It was Clement of Alexandria (150–215) who first distinguished between "image" and "likeness" and appropriated the above phrase and its cognates to describe the telos of the soul's ascetic journey to God.[33] By the mid–fourth century, Clement's soteriological conception would be taken on board by many Christians, most notably Gregory of Nazianzus (329–389) and Basil of Caesarea (329–379). Indeed, it was Basil who developed the pneumatological underpinnings of this idea, by arguing that a Christian can be "made like God, as far as

---

32. *Hom. Gen.* 8.9–10; Frederick G. McLeod, *The Image of God in the Antiochene Tradition* (Washington, DC: Catholic University of America Press, 1999), 59–61.

33. The phrase itself originates from Plato's *Theaetetus* and its usage was mediated to Clement through Philo of Alexandria. Plato, *Theaetetus* 17b; Clement, *Protr.* 12.122.4–123.1; *Strom.* 2.125.4–5.

it is possible for the human nature," only if he has the Spirit's help in his ascetic endeavors.[34]

When one surveys Chrysostom's writings, it is manifestly clear that his soteriology is shaped significantly by these Alexandrian-Cappadocian traditions. First, in his homilies elsewhere, Chrysostom is less rigid about the doctrine of the *imago Dei* that he develops in the Genesis homilies, and quite comfortable with ascribing the motif to both males and females. Moreover, he also identifies the *imago Dei* with the invisible human soul and thus differs from Theodore on this important respect.[35] On both counts, therefore, Chrysostom is quite in line with Clement and his successors. Second, not unlike Athanasius, Chrysostom asserts that the incarnation has enabled the divine nature to transform the human, thereby making possible the salvation of humankind:

> Through this name [of Christ], in fact, death was dissolved, demons imprisoned in bonds, heaven opened, gates of paradise thrown wide, the Spirit sent down, slaves made free, enemies became sons, strangers became heirs, human beings became angels. Why speak of angels? *God became man, and man [became] God*; heaven accepted the nature from earth, earth accepted the one seated on the Cherubim along with the angelic host.[36]

Furthermore, Chrysostom also taps into the broader soteriological traditions, both Alexandrian and Antiochene-Syriac, by emphasizing the role of Christ's recapitulative work.

> For Christ did not have sinful [flesh], but was like indeed to our sinful [flesh], yet sinless, and in nature the same with us. So also it is clear, therefore, that the nature of the flesh is not evil. For Christ did not take the other in the place of the former, nor did he exchange this same one in true essence, when he prepared it to renew the fight. Rather, he let it remain in its own nature [and] he made it bind on the crown over sin, and then after the victory, he raised it up and made it immortal.[37]

34. Basil, *De Sp. S.* 15.35–36.

35. For Theodore, the *imago Dei* is clearly a bodily and visible concept. *Hom. Col.* 3 (*NPNF*[1] 13:270); *Commentary on Colossians* 1.15.

36. *Exp. Ps.* 8, emphasis mine. Chrysostom's affinity with the Alexandrians is further confirmed by the fact that he understands the incarnation as the Word's assumption of human nature rather than the theory of *homo assumptus* propounded by Theodore. Lai, "Hermeneutics of Exemplar Portraits," 150.

37. *Hom. Rom.* 10. It is noted that Chrysostom uses the terms flesh (*sarx*) and body (*sōma*) interchangeably.

For Chrysostom, however, a Christian is not merely a passive recipient of the fruits of Christ's victory over sin. Rather, he is expected to participate in Christ's recapitulative work, so that he may be refashioned into the image of Christ.[38] This, as he so often puts it, is always achieved through the "superabundant grace" of God and his Spirit. It is in this way that Christians can surpass or transcend their human nature, so as to receive "health, comeliness, and honour and glory and dignities" that God has prepared for them.[39]

To summarize then, Chrysostom's soteriology coheres remarkably well with the Alexandrian-Cappadocian traditions in that he believes that Christ, by his incarnation, has made it possible for humanity to be united with God, and, by his recapitulative work, justified humanity before God. All these are achieved through the Spirit, who not only renews Christians by uniting them with Christ, but also enables them to embark on an ascetic journey towards divine likeness, or indeed, become the image of Christ. As to what this ascetic journey involves, we must now examine Chrysostom's psychology and the implications that this may hold for his ascetic ideals.

Chrysostom's Psychology and Asceticism

Like many of the Greek fathers, Chrysostom subscribes to a bipartite anthropology, whereby the human nature is constituted by a soul (*psyche*) and a body (*sōma* or *sarx*), both of which are naturally good.[40] The former, in addition, should govern the latter, like a charioteer having mastery over his horse, and not mislead the body into sin.[41] The dynamics of this psychology are worked out quite extensively in Chrysostom's homilies through his teachings on the *gnōmē*, or mindset. In his recent study of this subject, Laird demonstrates that the *gnōmē*, for Chrysostom, is a faculty or power of the soul that possesses "rational and emotional elements and features," and is also "the locus of personal autonomy with consequent authority in the soul." Alternatively, it may be regarded as "the set habit of the soul" or "the seat of personality." Functionally speaking, the *gnōmē* has authority over "desire, passions, impulse, intellect, moral choice, [and] conscience." After the fall, it is "flawed by a propensity toward evil" and often usurps the role of reasoning (*logismos*) in the soul. Based

---

38. *Hom. Col.* 8 (*NPNF*[1] 13:294–95).

39. *Hom. Rom.* 10 (*NPNF*[1] 11:403).

40. Chrysostom uses *sarx* and *sōma* interchangeably to refer to the body. Melvin E. Lawrenz, *The Christology of John Chrysostom* (Lewiston/Queenston/Lampeter: Mellen University Press, 1996), 114.

41. *Hom. Rom.* 13 and *Hom. Eph.* 5.

on this framework, sin occurs whenever the *gnōmē* directs the *proairesis*, or human choice, to comply by its distorted desires and habits.[42]

For Chrysostom, the transformation of the *gnōmē* begins at baptism, when a Christian receives an initial change to his mindset by the Holy Spirit. Thereafter, this change must be followed by a continual program of asceticism.[43] Like his pagan and Christian contemporaries, Chrysostom understood asceticism within the framework of Greco-Roman virtue ethics.[44] Essentially, if a human being is to become like God, one would have to attain the manifold virtues or excellences (*aretai*) reminiscent of God. As the means of achieving these excellences, asceticism is a continued and disciplined effort towards rehabituating one's *gnōmē*, so that one gradually develops the virtues of God, or as Chrysostom would put it, is transformed into the image of Christ.[45] As to how asceticism can yield such spiritual fruits, it is illustrated well in his discussion on the benefits of almsgiving.

> He that gives alms, as he ought to give, learns to despise wealth. He that has learned to despise wealth has cut up the root of evils. . . . but also in that his soul becomes philosophic, and elevated and rich. . . . And this lesson once fixed in his mind, he has gotten a great step toward mounting to Heaven and has cut away ten thousand occasions of strife, and contention, and envy, and dejection.[46]

Chrysostom, however, differs from his pagan counterparts in one important way. That is, he recognizes that the soul's rational capacity has its natural limitations or weaknesses and need not, by necessity, tend to things divine. For this reason, the soul is constantly in need of the Spirit's help so that a Christian can grow eventually into the likeness of Christ.[47]

Christian Rhetoric and Exemplar Portraits

The second half of the fourth century was a rare and remarkable period in church history. In a span of only fifty years, there arose several ascetic-bishops

---

42. Laird, *Mindset, Moral Choice and Sin*, 257–59.

43. Ibid., 257–59.

44. With regard to Chrysostom's reception of Greco-Roman ethics, see Lai, "Hermeneutics of Exemplar Portraits," 45–57.

45. *Hom. Eph.* 16 (*NPNF*[1] 13:126–27).

46. *Hom. Phil.* Introduction (*NPNF*[1] 13:183).

47. *Hom. Eph.* 5 (PG 62.41.31–32).

whose teachings would have a lasting influence on the Christian tradition and would rarely be superseded by subsequent generations.[48] Among these, the most prominent were Ambrose of Milan and Augustine of Hippo in the West, and the Cappadocian Fathers and Chrysostom in the East. Besides their common training in *paideia*—that is, Greek or Latin education—they were also well versed in Greco-Roman rhetoric, which they applied extensively to their pastoral work, creating what Averil Cameron calls a totalizing Christian discourse that provides "both the framework within which most people looked at the world and the words that they used to describe."[49]

Chrysostom's use of classical rhetoric in his preaching has been well documented since the early twentieth century.[50] As mentioned earlier, he also employed the same skills regularly to construct exemplar figures that would illustrate the angelic life he envisages for Christians. It was Mitchell, however, who first suggested that these exemplar portraits are no mere illustrations but hermeneutically important for an accurate understanding of Chrysostom's exegesis, theology, and ethics. Chrysostom's interpretations of the Pauline letters, she observes, are often accompanied by a myriad of Pauline portraits, ranging from epithets to large-scale portrayals of his soul, body, and external circumstances.[51] Contrary to popular opinion, these rhetorical constructs "are not sideshows to the 'main event' of the interpretation of the apostle's letters, but are themselves central to his [Chrysostom's] exegetical art."[52] As Rylaarsdam explains, this frequent use of exemplar portraits in scriptural interpretation and communication is a deliberate strategy on Chrysostom's part to create concrete mental images in the minds of his audiences so that they can grasp readily what can often be abstract theological and ethical ideas.[53]

Chrysostom's rhetorical hermeneutics, he adds, is due not to mere pastoral exigencies. Rather, it arises from his recognition that God himself, like a wise

---

48. Andrea Sterk, *Renouncing the World Yet Leading the Church: The Monk-Bishop in Late Antiquity* (Cambridge: Harvard University Press, 2004), 6; Stephen K. Black, "Paideia, Power and Episcopacy: John Chrysostom and the Formation of the Late Antique Bishop" (PhD diss., Graduate Theological Union, 2005), 223, 226.

49. Averil Cameron, *Christianity and the Rhetoric of Empire: The Development of Christian Discourse*, Sather Classical Lectures (Berkeley: University of California Press, 1991), 222.

50. See, e.g., Thomas Edward Ameringer, *The Stylistic Influence of the Second Sophistic on the Panegyrical Sermons of St. John Chrysostom: A Study in Greek Rhetoric* (Washington, DC: Catholic University of America Press, 1921); Hippolyte Delehaye, *Les Origines du Culte des Martyrs, Subsidia Hagiographica* (Brussels: Société des Bollandistes, 1933) and Wilken, *John Chrysostom and the Jews*.

51. Mitchell, *Heavenly Trumpet*, 69–377.

52. Ibid., 384.

53. David Rylaarsdam, *John Chrysostom on Divine Pedagogy* (Oxford: Oxford University Press, 2014), 231–43.

philosophical guide, has also been adapting his teachings rhetorically to the limits of human knowing.[54] Based on the psychagogic traditions of Greco-Roman philosophical rhetoric, this theology of divine adaptability both undergirds Chrysostom's biblical interpretation in general and informs his homiletical approach throughout his ministry. It is also the reason for the manifold and diverse exemplar portraits found throughout his writings. These portraits are rhetorical performances, if one may put it this way, or interpretations that actually elucidate and develop his didactic teachings.[55]

In light of this, it becomes obvious that a study of Chrysostom's didactic teachings on the angelic life is incomplete until we account for, if in a limited way, how his angelic vision is developed through his exemplar portraits. For this reason, the rest of this essay will be devoted to one of Chrysostom's favorite exemplars, King David, so that we may better grasp the intricacies involved in his vision of the angelic *politeia*.

David: The Angelic Christian

Despite being a figure of the Old Dispensation, David is regularly presented by Chrysostom as an exemplary Christian par excellence. This he achieves by frequently exalting the king as one who has attained virtues comparable to those of Christians, and thus he may be counted in their company.

> It is impossible . . . for someone in the Old Dispensation to show such sound values. . . . David had not heard the parable of the ten thousand talents and the hundred denarii; David had not heard the prayer that says, "Forgive people their debts as your heavenly Father also does;" he had not seen Christ crucified. . . . Instead he was raised on imperfect laws that made no such requirements, yet *he attained to the very summit of sound values of the age of grace*.[56]

It is within this context that David is regularly upheld as the exemplar of manifold *Christian* virtues, such as faith, forbearance, gentleness, clemency, re-

---

54. For a study of Augustine's appropriation of the psychagogic tradition, see Paul R. Kolbet, *Augustine and the Cure of Souls* (Notre Dame: University of Notre Dame Press, 2010).

55. Rylaarsdam, *Divine Pedagogy*, 6–7, 226.

56. *Dav. et Sau.* 3, emphasis mine. Elsewhere in *Homily* 1, he even speaks of David as one who has "surpass[ed] the norm of the commandments and attain[ed] to New Testament value." Translated by Robert Hill in John Chrysostom, *Old Testament Homilies*, trans. Robert C. Hill (Brookline, MA: Holy Cross Orthodox Press, 2003), 11, 43–44.

pentance, and humility. This rhetorical strategy operates on two levels. First, it enables Chrysostom to subvert or Christianize the Greco-Roman ethical framework that he employs by introducing a range of virtues that would have been unthinkable for his pagan peers but that he regards as important for the angelic life. Second, by having David "re-enact" a particular virtue in his own life, Chrysostom not only clarifies for his audience what he takes the virtue to be, but also offers rich insights as to how it may be operative in their lives. Take, for example, the virtue of humility (*tapeinophrosynē*), which he associates most often with David and the story of Absalom's rebellion (2 Sam 15). In one retelling of this tale, Chrysostom reminds his audience that, despite being a doer of "ten thousand good works," David had to suffer not only the betrayal of his son, but also flee like a refugee and endure the revilement of Shimei. Yet it was under such difficulties that David's humility was thrown into relief. This, Chrysostom articulates, through an imaginary speech of David. "If this pleased God . . . that I should be chased and wander and flee, . . . I acquiesce and accept it, and do thank God for His many afflictions." Clearly then, true humility, for Chrysostom, is no mere self-debasement, but a willingness to obey and be contented with whatever God brings to our lives, whether good or evil. It is for this reason he counts humility as "the first principle of philosophy" and a potent antidote for all sorts of sins, because he who is "humbled and bruised will not be vainglorious, wrathful, jealous for riches or harbour any passion."[57]

Other than a means of ethical reflections, David's life also becomes, for Chrysostom, a powerful demonstration of how a layperson can live out an angelic life comparable to those of the monks and ascetics. He notes, for example, that the king, along with Cornelius the centurion, Paul the worker of leather, and Job the landowner, could keep himself pure even though he practiced a secular vocation.[58] Indeed, David was able to remain humble and moderate throughout his life despite the fact that he spent most of it in army camps and, presumably, in the company of rowdy and violent men.[59] In a sermon series on David's encounter with Saul at the cave (1 Sam 24), the king is further invested with motifs commonly associated with the angelic lifestyle. In *Homily* 1, for example, Chrysostom recounts the incident where David struggled with his men's urges to kill Saul at the cave. Here, David is depicted as a martyr figure through a series of rhetorical devices commonly associated with martyrs, such as the arena, contest, and crown. Clearly, the aim here is to portray his present temptation as not unlike that of a martyr struggling for his spiritual crown.

---

57. *Hom. Matt.* 3.8–9 (PG 57.38.40–41).
58. Ibid., 61.3.
59. Ibid., 72.4.

The cave was an arena, and a kind of remarkable and surprising contest took place. . . . David entered the lists, resentment struck a blow, Saul was the prize, and God acted as a referee—or, rather, the battle was not against himself, and his desires but also against the soldiers present [who might slay him if he spares Saul].[60]

This being said, David is no mere martyr from the era of persecutions. Rather, he is the exemplary spiritual martyr or monk who no longer dies physically but spiritually to his ill passions.[61] Elsewhere, Chrysostom would develop further David's ascetic character by depicting him as a spiritual physician (*iatros*), another trait commonly among the monks. Speaking of Saul's persecution of David, he has the king choosing voluntary exile so that this may be a therapeutic means for "bring[ing] down the swelling, check[ing] the inflammation and allay[ing] the malice" in Saul's soul.[62] Later, against those who doubt whether David's struggles were real, Chrysostom asserts that "billows of resentment" did buffet him and "a great tempest of thoughts was stirred up." Nevertheless, the king managed to hold "the storm in check with the fear of God and subdued his thinking." This was possible only because he was watchful like the ascetics, who "before falling they get up, before proceeding to sin they get a grip on themselves since they are always watching and always on the alert."[63]

Earlier we mentioned that the central aspect of Chrysostom's soteriology is his doctrine of recapitulation: namely, Christ has saved humanity by becoming our representative before God and fulfilling his laws perfectly. Humanity should, in turn, follow in his footsteps by the power of the Spirit, so that they may be transformed into Christ's likeness. As in the case with his exemplar portraits elsewhere, Chrysostom's David is never a mere martyr or monastic figure who exemplifies divine virtues. More importantly, David's life often becomes, for Chrysostom, concrete demonstrations of how his soteriological vision may be worked out practically. Chrysostom's conclusion to *Homily* 1 is an excellent example. Speaking on David's prayer, "the Lord forbid," in 1 Samuel 24:6, Chrysostom expounds the prayer imaginatively by having the king declare,

> May the Lord be merciful to me, and if I actually had the intention may God *not allow* me to act on it *nor permit me* to proceed to the sin.

60. *Dav. et Sau.* 1 (Hill, *Old Testament Homilies*, 18).
61. Ibid., 18.
62. Chrysostom, *Old Testament Homilies*, 17.
63. Ibid., 21.

Through this creative reenactment, Chrysostom makes it clear that progress towards the angelic life is to be found in our consciousness of our own weaknesses and prayerful dependence on God. It is in this way that help is received from "grace from on high" and one can transcend oneself, so that "while still belonging to the human nature [he] is giving evidence of the angelic way of life."[64]

Apart from the above, the life of David also offers Chrysostom ample opportunities to reflect on the perils faced by an ascetic on his spiritual journey. No story helps him more on this than David's adultery with Bathsheba. Speaking on the story on two separate occasions, Chrysostom argues that the king's sin was due not to "a habitual practice of wickedness" but his being "carried away by circumstances."[65] On first glance, it would seem that Chrysostom was abiding by the ethical assumption common among Late Antique biographers. That is, to ascribe one's potential and moral behavior to one's nature and nurture.[66] Based on this logic, David, known for his piety, could not be thought of as a habitual sinner, but rather as one who had lapsed unexpectedly into sin. On closer analysis, however, a different picture emerges. Elsewhere in his comments on Matthew 7:17, Chrysostom explains that nature on its own does not determine one's moral ability, as though "there is no way for the wicked to change or that the good cannot fall away." Instead, one "may indeed change to virtue" as long as he forsakes his evil ways and vice versa.[67] Turning to the case of David, Chrysostom then asserts that the king's fall into sin was due largely to his abandonment of his virtuous habits, or as he puts it elsewhere, that he allowed his sexual desire to compromise his reason and dull his intelligence.[68]

Chrysostom, I believe, is not being contradictory here. Rather, he is bringing to bear his personal experience on the challenges and intricacies involved in ascetic practice. To be sure, the ascetic discipline does play a crucial role in helping a monk form virtuous habits. Nevertheless, a monk, or indeed, any Christian, remains constantly under threat, and it takes but a slight negligence on one's part before he is caught unexpectedly and slides into grave sin. This point he has already alluded to in his portrayal of the Edenic Adam discussed earlier. It is made even more poignantly in his *Adhortationes ad Thedorum Lapsum*. Here, he recounts the story of an aged ascetic who had led "an angelic life" for much of his life. On one occasion, however, the monk yielded to his lust and found himself visiting a brothel. Fortunately for him, his companion found

64. Ibid., 22.

65. *Hom. Rom.* 16 (PG 60.557); *Hom. Matt.* 26.8.

66. Patricia Cox, *Biography in Late Antiquity: A Quest for the Holy Man*, Transformation of the Classical Heritage (Berkeley: University of California Press, 1983), 80–81.

67. *Hom. Matt.* 23.8 (NPNF[1] 10:230).

68. Ibid., 60.1.

and convinced him to return to his ascetic regime.[69] Taken together, the spiritual insight from these Davidic and monastic portraits is clear: an ascetic must always be watchful against *rathymia* or careless negligence, lest he find himself being drawn away from the angelic life that the Spirit has nurtured in his life.

Vision of the Angelic Life

Momentous shifts in history often lead to momentous challenges to self-identity. This was certainly the case for Christians living in the late fourth century. As heirs of a four-hundred-year-old heritage, they could take pride in the courage of their martyrs, draw on the theological insights of spiritual luminaries, and rejoice that Christianity, a once minority religion, had now become the dominant faith in the Roman Empire. This being said, the fact that they were no longer the Church persecuted but the Church triumphant was problematic on two levels. The first is their sense of discontinuity from the past. One can no longer, for example, imitate the martyrs who died for their faith. Indeed, as members of a major religion, it was simply harder for Christians to grasp the pressures faced by their persecuted forefathers. Second, the fact that Christianity was now a religion with significant social, political, and cultural influence begs the question as to how one should live out one's faith in such new circumstances. This was the challenge posed to Chrysostom. As a pastor of this era, he must not only help his peers make sense of and identify with the past, but also appropriate this heritage in a way that would be relevant for their new spiritual climate. This he achieves through his rhetorical discourse about the angelic life. By contextualizing biblical and Christian figures creatively, Chrysostom not only familiarizes his audiences with their Christian past but also offers them rich and vivid suggestions as to how this heritage may be adapted for their present lives. In the twenty-first century, a similar momentous shift is taking place. Christianity is no longer a Western religion but one that is both multicultural and dominated by the Global South. Once again, the familiar question arises: how may we adapt our faith to these new cultural circumstances and still maintain our continuity and roots with our Christian past? Hopefully, Chrysostom's vision of the angelic life may offer us some helpful insights in this respect.

---

69. *Theatr.* 1.18–19.

Chapter 13

Augustine of Hippo:
The Christian Life, Then and Now

PAUL C. BURNS

Over his long life from 354 to 430 CE, Augustine wrote a voluminous amount of material in a variety of genres for diverse audiences. Since he was a highly trained rhetorician, he varied his argument, diction, and examples to address his immediate audience. Consequently the writings of Augustine have been invoked by very divergent groups throughout the history of Western Christianity from Carolingian monasteries, to the schools of Christian thought in the high Middle Ages, to participants on all sides of the Reformation controversies. Augustine continued to be a rich cultural resource for Enlightenment figures as diverse as Jean-Jacques Rousseau and Blaise Pascal. The range of appeals to his writings has clouded some of the nineteenth- and twentieth-century scholarship on Augustine, including those scholars preoccupied by competing claims of Catholic and Protestant perspectives. This collection of essays represents the new era of cooperation by scholars across Christian denominational identities.

More recently there have been at least three constructive developments in Augustinian scholarship. In the twentieth century scholars have attempted to provide more balanced analyses of Augustine's major debates with the Manichees[1] or the Donatists[2] or the Pelagians[3] against which he developed his understanding of the Christian person.[4] Then in the broader academy several

---

1. J. Kevin Coyle, *Augustine's De Moribus Ecclesiae Catholicae: A Study of the Work, Its Composition and Its Sources* (Freiburg: Freiburg University Press, 1978).

2. W. H. C. Frend, *The Donatist Church: A Movement of Protest in Roman North Africa* (Oxford: Oxford University Press, 1985).

3. Dominic Keech, *The Anti-Pelagian Christology of Augustine of Hippo, 396–430* (Oxford: Oxford University Press, 2012).

4. For a succinct, systematic assessment of current scholarship on aspects of Augustine's

distinguished cultural historians have focused on Augustine's use of the classical tradition of the liberal arts[5] with some scholars narrowly emphasizing his use of Neoplatonism.[6] Then some social historians have helped recover an understanding of the sensitivities of the Late Antique period.[7] As a result of these studies Augustine's *Confessions* (*Conf.*)[8] and his *City of God* (*Civ.*)[9] have become much more accessible to members of the modern academy. Although this represents significant progress in our understanding of Augustine, we need to incorporate Augustine's evolving understanding of Christian identity and mission.

To promote this distinctively Christian perspective, current studies on Augustine's massive *Expositions of the Psalms* (*Enarrat. Ps.*), compiled from 391 to around 418, certainly are helping complete our appreciation for the expansive range of his understanding of the Christian life.[10] Like his mentor Ambrose,

---

construction of the human person, consult Peter Burnell, *The Augustinian Person* (Washington, DC: The Catholic University of America Press, 2005).

5. Consult Henri Marrou, *A Brief History of Education in Antiquity* (New York: Sheed & Ward, 1956), and idem, *St. Augustin et la fin de la culture antique* (Paris: Editions E. de Boccad, 1958).

6. Consult A. H. Armstrong, *The Cambridge History of Later Greek and Early Medieval Philosophy* (Cambridge: Cambridge University Press, 1967). For a particularly narrowly focused discussion of the influence of Plotinus on Augustine, see the study by one of the editors of the Oxford Greek edition of Plotinus, Paul Henry, *The Path to Transcendence: From Philosophy to Mysticism in Saint Augustine* (Pittsburgh, PA: Pickwick Press, 1981).

7. Peter Brown, *Augustine of Hippo: A Biography* (London and Berkeley: Faber & Faber, and University of California Press, 1967 and 2000), James J. O'Donnell, *Augustine: Confessions*, 3 vols. (Oxford: Clarendon, 1992), and Robert Markus, *The End of Ancient Christianity* (Cambridge: Cambridge University Press, 1990). Robert Markus has offered the stimulating proposal of an emerging secular sphere during the fourth century of the empire. I think what is happening is the transition from the perspectives informed by Roman pagan culture to the expectations reflected in the emerging Christian society. For a helpful discussion of this phenomenon, consult Michele R. Saltzman, *On Roman Time: The Codex-Calendar of 354 and the Rhythms of Urban Life in Late Antiquity*, The Transformation of the Classical Heritage 17 (Berkeley: University of California Press, 1991).

8. The English translation employed in this paper is Saint Augustine, *Confessions*, trans. Henry Chadwick (Oxford: Oxford University Press, 1991).

9. The translation employed in this paper is *The City of God Against the Pagans*, trans. R. W. Dyson, Cambridge Texts in the History of Political Thought (Cambridge: Cambridge University Press, 1998).

10. The English translation used in this paper is from *Exposition of the Psalms*, trans. Maria Boulding, 6 vols., *The Works of Saint Augustine: A Translation for the 21st Century* (New York: New City Press, 2000). For a critical edition with notes, in progress, consult *Oeuvres de Saint Augustin: Les Commentaires des Psaumes 1–16, 17–25, 26–31: Enarrationes in Psalmos*, trans. and ed., Martine Dulaey, 57A, 57B, 58A (Institut d'Études Augustiniennes, 2009, 2011). For an excellent study of Augustine's treatment of the first 32 Psalms, consult Michael Cameron, *Christ Meets Me Everywhere: Augustine's Early Figurative Exegesis* (Oxford: Oxford University Press, 2012). For a

Augustine had demonstrated an attraction for the ascetical ideal for the Christian life. That influence shapes the prominence of celibacy in his conversion decision in his *Confessions* and is also reflected in his early initiatives in communal living both in Italy and immediately after his return to North Africa. After his ordination to the priesthood in 391 and his consecration as bishop in 395, however, Augustine becomes determined to forge an appropriate blueprint for the Christian life for believers who remain involved in the daily life of Roman society.

Construction of the "Self" in his *Confessions*

In both his *Confessions* and in his *City of God* Augustine demonstrates a comprehensive grasp of a range of Roman literary culture along with a selective pastoral appreciation for its value to the Christian. In his autobiography at 4.16, for example, Augustine comments that he expended time and energy on the liberal arts. In this passage he emphasizes the pleasure this provided, but now looking back, he regrets that he did not recognize the real truth and wisdom that is the source of this tradition. On a more positive note, in several passages in his autobiography, Augustine names a classical author who actually helped prepare him to accept the Christian life. In his student days at Carthage, he read Cicero's *Hortensius,* which prompted a longing "for the immortality of wisdom with an incredible ardour in my heart" (*Conf.* 3.4). Later at 5.3 he uses classical astronomy and the ability to predict dates, places, and scope of eclipses of the sun and moon to challenge the cosmic myths of the Manichees. Then in passages at 7.9, 10, and 16 he pays tribute to the Platonizing tradition he encountered in Milan. This provides Augustine with the language to describe a mystical ascent through material things and return to their ultimate source empowered by love. It is clear that Augustine is crediting a role for secular literature, science, and Neoplatonic philosophy in preparing him for the gift of Christian faith. This positive role is reflected in the advice to Monica from the unnamed cleric at 3.12 to let him continue with his reading. This secular literature is an important contribution to his own journey, and he is offering

---

very helpful overview of Augustine's treatment of the Psalms, consult Michael Cameron, "Enarrationes in Psalmos," in *Augustine through the Ages: An Encyclopedia,* ed. Allan D. Fitzgerald, OSA (Grand Rapids: Eerdmans, 1999), 290–96. For a comprehensive example of the growing scholarly interest in patristic exegesis of the Psalms, consult the fifteen articles in A. G. Andreopoulos, Augustine Casidy, and Carol Harrison, eds., *Meditations of the Heart: The Psalms in Early Christian Thought and Practice: Essays in Honor of Andrew Louth,* Studia Traditionis Theologiae 8 (Turnhout: Brepols, 2011).

his experience as an encouragement for his peers in Roman culture to do the same. His cameo life of Monica, however, makes it clear that he is not claiming that the use of secular authors is essential for every journey in the Christian faith. Monica is an example of a clear steadfast faith informed by common sense, probably without the benefits of any formal education. Her practical intelligence comes out sharply in the episode over the interpretation of her dream. She quickly objects to Augustine's attempts to invert subject and object and insists that "where you [Monica] are, he will be also" (*Conf.* 3.11). She defeats the master rhetorician at his own profession!

Moreover, from these cultural resources, Augustine is able to construct a dynamic notion of the human self. At the end of the first book on his infancy and boyhood, Augustine provides an impressive catalogue of the human gifts he has discovered in himself.

> I existed, I was alive and thought. An inward instinct told me to take care of the integrity of my senses. . . . I took delight in the truth. . . . I developed a good memory. I acquired the armoury of being skilled with words, friendship softened me, and I avoided pain, despondency, ignorance. . . . They are good qualities, and their totality is my self. (*Conf.* 1.20)

These values remain with him but he is increasingly disturbed by the disorder that exists in himself and causes intense inner tension that he later compares to a "house divided against itself" (*Conf.* 8.8).[11]

Pastoral Engagement with His Audience in *City of God*

Augustine returns to a much more comprehensive discussion of Roman culture in his *City of God*.[12] Here he is refuting the Roman claim that the city suffered at the hands of a barbarian attack in 410 because the citizens had stopped the traditional festivals and sacrifices as a consequence of the legislation of Theodosius in the East in 389 and extended to the West in 393 to 395.[13]

---

11. For this phrase I am borrowing the translation in *Saint Augustine: Confessions*, trans. R. S. Pine-Coffin (New York: Penguin, 1961), 170.

12. Gerard O'Daly, ed., *Augustine's City of God: A Reader's Guide* (Oxford: Clarendon, 1999), and Robert J. Dodaro, ed., *Augustine: Political Writings*, Cambridge Texts in the History of Political Science (Cambridge: Cambridge University Press, 2001).

13. At *Civ.* 5.24–26, Augustine expresses appreciation for the settlement of Constantine and the humility of Theodosius but he neither shares the naïve euphoria of Eusebius of Caesarea nor the aggressive agenda of Ambrose of Milan.

In dealing with the issues provoked by the sack of Rome, Augustine continues to demonstrate a pastoral concern not only for the Christians who invoked his help but also for the Roman citizens whom he regards as potential Christians. So in book 1 when he deals with the consequences of the assault on Rome, he identifies care for dead bodies, sanctuary for those under attack, sensitivity to rape victims, and response to the plight of captives. Throughout he demonstrates an informed awareness and a genuine appreciation for Roman practices, literature, and history. At the same time, in his discussion of the famous cases of Lucretia (*Civ.* 1.19) and Cato (*Civ.* 1.23), Augustine provides a sharp Christian critique of the Stoic advocacy of suicide. At 1.1 he points out that Christians must defend themselves against criticism from the enemies of the heavenly City. In that opening paragraph he reminds both Christians and also their critics that many found sanctuary from the marauding Goths in Christian basilicas. On the respect for the bodies of the dead, Augustine demonstrates an understanding and a respect for Roman customs.

> Their actual bodies, which we wear far more intimately and closely than any garment, should certainly not be despised. For they are not an ornament . . . , rather they belong to the very nature of man. To the righteous men of old, therefore, the last offices were rendered with pious care, and obsequies celebrated and sepulchres provided. (*Civ.* 1.13)

The Christian shares these values and practices and has the additional appreciation for the resurrection of the body. He goes on at 1.15 to speak of the plight of captives and invokes the powerful example of the Roman hero Regulus. At 1.16 Augustine expresses a sensitive view of the impact of rape and he attempts to remove the corrosive sense of shame in these victims.

For his critique of the decline in moral values within Roman culture, Augustine makes repeated use of Sallust and Cicero. For his definition of a true city, Augustine uses an extended passage from Cicero's *De Re Publica* at 2.21 and returns to it at 19.21. He also employs Cicero's requirement of justice for an authentic society. For Augustine this ideal cannot be realized without the power of Christ to transform the fallen human condition. Scholars have long acknowledged Augustine's sustained use of Roman voices to criticize many features of their culture. What deserves attention, however, is that in marshaling these criticisms, Augustine also appeals to Romans to consider joining the Christian faith. Near the end of book 1 after his sustained reply to Roman critics of the Christian church, he reminds Christians that these very people may find their way into the church.

> Let these answers . . . be made to their enemies by the redeemed family of
> the Lord Jesus Christ and by the pilgrim city of Christ the King. Remember,
> however, that among these very enemies are hidden some who will become
> citizens. (*Civ.* 1.35)

In fact, at the end of book 2 he addresses a compelling appeal to those who
embody the qualities of Roman heroes:

> Desire these things, then, O admirable Roman character—O offspring of the
> Reguli, Scaevolae, Scipios and Fabricii: desire these things instead. (*Civ.* 2.29)

Augustine continues to provide an informed review of many components of
Roman culture. He makes extensive use of Marcus Terentius Varro to identify
three types of Roman religion: the scurrilous activities of the gods in Roman literature, the contrived social festivals in the annual cycle of the Roman calendar,
and finally the divinity refined by philosophical thought (*Civ.* 4.22, 27, 31; 6.2–7,
10; and 7.17, 26). Some philosophical traditions were moving towards a sense
of a single divine principle, which Varro, much to the delight of Augustine,
would have preferred (*Civ.* 4.31). A final component in this cultural analysis is
Augustine's appreciation for the Platonic tradition (*Civ.* 8.4, 5, 9), specifically
the Neoplatonism represented by Plotinus (*Civ.* 10.2, 14, 24).

> The Platonist philosopher Plotinus indeed discusses providence (*Enneads*
> 3.2.13). He infers from the beauty of flowers and leaves that providence ex-
> tends downwards even to these earthly things from the supreme God, to
> Whom belongs intelligible and ineffable beauty. (*Civ.* 10.14)

He continues to distinguish this useful intellectual tradition from the salvation
accomplished through the incarnation of Jesus Christ. In his assessment of
this philosophical tradition, Augustine points out that Christians identify the
source of salvation as the three persons in the Godhead accomplished through
the incarnation of Jesus Christ rather than the impersonal "principia" of the
Platonic tradition (*Civ.* 10.24).

Experience of the Christian "Self" in His *Expositions of the Psalms*

In this essay I am building upon contemporary scholarship but with a focus on
themes and methods Augustine employed in his *Enarrationes in Psalmos*, which
he began soon after his ordination to the priesthood and continued through to

about 418. In his autobiography he has over 200 quotations from the Psalms, far more than any other source. The language of the Psalms also influenced key themes and perspectives in his *City of God.*

It is clear from passages in the *Confessions* that Augustine was impressed with the practice of Psalm recitation or singing that he experienced at the church in Milan (*Conf.* 9.7). Then he raises his reservations about this practice at 10.33. There he expresses his concerns over the power of music to appeal to the emotions but ultimately he approves of the recommendations of Athanasius at Alexandria to focus on the text supported by a subtle musical setting. He ends with his recollection of the power this practice had on him during a critical stage in his struggles towards the Christian faith. In the introduction to his sermon on Psalm 18.2.1, Augustine addresses his congregation with similar concerns about the use of music for the Psalms. He is worried about the popular use of music that is inappropriate to express the faith of the believer. To warn his people he employs an extended contrast between the singing of blackbirds, parrots, crows, magpies, and other species with humans who can understand what they are singing. Birds focus on sound and rhythm; people in the congregation must subordinate the music to the sense of the revealed words. Against this tentative background, Augustine's respect for the significant power of the recitation and singing of Psalms at this critical stage in his life and at the death of his mother is all the more impressive (*Conf.* 9.12). In book 9, Augustine highlights the contribution of the Psalms at a critical time in his preparation for baptism:

> My God, how I cried to you when I read the Psalms of David, songs of faith, utterances of devotion . . . I was but a beginner in authentic love of you, a catechumen resting at a country villa. . . . How I cried out to you in those Psalms, and how they kindled my love for you! I was fired by an enthusiasm to recite them, were it possible to the entire world. (*Conf.* 9.4)

This passage is significant for our theme. The power of the Psalms to instill and to express a profound and passionate love for God is an important corrective to those modern scholars who attribute the origin of the affective component in Augustine's view of the human person to Neoplatonism. This contribution of the Psalms also informs the mystical ascent of Monica and Augustine as they overlook the garden. After invoking the words of Psalm 35:10 (36:8), as "we drank in the waters flowing from your spring" (*Conf.* 9.10) they began their mystical ascent. "Our minds were lifted up by an ardent affection towards eternal being itself" (*Conf.* 9.10). We passed beyond earth and the heavens above; we approached uncreated heavenly Wisdom, and "we touched it in some small degree by a moment of total concentration of the heart" (*Conf.* 9.10).

In Augustine's mind, the Psalms have become the appropriate text to provide a map and inspiration for the Christian life. In practice, too, the Psalms have become the people's biblical text, of which they chant or sing at least one verse as a refrain. Throughout his work on the Psalms, Augustine provides information about the importance of the daily recitation, which he does himself and which he recommends to the congregations to whom he preaches. Augustine uses the metaphor of a mirror (*speculum*) to depict the correspondence between the text of the Psalms and one's personal experience.

> If the psalm is praying, pray yourselves; if it is groaning, you groan too; if it is happy, rejoice; if it is crying out in hope, you hope as well; if it expresses fear, be afraid. Everything written here is like a mirror held up to us. (*Enarrat. Ps.* 30.4.1)

On Psalm 49:23, Augustine mentions the practice of singing or recitation at church in the morning and in the evening and then at home at the third or fourth hour of the day. A little later on Psalm 66, Augustine makes use of an extended metaphor of a colony of ants.

> Think of God's ants. They rise daily and hurry to church, pray, listen to the reading, sing the hymn, ruminate on what they have heard, think over it at home and store within themselves whatever grains they have collected from the threshing-floor. (*Enarrat. Ps.* 66.3)

The Pilgrim "Self" in the *Exposition of the Psalms*

Unlike one of his Latin predecessors in Psalm commentary, Augustine does not employ a clear organizational schema to construct a clear structure and sequence for his extended treatment of the Psalms.[14] There are, however, some key terms from the Latin text of the Psalms that he adapts to provide guidance to his interpretation of the Psalms. These terms also provide a helpful key to his autobiography, as well as to his extended assessment of Roman culture. For our purposes, I will concentrate on "pilgrimage" (*peregrinor*)[15] and "confes-

14. For a study of the stages of the Christian life for each cluster of fifty psalms in Hilary of Poitiers's *Treatise on the Psalms*, composed in the middle 360s, consult Paul C. Burns, *A Model for the Christian Life: Hilary of Poitiers' Commentary on the Psalms* (Washington, DC: The Catholic University of America Press, 2012).

15. For an analysis of the sources and the meanings of the pilgrim language, consult M. A. Claussen, "'Peregrinatio' and 'Peregrini' in Augustine's 'City of God,'" *Traditio* 46 (1991): 33–75.

sion" (*confiteor*) and their respective cognates. In his treatment of the Psalms, in particular, Augustine forges a scriptural perspective upon which to ground the journey of the Christian life to its ultimate goal into glory. For this critical relationship to Christ, Augustine uses a range of terms, including "body of Christ" (*corpus Christi*) and "the whole Christ" (*totus Christus*).

In his Commentary on Psalm 42, Augustine uses the desire for God to motivate the search for or journey to God. *As the deer longs for running streams, so my soul longs for you, my God.* In several passages in his discussion of this Psalm, Augustine uses the terminology of pilgrimage[16] and its cognates. This terminology reflects the condition of a stranger in an alien land moving towards a goal that lies in the future. This language with its eschatological emphasis on longing for a goal in the future marks a departure from his Neoplatonic "return to a homeland" lost in the past.[17] At the outset of his treatment, Augustine points out that even baptism will not satisfy the candidates' desire for the goal of their pilgrimage (*peregrinentur*) but only sharpen their longing for it (*Enarrat. Ps.* 41.1).

In a passage reminiscent of the mystical ascent with Monica in *Confessions* 9.10 he sets out the pattern of an extended ascent through the natural wonders of the world to a consideration of the complex mystery of the human self to God who resides above all. In this passage on the Psalms, however, he expands on his appreciation for divine providence active throughout his journey. Here on the Psalms, Augustine makes the theme of divine providence very vivid with a series of active verbs with a direct impact on him.

> *I poured out my soul above myself*, and now there is nothing left for me to touch, except my God. For there, above my soul, is the home of my God; there he dwells, from there he looks down upon me, from there he created me, from there he governs me and takes thought for me, from there he arouses me, calls me, guides me and leads me on, and from there he will lead me to journey's end. (*Enarrat. Ps.* 41.8)

He goes on in the very next section to associate this pilgrim status to the Church, the community of faith on the way to the heavenly City.

On page 62, Claussen points out that "peregrinatio" and its cognate forms appear over 800 times in the works of Augustine with 300 in *Enarrat. Ps.* and 100 in *Civ.*

16. For a systematic analysis of Augustine's three stages of the human journey, "Garden, this world, and heaven," consult Burnell, *The Augustinian Person*, in his chapter entitled "The Stages of the Human Condition," 71–96.

17. For a discussion of Augustine's shift, around 412, from a Neoplatonic "return to a homeland" to a more pronounced focus on the eschatological future, consult Claussen, "Peregrinatio," 71–73.

For he who has his most lofty home in a secret place has also a tent on earth. His tent is the Church, the Church which is still a pilgrim [*peregrina*]; yet he is to be sought there, because in this tent we find the way that leads to his home. (*Enarrat. Ps.* 41.9)

He continues the theme of the pilgrim still far from the Lord but on the journey to him. When Augustine begins to consider the "Gradual Psalms" 119–133, the reality of the destination comes into sharper focus.

The psalmist is one who is beginning to make progress. He therefore notices bad people and many evils of which he was previously unaware; and cries out to God, *Alas, alas how drawn-out is my exile*! I have gone so far from you. My pilgrimage is so wearisome! I have not yet arrived in that homeland where I shall live untroubled by any evil. . . . An "exile" implies a pilgrimage or journey abroad. A person who lives in a foreign land, away from his own country, is called an exile. . . . *Alas* is a word that indicates misery; . . . yet it also expresses hope, because the one who uses it has at last learned to grieve. There are many others, just as wretched, who do not grieve; they are exiles too, but have no desire to go home. (*Enarrat. Ps.* 119.6–7)

He goes on to apply the pilgrimage theme to the soul rather than simply a physical journey.

My soul has been on a pilgrimage for a long time. He says that it is his soul that has been on a pilgrimage, to make sure you do not think only of bodily journeys. The body travels from place to place; the soul travels by its affections. . . . If you are in love with God, you are climbing towards him. . . . Where does he ascend? *The ascents are in his heart* we were told in another psalm (83.6 [84:5]). If he is to ascend in his heart, there can be no ascent for him unless his heart is on pilgrimage. (*Enarrat. Ps.* 119.8)

The heavenly City, Jerusalem, becomes the community to which we should look forward.

The psalmist is someone who wants to ascend. . . . In heaven is the eternal Jerusalem, where dwell the angels, our fellow-citizens. For a little while we are absent from those compatriots of ours, while we are journeying [*peregrinamur*] on earth. On our pilgrimage [*peregrinatione*] we sigh, but in our own city we shall rejoice. (*Enarrat. Ps.* 121.2)

So in the Psalms Augustine has come to locate the goal of the Christian journey in the eschatological future at the end of time and not simply the Neoplatonic return to a homeland.

The Confessing "Self" in the *Exposition of the Psalms*

Throughout his treatment on the Psalms, Augustine employs another key word, "confession" and its cognates, to express the perspectives of the person on this pilgrimage to the heavenly city. Early on in that commentary, Augustine offers a very succinct distinction in the term "confession." "Confession is twofold; it can be either of sin or of praise" (*Enarrat. Ps.* 29.2.19). He repeatedly returns to this double meaning as especially appropriate in Scripture.

> *Let us forestall him by coming into his presence* confessing. "Confession" is understood by Scripture in two senses: there is the confession of one who praises, and the confession of one who groans. . . . Men and women confess when they praise God, and they confess when they accuse themselves; and the tongue has no nobler function. (*Enarrat. Ps.* 94.4)

Within several of these passages based on the double meaning of *confiteor*, Augustine develops some applications that would resonate with members of his congregation. On Psalm 66:5 (4), for example, Augustine links the double activity of *confiteor* with the theme of "singing a new song." Here he alludes to popular practice of singing on a journey to pass the time and especially at night to ward off threats. Then in the very next passage on the same Psalm, Augustine contrasts the brutal experience of confession in front of a human tribunal with confession to God.

> *Let the Gentiles be glad and exult.* Robbers who have confessed their guilt wail before a human judge, but let believers who have confessed be glad before God. In a human tribunal, there is collaboration between a torturer and fear to elicit a confession from a criminal; or, again, fear sometimes suppresses the confession which fear is trying to extort, for the accused person, though screaming in torments, is afraid he will be killed if he confesses. He therefore bears the torments as best he can; but if the pain is too much for him, he blurts out his confession, and in so doing pronounces his death sentence. . . . when he [the criminal] has confessed he is condemned and led away by the executioner. (*Enarrat. Ps.* 66.7)

Augustine completes his contrast between confessing before a human tribunal and confessing before God with an appeal to medical healing.

> [O]nce you confess, dance for joy; because now you have the prospect of healing. The physician uses a medicinal knife to correct the trouble. . . . Confess. Let all the pus come out and flow away in your confession; then dance for joy and be glad. (*Enarrat. Ps.* 66.7)

Thus the combined activities of "confession" and "profession" reflect the dynamic perspectives that characterize Augustine's assessment of the current stage in this life of the human journey or "pilgrimage."

> We are captives still, burdened by the luggage of our mortal bodies as we walk our pilgrim way and sigh for the great city, Jerusalem. When she is finally made new, we shall be at home in her, exulting in the city we sighed for on our pilgrimage. Anyone who does not sigh as a pilgrim will never rejoice as a citizen, for there can be no desire in him. (*Enarrat. Ps.* 148.4)

The Pivotal Role of Christ in the Christian "Self" in His *Exposition of the Psalms*

To accomplish the journey and to receive healing and mercy for confession, Augustine, in his writing on the Psalms, increasingly expands his appreciation for the pivotal role of Christ. He does have a clear sense of the divinity of Christ united with his human soul and human body. At times, in his commentaries, Augustine does assign the voice of Christ to one aspect of this complex identity. But as one recent insightful scholar observes, in his work on the Psalms Augustine tends to emphasize the unity of Christ.[18] He also tends to avoid technical theological language and instead use diction and examples to engage the broad demographics of his congregations at Hippo, Carthage, and other centers.

From his treatment of Psalm 21 onwards, Augustine tends to identify the body of Christ with the humility of the incarnation, the taking up of the fallen humanity, and the appeal to ordinary people.[19]

18. See Cameron, "Enarrationes," in *Augustine through the Ages*, 292–93.
19. See Cameron, *Christ Meets Me Everywhere*, especially in "The Keystone Exegesis of Psalm 21," 197–99.

To the end, for his taking up in the morning, a psalm of David. To the end, because the Lord Jesus Christ speaks here, praying for his own resurrection, for he was raised in the morning, on the first day of the week. On that day Jesus Christ was taken up into eternal life, and death will never hold sway over him again; but the words of this psalm are spoken in the person of the crucified one, for here at its beginning is the cry he uttered while he hung on the cross. He speaks consistently in the character of our old self, whose mortality he bore and which was nailed to the cross with him. (*Enarrat.* 21.1.1)

A little later, Augustine distinguishes between the voices employed by Christ. Occasionally he speaks as the Head, but at other times he speaks in the person of the body, the Church that he has taken up. Here he also identifies the conditions for our presence in this extended body of Christ.

There is no peace in my bones in the face of my sins. The question usually asked is, "Who is speaking here?" Some take this to be Christ's voice, on account of all that is said a little later about the passion. . . . The need to make sense of this forces us to recognize that "Christ" here is the full Christ, the whole Christ, that is, Christ, Head and body. When Christ speaks, he sometimes does so in the person of the Head alone, the Savior who was born of the virgin Mary; but at other times he speaks in the person of his body, the holy Church diffused throughout the world. We are within his body, provided we have sincere faith in him, and unshakable hope, and burning charity. We are within his body, we are part of it, and we find ourselves speaking these words. (*Enarrat. Ps.* 37.6)

So this reflection on the pain provoked "in the face of our sins" connects us with the person of Christ present in his extended body. Our inspired confession is made possible through this unity we have in Christ. Later he shows that, through being recalled to the humility of his suffering, the lost pilgrim will find the way.

Two disciples wanted to sit beside the Lord, one at his right, the other at his left. The Lord saw that they were getting things back to front and thinking about honors prematurely, for they should have been learning first of all how to be humbled in order to be exalted. So he said to them, *Are you able to drink the cup I am to drink* (Mt 20.22)? He was destined to drink the cup of suffering in the valley of weeping; but they, paying no heed to Christ's humility, wanted to seize the high dignity of Christ. He recalled them to the way like

221

lost travelers, not because he meant to refuse them what they wanted but in order to show them how to reach it. (*Enarrat. Ps.* 119.1)

On the very next Psalm, Augustine has Jesus not only showing followers how to reach the goal, the humility of his body, but also the way to accomplish that journey.

If you have believed in what Christ afterward became for you, if you have believed in what Christ afterward assumed for you, if you believe in what the Word became for you, if you believe that he rose in the flesh to save you from despairing about your own flesh, you will become Israel. [He had just explained Israel as "the one who sees God."] (*Enarrat. Ps.* 120.6)

Later in the same Psalm, he states that the humility of Christ's body is appropriate for the simple and the little ones in his congregation.

To the little ones the humility of Christ is preached, and the flesh of Christ and the crucifixion of Christ, because this is the milk suited to little ones. These little ones are not abandoned in the night, because the moon shines then; this symbolizes the Church which is preached through the reality of Christ's flesh; for the very flesh of Christ is the head of the Church. (*Enarrat. Ps.* 120.12)

Through trends in recent scholarship on Augustine, we have come to recognize the influence of the Psalms on him. These reflections provide him with a structure for the human predicament. When the pilgrim confesses sin, Jesus Christ, who has taken up human sin, weakness, and death, receives that person into his body through which we enter the heavenly Jerusalem. Empowered by this Christian faith and understanding, Augustine used his knowledge of Latin literary, historical, and philosophical culture to engage constructively with his educated peers in both his *Confessions* and in his *City of God*.

Chapter 14

Gregory the Great:
Conversionis Gratia—Ipse Becoming *Idem*

RYAN S. OLSON

Sed . . . retraxit pedem. So Gregorius introduces his icon, Benedict, to a popular audience. "But he withdrew his foot." Raised in a noble family with an elite Roman education, Gregorius narrates to his friend Peter in his *Dialogues*: gracious Benedict forsook his father's estate and went to the desert. *Sed . . . mutati sunt.* The visitors who became acquainted with Benedict, the servant of God in the desert, are transformed to piety and grace. They, too, forsook their nondesert life and were transformed. What caused such a sudden rupture from previous habits of life for Benedict, for his desert companions, and for the author of the *Dialogues*?[1]

The questions that the authors of this volume have been assigned are, What is the Christian identity of the historical figure, and What would he or she teach late-modern Christians about having an identity in Christ? To wrestle with these in a way that does justice to Gregory I, or Gregory the Great (AD 540–604), and comports with late modern, North Atlantic cultures, one can hardly do better than invoke the philosopher Paul Ricoeur. Ricoeur's insights about the nature of identity will help us to understand how Gregory appears to have been thinking about identity.

The basic problem with which Gregory wrestled in his several public roles—within the vicissitudes of active life—was how to maintain a coherent identity or soul, nurtured by rootedness in Christ, through contemplation of the triune God of grace. Though he at least occasionally strays from St. Augustine into synergism in ways that would be clarified by the sixteenth-century reformers,[2]

---

1. In J.-P. Migne, ed., *Patrologiae cursus completus: Series Latina* (PL) 66: *S. Benedicti* (Paris: apud Garnier fratres, 1859), 126.

2. Roger Olson, *The Story of Christian Theology: Twenty Centuries of Tradition and Reform* (Downers Grove, IL: InterVarsity Press, 2009), 287–89.

particularly by Martin Luther,[3] we will see that Gregory's understanding of the integration of identity in his own life requires habits and stand-taking that have not been sufficiently appreciated. *Standing up to habituation and forming new habits in the company of like-hearted friends for the benefit of serving one's neighbors more faithfully: this is the identity formation in Christ through the word of God that Gregory himself lived and that he urged upon his hearers.*

Gregory wrestled with this because, in his as in any epoch, an adequate understanding of oneself entails *time* as the background on which one's life is experienced and enacted. Specifically, the problem time introduces is how one remains *the same* despite bodily, intellectual, circumstantial, spiritual, and other changes, which, for Gregory, involved the acute pull from sameness occasioned by changes in life's demands in different career stages or even in momentary shifts from prayer to activity. Put philosophically, How is one (in some sense) the same person one was twenty years ago, or the same person who adored Christ in one's cell but now confronts a routine human conflict needing adjudication? In other words, How can another person identify one as the same person at different times and in diverse circumstances?

Yet a person is not only self-same, identifiable based on patterns from childhood, family, upbringing, friends, social groups, and so on. The self can change; the self can take a stand. Ricoeur meditated on this basic reality of the self by invoking Latin terms for "I": *idem* and *ipse*. *Idem* is the term for sameness, from which we receive the English word "identity," related to identifying or equating. *Idem*-identity allows one to remain coherent as one person over time despite many kinds of change and to identify oneself with another. *Ipse* is selfhood, unique from others and from background.[4] Hence human beings have a split identity, the parts of which overlap in the concept of *habit*. Sedimentation of actions reifies as traits that cover over the innovation of the new action that became a habit and *acquired identifications* (attachments to external "values, norms, ideals, models, and heroes in which the person identifies herself"). There are, then, two dialectics—the dialectic of habit acquisition between sedimentation (*idem*) and innovation

3. "Augsburg Confession, Article IV," in R. Kolb, T. J. Wengert, and C. P. Arand, eds., *The Book of Concord: The Confessions of the Evangelical Lutheran Church* (Minneapolis: Fortress, 2000): 38–39; see also A. Köberle, *The Quest for Holiness: A Biblical, Historical and Systematic Investigation*, trans. J. C. Mattes (Eugene, OR: Wipf & Stock, 2004), 48–83.

4. Paul Ricoeur, *Oneself as Another*, trans. Kathleen Blamey (Chicago: University of Chicago Press, 2008), 1–3; see the helpful summary of Ricoeur's hermeneutics of the self in David Vessey, "The Polysemy of Otherness: On Ricoeur's Oneself as Another," http://www.davevessey.com/Vessey_Ricoeur.html, accessed December 1, 2015.

(*ipse*), and the dialectic of identification between otherness (*idem*) and internalization (*ipse*).[5]

Here we require a concept central to Gregory's *oeuvre*: character oriented toward the virtues. Character is a way of being that is deeply etched[6] over time through virtuous habits, prayer, contemplation of Scripture, decisions, beliefs, emotions, institutions, commerce, friendships, personal reflections, service to others, and innumerable other influences. Character is fundamentally relational, expressed in social bonds as dependability. A person of good character can be expected to "walk" in certain predictable ways because of her identity with the good and by habituation of action.[7]

Character is *ipse* normalizing as *idem*. Taking a stand, being converted, making a dramatic break from what went before in one's life, these expressions of aliveness, of *ipse*, then lead to new habits that sediment and become *idem*, becoming dependable in one's relationships and responsibilities. Consider that "awareness that we can take up a stand towards our character, preserving it, strengthening it, and revising it[,] reveals the connection with *ipse*-identity. But these attitudes towards our character are themselves implicated in our character so the dialectical relation between *idem*-identity and *ipse*-identity is particularly apparent here. Character is *ipse* becoming *idem*, but *idem*-identity is only recognized as possessing certain traits appearing in certain ways, reflecting certain values, that is, as a product of our character."[8]

These dynamics are revealed throughout Gregory's large, diverse textual corpus. But their focal point is a letter addressed to a friend appended to the beginning of one of his most important works, a commentary on the biblical book of Job. The epistolary prologue's dramatic story—Gregory's *gratia conversionis*—becomes a turning point, a *metanoia*, in which *ipse* overcomes *idem* and "re-sediments," through friendship and contemplation, then to reengage in a renewed active life that drives one back to *contemplatio* or *theoria*. After providing biographical and historical context, we will analyze the letter and review echoes of that letter throughout the Gregorian corpus while cursorily

---

5. Ricoeur, *Oneself as Another*, 120–22.

6. Søren Kierkegaard picks up the meaning of the Greek word from which our English word derives: "Morality is character; character is something engraved (*charassō*), but the sea has no character, nor does sand, not abstract common sense, either, for character is inwardness." Søren Kierkegaard, *Two Ages: The Age of Revolution and the Present Age, a Literary Review*, ed. Howard V. Hong and Edna H. Hong, Kierkegaard's Writings, vol. 14 (Princeton: Princeton University Press, 1978), bk. 7, 73.

7. For a rigorously philosophical and existentially relevant discussion, see Ricoeur, *Oneself as Another.*

8. Vessey, "The Polysemy of Otherness," para. 4.

considering implications for Christian identity in late modernity for the North Atlantic world.

To Gregory the Great are attributed innovations in liturgy, the privileging of monastic vocations and the Benedictine rule, the evangelization of Britain and parts of Europe, and improvements in the management of the church's possessions, especially its extensive land holdings.[9] That he became pope, though reluctantly,[10] attests to his administrative, diplomatic, and leadership skills. His novel route there led through a monastery, a perhaps unlikely, out-of-the-way place for his soul to dwell, a solace from the monumental successes of his ever-ascendant public career. That career seemed to terminate when as *praefectus* at Rome, Gregory sold his father's estates upon the elder's death and began a monastery, St. Andrew's, into which he moved as a monk under an abbot.

After at least two monastic years, Gregory again reluctantly entered the public arena, this time as a papal diplomat to Constantinople and then again reluctantly (*Ep.* 1.4) as the bishop of Rome, where he served from 590 until his death in 604. Reentering from St. Andrew's, though, marked a change. He now embarked on what later commentators have called the "mixed life," a life of activity as before his monastic experience, but this time with contemplative posture and practices, as well as the community of the monastery around him as he went to the capital.

Gregory's Conversion

So far from being simply a "mixed life," however, Gregory's identity was integrated, not schizophrenic;[11] it was a sedimentation of habits and innovation. As we shall see, with Job, Gregory unified action and prayer, in the way of Cassian before him. A conversion must be understood within the framework of a

9. For a summary of possible liturgical improvements, which are much more modest than tradition holds, see Jeffrey Richards, *Consul of God: The Life and Times of Gregory the Great* (London and Boston: Routledge & Kegan Paul, 1980), 123–25; see also Constant Mews, "Gregory the Great, the Rule of Benedict and Roman Liturgy," *Journal of Medieval History* 37, no. 2 (June 2011): 125–44; for property management, R. A. Markus, *Gregory the Great and His World* (Cambridge: Cambridge University Press, 1997), 112–24, arguing it was "complex, well controlled . . . efficient and humane."

10. Though such reluctance was a trope, it appears to have been true at least with Gregory. Joan M. Peterson, *The Dialogues of Gregory the Great in Their Late Antique Cultural Background*, Studies and Texts (Toronto: Pontifical Institute of Mediaeval Studies, 1984), 70.

11. Markus, *Gregory the Great and His World*, 17–23, gives the historical trajectory of integration or blurring of active and contemplative in which Gregory finds himself.

biographical narrative, and so it is to the outline of Gregory's narrative and its sixth-century historical context that we now turn.

Biography

Gregory was born in 540 to Gordianus and Sylvia[12] into a tumultuous time of decline.[13] Italy had endured thirty years of war with the Ostrogoths before Belisarius conquered Sicily in 535, and then took Naples to advance through central Italy toward Ravenna, which Belisarius captured from Vitigis in the year of Gregory's birth.[14] Eleven years later, after Totila had recaptured many of Belisarius's conquests, Justinian's long war with Persia came to an end by a treaty. Justinian's focus turned to Gregory's homeland, Italy, which Justinian captured in 565 and celebrated with a well-known inscription declaring the restoration of freedom and happiness to Italy,[15] and, according to Procopius, thereby concluded the Gothic war,[16] leaving Gregory's Rome at least partially destroyed[17] in his twenty-fifth year. Not five years later, much of the Po Valley had fallen to the Lombards, who used raids to capture territory for fortifications and transportation routes.[18] By looting churches, razing cities, killing nobles, and taking greater swaths of territory, the Lombards' strength grew in several areas including Spoleto,[19] whose nearness threatened the city of Rome

12. Anonymous Monk of Whitby, *[Vita Gregorii]. The Earliest Life of Gregory the Great*, ed. and trans. Bertram Colgrave (Lawrence: University of Kansas Press, 1968), 1; for an excellent discussion of Gregory's biographers and their sources, Walter A. Goffart, *The Narrators of Barbarian History, AD 550–800: Jordanes, Gregory of Tours, Bede, and Paul the Deacon* (Princeton: Princeton University Press, 1988), 370–73; for a biographical summary, Robert Gillet, "Grégoire le Grand," in *Dictionnaire de spiritualité: Ascétique et mystique, doctrine et histoire*, ed. Marcel Viller et al. (Paris: G. Beauchesne et ses fils, 1995 [1932]), 872–76.

13. For a fuller historical narrative, see James J. O'Donnell, *The Ruin of the Roman Empire* (New York: Ecco, 2008), 364–84.

14. Gregory's birthdate was in the 540s, but the ages I provide for various stages of Gregory's life are based on a birth year of 540.

15. *CIL* 6.1199; Mark Humphries, "From Emperor to Pope? Ceremonial, Space, and Authority from Constantine to Gregory the Great," in *Religion, Dynasty, and Patronage in Early Christian Rome, 300–900*, ed. Kate Cooper and Julia Hillner (Cambridge: Cambridge University Press, 2007), 54.

16. Procopius, *History of the Wars*, 8.35.36–38; but cf. Agathias, *The Histories*, 1.1; see Mark Humphries, "Italy, AD 425–605," in *The Cambridge Ancient History*, ed. Averil Cameron, Bryan Ward-Perkins, and Michael Whitby (Cambridge: Cambridge University Press, 2001), 534.

17. Procopius, *History of the Wars*, 8.33.14.

18. Neil Christie, *The Lombards: The Ancient Longobards* (Oxford: Blackwell, 1995), 77–81; see also Markus, *Gregory the Great and His World*, 97–111.

19. Christie, *Lombards*, 82–83.

itself just as Gregory achieved the highest imperial office in Rome by 573, as *prafectus urbi*.

That he achieved such a position indicates his lineage, his skills, and his education. He would have received a rigorous classical *paideia*, including grammar, rhetoric, and rehearsing the *personae* and virtues befitting a noble male who would serve in the bureaucracy.[20] While it is a subject of some scholarly dispute how well Gregory knew Greek, his Latin composition was good for its time, and his attitude to learning pagan authors of the classical tradition was favorable, even if such knowledge was subservient to his study of Augustine, Cassian, Cassiodorus, and the Desert Fathers, all of whom seem to have influenced Gregory's formation.[21] The built environment surrounding Gregory testified to the memory of classical Rome, now in neglect and decay from Gordianus's and Sylvia's palatial perch on the Caelian Hill in central Rome,[22] as well as to the vitality of the historical Christian aristocracy, including Jerome's home, a library of the Christian fathers[23] founded by Gregory's relative Pope Agapetus, and magnificent churches.[24] In addition to the memory of Agapetus, others of Gregory's family must have influenced his upbringing, such as his great-great-grandfather, pope Felix III, and his paternal aunts, who were ascetics living in the family's home, well-enough known to Gregory to have had a significant influence on him.[25]

20. W. Martin Bloomer, "Schooling in Persona: Imagination and Subordination in Roman Education," *Classical Antiquity* 16, no. 1 (1997): 57–78.

21. On Gregory's education and attitudes, see Markus, *Gregory the Great and His World*, 34–41; on the important influence of Cassiodorus, see Peter Brown, *The Rise of Western Christendom: Triumph and Diversity, AD 200–1000*, 2nd ed. (Malden, MA: Blackwell, 2003), 196–98; for influences on the *Moralia*, Robert Gillet, "Introduction," in *Grégoire le Grand: Chantilly, Centre culturel Les Fontaines, 15–19 septembre 1982: Actes*, ed. J. Fontaine, R. Gillet, S. Pellistrandi, and Centre national de la recherche scientifique (France) (Paris: Editions du Centre national de la recherche scientifique, 1986), 81–109; on the influence of the Desert Fathers, Petersen, *Dialogues of Gregory the Great*, 151–88.

22. See the eloquent description in Brown, *Rise of Western Christendom*, 198–99; but note the nuanced picture of decline and renewal in Humphries, "From Emperor to Pope?" 45–46.

23. James J. O'Donnell, "The Holiness of Gregory," in *Gregory the Great: A Symposium*, ed. John C. Cavadini, Notre Dame Studies in Theology 2 (Notre Dame: University of Notre Dame Press, 1995), 79 n. 23; Giovanni Battista de Rossi and Giuseppe Gatti, *Inscriptiones Christianae urbis Romae septimo saeculo antiquiores* (Rome: Ex Officina Libraria Pontificia, 1888), 2:28 (inscription 55).

24. Jacques Fontaine, Robert Gillet, Stan Pellistrandi, and Centre national de la recherche scientifique (France), eds., "Les Monuments de Rome à l'èpoque de Grégoire le Grand," in *Grégoire le Grand: Chantilly, Centre culturel Les Fontaines, 15–19 septembre 1982: Actes*, Colloques internationaux du Centre national de la recherche scientifique (Paris: Editions du Centre national de la recherche scientifique, 1986).

25. Gregory's detailed knowledge of his aunts appears in his *Gospel Homily* 38, about the para-

One cannot overestimate the formative influence of these relatives on Gregory as models, at least as much as formal teaching,[26] especially as one aunt, Tarsilla, had prayed so fervently throughout her life that the skin of her elbows and knees had calloused and become tough. "Her dead body bore witness to what her living spirit had been," said Gregory, admiringly.[27] Perhaps in his youth, habits had been introduced that would later recur.

At age thirty-two, though, Gregory's primary habits were civic. To hold office by that time, he likely held lower offices and "climbed the bureaucratic ladder" successfully, leading possibly to *quaestor*, then *praetor urbanus* before he likely became *praefectus urbi Romanae* at age thirty-four.[28] Such offices were open to aristocratic families and, by Gregory's time, seem to have required resolving legal disputes, deciding appeals, handling urban administrative matters, supervising the Roman senate, as well as administrators with responsibilities for grain and water supply, and delivering public speeches.[29] He may have held this office for one year; but by 576, he had taken a turn. Gregory had become a monk.

We will consider Gregory's *metanoia* below, but to finish the *curriculum vitae*: he lived as a monk for about two years, was ordained a deacon in 578, and was drafted from the monastery by Pope Pelagius II to serve as *apocrisarius* to the Byzantine emperor Tiberius II in Constantinople, from 579 until 585, especially to plead for assistance against the Lombards.[30] After moving back to

---

ble of the marriage feast in Matthew 22: see Gregory the Great, *Forty Gospel Homilies*, trans. David Hurst, Cistercian Studies Series 123 (Kalamazoo, MI: Cistercian Publications, 1990), 352–54. The aunts were not nuns but were "pious, leisured ladies" who both equaled men and were "unspoken models of male behavior," according to Brown, *Rise of Western Christendom*, 20.

26. Ville Vuolanto, "Elite Children, Socialization, and Agency in the Late Roman World," in *The Oxford Handbook of Late Antiquity*, ed. Scott Fitzgerald Johnson (Oxford and New York: Oxford University Press, 2012), 583, 590–92.

27. Gregory the Great, *Forty Gospel Homilies*, 353.

28. The most concise discussion is John R. C. Martyn, ed. and trans., *The Letters of Gregory the Great*, Mediaeval Sources in Translation 40 (Toronto: Pontifical Institute of Mediaeval Studies, 2004), 1:3, 1:3 n. 13, 1:288 n. 7, which discusses the primary evidence for Gregory's pre-papal offices, i.e., *Ep.* 4.2, with textual variants.

29. On responsibilities, Andreas Gutsfeld, "Praefectus Urbi," in *Brill's New Pauly Encyclopaedia of the Ancient World: Antiquity*, ed. Hubert Cancik and Helmuth Schneider (Leiden: Brill, 2002); William Gurnee Sinnigen, *The Officium of the Urban Prefecture during the Later Roman Empire*, vol. 17, Papers and Monographs of the American Academy in Rome (Rome: American Academy in Rome, 1957), 5–9, 109–14; if Symmachus's role in AD 384 is any indication, see also H. A. Pohlsander, "Victory: The Story of a Statue," *Historia* 18, no. 5 (1969): 594–95.

30. Bernard Bavant, "Le duché byzantin de Rome: Origine, durée et extension géographique," *Mélanges de l'Ecole française de Rome. Moyen-Age, Temps modernes* 91, no. 1 (1979): 53–55; on *apocrisarius*, see Humphries, "From Emperor to Pope?" 55.

his monastery for perhaps five years, Gregory became pope at age fifty, on September 3, 590, an office that he took during a plague[31] and that he served until he died, on March 12, 604, aged sixty-four. He was not uncontroversial,[32] nor perfect,[33] but he is generally thought by modern commentators to have been faithful to the monastic way of life, even to the point of destroying his health.[34]

Letter to Leander

In July 595, nearly five years after he became pope, Gregory sent a letter to his friend Leander, arguably the most important epistle for understanding what he calls his *conversionis gratia*.[35] This letter appears as a cover to the *Moralia in Iob*, Gregory's commentary on Job that he delivered first as lectures through his homilies (*dicta . . . per homilias*).[36] In it, Gregory offers a rare description of his life before becoming pope. The experience he describes occurs when he was in Constantinople representing the pope to the emperor. The "conversion" to which Gregory refers does not seem to be initial belief in Jesus Christ through baptism either as an infant or when he publicly professed faith. Even if he had not been baptized as an infant, his profession would likely have occurred several years earlier.[37]

Narrating this new conversion, then, Gregory says that he met Leander, a Spaniard who became archbishop of Seville, and disclosed to his friend his

---

31. Robert Sallares, "Ecology, Evolution, and Epidemiology of Plague," in *Plague and the End of Antiquity: The Pandemic of 541–750*, ed. Lester K. Little (New York: Cambridge University Press, 2007), 263–64.

32. Gregory is often criticized for supporting the usurping Phocas, the Byzantine emperor who murdered Maurice, with whom Gregory had enjoyed a collegial relationship; see Humphries, "From Emperor to Pope?" 57–58. As the first monk to become pope, he also advocated for the primacy of the monastic life, which was not accepted by clergy in his day: George E. Demacopoulos, *Gregory the Great: Ascetic, Pastor, and First Man of Rome* (Notre Dame: University of Notre Dame Press, 2015), 113–23.

33. Markus, *Gregory the Great and His World*, 131; O'Donnell, "The Holiness of Gregory," 64.

34. Martyn, *Letters of Gregory the Great*, 1:5–6; Carole Ellen Straw, *Gregory the Great: Perfection in Imperfection* (Berkeley: University of California Press, 1988), 184–85. The literature on Gregory I is far more vast than can be discussed here; for a helpful summary, see ibid., 261–66.

35. On this friendship and letter, now see John R. C. Martyn, *Gregory and Leander: An Analysis of the Special Friendship between Pope Gregory the Great and Leander, Archbishop of Seville* (Newcastle upon Tyne: Cambridge Scholars, 2013).

36. Ep. 5.53a appears in Adriaen, *S. Gregorii Magni Moralia in Iob Libri I–X, Ad Leandrum*; with English translation in Martyn, *Letters of Gregory the Great*, 2:379.

37. Andrew Louth, "Fiunt, Non Nascuntur Christiani: Conversion, Community, and Christian Identity in Late Antiquity," in *Being Christian in Late Antiquity*, ed. Carol Harrison, Caroline Humfress, and Isabella Sandwell (Oxford: Oxford University Press, 2014), 113–14.

resistance to becoming a monk, which displeased Gregory about himself (*omne in tuis auribus, quod mihi de me displacebat*). Specifically, he had delayed his "grace of conversion" (*conversionis gratiam*) and supposed it to be better to wear secular clothing (*saeculari habitu contegi melius putavi*), even though he had been inspired by a desire for heaven (*et postquam coelesti sum desiderio afflatus*) and though what he was seeking about a love for eternity (*de aeternitatis amore quid quaererem*) was already being revealed to him (*aperiebatur mihi iam*). Despite his desire and love being awakened and revealed, he still found that an ingrained habit was preventing him or holding him in bondage (*inolta me consuetudo devinxerat*) from changing his way of life or attire (*exteriorem cultum mutarem*). Gregory continues to disclose to Leander, in Constantinople then and again now in his letter of 595, that his mind (*animus*) was forcing him to serve the present world (*praesenti mundo*) and that his worldly concern (*mundi cura*) was building up against him (*contra me . . . succrescere*). He stresses again that he was held back by his mind (*mente retinerer*). He uses dire terms for his earlier life: it was a shipwreck (*naufragio*),[38] and he now emerged naked (*nudus*).

Quae tandem cuncta sollicite fugiens, portum monasterii petii, et relictis quae mundi sunt: "Finally I fled anxiously from all of this and sought the harbor of the monastery." After Gregory's worldly successes and achievements, he retired to the monastery for a life of labor, Bible reading, and prayer, not even to become an abbot. This is the more striking because the monastery, St. Andrew's, is one he founded on the family's Roman estate when his father died.[39] Fleeing indicated or enacted a decisive break with his previously ingrained habit, a change in Gregory's identity.

Two points are important for understanding Gregory's changing identity and the stand he took to disrupt his former habits. First is the importance of friendship. Using personal conversation and remembering the event in this personal letter, Gregory self-disclosed to his friend Leander the displeasure of his own sin, his resistance to grace, and, specifically, his reluctance to seek the repose of the monastery (*quietem monasterii*). Gregory does not refer to any friends supporting him to enter the monastic life. Perhaps seeds planted by his family early in his life—his contemplative aunts, his pious father, memories of other relatives, and a loving, supportive mother—flourished in that premonastic period. But Gregory does refer to the importance of his friends in taking

---

38. For the frequent use of nautical imagery, Martyn, *Letters of Gregory the Great*, 1:106–7.

39. See evidence for the monastery in Guy Ferrari, *Early Roman Monasteries: Notes for the History of the Monasteries and Convents at Rome from the V through the X Century*, Studi di Antichità Cristiana 23 (Vatican City: Pontificio Istituto di archeologia cristiana, 1957), 138–51.

the life of contemplation with him when he was again pressed into service as a priest (*altaris ministerium, curae pastoralis*). His contemplative habits were not self-willed or self-dependent. Rather, his community of brotherly friends went with him (*ubi me scilicet multi ex monasterio fratres mei*). He was then able to follow his friends' example in prayer (*exemplo ad orationis*), which held him fast as a rope secures a boat to an anchor (*anchorae fune restringerer*). So now rather than flee his incessant earthly business (*curis exteriorbus; causarum saecularium incessabili, actus volumina fluctusque fugiebam, mucrone suae occupationis exstinxerat*), he sought his friends' fellowship (*consortium*) and discussed learned reading (*per studiosae lectionis alloquium*), which quickened his compunction (*aspiration compunctionis animabat*). His friends encouraged him to write (*exponere*) about Scripture, particularly in this case, about the biblical book of Job. These studies and daily readings led by Gregory, then, became the *Moralia in Job*.

In addition to friendship, this new way of life that demonstrated Gregory's identity requires recognition of the importance of habit and of innovation. His impediment was an ingrained habit (*inolta consuetudo*), especially, he says, in his mind. His years of earthly cares and burdens, and habits he had adopted to succeed spectacularly in Roman civic life, prevented him from seeking a life of peace in the monastery. The habits he had built were apparently extraordinarily useful to others, because his friends and superiors continually pressed him into service, whether to write meditations on Scripture, to serve as deacon or priest, or to represent the pope in the imperial capital. But then the moment of *metanoia*, of changing direction, was fleeing to the monastery, founding St. Andrew's on the family estate. To that point in his life, Gregory had identified with civic or "external" cares, which imposed a certain shape and disposition on his life. This is *idem*-identity, the sedimentation of habits over time that become one's character. Gregory was dissatisfied with his character, as he disclosed to his friend Leander. So he took a stand, after much anxious struggle, and innovated, which is his *ipse*-identity. The existential breakthrough of *ipse* led to new habits that also then sedimented in his character: friendship, monastic community, prayer, regular divine reading, writing about the senses of Scripture, compunction.

The nature of this new life—often called by modern commentators a "mixed life" because Gregory was now a monk even as he resumed civic and ecclesial duties—is worth much more discussion. First, however, we must see how this pattern of "gracious conversion" from previous habits is elsewhere present in Gregory's corpus, though discussion of each work must be brief.

Conversion in Gregory's Works

Gregory's commentaries and sermons on biblical books describe the various factors involved in forming new habits that reflect gracious conversion.[40] These include human effort, divine help, the preacher of the word of God, and the hands of Christ himself. Gregory is clear that Christ has satisfied God the Father's wrath over human sin.

Gregory's audience usually seems to have been other clergy, though the *Dialogi* and the Gospel homilies seem to have been aimed at a more popular audience, including lay people. But Gregory wrote in an engaging and accessible way, such that he often seems to communicate over his first audience and be relevant to all times.[41]

Pastoral Rule

Published early in Gregory's papacy, the *Regula curae pastoralis* outlines the qualifications for those who care for souls and the ways in which they should live, as well as instructs them on how to personalize the Scriptures for their hearers. In part one, about qualifications, Gregory discusses who should not be allowed to lead, particularly one who allows vice to reign in himself (*in se . . . regnat*) (1.11). The summary Gregory provides in this chapter could serve as a guide to much of his corpus, emphasizing *contemplatio, consuetudo*, and *discretio*. Gregory meditates on the instructions to Aaron in Leviticus 21 about disqualifications for priests, and explains a moral meaning for the physical ailments listed in Leviticus. One is blind, as a Hebrew priest could not be, says Gregory, if he is ignorant of the light of divine contemplation (*supernae contemplationis lumen ignorat*), and lame if he cannot keep the perfect way of life he sees (*vitae viam perfecte non ualet tenere quam videt*) because of weak or unstable habits (*fluxa consuetudo*). This certainly fits Gregory's earlier admonition that an unqualified person does not practice (*non opere*) what he preaches or studies (1.2). That person runs the risk of misleading his hearers, earning Jesus's warning in Matthew 18 about having a millstone tied around his neck and being cast into the sea because of his worldly character (*exteriori habitu*). Here

---

40. For a systematic, concise overview of the works, see Gillet, "Grégoire le Grand," 876–81; a more systematic, fulsome interpretation of contemplation and action than can be provided here can be found in Straw, *Gregory the Great,* 128–45, 213–35; G. R. Evans, *The Thought of Gregory the Great,* Cambridge Studies in Medieval Life and Thought (Cambridge: Cambridge University Press, 1986), 105–11.

41. For Gregory's audience, O'Donnell, "The Holiness of Gregory," 68–69, 79 n. 26.

Gregory emphasizes the importance of contemplation and developing stable habits based on what one contemplates and then teaches in a personalized way for one's audience.

Moralia in Job

Gregory's letter to Leander that introduces his commentary on Job (*Moralia in Job*), discussed above, includes in microcosm what Gregory explicates throughout the rest of that work. Gregory teaches that Holy Scripture is a mirror (*speculum*) that reveals to the eyes of our mind (*mentis oculis*) our ugliness and beauty (2.1). He explicates how sin dims the mind: "The blindness of the mind engendered by the habit of sin is a frequent theme of the Moralia,"[42] according to Matthew Baasten. Commenting on Job 36:16, Gregory reflects on the meaning of the promise that God will bring Job from a narrow opening (*ore angusto*) to the broadest (*latissime*) one. The narrow opening is made narrow or inescapable by oppressive evil habit (*ab opprimente mala consuetudine exsurgere velle*) that one wishes to rise from, but is not able to (*nec posse, Moral.* 26.66), despite heavenly desire (*desiderio ad superna*). It is only when a soul, by the hand of grace (*manu gratiae*), overcomes his difficulties (*victis difficultatibus*) that he can complete the good works he desires (*opera bona perficit quae concupiscit*).

Doing this requires one to break from common habits to which people are given over (*populi . . . qui quasi vulgari consuetudini dediti, Moral.* 26.77). Gregory meditates on the moral sense of Job 36, noting in *Moral.* 26.79 how the human mind is characterized by innumerable motions (*innumeris motibus*) and fluid change (*fluxa mutabilitate*), unable to focus on that which it ought. But in contemplation of the creator (*in contemplatione creatoris, Moral.* 26.80) one always has stability of mind (*semper mentis stabilitate*) and unity (*unitati*), and deviations from this stability are addressed by collecting (*colligant*) one's mind efficiently (*sparsam mentem*).

Gregory taught that a busy person would practice a contemplative active life by creating a quiet place in his heart. Reflecting on Moses's self-exile in the desert after killing an Egyptian and then becoming Israel's leader, he notes that Moses ascended Mount Sinai to receive God's will as his law, thereby finding a hiding place from the tumult of external things and an entry point to internal things (*interna penetret, ab externis tumultibus occul-*

---

42. Matthew Baasten, *Pride according to Gregory the Great: A Study of the Moralia*, Studies in the Bible and Early Christianity 7 (Lewiston, NY: Mellen Press, 1986), 71.

tatur).[43] Similarly, those who must be active always take refuge in the secrets of their heart (*semper ad cordis secreta refugiunt*).[44] Like Moses entering the tabernacle, the active person leaves the crowd, puts aside the noise of the outward world (*exteriorum tumultibus*), and enters into the secret place of the mind (*secretum mentis intrare*). This is not a retreat of the person with himself, but a consultation with God (*ibi enim Dominus consulitur*) where one hears internally and silently, and then makes one's contemplations known to the world through one's behavior (*agentes innotescunt*). Gregory believed that good leaders pursue this habit daily (*quotidie*) as they are faced with uncertainties (*res dubias*).

The cross-pressures of the rational Enlightenment and the Romantic Enlightenment,[45] the pitched battle between relativism and fundamentalism,[46] the disruptive effects of technology and globalization, these destabilize and create opportunities in the daily lives of late modern people of the North Atlantic world—*res dubias* indeed, and in more far more complex ways than Gregory envisaged. In view of these realities, Gregory's diagnosis and prescription of taking rest from the pressures of the world so as to perceive in a lively way inward matters (*vivacious interna cognosco*) would repay sustained, purposeful reflection.

On Scripture: Gospels, Song of Songs, Ezekiel

In his *Homiliae in Evangelia* (*Homilies on the Gospels*),[47] Homily 5, Gregory takes Matthew 4:18–22 as his text, in which Jesus calls his first disciples, Simon and Andrew. The calling of Jesus, now ascended to heaven, is an admonition to conversion (*de conversione nos admonet*). Despite the fact that the first apostles had seen no miracles nor received any threat of hell, at one command of the Lord (*unum Domini praeceptum*), "they forgot everything they seemed to possess" (*hoc quod possidere uidebantur obliti sunt*).[48] Gregory exhorts his hearers

---

43. Adalbert-G. Hamman and J.-P. Migne, eds., *Patrologiae cursus completus: Series latina* (PL) 76: *Sancti Gregorii Papae I* (Paris: apud Garnier fratres, 1857), 33.37.

44. Ibid., 33.38.

45. Charles Taylor, *Sources of the Self: The Making of the Modern Identity* (Cambridge: Harvard University Press, 1992).

46. James Davison Hunter, "Fundamentalism and Relativism Together: Reflections on Genealogy," in *Between Relativism and Fundamentalism: Religious Resources for a Middle Position*, ed. Peter L. Berger (Grand Rapids: Eerdmans, 2010).

47. See the introduction by Hurst in Gregory the Great, *Forty Gospel Homilies*, 1–4.

48. The translation is the very good one in ibid., 10, which appears as Homily 2.

not only to give up their possessions, but their desires (*desideriis renuntiatis*), and to offer God their heart (*oblatione cordis*) and good will (*uolantate bona*). He embellishes his meaning of good will:

> to experience fear for the adversities of another as if they were our own, to give thanks for a neighbor's prosperity as for our own advancement, to believe another's loss is our own, to count another's gain our own, to love a friend not in the world but in God, to bear even with an enemy by loving him, to do to no one what you do not wish to suffer yourself, to deny no one what you rightly desire for yourself, to choose to help a neighbor in need not only to the extent of your ability but even to assist him beyond your means. What is richer and more substantial than this whole burnt offering, when what the soul is offering to God on the altar of its heart is a sacrifice of itself?

This beautiful exposition of self-sacrificing love is the crux of contemplation and action as new habits in an active life, the identification of one's desires and one's will with one's neighbor through habitual service.

In his *Commentary on the Song of Songs* (*Expositio in Canticum Cantico-rum*),[49] Gregory discusses the need for divine help to pursue a life of *contemplationis*. Gregory arrives at Song of Songs 1:4: "*Trahe me*, draw me . . ." Here he sees the contemplative's will to be united with Christ. Human nature wants to follow God (*natura humana sequi deum uult*),[50] but "overcome by a habit of weakness, it is incapable of following as it should" (*infirmitatis consuetudine superata, sicut debet, sequi non praeulet*).[51] Thus, there is one thing in us that urges us forward and another that draws us back (*aliud est in nobis quod nos incitat, aliud quod gravat*). So Gregory urges his reader to pray *trahe me* because it indicates that one desires to be devoted to Christ, but requires divine help to do that which his frail human will is incapable of doing.

In one of his sermons on Ezekiel (*Homiliae in Ezechielem*), Homily 3, Gregory meditates on the meaning of the image in Ezekiel 1, of a bronze winged figure. The winged figure has human hands under its wings, and Gregory takes these two images—wings and hands—to correspond to the contemplative and

---

49. See the introduction in Mark DelCogliano, *Gregory the Great on the Song of Songs*, Cistercian Studies Series 244 (Collegeville, MN: Liturgical Press, 2012).

50. Gregory I, *Sanctus Gregorius Magnus In Canticum canticorum, In librum primum Regum*, 44:1.24; PL 79, 482.

51. DelCogliano, *Gregory the Great on the Song of Songs*, 126–27; cf. Denys Turner, *Eros and Allegory: Medieval Exegesis of the Song of Songs*, Cistercian Studies Series 156 (Kalamazoo, MI, and Spencer, MA: Cistercian Publications, 1995), 232, where *infirmitatis consuetudine* is rendered "acquired weakness."

the active. Gregory sees the hearts of a preacher's hearers as being inflamed (*eos quos in corde tetigerint incendunt*)[52] with love for God (*Dei amore*) such that one who intends to continue in the active life (*in activa disposuit vita perdurare*) takes the preacher's teaching about the words of the ancient fathers (*antiquorum patrum*) and the sharpness of the word (*uerbi acumine*) through all he does (*per omne quod agit*).

Building upon the importance of preaching, Gregory emphasizes two further images related to conversion to the contemplative identity. He takes one from Exodus 21:6, of a slave's ear being pierced by an awl. He interprets the piercing as occurring when one's mind (*mens*) is shocked (*percutitur*) by the acuteness of the fear of God (*timoris Dei subtilitate*), presumably in preaching. That person is a slave to all, serving all through his active life (*per activam vitam hominibus servire*), and he experiences through the contemplative life a freedom of mind (*libertatem mentis*). Gregory meditates on how this is possible by means of another image, one he takes from his Ezekiel text: of the hand of a man under the wings of the creature that appears to Ezekiel. Whereas earlier Gregory had taken the hands to indicate the active life and the wings to mean the contemplative, here Gregory interprets the hands as those of Christ our Savior (*Redemptor noster*). Through the incarnation of the Word (*Verbum*), Christ's hand upholds our hearts (*manus corda nostra portat*) and lifts us in contemplation (*contemplatione nos sublevat*).

Hence, while Gregory takes a stand, making a break with his former identity and the habits of an exclusively active life, he does not do so, nor does he advocate that his readers do so, through their own self-generated effort. Gregory far predates the therapeutic quest and an understanding of character as various comportments of will. Rather, he emphasizes the need for human decision and will, but with God's help through prayer, by hearing the word of God through the preacher, and by the hands of Christ the Savior.

Friendship between *Vita activa* and *Vita contemplativa* in Gregory's Letters

So far, we have cursorily surveyed Gregory's explanations of gracious conversion in his literary works, especially as an overcoming of former habits in taking a stand in a new identity. We have yet to see how he discourses about living out one's new identity in his daily life of responsibilities. The most reliable evidence for this is his corpus of letters, the *Registrum Epistularum*. These 854 letters appear in 14 books, beginning from September 590, when Gregory became

---

52. The text discussed here is quoted from PL 76, 807–812.

pope. All bear Gregory's name, if they were not all written by him personally but produced by his office, and they address matters of administrative, political, economic, and theological importance, a trove of documentary evidence for historians of Late Antiquity.[53] Rather than providing theological treatises or philosophical reflections, the letters show us Gregory's *vita activa*, addressing bishops, emperors, political officials, and the like, about his concerns and responses.

At the very least, the letters reveal that Gregory stands against convention, when one's mind is not brought into harmony with one's faith. For example, he writes to the empress Constantia in 595 requesting her intervention in matters affecting Christians (*Ep.* 5.41).[54] Pagans on Sardinia had been converted beginning in the previous year. But they were continuing to pay a tax that was required after sacrificing to idols, even after they had been baptized (*post baptismum*), which they had been accustomed (*consuervant*) to paying. The solution, Gregory suggested, was to have the judge stop requesting the tax be paid. Simply following the Sardinian habits, continuing to pay the tax without protest, was not acceptable: a stand should be taken.

For Gregory, aliveness exists in the dialectic between action and contemplation. The two patterns of life are inseparable, and they are united by friendship. As his epistolary preface to the *Moralia* narrated, friendship provides the context in which disgust toward his own habits and gracious conversion toward his Lord are disclosed. Moreover, a community of friends provides the context in which Gregory's newly discovered contemplative life was put into action when that community traveled with him to his Constantinopolitan assignment. Within that context, habits were of great importance: breaking sinful habits that threaten one's salvation and union with Christ, and establishing new contemplative habits that can be applied in a life of action. This process involves innovation and sedimentation, *ipse* and *idem*, the uniqueness of the self taking a stand in a moment, and the constancy of habit oriented toward virtue over a lifetime. Rather than a retreat from the burdens of responsibility, Gregory sees contemplation as a mode of active life, the highest form of aliveness.[55]

In letters of friendship, the connection between active and contemplative, internal and external, is made concrete. A letter early in his papacy (591) to his friend Andrew, an advisor to the emperor Maurice, affirms Gregory's love

53. See the excellent English translation and introduction now provided by Martyn, *Letters of Gregory the Great*, 1:15–116, a superb introduction covering historical context and philological issues; on the letters' destinations, Markus, *Gregory the Great and His World*, 206–8.

54. PL 77, 5.41; in Martyn, *Letters of Gregory the Great*, 2:354; the translation appears as letter 38 in book 5.

55. Petersen, *Dialogues of Gregory the Great*, 69–73.

(*charitate*) for his friend and remembers his friend's goodness (*bona*). Gregory asks Andrew—if he loves (*diligitis*) him—to mourn (*plangite*) for him because his ecclesiastical burdens seem to separate him from the love of God (*ab amore Dei me videam esse separatum*). Gregory laments his position continually (*incessanter defleo*) and pleads for Andrew's prayers on his behalf (*pro me Dominum exoretis rogo*).[56] Here Gregory laments his separation from contemplating God while being active in his vocation, so he seeks support and aid from his friend.

In another letter, to Leander who was bishop of Spain and a friend from his circle of brothers in Constantinople, Gregory begs forgiveness for neglecting Leander's letters and even for the tone of the letter he was then composing, for he seemed to communicate indifference to his beloved friend (*negligenter loquor, quem vehementer diligo*). Gregory likens himself to a ship in fierce seas, with waves overtaking him on all sides, so that he is unsettled (*turbatus cogor*). Furthermore, he confesses that, "through my negligence, a bilge water of vices is rising" (*sentio quod negligente me crescit sentina vitiorum*). Here the very situation of an unstable mind that Gregory warns of in his teaching is his own situation; he writes based on his own sufferings. As the "winds of duties blow against him," Gregory's response is again to plead with his friend for prayer (*orationis*) so that they might both stand strong in their troubles.[57] After this self-disclosure and plea, Gregory turns to routine ecclesiastical issues, his *vita activa*, in the rest of his letter. Gregory's affection and attachment to Leander is clear in the letter's conclusion, and he closes finally with a prayer that God would keep his friend safely.

While the level of intimacy expressed to his very close friend Leander is not a surprise, Gregory expressed much kind regard and warmth to his correspondents[58] as an expression of the love of God he contemplated in moments of quiet prayer.[59] One letter, in 596 to the bishop of Carthage, recalls Christ's incarnation and sacrifice and exhorts Dominic not only to praise divine love but also to confess it with a hand (*fateamur manu*) by showing compassion in action.[60] Their action includes sustaining friendship with each other, loving their enemies, and loving those under their pastoral care (*pastoralis curae*).

---

56. PL 77, 1.30; Martyn, *Letters of Gregory the Great*, 1:150 (1.29).

57. Martyn, *Letters of Gregory the Great*, 1:160 (1.41), 160–61 n. 223.

58. See, e.g., Martyn, *Letters of Gregory the Great*, 1:265–66 (3.47), 266–67 (3.48), 318–19 (4.38); 2:462 (7.8); 3:790 (11.44), 806 (12.1).

59. Martyn, *Letters of Gregory the Great*, 1:286 (3.65). This letter reveals the connection between the love that Gregory knew in contemplation and gratitude to God, who "fills the innermost parts of your mind with the grace of his love." See also Martyn, *Letters of Gregory the Great*, 2:416 (6.19).

60. Cf. Martyn, *Letters of Gregory the Great*, 2:683–88 (9.219).

From these concerns flows an exhortation to be engaged in holy works (*piis versemur operibus*) and to be rich in virtues (*virtutibus polleamus*), providing examples (*praebeamus exempla*) to their flock (*gregi*). Gregory calls his friend to the earthly work he has been given to do, yet also to leave earthly affairs (*relinquentes terrena negotia*) and to long for heavenly ones (*coelestibus anhelemus*). In a characteristic expression, he exhorts himself and Dominic not to let their "mind flow away in the dissipation of the secular [*mens nostra in saeculari varietate non diffluat*], but to hasten and flow on to just one end, which David considered with amazing sweetness: 'One thing have I desired of the Lord; that will I seek after: that I may dwell in the house of the Lord all the days of my life' (Ps. 26 [27]:4)."[61] Gregory's definition of friendship is not the utilitarian type of the Greco-Roman world. Rather, the friend is the guardian of one's soul.[62]

We may note here some growth, whereas initially Gregory's correspondence to his friends expresses great lament for his divided will and dissolute mind, for which he needs his friends' prayer, it flowers some years later into exhortation to his friends to seek contemplative prayer intermixed with their daily duties,[63] including a letter to the praetorian prefect of Africa whose request for the *Moralia*, which would refocus the prefect when distracted by secular cares, was redirected to Augustine's works instead of Gregory's own.[64] Such growth of character was due to developing new habits of contemplation, of action, and of the life of friendships that held together an identity with the two ways of life in service to the neighbor that Gregory could scarcely resist because of his *conversionis gratia*.

---

61. The translation is from Martyn, *Letters of Gregory the Great*, 2:447–48 (6.63); PL 77, 847–48 (6.64).

62. Brian Patrick McGuire, *Friendship & Community* (Ithaca, NY: Cornell University Press, 2010), xv; PL 76, 1207 (*Hom. Ezech.* 27.4). Gregory's full definition there is "Amicus enim quasi animi custos vocatur."

63. Though letters of distress and prayer requests are never entirely unnecessary: Martyn, *Letters of Gregory the Great*, 2:500 (8.2), with its request of prayers for his heart, mind, and eternal peace (PL 77, 907 [8.2]).

64. Martyn, *Letters of Gregory the Great*, 3:726 (10.16).

Chapter 15

Captives in Late Antiquity:
Christian Identity under Foreign Rule

ANDREA STERK

"God chose what is weak in the world to shame the strong; God chose
what is low and despised in the world, things that are not, to reduce to
nothing things that are."

—1 Corinthians 1:27–28

The writing of Christian history, both premodern and modern, is changing focus: from great geographic centers, like Rome and Constantinople, to regions
once considered peripheral; and from the thought of great theologians and bishops to the lived experience of everyday believers.[1] To be sure, we know a great
deal about the theological debates of the patristic era, the age of the great fathers
of the church, and, increasingly, about the lives of a few outstanding women have
come into focus. Yet the day-to-day experiences of the mass of Christians in late
antiquity, both men and women, continue to elude us; much less do we know
about those who lived on the peripheries or beyond the frontiers of the Roman
Empire. While most of the chapters in this volume examine the lives and thought
of well-known Christians who have shaped the church and society through their
writings, the individuals and groups I discuss in this essay were neither famous
leaders nor theologians. Rather, they were mostly anonymous captives, nameless
victims amid massive population movements, part of a great "centrifugal force"
that characterized the Eurasian world in late antiquity.[2] For this was an era of

1. The seven-volume series edited by Denis R. Janz, *A People's History of Christianity* (Minneapolis: Augsburg Fortress, 2014) provides a good example of this shift in historiography.
2. Glen Bowersock, "Centrifugal Force in Late Antique Historiography," in Richard Lim and
Carol Straw, eds., *The Past Before Us: The Challenge of Historiographies of Late Antiquity* (Turnhout:
Brepols, 2004), 19–23.

dislocation, an age of slavery, captivity, deportation, and human trafficking that dwarfs these realities today.[3]

These men and women have in most cases left no writings of their own, but we catch glimpses of their lives through brief accounts in hagiographical as well as historical sources. Though the sources pose interpretive challenges and must be used with caution, we have abundant evidence of Christian prisoners of war, deportees, refugees, and slaves, including whole communities of captives, who practiced their faith under foreign regimes or oppressive masters. Despite considerable study of the church's role vis-à-vis captives and slaves in late antiquity,[4] there has been exceedingly little treatment of those Christians who actually lived as captives under foreign rule. Drawing from Syriac and Arabic as well as Greek and Latin sources, I hope to shed light on the lives of Christian captives on or beyond the eastern frontiers of the Roman Empire. My focus will be the ways in which they maintained, cultivated, and even spread their faith in diverse contexts of captivity and oppression.

Captive Communities among the Persians

From the time of the Babylonian exile, slavery and mass deportation were a customary feature of warfare in the ancient Near East. In late antiquity both Romans and barbarians regularly enslaved their captives, but the Sasanid Persians, rulers of the last great Iranian Empire before the rise of Islam, were especially known for the deportation and resettlement of entire cities, armies, and civilians in Persian territory.[5] As the trilingual inscription *Res Gestae Divi Saporis* proclaims regarding a campaign of the Iranian shah, Shapur I (reigned ca. 240–270): "We led away into captivity men from the Empire of the Romans, non-Iranians, and settled them into our Empire of Iran, in Persia, in Parthia, in Susiana and in Assuristan [Iraq]."[6] The first of many similar deportations

3. Kyle Harper, *Slavery in the Late Roman World, AD 275–425* (New York: Cambridge University Press, 2011), especially chapter 2, "The Endless River" (a quote from a letter of Augustine on the horrors of the slave trade).

4. See, for example, Carolyn Osiek, "The Ransom of Captives: Evolution of a Tradition," *Harvard Theological Review* 74:4 (1981): 365–86.

5. Foundational on this topic is Samuel N. C. Lieu, "Captives, Refugees, and Exiles: A Study of Cross-Frontier Civilian Movements and Contacts between Rome and Persia from Valerian and Jovian," in *The Defence of the Roman and Byzantine East*, vol. 2, ed. P. Freeman and D. Kennedy (Oxford: BAR International Editions, 1986), 475–505.

6. Translated in M. H. Dodgeon and S. N. C. Lieu, *The Roman Eastern Frontier and the Persian Wars: A Documentary History* (New York: Routledge, 1991), 57.

during the Sasanid era, the movement of whole populations of captives entailed tremendous human misery. According to the Arabic *Chronicle of Seert*, also known as the Nestorian Chronicle, those who survived the arduous journey from Roman cities like Antioch, Nisibis, and Carrhae were spread out and settled in newly founded or restored cities in sgy Eranshahr (Iran). Among the deportees were not only soldiers, but builders, engineers, artists, craftsmen, doctors, and scholars who were needed for the shah's major construction projects and formed "the professional and artisan core" for newly founded cities like Gandeshapur and Bishapur.[7] Later Roman deportees under Shapur II were especially involved in the development of glass, metalwork, and textile industries, and succeeding centuries saw similar deportations and resettlement of Roman captives in Persia.[8]

In each of these deportations Christians comprised a substantial number of those captured and resettled, adding to the Sasanians' already "vibrant native Christian populations."[9] Persian rulers often kept families together and community structures intact, recreating whole towns and cities that were named in honor of the shah. They even transplanted ecclesiastical structures, as priests and bishops along with their flocks were numbered among the deportees. On the deportation from Antioch under Shapur I, the *Chronicle of Seert* reports that "Christians also multiplied in Persia, building churches and monasteries. Their number included priests who had been taken prisoner at Antioch. They colonized Gundeshapur and elected Azdaq of Antioch as their bishop, owing to Demetri(an)us, the patriarch of Antioch, having fallen ill and died of sorrow."[10] Some have suggested the number of Christians among Shapur's deportees has

---

7. Lieu, "Captives," 478–79. Lieu draws primarily from the medieval Arabic *Chronicle of Seert*, ed. and trans. Addai Scher, *Histoire nestorienne (Chronique de Séert)*, Patrologia Orientalis 4.3, 5.2, 7.2, and 13.4 (Turnhout: Brepols, 1908, 1909, 1910, 1918). On this important chronicle, composed in the tenth century largely based on earlier Syriac Christian sources, see Philip Wood, *The Chronicle of Seert: Christian Imagination in Late Antique Iraq* (Oxford: Oxford University Press, 2013).

8. See Michael G. Morony, "Population Transfers between Sasanian Iran and the Byzantine Empire," in *Convegno internazionale la Persia e Bisanzio (Roma, 14–18 ottobre 2002)* (Rome: Academic Nazionale dei Lincei, 2004), 161–79, and Beate Dignas and Englebert Winter, *Rome and Persia in Late Antiquity: Neighbors and Rivals* (Cambridge: Cambridge University Press, 2007), 254–63; for a survey of the deportations according to period, Erich Kettenhoffen, "Deportations, ii," in *Encylopaedia Iranica* VII/3, 297–308; available online at: http://www.iranicaonline.org /articles/deportations#pt2.

9. Matthew P. Canepa, *Two Eyes of the Earth: Art and Ritual of Kingship between Rome and Sasanian Iran* (Berkeley: University of California Press, 2010), 28.

10. *Chronicle of Seert* 2, Patrologia Orientalis 4, 220–21; Dodgeon and Lieu, 297. The *Chronicle*'s reference to "monasteries" in the third century is anachronistic and one example of the challenges of using this source. Philip Wood's recent work (n. 7) is a helpful guide.

been exaggerated. Yet their number certainly multiplied in exile, and the "captivity," as the Christian community called itself, played a critical role in the spread of Christianity in Persia.[11] Writing in Persian-controlled Armenia, the historian Elishe also testifies to the influence of Christians under Shapur I, emphasizing their faithful service to the shahanshah.[12] Though we know very little about individual Christians in this earliest phase of Sasanian deportation, a few men and women stand out among the captives raised in exile. The *Martyrdom of Candida*, for example, introduces a young Christian woman in the later third century "who belonged to those deported from Roman territory" and was "raised as a Christian by her parents."[13] Because of her great beauty Candida was taken as one of the king's wives; but the jealousy of the other royal wives eventually led to her downfall, and she was persecuted, tortured, and martyred when she refused to apostasize.

Though most deported Roman captives in the third and early fourth centuries would have certainly been pagans, many converted en route to their new land through the influence of the Christian community-in-exile. Regarded as the leader of the entire captive community, the bishop sustained morale on the long journey south such that "those who were not Christians when taken captive would probably have become so in the course of the march."[14] The Syriac "Martyrdom of the Captives" refers to the important role of Bishop Heliodorus, who numbered among the nine thousand deported prisoners following Shapur II's capture of Bezabde.[15] He died during the journey, but not without first consecrating a priest as his replacement. Following the death of Heliodorus, the captives "began to come together as one congregation and to recite psalms in choirs," which united the prisoners but also incited hostility and shortly thereafter persecution from the Zoroastrian mobed (priest).[16] It ultimately led to the martyrdom of 275 Christian captives including many

11. On Christianity in Persia see S. P. Brock, "Christians in the Sasanian Empire: A Case of Divided Loyalties," in S. Mews, ed., *Religion and National Identity* (Oxford: Blackwell, 1982), 1–18. Morony, "Population Transfers,"167–69, critiques the exaggerated numbers of Christians deported under Shapur I; yet he concurs with Lieu's interpretation of the *Chronicle* regarding the spread of Christianity in exile.

12. Elishe, *History of Vardan and the Armenian War*, trans. and commentary by Robert W. Thomson (Cambridge: Harvard University Press, 1982), 97.

13. For a translation of the Syriac account of the martyrdom of Candida see Sebastian Brock, "A Martyr at the Sasanid Court under Vahran II: Candida," *Analecta Bollandiana* 96/2 (1978): 167–81.

14. Lieu, "Captives," 497.

15. Bedjan, *Acta Martyrum et Sanctorum Syriace* 2.316–24; English translation in Dodgeon and Lieu, *The Roman Eastern Frontier*, vol. 1, 215–19.

16. Dodgeon and Lieu, *The Roman Eastern Frontier*, vol. 1, 215.

"daughters of the Covenant," female ascetics who refused to renounce their worship of Christ.

Under Shapur II (309–379), considerably less tolerant than his great grandfather, martyrdom accounts reveal the continuing strength of the Christian "captivity" and the important social and economic roles these captives and their descendants played in Sasanian Iran. The *Acts of Pusai* recounts the life and martyrdom of the king's "chief craftsman," a Christian descended from Roman prisoners whom Shapur I had deported and resettled in Bishapur. Introducing Pusai, the son of a Roman father and a Persian mother,[17] the author also describes Shapur II's failed plans regarding the captives:

> [Pusai] took a Persian from the city, converted her, baptized his children, and brought them up in and taught them Christianity. When Shapur had built the city of Karka de Ladan and settled there captives from various places, he also thought of bringing and settling about thirty families apiece from each of the ethnic groups living in the various cities of his empire among them, so that as a result of inter-marriage, the captives would be bound by family ties and affection, and it would therefore not be easy for them to flee gradually back to their homeland. This was Shapur's clever plan; but God in his mercy used it to the good, so that through this mixing of those deported with the pagans, the latter were caught in the recognition of truth and converted to knowledge of the faith.[18]

Pusai and his family were among those captives moved from Bishapur to Karka, where the skilled craftsman, a master weaver and embroiderer, won the favor of the King of Kings. He was soon appointed head of the royal workshop next to the palace with supervisory responsibility over similar establishments in other Persian cities in which Christian artisans worked for "the material improvement of the communities in which they settled."[19] Pusai eventually ran afoul of the mobeds, the Zoroastrian religious establishment, who convinced the shah of his servant's disloyalty. Shapur himself pleaded with the mobeds to bring Pusai to

17. Basing his idea on the Iranian name, Lieu, "Captives," 484, suggests that he was born in Persia to parents captured by Shapur I. He dates his martyrdom ca. 341.

18. *Acta Martyrum et Sanctorum Syriace* 2.208–9: Dodgeon and Lieu, *The Roman Eastern Frontier*, vol. 1, 163. For further discussion of Pusai and Shapur's strategy as reflected in this passage see Richard Payne, *A State of Mixture: Christians, Zoroastrians, and Iranian Political Culture in Late Antiquity* (Berkeley: University of California Press, 2015), 65–66; on the role of several other of Shapur II's deportees see Lieu, "Captives," 483–87.

19. Lieu, "Captives," 486. On the importance of the deportees for the development of the textile industry, see also Morony, "Population Transfers," 170.

reason, explaining that "he is one of the most useful men of my kingdom," but the shah's chief craftsman was ultimately put to death.[20] The next day, Pusai's daughter Martha, after refusing the mobed's offer either to renounce her faith or to marry, was also martyred at the king's order.[21] Despite their distinctive identity as captives, in the trial before their martyrdom both Pusai and Martha identified themselves not as captives but as Christians or servants of the living God.[22]

Another prominent member of the captivity under Shapur II was the ascetic physician Bar Shabba, whose story is narrated in the *Chronicle of Seert*.[23] Having mastered both Syriac and Persian after his deportation, the young doctor gained a reputation as a healer and in this way came to the attention of the shahanshah. He not only healed one of the shah's concubines but also cured his sister, Sirwan, after which she became a devout Christian. Rather than put her to death for conversion from Zoroastrianism to Christianity, the shah exiled his sister to central Asia, giving her in marriage to the provincial governor of Merv. Bar Shabba was later permitted to visit Sirwan in Merv, where he consecrated a church, was himself eventually ordained bishop of Merv, and effectively evangelized the region of Khorasan, making disciples in all the villages. Although she was not allowed to bring up her son as a Christian, Sirwan made certain that he would be sympathetic to the Christian cause.[24] Bar Shabba himself, a deported ascetic doctor who established his reputation through his medical expertise in the service of Shapur II, is one of the most remarkable examples of the social and religious impact of Christian captives in the Iranian Empire and even beyond the Persian frontiers.

Indeed in the fourth century Christian captives seem to have particularly flourished under their Iranian overlords even amid intense persecution. In his narration of a similar persecution during the reign of Yazdegard II

20. *Acta Martyrum et Sanctorum Syriace* 2.211; cited in Alan V. Williams, "Zoroastrians and Christians in Sasanian Iran," *Bulletin of the John Rylands University Library* 78:3 (1996), 50.

21. The account of the martyrdom of Martha is translated in *Holy Women of the Syrian Orient,* ed. and trans. Sebastian P. Brock and Susan Ashbrook Harvey (Berkeley: University of California Press, 1987), 67-73.

22. For further discussion of Pusai and the coincidence of religion and "national" identity for Christians in Sasanian Iran, see Brock, "Divided Loyalties," 12–18.

23. Patrologia Orientalis 5, 253–58. See also Sebastian P. Brock, "Bar Shabba/Mar Shabbay, First Bishop of Merv," in *Syrisches Christentum weltweit: Studien zur syrischen Kirchengeshichte,* ed. Martin Tamcker, Wolfgang Schwaigert, and Egbert Schlarb (Münster: Lit, 1995), 190–201.

24. Lieu, "Captives," 486–87, also notes that the missionary work may not have begun in earnest until after the death of Shapur II. See also Christelle Jullien and Florence Jullien, *Apôtres des confins: Processus missionaires chrétiens dans l'empire Iranien,* Res Orientales 15 (Bures-sur-Yvettes: Groupe pour l'Étude de la Civilisation du Moyen-Orient, 2002), 177.

(438–457), the Armenian historian Elishe included a letter from the chief Magian priest describing the influence of earlier Christians under the reign of the shah's ancestor Shapur II. The magus emphasizes their relentless expansion, their inexplicable wealth, lavished especially on the building and decoration of churches, and their endurance in the face of persecution. In this light, he counsels against continued persecution in the present for, he recalls, "the more he [Shapur] wished to restrain and prevent them the more they increased and expanded."[25] The deportation of Roman captives in Persia declined in the fifth century, though Christian communities continued to exist despite periods of intensified persecution.[26] They distinguished themselves as "captives," a term used interchangeably with "Christians" in East Syrian hagiography, in order to affirm their religious difference from Persian Zoroastrianism; at the same time, however, Christian captives increasingly identified with the indigenous people of the region in which they lived and worked.[27] Deportation became important again in the sixth and early seventh centuries, largely due to the resumption of Sasanian economic activities, especially during the reign of Khusau I.[28] Following sieges and gruesome massacres, whole Roman civilian populations were deported, new cities were built by the shahs, and captives were put to work in agricultural labor or as skilled craftsmen and artisans. Christian sources understandably speak of the misery of Christians, and hagiographical texts exalt the great saints and martyrs. Yet throughout late antiquity the mass of captive Christians resettled in the heartland of Iran continued to worship their God, develop their ecclesiastical institutions, serve their communities, and ingratiate themselves with the rulers and the people of Eranshahr.

25. Elishe, *History of Vardan and the Armenian War*, 111.

26. See S. J. McDonough, "A Question of Faith? Persecution and Political Centralization under Yazdgard II (438–457 CE)," in Harold Allen Drake, ed., *Violence in Late Antiquity: Perceptions and Practices* (Burlington, VT: Ashgate), 69–82. McDonough attributes intensified persecution of non-Magians, both Christians of the Church of the East and Armenians as well as Jews in Babylonia, to Yazdgard's centralizing policies, an effort to spread a uniform Magian religious identity among his subjects.

27. Payne dates the prevalence of the term "captives" for Christian communities in the Iranian Empire to the fifth century as part of this complex process of differentiation alongside assimilation. See Payne, *State of Mixture*, 64–72.

28. Morony, "Population Transfers," 171–75. The outbreak of plague in 540 further intensified the shortage of labor. For an overview of deportations in this period see Kettenhoffen, "Deportations, II."

Among the Goths, Arabs, and Huns

While exchanges of captives between Romans and Persians were a product of political relations between the two great late antique empires, other groups took captives for different reasons. Around the time of Shapur I's capture and deportation of Roman citizens to the Iranian Empire, tribes of Goths, called Scythians in the earliest Greek sources, were raiding cities along the eastern frontiers of the Roman Empire. The conversion of the Goths is most often identified with their fourth-century "apostle" and first bishop, but Christianity actually reached the Goths in the third century, and again captives played a key role. The church historian Philostorgius presents the fullest account of their capture and resettlement. During the reign of Emperors Valerian and Gallienus, raiding Goths attacked and plundered Galatia and Cappadocia, taking many captives, including members of the clergy, and transplanting them north of the Danube. Among the prisoners were the forebears of Ulfila, abducted from the village of Sadalgothina in Cappadocia. By living among the barbarians, Philostorgius explains, "the faithful throng of captives . . . converted not a few of them to the faith and brought them over from paganism to Christianity."[29] Similarly, the historian Sozomen emphasizes the virtuous lives and wonderful deeds of these captives that amazed their Gothic captors and led eventually to their conversion and baptism.[30]

We should not imagine, of course, that all Christians remained steadfast in their faith through the harrowing ordeal of invasion and captivity. Describing the Gothic raids in Cappadocia (ca. 260), Bishop Gregory Thaumaturgus laments that not only had houses been pillaged, women raped, and many killed or captured, but some Roman Christians had actually "enrolled among the barbarians . . . forgetting that they were men of Pontus, and Christians." These Christians robbed and plundered fellow Christians, detained captives who had escaped, and collaborated with the enemy to the point of executing prisoners or betraying their own former neighbors.[31] Yet many faithful Christians survived the raids and continued to practice their religion in their new land. Ulfila

---

29. Philostorgius, *Historia ecclesiastica* 2.5.

30. Sozomen, *Historia ecclesiastica* 2.6.

31. Gregory Thaumaturgus, *Canonical Letter*, canon 7, in Peter Heather and John Matthews, *The Goths in the Fourth Century*, Translated Texts for Historians 11 (Liverpool: Liverpool University Press, 1991), 8–9. For a contextualized discussion of Gregory's letter see also Herwig Wolfram, *History of the Goths* (Berkeley: University of California Press, 1998), 49–51. A century later Basil of Caesarea would describe how Cappadocian Christians taken captive by the Isaurians had lapsed and sacrificed to pagan deities. See *Ep.* 217.81 and N. Lenski, "Basil and the Isaurian Uprising of 375," *Phoenix* 53 (1999): 308–29.

himself was a descendant of those captives who had maintained their faith in captivity and played a major role in the Christianization of the Goths in the fourth century. Judging from his name, he was the son of a Gothic father and a mother of Cappadocian descent.[32] Most of these captives had gradually integrated into Gothic society, giving their children Gothic names and, as we may surmise from Ulfila's disciple and biographer, Auxentius, spoke fluent Gothic.[33] An assimilated Gothic descendant of Cappadocian Christians abducted two generations earlier, Ulfila became a leader of the faithful in exile. Ordained bishop of the Goths, he translated the Scriptures into the Gothic language, taught and evangelized, and led a large group of Gothic Christians from persecution in barbarian lands to the safety of Roman soil. From his location just over the frontier he continued to oversee missionary efforts among the Goths. At the same time many other Christians, largely descendants of Roman captives taken in the third century, remained in Gothia, where Christianity continued to spread.[34]

Meanwhile the Saracens, nomadic Arabs who began to cohere in powerful tribal confederations in late antiquity, put pressure on both the Roman and Persian frontiers. A people known for the capture of prisoners, their location on the frontiers placed them in an ideal situation to buy captives from one empire and sell them to the other.[35] To be sure, their main motivation was not political but economic. Some captives were executed, others were ransomed, especially high priced ones, but many were sold into slavery or kept for the labor-intensive work of tending flocks and herds for their Saracen pastoralist masters. Unlike the Persian rulers who often kept captive families together, the Saracens very

32. On Ulfila see Neil McLynn, "Little Wolf in the Big City: Ulfila and His Interpreters," in *Wolf Liebeschuetz Reflected: Essays Presented by Colleagues, Friends, and Pupils*, ed. John Drinkwater and Benet Salway (London: Institute of Classical Studies, 2007), and Hagith Sivan, "Ulfila's Own Conversion," *Harvard Theological Review* 89:4 (1996): 373–86, regarding distortions in the historiography.

33. Auxentius, 33[53] in Heather and Matthews, 140. Best on this whole process is Knut Schäferdiek, "Die Anfänge des Christentums bei den Goten und der sog. gotische Arianismus," *Zeitschrift für Kirchengeschichte* 112; also (2001): 295–310. See also Noel Lenski, "The Gothic Civil War and the Date of the Conversion," *Greek, Roman and Byzantine Studies* (Spring 1995): 76–77 on Christians and ecclesiastical institutions in Gothic society.

34. For Ulfila's continued evangelistic work from his base in the Roman Empire, where the emperor gave the Goths land to settle, see Auxentius 35[58] in Heather and Matthews, 141; Philostorgius 2.5: Amidon, 20–22; Socrates, *Historia ecclesiastica* 4.33.7. See also Lenski, "Gothic Civil War," 77–80 and 82, and Wolfram, 75–76.

35. Noel Lenski, "Captivity and Slavery among the Saracens in Late Antiquity (ca. 250–630 CE)," *Antiquité Tardive* 19 (2011): 237–66. On the earliest uses of the term "Saracens" for Arab nomads, 239 and 243–44.

purposefully separated captured husbands and wives and forced marriages as a strategy to lower the odds of escape.[36]

Some eastern Christian monks cultivated friendly and mutually benefi-cial relations with tribes of Arab nomads, but neither were they exempt from violent attacks involving captivity and enslavement. In fact, several accounts of ascetics or monks captured by Saracens throw light on the whole process of Saracen slave-raiding as well as its reality for Christians. St. Jerome's *Life of Malchus*, deemed historically plausible if not literally true, tells the story of a young Syrian monk taken captive by raiding Arab nomads.[37] He was assigned to a Saracen master who put him to work tending sheep. Malchus lived and dressed as a Saracen, yet managed to retain his monastic way of life, praying continually and singing psalms in the desert. When Malchus was forced by his master to take a wife, a pious Christian woman who had been separated from her husband when they were both captured, the two agreed to live together in chastity and eventually escaped. As they were chased through the desert and on the point of being slain, a lioness intervened, killing their Saracen master and another slave but leaving Malchus and his female companion unharmed. Malchus's life, Jerome concludes his account, shows that "in the midst of swords, and wild beasts of the desert, virtue is never a captive, and that he who is devoted to the service of Christ may die, but cannot be conquered."[38]

A tradition passed down by medieval Muslim authors recounts the story of Faymiyun, a Christian bricklayer-turned-ascetic, who was captured by a caravan of Arab nomads and sold into slavery in Najran. His holiness and prayer drew the attention of his master who asked Faymiyun about his reli-gion; and after miraculously destroying a palm tree sacred to the pagan Naj-ranis, the slave converted his master and soon after all the inhabitants of Na-jran to the Christian faith.[39] In a similar account, which may have served as the basis of the stories of Faymiyun, the ascetic bishop Paul and the priest John

---

36. Lenski, "Captivity and Slavery among the Saracens," 258–59.

37. Jerome, *Life of Malchus, the Captive Monk*, trans. W. H. Fremantle, *Nicene and Post-Nicene Fathers*, 2, vol. 6 (New York, 1983), 315–19.

38. Jerome, *Life of Malchus*, 319.

39. *The History of Al-Tabari*, vol. 5: *The Sasanids, the Byzantines, the Lakmids, and Yemen*, trans. Clifford Edmund Bosworth (Albany: SUNY Press, 1999), 195–99. See also Ibn Ishaq, *The Life of Muhammad*, trans. A. Guillaume (New York: Oxford University Press, 1955), 14–16. For parallels between this account and John of Nikiu's account of the virgin Theognosta, captured from a convent on the Roman frontiers and given to the king of Yemen, whom she soon converts to Christianity, see Andrea Sterk, "'Representing' Mission from Below: Historians as Interpreters and Agents of Christianization," *Church History* 79:2 (2010): 297–300.

were captured by nomadic Arabs near Mt. Sinai and sold as slaves in Himyar, where they narrowly escaped serving as human sacrifices. After Paul cured his master's daughter and cursed a sacred palm tree, the king of Himyar and all the people were baptized.[40] As Noel Lenski has recently demonstrated, these tales throw light on patterns of human trafficking in late antiquity and the all-too-familiar plight of captivity to Arab nomads.[41] But they also illumine the influence of Christian captives and slaves in the religious history of the Arabian peninsula.

Yet another example of the slave trade as well as the role of captives in Christianization concerns the Hepthalite Huns in the sixth-century Syriac chronicle of Zacharias of Mytilene.[42] Once again a Sasanid king, Kavad I, took Roman prisoners of war into Persia following the siege of the frontier city of Amida in 502–503. Rather than deport them to a Persian city, however, he sold the captives to the Huns, a particularly feared barbarian tribe. Among these prisoners were Christians, who "took wives and made families there," yet also continued to practice their faith in captivity. Drawing from the testimony of former captives who had returned to Amida after its reconquest by the Romans, the chronicler reports that they had lived among the Huns for more than thirty years when an angel appeared to the Armenian monk-bishop Kardutsat telling him of God's sovereign authority over "these captives who have gone into the nations from the land of the Romans." The angel instructed him to go to the captives, ordain priests, give them the sacraments, encourage them, "and perform signs there among the nations." In fulfillment of this commission Kardutsat and his missionary colleagues ministered to the captives, who had intermarried with the Huns during their thirty-year captivity, "and many of the Huns were baptized and became disciples." They remained there seven years and "translated books" into the Hunnic language.[43] Immediately following this account we learn of the Armenian bishop, Macarius, who was so inspired by his predecessor's mission that he, accompanied by some of his priests, went to their country "of his own accord . . . and baptized many." He

40. The Syriac text is translated and edited by Hans Arneson et al., *The History of the Great Deeds of Bishop Paul of Qentos and Priest John of Edessa*, Texts from Christian Late Antiquity 29 (Piscataway, NJ: Gorgias Press, 2010). See the editors' discussion of parallels with the story of Faymiyun and Salih and other accounts of the origins of Christianity in Yemen (9).

41. Lenski, "Captivity and Slavery among the Saracens," 260–63.

42. Also known as Zacharias Rhetor, Zacharias Scholasticus, and Pseudo-Zachariah Rhetor. His Syriac chronicle was recently published with helpful introductory material in *The Chronicle of Pseudo-Zachariah Rhetor: Church and War in Late Antiquity*, ed. Geoffrey Greatrex, trans. Robert R. Phenix and Cornelia B. Horn, with contributions by Sebastian P. Brock and Witold Witakowski.

43. *Chronicle of Pseudo-Zachariah* 12.7, trans. Phenix and Horn, 452–53.

not only constructed a brick church among the Huns but also taught them the rudiments of agriculture; and the missionaries were still living among them at the time the Chronicle was written.[44] Although Armenian bishops and priests led these sixth-century missions to the Huns, captive Christians had lived and worshiped among them for decades and formed the foundation for further missionary work in their land.

Captive Women in the Caucasus

So far we have caught glimpses of a few female exiles, captives, and slaves in late antiquity alongside their male counterparts: the faithful virgin martyr Candida, the shah's exiled sister Sirwan, the female companion of the enslaved monk-turned-goatherd, Malchus. Yet a peculiar group of captive women is particularly associated with the origins of Christianity in lands on the east Roman frontiers, specifically the Caucasian countries of Armenia and Georgia.[45] According to the fifth-century Armenian historian Agathangelos, Gregory the Illuminator, the noble credited with converting the king and people of Armenia from paganism to Christianity, was aided in his work of evangelization by a group of female refugee nuns fleeing persecution under the Roman emperor Diocletian. Most prominent among them was the beautiful virgin Rhipsime, who was chosen to wed the Armenian King Trdat. Proclaiming her faith through loud prayers while being dragged from her hiding-place to the royal chamber, Rhipsime continued her prayers in captivity. She then endured attempted rape by the king, yet overpowered the ruler and temporarily escaped before being recaptured and executed with her female companions.[46] This led to King Trdat's madness, the preaching of Gregory, and ultimately the king's restoration and conversion. In a long sermon to the king and his court Gregory attributes Armenia's conversion

44. *Chronicle of Pseudo-Zachariah* 12.7, trans. Phenix and Horn, 452–53. The writing of this part of the chronicle dates to ca. 555, at which point the missionaries are said to have been among them. The name of the second Armenian missionary bishop, Macarius (Syriac *mqr*), is often mistranslated Maku (453, n. 229). On missionary efforts to the Huns see E. A. Thompson, "Christian Missionaries among the Huns," *Hermathena* 67 (1946): 73–79, who comments on the "economic insight" of Macarius in building a church and teaching the Huns agricultural skills which could wean them from their nomadic lifestyle.

45. For a full analysis see Andrea Sterk, "Mission from Below: Captive Women and Conversion on the East Roman Frontiers," *Church History* 79:1 (2010): 1–39, and Sterk, "'Representing' Mission from Below," *Church History* 79:2 (June 2010): 271–304.

46. *Agathangelos: History of the Armenians*, ed. and trans. Robert W. Thomson (Albany: State University of New York, 1976). For Rhipsime's struggle with the king, §§178–96; for the martyrdom, §§197–210.

to the faith and witness of the captive virgin and martyr Rhipsime,[47] who with Gregory became the apostle of a new Christian land.

If the virgin Rhipsime and her companions were martyred for their witness to Christ, an anonymous captive woman played an even more prominent role in the Christianization of neighboring Georgia.[48] The nameless female captive, known as St. Nino in medieval Georgian tradition, attracted the attention of her community by her modest, sober lifestyle and her relentless devotion to prayer. When news of her efficacious prayer for the sick child of a local woman reached the queen, who was suffering from a grave illness, the desperate queen insisted that she be brought to the captive woman's hovel. The woman's prayer for the queen effects an immediate cure, she attributes the healing to Christ, teaches the queen about him, and urges her to worship him. The queen returns joyfully to the king, who wants to repay the captive with silver and gold but declines to follow the queen's advice "to worship as God the Christ who cured me" until he himself experiences the power of the captive's God in a moment of crisis. He too then converts and is instructed by the captive, who advises the king to have a church built and describes how it should be designed.[49] After a miraculous placement of an immovable column in the church, all the people of Georgia follow the king and queen in their conversion to the Christian God and thirst for a deeper knowledge of the faith. At the captive's advice, envoys are sent to the Roman emperor to request priests for instruction. Yet in Theodoret's rendering the captive woman herself is clearly a teacher endowed with the gifts of an "apostle."[50]

Though all four early fifth-century accounts identify the woman as a "captive" or even a "prisoner of war," her political and ethnic identity is unclear.[51] To be sure, however, she would have had three strikes against her in any ancient culture: she is a captive, a foreigner, and a woman. The church historian Rufinus describes her as an ascetic whose devotion to prayer and fasting provoked

---

47. *The Teaching of Saint Gregory*, trans., comm., and intro. Robert W. Thomson, rev. ed. (New Rochelle, NY: St. Nersess Armenian Seminary, 2001), especially §514, §541, §562, §564, and §572.

48. The earliest account of the Christianization of Georgia is that of the monk and historian Rufinus, writing ca. 400. See Philip R. Amidon, SJ, trans., *The Church History of Rufinus of Aquileia*, Books 10 and 11 (New York: Oxford University Press, 1997), 20–23. The three fifth-century Greek historians, Socrates, Sozomen, and Theodoret, all narrate similar accounts of the captive woman.

49. Rufinus, *Historia ecclesiastica* 10.11.

50. Theodoret, *Historia ecclesiastica* 1.24.1.

51. Assumed to be Roman, she may have been a victim of disputes between Armenia and Georgia contemporaneous with Roman-Persian conflict. See Balbina Bäbler, "Die Blick über die Reichsgrenzen: Sokrates und die Bekehrung Georgiens," in *Die Welt des Sokrates von Konstantinopel*, ed. Balbina Bäbler and Heinz Günther Nesselrath (Munich: Saur, 2001), 163–64.

the curiosity of the "barbarians" among whom she lived, starting with certain "common" or "weak" women in her community.[52] She is characterized by humility, asceticism, gifts of healing, evangelistic preaching, and apostolic gifts. She proclaims a simple message ascribing healing to Christ and calling the queen, the king, and all the people to worship him. While the details of such narratives are difficult to confirm and some parts are surely semi-legendary, they underline the important function of captives in the religious history of the premodern world. Moreover, stories and texts about them continued to play a role in building the identity of newly Christianized peoples beyond the frontiers and in illustrating important aspects of the Gospel message: the weak overcoming the strong and God's choice of the lowly and despised of the world as ambassadors. These accounts also remind us that both before and after the Roman Empire was officially Christianized, many Christians living beyond its borders maintained and even spread their faith under foreign regimes—as refugees, captives, or slaves.

Conclusion

Among the multitudes of captives in late antiquity, a few played more prominent roles in Christian history.[53] But I have sought to bring into relief the lesser known and often nameless victims of deportation, enslavement, or captivity. I have also focused on regions beyond the eastern frontiers, where whole Roman populations were deported and resettled.[54] Yet Christians in the west were by no means exempt from the harsh realities of captivity and slave trading, aptly described as an "interethnic collusion in human misery."[55] St. Augustine detailed the horrors of human trafficking in North Africa in several late sermons and letters, noting that at least one member of his own congregation was complicit in luring fellow citizens to the slave ships.[56] In another letter on the terrifying

---

52. Rufinus, 10.11: Amidon, 20, translates *mulierculae* as "common women," but it might equally be rendered "weak" or "foolish women."

53. For example, the young captive Frumentius, credited with planting the seeds of Christianity in the ancient kingdom of Axum. Rufinus, *Ecclesiastical History* 1.9–10.

54. For further discussion of the distinctive situation of Christianity and the eastern frontier with Persia see Graham, *News and Frontier Consciousness in the Late Roman Empire* (Ann Arbor: University of Michigan, 2006), 159–62, and A. D. Lee, *Information and Frontiers: Roman Foreign Relations in Late Antiquity* (Cambridge: Cambridge University Press, 1993), 49–66.

55. Noel Lenski, "Captivity and Romano-Barbarian Interchange," in Ralph W. Mathisen and Danuta Shanzer, eds., *Romans, Barbarians, and the Transformation of the Roman World: Cultural Interaction and the Creation of Identity in Late Antiquity* (Burlington, VT: Ashgate, 2011), 197.

56. See Augustine, Letter 10*, describing the "continuous flood" of free Roman men, women,

capture of Christians by barbarians he refers to a young virgin, carried off by three barbarian brothers, who won her freedom by her efficacious prayer for their healing.[57] St. Patrick, himself a former captive turned missionary, bemoaned the killing and capture of baptized Christians in Ireland and their sale "to foreign peoples who have no knowledge of God."[58] Writing in the mid-fifth century, Prosper of Aquitaine put a more positive spin on the plight of Christian captives, noting that "some sons of the church, made prisoners by the enemy, changed their masters into servants of the Gospel. . . . Thus, where the church feared danger, there she finds her expansion."[59]

The vast majority of these Christians remain completely unknown to us. How did they understand their faith or their own identity as Christians in captivity? What were their hopes and fears? We have far too few sources that reflect on such questions, much less the writings of Christians themselves about their inner lives. Yet certain patterns emerge in both historiographical and hagiographic narratives of Christian captives. First, we find the centrality of prayer and worship. Whether entire captive communities, deportees en route to foreign settlements, isolated ascetics enslaved by harsh masters, or female refugees under hostile rule, Christian captives continued to pray and to worship their God; and whenever possible they constructed a church, a physical place of worship, which served as a focal point for captives in exile. Second, narratives of Christian captives emphasize the quality as well as the faithfulness of their service. Some gained reputations for specialized labor—as artisans, builders, textile workers, or doctors; but whether applying special expertise or tending herds in the desert, they did their work well and often went beyond the call of duty. Third, and closely connected to their lives of worship and faithful service, they drew others around them to their religion. Whether celibate ascetics or professional elites, kept together with spouses and kin or forced to intermarry with Persian Zoroastrians, individual Christian captives or whole captive communities attracted both the high and the lowly. Few in the east, if they had gained their freedom, returned to their captors as active missionaries

---

and children being sold into slavery, such that Africa was being "emptied of its native inhabitants." For a recent analysis of this letter see Aaron D. Conley, "Augustine and Slavery: Freedom for the Free," in *Augustine and Social Justice*, ed. Teresa Delgado, John Doody, and Kim Paffenroth (Lanham, MD: Lexington Books, 2015), 131–44.

57. Augustine, Letter 111.7. The parallel with accounts of the Georgian captive woman is noteworthy.

58. *Ep. ad Coroticum* 14; *Studies in Church History* 249:144–46.

59. *De Invoc. Omnium Gentium* 2.33, in St. Prosper of Aquitaine, *The Call of All Nations*, trans. P. De Letter, Ancient Christian Writers 14 (Washington, DC: Catholic University of America Press, 1978), 146.

like St. Patrick; but the sources repeatedly feature conversion through inter-action between captives or slaves and their masters.[60] Amid centrifugal forces that dominated the Eurasian world in this era, Christian captives functioned as countervailing centripetal forces—changing the notion of Roman-ness, blurring the meaning of frontiers,[61] and attracting their foreign masters to the greater Lord they claimed to serve.

60. As has recently been noted, "the degree to which the sources feature conversion to Christianity by barbarian peoples as a product of slave–master interchange is remarkable." Lenski, "Captivity and Romano-Barbarian Interchange," 195.

61. Regarding these two phenomena see Graham, *Frontier Consciousness*, 155–63.

Chapter 16

Timothy I of Baghdad: A Stranger in His Own Land

Robert A. Kitchen

During the late fourth century in the province of Adiabene of northeast Iraq, then a part of the Sasanian Empire, an enigmatic community of Christians lived in the wake of the severe persecutions of the Zoroastrian Shapur II. The spiritual leader of this community wrote a collection of thirty discourses or *mēmrē* entitled by later scholars as *The Book of Steps*.[1] Some were sermons, other works provided a basic rule of life and behavior, still others responded to theological issues and challenges. It is one of the earliest major works in Syriac, but there are no historical references, no names are used except those of biblical personalities, and the author remains intentionally anonymous.

There is a lot of conversation about perfection. The author's configuration of the church necessitates a two-level order: the Upright and the Perfect. The former are laity who marry, have jobs, own property and perform the traditional acts of charity within the church and the community. The latter are virtually monks, although the formal institution of monasticism had not yet appeared this deep into the Persian Empire. The Perfect are celibate, do not own property or work, pray unceasingly, teach and mediate conflicts. *The Book of Steps* chronicles the development and the difficulties of Perfection, but at one point the author makes a surprising observation and judgment. A bishop can never be Perfect, by definition. A bishop, after all, has to be deeply involved in the worldly administration of the church, its clergy and laity, and so inevitably has to mete out punishment, often corporal.[2] This is not the prayerful, nonjudgmental way of life of the Perfect, at least as Perfection is perceived by the anonymous author.

---

1. *The Book of Steps: The Syriac Liber Graduum*, trans. and intro. R. A. Kitchen and M. F. G. Parmentier (Kalamazoo, MI: Cistercian Publications, 2004).

2. *Book of Steps*, Mēmrā 19 (Kitchen and Parmentier, 199).

This raises an important question: in a church dominated by monastic endeavors to attain perfection, holiness, purity, should not the leader of the church be a holy man? But, as the author of *The Book of Steps* emphatically declared, how can he be?

Four centuries later (780) in the same geographical region, now the realm of the relatively new 'Abbāsid Caliphate, Timothy I became the catholicos or patriarch of the Church of the East. Timothy would lead the church for forty-three years, and has been generally acknowledged as the greatest catholicos in the Church of the East's long history.

An extraordinarily multitalented person, Timothy was a translator of classical Greek texts into Arabic at the beginning of the Translation Movement initiated by the 'Abbāsids, a capable administrator of the Church of the East and an enthusiastic promoter of missionary work to Central Asia and beyond to China. He also was a theologian of great depth, well suited to engage in dialogue with the Islamic leadership and intelligentsia, but also one who rooted out perceived heretics from influence in the church. A codifier of a new system of law, his influence lasted well beyond his own reign.

All these accomplishments and gifts did not make him holy in the eyes of many of his contemporaries or of his successors. He used power efficiently and sometimes brutally, so Perfect he was not. Does it matter, in so far as the church prospered and grew and spread the Holy Gospel? Most historians note that the Church of the East during this period was the largest church in the world, both in members and adherents, as well as in geographical territory. A complex personality, Timothy I of Baghdad enabled the Church of the East to coexist uneasily with its Muslim rulers as strangers in their own land, and that required a different set of skills from most bishops. In order to create and maintain a holy church, personal holiness did not appear to be the primary characteristic of the catholicos. Timothy I has eluded full examination by scholars for centuries, but his legacies are seldom remembered without passionate opinions. The following will attempt to sort out a prelude to the achievements and personality of Timothy, certainly not a definitive assessment.[3]

Early Life and Election

Timothy was born in Hazza in Adiabene (twelve kilometers from modern Erbil) in 728, a little past one century AH in the new reality of Islam's presence under

---

3. The best summary of Timothy I's life is Martin Heimgartner, "Timothy I," in D. Thomas and B. Roggema, *Christian-Muslim Relations: A Bibliographical History I*, 600–900 (Leiden, 2009), 515–19.

the Ummayad Dynasty. The Muslims were still in the minority, but they were not going to go away. The first century of Islam saw subject Christian communities hoping that the new rulers and their faith would eventually fade away, and so for the time being many Christians tried to ignore them. Following the assumption of the 'Abbāsid dynasty in 750 and the building of the new capital, Baghdad, the new reality had sunk in. By the time of Timothy's ascension to the patriarchate, there was no longer any doubt or speculation about the foreseeable future of religious hegemony. The question was whether Christianity would be the faith to fade away.

Timothy's uncle, George, bishop of Beth Bagash, took charge of his nephew's education, sending him at first to the school at Bashosh under Abraham bar Dashandad. Abraham would move to Marga and later to the monastery of Mar Gabriel in Mosul with Timothy following him. Timothy was a strong advocate of education, especially in the schools and monasteries where a rigorous curriculum could be ensured, and as a positive consequence control unorthodox and heretical thinking.[4]

Timothy came to full public attention while he was still serving as bishop of Beth Bagash in the rural metropolitan province of Adiabene. The Catholicos Ḥenanisho died in 780 after a mere seven-year reign, and the circumstances of his death seemed abnormally normal for that era, a sudden death after minor surgery. Rumors circulated that the surgeon's scalpel was coated with poison.[5] As has been witnessed in countless oppressed ethnic, racial, and religious groups, there is a marked tendency towards vicious in-fighting for the crumbs of power rather than daring to challenge the true oppressor.

Timothy was no novice at the power game and openly sought the highest post with no holds barred, and he was not the favorite. There were two other candidates: the first, Ishoyahb, superior of the monastery of Beth Abē, was an older man, and Timothy advised him that he was too old for the position; the second, Giwargis, a renowned linguist who had been defeated by the previous patriarch Ḥenanisho, died shortly before the election, raising a few eyebrows in Timothy's direction, yet there was never any proof of his involvement.[6] Timothy appeared to have engaged in the ancient practice of simony, promising favors of ecclesiastical office for support or for withdrawal from the process. He did win, but several of his opponents doggedly attacked the legitimacy of the election. Joseph, former metropolitan of Merv, and now a famous convert to Islam, was

4. Sebastian P. Brock, *A Brief Outline of Syriac Literature* (Baker Hill, Kottayam, Kerala, India: St. Ephrem Ecumenical Research Institute, 1997), 63–65.

5. David Wilmshurst, *The Martyred Church: A History of the Church of the East* (London: East & West Publishing, 2011), 140–42.

6. Wilmshurst, *Martyred Church*, 141.

relentless until he went too far. By hinting to the caliphate's office that Timothy was a secret supporter of the Byzantine government, and therefore treasonous, Joseph meant to undermine Timothy's position with the caliph—and would have undermined the status of the Church of the East as well. Timothy's supporters responded by saying that the Byzantines (Chalcedonians) reviled the Church of the East much more than the Jews. The caliph tentatively accepted Joseph's version, but a subsequent prisoner of war from Constantinople confirmed that, yes, he considered the Nestorians vile and that the Byzantines were much closer to the Arabs. Joseph of Merv was completely discredited.[7]

Only then was Timothy able to initiate some new directives. The beginning of a term is a good time to take a risk. He reversed the long-time custom of marriage for clergy by insisting that while regular clergy could remain married, monks and bishops should not. It has often been claimed that Timothy made the decision to move the patriarchal see from the ancient capital of Seleucia-Ctesiphon on the Euphrates, but it was actually his predecessor Ḥenanisho four years earlier. No matter who claimed credit, it was a shrewd strategy to be close to the people and institutions of the 'Abbāsid dynasty, and Timothy would take full advantage.

Theological Engagement with Islam

Timothy's forty-three-year patriarchal reign involved innumerable activities, events, and skills, but his enduring legacy is found in his theological writing, the great majority being in letters written to diverse audiences, the surviving majority to a friend and colleague Sergius, metropolitan of Elam. There is an extant corpus of fifty-nine letters, although 'Abdisho of Nisibis, a thirteenth-century historian of Syriac literature, observed that there were about 200 letters, which would be believable, but most have not been located. Two-thirds treat various issues in ecclesiastical matters; fifteen inquire about the availability of manuscripts from Greek patristic writers; three deal with topics of Aristotelian philosophy—translations from Greek into Syriac, and a discussion with a Muslim Aristotelian philosopher; theological topics addressed to monks; one concerning ecumenical relations, and others on baptism, the soul, a letter of consolation, a new grammar, and miscellaneous topics.[8]

The most influential and widely circulated of his writings is the transcript of a reputed two-day conversation with the Caliph al-Mahdi (ca. 781–782) at

---

7. Wilmshurst, *Martyred Church*, 142–43.
8. Brock, *A Brief History*, 63–64.

the beginning of Timothy's patriarchate.[9] It is a lengthy and detailed defense of Christianity in response to the subtle critiques and challenges of the caliph. Many have been skeptical whether this text records an authentic conversation between Timothy and al-Mahdi, although recent scholars have been inclined to consider it genuine. The text is written in Syriac, but the conversation was conducted in Arabic. The dialogue was translated quickly into Arabic and utilized for centuries as a basic apology for Christians in the Muslim world. The first language for Christians had soon become Arabic, so this Apology enabled successive generations with the language and logic to maintain their faith as a minority against a sophisticated and daunting opponent.

The tone of the conversation and debate between the caliph and the catholicos is marked by mutual respect, although it is apparent that the caliph knows that he and his faith possess the fuller measure of power. The caliph's questions and repartees to Timothy's explanations sometimes evidence a populist criticism of the Christian narrative, while the catholicos's responses are subtle and deft, yet offering commonplace examples. The sticking points from the Islamic side are the Christian understanding of God and his providence, Christ and his nature along with that of the Trinity, the function of the cross and resurrection in the salvation narrative, and why Christians do not accept Muhammad as a prophet. Timothy never challenges a fundamental principle of Islamic theology, although he does not shrink from explaining why it is not necessary for Christians to accept Islam and its conceptual view of the world.

Disputation and Apology

No matter whether this text was an authentic transcription of an actual conversation between Timothy and al-Mahdi or a literary re-creation of what such a conversation should have said, Timothy's Apology was primarily a pastoral initiative for Christians living amongst Islam. It gives its readers the intellectual tools and logic to respond to denunciations of their faith and to develop pride in the integrity and truthfulness of Christianity while the powers-that-be are insisting they are wrong, if not heretical and blasphemous. Timothy's format and language is courteous, but firmly grounded with a confidence in the Christian faith that must have bolstered flagging spirits over the centuries. At the end of the conversations, Timothy appears to have won the respect of al-

9. Alphonse Mingana, *Timothy's Apology for Christianity*, vol. 2 of Woodbrooke Studies: Christian Documents in Syriac, Arabic, and Garshūni, Edited and Translated with a Critical Apparatus (Cambridge: W. Heffer & Sons, 1928), 11–90 (English translation).

Mahdi, but in terms of arguing for the primacy of one religion versus another, Timothy did not win. Nor did he lose. That would be the optimum result for his readers as well.

Recurring themes are worth recounting in the seventy-five-page text, and several of the challenges to Christian practice and doctrine sound uncannily modern. The pattern throughout the two days is the caliph asking a pointed question, "Why don't you . . . ?" and Timothy responding with an explanation, an apology of "why" and "how." For most Christians this would be the kind of situation they would find themselves in, so the imperative to explain oneself would be the norm for his readers.

Some questions treat what appear to be less significant matters. The caliph asks, "Why are you not circumcised? After all, Jesus Christ was circumcised." Timothy replied that the Torah and its laws were the image of the gospel, and the sacrifices of the Law were the image of the eventual sacrifice of Jesus Christ, and finally physical circumcision was the image of Christ's spiritual circumcision performed not by human hands, but by the power of the Holy Spirit. In essence, Christ had abolished the physical Law and superseded its requirements by spiritual transformations in the actions and hearts of Christians.[10] A subtle shift is effected by Timothy to move his readers from a defensive position to one of spiritual superiority without saying so.

The caliph proceeds to entrap Timothy and Christianity in an illogical practice. Al-Mahdi asks, "Where did Jesus worship and pray in the years between his birth and ascension to Heaven? Was it not in the Jerusalem Temple?" When Timothy answers, "Yes," the caliph probed deeper, "Why then do you worship God and pray in the direction of the East?" Jerusalem was to the west of Baghdad. Timothy does not hesitate, declaring that true worship of the Omnipotent God will be ultimately performed in the Kingdom of Heaven, and the Kingdom of Heaven's earthly image is the Paradise of Eden, which is in the East. Again, a subtle nudge, for the Muslims pray in the direction of Mecca, an important holy city, but nevertheless a mere city when compared to the Paradise/Garden of Eden.[11] Timothy was not always so polite about Islam. He once wrote that the Muslims are "the new Jews," which was no compliment.

The most controversial issue between Christians and Muslims is the Trinitarian conception of the nature of God, and the disputation between al-Mahdi and Timothy keeps returning to the problem from different positions throughout the conversation. The caliph begins bluntly with a comment likely to be heard on the street, "Why do you believe in three gods?" Timothy's description

10. Mingana, *Timothy's Apology*, 27–28.
11. Mingana, *Timothy's Apology*, 29–30.

of the Trinity is the One God with his Word and Spirit that are indistinguishable and inseparable from the Godhead, just as the sun is not distinguishable from its light and heat and therefore is not three suns.[12]

The caliph does not budge, for the idea of Three in One remains incomprehensible to him, and so attacks from different angles. He keeps coming back to insist that the Word (Christ) and (Holy) Spirit have to be in some fashion distinct from God and therefore three distinct entities, three gods. Timothy's most insightful response posits that "If one ventures to say about God that there was a time in which He had no Word and no Spirit, such a one would blaspheme against God, because saying that would be equivalent to asserting that there was a time in which God had no reason and no life."[13]

Exasperated, but still not yielding, al-Mahdi pulls out a fundamental challenge, "Tell me from which books you can show me that the Word and the Spirit are eternally with God?" (23) Timothy gives an extensive answer, beginning with a number of Psalms, then Isaiah, and the Gospels of John and Matthew.[14] The caliph would have been more convinced if Timothy could have demonstrated such a proof from the Qur'an. Note that the understanding of these most fundamental of concepts do not derive from our rational thinking, but from the sacred books, a source that points to the designation People of the Book, by which Islam associated itself with Christianity and Judaism.

The Trinity is still not settled, as the caliph shifts to the difference between the Son and the Spirit; how are they not equal? They differ in their relationship to one another, Timothy states and then treads on familiar Trinitarian concepts. The first (God) is unbegotten, the second (Word/Son) is begotten, and the third (Holy Spirit) proceeds.[15] God begat the Son and made the Spirit proceed from him—the *filioque* is not considered here.

The final chapter, though not a conclusion, comes with al-Mahdi's subtle observation, "If the Father and the Spirit did not put on a human body with the Son, how is it that they are not separated by distance and space?" Timothy offers an analogy of the caliph's own person. "As the word of the king (the caliph) clothes itself with the papyrus on which it is written, while his soul and his mind cannot be said to do the same, and as his soul and his mind, while not separated from his word, cannot nevertheless be said that they clothe themselves with the papyrus, so also is the case with the Word of God."[16] After Timothy completed

---

12. Mingana, *Timothy's Apology*, 22.
13. Mingana, *Timothy's Apology*, 23.
14. Mingana, *Timothy's Apology*, 23–25.
15. Mingana, *Timothy's Apology*, 25.
16. Mingana, *Timothy's Apology*, 27.

his explanation, al-Mahdi changed the subject to the above-mentioned query about Christian noncircumcision.

The cross also proved difficult for the caliph and other Muslims to comprehend. "Why do you worship the Cross?" is a question of incredulity regarding the disgracefulness of that kind of death. Timothy's counter was that "the Cross is the cause of death, as you say, but death is also the cause of resurrection and resurrection is the cause of life and immortality. . . . We honour the Cross as the root of which the fruit of life was born to us, and from which the ray of immortality shone upon us."[17]

The caliph has a larger theological purpose in probing about the cross, and so next asks his impossible question, "Can God then Himself die?" Timothy immediately states the distinctive Christology of the Church of the East: "The Son of God died in our nature, but not in His divinity."[18] This is the shorthand rendering of the so-called Nestorian explanation of the nature of Christ, which the Church of the East generally adopted. Christ has two natures and two persons (qnōmē in Syriac), one human and one divine, as opposed to the Chalcedonian or "Melkite" definition of one person (qnōmā) and two natures, and to the Miaphysite or "Jacobite" understanding of one person and one nature (divine-human). The source of the problem lies in part in the definition and connotation of the term for person (qnōmā), which for the Church of the East requires a nature. The two natures, human and divine, each require a person. This does not mean that there were two Christs walking around, but the intent is to preserve the humanity of Jesus from being overwhelmed by his divinity—and consequently rendering it impossible for a normal human being to imitate Christ.

Complex as it appears, this definition of the nature of Christ had an appeal to Muslim theology since the Church of the East was not saying that Jesus was God. In some of his behavior, Jesus was being fully human, such as on the cross, and fully divine in others. The thought of a human becoming divine was simply blasphemous to Islam. Whereas Timothy and the contemporary Church of the East did not devise these definitions themselves, he was well aware of the distinctive and positive position in which it placed the Church of the East with respect to orthodox Islamic thought. At the conclusion of the conversation, al-Mahdi asked pointedly again, "Who are those who say that God suffered and died in the flesh?" Timothy is blunt, "The Jacobites and Melkites say that God suffered and died in the flesh, but as for us we not only do not assert that God suffered and died in our nature, but He even removed the passibility of our

17. Mingana, *Timothy's Apology*, 40.
18. Mingana, *Timothy's Apology*, 40–41.

human nature that he put on from Mary by His impassibility, and its mortality by His immortality, and He made it to resemble divinity, to the extent that a created being is capable of resembling his Creator."[19] The caliph found Timothy's assertion more palatable in contrast to the others.

The elephant in the faith remained, but inevitably was named, as Christians in Baghdad heard regularly from their Islamic neighbors, "Why do you not accept Mohammed?" Al-Mahdi makes it specific, asking why is it that Timothy accepts Christ and the gospel from the testimony of the Torah and the prophets, but does not accept Mohammed from the testimony of the Christ and the gospel.[20] There was a claim that the name of Mohammed was indeed found in Jewish and Christian books. Timothy goes through the various witnesses, but as for Mohammed comes up empty-handed with no references. The caliph does not relent and asks what is the Paraclete, to which Timothy replies that it is the Spirit of God, the fullness of the Spirit which proceeds from the Father. After Timothy offers a few more characteristics and cites the words of Christ in John about it, the caliph interrupts, "All these [characteristics] refer to Mohammed."[21] Timothy gently proceeds by noting that the Paraclete is the Spirit of God and so Mohammed would have to be the Spirit of God. That means that Mohammed would be uncircumscribed and un-composed like God, invisible, and without a body. Mohammed is not God, but a created human being—a basic understanding of Islam—and therefore, Mohammed is not the Paraclete.[22]

The final argument of the caliph, a convenient intellectual strategy when all other arguments do not succeed, is that the Christians have corrupted and distorted their Scriptures so that Mohammed is omitted. Timothy's response is a practical one: Jews and Christians do not get along in a civil manner and the resulting hostility guarantees that both sides have been vigilant in making sure that their respective Scriptures are not tampered with.[23] Wisely, Timothy affirms that the Muslims are different, people of great integrity, intellect, with uncompromising devotion to the One God.[24]

Remarkable as the learned nature and theological nimbleness of both participants are in this conversation, this is not in the first instance an academic treatise on theological doctrine. For the Caliph al-Mahdi, this is still the youth of Islam (ca. AH 160). Islamic thought had reached a level of maturity and self-assuredness, particularly in its conviction that it represented the final revelation

19. Mingana, *Timothy's Apology*, 87.
20. Mingana, *Timothy's Apology*, 32–33.
21. Mingana, *Timothy's Apology*, 33.
22. Mingana, *Timothy's Apology*, 33–35.
23. Mingana, *Timothy's Apology*, 55–58.
24. Mingana, *Timothy's Apology*, 59.

of God that superseded those of Judaism and Christianity. Nevertheless, it was acknowledged that Christian scholars knew a great deal more about the things the Muslims wished to learn, especially classical Greek philosophy, mathematics, science, and medicine. The ʿAbbāsid dynasty possessed the superior hand of power and government, and now it wanted to assume that advantage theologically and intellectually.

Timothy's record of his two-day conversation is not intended as systematic theology. Most of his answers to the challenges against Christianity are brief and easy to understand, memorize, and recite. It is a pastor's guide for the people of the church living around him on how to maintain the integrity and accuracy of the Christian faith in a society that has moved beyond one's way of life and thinking—a modern dilemma as well. Except for the references to the specific role of Mohammed, the questions asked by the caliph could still be tendered by contemporary cultured despisers of religion.

Messalianism and Wrong Christian Thinking

The other eye of Timothy's theological vision was turned inwardly towards Christian theology, especially inaccurate or heretical thinking, but even here he was always sneaking a look back over his shoulder at how Islam judged what he was seeing and judging.

The openness and graciousness for dialogue with Islam that Timothy helped pioneer finds a contrast in his internal dealings with Christian theology he deemed to be dangerous to the church's faith and survival. In the year 786/787, Timothy convened a council that anathematized three Church of the East mystical theologians: John of Dalyatha, Joseph Ḥazzaya, and John of Apamea. The writings of this trio were banned from being kept in monasteries, and copies, particularly of John of Dalyatha's works, have been found only in the collections of other confessions. Drastic decisions such as these do not occur without some political factors, for Timothy's successor, Išōʿ bar Nūn (823–827), immediately rescinded the anathema on John, finding nothing objectionable in his writings.[25] The new patriarch had had a lengthy rivalry with Timothy, but obviously did not have the position or power to express his disagreements earlier.

The problem with John of Dalyatha was that he allegedly had written that

25. Alexander Trieger, "Could Christ's Humanity See His Divinity? An Eighth-Century Controversy between John of Dalyatha and Timothy I, Catholicos of the Church of the East," *Journal of the Canadian Society for Syriac Studies* 9 (2009): 3–21.

Christ in his humanity was able to see his divinity. In a passage in his Letter 14, John rephrases the Beatitude (Matt 5:8) to "Blessed are the pure, for it is in their hearts that they shall see God."[26] It is at the height of mystical contemplation during this life that one is able to see God. John was influenced significantly by Evagrius Ponticus and Pseudo-Dionysius. From the latter John apparently adapted the concept of "unknowing, which is higher than all knowledges and all those who know."[27] These exalted concepts became uncomfortable for the orthodox Church of the East leadership, for these did not sit well with Islamic discouragement of mystical types of thinking. A human being not only cannot become divine or pretend to be, but cannot claim to sense the divinity through human faculties. However, there was more to this anathematization than doctrine with Timothy.

Alexander Trieger has unveiled some later correspondence of Timothy that indicates the real problem with John was that he did not clear his writings with Timothy for his imprimatur.[28] In addition to the charge that John had written that a created being can see its Creator, Timothy added John's statement that the Son and the Spirit are not hypostases, but (merely) powers, and further that the Word is called Son because through the Son the Father created all things, not because the Son was begotten of the Father.[29]

Timothy's principal target was a fourth- and fifth-century movement or controversy labeled "Messalianism." The term comes from the Syriac word "to pray" or "those who pray" (*mṣallyānē*).[30] There never was an organized "church" or sect of Messalians, tending to be various wandering groups with the common thread of a charismatic understanding of the efficacy of prayer alone. Neither the sacraments nor the clergy were of any assistance in encountering the divine. Antoine Guillaumont had depicted these wandering, begging groups as "sorte de hippies" who scandalously included men and women in their traveling caravans. They thought that dreams during sleep were instances of "unceasing prayer," so unceasing sleep was considered an efficient technique.[31] Their re-

---

26. Trieger, "Could Christ's Humanity," 4; *The Letters of John of Dalyatha*, trans. and intro. Mary Hansbury, Texts from Christian Late Antiquity 2 (Piscataway, NJ: Gorgias Press, 2006), Letter 14, 68.

27. Trieger, "Could Christ's Humanity," 4–5.

28. Trieger, "Could Christ's Humanity," 7.

29. Trieger, "Could Christ's Humanity," 7–9.

30. See Columba Stewart, *Working the Earth of the Heart: The Messalian Controversy in History, Texts and Language to A.D. 431* (Oxford: Clarendon, 1991); Marcus Plested, *The Macarian Legacy: The Place of Macarius-Symeon in Eastern Christian Tradition* (Oxford: Oxford University Press, 2004); and Daniel Caner, *Wandering, Begging Monks* (Berkeley: University of California Press, 2002).

31. Antoine Guillaumont, "Un mouvement de 'Spirituels' dans l'Orient chrétien," *Revue de*

jection of ecclesiastical structures and practices naturally did not endear them to the church's hierarchy, and several early councils condemned the enigmatic collage of individuals. People of the Book always, there was an earnest search for an *asceticon* of Messalianism, and while some pointed to *The Book of Steps*, no book ever convincingly materialized.[32] Other theological errors and blasphemies were claimed at different councils, but given the anti-institutional nature of these wanderers in the faith, such sophisticated ideas were not convincingly authentic. Nevertheless, Messalianism proved a convenient label with which to convict a number of perceived heresies for centuries, and Timothy appears to have designated Messalianism as the primary theological nemesis, issuing a proclamation in the second year of his patriarchate that required all those convicted of this heresy to submit a written renunciation of its teachings before being allowed to participate and serve in the church and receive the sacraments.

John of Dalyatha conveniently fell within these errors, particularly those that propose to commune with the divine without the agency of the church. Trieger pulls together the evidence to show that Timothy's anti-Messalian diatribe and requirement of his imprimatur provoked a defiant response from John in his Letter 25, "On the Incomprehensibility of God."[33] Timothy reacted with an anathematizing council in several years. Timothy's concerns were to present the Church of the East as the only theologically compatible Christian confession with Islam, in that Christ was not a blasphemous human-god, but a fully human being conjoined with the Word, but not identical to it. The Melkites and Jacobites did not make this distinction and were susceptible to the charge of idolatry under Islam's gaze.

Behind the scenes, John's defiance was deeply worrying and subversive to Timothy since he was afraid other clergy and laity might apostatize and convert to Islam, as they were under intense pressure to do. Theology for Timothy was not a straightforward matter of proclaiming the good news of Jesus Christ as attested by the Scriptures and by the thinking and practice of the church. He needed to be alert at every juncture regarding who his audience would be and what they needed to hear first. Timothy's theological messages had to be precise, not only from the perspective of the Christian faithful, but from that of their opponents as well.

---

l'Histoire des Religions 189 (1975): 126; Stewart, *Working the Earth*, "Themes 7 and 8: Avoidance of Work and Desire for Sleep," 62–63.

32. R. A. Kitchen, "Becoming Perfect: The Maturing of Asceticism in the *Liber Graduum*," *Journal of the Canadian Society for Syriac Studies* 2 (2002): 30–45, esp. 33–34.

33. Trieger, "Could Christ's Humanity," 11; Hansbury, *The Letters*, Letter 25, 118–23.

Translating Wisdom

During the reign of Timothy I in Baghdad at the turn of the eighth and ninth centuries, Syriac Christians found themselves immersed in a critical venture that some believe changed the course of civilization. The 'Abbāsid dynasty possessed an ambitious and inventive spirit, intent in one aspect upon creating "a knowledge economy." They were intelligent enough to know that they did not know everything, but quickly learned where to go to find the right kind of knowledge—from the Greek classics of antiquity of philosophy and ethics, almost exclusively Aristotle, mathematics, astronomy, science, and medicine. The 'Abbāsids did not know Greek, so they turned to Syriac Christians for their help and expertise. For centuries Syriac scholars and monks had been translating the Greek New Testament into Syriac, first for the Peshiṭta, and later on for versions (Philoxenian, Harklean) increasingly precise about the correspondence of the Greek to Syriac. The intent was to create "mirror image" translations in which the Syriac was equivalent to the Greek in form and grammar. The result was that after five centuries of intimate engagement with Greek and Syriac, a large cadre of Syriac scholars existed across confessional traditions who could handle any Greek text of antiquity. Their method was to seek out the best available Greek manuscripts over an exceedingly wide territory and translate the Greek first into Syriac, utilizing the linguistic skills passed down through the centuries. Then the translators would translate Syriac into Arabic, both being cognate Semitic languages.[34]

The House of Wisdom (*Bayt al-Hikma*) was established in Baghdad by the Caliph al-Rashid in 786 as the center for research and the accumulation of knowledge. It would come to full fruition under al-Rashid's son, Caliph al-Ma'mun (813–833).[35] Timothy was the catholicos during both of their reigns and would take a significant role in translating the *Topics* of Aristotle, reputedly at the request of al-Mahdi, the learned conversational partner with Timothy in the Disputation and Apology described above. Timothy had the advantage that the *Topics* had been translated into Syriac and manuscripts were located in several Syrian monasteries, having been in use in the monastic curriculum for about a century. One of his letters to the abbot of one such monastery asks whether there were any commentaries or scholia on this and several related texts.[36] That

34. See Sebastian P. Brock, "Changing Fashions in Syriac Translation Technique: The Background to Syriac Translations under the Abbasids," *Journal of the Canadian Society for Syriac Studies* 4 (2004): 3–26.

35. See Wilmshurst, *Martyred Church*, 183–86.

36. Sebastian P. Brock, "Two Letters of the Patriarch Timothy from the Late Eighth Century on Translations from Greek," *Arabic Sciences and Philosophy* 9 (1999): 233–46.

there were none indicated the text was considered of minor importance, although Aristotle's logic in Arabic immediately attracted a rabid readership.

The translation movement would spur a great renaissance of learning and scholarship under 'Abbāsid encouragement. The interest did not cover all the fields of study, ignoring for the most part the classical literature of the Greeks and their renowned playwrights. Logic, science and mathematics were their foci and this would inevitably benefit societies well beyond Baghdad. Given the noted rivalry between the Church of the East, Syrian Orthodox/Jacobites, and Chalcedonian/Melkite confessions for preeminence in the 'Abbāsid court, the translation movement was open and ecumenical. Timothy's letter requested copies of manuscripts translated by Jacobites and Chalcedonians,[37] and the most renowned of the translators at the House of Wisdom was Hunayn ibn-Ishaq (808–873) of the Church of the East. Few, if any of these translated texts could be categorized as religious or theological, but learning and education serviced a theological worldview advocated by Timothy and others. Philosophy during that era did not refrain from inquiring about God and the questions of meaning.

Jesus Shall Reign Where'er the Sun

The era of Timothy I's patriarchate occurs during a high point of the great missionary expansion of the Church of the East. Timothy played a role at the center of this movement, but was not its originator. In the first year of Timothy's reign (781), the famous stele at Xian in China was erected with inscriptions in Chinese and Syriac describing the coming of Christianity, "the Luminous Religion," beginning in 635. The catholicos listed was Henanisho II, Timothy's predecessor, but communication was not yet adequate for the tremendous distances, so that the inscriber, the priest and bishop Adam, had not yet received word of the catholicos's death and of his successor.[38]

The missionaries were already well on their way, but Timothy's contributions were administrative, diplomatic, and pastoral. Administratively, Timothy's strategy was to create, expand, and merge a number of metropolitan regions in the "exterior provinces." Often it was a calculated risk to send a metropolitan bishop where Christians had barely established themselves. Many outposts met hostile resistance from locals, others indifference and isolation; some vanished in a matter of a few years, others took hold for much longer. Timothy commis-

37. Brock, "Two Letters," 236–37.
38. Wilmshurst, *Martyred Church*, 167–69.

sioned some monks and a metropolitan to initiate evangelization in Dailam, a region between Armenia and the Caspian Sea largely inhabited by Zoroastrians and pagans. There were some successes and converts, although the metropolitan Ubališō' was murdered.[39] Other metropolitans were sent and survived, and their descendants would continue for a couple of centuries. Nevertheless, by the twelfth century, the region was almost entirely Islamic.

As with many of his other duties, an important part of his missionary ventures was carried out through his letter writing. His correspondence communicated with and referred to the existence of metropolitanates in India (*Beth Hinduwāyē*), China (*Beth Ṣināyē*), Tibet (*Beth Tuptāyē*), and among the Turks (*Beth Ṭurkāyē*), in all a sizeable piece of territory. David of Beth Abē monastery was the metropolitan of Beth Ṣināyē in Ch'ang-an during Timothy's reign, and the atmosphere was comfortable and receptive. A generation after Timothy, however, matters turned badly for Christians and other non-Chinese religions as the Chinese emperor formally decreed their expulsion. The Xian stele probably was buried at this time, and by the end of the ninth century, there was little evidence of Christians in the region.[40]

Timothy is sometimes credited with having converted the Turks, but there is no direct evidence, and moreover, the label of Turks was used to describe an extremely diverse collection of peoples. Beth Ṭurkāyē is an ambiguous designation, referring sometimes to a geographical region, to an ethnic group, or to an ecclesiastical gathering. Mark Dickens suggests that the Qarluq Turks were likely candidates in the late eighth century for his references to the Turks.[41] Nevertheless, Timothy's administrative initiatives through appointments and correspondence nurtured a broad territory in the faith.

A good instance of Timothy's ambition and imagination was in his written intention to appoint a metropolitan in Tibet or Beth Tuptāyē. Tibet was a large and independent kingdom in the eighth and ninth centuries, and it is possible that Christianity was introduced into the country via Silk Road merchants. Unfortunately, beyond mention in several of Timothy's letters, there is no evidence of a metropolitanate ever being established in Lhasa or one of the other Silk Road cities. A mid-ninth-century reaction by Buddhists apparently eliminated Christian and Muslim presence in Tibet.[42]

---

39. Wilmshurst, *Martyred Church*, 165–67.

40. Wilmshurst, *Martyred Church*, 168–69.

41. Mark Dickens, "Patriarch Timothy I and the Metropolitan of the Turks," *Journal of the Royal Asiatic Society of Great Britain & Ireland* 20 (2010): 117–39.

42. Dickens, "Patriarch Timothy I," 117–21; Wilmshurst, *Martyred Church*, 169.

Lawgiver

In the twenty-sixth year of his reign, 805, Timothy compiled a collection of laws for the East Syrian Church, *The Order of Ecclesiastical and Succession-Related Rulings*.[43] Several versions of this work survived to become part of a larger corpus of East Syrian legal principles stretching from the fifth to the eleventh centuries.[44] Some of these were what later generations would call "canon laws," regulations and rulings related to ecclesiastical matters, but many went beyond church concerns into secular arenas. The impetus for this compilation were repeated requests by other bishops and priests to provide some structure and resource for various legal situations for Church of the East members, who in the absence of a code sanctioned by the church were increasingly resorting to Islamic courts.

Timothy recognized the theological problem of a cleric becoming involved with prescribing laws. The preface to his legal collection describes the dilemma: "If Christians were in the kingdom of heaven . . . there would be not a single dispute or strife. Where there is no dispute or strife, neither is there any need for the decreeing of judgments. Among Christians [i.e., true Christians in heaven], then, worldly judgments are superfluous and useless. For judgments and prescriptions are useful to the men of the world."[45] Nevertheless, the gospel, not the law, is the operating principle of the church, and even when there are disputes, Timothy knows that Paul's admonition in 1 Corinthians 6:1–3 for Christians to restrict their legal disputes within the community of saints is still the preferred method. "Few and rare are those heavenly ones," Timothy admits, and so decides to provide a temporal solution for Christians until the world to come arrives.

The text comprises ninety-nine judicial decisions in question-and-answer format, which are grouped in sections treating church order, ritual administration, and matters of ecclesiastical hierarchy; marriage; succession/inheritance issues; ecclesiastical property. Lev Weitz observes that a number of features indicate that Timothy did not write original judgments or rulings, but compiled a series of case-specific rulings instead of more general legal principles or rules.[46] Weitz sees that a portion of the judgments were actual decisions determined by Timothy, or his responses to other cases and questions of legal procedure

43. E. Sachau, ed. and trans., *Syrische Rechtsbücher*, 3 vols. (Berlin, 1907–1914).

44. This is found in a single manuscript, Baghdad Chaldean Monastery 509. Cf. Lev Weitz, "Shaping East Syrian Law in 'Abbasid Iraq: The Law Books of Patriarchs Timothy I and Išō' Bar Nūn," *Le Muséon* 129, no. 1–2 (2016): 73–76.

45. Sachau, *Syrische Rechtsbücher*, 2:54.6–11.

46. Weitz, "Shaping East Syrian Law," 83.

sent to him and then collected. There are redundancies and contradictions that indicate that Timothy did not consolidate his judgments, but simply gathered them together. The question-and-answer format is seen as Timothy's method of rewriting and reorganizing his materials. In matters for which there is not a heritage of East Syrian precedents, Timothy relies upon common Near Eastern legal practices and blesses them as law for the Church of the East.[47]

The betrothal contract and succession/inheritance laws occupy a significant part of Timothy's attention, both relying upon traditional Near Eastern practices for there were no distinctive East Syrian traditions at play. The betrothal (*mkūrē*) is not just a simple pledge to marry at a future time—an "engagement" in modern Western terms—but the establishment of a legal relationship involving specific rights and obligations. *Mkūrē* is then a virtual full marriage, and breaking the betrothal agreement would involve serious penalties. Timothy states that a betrothal can be dissolved only in the instance of one partner committing adultery, just as in a marital divorce.[48]

Succession or inheritance laws, closely related as well to dowry customs, take up the majority of space in Timothy's law book. The anecdotal situations all involve the death of a man who ideally has living children surviving him. His property is usually divided among the sons, but if there are unmarried daughters, they are to be given a lesser portion for their support. If the daughters are married, the dowry becomes their only tangible inheritance and they are no longer considered under their father's responsibility.[49]

This mixture of ecclesiastical and civil traditions in the construction of a Church of the East system of laws that cannot ignore the dominant Muslim system, but seeks a particularly Christian way to settle a number of problematic life-situations, is both to be expected for a patriarch as the leader of a minority population, yet contrary to his ecclesiastical calling. During his lengthy tenure of forty-three years, Timothy I seldom was able to keep ecclesiastical roles distinguished from civil, and perhaps did not want to do so.

Can the Catholicos Be Holy?

For the record, the Church of the East has its canon of saints, and Timothy I is not one of them. That is no injustice or slight of Timothy's contributions, but it refers us to another category of contribution. The late Swiss Catholic theologian

47. Weitz, "Shaping East Syrian Law," 80–81.
48. Weitz, "Shaping East Syrian Law," 94.
49. Weitz, "Shaping East Syrian Law," 101.

Hans Urs von Balthasar, in an article "Theology and Sanctity," expressed his sadness and regret that following the medieval Scholastic period, theologians stopped being saints.[50] Not intentionally, of course, but the connection between holiness and writing theological works started to fade as philosophy and the development of the natural sciences increased the scope of knowledge for the theologian to absorb. Von Balthasar noted that in the early church the offices of teacher and pastor or pastoral care and service were seamlessly intertwined, so that there was no distinction between Christian life and Christian doctrine.[51]

Timothy I was a priest, bishop, and catholicos/patriarch, who became an exemplar of the church statesman, immersed deeply in the pastoral and institutional concerns of the church and how those concerns inevitably intersected with the affairs and culture of the state outside the church. Nonetheless, Timothy was a theologian and philosopher of significance, whose writings were generally occasional for the benefit of the church and its members, rather than systematic constructions. Timothy's detractors focused upon the reputed manipulation of his own election to the patriarchate, and subsequently other administrative decisions would raise the ire of his opponents within the church. Augustine also periodically endured similar controversy regarding his episcopal decisions. The lasting merit of Timothy's patriarchate was in his long service to his church and people in the midst of a ruling government that tolerated his church, but did not enable it. His pastoral concern was evidenced through his theological writings enabling Christians to possess confidence and religious dignity as a minority. His efforts to expand the geographical range of his church are well known and heralded, even if history did not preserve his efforts. Timothy cobbled together a code of law so that his church had some resources to regulate its own affairs, rather than have to live under somebody else's laws. The grace of Timothy's patriarchate lay not in his personal holiness, but in how he worked to enable the people of the Church of the East to encounter the presence of Christ and maintain that presence in their lives and communities.

---

50. Hans Urs von Balthasar, "Theology and Sanctity," in *The Word Made Flesh*, vol. 1 of *Explorations in Theology* (San Francisco: Ignatius Press, 1989), 181–209.

51. Cf. David Moss, "The Saints," in *The Cambridge Companion to Hans Urs von Balthasar*, ed. Edward T. Oakes, SJ, and David Moss (Cambridge: Cambridge University Press, 2004), 79–92, esp. 83.

PART FOUR

Identity in the Middle Ages

Chapter 17

Anselm: The Integrated Theologian

STEVEN L. PORTER

The church needs Anselmian theology today, not so much for its content but for its methodology, which was exemplified in Anselm. Indeed, Anselm of Bec and then Canterbury (ca. 1033–1109) is an especially important figure of whom to take note in our particular time and place. Chastened by philosophical postmodernism, we rightly decry theological investigation that is overly rationalistic, individualistic, and needlessly abstract such that it is practically irrelevant to the spiritual life and witness of the church. By contrast, in Anselm we find a theologian who is intellectually rigorous, interpersonally connected, and demonstrates a way of doing theology that while at times abstract is also embedded within a life of eager devotion to God. Intellectual rigor, interpersonal connectedness, and passionate spirituality are not often found in one and the same person. As such, Anselm embodies an antidote to some of the dichotomization and disintegration that can plague theological work today.[1] Or, perhaps better said, Anselm found his way into an integrated identity that allowed him to resist the dichotomization and disintegration that can plague theological work, and it would be good for us to find our way into a similar integrated way of being.

In this essay, we briefly explicate Anselm's intellectual rigor, spiritual devotion, and interpersonal connectedness with the aim of showing how these three aspects of Anselm's life formed a whole. Second, we touch on some of what influenced Anselm in his time and place such that he could hold together these important dimensions of human life. For, as Sir Richard Southern states

---

1. Kelly Kapic addresses some of the fragmentation within contemporary theology in his *A Little Book for New Theologians: Why and How to Study Theology* (Downers Grove, IL: InterVarsity Press, 2012).

it, "Anselm is an original thinker of great stature, and we can easily forget that he was not always original nor always a thinker."[2] Anselm became, as we all must become, the person that he was. And so, we conclude with some thoughts on how persons today might find their way into the same sort of formative influences that we see in Anselm.

Anselm's Intellectual Rigor

When it comes to theological study, we might think of intellectual rigor as the process of careful and sustained reflection on a theological reality (e.g., the incarnation of Jesus) that acquaints one with the nature of that reality, the sources and conditions through which it can be known, and the reasons for understanding that reality one way rather than another. So intellectual rigor includes the intellectual traits of carefulness, perseverance, thoroughness, attentiveness, and autonomy (i.e., thinking for one's self), which become the seedbed for both intellectual courage and humility.[3] Courage arises in that the rigorous theologian has seen the truth for herself, knows when to take a stand for that truth, and has something solid on which to take a stand. But humility also results in that rigor acquaints one with the complexities of theological matters and the limitations of the knower as well as the importance of trusting sources of knowledge more well-positioned vis-à-vis the truth than one's individual self. On this way of describing things, Anselm was clearly a rigorous thinker: careful, tenacious, thorough, attentive, autonomous, courageous, and humble. This can be seen in several ways.

First, Anselm highly valued clarity and logical coherence in his theological arguments. For instance, no one doubts whether the argument of the *Proslogion* takes a logically valid form.[4] While the soundness of the argument has been questioned by many, the logical validity of the argument form is clear. To clarify, a "valid" argument is one in which the conclusion logically follows from the premises, while a "sound" argument is one in which the conclusion follows logically from the premises *and* the premises are true. Even the likes of Bertrand Russell reports:

2. R. W. Southern, *Saint Anselm and His Biographer: A Study of Monastic Life and Thought* (Cambridge: Cambridge University Press, 1963), xi.

3. For a discussion of intellectual virtue concepts such as these, see Jason Baehr, *The Inquiring Mind: On Intellectual Virtues and Virtue Epistemology* (Oxford: Oxford University Press, 2012), and Phillip E. Dow, *Virtuous Minds: Intellectual Character Development* (Downers Grove, IL: IVP Academic, 2013).

4. See A. D. Smith's recent assessment in his *Anselm's Other Argument* (Cambridge: Harvard University Press, 2014).

I remember the precise moment, one day in 1894, as I was walking along Trinity Lane, when I saw in a flash (or thought I saw) that the ontological argument is valid. I had gone out to buy a tin of tobacco; on my way back, I suddenly threw it up in the air, and exclaimed as I caught it: "Great Scott, the ontological argument is sound."[5]

Of course, Russell eventually rescinded his conclusion that the argument was sound, but that the argument form is valid was and remains clear. Such clarity and logical coherence was Anselm's practice in a period in which theological work often utilized rhetorical argumentation that lacked logical coherence.[6] Eileen Sweeney writes: "The audacity of Anselm's willingness to submit not just the existence of God but the Incarnation, Virgin birth, and *filioque* controversy to the bar of reason, seeking necessary and indubitable conclusions, is unparalleled. His faith in reason and in the power of words and arguments is seemingly boundless."[7] Indeed, Anselm boundlessly labored for clarity and coherence in his thinking, teaching, and writing, often redrafting his treatises several times and welcoming the critiques of others as a means to that end.[8]

But intellectual rigor is not simply seen in Anselm's carefully constructed theological treatises. Another indication of Anselm's rigor is that he approached theological issues with sustained and thorough attentiveness to the issue at hand. Sustained and thorough attention to a matter can help one get to the bottom of an issue and discern when something of substance is at stake and when it is not. An example of this is Anselm's response to Walram, the bishop of Naumburg, who wrote to Anselm alarmed by differences amongst Palestinian, Armenian, Gallic, and Roman Christians when it came to administering

5. Bertrand Russell, "The Philosophy of Bertrand Russell," in *The Many Faces of Philosophy: Reflections from Plato to Arendt*, ed. A. O. Rorty (New York: Oxford University Press, 2003), 406.

6. One example of the sort of argumentation that was typical of Anselm's age is that of Walram, bishop of Naumburg, which will be treated below.

7. Eileen Sweeney, *Anselm of Canterbury and the Desire for the Word* (Washington, DC: Catholic University of America Press, 2012), 1.

8. One charge against Anselm's ontological argument is that it begs the question in that it assumes God's existence in its first premise. If Anselm is guilty of begging the question in this sort of obvious way, this would count against his intellectual rigor. But Anselm was well aware of this objection—indeed, it was the objection of Gaunilo—and Anselm thought he had an answer in that existential statements (at least regarding God) can be necessarily true. Indeed, Alvin Plantinga contends that "although the argument looks at first sight as if it ought to be unsound, it is profoundly difficult to say what exactly is wrong with it. Indeed, it is doubtful that any philosopher has given a really convincing and thorough refutation of the ontological argument." See Plantinga, *God and Other Minds* (Ithaca, NY: Cornell University Press, 1980), 27.

the Eucharist.[9] Walram pointed out that some blessed the chalice and bread separately making the sign of the cross twice, while others blessed the chalice and bread together with one sign of the cross. Walram took the two separate blessings to be correct because he maintained that this was Christ's practice in 1 Corinthians 11:23–25, where Christ also commanded, "Do this, as often as you drink it" (1 Cor 11:25 ESV), such that, Walram concluded, to bless only once was a departure from the imitation of Christ.[10] Still another difference Walram noted was that some covered the Eucharistic chalice with a folded cloth at the start of the celebration and others only at the end as a way to keep the consecrated elements clean. While Walram was open to covering the chalice at the end of the celebration, he thought covering the chalice at the beginning failed to imitate Christ in that Christ was naked (uncovered) on the cross. Walram wrote, "Let Jesus, who was naked on the altar of the cross, appear naked on the altar of our immolation."[11]

While Walram's specific concerns might now seem a bit petty, Walram certainly did not see them that way. As well, there were substantive issues intertwined with Walram's questions of practice. Without thorough and sustained attention on the part of the respondent, responses to these sorts of theological questions can fail to discern what is of substance and what needs correcting. As many a church leader can attest, the quick and easy retort to objections like these can easily muddy the waters and lead to greater dissension.

The attentiveness and thoroughness of Anselm's thinking can be seen in his response to Walram. Anselm first located what good there was in Walram's concern, agreeing with Walram that "it would be a good and praiseworthy thing" if the church were uniform in how it administered the Eucharist. "However," he went on to write, "there are many differences which do not conflict with the fundamental importance of the sacrament or with its efficacy or with faith in it. . . . Accordingly, I think that these differences ought to be harmoniously and peaceably tolerated rather than being disharmoniously and scandalously condemned."[12] Here Anselm saw that the substantive issue had to do with maintaining unity on the value of the Eucharist, its efficacy, and confidence in it. Such unity on the essential meaning of the sacrament allowed for divergent ways of administering the sacrament that did not affect its "fundamental importance."

9. "Three Letters on the Sacraments," in *Complete Philosophical and Theological Treatises of Anselm of Canterbury*, trans. Jasper Hopkins and Herbert Richardson (Minneapolis: Arthur J. Banning Press, 2000), 523–27.
10. Letters on the Sacraments 2.3.
11. Letters on the Sacraments 2.4.
12. Letters on the Sacraments 3.1.

While that response alone should have been adequate to enable Walram to see the error in his thinking, Walram might have persisted in thinking that whether one blessed the bread as well as the cup and whether one covered the consecrated cup at the beginning of the Eucharist or just the end were essential to the "fundamental importance" of the sacrament. Anticipating that line of thinking, Anselm thought through these matters to their end, showing that Walram's manner of reasoning regarding the problematic nature of these divergent practices was faulty.

First, Anselm defended those who made only one sign of the cross over both the bread and the cup since Christ is one person and so there is one offering or victim in the bread and cup to receive the one blessing. Moreover, to depart from Christ's apparent blessing of the bread separately from the cup in 1 Corinthians 11 does not count as a problematic difference. Of those who practice a single blessing of bread and cup, Anselm wrote:

> I do not see that in doing this these latter dissent more from Christ, who blessed each individually, than all those dissent who do not consecrate the chalice after a supper, as Christ did, and who do not always do it in the evening, as Christ did, and who call both together by one name—"offering" or "victim"—which Christ did not do. From this we may conclude that in such an action, provided we mutually preserve the truth of the thing, we may differ from one another without blame, since we differ from the very author of the sacrifice itself without offense.[13]

Anselm's reasoning here was clear: there were many ways in which the administration of the Eucharist was unlike Christ's administration, and yet those divergences did not undermine the fundamental meaning of the sacrament.

Anselm went on to offer a similar response to Walram's objection to the covering of the chalice. Yes, Anselm replies, Christ suffered naked on the cross, but also he suffered "outside the city, outside a house, and under the open sky."[14] It did not follow from this that the Eucharist must be performed outside the city, outside a house, and under an open sky. These are not elements that are essential to the meaning and efficacy of the Eucharist. Therefore, neither does Christ's nakedness need to be represented in leaving the chalice uncovered. Moreover, Anselm contended that Christ's nakedness on the cross had far greater implications when it came to the imitation of Christ. Christ's nakedness was part of Christ's overall example of "enduring incomparable contempt

---

13. Letters on the Sacraments 3.2.
14. Letters on the Sacraments 3.3.

and poverty for the sake of justice."[15] In this way, Anselm holds that one should imitate Christ's self-sacrificial way of life for the sake of justice in "one's life by deeds" rather than an uncovered chalice.[16] In this way, Anselm not only showed that Walram was not seeing the forest for the trees, but that he was not seeing the trees correctly either! Anselm's intellectual rigor brought about sustained and thorough attentiveness that made possible clear and penetrating theological analyses.

But Anselm's rigorous mind was most clearly on display in his appreciation of and ability to maintain a stance of "faith seeking understanding" (*fides quaerens intellectum*).[17] As the history of Christian thought has shown, many Christian thinkers split over faith and reason, faith understood here as acceptance of a view solely based on authoritative tradition and reason understood as reflection on the rational grounds for one's theological position.[18] Those who submit to traditional theological views on the basis of the authority often feel threatened by taking questions and doubts about such views seriously, let alone the attempt to rationally consider the evidence available. In contrast, those who are most eager to bring rational considerations to bear on theological matters are often pained by any appeal to authoritative tradition.

While many might fall somewhere on the continuum between the fideist and the rationalist, it takes a keen and flexible mind to find equipoise between faith and rational understanding. It was precisely Anselm's rigorous approach to theology that allowed him to remain confident that reason could rationally undergird the truths of faith by bringing one to understand that which one already believed, while at the same time it acquainted him with the complexity of theological realities and the limitations of reason such that he was content to pursue rational understanding all the while submitting to the authority of Scripture and church teaching. Anselm wrote:

> Indeed, no Christian ought to argue how things that the Catholic Church sincerely believes and verbally professes are not so, but by always adhering to the same faith without hesitation, by loving it, and by humbly living according to it, a Christian ought to argue how they are, inasmuch as one can

15. Letters on the Sacraments 3.3.

16. Letters on the Sacraments 3.3.

17. See the preface to Anselm's *Proslogion*, and Brian Davies and G. R. Evans, *Anselm of Canterbury: The Major Works* (Oxford: Oxford University Press, 1998).

18. For a treatment of Anselm's notion of faith seeking understanding in the context of discussions of faith and reason, see Paul Helm, *Faith and Understanding* (Grand Rapids: Eerdmans, 1997), 28–35.

look for reasons. If one can understand, one should thank God; if one cannot, one should bow one's head in veneration rather than sound off trumpets.[19]

Anselm had the kind of rigorous mind that could simultaneously hold the value of authority and reason, not allowing a tension to arise between these two compatible sources of knowledge.

Anselm's Spiritual Devotion

Much more could be said about Anselm's intellectual rigor, but what is poignant for the purposes of this essay is that Anselm integrated that rigor with a serious connection to the person of God. It can be unfortunately difficult in theological study today to even get a hearing for the pairing of theological investigation and communion with God. At times it is almost taken for granted that, for instance, seminary training is necessarily deadening to one's spiritual life.[20]

As a case in point, I regularly teach systematic theology to graduate students who have gathered for a degree program in Christian formation. These students tend not to be inclined to systematic theology; rather, they are inclined to spiritual theology. They are not primed to adore Aquinas, Calvin, and Warfield; instead, they are primed to adore Bernard, Theresa, and Merton. When teaching this group, I am often concerned that theological analysis will be seen as distant from and irrelevant to the immediacy of the students' desired communion with God and transformation in the way of Jesus. I seek to exhort the students that there is a place for rigorous and systematic investigation of God's self-revelation as that has been understood down through church history. But I do not want to carve out that space by turning too quickly to the practical or personal application of each doctrine, for in turning too quickly I am liable to lose the depth of understanding that is an essential part of practical application and personal internalization. And so, as a preliminary way to address this concern, I often begin the first session of my systematic theology classes with each student in the class reading aloud one line at a time from Anselm's *Proslogion*:

> Come now, insignificant man, fly for a moment from your affairs. . . . Abandon yourself for a little to God and rest for a little in Him . . . Come then, Lord

19. *De Incarnatione Verbi* 1.1. All quotations from Anselm's works are from Davies and Evans, *Anselm of Canterbury: The Major Works*, unless otherwise noted.
20. Of course, seminary training is not automatically conducive to spiritual growth, but that it is deadening is not necessarily the case.

my God, teach my heart where and how to seek You, where and how to find You. . . . Look upon us, Lord; hear us, enlighten us, show Yourself to us. . . . I do not try, Lord, to attain Your lofty heights, because my understanding is in no way equal to it. But I do desire to understand Your truth a little, that truth that my heart believes and loves. For I do not seek to understand so that I may believe; but I believe so that I may understand. For I believe this also, that "unless I believe, I shall not understand" (Isa 7:9). Well then, Lord, You who give understanding to faith, grant me that I may understand, as much as You see fit.[21]

After reading together the longer passages from which the lines above were extracted, I go on to quote Anselm a bit further along in his same treatise. This humble, passionate, prayerful, God-thirsty theologian represented in the initial section of the *Proslogion* is the same author who a few lines later puts forth the following proof:

And surely that-than-which-a greater-cannot-be-thought cannot exist in the mind alone. For if it exists solely in the mind, it can be thought to exist in reality also, which is greater. If then that-than-which-a greater-cannot-be-thought exists in the mind alone, this same that-than-which-a greater-cannot-be-thought is that-than-which-a greater-can-be-thought. But this is obviously impossible. Therefore there is absolutely no doubt that something-than-which-a greater-cannot-be-thought exists both in the mind and in reality.[22]

And thus, one of the most seemingly overly rationalistic and needlessly abstract bits of theologizing ever reflected upon comes into existence. It is often surprising to my students that what has come to be called the ontological argument for God's existence was formulated in the midst of passionate prayer. Indeed, Eadmer, Anselm's biographer, reports that during Matins "the grace of God illuminated" Anselm's heart and he received the ontological argument as a flash of insight.[23] From that prayerful origin, Anselm continued to pray his way through the complex, rigorous treatise. As Benedicta Ward states, "Anselm himself prayed his theology till there was no difference between theology and prayer."[24] In the *Proslogion*, Anselm never paused or hesitated to think that

---

21. *Proslogion* 1.1.

22. *Proslogion* 1.2.

23. As quoted in Benedicta Ward, "Anselm of Canterbury and His Influence," in *Christian Spirituality: Origins to Twelfth Century*, ed. Bernard McGinn, John Meyendorff, and Jean Leclercq (New York: Crossroad, 1993), 200.

24. Benedicta Ward, trans., *The Prayers and Meditations of Saint Anselm with the Proslogion* (London: Penguin, 1973), 77.

in the rigor he had somehow moved from heart to head. No, Anselm was, as Michael Ramsey put it, "all of one piece. The monastic life, the praying, the reasoning, the caring for people . . . all had a single root, and the separation of them would have been for Anselm impossible and without meaning. . . . Every human faculty is drawn into this quest for God: praying, caring, and reasoning well."[25]

Indeed, for Anselm, the contemplation of God is partly constituted by seeking to rationally understand what one already believes. Marilyn McCord Adams makes the point that in the *Monologion* Anselm had already concluded that loving God above all other goods is the highest good for humans and that since love seeks the good with all of its powers, "a rational creature ought to devote all its powers and will to remembering and understanding and loving the Highest Good—the [end] for which it knows itself to exist."[26] Adams goes on to argue that Anselm's theological method in the *Proslogion* involved "asking questions of, addressing puzzles to, and/or begging help from God" and then articulating what God revealed with "explicit acknowledgments of Divine collaboration."[27]

But not only did Anselm's theological work flow out of a life of prayerful devotion, Anselm's life of prayerful devotion was also informed by his theological conclusions. In Anselm there is a "balance of intellect and spirituality," and his prayers are "at once devotional and theological."[28] Referring to the *Proslogion* and the *Meditation on Human Redemption*, Ward writes, "This combination of theological veracity and personal ardour is what most distinguishes Anselm's writings from similar prayers, and makes him both traditional and revolutionary."[29] Ward contends that there was a new intensity in eleventh-century spirituality of tenderness and compassion towards Jesus and his mother that arose partly due to Anselm's role in developing a new doctrine of the atonement. In *Cur Deus Homo*, Anselm turns atonement theorizing from an exchange between Christ and Satan that releases human persons from bondage to Satan to an exchange between the Father and the Son that places humans face-to-face with God.[30] On Anselm's view of the atonement, Christ's death and Mary's loss were more sacrifice to God

25. Michael Ramsey, "Anselm of Bec and Canterbury," in *Anselm Studies: An Occasional Journal* 1 (Millwood, NY: Kraus International Publications, 1983), 1. A more recent argument for a unified view of Anselm is Sweeney, *Anselm of Canterbury and the Desire for the Word*.

26. As quoted in Marilyn McCord Adams, "Praying the *Proslogion*: Anselm's Theological Method," in *The Rationality of Belief & the Plurality of Faith*, ed., Thomas D. Senor (Ithaca, NY: Cornell University Press, 1995), 15.

27. Adams, "Praying the *Proslogion*," 18, 20.

28. G. R. Evans, *Anselm* (London: Continuum), 27, 28.

29. Ward, *Prayers and Meditations*, 76.

30. On this point, see Southern, *Saint Anselm and His Biographer*, 92–102; and Ward, *Prayers and Meditations*, 58–59.

for rebellious injury to him than ransom to Satan for escape from bondage. Jesus was victim of suffered loss as opposed to Jesus as triumphant hero. We can see Anselm's atonement theology informing his *Prayer to Christ*:

> So, as much as I can, though not as much as I ought,
> I am mindful of your passion,
> your buffeting, your scourging, your cross, your wounds,
> how you were slain for me,
> how prepared for burial and buried . . .
> All this I hold with unwavering faith,
> and weep over the hardship of exile,
> hoping in the sole consolation of your coming,
> ardently longing for the glorious contemplation of your face.[31]

Anselm's theology of the cross places him in a position of compassion for his savior and ardent desire to fulfill the purpose for which the cross was required.

Ironically, G. R. Evans makes the point that it is precisely Anselm's integration of spirituality and theology that limited the range of his influence. She writes, "Anselm saw theological truths with a directness compounded of spiritual and intellectual insight. He unites the virtues of the monastic and scholastic traditions which were increasingly to diverge in the twelfth century."[32] Evans maintains that it was Anselm's unification of these two traditions that made "the style of his theology incompatible" with the scholastic theologians that followed him in the twelfth-century schools (e.g., Peter Abelard).[33] Anselm was able to hold together spiritual contemplation and theological speculation in a manner that many theologians since have found difficult.[34]

Anselm's Interpersonal Connectedness

Southern has argued that Anselm's spirituality expressed the "urge towards a greater measure of solitude, of introspection and self knowledge."[35] For Anselm, it was not so much in the liturgical prayer of the monastic community that God was to be found but through prayers that touched the "innermost recesses of

---

31. "Prayer to Christ," as translated in Ward, *Prayers and Meditations*, 62–72.
32. G. R. Evans, *Anselm and a New Generation* (Oxford: Oxford University Press, 1980), ix.
33. Evans, *New Generation*, 8.
34. See also, Evans, *Anselm*, 66.
35. R. W. Southern, *The Making of the Middle Ages* (New Haven: Yale University Press, 1992), 227.

the conscious and awakened soul."[36] Hence, it might be thought that while Anselm integrated theological reflection and spiritual devotion, he did so in a privatizing, individualistic manner. And yet, we see that in both his theological reflection and spirituality, Anselm lived in loving connection with persons.

For one, even in the development of his prayers for private devotion, Anselm was relationally integrated. First, the motivation for Anselm's writing prayers that bring the individual before God was his concern for the spiritual welfare of others, both his monastic brothers (e.g., Gundolph) and those outside of monastic communities (e.g., Princess Adelaide and Countess Mathilda) who desired to pursue a deeper spiritual life. Hence, he developed these private prayers not out of his own self-referenced spiritual needs, but rather out of his concern for others. For instance, to Countess Mathilda he wrote, "It has seemed good to your Highness that I should send you these prayers, which I edited at the request of several brothers. . . . They are arranged so that by reading them the mind may be stirred up either to the love or fear of God."[37]

Second, Anselm's prayers are deeply interpersonal in nature. Anselm's emotional displays of affection for God, for the saints, for his friends, and even his enemies represent a significant interpersonal drive within his spiritual life. In his "Prayer for Friends" he writes, "Love them, Author and Giver of love, for your own sake, not for mine, and make them love you with all their heart, all their soul, and all their mind, so that they will and speak and do only what pleases you and is expedient for them." As Ward points out, in these prayers, Anselm "has not withdrawn from the *koinonia*; he has only entered more deeply into the fullness of the people of God, where he talks with Christ and the saints as a man talks with his friends."[38] Moreover, Ward notes that when Anselm "addresses the saints he is interested only in two things, what God has done in them and how they have experienced his work. It is not their miracles, their appearance, their glory even, but themselves as people that Anselm cares about."[39] Anselm was thoroughly personal in his spiritual life.

The same holds true in Anselm's theological treatises. Anselm is constantly writing for the sake of others, responding to requests and questions and controversies that others have brought before him. Anselm writes as a pastor, as a shepherd of those under his care. He writes the *Monologion* "at the pressing entreaties of several of my brethren"; he writes *Proslogion* so that "what had given me such joy to discover would afford pleasure, if it were written down,

---

36. Southern, *Making of the Middle Ages*, 226. See also Ward, *Prayers and Meditations*, 51.

37. Letter of Anselm to the Countess Mathilda of Tuscany, as translated in Ward, *Prayers and Meditations*, 90.

38. Ibid., 52.

39. Ibid., 58.

to anyone who might read it"; he writes *Cur Deus Homo* at the earnest request "both by word of mouth and in writing, by many people, to set down a written record of the reasoned explanations with which I am in the habit of answering people"; he writes *De Incarnatione Verbi* in order to respond to Roscelin's charges against him; he writes *De Conceptu Virginali* to comply with the interests and curiosity of "my brother and dear son Boso."

But perhaps nothing else better demonstrates Anselm's interpersonal connectedness than his emphasis on and practice of friendship. While much has been written on Anselm's affectionate letters of friendship, even beyond these letters, there is repeated evidence that Anselm was well loved by and loved well those with whom he came into contact, whether fellow monks or lay persons.[40] Eadmer, William of Malmesbury, Gundulf, Alexander, Boso, Gilbert Crispin, and various others recount having been meaningfully influenced by Anselm's presence and teaching. Evans writes, Anselm "was clearly much loved and admired in his generation, at least by those in his small but close circle of the monks at Bec and a few others who later had the experience of living with him in community at Canterbury."[41]

Anselm's Formative Influences

So, we have in Anselm a unique Christian identity—an integrated identity of keen intellect, passionate spirituality, and rich relationality. And yet, if we are to have more than an ideal to inspire us, we must know something of the form of life that made Anselm what he was. While Anselm's formative influences are no doubt complex and, to some degree, lost to history, there are several intriguing facts that can be briefly noted.

First, we cannot underestimate the impact of the Benedictine Rule on Anselm's development. He was no reluctant participant in the Rule, but rather an ardent defender and a "scrupulous observer of the monastic routine."[42] Of the Rule at this time in history, Southern writes, "The life it enjoined was ceaseless discipline, an unvaried round from year to year, a communal life where the individual was lost in the crowd and stripped of those eccentricities which we

---

40. On Anselm's letters of friendship, see R. W. Southern, *Saint Anselm: A Portrait in a Landscape* (Cambridge: Cambridge University Press, 1990), 138–65; and Sweeney, *Anselm of Canterbury and the Desire for the Word*, 70–73.

41. G. R. Evans, "Anselm's Life, Works, and Immediate Influence," in *The Cambridge Companion to Anselm*, ed. Brian Davies and Brian Leftow (Cambridge: Cambridge University Press, 2004), 24.

42. Southern, *The Making of the Middle Ages*, 227.

call his personality."[43] At Bec, Anselm would have prayed through the entire psalter every week in addition to additional psalms, prayers, and offices such that a large part of the day would have been spent in liturgical contemplation.[44] "This continuous round of psalmody gave the monk a rich and deep knowledge of the psalter, which would be absorbed almost unconsciously."[45] For over fifty years, Anselm lived in one of two Benedictine communities, maintaining close relations with those from Bec even after moving to Canterbury. This Rule of life framed Anselm's theological development, his dependence on God, as well as his connection to others.

Second, while Anselm's Benedictine way of life stripped him of his individual identity, it was simultaneously an introspective spirituality for the purpose of self-knowledge and compunction. Anselm's prayers to St. Peter, St. Benedict, for any Abbot, for any Bishop, as well as others demonstrate that Anselm was keenly aware of his own failings and places of weakness.[46] Anselm's meditations attempted to rouse the mind from its slumber in order to awaken the soul to its need for God and for his forgiveness. In this way Anselm was formed by a spirituality that included a penetrating knowledge of self for the purpose of coming to have a deep awareness of his utter dependence on God.

Third, Anselm gave himself up to a relational existence with others. In this vein, it is important to note that while Anselm's relationship with his father became increasingly strained after the death of his mother and we know little of his interactions with his sister, he did live at home until age twenty-three and did not enter the cloistered life until age twenty-seven. Unlike Aquinas, for instance, who entered the monastery at age five, Anselm developed as a person within his biological family and then in his young adulthood as a traveling student. In other words, before he was Anselm of Bec or Canterbury, he was Anselm of Aosta. What this early relational experience did for Anselm would be mere speculation, but it is striking that he had time to develop outside monastic life. Upon entering the monastery at Bec, he entered fully into what can be described as an intense connection to his fellow monks and an unwavering submission to his prior, Lanfranc. As mentioned earlier, Anselm maintained long-standing friendships with several of his monastic brothers.

An additional formative influence on Anselm was precisely his pursuit of

43. Ibid., 223.

44. Ward, *Prayers and Meditations*, 27–28.

45. Ibid., 28.

46. See Benedicta Ward, review of Sally Vaughn, *Archbishop Anselm, 1093–1109: Bec Missionary, Canterbury Primate, Patriarch of Another World*, in *Journal of Theological Studies* 64, no. 2 (2013): 771–772.

theological understanding that provided him experiential knowledge of theological truths.[47] Anselm writes:

> There is no room for doubt about what I say: one who has not believed will not understand. For one who has not believed will not experience, and one who has not experienced will not know. For as much as experiencing a thing is superior to hearing about it, so much does the knowledge of someone who has experience surpass that of someone who merely hears.[48]

In his appreciation of experiencing the truth for one's self—knowledge by acquaintance—as opposed to the mere hearing of the truth from others, Anselm finds an echo in Aquinas, who writes that the purpose of theological disputations is

> less to push error out than to lead listeners into the truth they strive to understand. Accordingly they must be carried by reasonings in order to get to the root of the matter, and helped to see for themselves how what is asserted is true. Otherwise, if the appeal is merely to bare authorities, then all the teacher does is to certify to his listeners that such in fact is the answer to the problem; apart from this they have gathered no reason for it and no understanding, and so go empty away.[49]

Anselm's methodology was to be "carried by reasonings" and get to the "root of the matter." He saw rational reflection and the understanding it brings as a mediating pathway from faith to final revelation. For Anselm, writes Paul Helm, "in seeing how it is true the mind comes to grasp something of the divine reality itself."[50] Anselm described coming to have such understanding as bringing joy, pleasure, and nourishment. At the conclusion of Anselm's argument in *Cur Deus Homo*, Anselm's dialogue partner in the treatise, Boso, reports, "I receive such confidence from this that I cannot describe the joy with which my heart exults."[51]

47. For a discussion of this, see Sandra Visser and Thomas Williams, *Anselm* (Oxford: Oxford University Press, 2009), 20–21.

48. As quoted in Visser and Williams, *Anselm*, 20.

49. Thomas Aquinas, *Quaestiones quodlibetales*, 4 q. 9 a. 2; as quoted in Thomas Gilby, OP, introduction to St. Thomas Aquinas, *Summa Theologiae*, ed. Thomas Gilby, OP, et al. (Cambridge: Blackfriars, 1964), 1:xxi. Thanks to Alfred Freddoso for directing me to this source.

50. Helm, *Faith and Understanding*, 29.

51. *Cur Deus Homo* 2.19, quoted in Sweeney, *Anselm of Canterbury and the Desire for the Word*, 2.

This sort of experiential knowing—seeing the truth for one's self—is an important feature of Anselm's formation. Taking steps to come to have a deeper degree of confidence in God and his ways brings with it an increasing sense of security, contentment, peace, and joy in the kingdom of God. As Evans puts it, Anselm was "at the end of an era of quiet reflective confident trust in divine leading toward the truth."[52]

Following Anselm as He Follows Christ

Having considered Anselm's integrated identity and some of the elements that formed his identity, we are now in the position to consider the ways of Christ of which we are reminded in Anselm that we can take on today. I will mention three salient ones of what could be many.

First, we would be wise to take on Anselm's practice of rigorous theological study coupled with prayer. Those who write theological papers, sermons, Bible study notes, and the like are wise to experiment with Anselm's practice of writing out a prayer to God that guides, informs, and orients one's theological work. While theological writing today does not typically lend itself to be written in the form of an extended prayer, a short, written prayer at the start of theological study to which one returns throughout one's study can help ingrain the God-ward companionship amidst one's study that Anselm enjoyed. For instance, in some of my theology classes I have a written prayer that I utilize to orient me to God as I prepare for that class. Occasionally I ask my students to write out their own prayer for the course, and we begin each class session with one of us praying aloud our written prayer.

A second Anselmian practice is to find our way into a place of faith seeking understanding. I say "find our way into" because this is something that must be developed over time. Anselm maintained that there was a joy in finding confirmation for our faith through reasons for our faith, and in that vein we might consider reflecting on reasons in favor of certain theological issues as a spiritual discipline.[53] As mentioned earlier, this is to approach theological study with intellectual rigor. Given that intellectual rigor involves characteristic ways of thinking (e.g., perseverance, carefulness, attentiveness, etc.), rigor can be practiced and developed. For instance, we can make choices to persevere

---

52. Evans, "Anselm's Life," 28.

53. See Steven L. Porter, "What Do the *Five Ways* Have to Do with the *Ascent of Mt. Carmel*? Apologetics as a Modern Day Spiritual Discipline," *Philosophia Christi* 9, no. 1 (March 2007): 189–202.

in theological study even when the content challenges our intellectual powers and energy; we can resist diminishing the importance of questions and views when we find those questions or views frustrating or difficult to grasp; we can practice careful, slow, interactive reading of theological texts; we can learn to ask good questions and receive guidance from those who are further along in theological study; we can place ourselves in teaching situations that will force us to go further in our understanding as we prepare; and so on.

Of course, it is important to pursue understanding with an Anselmian attitude of "grant me that I may understand, as much as You see fit."[54] Anselm only wanted to understand as much as God intended him to understand—nothing more, but also, nothing less. Some of us will be inclined for more understanding than God sees fit for us, while others of us will tend to settle for less understanding than God sees fit. There is no one answer for what degree of understanding is fitting for this or that person. Much depends on one's calling, how one's mind works, the availability of training, and so forth. And we must not forget that we attempt to rationally understand matters of faith about which we already have grounds to believe via the authority of Scripture, church traditions, and the testimony of the Holy Spirit. Anselm shines forth as an example, as do others, of the spiritual benefits of developing a posture of faith seeking understanding.

Lastly, Anselm did theology for the sake of others and in close relationship with others. He wrote within a Benedictine community of close, interconnected lives. These men were bound by prayer and by long-established, daily rhythms. He wrote often for the needs and concerns of others, sharing his work with those around him. He regularly invited interlocutors into his thinking and writing: Guanilo, Boso, Eadmer, Lanfranc. We do well to do the same. Again, for those in formal theological training, cultivating friendships around theological education is essential.

"All of One Piece"

In his preface to the first edition of *Anselm: Fides Quaerens Intellectum*, Karl Barth references his "love for Anselm" and positions his book as a statement of some of the reasons why he finds "more of value and significance in this theologian than in others."[55] While a consideration of Barth's reading of Anselm cannot be accomplished here, Barth's clearly articulated appreciation of Anselm

---

54. *Proslogion* 1.2.
55. Karl Barth, *Anselm: Fides Quaerens Intellectum* (Cleveland: World Publishing Company, 1960), 7.

is suggestive of a long line of persons who have caught a glimpse of something significant in Anselm that is to be loved and valued. Against the backdrop of the fullness of Anselm's significance, this essay has highlighted his intellectual rigor, spiritual devotion, and interpersonal connectedness that were "all of one piece." Anselm's integrated identity stands before us today as an example of what is possible, and his way of life shines light on a pathway towards the realization of that possibility in Christ. We pray with Anselm to Christ:

Hope of my heart, strength of my soul,
help of my weakness,
by your powerful kindness complete
what in my powerless weakness I attempt.[56]

56. "Prayer to Christ," in Ward, *Prayers and Meditations*, 93.

Chapter 18

Bernard of Clairvaux: Lover of God as the Lover of Jesus

JAMES M. HOUSTON

Bernard of Clairvaux (1090–1153) is the great interpreter of the Fathers such as Origen, Augustine, and Gregory the Great. He is also the great monastic reformer, maintaining continuity between the original Benedictine order and the monastic reforms of his times. Whereas the original monasticism tended to become a *centripetal* institution as a shelter from paganism, Bernard led forward the later Cistercian renewal *centrifugally* to institute major cultural changes and to become strongly countercultural against feudalism, chivalry, and courtly love. Claimed justifiably as "the Last of the Fathers,"[1] he can also be called "the First of the Reformers," for he was thus appreciated by Martin Luther and later endorsed by John Calvin. In all reform movements, including those today in the rapid sequence since Vatican II, he remains a uniquely pivotal presence.

Bernard's Many "Identities"

Much has been said about the many aspects of Bernard, a man who dominated the first half of the twelfth century in sanctity, politics, and cultural influence. He is still a controversial figure that daunts personal identification—as all charismatic figures do. For medieval saints, like Hollywood stars today, share a certain charisma, which makes them inevitable leaders who bedazzle and mystify

---

1. Mabillon, who first collected Bernard's work (later published in J.-P. Migne, ed., *Patrologia Latina*, vols. 182–85), originally gave Bernard this title, though it was popularized more recently by Thomas Merton, *The Last of the Fathers: Saint Bernard of Clairvaux and the Encyclical Letter, Doctor Mellifluus* (New York: Harcourt Brace, 1954).

to identify uniquely. As Thomas Merton noted in honoring the anniversary of Bernard's death (1153–1953): "He left his mark on schools of spirituality, on Gregorian chant, on the clerical life, and on the whole development of Gothic architecture and art."[2] From politics to the *roman courtois,* and its deteriorating trend into the "courtly love" of medieval chivalry, as well as with heresies of scholasticism[3] and the Cathars[4]—with all of these Bernard was involved voluntarily and involuntarily.

Appropriately on the nonacentenary of his birth (1990), the great Bernardian scholar, Jean Leclerc contributed his own mature views in an article entitled "Towards a Sociological Interpretation of the Various Saint Bernards."[5]

The Legendary Identities of Bernard

First, there are the various "legendary views" of Bernard, initially put forth by his friend William of St. Thierry. Knowing Bernard would frown upon such hagiography, he nonetheless began circulating various legends of Bernard in order to initiate the process of canonization.[6] These accounts highlight both William's own needs of his friend as well as what Bernard was really like in his love for God. Another admirer—though outside of his circle—was Arnold of Bonneval, who continued the legendary account of Bernard's life, along with other legends about Bernard's mystical experiences with the Virgin Mary. The picture of Bernard emerging from these portraits has become a complex, multilayered receptivity of portraits—like entering into a tunnel of walled mirrors.

The Personality of Bernard

Another approach, put forward by Michael Casey, is that we learn of Bernard's personality through his letters and *sermones,* or informal discourses, which he gave to his novitiates in the chapter room. Secure in his own identity, Bernard was humorous and self-deprecating; he was aware of his own limits and ready

---

2. Ibid., 29.

3. The most helpful source is John R. Sommerfeldt, *Bernard of Clairvaux, On the Life of the Mind* (Mahwah, NJ: Newman Press, 2004), 40–54.

4. Bernard saw the heresy as a sinister spirit of evil, with no leader, but a grave threat to orthodox Christianity. See Malcolm Lambert, *The Cathars* (Oxford: Blackwell, 2009), 38–40.

5. Jean Leclercq, "Towards a Sociological Interpretation of the Various Saint Bernards," in *Bernardus Magister,* ed. John R. Sommerfeldt (Spencer, MA: Cistercian Publications, 1992), 19–34.

6. St. Bernard was swiftly canonized in 1174, just twenty-one years after his death.

to admit mistakes (he could be quite hasty in temper); he was collaborative and appreciative of others, delegating much of the abbot's administration to his brother Gerald.[7] He was a spell-binder because of the purity of his heart, his generosity, his enthusiasm, the attractive power he had to transform others, and his love—for he indeed was so lovable.[8]

The Historical Accounts of Bernard

Third, there are various "historical accounts" of Bernard, past, present, and yet future ones. These histories, however, often disclose more about the historical premises of the historians writing them as a continued industry of professional scholarship. Indeed, the paradox today is that without accepting that "truth is the daughter of time" (Bernard of Chartres)[9] and that "history is mystical tropology" (Henri de Lubac),[10] contemporary historians who do not understand the spiritual nature of history will struggle in vain to study Bernard "historically." Such are the recent scholarly studies of M. B. Pranger and Willemien Otten, and doubtless many more to come.[11]

Involved culturally in a remarkable twelfth-century "renaissance," Bernard has been associated with "the rise of the individual,"[12] "the rise of scholasticism,"[13] the first major medieval urbanization movement, and its supportive "agricultural revolution," "the confused role of the divided papacy," and "the expansive spread of the Crusades against Islam."[14] This was the age of the revival

7. Michael Casey, "Reading Saint Bernard: The Man, the Medium, the Message," in *A Companion to Saint Bernard of Clairvaux*, ed. Brian Patrick McGuire (Leiden/Boston: Brill, 2011), 62–107.

8. Ibid., 83.

9. Cited by M.-D. Chenu, *Nature, Man, and Society in the Twelfth Century*, ed. and trans. Jerome Taylor and Lester K. Little (Toronto: University of Toronto Press, 1997), 162.

10. See Henri de Lubac, "Mystical Tropology," chap. 9 in *Medieval Exegesis: The Four Senses of Scripture*, trans. Mark Sebanc and E. M. Macierowski (Grand Rapids: Eerdmans, 1998–2009), 2:127–78.

11. M. B. Pranger, *Bernard of Clairvaux and the Shape of Monastic Thought* (Leiden/Boston: Brill, 1994); Willemien Otten, *From Paradise to Paradigm: A Study of Twelfth-Century Humanism* (Leiden/Boston: Brill, 2004).

12. Colin Morris, *The Discovery of the Individual, 1050–1200* (New York: Harper Torch, 1972). See now also Larry Siedentrop, *Inventing the Individual: The Origins of Western Liberalism* (Milton Keynes: Penguin, 2014).

13. M.-D. Chenu, *Nature, Man, and Society*, 270–309.

14. Bernard's controversial role in the crusades is clarified if it is recognized that he praised only the Knights Templars and their "spiritual role." For the feudal knights of his day, however, he was filled with contempt. See Richard W. Kaueffer, *Chivalry and Violence in Medieval Europe*

of the Latin classics—especially of Cicero and his great theme of friendship—as well as the dawn of courtly love and the later troubadours.[15] In this cultural maelstrom, Bernard is caught up, having no influence with power-hungry potentates, and yet having great spiritual influence with saintly leaders.

The Monastic Reformer

Fourth is Bernard "the Mellifluous Doctor," celebrated in voluminous scholarship on the basis of his own meditative writings.[16] This certainly gets us closer to the biography and to the mind of Bernard, but again it is a moving target, for there have been no less than five periods identified in the life of Bernard: his family life from his birth (ca. 1090/1–1113); his entry into the monastic order of Citeaux, his entry into the community of Clairvaux, and the spread of that order (1113–1130); the intense political life of Bernard—especially the schism of Rome (1130–1140); the mature, scholarly life of Bernard with his major writings and disputations (1140–1143); and, finally, the elderly Bernard, commissioned to preach the Second Crusade in the midst of a confused and tumultuous culture (1143–1153).[17]

Bernard's life as a monastic reformer thus remained paradoxical: he was both the servant of the church—ecclesiastically and politically—and the servant of God—mystically and personally. Understanding the nature of this paradox gets us close to the heart of Bernard's Christian identity.

Bernard the Theologian

Various choices for understanding St. Bernard still remain, especially when one focuses upon his writings. One of the most promising interpretations is "Bernard the Theologian." Martin Luther was one of the first to select him as "the theologian of the Love of God,"[18] with John Calvin quickly following suit. Many

---

(Oxford: Oxford University Press, 1991), 76–77; see also C. H. Haskins, *The Renaissance of the Twelfth Century* (Cambridge: Harvard University Press, 1927), viii–ix.

15. Etienne Gilson, *The Mystical Theology of St. Bernard* (New York: Sheed & Ward, 1940), 170–97.

16. Mellifluus, a medieval term to refer to one who extracted the spiritual meaning of Scripture, as distinct from the literal meaning of the text.

17. These are the stages divided by the Abbe Theodore Ratisbonne, *St. Bernard of Clairvaux* (Charlotte, NC: Tan Books, 1991).

18. Franz Posset, "*Divus Bernhardus:* Saint Bernard as Spiritual and Theological Mentor of

Catholic theologians have adopted from him the reforming motives of their differing periods, during which the writings of his scholarly friend William of St. Thierry were almost totally eclipsed for being too "Bernardian"—that is, at least until their rediscovery by A. Adam and Dom A. Wilmart in the early twentieth century. As Etienne Gilson was later to say: "For William of Saint-Thierry has everything: power of thought, the orator's eloquence, the poet's lyricism, and all the attractiveness of the most ardent and tender piety."[19] Why then did Gilson still choose to focus upon *The Mystical Theology of St. Bernard*? Leading up to Vatican Council II, it was becoming clear that modern Catholic scholasticism also needed reform, a fact that scholars such as the historian Henri de Lubac and the theologian Hans Urs von Bathasar were also pointing toward with the start of the *theologie nouvelle* movement. Like the more recent "spiritual theology," "mystical theology" had become a critique of abstract theological scholarship being pursued as an end in itself, instead of being for the transformation of its readers and pupils. This theological process continues, as evidenced now by the way in which such scholars as the evangelical theologian A. N. S. Lane have adopted Bernard to be the medieval defender of the doctrine of justification by faith alone.[20]

Bernard, the Chimera of His Culture

But Bernard was not conscious of being either a scholar or a writer in the way we professionalize these roles today. "My monstrous life, my troubled conscience, cries out to you," confesses Bernard. "I am something like the chimaera of my age—neither cleric or lay. For I have cast off the life of a monk, though not the habit."[21] Though he travelled extensively throughout western Europe, Bernard devoted much time to producing what amounted to a massive literary output, now collected in the nine volumes of the critical edition of his works. He wrote eight treatises, some 138 liturgical *sermos* (for a total of 718), various homilies, parables, some 358 "sentences" as notes and fragments, and a growing collection of letters, now numbered at 547.[22] He was constantly revising his

the Reformer Martin Luther," in *Bernardus Magister*, ed. John R. Sommerfeldt (Spencer, MA: Cistercian Publications, 1992), 517–32.

19. Gilson, *The Mystical Theology of St. Bernard*, 198.

20. A. N. S. Lane, "Bernard of Clairvaux: A Forerunner of John Calvin?" in *Bernardus Magister*, ed. John R. Sommerfeldt (Spencer, MA: Cistercian Publications, 1992), 533–46.

21. John R. Sommerfeldt, *Bernard of Clairvaux: On the Life of the Mind* (New York: Newman Press), 107.

22. Adriaan Bredero, "Conflicting Interpretations of the Relevance of Bernard of Clairvaux to the History of His Times," *Citeaux* 31 (1980): 53–81.

writings throughout his life, since rhetoric and the polish of his words he perceived as a moral obligation to honor "the Word who became flesh." Many of his writings are responses to the requests of others to compose letters, to write treatises, and to record his sermons. Obedience was his saintly motive, not self-promotion as is the common habit of our fallen nature. The motivation behind Bernard's desire to preach, teach, write, and revise was Jesus, together with the obedient example of Mary. Certainly, it was not flattery, egotism, ambition, vainglory, or even scholarship.

Rather like C. S. Lewis—a sound scholar who wrote Christian literature on the side—Bernard was not "the star turn of the twelfth century." (It was only later that Lewis-mania became an American industry.) Likewise, Philip Hughes, a fellow Englishman, notes that Pope Alexander III dominates the second half of the twelfth century, whereas Bernard had done so in the first half.[23] So when Adrian Bredero started in 1978 to rewrite a life of Bernard as his contemporaries viewed him, Bredero hesitated for some time because of the conflicting evidence he was gathering from over twenty-five other notable chroniclers who were all Bernard's illustrious contemporaries.[24]

In the light of all these considerations, Bernard would no doubt have liked us to see his identity as a maturing one—from childhood, through youth and maturity into eldership. Bernard's understanding of identity can be characterized by twin poles, encapsulated by the apostles he so loved: Paul for his articulation of being "in Christ," and John for his three categories of child, youth, and father (1 John 2:1–10).

Embraced by the Sweet Name of Jesus

Bernard was born in 1090/91, as the third son of a noble knight Teclin, Lord of Fontaines, near Dijon, close to the person of the Duke of Burgundy, and to Elizabeth, his young mother, whose godliness was enveloped in mystical experiences. When one attempts to focus upon "the inner life of Bernard," it is his love of Jesus that is the consistent theme of his life. It is like a hidden spring of water, from which flowed the later Franciscan and Dominican spirituality of poverty, accumulatively swelling into the late medieval renewal of *devotio moderna* as "the imitation of Christ," now domesticated in vernacular language and home life.

Even as a child, Bernard is reported to have had a mystical vision of Jesus at his Nativity. By contrast, the apostle Paul in full manhood as a zealous persecu-

---

23. Philip Hughes, *A History of the Church* (New York: Sheen & Ward), 2:291.
24. Bredero, "Conflicting Interpretations."

tor of the Christians was smitten on the Damascus road by the exalted vision of *the transcendent Christ*. Ever after, Paul saw his identity wholly "in Christ." But Bernard experienced an imminent experience of the birth of Jesus. Still a small child, falling asleep one Christmas eve while waiting for the midnight vigil to begin, Bernard is reported to have dreamt he saw the birth of Jesus coming from the Virgin Mary. From then on, "Bernard the child" loved Jesus passionately in all his humility and humanity. Bernard's identity discretely and gradually grew to maturity as a lover of the name of Jesus. He was nurtured by his saintly mother, Elizabeth, who had dedicated herself as a child to become a nun but was instead wedded at age fifteen. Yet she sweetly accepted her new role as a mother, adoring the Virgin Mary, who had exemplified her obedience. The church within the grounds of Fontaine was dedicated to St. Ambrose, and strangely, while appearing still in good health, Elizabeth announced that she would die on the feast day of St. Ambrose; amazingly to all her family she died that day!

Another powerful event occurred on a visit to his elder brothers serving with the Duke of Burgundy, at the siege of Grancey. As Bernard rode, deep in reflection, the words of Matthew 11:28–29 entered his heart with new depth: "Come to me all you that labor and are burdened and I will refresh you; take up my yoke upon you . . . and you shall find rest to your souls." Entering a nearby chapel, thrilled to the very marrow of his bones and praying with many tears prostrate on the ground, "a deep calm fell upon his soul . . . and Bernard all on fire with love, consecrated himself forever to God, and joyfully took upon him the yoke of Him who is meek and humble of heart."[25] Later, whenever he felt cold and distanced from the presence of Jesus, he would recall this life-changing moment, reflecting with the Psalmist, "Who can endure such cold?" (Ps 147:17).

A gifted student, he was sent to one of the new "secular schools," reading and writing Latin with ease, engaging in dialectics, yet chilled by the often casual way in which the Holy Scriptures were treated with logic, analysis, and irreverence. Upon turning nineteen, he had his first and last sexual temptation, which both horrified and strengthened him for the rest of his life against the sensual life: whether in sex, carnal passions, and desires, or indeed in scholarship that was secular rather than spiritual. Bernard as a youth had great natural beauty, and so was tempted to be vain and sensuous. Yet he remained a passionately studious and intellectual youth. He had all the world at his feet, especially with such a wealthy, chivalrous knight as his father. He could have easily been tempted to disobey the call of God.

Then, however, to the astonishment of all, his uncle, the valiant knight Gauldry Count of Trouillon, decided to attach himself to his nephew, Bernard,

25. Ibid., 18–19.

in preparation to enter this new spiritual world of the cloister. Bernard's elder brother, Bartholomew, then on the point of entering the service of the Duke of Burgundy, decided soon thereafter to follow, and soon after his younger brother Andrew—now already received as a knight—decided also. The oldest brother Guido followed suit, then Gerard, and thus an amazing spiritual revival began to affect the whole feudal family, as well as their small community of friends. It was all just too much for Bernard's younger sister, who was a mixture of anger and anguish. She begged her brothers not to leave the ancestral home. Yet as this amazing change was occurring within the family, they remained uncertain where all this was leading. Citeaux was not yet their "star of guidance." But sitting in church one day, they heard the text read from Paul's epistle: "He who has begun a good work in you will perfect it unto the day of Jesus Christ" (Phil 1:6). Reignited, their faith was fired to move forward. For we can all have the experience of spiritual wavering when we ponder "can I really know if God is actually speaking to me personally?"

Freed from Chivalry, Feudal Love, and Scholasticism

Bernard of Clairvaux, who inherited a youthful and active knighthood "for Christ," had a *metanoia* encounter, to become adopted to live meditatively as a "Child of God," "in Christ Jesus, the Child Jesus."

The Recovery/Reform of the Benedictine Way of Life

Bernard was not devising a new form of monasticism in joining the Cistercians. He was simply initiating a reform or return to the original Rule of St. Benedict, for it had been abused as the demographic device to sustain the growth of feudalism, which it did by admitting children into cloisters who were too many in a feudal family to marry off to neighboring barons; this was the privilege of the older children. But now the knightly youth who entered of their own free will to the life of the *conversi* were—like his own band of brothers and friends—all freely seeking the cloister in order to accept a life of obedience through personal humility. "Conversion" for them was their conversion from pride to humility, and more specifically within the monastic setting as a daily perseverance in the humility of "the cloister of the heart."[26]

---

26. Bernard Bonowitz, OCSO, *St. Bernard's Three-Course Banquet* (Collegeville, MN: Liturgical Press, 2013), 5.

Bernardian Hymnody on the Name of Jesus

Perhaps even before the dignity of German Gregorian chant, Bernardian hymnody first filled the cloisters of Citeaux soon after Bernard and his youthful associates began their new life as "conversi." Early hymns about the name of Jesus are all Bernardian, since they are the hymns a child like Bernard learned to sing on his mother's knees. Such is the hymn: "Jesu, the very thought of Thee / With sweetness fills my breast; / But sweeter far thy face to see / And in its presence rest." For in all the cosmos there is "no sweeter sound than thy blest name, / O Saviour of mankind." Ever since the twelfth century, *Jesu, dulcis memoria* has been continuously translated time and again, until in the Olney Hymns of 1779, John Newton finally rephrased it: "How sweet the name of Jesus sounds in the believer's ear." These hymns all echo the Song of Songs 1:3, continually dear to Bernard's own meditations, from childhood to maturity:

> How shall we explain the world-wide light of faith, swift and flaming in its progress, except by the preaching of Jesus' name? Is it not by the light of this name that God has called us into his wonderful light, that irradiates our darkness and empowers us to see the light? To such as we Paul says: "You were darkness once, but now you see the light." . . . But the name of Jesus is more than light, it is also food. Do you not feel the increase of strength as often as you remember it? What other name can so enrich the one who meditates? . . . Jesus is to me honey in the mouth, music in the ear, a song in the heart. Again, it is a medicine. Does one not feel sad? Let the name of Jesus come into one's heart . . . and invoke this life-giving name and his will to live again will be at once renewed.[27]

Appropriately, the 1953 encyclical Letter of Pope Pius XII, commemorating the eighth centenary of the saint's death, ascribed to him *Doctor Mellifluis* because of his wise theology. But Bernard himself never separated biblical wisdom from meditation upon the humanity of Jesus, all summarized in the sweetness of his name.

27. Bernard of Clairvaux, "Sermo 15," in *On the Song of Songs*, trans. Kilian Walsh, 4 vols. (Spencer, MA: Cistercian Publications, 1971–1980), 109–10.

Communicating the Humility of Jesus through "the Apple Tree"

The community of believers as the Bride—whether as the Church Universal, or as mirrored in the small Cistercian communities that Bernard and his associates fostered—identified their Beloved Spouse, Jesus, with "the Apple Tree." The Christmas carol composed by Poston, "Jesus Christ the Apple Tree," echoes this medieval carol, again traceable to Bernard:

> For happiness I long have sought,
> And pleasure dearly have I bought:
> I missed of all; but now I see
> 'Tis found in Christ the apple tree.

With Bernard the monks confess in the final verse:

> This fruit doth make my soul to thrive,
> It keeps my dying faith alive;
> Which makes my soul in haste to be
> With Jesus Christ the apple tree.

Much later in life, Bernard asked in his forty-eighth *sermo*, on Song of Songs 2:3, why does the Bride of Christ Universal, as also the Bride represented by the small Cistercian communities, "compare Jesus to the apple tree surrounded—perhaps smothered by all the stately trees of the forest?" "Why" he asks,

> when the finer and nobler trees were ignored, was the insignificance of "this" tree brought forward to be eulogized as "the Bridegroom"? . . . For to compare Him with that tree seems to indicate that He who has no equal has a superior. What shall we say to this? I say the praise is little for one who is little. The proclamation made here is not, "Great is the Lord and greatly to be praised," but "Little is the Lord and greatly to be loved"; namely the child who is born unto us.[28]

The deeper meaning that Bernard and his successors continued to celebrate in the apple tree was the humility of Jesus, which escapes the notice of the proud. Bernard further marvels at "the wonderful way in which the Son both subjected himself as a man to the angels and yet, remaining God, retained the angels as his subjects. Because the littleness of Jesus gives sweeter relish to the bride . . .

28. Bernard of Clairvaux, "Sermon 48," *On the Song of Songs*, vol. 2, 109–10.

happy to contemplate Him as a man among men, not as God among the angels."[29] Later, John of Ford, commenting in the same vein as Bernard, quotes from the Epistle to the Hebrews: "He did not concern himself with angels, but with the sons of Abraham" (Heb 2:16).

Perhaps the rich fruits of a lowly apple tree were a boyhood's memory of delight for Bernard playing in his family's castle grounds. Certainly they were later for John of Ford, coming from the cider West country of Devon, Somerset, and Dorset. Such fruit are easily shaken down, which any small boy can do. A child's simple prayer has a like efficacy in humility—to wait upon the Lord, to fulfill the desires of the heart, all in a richness given only to the humble in heart.[30] Thus did Bernard the child grow into the youthful lover of Jesus.

Bernard's Progressive Reflections on the Freedom of Humility

Now grown up, Bernard wrote "The Steps of Humility and Pride," as one of his first treatises in 1125/26. Humility had always been countercultural, but Bernard made it more positively an expression of freedom, by relating it to the symbol of Jacob's ladder, the voluntary descent of the humble God to provide our ascent in the steps of humility.

St. Benedict had set out twelve ascending degrees of humility. Now in his commentary on this section of *The Rule*, Bernard taught freshly on the renunciation of self-will in contempt of self. For this, what was needed was "biblical" self-knowledge, not in the Socratic way, nor as advised by the Delphic Oracle, but in knowing ourselves as sinners before God. Only then would "the fear of the Lord" lead to wisdom, towards knowing God in the light of knowing ourselves: this is "the double knowledge" traceable back to the early Fathers.[31]

Bernard's Maturing Identity into Deeper Freedom

While the troubadours and later courtly love only began to flourish in the generation after Bernard, their roots are traceable to the 1090s.[32] As feudal lords,

29. Ibid., *Song of Songs*, vol. 3, 14.

30. See the suggestive essay of Elizabeth Oxenham, "Under the Apple Tree," in *Bernardus Magister*, ed. John R. Sommerfeldt (Spencer, MA: Cistercian Publications, 1992), 277–86.

31. James M. Houston, "The 'Double Knowledge' as the Way of Wisdom," in *The Way of Wisdom: Essays in Honour of Bruce K. Waltke*, ed. J. I. Packer and Sven Soderlund (Grand Rapids: Eerdmans, 2000), 308–26.

32. Gilson, *Mystical Theology of Bernard*, 170.

Bernard's family were surrounded by its culture. Therefore, Bernard's deepening sphere of reform involved a critique of the widely popularized sources of classical love and Ciceronian friendship, immensely appealing as they were. Even if unrequited, Plato taught that love was a spiritual and intellectual beauty, not a personal relationship with a human being, let alone with God. Ovid and Horace were much more crudely sensual and erotic in their love poems. But how could Cicero be faulted in his highly popular *De amicitia* when he was teaching that the love of a friend must be selfless? Thus *De amicitia* was particularly deceptive to the majority of monks, since it was a practical manual on the ethics of such friendship. Happily secluded in a Yorkshire dale, Bernard's friend Aelred of Rievaulx composed his charming treatise *On Spiritual Friendship* under the influence of Cicero. He wrote this knowing that Cicero had also profoundly influenced Augustine, Gregory the Great, and Jerome before him.

Now some twenty years after moving into the cloister of Citeaux, when his followers were spreading into ever widening circles of other Cistercian communities, Bernard began his mature period of writing, with a deeper focus upon the love of God. This meant more engagement with the popular culture in development from poetic and philosophical love, to the troubadours and then to courtly love. There was an itinerant scholar Peter Abelard who had become its hugely popular spokesman, with audiences of youthful thousands throughout France and beyond who were enraptured by his message. We do not know when Bernard first heard of Peter Abelard (1079–1142). Abelard had been already condemned by the Council of Soissons (1121) for his treatise *Introductio ad Theologiam*, where he defined the love of God as being a love for God because of his own perfection, following on Cicero's pagan doctrine of "pure love." In this Abelardian practice, one does not have a personal, reciprocal relation with God, any more than he had with his lover, Heloise. It was the love of an abstracted philosophical god, from whom one could expect no response.[33] Love of god and love of a human like Heloise were really no different. So Heloise's intellectual abilities could be isolated and "loved" apart from her person. After he had violated her virginity, and with no concept of marriage—which would impede his scholarly pursuits—he was forced callously to "marry" her on the birth of their illegitimate son.

Yet Abelard had long pursued Heloise with love songs he had composed, verses well popularized among the youth of France by the 1130s. Much like our contemporary culture, the songs expressed the zeitgeist. As Etienne Gilson has paraphrased Abelard's distorted view of love of God (or indeed his love of Hel-

---

33. An interesting parallelism can be made between Abelard-Heloise in the worship of philosophy in the twelfth century, and of Jean-Paul Sartre and Simone de Beauvoir in our modern age.

oise), each was to be interpreted abstractly: "I never loved Heloise; what I loved in her was my own pleasure."[34] Likewise, he distorts through a Ciceronian lens the apostle Paul's passage of 1 Corinthians 13:7—"love bears all things, believes all things, hopes all things, endures all things"—to express this distorted ideal of selflessness. When he then offers to marry Heloise, she dances around with her own alternative, which is now to embrace willfully the cloister as a nun. This was "to make it plain to everyone that she was the absolute mistress of her own heart and body," even if it meant humiliation and contempt in order "to love the beloved," on her own terms.[35] Perhaps never before had there arisen such ingeniously destructive concepts by which to distort the Christian gospel of God's love for all humanity.

Bernard's Recovery of Biblical Love

Mercifully, Bernard was grounded solidly on the biblical understanding of love. It was expressed clearly to him through his meditations on 1 John 4:8: "love is of God." It was not sourced in friendship, humanly attractive as that is. It comes alone from God. As such, it is gifted to us only by the Holy Spirit (1 John 4:13).[36] Love, then, has no metaphysical cause, nor can it be interpreted by a logician. For it is God who is love, he whom we have not seen but whose presence is evidenced humanly by acts of charity, and by the freedom from fear (1 John 4:18). God's love then provides multiple freedoms—from self, from human sources, and above all, from fear.

Only now are neuroscientists beginning to teach us that fear is the basic human emotion, from which all kinds of negative emotional responses develop to shape our brain actions.[37] It is fear that drags us downward into such egotistical reactions. This can now be mapped by neuroscientists, but what they can never tell us scientifically is how we gain freedom from fear and its addictive consequences. That is the discovery Bernard found in 1 John 4:18: "For perfect love casts out all fear."

But the word "freedom"—like "love"—had many facets for Bernard. He started with the human consciousness of having self-knowledge, free from an instinctual life like the animals, free to make choices and to have knowledge of one's own dignity. But when the source of this dignity is ignored or forgotten,

34. Gilson, *Mystical Theology of Bernard*, 163.

35. Ibid., 164.

36. Matthew Knell, *The Immanent Person of the Holy Spirit from Anselm to Lombard* (Eugene, OR: Wipf & Stock, 2009), 61–78.

37. Theodore George, *Unfolding the Emotions* (New York: HarperCollins, 2014).

as coming from God his Creator, then one's freedom is lost in false choices, in some form of idol-worship, and worst of all, in self-glorification. For human pride is the worst form of idolatry, as the worship of the self. This becomes the sabotage of love, which is only sourced in and from God, as freedom also is.

Our first condition then is the bondage of egotistical love, of "loving ourselves for our own sake." Its reversal or emancipation is not in the annihilation of the self, as in the Buddhist way, but the restoration of the human dignity of free-will, recognizing that it is "love of self" as being God's gift to us. The motive for love of self must then be reoriented, to be sourced in God's love for us. Bernard based this on his reading of 1 Corinthians 15:46: "it is not the spiritual that is first but the natural, and then the spiritual." We may think we are made in our own image and likeness—this is "natural." In fact, we bear God's image and likeness—that is "spiritual." A newborn child can only revolve around all that is of the body, as our contemporary secularists can only be obsessed by what is body fitness, since for them there is no prospect of immortality.

Since we are body-spirit, excessive asceticism will not do either, as we do need to "love the body." Nor can this be confused with what the Fathers called *concupitas*, or concupiscence, for this is love of sensual pleasure, which entails a bondage to sensual appetites. Rather, we need *metanoia* as a change of heart and mind that gives us the freedom to love God—not by our own efforts but as the gift of the Holy Spirit. Bernard never ceased to demonstrate the constant misery and bondage that is addictive of cupidity. For as Bernard would see it, "cupidity is but a love of God become unaware of itself."[38]

Living outside the awareness of God's love and freedom is like being exiled in a strange land; all the while we still bear God's image and likeness. Augustine interpreted this to be within our intelligence, but Bernard saw it more in the exercise of freedom—freedom from necessity—for we don't need to go on living with the misery of the status quo. The "image" of the *imago Dei* is never lost, although we may forfeit the "likeness." We can call upon God at any time for conversion, to love differently. But Christ alone is "the Image," the Word of God, the unique and transforming power by which we are changed into our true likeness. So Bernard quotes the psalmist, "Lord, who is like unto Thee?" (Ps 35:10).

All this is prelude to Bernard's treatise *On Loving God* (*De diligendo Deo*) written sometime after 1127. Whether he knew of William of St. Thierry's treatises on similar countercultural themes—*On Contemplating God* and *On the Nature and Dignity of Love,* written between 1118 and 1135—we don't know. Certainly later these treatises were exchanged with each other,

---

38. Gilson, *Mystical Theology of Bernard*, 45.

to reinforce each other's biblical convictions when both attacked Abelard for heresy in the Council of Sens (1140–1141). But this occurred in the last stages of Bernard's life.

Bernard's Pursuit of the Contemplative Life

Already at age twenty-five, Bernard had been appointed abbot of his community of Citeaux. Since then, he had led a conflicting life between the cloister and his occupation as ecclesial adviser. On one of his journeys, he stopped off in Paris to deliver a powerful recruiting address to its itinerant scholars, encouraging them to consider becoming *conversi*, or members of the cloister. *On Conversion* is a powerful scriptural appeal to experience this personal *metanoia* as a new way of living. In contrast to the way the cited texts of Scripture had arrested Bernard from time to time in his Christian growth, now he began much more to "masticate" the words of Scripture, allowing them to flow into all his speech and written texts. In *On Conversion*, he cites over four hundred biblical texts—largely from the Psalms, which were deeply ingrained in him through the daily chant, and from the epistles of Paul and John. So he begins his address: "To hear the Word of God, I believe you have come. . . . I entirely approve this desire and I congratulate you on your zeal. . . . 'Blessed are they who hear the Word, but only if they observe it.'" Then he began to explain what it means to be a *conversus*: it is simply wanting to live God's will.[39] What follows is an exposition of what we might now call a Theo-anthropology—that is, an understanding of the nature of God's relation with human beings. This was not just a call for recruitment to the monastic way of life but the advocacy of what all people need: a radical understanding of what it means to have a Christian identity. Of course, church and Christ were inseparable to Bernard, as they should be for us. But there was a particular cultural challenge in the twelfth century, which was to address the confusion felt by the youth of society (in this there is also a striking parallel to our own day). *But it has always been about being truly human in the humanity of Jesus Christ.* So Bernard addresses the lamentably corrupt state of the church in his day, calling for repentance. But he concludes that the one who exposes and rebukes the greed, ambition, and avarice of a culture's leaders is bound to face persecution, to suffer for Christ's sake.[40]

39. Bernard of Clairvaux, *Sermons on Conversion: On Conversion, a Sermon to Clerics*, trans. Marie-Bernard Said, OSB (Kalamazoo, MI: Cistercian Publications, 1981), 31.
40. Ibid., 69–79.

Bernard's Growing Discernment in His Adoration
of the Humanity of Mary (Letter 146)

As previously mentioned, Bernard had received a mystical experience of the Virgin Mary as a child, which remained unforgettable. Later, in his *Sermons on Advent*, he attributes in a prayer to "Queen Mary" the titles of "Queen," "Dame," "Mediator," and "Advocate." She is called upon in the juridical usage of these terms in the twelfth century (which are not necessarily equivalent to our terms today) in order to recommend us, to exercise her influence, to show us her mercy as "exiles," "citizens of another country," and as those who are "helpless." All this she does because she shares our humanity, as Jesus does. Cautiously though, we also need to interpret this Marian understanding in the context of twelfth-century feudalism.

Mary herself acts at times in uncertainty over the mystery of her human son, Jesus, as the Gospel writers report. Jesus too, is caught up in human events, such as the wedding arrangements in Cana of Galilee, when Mary points out to Jesus, "They have no wine!" (John 2:3). Yet Jesus faces uniquely the human tension: "his Father in heaven" or his earthly Mother (v. 4)? Bernard's friend Aelred of Rievaulx later pondered over the temple incident of Jesus at the age of twelve, reflecting on Mary's response to the boy Jesus, "Why have you treated us so?" and on his response, "Did you not know I must be in my Father's house?" (Luke 2:41–51). If then the Gospel record leaves the reader confused about the role of Mary with both her Son and with the disciples, is it any wonder that two millennia of Marian adoration, of ecclesial Mariology, and of pagan Mariolatry have intensified centuries of confusion? Thankfully, biblical and historical scholarship is now melting it quietly away, to genuinely restore our reverence for the unique Motherhood of Mary.

But for Bernard, in his day, all the glory of Mary is reflected from the mystery of her Son, from whom are the ultimate intercession, mediation, and redemptive grace. She is but the aqueduct through which flows Jesus the spring of Eternal Life. Later this will develop into an "ecclesial Mary"—like Beatrice guiding the youthful Dante out of "the dark woods" (*selva obscura*). Mary was for Bernard the emancipator from the sexual passions of youth. We remember too that Bernard had lost his mother as a child, so the mothering role of Mary always remained special for him. Yet Mary is always pointing to her Son as the motive and destiny of the heart's desire, guiding the youthful Bernard to escape the snares of sexual passion.

Now in his maturity Bernard hears that the canons of Lyons have announced a new doctrine, "the Immaculate Conception of the Virgin Mary." As a theological exile himself, Bernard had trusted the company of his friends as "fellow exiles." But they have betrayed him with this new doctrine, and so he writes strongly in rebuke. Three times now he has been betrayed by them, and now he is an old sick man, wondering how long he has to live.[41] In all Bernard's sermons on the Assumption, Bernard had never included Mary, for he followed strictly the biblical account of the Gospels. Yes, he honored the Virgin Mary with unique titles, in her unique purity, her virginal fecundity, her divine obedience. Yes, she has a unique role in God's salvation, but none of the prophets in anticipating her unique mission make mention of her "immaculate conception." So Bernard again is a prophetic voice against the diverse Mariological heresies of his contemporaries. Yes, Bernard can address hymns and prayers to Mary, but not as "immaculate in her conception." It is human speculation that leads downwards from such "speculative Mariology" into crude "Mariolatry."

Bernard the Aged

As all who are aged experience the death of family and friends, so Bernard the aged lost his friend William of St. Thierry, his brother Gerard, and in 1148 the Archbishop of Armagh, Malachia O'Morghair, whose life he had written. Abelard had died in 1142. In rewriting and adding to his collection of *Sermons on the Song of Songs*, it is no surprise that he alludes frequently to death.[42] The cloister was itself a form of "the angelic life"—as an anticipation of heaven and of the final bridal reunion of the Christian with Christ. He cites the apostle Paul's words: "For you have died, and your life is hidden with Christ in God" (Col 3:3). This is his meaning of "angelic death," not that the immortal state of the angels ever "dies," but it is the perfect state of selflessness. Yet the human tension remains for Bernard: he mourns the death of his brother Gerard (in *Sermo* 26) as a very human grief, now seeing his own life as "shadowy" within the valley of death, alone without his brother's presence.

Bernard had long struggled to distinguish between and teach on meditation and contemplation. There was a long tradition traceable to Origen at the end of the second century to use the Song of Songs as the text par excellence for meditation by use of "allegorical" or "spiritual" reading. The sensual reader still cannot read the Canticles "spiritually," so it remains only the realm for the mature Christian. Bernard made use of at least thirty-two of Origen's sermons,

41. *The Letters of St. Bernard*, trans. and ed. Bruno Scott James (Chicago: Henry Regnery, 1953), 214–15.

42. Burcht Spranger, "The Concept of Death in Bernard's *Sermons on the Song of Songs*," in *Bernardus Magister*, ed. John R. Sommerfeldt (Spencer, MA: Cistercian Publications, 1992), 85–93.

which he incorporated into his own homilies. Then a whole series of commentaries followed—from Gregory of Nyssa, Jerome, Gregory the Great, all of whom Bernard used. Thanks to the research of the medieval historian Henri de Lubac, we now can appreciate this long history of such meditative reading.[43] We sorely need its recovery today.

In his homily *Sermo 74*, Bernard summarizes his use of spiritual rhetoric as being "to enlighten" the mind of his audience and to root our affection "in God."[44] So, like Cicero, Bernard's intent was not merely stylistic but concerned with judging the truth about what has to be acted upon. Knowledge for its own sake is merely "curiosity" (*curiositas*). As Cicero was so close to the truth about "love," so too was he near the mark in his understanding of "rhetoric." Bernard had to struggle against such subtle classical seduction. He succeeds by giving priority to "love" over "knowledge." As he asserts: "It is in vain for anyone who does not love to listen to this song of love, or to read it, for a cold heart cannot catch fire from its 'eloquence'"[45]—that is, its Ciceronian rhetoric. "Have you seen Him whom my soul loves?" asks the Bride, for if not, you cannot appreciate the whole love song.

But preliminary to reading the Song of Songs is the text of Ecclesiastes, which depicts the vanity of the world before the reader's heart, and the book of Proverbs, which places specific truths before the reader's mind. Both of these works one must read prior to entering into "the Bride's chamber in the Canticle," where humble self-knowledge, the fear and knowledge of God, and the experience of his love personally all lead to a transforming spiritual appetite in pursuit of the beloved Christ. This teaching then is even deeper than knowing prudential truth for a virtuous life or for the needs of salvation—vast as these are also! Multiple metaphors are skillfully woven into all Bernard's homilies upon the Song of Songs in order to enflame the hearer/reader with an ever-increasing desire for God alone. For once Christ's presence is personally experienced, it can never be satiated. The reader today is left aware just how far ahead of us is Bernard in being called a "Christian." Yet he leaves us comforted that we, too, like the disciple leaning on Jesus's bosom, can rest upon Christ's two breasts of his patience with us and his mercy to us.

---

43. See esp. de Lubac, "Mystical Tropology" in *Medieval Exegesis*, Vol. 2: *The Four Senses of Scripture* (Grand Rapids: Eerdmans, 2000), 127–79.

44. St. Bernard, *On the Song of Songs*, 4:85–96.

45. Sermo 79.1, in *On the Song of Songs*.

Chapter 19

Dominic of Caleruega (d. 1221), Jordan of Saxony (d. 1237): The Formation of Dominican Identity

Steven Watts

Dominic of Caleruega (ca. 1170–1221) was the founder of the Order of Preachers—or, as they would later be called, the Dominicans. Dominic was born in Castile and studied in Palencia, but the origins of his order are best situated in the south of France. In 1206, his bishop, Diego of Osma (d. 1207), organized a preaching mission characterized by apostolic poverty against the dualist heresy he encountered in Toulouse and the surrounding region. Dominic assumed leadership of the mission following Diego's death in 1207. Over the course of the following decade, having been encouraged by the papacy, he would transform an informal group of clerics into a religious order of friars whose remit would include the pastoral care of all of Christendom and beyond.[1]

According to our earliest sources, Dominic was winsome, courageous, and perhaps even a little impulsive.[2] He valued education and organization, and was adept at finding and mobilizing talented men. He also took a particular interest in the pastoral care of devout and religious women. He proved capable of persevering through even the most difficult circumstances and showed a willingness to improvise. Above all, however, Dominic was animated by a desire to save souls. At his death on August 6, 1221, only a few years after his order's official

---

1. For the institutional transformation of the order see Simon Tugwell, "Notes on the Life of St. Dominic," *Archivum Fratrum Praedicatorum* [hereafter *AFP*] 65 (1995): 5–169, at 6–53.

2. Beyond the *Libellus* (for which, see n. 15 below), the most important of these early sources are the collected depositions during Dominic's canonization process (1233), Peter Ferrandus's *Legenda* (ca. 1237–1242), and Cecilia of Cesarini's *Miracula* (ca. 1272–1288). For the depositions see Angelus Walz, ed., *Acta Canonizationis S. Dominici* [hereafter *Acta*], Monumenta Ordinis Fratrum Praedicatorum Historica [hereafter MOPH] 16 (Rome, 1935), 89–194. For the *Legenda* see Simon Tugwell, ed., *Petri Ferrandi Legenda Sancti Dominici*, MOPH 32 (Rome, 2015). For the *Miracula*, see Simon Tugwell, "Scripta quaedam minora de sancto Dominico," *AFP* 83 (2013): 64–105.

recognition, the seeds he had sown had already produced the first fruits of a remarkable harvest.[3] Predominantly urban, highly educated, and institutionally flexible, his friars numbered among the finest preachers, scholars, and mystics of the later Middle Ages.

Dominic's successor and first biographer, Jordan of Saxony (d. 1237), was both emblematic of and instrumental in the order's transformation in the 1220s and 1230s. Born to parents hailing from Burgberg in the diocese of Mainz, Jordan entered the order in 1220 while studying as a bachelor in theology at the University of Paris. Following his rapid rise through the order, which culminated in his election as general master in 1222, he travelled tirelessly throughout Europe, focusing especially on the university towns where he was estimated to have drawn more than a thousand recruits into the order.[4] He was a consummate preacher and an assured leader who was determined to meet the pastoral needs of the Church.[5] He was also deeply concerned with the order's responsibilities toward the great number of religious and devout women who increasingly sought the friars' pastoral care. His letters to Diana d'Andalò (d. 1236) and her religious community at St. Agnese, Bologna, are one of the treasures of medieval correspondence.[6] Tragically, on his return from the Holy Land, Jordan drowned off the coast of Antalya on February 13, 1237.

A Saint Discovered

In the late spring of 1233 the cities of northern Italy were in the thrall of spiritual renewal. The "Alleluia" or "Great Devotion," as this renewal would be known, was characterized by a remarkable convergence of religious and political activity, led principally by members of the newly arisen Dominican and Franciscan orders.[7] Charismatic preachers drew great throngs to miracle-laced sermons

3. The traditional date of the order's formal recognition is 1216, but a papal bull issued on January 21, 1217, still refers to Dominic's mission as a local affair. See Vladimir J. Koudelka, ed., *Monumenta Diplomatica S. Dominic*, MOPH 25 (Rome, 1966), 78–79.

4. B.-M. Reichert, ed., *Vitae Fratrum Ordinis Praedicatorum necon Cronica Fratrum Ordinis ab anno MCCIII usque MCCLIV*, MOPH 1 (Rome, 1896), 102.

5. For the sermons that can be unequivocally attributed to Jordan see Paul-Bernard Hodel, ed., *Beati Iordanis de Saxonia Sermones*, MOPH 29 (Rome, 2005).

6. The most recent edition of the letters is Angelus Walz, ed., *Beati Iordani de Saxonia Epistulae*, MOPH 23 (Rome, 1951).

7. The primary work on the Alleluia is Augustine Thompson, *Revival Preachers and Politics in Thirteenth-Century Italy: The Great Devotion of 1233* (Oxford, 1992). See also André Vauchez, "Une campagne de pacification en Lombardie autour de 1233: L'action politique des ordres mendiants d'après la réforme des status communaux et les accords de paix," *École française de Rome: Mélanges*

on charity, penance, and—above all—peace. Processions were led through the streets under the banners of saints. Hymns sung by soldiers, young women, and children resounded in the piazzas. Heresy, previously thought by pro-papal writers to have grown unchecked within these fiercely independent and characteristically fractious cities, was forcefully repressed. Most significantly, political, ecclesiastical, and familial rivalries were publicly reconciled. And in Bologna, at the height of this excitement, the famed Dominican friar John of Vicenza began testifying that he had received special revelations about the sanctity of his own order's founder, Dominic of Caleruega.[8]

Dominic's body had been laid to rest at the order's church at San Nicolò delle Vigne, Bologna, in early August 1221. For almost twelve years it had remained largely untroubled by the cult of sanctity—apparently due to the friars' reticence to encourage it.[9] But as the community grew, the church needed expanding, with the result that Dominic's bones had to be moved, or "translated," to a new tomb. What was otherwise a practical necessity took on a special significance during the Alleluia, where John's revelations were like a lit match to tinder. He ignited the imaginations and expectations of the order, the pope, and Bologna's leading citizens—all of whom had much to gain from the appearance of a new saint in their midst.[10] Already in competition with the Franciscans—who counted two of their order among the Blessed, the Preachers could finally attain a saint of their own.[11] Pope Gregory IX (d. 1241), taking advantage of a newly formed peace with Emperor Frederick II (1194–1250), could gain a powerful instrument in his quest to rid Christendom of the scourge of heresy.[12]

---

d'archéologie et d'histoire 78 (1966): 503–49; and Daniel A. Brown, "The Alleluia: a Thirteenth-Century Peace Movement," Archivum franciscanum historicum 81 (1988): 3–16.

8. For a helpful study on John of Vicenza see Marco Rainini, "Giovanni da Vicenza, Bologna e l'ordine dei Predicatori," in L'origine dell'Ordine dei Predicatori e l'Università di Bologna, ed. Giovanni Bertuzzi (Bologna, 2006), 176–93.

9. Brother Ventura attests that some brothers in Bologna did not want to attract a multitude or be perceived as encouraging the cult for their own gain. See Ventura's deposition during Dominic's canonization process in Acta, §9.

10. Brother Stephen of Spain credits John with instigating devotion to the cult (Acta, §39). The late-thirteenth-century Franciscan chronicler Salimbene de Adam (d. ca. 1290) gives a similar account. See Salimbene de Adam Cronica I a. 1168–1249, ed. Giuseppe Scalia, Corpus Christianorum Continuatio Mediaevalis 125 (Turnhout, 1998), 104–5.

11. Francis of Assisi (d. 1226) and Anthony of Padua (d. 1231) were canonized in 1228 and 1232, respectively. See M.-H. Vicaire, Histoire de Saint Dominique 2. au coeur de l'Eglise (Paris, 1982), 329–31.

12. A text, falsely attributed to Jordan, which describes Dominic's translation in 1233, implies that Pope Gregory IX initiated the process. See Simon Tugwell, The So-Called "Encyclical" on the Translation of St Dominic Ascribed to Jordan of Saxony: A Study in Early Dominican Hagiography

The leading members of the city could secure both a powerful patron and a totem of civic pride.[13]

But who was Dominic that he might fulfill the expectations of a growing religious order, an energetic pope, and a hopeful citizenship? No biography was extant, and such was the order's growth in the years following Dominic's death that most friars in the 1230s would have never met him. It was in this charged atmosphere, then, that Jordan of Saxony, Dominic's successor, assumed the responsibility for issuing an official statement. At the General Chapter in May 1233, Jordan produced two works—a *Libellus*, or little book, on the history of the order's foundations, and an encyclical letter, both of which dealt with the question of who Dominic was, and perhaps more importantly, what he meant for the brothers of his order going forward.[14] Both texts mark the transformation of Dominic into a model to be imitated, a spiritual father whose steps were to be followed by his spiritual sons. In short, they reveal what Jordan sought to teach his brothers about what it meant to be *Dominican*.

Evangelical Portraiture

Jordan introduces the *Libellus*, the more substantial of the two texts, as being produced at the request of many in the order who sought an account of its beginnings, institutions, and first brothers (§2). It was intended for the benefit of future friars so the past would not be forgotten (§3). It was also meant to be a source of consolation and edification (§3). Most importantly, it was to be accepted in a spirit of devotion, so that it might stir up a desire to emulate the first love (*caritas*) of the brothers who had come before (§3). It was Dominic, however, who was to be the work's set piece. He was the order's "first founder, master and brother" (§2). It was his path, his example that the brothers were to follow (§109).

(Oxford, 1987). This so-called encyclical of 1234 ought not to be confused with Jordan's encyclical letter of 1233.

13. The role of the leading citizens, as well as local bishops and the podestà, in the translation is attested in *Acta*, §§10, 15, 23, 40, 44.

14. The standard edition is *Libellus de principiis Ordinis Praedicatorum*, ed. H.-C. Scheeben, MOPH 16 (Rome, 1935), 1–88. Until otherwise noted, references (§) found in the body of the essay refer to this text. My translations, however, follow the Latin text in Simon Tugwell's unpublished critical edition, which is based on a better survey of the manuscript tradition. For this edition, and for much else besides, I am in Fr. Simon's debt. The most recent edition of the encyclical of 1233 is Elio Montanari, ed., *Iordanis de Saxonia Litterae Encyclicae annis 1233 et 1234 datae* (Spoleto, 1993), 67–73. All translations are my own.

It is significant, too, that Jordan appointed himself to tell Dominic's story, even though he was not among the first friars (§3). Saints' biographers conventionally describe their own unworthiness to undertake such a task—but not Jordan. He writes as one responsible for shaping the spiritual identity of the brothers under his care, and insofar as Dominic's memory is to contribute to that identity, the story of the saint likewise falls within Jordan's prerogative.

And yet, for all its importance as a record of early Dominican history, the *Libellus* is a peculiar work.[15] The text undergoes significant changes in tone and literary form. It shifts between hagiography, anecdote, narrative, and *exordium ordinis*—that is, the foundation story of a religious order. It also concludes not, as one might expect, with an edifying summary of Dominic's life, but with a peculiar story of a demonically-possessed brother (§§110–20).[16] Furthermore, the majority of what the *Libellus* records takes place no later than 1221. Primarily on this basis, Tugwell has convincingly shown that Jordan initially stopped writing what would become the *Libellus* in 1221, and it was not until around 1233 that he quickly polished it up—partly in response to Dominic's newfound popularity, partly to contribute something of substance to the dossier being prepared for Dominic's canonization process.[17]

Before 1233, the text probably looked more like a series of notes and exemplary stories, which Jordan may have used for the pastoral formation of Dominican novices.[18] This, at least, helps to explain the tonal and formal variety in the finished product. Another peculiar quality of the text is that when compared to other saints' *vitae* Dominic seems to cut a relatively unremarkable

15. Much work has been done on the *Libellus*. The most important of which is C. N. L. Brooke, "St. Dominic and His First Biographer," *Transactions of the Royal Historical Society* 17 (1967): 23–40; Simon Tugwell, "Notes on the Life of St. Dominic," *AFP* 68 (1998): 1–116, at 5–33; Giulia Barone, "Il Libellus de initio Ordinis fratrum Predicatorum e lo sviluppo dell'Ordine nel primo cinquantennio," in *Domenico de Caleruega e la nascita dell'ordine dei frati predicatori*, Atti del XLI Convegno storico internazionale, Todi, 10–12 ottobre 2004 (Spoleto, 2005), 431–40; and Luigi Canetti, "La Datazione del Libellus di Giordano di Sassonia," in *L'origine dell'Ordine dei Predicatori e l'Università di Bologna*, ed. Giovanni Bertuzzi (Bologna, 2006), 176–93.

16. It is important to note that Jordan's original text concludes at this point. In the critical edition, Scheeben adds several more paragraphs of a separate text describing the translation of Dominic's bones (§§121–30). This text is only found in one manuscript, and besides not being written by Jordan, was not part of the original work. See Tugwell, "Notes," *AFP* 68, 8, n. 9. For the most recent attempt to understand the role of the "possession" story see Steven Watts, "Diabolical Doubt: The Peculiar Account of Brother Bernard's Possession in Jordan of Saxony's *Libellus*," in *Doubting Christianity: The Church and Doubt*, ed. Frances Andrews, Charlotte Methuen, and Andrew Spicer, Studies in Church History 52 (Cambridge, 2016), 105–21.

17. Tugwell, "Notes," *AFP* 68, 5–33.

18. See Barone, "Il Libellus," 439–40; and Reichert, *Vitae Fratrum*, 126.

figure.[19] His life is relatively devoid of the miraculous. In fact, in one of the two miracles that Jordan does report, it is unclear whether the "revived" young man was actually dead in the first place (§100). Dominic is also by no means the most effective preacher in the narrative. Reginald of Orleans (d. 1220) and Henry of Cologne (d. 1227?) elicit much more powerful responses from their audiences (§63 and §77).

Scholars have posited that Jordan, perhaps following the inclination of the founder himself, consciously "submerged" Dominic within the order.[20] It is possible that Jordan sought to sidestep both John of Vicenza's enthusiasms and Francis of Assisi's divisive legacy, but as Canetti notes, if the *Libellus* was "rushed to the presses" in 1233, there was little opportunity to shape the text accordingly.[21] Moreover, the language of "submersion" overstates the matter considerably. As we shall see, Jordan both positions Dominic as the principal exemplar for the order going forward and presents the behavior of later brothers—such as Reginald and Henry—in terms that implicitly evoke Dominic's example.

However ironic it might appear to the modern reader, Jordan's first task in presenting Dominic as the primary exemplar for the order was to show that the founder was ultimately inimitable. That is to say, he needed to demonstrate Dominic's particular, divinely ordained sanctity. For just as a medieval scribe would set up a textual exemplar from which to base his copy, so too did the thirteenth-century hagiographer produce portraits of saints. The exemplar was necessarily as close to perfect as could be, otherwise it was an unreliable guide. The imitation, without divine assistance, could only ever be a faithful attempt. In the *Libellus*, Jordan communicates Dominic's holy singularity principally through a thematic employment of light. Dominic's blameless life and celibacy are said to have shone into "the foul darkness of the world" (§2). His mother's vision of the moon upon her child's forehead signified that he was to be a "light of the gentiles" (Acts 13:47) and that he would "illumine those remaining in darkness and in the shadow of death" (Luke 1:79) (§9).[22] Light and its cognates are then used to describe his many virtues, including his innocent life (§11), his contemplation (§13), his goodness (§36), and joy (§103). It is clear, however, that Jordan is also keen to show that Dominic's particular light has the capacity to illuminate those who follow after him. It is "by means of the light" of Dominic's

---

19. Brooke, "St. Dominic," 23–24.

20. Brooke, "St. Dominic," 39–40; and Tugwell, "Notes," *AFP* 68, 14–18.

21. Canetti, "La Datazione," 192.

22. The earliest account of Dominic's mother's vision is that she saw a moon on his forehead. In later hagiographical tradition this would be remembered as a star. Another vision of a small dog with a burning torch in its mouth would also be added.

manner of living, Jordan explains, that Christ regenerates those who follow after him (§109).

While the multivalent use of light illustrates Dominic's particular holiness, the *Libellus* contains a number of other key themes and virtues that more readily invite imitation. Foremost among these is Jordan's presentation of Dominic's love or *caritas*. Jordan explicitly intends the *Libellus* to stir up a desire among his audience "to imitate fervently the first *caritas* of our brothers" (§3). In its medieval religious context, the meaning of *caritas* drew especially from 1 Corinthians 13 and Augustine's influential definition in *De doctrina christiana*.[23] *Caritas* was divine in origin, selfless, and especially in the Dominican tradition, directed towards the other—as in the modern sense of the word *charity*. Jordan notes that it was Dominic's frequent and special prayer to God that he would be granted the gift of true *caritas* to enable him to labor for and to win salvation for others (§13). He later writes that "all were swept into Dominic's embrace of *caritas*," and "since he loved everyone, everyone loved him" (§107). It is also evidently on the strength of this same *caritas* that Dominic kept preaching in the Languedoc despite laboring "as though he were alone" for many years and with little success (§37).

Caritas tends to be described in medieval religious and scholastic literature as a capacity of the will, rather than of the emotions, but in the *Libellus* we should not take it to infer a lack of feeling on Dominic's part. In fact, Jordan presents his *caritas* most often in terms of *compassio*, a word that evokes an intense, at times physical, feeling of "fellow-suffering." This is aptly demonstrated in one account where Dominic's Christ-like *caritas* leads him to have *compassio* for a man indentured to heretics, such that he attempts to sell himself into slavery to set the other free (§35). We find a similar expression of *compassio* earlier in the text when Dominic decides to sell his possessions and set up a charitable center for the poor during a time of severe famine in Palencia (§10). Jordan makes a point of underlining the exemplary nature of this story. Thanks to Dominic's actions, both students and masters at Palencia were inspired to increase their giving.

Jordan also closely associates Dominic's *compassio* with the latter's lachrymosity. He writes that God granted Dominic the special "gift of tears" for sinners, the miserable, and the afflicted—whose sufferings the latter felt with pro-

---

23. *De doctrina christiana*, 3.10.16: "I call *caritas* the motion of the mind towards delight in God, for his own sake, and delight in one's self and in one's neighbor for God's sake." For a broader treatment on the development of *caritas* into the Later Middle Ages see Mirko Breitenstein, "Is There a Cistercian Love? Some Considerations on the Virtue of Charity," in *Aspects of Charity: Concern for One's Neighbour in Medieval* Vita Religiosa, ed. Gert Melville, Vita Regularis 45 (Berlin, 2011), 55–98, at 58–62.

found compassion (§12). The "gift of tears" has a venerable heritage in Christian spirituality, but it became increasingly common among male and female saints in the later Middle Ages, when it was typically associated with Christo-centric penitential devotion.[24] In the *Libellus*, however, Dominic's tears are primarily explained as a manifestation of his God-given desire for the relief and salvation of others (§12).

Caritas and *compassio* are the principal means by which Dominic is animated toward the saving of souls. Yet for the salvation of Dominic's own soul, a different, if complementary, picture emerges. Dominic's sanctity may have been predestined (§5), but Jordan nevertheless shows Dominic to have sought progress in the spiritual disciplines. And it is here, above all else in the *Libellus*, where the new tide of evangelistic fervor, embodied by the Dominicans and Franciscans, meets the ancient shores of desert spirituality. Jordan remarks that Dominic loved to read John Cassian's *Conferences of the Fathers*, which dealt with "the vices and all matters of spiritual perfection" (§13). The early-fifth-century *Conferences* is a collection of recorded conversations with notable desert ascetics, which was later reconstituted for a western ascetic audience. Thanks in large part to the sponsorship of Benedict of Nursia (d. ca. 547), the text was established within the Western monastic canon.[25] Jordan writes that Dominic strove to study this book and to imitate the paths of salvation found therein with all his strength (§13). His progress is thus described in terms of desert disciplines both external—"unceasing prayer" and nocturnal vigils (§§13, 105–6)—and internal: moderation (§108), purity (§13), and a serene and undivided mind (§§62, 103). These qualities, too, could be studied and practiced by the brothers under Jordan's care.

Beyond *caritas* and *compassio*, there are two further virtues to which Jordan draws particular attention in Dominic's life: *humilitas* (humility) and *paupertas* (poverty). Humility was the contrary virtue to pride, Satan's signature vice. Poverty, in the collective sense, had been espoused by the earliest cenobites and was modeled on the early Christian community described in Acts 2:44. And yet, in the religious climate of Jordan's day, which prioritized the literal imitation of Christ and his disciples, they took on a special evangelical resonance.[26] For just as

---

24. The critical study on the "gift of tears" in the Middle Ages is Piroska Nagy, *Le Don des larmes au Moyen Âge: Un instrument en quête d'institution, Ve–XIIIe* (Paris, 2000). For the role of Dominic's tears in Dominican hagiography see Kimberley-Joy Knight, "Blessed Are Those Who Weep: *Gratia lacrymarum* in Thirteenth-century Hagiographies" (PhD thesis, University of St. Andrews, 2014), 137–224.

25. See Owen Chadwick, introduction to John Cassian, *Conferences*, ed. Colm Luibheid, The Classics of Western Spirituality (New York, 1985), 1–36; and *Sancti Benedicti Regula*, chap. 42.

26. M.-D. Chenu, *Nature, Man, and Society in the Twelfth Century: Essays on New Theolog-*

the disciples were sent out to preach the gospel, barefoot and without possessions (Luke 9–10), Dominic followed his bishop Diego of Osma in the latter's embrace of poverty and humility for the sake of evangelizing the heretics in southern France (§20). But Jordan indicates that these virtues were not simply of instrumental value. They lay at the core of what it meant to be a preaching friar in the 1220s and 1230s. In the introduction added to the order's Primitive Constitutions in 1228, the renunciation of possessions and revenues is established as one of only three immutable laws of the order.[27] These same Constitutions institute that the master of novices must teach "humility of heart and body" to those under his care.[28] Even the head of the order, Jordan explains, was chosen by the brothers to be called "master" rather than "abbot" so as to demonstrate his humility (§48).

Dominic's humility is likewise described as a quality of the heart. Jordan notes that it allowed him to penetrate difficult theological questions (§7). It also contributed to the beneficial influence he had upon his fellow canons in Osma (§12). As for poverty, Dominic is described as its "true lover" (§108). He adopted a life of simplicity, intentionally wearing cheap clothing and eating and drinking only in the strictest moderation (§108). As noted above, while he was a student in Palencia he sold everything he had, including his books, to provide for the poor (§10). And when Dominic sought to persuade Reginald of Orleans to join the order, he exhorted him "to imitate the poverty of Christ" (§56).

The apostolic, evangelical resonance of humility and poverty was likewise evident in the order's approach to *caritas*. In fact, a number of early-thirteenth-century texts—including a *Testament* attributed to Dominic—group these three virtues together as constituting "the way of Christ."[29] For traditional monastic communities, *caritas*—insofar as it was directed towards one's neighbor—tended to govern social interactions within the walls of the monastery.[30] For the Preachers, *caritas* still informed relationships within the priory, but it was ultimately intended for the benefit of those outside.[31] To externalize that *caritas* was primarily, in their case, to preach—and preaching required study.

---

ical Perspectives in the Latin West, ed. and trans. Jerome Taylor and Lester K. Little (1968; repr., Toronto: University of Toronto, 1997), 202–69.

27. The critical edition of the Primitive Constitutions (hereafter PC) is in *Constitutiones antiquae ordinis Fratrum Praedicatorum,* ed. A. H. Thomas, in *De oudste Constituties van der Dominicanen: Voorgescheidensis, Tekst, Bronnen, Onstaan en Ontwikkeling, 1215–1237* (Leuven, 1965), 304–69.

28. PC 1:12.

29. Raymond Creytens, "Le 'Testament de S. Dominique' dans la littérature dominicaine ancienne et moderne," *AFP* 43 (1973): 29–72.

30. Breitenstein, "Is There a Cistercian Love?" 94–95.

31. Rudolf Kilian Weigand, "Proclaiming *Caritas*: The Propagation of a Way of Life in Sermons," *Aspects of Charity,* 147–66, at 150.

It is no wonder then that Jordan goes into great detail about the nature of Dominic's commitment to education. One can imagine him reading the passage to a group of eager novices, fresh from their classes at the university of Paris. The *Libellus* reports that Dominic initially studied the "liberal sciences," but once he found that he was satisfactorily competent at these he abandoned them to study theology (§6).[32] Indeed, Dominic considered theology a more profitable use of his limited time on earth (§6). But rather than positioning study as a necessary obligation, Jordan waxes eloquent about Dominic's growing taste for the divine words of Scripture, which were to him something sweeter than honey, and about the long nights he spent satisfying his unremitting eagerness to learn (§7). He goes on to add that Dominic stored the truth in his memory and put what he learned into practice—the latter, Jordan notes, being more commendable than the former (§7). Those things Dominic easily understood were thus "watered by the love of his devout nature and so blossomed into works of salvation" (§7). And because Dominic had received the commands of God with such fervent passion and followed the voice of the Spouse—that is, Christ—with good will, "the God of the sciences" granted him the grace to penetrate difficult and mysterious theological questions (§7).

Jordan's description of Dominic's approach to study, with his own extended reflection on its benefits, is consonant with, and indeed reinforces, the order's approach to education in its early years. As soon as arts students were recruited to the order, they were immediately directed toward theology, as that was the means by which they would be most useful to their neighbors.[33] Even the Divine Office was attenuated for the purposes of learning.[34] But rather than subordinating prayer to study, Jordan describes Dominic's study as a kind of prayer. Indeed, Dominic's fervent and tireless labor that extended long into the night evokes the "unceasing prayer" and nocturnal vigils described in other parts of the *Libellus*. It is as if the spirituality of the desert had been transposed, by means of evangelical necessity, into the thirteenth-century Dominican *studium*.

In the *Libellus*, the ardent commitment Dominic devotes to learning is also evidenced in other facets of his life. It is evident in his study of God's commands (§7), his desire to win his heretical host in Toulouse back to the catholic fold (§15), his passion for saving as many souls as he could for Christ (§34), and his constant prayer (§106). On his deathbed, Dominic exhorts his brothers to that

32. The "liberal sciences" or "liberal arts" provided the basis of education in the Middle Ages. The three foundational liberal arts (the *trivium*) were related to language: grammar, rhetoric, and logic.

33. M. Michèle Mulchahey, *"First the Bow Is Bent in Study . . ."*: Dominican Education before 1350 (Toronto, 1998), 54–59. See also the prologue to the PC.

34. PC 1:3.

same fervency, particularly in their promotion of the order and their perseverance in holiness (§92).

In sum, the multifaceted portrait of Dominic that emerges from the *Libellus*
may be distilled into a number of complementary qualities. Beyond the singularity of his illustrious election—which makes him a model to be imitated,
however imperfectly—Dominic is shown to exemplify an evangelical *caritas*
and Christ-like *compassio*. He progresses in ways characteristic of the desert
spirituality espoused in Cassian, while embodying the virtues of poverty and
humility as understood within the apostolic character of thirteenth-century
devotion. He attends to his studies with the same ardent commitment as he
does to prayer. Indeed, the former seems barely distinguishable from the latter
in Jordan's rendering. And, last but not least, a passionate fervor permeates all
aspects of his life and work—most especially for the sake of saving souls for
Christ. To what extent, then, was Jordan's audience expected to imitate this lofty
example of holiness, to follow this path set before them?

Imitating the Inimitable

As noted earlier, not everything in Jordan's portrait of Dominic in the *Libellus*
could be imitated by the order's rank and file. His innocence from youth (§8), his
mother's vision (§9), the odor of sanctity that surrounded him (§5), the gift of tears
(§12), his acceptance of potential martyrdom at the hands of heretics (§34), his
gathering of twelve or so brethren around his deathbed (§92), and his promise that
he would be of more use to his brothers dead than alive (§93), are all typical characteristics of a saint's *vita*.[35] And even though Jordan was, by medieval standards,
more reticent than others to communicate the miraculous, he still mentioned two
miracles that Dominic accomplished during his lifetime: his reviving of the young
man in Rome (§100) and his prevention of rainfall by the sign of the cross (§101).

But as a means of helping his brothers seek to imitate the otherwise inimitable, Jordan points out that Dominic's miracles were outshone by the integrity
of his way of life and the vigor of his divine passion (§109). This, Jordan says, is
also perhaps too difficult to imitate perfectly, unless one is given a special grace
of God's merciful goodness:

> Yet, brothers, let us follow the steps of our father as much as we can, and let
> us also ask for the graces of the Redeemer, who presented such a great leader

---

35. See André Vauchez, *Sainthood in the Later Middle Ages*, trans. Jean Birrel (Cambridge,
1997, originally published in 1988), 507–26.

to his servants on this road that we travel upon and who is regenerating us through [Dominic], in the light of his manner of living. (§109)

Dominic's example is meant to be followed. Evidently this does not refer to his holy singularity or his miracles, but the *Libellus* provides many occasions— many of which we have already seen above—where this was shown not only to be possible, but also to have occurred among the first brothers who followed in Dominic's steps. Indeed, Dominic himself was following a prior example.

The phrase "following in the steps of the fathers" appears to draw ultimately from Romans 4:12 ("walk in the footsteps of the faith that our father Abraham had"), but its medieval significance owes especially to the desert tradition. In this setting it was primarily concerned with the way in which a novice was to learn the monastic life by obediently imitating the example of an older, wiser monk—an *abba*, or father. We find it similarly employed in twelfth-century works that describe the origins of the Cistercian and Premonstratensian orders, both of which exerted an influence on the first Preachers.[36]

In the *Libellus,* Dominic's salutary practice of imitating the paths set before him is implicit in his reading of Cassian's *Conferences* and in the way his example mirrors that of Diego, his bishop. For instance, in a move that has struck a number of scholars as peculiar, the narrative introduces Diego *before* Dominic. Diego's love for God is said to have so completely absorbed him that he turned his mind entirely to the task of winning souls (§4). He began the preaching mission out of compassion for those he found deluded by heresy (§15). And it was on his initiative that the preachers embraced humility and poverty for the sake of evangelism (§20). In all these respects, Dominic clearly followed in the steps of his bishop.

Dominic's example is then reproduced in turn by those who gathered around him. The brothers in Toulouse are described as growing further in humility (§38). Bishop Fulk of Toulouse (d. 1231) notes the brothers' fervor in preaching and is thankful for this "new light" in his diocese (§39). We also see Dominic's virtues embodied in the lives of individual brothers. Brother Dominic of Spain is lauded for his exceptional humility (§49). Reginald of Orleans is remembered to have said that he did not deserve the habit of the order (§64). Reginald (§63), Bertrandus (§51), and Tancred (§100) are all noted for their fervor. Henry of Cologne appears almost as a second Dominic. Like the prospective saint (§3), Henry is described as an "instrument of election" (Acts

36. Prologue to *Exordium Magnum Cisterciense sive Narratio de Initio Cisterciensis Ordinis,* ed. Bruno Griesser, Corpus Christianorum Continuatio Mediaevalis 137 (Turnhout, 1994); and *Vita S. Norberti,* PL 170, cols. 1253–1350, at col. 1253B.

9:15) (§77). He is said to have demonstrated *caritas*, purity of heart, humility, poverty, and virginity (§78). He was also an excellent and "fervent" student whose preaching—like that of Reginald—made a powerful impression on his audience (§77).

An Uncompromising Challenge

In his final word on Dominic in the *Libellus* (§109), Jordan encouraged his brothers to follow in their father's steps, but there is little explicit direction in terms of what that meant in practice.[37] This we find in Jordan's encyclical letter, which was composed shortly after the *Libellus* was completed.[38] The lone extant copy of the encyclical was addressed to the brothers in the province of Lombardy, but the letter probably circulated throughout the various provinces of the order.[39] It is, in short, a master's *visitatio* in writing.

Typically, each Dominican priory could expect to receive a *visitatio* by one of four brothers who were elected by the relevant provincial chapter.[40] These "visitators" were to report to the chapter whether the brothers were living in peace, diligent in study, and fervent in preaching.[41] This included commenting on the reputation of the house, the fruit of the brothers' labors, and whether the house was following the order's constitutions appropriately. These *visitationes*, like receiving a doctor's annual checkup, were designed more to diagnose and correct what was wrong than to celebrate what was right, and it is within this setting that we can best understand Jordan's encyclical. For while we might expect an encomium, especially in a letter directed to a province in the midst of the Alleluia, what we find instead is a combination of rebuke and exhortation, both centered upon Dominic's example.

Jordan begins the encyclical by explaining to the brothers that while he is unable to visit them in person, *caritas* invites him and usefulness urges him to

---

37. See John Van Engen, "Dominic and the Brothers: *Vitae* as Life-forming *exempla* in the Order of Preachers," in *Christ among the Medieval Dominicans: Representations of Christ in the Texts and Images of the Order of Preachers*, ed. Kent Emery Jr. and Joseph Wawrykow (Notre Dame: University of Notre Dame Press, 1998), 7–25, at 8.

38. The encyclical refers to the translation of Dominic's bones, which occurred after the *Libellus* was completed. See *Litterae Encyclicae*, §4. The following references (§) in the essay refer to the text of the encyclical.

39. Thomas Kaeppeli, "B. Iordani de Saxonia Litterae Encyclicae," *AFP* 22 (1952): 177–85, at 181–82.

40. PC 2:19.

41. PC 2:18.

take the opportunity to pay them "a kind of visitation in writing" (§2). He tells them that in "this place of pilgrimage" it is all too easy to grow lethargic, and so he seeks to encourage them, with all his strength, not to forget their holy purpose and profession (§2). He urges them to be mindful of those "ancient paths" by which their predecessors "hastened to their rest with a vigorous spirit" (§2). These predecessors were "imitators of the Spirit, scorners of themselves, despisers of the world, seekers of Heaven, strong to endure, willing for poverty, and fervent with love" (§2). Dominic, he notes, was surely one of these. Jordan continues the passage with a celebration of the founder, a summary of his virtues, and an exhortation that the brothers ought to follow his example.

Dominic is described as displaying a true spirit of poverty (§3). He is remembered as being constant in prayer, exceptional in "fellow-suffering" (*in compassione*), and lavish in the shedding of tears—all on account of his fervent desire for souls (§3). He was undaunted by difficulties, nor did obstacles worry him (§3). Jordan singles out Dominic's true humility of heart, voluntary poverty, lack of self-indulgence, "jealousy with a divine jealousy for all" (2 Cor 11:2), and life-long virginity (§4). Then, in an important rhetorical turn, Jordan employs a series of collective pronouns. He gives thanks to Christ for choosing such a man to be "our" father, whose religious instruction informs "us" and whose example of shining sanctity inflames "us" (§4). He, too, is a fellow spiritual son of Dominic of Caleruega.

For the careful reader of the *Libellus*, this should all sound very familiar. Jordan has effectively distilled its exemplary portrait of Dominic. But the encyclical does not simply summarize Dominic's qualities, it recasts them as the rule by which the brothers are to be measured. The result is a litany of withering criticisms concerning those who effectively practice the opposite of all that Dominic exemplified. Jordan censures those who are proud, who seek comfort, and who falsely profess poverty (§5). He denounces those who, rather than being untroubled by obstacles, are feebly seized by unimportant things undeserving of their attention (§5). Those with God-given talent are not using it (§5). Teachers and students have been negligent. Superiors fail to encourage study, mismanage those who have ability, or distract talented brothers from studying (§5). Teachers are so half-hearted that the students become even more unenthusiastic than those who are instructing them (§5). And the students themselves are said to be uninterested in their study, undisciplined, lazy, and stupid in their debates (§5). Some of them are too distracted by "excessive devotions"; others have a destructive appetite for leisure (§5). While the negligence and laziness of the brothers puts them at odds with Dominic's rigorous approach to study, the fundamental issue for Jordan is that they are not following "the father's rule of *caritas*" (§5). Their lack of effort deprives many of the chance for salvation.

Jordan's solution to the ills of those brothers being "visited" also draws from Dominic's example. Happy, Jordan writes, is the one who keeps to the middle way—that is, who shows discretion in giving each its appropriate due (§6). It is this, he argues, which allows the brothers to help their neighbor without sacrificing self-knowledge and self-criticism in the process. The point is not to be motivated by human approval, but to be urged on by *caritas* (2 Cor 5:14) and guided by the Spirit of God (§6). The one who does this, Jordan explains, will look purely and simply to the glory of God, to the spiritual benefit of his neighbor, and to his own salvation in every situation.

Shifting back to the collective pronoun, and thus continuing to reaffirm his identity as one of Dominic's spiritual sons, he asks, "Oh, how often does the base, uncertain meandering of our affections lead us off the path? It is neither directed toward truth nor focused on the proper goal" (§7). Jordan maintains that if *caritas* abounds in "our" hearts then "our" work will prove richer in virtue and more fruitful in merit (§7). It is *caritas*, demonstrated fully in Dominic's example, that directs and orders everything towards God, the brothers' true end. And here, just as in the *Libellus*, we find in Dominic a confluence of desert spirituality and of the evangelical impulse of the thirteenth century. Discretion and an observance of "the middle way"—an ethos classical in origin but baptized among the desert monks—prove necessary in making sure that the evangelical impulse remains focused on its proper goal. The encyclical, therefore, is a companion piece to the *Libellus*. In contrast to the exemplary stories found in the longer text, Jordan's *visitatio* in writing distills their central message—centered upon Dominic's example—into an uncompromising pastoral challenge.

An Opportunity Seized

In 1233 Jordan was granted an opportunity. Dominic was no longer simply the founder of an order, but would soon be recognized as one of God's chosen saints. His example, therefore, had a divine stamp of approval. But Jordan did not seem interested in relishing in the excitement surrounding Dominic's cult or in satisfying the heightened expectations of the pope, Bologna's leading citizens, or even some within his order. These expectations would be satisfied later, but not by him. In later Dominican hagiography, Dominic became a wonder-worker par excellence.[42] Gregory IX's bull of canonization, issued in the summer of 1234, portrays Dominic in apocalyptic terms as God's chosen

---

42. See Constantine of Orvieto's *Legenda* (ca. 1246) in MOPH 16, 261–352.

instrument against heresy.[43] In the following decades, the citizens who eagerly watched the opening of Dominic's tomb in 1233 would offer prayers appropriate to a saint the city could call its own.[44]

Jordan's portrait of Dominic tells a different story—one that is primarily interested in how the brothers in the order ought to imitate their spiritual father. It was about forging a *Dominican* identity. The singular "light" of Dominic's sanctity was shown to reveal a path to salvation governed primarily by *caritas* and expressed in qualities and virtues such as *compassio*, humility, poverty, and "the middle way." It was a path that had already been travelled by the desert fathers and, more recently, by his bishop. It was also a path that had been followed by those brothers who had already "hastened to their rest," such as Reginald of Orleans and Henry of Cologne. Jordan's encyclical emphatically set that same path before the brothers under his care. They, too, were to follow their father's rule of *caritas* with an evangelical fervency that was to enflame their study, prayer, and preaching.

Prior to the heady days of the Alleluia in 1233, Dominic's followers had let their founder rest in peace. Yet when Jordan chastises them in the *Libellus* for having both "neglected the general progress of the Church" and "buried the divine glory" (§98), he is not talking about the brothers' failure to promote Dominic's cult. What they had needlessly left in the tomb was Dominic's holy example. In the *Libellus* and, more succinctly, in the encyclical, Jordan brought that example into the light. He illuminated those "steps of the father" that he and his brothers ought to follow to the best of their ability, through grace, for *caritas*.

43. See Simon Tugwell, ed., *Humberti de Romanis Legendae sancti Dominici: Necnon materia praedicabilis pro festis sancti Dominici et testimonia minora de eodem: Adiectis miraculis rotomagensibus sancti Dominici Gregorii IX bulla canonizationis eiusdem*, MOPH 30 (Rome, 2008), 563–75.

44. Diana Webb, *Patrons and Defenders: The Saints in the Italian City-States* (London: Tauris Academic, 1996), 176 and 178–79.

Chapter 20

Aquinas: Participating in Christ's Poverty, Mission, and Life

Yonghua Ge

Thomas Aquinas was born in 1224/25[1] in Roccasecca, a small town in southern Italy. At the age of five, he was sent to study at the Benedictine abbey of
Monte Cassino, where he spent the next ten years of his life. In 1239, when the
monastery was evacuated by Fredrick II, Thomas was transferred to the newly
founded University of Naples, where he studied Aristotelian philosophy. It
was there that he became attracted to the Dominican Order and received
the mendicant habit in 1244. On his way to Bologna, however, Thomas was
kidnapped by his brothers and was held in confinement for a year. After being released, he proceeded to study in Paris and later became the assistant to
Albert the Great in Cologne.

In 1252, Thomas began to teach as a bachelor at Paris, but was soon caught
in the conflict between secular and mendicant masters, which was so intense
that the pope had to command the university to grant Thomas the license to
teach in 1256, and later his master's degree in theology. During this period, he
wrote some significant works such as *De veritate* and commentaries on Boe-
thius. From 1259 to 1265, Aquinas stayed in Italy and taught at various houses
of study. There, he continued to work on *Summa contra gentiles* and completed
Catena aurea. It was also during this period that the plan of writing the *Summa
theologiae* (*ST*) was conceived.

In 1269, Thomas returned to Paris for the second regency and was again
engaged in severe disputes. On the one hand, he defended the Dominican the-

---

1. The general consensus among the scholars on Aquinas's year of birth is 1224/25, although
some secondary sources propose 1226 or 1227. Jean-Pierre Torrell, *Saint Thomas Aquinas*, vol. 1,
The Person and His Work, trans. Robert Royal (Washington, DC: Catholic University of America
Press, 1996), 1.

ology against conservative theologians of the Augustinian tradition. On the other hand, he attacked the Latin Averroists, represented by Siger of Brabant, who was condemned by the bishop of Paris in 1270. This was a period of great literary output for Thomas: the larger portion of the Aristotelian commentaries was finished or elaborated, and work on *Summa theologiae* progressed steadily. There is no doubt that Aquinas's most original contribution to theology was made in his second Parisian period.

Thomas left Paris in 1272 and moved to Naples to help erect a Dominican *studium generale,* in which he held class, lectured, and directed disputations. His literary activity slowed down until he completely stopped writing after a mysterious experience on December 6, 1273. Not long after that, he fell ill and died in the Cistercian Abbey of Fossanuova at the age of forty-nine.[2]

Aquinas is widely known as a master of theology.[3] His personal life, however, especially his Christian identity, is often overlooked.[4] In fact, his theology cannot be understood apart from his profound sense of following the call of Christ; his life and works were but the unfolding of his Christian conviction. Like Christian theologians before him, such as Augustine and Anselm, Thomas was a man of deep faith. Yet unlike Anselm, a monk in the monastery, Aquinas was an itinerant friar and academic theologian in the university. This difference to some extent reflects the difference between the world in which Aquinas lived and that in which Anselm lived. While Aquinas shared the Christian identity with his predecessors, he embodied this identity in a new way, namely, as a response to the new social, cultural conditions. In this chapter, I will argue that, in the face of the new developments in thirteenth-century Europe, Aquinas chose to express his Christian identity as a Dominican mendicant and teacher of the Word of God. In other words, for Aquinas, to be a Christian meant to participate in Christ's poverty and mission—and as a Dominican, he was particularly concerned about preaching God's Word to the world.

At the end of his life, however, Thomas sensed that his mission as a teacher

2. Thomas's first biographer indicated that he died on the morning of March 7, 1274, in his forty-ninth year. See *Vita S. Thomae Aquinatis auctore Guillelmo de Tocco* 65, 139.

3. In fact, Aquinas is also considered by many to be one of the greatest philosophers in history. Norman Kretzmann and Eleonore Stump, eds., *The Cambridge Companion to Aquinas* (Cambridge: Cambridge University Press, 1993), 1.

4. There are a number of works that explore Aquinas's spirituality: see, for instance, Jean-Pierre Torrell, *Saint Thomas Aquinas,* vol. 2, *Spiritual Master,* trans. Robert Royal (Washington, DC: Catholic University of America Press, 2003); and Robert Barron, *Thomas Aquinas: Spiritual Master* (New York: Crossroad, 1996). Both explore the way in which Aquinas's theology embodies and is permeated by his spirituality. Not enough attention, however, has been given on how Aquinas's life and work as a theologian reflects his Christian identity.

had come to an end, as he was anticipating a deeper participation—union with Christ himself. Thus, parallel to the three stages of man's knowledge of God,[5] Aquinas's participation in Christ may also be seen in three phases: in youth as a poor man in Christ; in middle age as a theologian in Christ; and in old age as a mystic ready to be in union with Christ.[6] In what follows, then, I will first briefly discuss the social changes of the thirteenth century in connection with the rise of the Dominican Order. Then I will trace the three phases of Thomas Aquinas's identity in Christ: participating in Christ's poverty, participating in Christ's mission of teaching, and participating in Christ's very life.[7]

Social Developments and the Dominican Order

Thomas lived in a time of profound social, cultural, and intellectual changes, which in certain ways occasioned the emergence of the Dominican Order. Diarmaid MacCulloch suggested that, like the Reformation in the sixteenth century, "an equally crucial Reformation" took place in Western Christendom during the first three centuries of the second millennia. A significant part of this reformation was the creation of a grand unified vision of reality, in which the Church, with the pope, would unify and rule over the whole world.[8] The Church's influence, therefore, would not limit itself within the walls of monasteries; all domains of the society must be brought under its reign so that Christ can have dominion of all things. This vision made a lasting and profound impact on the medieval ages. To a certain degree, crusades against the pagans and heretics were a response to that aspiration, and the Dominican fervor to win heretics back was stimulated by a similar passion, although they used the Word of God—rather than swords—as their weapon. In a sense, Aquinas's incorporation of Aristotelian philosophy into theology and his construction of *Summa theologiae* also reflected this vision of bringing all things into unity under Christ.[9]

Fundamental shifts also occurred in economic and social realms. The elev-

---

5. *ST* 1.93.4.

6. Of course, these three stages are not clearly separable; rather, they are like three themes that run through Thomas's life. Nevertheless, it is possible that in each phase of his life Thomas had an emphasis on a particular theme.

7. Focus will be given to the first two, and my discussion of the last theme will be brief.

8. Diarmaid MacCulloch, *Groundwork of Christian History* (London: Epworth, 1987), 125.

9. Indeed, Christ plays an absolutely primary role in Aquinas's system of theology. For Christ's role in his spiritual theology, see Jean-Pierre Torrell, *Christ and Spirituality in St. Thomas Aquinas,* trans. Bernhard Blankenhorn (Washington, DC: Catholic University of America Press, 2011), chap. 5.

enth and twelfth centuries witnessed a series of developments that profoundly reshaped the European landscape. Territorial expansion and innovations in agriculture not only brought economic prosperity but also rapid urbanization. Accompanying the fast growth of towns and cities was the considerable expansion of trade, commerce, and urban organizations, particularly various guilds of craftsmen and merchants. Along with such guilds emerged scholastic guilds of masters and students, which eventually became universities. These universities were "spontaneous products of the instinct of association which swept like a great wave over the towns of Europe in the course of the eleventh and twelfth centuries."[10] Together, these new developments brought about radical changes in the society. In contrast to the relatively stable feudal system, the society was now full of restlessness and challenges. On the one hand, the increased prosperity not only increased the gap between the rich and the poor but also fostered spiritual indolence among the people. On the other hand, the rapid urbanization "made it difficult for the traditional parish ministry to fill the needs of those who flocked to the towns."[11] "The desperate plight of the people, divided by heresy, animated either by the desire for material security or by the inordinate greed for wealth and power, corrupted by sin, demanded a radical remedy. This was provided by the preaching of men who renounced the world only to possess it again for Jesus Christ."[12]

This was the context in which the Dominican Order emerged.[13] Dominic was involved in the campaigns to convert the Albigensians in southern France, but soon he realized such efforts were inefficient, since the comfortable life of many orthodox priests had compromised the gospel they preached. As such, Dominic emphasized that the preaching of the Word of God must accompany gospel living. Called by his biographer "*vir evangelicus*—man of the gospel,"[14] Dominic sought to renew the gospel by simultaneously preaching God's Word and imitating Christ's poverty. This vision blossomed into the new Order of Preachers, which devoted itself to teaching and living the Word of God.

10. Hastings Rashdall, *The Universities of Europe in the Middle Ages* (Oxford: Clarendon, 1895), 17–18.

11. Justo L. González, *The Story of Christianity*, vol. 1, *The Early Church to the Dawn of the Reformation* (New York: HarperCollins, 1984), 302.

12. William R. Cannon, *History of Christianity in the Middle Ages* (Nashville: Abingdon, 1960), 224.

13. Needless to say, the Franciscan Order also arose around this time. While both mendicant orders shared the conviction on evangelical poverty, the Dominicans had a stronger passion for preaching the Word of God.

14. John of Saxony, *Libellus on the Beginnings of the Order of Preachers*, in Monumenta Ordinis Praedicatorum Historica, ed. H. C. Scheeben (Rome: MOPH, 1935), 16:75.

While maintaining a kind of spiritual continuity with monasticism, the Dominican Order—as a response to the new social developments—was a radically new way of following Christ, which "turned the ecclesiastical world of the early thirteenth century upside down."[15] Living outside the orderly monastic communities, the friars provided a challenge to the traditional monastic foundations. While monasteries were economically and politically powerful in the feudal system, the friars resolutely rejected wealth and power and pursued poverty in order to witness to Christ in a world that became increasingly preoccupied with wealth. Moreover, while monasteries were committed to stability, the mendicants forsook all forms of stability; they roamed around begging, so as to place themselves completely in God's hands. Because of their mobility, the Dominicans were able to minister to the moving population. Whereas monasteries remained in rural areas, the mendicants were actively involved in the cities, especially in the universities. Turner sums up the contrast nicely:

> Dominicans engage in no economically productive activity, the monks farm; Dominicans are beggars, the monks are economically self-supporting; Dominicans can count on no permanence of place, and if they preach, they preach to all corners of the street, whereas the monks are vowed to the stability of place and belong to the settled communities; Dominicans are city dwellers, the monks commonly rural; Dominicans are universities, their learning that of the schools; the monk's *schola* is the cloister. But above all, the Dominicans for the most part talk, and the monks, when not singing, are for the most part weeping those silent tears.[16]

In becoming a Dominican friar, therefore, Thomas Aquinas chose to commit himself to this way of life. In the tumult of thirteenth-century Europe, he decided to identify himself as a Christian—a follower of Christ—by participating in Christ's poverty and by teaching the Word of God in order to win the world back to Christ.

Participating in Christ's Poverty

Aquinas's life cannot be understood apart from his Dominican identity as a participant in the poverty of Christ. From his first decision to join the Dominican Order to his final breath, Thomas constantly pursued evangelical poverty as a

---

15. Denys Turner, *Thomas Aquinas: A Portrait* (New Haven: Yale University Press, 2013), 11.
16. Turner, *Thomas Aquinas*, 17.

way of following his Lord, who became poor so that the world might become rich; who came to save the world but was rejected by the world, having nowhere to lay his head.

Becoming a Dominican Friar

Given his family background, Thomas's decision to become a Dominican friar was radical and even scandalous. His father, Count Landolf, was a feudal lord of the town of Roccasecca and hoped that his youngest son would become the abbot of the Benedictine Abbey, since "the abbot, a true feudal lord, had great prestige in a society where religion was able to sacralize political power."[17] It was the family's plan for Thomas to become a socially, economically, and politically influential figure in the local region. This dream, however, was in danger of being shattered when they heard about Thomas's decision to become a mendicant, that is, a beggar! In the eyes of such a well-to-do and respected family as Thomas's, the friars were hardly distinguishable from vagabonds—"gangs of self-promoting tramps," in Turner's colorful phrase.[18] In an attempt to bring Thomas back to sanity, Thomas's family kidnapped him and put him under house arrest.

We have to note that "Thomas was no adolescent rebel anxious to free himself of parental influence."[19] On the contrary, he highly valued family loyalties, arguing that we ought to love parents before all others, even spouses.[20] So it must have taken tremendous courage for him to defy his family's wishes. He knew that his choice would deeply disappoint his family, and yet he made it nonetheless. To make this decision, Thomas might have gone through intense emotional struggles. He was probably torn between the duty to honor his parents and the call to follow Christ. But the Dominican zeal seems to have kindled in Thomas's young heart such a fervor that he was willing to abandon everything, including family duties, for the sake of Christ, who, after all, commanded: "Whoever loves father or mother more than me is not worthy of me" (Matt 10:37). Thomas chose to honor Christ rather than his parents. He justified this position later in *Summa theologiae*: "Better to obey the *Father of spirits* (Heb 12:9) through whom we live than to obey the generators of our

17. Marie-Dominique Chenu, *Aquinas and His Role in Theology*, trans. Paul Philibert (Collegeville, MN: Liturgical Press, 2002), 4.

18. Turner, *Thomas Aquinas*, 12.

19. Ibid., 13.

20. *ST* 2–2.26.11.

flesh."[21] For sometimes families may become an obstacle to one's commitment to God, and "in this domain," he asserted, "our relatives according to the flesh are more enemies than friends."[22] From this, we can see that Thomas was no Stoic; rather, he was a man of deep passion and emotion, which was behind his resolution to forsake all things for Christ. But to abandon the world for Christ was essentially to participate in the poverty of Christ, and so, in this sense, Thomas's refusal of his family's wishes was "the exact parallel to Francis of Assisi's gesture of renunciation."[23] His decision to become a Dominican friar against his family's will was an outward manifestation of his inner resolution to identify with Christ's poverty.

Thomas's family, however, did not understand his profoundly evangelical conviction. They had thought that perhaps his youthful excitement would dissipate over time, and so kept him confined in a castle, hoping he would change his mind. What they did not realize was that Thomas already lived in a world sharply different from their own. Theirs was the traditional feudal world, in which religion was integrated with social and economic stability. But Thomas lived in a world where a profound revival of the gospel was taking placing and many were called to forsake material comfort in order to imitate Christ's poverty. Once he made up his mind to follow Christ, Thomas was absolutely firm on his conviction and refused to change his mind—even after long confinements. He guarded this commitment with such fervor and seriousness that when a prostitute was brought to seduce him away from his calling, Thomas chased her out with a flaming stick![24] After retaining him for over a year, Thomas's family finally gave in, realizing that his decision was not an impulsive one but a life-long dedication—the dedication to a life of poverty as his way of identifying with Christ, who gave up all things, even his own life, in order to save the world.

Defending the Dominican Order

The radical Dominican commitment to poverty was not only scandalous for individuals and families; it was also deeply disturbing for institutions. It was for this reason that the presence of mendicants in the University of Paris met

---

21. *ST* 2–2.189.6.

22. *Contra Retrahentes* 9, Leonine, vol. 41, C 57, quoted in Torrell, *Person and Work*, 17.

23. Chenu, *Aquinas and His Role*, 7.

24. Bernard Gui, "The Life of St. Thomas Aquinas," in *The Life of Saint Thomas Aquinas: Biographical Documents*, ed. and trans. Kenelm Foster (Baltimore, MD: Helicon; London: Longmans, Green, and Co., 1959), chap. 7.

fierce resistance from secular masters. In particular, William of Saint-Amour, with the support from several bishops, launched several sustained attacks. One of his main critiques was that the mendicant practice of poverty endangered the social order and private property.[25] Again these accusations, Thomas engaged in impassioned debates, defending the legitimacy of the Dominican identity. Particularly telling was his defense of the Dominican commitment to evangelical poverty, which, he argued, was absolutely essential to the imitation of Christ.

> Of all that Christ did or suffered during his mortal existence, His venerable Cross is offered to us as the prime example that we must imitate. . . . Now, of all that he teaches us, *absolutely first is poverty* [*omninoda paupertas*]; Christ was deprived of every exterior good, even to the point of bodily nakedness. . . . It is that nakedness on the Cross that those who embrace voluntary poverty wish to follow, particularly those who give up all gain. . . . Clearly, therefore, the enemies of poverty are also the enemies of Christ's Cross.[26]

For Aquinas, it is paramount that Christians participate in the poverty of Christ. To be a disciple of Christ means to imitate him, and the first task of imitation is to identify ourselves with Christ's poverty—especially the ultimate poverty of the cross: "If anyone would come after me, let him deny himself and take up his cross daily and follow me" (Luke 9:23). For Aquinas, therefore, the first fundamental act of Christian discipleship is to die to the world and to oneself in order to be united with the crucified Christ—this is at the very heart of evangelical poverty. Participating in Christ's poverty was intrinsic to Thomas's vision of Christian identity. His defense of evangelical poverty was essentially a defense of his Christian identity.

The Silence of Thomas[27]

Thomas's commitment to poverty is more thoroughly manifested in the dramatic period of silence that came toward the end of his life. At the height of his literary output, Thomas, after a mystical experience, decided to stop writing completely. While we cannot be certain of what exactly this entailed, we can see that it must have been so significant that Aquinas decided to leave his great

25. Chenu, *Aquinas and His Role*, 10.

26. *Contra Retrahentes* 15, Leonine, vol. 41, C 69, quoted in Torrell, *Person and Work*, 16, emphasis added.

27. I am borrowing the phrase from the title of Josef Pieper's *The Silence of St. Thomas: Three Essays*, trans. John Murray and Daniel O'Connor (South Bend, IN: St. Augustine Press, 1999).

Summa theologiae unfinished. Like his initial decision to become a friar against his family's will, this decision must have been a hard one. As Turner speculates, "Having got so far with it, seven-eighths of the way through, he must desperately have wanted to finish it—which author would not have felt the power of the imperative to finish it?"[28] Given all the time and energy poured into that work and the fact he could complete it in a few months at his work rate, it must have required an enormous amount of emotional power and strength for him simply to put down his pen.

There may be a host of explanations behind this radical decision, but one crucial factor cannot be ignored: Thomas's commitment to evangelical poverty. Just as in his youth he abandoned everything to follow the Lord, toward the end of his life Thomas chose once again to abandon everything—in this case even his writing—in order to identify himself with the impoverished Christ—even, as he puts it, "to the point of nakedness." As Turner elegantly describes it,

> The silence of Thomas in those last three months of his life was a final response to the demands of mendicant poverty, for on that December day he laid down the one scrip that as a Dominican he could legitimately carry and call his own, his personal work as a theologian. That elected incompleteness of his life's work was, therefore, a form of silence that was Thomas's last word as a Dominican theologian, his response to the last and ultimately self-denying demand that the poor Christ could make on him.[29]

Participating in Christ's Mission of Teaching

As a Dominican, Thomas's commitment to poverty was inseparable from his commitment to proclaiming the Word of God to the world. Just as Christ became poor even to the point of death in order to save and enrich the world, Thomas lived a life of poverty in order to more effectively participate in the redemptive work of Christ. For Thomas, as for other Dominicans, to participate in this redemptive ministry meant, above all, to preach the Word of God. This conviction, as we have seen, was consistent with the original motivation for the formation of the Dominican Order. Dominic's chief concern was the salvation of souls, but noticing how the wealth and corruption of many orthodox priests were offensive to heretics, he emphasized that preaching must

28. Turner, *Thomas Aquinas*, 44.
29. Ibid., 45–46.

go hand in hand with a life of poverty.[30] In this sense, "Dominicans had seen poverty as an argument that strengthened and facilitated their task of refuting heresy. Their main objective was preaching, teaching, and study, and poverty was seen as a mean to that end."[31] While this might be an overstatement for Thomas,[32] there is an element of truth in it: his participation in Christ's poverty undergirded his participation in Christ's redemptive work of preaching and teaching the Word of God. A Christian must identify oneself with Christ in his life and resurrection as well as in his death. To identify fully with Christ, one must not only imitate Christ's poverty; one must also participate in his core mission: the redemption of the world. Hence, Thomas's commitment to preaching the Word of God as a life-long vocation was an essential way of his identifying with Christ the savior, just as his commitment to poverty was his way of identifying with the crucified Christ. Such are the two sides of the paradoxical nature of Christian identity. Those who belong to Christ are "set apart from the world, yet still present to it."[33] In the midst of the radical social changes in the thirteenth century, Thomas, along with the Dominican Order, caught a deep sense of the revival of the gospel. Christians were called to be "separate" from the world only to be "present" to it. Thomas's simultaneous commitment to poverty and to preaching was therefore his participation in the mystery of the gospel of Christ.

For this reason, Thomas's role as a Master of Sacred Doctrine and Teacher of the Word was an essential part of his Christian identity. Just as Jesus functions as the Mediator between God and humanity, the teacher, in imitation of Christ, also functions as a bridge between the two. But like Jacob's ladder, the bridge must be anchored in both sides—heaven and earth—and involve a two-way movement. Hence, the teacher must first constantly seek, study, and contemplate the truth in order to communicate it faithfully to the world. This is why Aquinas as a teacher was first of all a diligent student of the truth. Second, the teacher must pass on the truth to the people so that they can be enriched and brought back to God. Hence, Thomas was not only a contemplative but also one who wrote and lectured unceasingly. As his biographer William of

---

30. This is confirmed by Pope Honorius in his recommendation letter for the Preachers. He writes: "we recommend to you our dear sons, the Preachers who by the profession of *poverty* and of the regular life are *completely dedicated to the proclamation of God's Word.*" The pope also states that "the desired outcome of their work and their goal . . . is *the salvation of souls.*" Quoted in Chenu, *Aquinas and His Role*, 12–13, emphases added.

31. González, *Story of Christianity*, 1:305.

32. As we discussed above, poverty for Thomas is perhaps more than a means to an end; it is at the heart of his way of identifying himself with Christ.

33. Chenu, *Aquinas and His Role*, 11.

Tocco testifies: "His whole life was nothing but prayer, contemplation, lectures, sermons, disputations, writings, and dictations."[34]

Indeed, Thomas's life was a juxtaposition of contemplation and action. He contemplated as he sought divine wisdom; he acted as he passed the truth on to the world.[35] This picture of a two-way engagement was clearly presented in Thomas's inaugural sermon as a Master of Theology at the university, which was essentially his manifesto as a teacher of God's Word. Reflecting upon Psalm 104:13—"From your lofty abode you water the mountains; the earth is satisfied with the fruit of your work"—he wrote, "In the same way the divine light illuminates the minds of Masters and Doctors through whose ministry this light is then passed on to the minds of the students."[36] After discussing the nature of sacred teaching ("lofty abode"), Thomas expounded on the duty of teachers:

> Consider the nobility of those who teach, who are symbolized by mountains. Mountains are high, and like them the teachers of sacred doctrine are straining toward the things of heaven. . . . They are radiant: the mountains are the first to catch the sun's light, and holy teachers are the first to catch divine light in their minds. . . . They are a stronghold: like mountains which protect the surrounding countryside, holy teachers protect the faith against errors. So all teachers of holy doctrine ought to be "lifted up" because of the excellent witness of their lives, incandescent in their teaching, and strong in their defense of truth. These are precisely their three functions: preaching, teaching, and disputing.[37]

The first movement—"straining toward the things of heaven"—well characterizes Thomas's intellectual life, which was dedicated to the pursuit and contemplation of wisdom, especially the divine truth. As a child he had asked the question, "What is God?"—a question that could well characterize the remainder of his life. His intense preoccupation with divine truth often kept him in such a state of mystical speculation that he came to be known by many as a profound contemplative. His contemplation was inseparable from prayer and fervent petition for insights. William of Tocco reported:

> Thomas did not acquire his knowledge by natural ingenuity, but rather through the revelation and infusion of the Holy Spirit; for he never began

34. Quoted in Martin Grabmann, *The Interior Life of St. Thomas Aquinas*, trans. Nicholas Ashenbrener (Milwaukee, WI: Bruce, 1951), 12.

35. For Aquinas, the relation between contemplative life and active life is the relation between love for God and love for neighbors. *ST* 2–2.182.2.

36. Thomas Aquinas, *Inaugural Lecture* (1256), quoted in Chenu, *Aquinas and His Role*, 60.

37. Ibid.

to write without previous prayer and tears. Whenever a doubt arose, he had recourse to prayer. After shedding many tears, he would return to his work, now enlightened and instructed.[38]

Yet this profound, sometimes abstract thinker was never so absorbed in his pursuit of heavenly wisdom as to withdraw from mundane duties. On the contrary, as a teacher, he worked hard to communicate the truths he received to others. As in the Dominican motto, *contemplata aliis tradere*, Thomas believed that "it is better to cast light for others than merely to shine oneself."[39] For this reason, Thomas devoted himself not only to contemplation but also to lecturing and writing. Given his relatively short life, his literary output was staggering—made possible in large part due to a profound work ethic. As Robert Barron puts it, "He was, I think it would be fair to say, something of a workaholic, rarely resting or turning away from the tasks at hand. . . . Thomas pushed himself relentlessly and probably dangerously."[40] Given the fact that he so highly valued contemplation and abstract thought,[41] it is remarkable that Thomas spent so much of his life writing works for nonexperts. It is telling that his *magnum opus*, the *Summa theologiae*, was in fact written for novices. In the preface, Thomas writes:

> Because the doctor of Catholic faith ought not only to teach the proficient, but also to instruct beginners (according to the Apostle: *As unto little ones in Christ, I gave you milk to drink, not meat*; 1 Cor 3:1–2), we purpose in this book to treat of whatever belongs to the Christian religion, in such a way as may tend to the instruction of beginners.[42]

So, while he could have spent most of his life in the upward movement of "straining toward the things of heaven," Thomas never neglected his duty as a teacher, and instead dedicated himself to the "downward movement" of passing on the truths he sought in contemplation to the world around him. Thomas's commitment to this double movement was, indeed, his participation in Christ's two natures. If the upward movement was his participation in Christ's divinity, the downward movement was his participation in Christ's humanity, through which divine truths reached the earth so that the world may be turned back towards God.

38. Quoted in Grabmann, *Interior Life of Aquinas*, 12.
39. Turner, *Thomas Aquinas*, 6.
40. Barron, *Thomas Aquinas*, 23.
41. *ST* 2–2.182.1.
42. Preface to *ST*.

Participating in Christ's Own Life

In the tumult of social, cultural changes of the thirteenth century, Thomas chose to follow Christ through participating in his poverty and redemptive mission. As such, Thomas dedicated his life to evangelical poverty and the mission of teaching the Word. Most of his life was a mixture of action and contemplation. However, toward the end of his life, a mysterious experience brought an abrupt end to this pattern. His active life—his participation in Christ's mission through teaching the Word—came to a stop. We argued earlier that this silence was a statement of Thomas's identity in Christ's poverty. But there is also something more. Thomas underwent such a profound experience that he confessed, "Everything I have written seems to me as straw in comparison with what I have seen."[43] This is sometimes interpreted as Thomas's repudiation of his writing. It can be argued, however, that the focus of the statement is not about the quality of his works but about the radical superiority of the mystical vision. Thomas had devoted his life to the participation in Christ's poverty and mission, but he was now on the verge of a more much direct and intimate participation—a participation in Christ's very life, compared to which everything else paled. Hence, at the end of his life, Thomas was ready for the highest level of participation—the mysterious union (*koinōnia*) with Christ himself. Although this may be seen as a third—and thus new—phase of Thomas's Christian identity, this kind of participation in Christ was never foreign to him. In fact, this yearning for Christ himself—the ultimate identification with Christ—was Thomas's lifelong passion and indeed the very foundation of his life and work. For when Christ confirmed that Thomas spoke well of him, and asked what he desired in return, the mystic Aquinas responded simply: "*Non nisi Te* (nothing but yourself, Lord)!"[44]

43. Quoted in Torrell, *Life and Works*, 289.
44. Quoted in Pope Benedict XVI, *Holy Men and Women of the Middle Ages and Beyond* (San Francisco: Ignatius Press, 2012), 70.

Chapter 21

Julian of Norwich: The Inclusive Christian

ELEANOR McCULLOUGH

Julian of Norwich (ca. 1343–ca. 1416) was a female theologian, famous for writing two accounts in English of sixteen visions that she received while contemplating a crucifix.[1] These visions took place on May 13, 1373, at the age of thirty, while receiving the last rites during a severe bout of sickness from which she nearly died. Even though Julian reveals deep insights about her revelations in her two books, she says nothing about her family, social background, or current circumstances; even the name given to her at baptism is unknown. We now know her by her adopted name, Julian of Norwich, conferred upon her when she attached herself as an anchoress to the Church of St. Julian at Conesford in Norwich. We also know through other sources that Julian became an anchoress at some point between experiencing her visions and writing her first account of them, probably soon after her experience.[2] Four wills bequeathing money to

1. There is extant one mid-fifteenth-century manuscript of the shorter text, London, British Library MS Additional 37790, fols. 97–115. The three complete extant manuscripts of the longer text are all copies: London, British Library MS Sloane 2499 (17th c.); London, British Library MS Sloane 3705 (perhaps an eighteenth-century derivative of Sloane 2499); and a 1670 Cressy printed edition, Paris, Bibliothèque Nationale MS Fonds anglais 40. A fifteenth-century series of excerpts from the longer text appears in London, Westminster Cathedral Treasury MS 4, fols. 72v–112v. See Edmund Colledge and James Walsh, eds., *A Book of Showings to the Anchoress Julian of Norwich*, 2 vols., Studies and Texts 35 (Toronto: Pontifical Institute of Mediaeval Studies, 1978), 1–18, supplemented and corrected by Marion Glasscoe, "Visions and Revisions: A Further Look at the Manuscripts of Julian of Norwich," *Studies in Bibliography* 42 (1989): 103–20.

2. There seems to be some discrepancy as to when the first account was written. The consensus is that it was written soon after the visions themselves, e.g., Colledge and Walsh, *A Book of Showings*, 19; and Georgia Ronan Crampton, *The Shewings of Julian of Norwich*, TEAMS Middle English Texts (Kalamazoo, MI: Medieval Institute Publications, 1994), 1. Watson argues that the date of the final form of the first version may be as late as the late 1380s, in part due to Julian's

Julian survive.[3] Together, they confirm that she had become an anchoress in the Church of St. Julian by the year 1393 and that she was still alive in 1416, when she would have been seventy-three. The only direct written account of Julian is contained in Margery Kempe's biography.[4] The younger Margery records that she went to seek advice from Julian in her cell at Norwich, around 1413, when Julian was seventy. Julian gave her sound advice, telling her she could trust that the younger woman's visions were from the Holy Spirit. The bequests and Margery's account together indicate that Julian had gained a reputation as an anchorite and counselor by the end of her life.[5]

Although we know nothing of her family status, Julian's writings suggest that she may have received formal elementary schooling. Given her understanding of Christian doctrine, passed down both through the church fathers and the eremitic Desert Writers of the early church, some scholars believe she could have been a nun at a local Benedictine convent at the time of her revelations.[6] Alternatively, others are of the opinion that Julian was at the time of her visions, as she claims in her second book, "a simple creature unletterde" (*Revelation* 2.1),[7] but that by the time of writing her second version of the events, at least twenty years later, she had educated herself.[8] Regardless of her level of

repeated defense of her visions as being in accordance with "holy Church." She is, according to him, anxious to refute the heretical teachings against the use of images, which were associated with the Lollards and officially condemned in 1382. Watson goes on to argue that the longer version may be a fifteenth-century account rather than the accepted position that it was written ca. 1393, based on Julian's own recollection of the initial vision as being "[f]or twenty yere after the time of the shewing, save thre monthes" (*Revelation* 51:l.73). See further, Nicholas Watson, "The Composition of Julian of Norwich's *Revelation of Love*," *Speculum* 68, no. 3 (July 1993): 664, 678.

3. Nicholas Watson and Jacqueline Jenkins, eds., *The Writings of Julian of Norwich: "A Vision Showed to a Devout Woman" and "A Revelation of Love"* (Turnhout, Belgium: Brepols, 2006), 5.

4. Lynn Staley, ed., *The Book of Margery Kempe*, TEAMS Middle English Texts (Kalamazoo, MI: Medieval Institute Publications, 1996), chap. 18.

5. Margery recounts that "[t]hys creatur schewyd hyr maner of levyng to many a worthy clerke, to worshepful doctorys of divinyté, bothe religiows men and other of seculer abyte, and thei seyden that God wrowt gret grace wyth hir and bodyn sche schuld not ben aferde, ther was no disseyte in hir maner of levyng." *The Book of Margery Kempe*, chap. 18, ll. 988–91.

6. E.g., Edmund Colledge and James Walsh, trans. and eds., *Julian of Norwich: Showings*, Classics of Western Spirituality (New York: Paulist Press, 1978), 20. Dutton disputes this belief, instead arguing that she, like many lay women of the period, was probably literate in English and educated in the vernacular teachings of the Church. For a fuller discussion, see Elizabeth Dutton, *Julian of Norwich: The Influence of Late-Medieval Devotional Compilations* (Cambridge: D.S. Brewer, 2008), 7–12.

7. The full title of her second book is *A Revelation of Love that Jhesu Christ, Our Endles Blisse, Made in Sixteen Shewinges*. The edition cited throughout is that of Watson and Jenkins.

8. Julian may have declaimed her ability to impart spiritual truths as a means of modesty, a device common in medieval visionary writings. This accorded with biblical tradition that God

education, Julian's two works can be firmly placed within the corpus of English spiritual writers of the mid-late fourteenth century, both because of the quality of her literary style and the depth of her theological exploration on the meaning of the visions she encountered while on her sickbed. The first, shorter, account of her visions (*Vision*)[9] stands in the personal meditative tradition, relating back to Anselm and the thirteenth-century *Wooing Group* writers. Her second and much fuller account, *Revelation,* places her within the tradition of English mysticism that combined deep reflection on the mysteries of God with a theology of the self-giving love of God through the incarnation.[10] Unlike many Latin writers, the emphasis for the vernacular theologians such as Julian was not so much on how one could achieve union with God as on the relevance of God's message of salvation to contemporary lay Christians.[11]

Julian's Place in the English Spiritual Tradition

Julian was living in a period of immense cultural change. The hierarchical structures of both religion and society were being eroded in the wake of the Black Death;[12] a new mercantile and skills-based sector was being formed, and as laypeople were becoming increasingly textually literate there was a growing demand for texts in English.[13] Around the time she was writing about her revelations, Langland and Chaucer were respectively composing *Piers Plowman* and *The Canterbury Tales*, and John Wycliffe was translating the Bible into

---

often chose the humble as a vehicle for imparting spiritual truths (e.g., Jacob, Isaiah, Mary, and even Jesus himself, who took on the form of a servant [Phil 2:6–8]). See, e.g., Watson and Jenkins, *The Writings*, 7–8; Dutton, *Julian of Norwich*, 6–7.

9. The full title is *A Vision Showed to a Devout Woman*. The edition cited throughout is that of Watson and Jenkins.

10. The anachronistic term "mysticism" implies that there was one strand; however, writers held different perspectives within the tradition. See further, Nicholas Watson, "The Middle English Mystics," in *The Cambridge History of Medieval English Literature*, ed. David Wallace (Cambridge: Cambridge University Press, 2002), 538–41.

11. Watson, "The Middle English Mystics," 544–46.

12. This bubonic plague swept over Europe in 1347–1350, making its way into England by 1348 and killing up to a third of the population in some areas. There is some speculation that Julian may have been widowed as a result of the plague. See, e.g., Santha Battacharji, "Julian of Norwich, 1342–ca. 1416: Anchoress and Mystic," *Oxford Dictionary of National Biography* online ed., Oxford University Press (last updated 2017).

13. Jo Ann Hoeppner, "Literacy and the Laicization of Education," in *The Growth of English Schooling, 1348–1548* (Princeton: Princeton University Press, 1985), 150; M. B. Parkes, *Scribes, Scripts and Readers: Studies in the Communication, Presentation, and Dissemination of Medieval Texts* (London: Hambledon Press, 1995), 275–86.

the vernacular. Her contemporaries the hermit Richard Rolle, the Augustinian canon Walter Hilton, and the anonymous *Cloud of Unknowing* author were also choosing to write in the English vernacular for an audience that included the laity. These writings, combined with many vernacular prayers and hymns and treatises translated from Latin that were incorporated into books of hours and religious anthologies of the period, provide evidence that the laity were taking an active role in their spirituality.[14] This resurgence in vernacular expression was not, however, without its dangers. Wycliffe and the Lollards were being accused of heresy, and it was important for spiritual writers to be seen to be writing within the parameters of orthodoxy.[15]

Julian's Theology of Love

Julian is placed within the English spiritual tradition of writers who based their theology on the Bible and the teachings of the church fathers, and is therefore considered orthodox.[16] Yet she is also distinctive, not only because she was the first female theologian to write in English but also because of her inclusive view of the love of God for all of humanity. She often turns on their head language and theology that discriminate against women and laypeople and, using equalizing terminology, addresses all "that shal be savid"—male and female, contemplative and lay—referring to them as "even cristene." She continuously weaves positive phrases concerning God's love through her narrative, culminating in her insistence at the end of *Revelation* that "love was his mening." Her most famous recollection of Christ's words to her, "Alle shalle be welle, and thou shalt see it thyselfe that alle manner thing shall be welle" (63:39–40), is often used in conjunction with her understanding of sin as a necessary part of God's plan to help us understand the nature of his mercy and grace, which are

14. For a fuller discussion see my "Praying the Passion: Laypeople's Participation in Medieval Liturgy and Devotion" (PhD thesis, University of York, 2011).

15. Lollards, under the leadership of John Wycliffe (ca. 1330–1384), were considered heretical because of their rejection of the doctrine of transubstantiation. They were also regarded as subversive because they exposed the hypocrisy of the Church and argued for the translation of the Bible into English so that the laity could have greater access to scriptural truths and a freer expression of worship.

16. Julian was highly regarded by doctors of divinity and members of the religious orders, according to Margery Kempe, suggesting that she was considered orthodox by the ecclesiastical authorities in her own time. Julian would, however, have been aware that speaking as a woman and as a visionary may have raised suspicion from the religious authorities. She is repeatedly at pains to point out that her teachings are in accordance with those of "holy Church." See Watson, "Composition of Julian of Norwich's *Revelation of Love*," 647–52.

the qualities that direct us to God. The words were not used lightly by Julian but were borne out of her own physical suffering and deep contemplation over many years on the wounds of Christ. They would undoubtedly have provided solace for her lay contemporaries who would have had an acute awareness of sin and suffering but were perhaps less well steeped in an inclusive theology of mercy and grace.[17]

Julian's inclusive theology of love is most explicitly expressed in her elaborate metaphor of the Lord (representing God) and his servant (sometimes representing Adam and sometimes Christ, the second Adam), beginning in chapter 51 of *Revelation*. The story is partly based on the Parable of the Good Samaritan and Philippians 2:5-11 and is recounted in order to explain the intimate relationship of the triune God with his creatures. In this section, Julian uses everyday terminology to explain how, just as Christ is both very God and very man, as human beings we have two aspects to our nature, "wel and wo," or sorrow and joy. Joy is linked with Christ and his rising, whereas sorrow is linked with Adam and his fall. We constantly move between the two extremes of rising and falling, just as Jesus the servant fell in coming to earth and struggling as we do, yet rose in revealing his wisdom: "And thus in the servant was shewde the blindhede and the mischefe of Adams falling: and in the servant was shewde the wisdom and the goodnesse of Goddes son" (52:33-34). God relates to both aspects of our humanity, on the one hand revealing to us our excusing of ourselves, but on the other, our worship. By his grace, he then goes about "torning all oure blame into endlesse worshippe" (52:82-83). The end process is that we are knit and joined ("this rightful knitting and this endlesse oning," 53:18) to God in love.

Julian's Doctrine of the Soul

After introducing the theme of God's intimate relatedness with humanity through the parable of the Lord and his servant, Julian goes on to elaborate more fully on the nature of the soul, this time using theological terminology derived from Latin: "*sensualite*" and "*substance*." She likens *sensualite* to our bodily form, whereas *substance* conforms to our inner aspect. This division of human nature into two parts is based on Neoplatonic teachings and transmit-

17. For medieval Christians, emphasis was on the fear of hell and on doing penance and reciting prayers in order to spend less time in purgatory, where it was believed that all Christians had to spend some time in order for them to be purged of their sins and rendered fit for heaven. See for example, Eamon Duffy, *The Stripping of the Altars: Traditional Religion in England, c. 1400-c. 1580* (1992; 2nd ed., New Haven and London: Yale University Press, 2005), chaps. 9-10.

ted through the church fathers. Whereas they tend to regard the sensual or bodily aspect of human nature as inferior to the spiritual or inner one, Julian connects both aspects with the twofold role of the second person of the Trinity. In becoming man, the incarnate Jesus was enclosed in our sensuality, while our substance is enclosed in Christ, the second person of the Trinity. In coming to earth, Jesus began the process of redeeming the lower part of humankind, but he was still joined to the higher part of his being, as the second person of the Trinity:

> the seconde person in the trinite had taken the lower party of mankind, to whome that hyest was oned in the furst making. And theyse two perties were in Crist, the heyer and the lower, which is but one soule. The hyer perty was ever in pees with God, in full joy and blisse. The lower perty, which is sensualite, suffered for the salvation of mankind. (55:49–53)

Although Julian connects *sensualite* with the lower aspect of the soul, and *substance* with the higher, she explains that both parts are connected with Christ: the lower with his humanity and the higher with his divinity. Our sensuality is separated from God because of its fallenness, but by God's grace and mercy working in us, both aspects of our nature are restored to union with the Trinity: "For I saw full sekerly that oure substance is in God. And also I saw that in oure sensualite God is" (55:19–21). Julian goes on to explain, using the image of the womb closely associated with the anchoritic cell, that just as Jesus was enclosed in Mary's womb, so we are enclosed in him:

> For in that same time that God knit him to our body in the maidens wombe, he toke oure sensual soule. In which taking—he us all having beclosed in him—he oned it to oure substance, in which oning he was perfit man. For Criste, having knitt in Him ilk man that shall be savid, is perfit man. (55:35–38)

Julian never refers to any theologian in *Revelation*, and yet her account of union with God is steeped in the theology of the church fathers, presumably mediated through vernacular treatises and lyrics. In her usage of the words *sensualite* and *substance* she draws on Augustine's theology of the soul. However, whereas Julian speaks in terms of "beclosed," "oning" and "knitt[ing]" ("enclosing," "joining," and "knitting"), Augustine used the language of division. The higher, intellectual and spiritual part, which he termed "*animus*," a masculine noun, is uncontaminated by the inferior body, while the lower, sensual faculty, "*anima*," a feminine noun, is in contact with external material reality and thus occupies an intermediary position between the intellect and carnality.[18] Augustine's suspicion of female flesh was embedded in the doctrines of the Church regarding the creation and fall, in which Eve was blamed for using her sensuality to beguile the more rational Adam.[19]

Julian's contemporary, Walter Hilton (1343–1396), also spoke of the soul as being split into two parts:

> The overe [upper] partie and the nethere [lower] partie. The overe is likned to a man, for it schulde be maister and sovereyne, and that is propirle the ymage of God, and bi that oonli the soule knoweth God and loveth God. And the nethere is likned to a woman, for it schulde be buxom [obedient] to man.[20]

Hilton makes explicit what was implied in Augustine's theology: the higher aspect of the soul accords with the male and the lower with the female. As we have seen, Julian also sees the soul as consisting of two parts, sensuality and substance. However, they are never fully separated from each other. According to Julian, all humans, male and female, comprise both natures, sensuality and substance, and both male and female are knitted to God by the bonds of love. There is no gender differentiation, either in her terminology or her understanding of the position of the human being in relation to God.

Julian's Doctrine of the Trinity

Julian's explanations of human nature and its relation to the Trinity are intricately linked with a discussion on the properties of the Trinity. Through means of a series of triads in chapter 58, she balances a profoundly Trinitarian view of God with male and female imagery, but again, this is relational. She explains that we are "knitted" to God, the second person of the Trinity, because of his identification with us in his indwelling of human flesh. Using Bernardine terminology of Christ the lover of the soul based on the Song of Songs, she states that Christ has chosen to image himself in relational terms as Father, Mother, and Spouse:

18. St. Augustine, *Concerning the City of God against the Pagans*, trans. Henry Bettenson, ed. David Knowles (Middlesex, England: Pelican Classics, 1972), 536.

19. "For we were all in that one man, seeing that we all were that one man who fell into sin through the woman who was made from him before the first sin" (8.14, trans. Bettenson, 523). Augustine does, however, acknowledge that sin passed through Adam.

20. Walter Hilton, *The Scale of Perfection*, ed. Thomas H. Bestul, TEAMS Middle English Texts (Kalamazoo, MI: Medieval Institute Publications, 2000), 159.

And thus in oure making God almighty is oure kindly fader, and God alle wisdom is oure kindly mother, with the love and the goodnes of the holy gost, which is alle one God, one Lorde. And in the knitting and in the oning he is oure very tru spouse, and we his loved wife and his fair maiden, with which wife he was never displeased. (58:9–13)

In her discussion on the properties of God, Julian is in keeping with received tradition, imparted from scriptural and Church teachings. While her depiction of God as Mother may seem strange to modern ears, it would have been readily understood and accepted by her contemporaries. The feminization of religious language was present as early as the writings of the church fathers, particularly Clement of Alexandria (c. 150–215)[21] and St. Augustine (354–430),[22] both of whom drew from Old Testament images of God as nurturer and provider, as well as from Christ's depiction of himself as a mother-hen in the Gospels of Matthew and Luke.[23] A few centuries later, Anselm of Canterbury (ca. 1033–1109) incorporated images of Christ as Mother into his many poems and prayers that were widely disseminated for use in daily devotions. In his *Prayer to St. Paul*, he utters: "And you, Jesus, are you not also a mother? / Are you not the mother, who, like a hen, / gathers her chickens under her wings? Truly, Lord, you are a mother."[24]

By the twelfth century, feminized images of Christ became increasingly linked with devotion to his suffering on the cross. Aelred of Rievaulx (1109–1166), the founder of the English-based Cistercian order, compares the literal nursing of a mother with the metaphorical nursing of Christ as portrayed in the crucifix that adorned every altar in anchorholds:

And as touchyngge holy ymages, haue in þyn awter þe ymage of þe crucifix hangynge on þe cros, which represente to þe þe passioun of Crist, which þu schalt folwe. Al-to-gydere he is ysprad abrood to bykleppe þe in his armes, in which þu schalt haue gret delectacioun; and hys tetys beþ al naked ischewd to þe to gyue þe melk of spiritual deletacioun and confortacioun.

(And regarding holy images, have on your altar the image of the crucifix

21. Clement of Alexandria, *Christ the Educator*, trans. Simon P. Wood, FC 23 (Washington, DC: The Catholic University of America Press, 1954), 40–41.

22. Augustine of Hippo, *Questiones Evangeliorum* 2.26 (PL 35:1330). Cited by Ritamary Bradley in "Patristic Background of the Motherhood Similitude in Julian of Norwich," *Christian Scholars Review* 8 (1978): 102–3.

23. Matt 23:37; Luke 13:34.

24. Benedicta Ward, trans., *The Prayers and Meditations of Saint Anselm with the Proslogion* (London: Penguin, 1973), 153 (11.397–99).

hanging on the cross, which represents to you the passion of Christ, which you shall follow. He is totally spread out to clasp you in his arms; you will experience great delight in this. And his teats are made bare to you to give you the milk of spiritual delight and comfort.)[25]

One of the earliest English expressions of devotion to the wounds in Christ's side based on the clefts of the rock of Song of Songs 2:14 is cited in *Ancrene Wisse*, a guide for female anchorites written in the early thirteenth century. Drawing from Bernard of Clairvaux's sermons on the Song, the anonymous author writes: "Flee to his wounds. He must have loved us very much to let such holes be pierced in him to hide us in. Creep into them with your thought—are they not all open?"[26] The author goes on to transliterate verse 2:14 of the Song of Songs as "My dove . . . come and hide yourself in the holes in my limbs, in the opening in my side."[27] Although the language is not explicitly feminized, the writer deals with the theme of enclosure as it relates to the situation of female anchorites. They regarded themselves as devotees committed to living in womb-like cells in imitation of Christ, who chose to dwell in his mother's womb.

As well as being linked with the safety of the clefts of the rock, enclosure imagery was further based on descriptions of the bride as an enclosed garden in the Song of Songs 4:12 and was closely connected with female virginity. Throughout *Ancrene Wisse*, anchorites are exhorted to keep their bodies closed, not only sexually, but also through strict dietary and dress codes in accordance with the anchoritic rule. However, as with Aelred of Rievaulx's text where the body of Christ is spread out in a posture of welcome, the invitation to enter into Christ the Bridegroom's open body represents a subversion of the enclosure concept and a corresponding transgression into a forbidden area of ecstasy.

The feminization of religious terminology implied in *Ancrene Wisse* and *De Institutione Inclusarum* is more explicitly expressed in *Revelation*, chapter 60, where Julian speaks of how the loving, nurturing, and serving properties of earthly mothers are imaged in our "Moder Jhesu." He, in turn, lovingly sustains and nourishes us with the spiritual milk of the Eucharist:

The moder may geve her childe sucke her milke. But oure precious moder Jhesu, he may fede us with himselfe, and doth full curtesly and full tenderly

25. Aelred of Rievaulx, *De Institutione Inclusarum: Two English Versions*, trans. John Ayto and Alexandra Barratt, Early English Text Society, Original Series 287 (London: Oxford University Press, 1984), 35 (my translation).

26. *Ancrene Wisse: Guide for Anchoresses*, trans. Bella Millet (Exeter: Exeter University Press, 2009), pt. 4, 111.

27. Ibid., pt. 4, 111.

with the blessed sacrament that is precious fode of very life. And with all the swete sacramentes he sustaineth us full mercifully and graciously. . . .

The moder may ley her childe tenderly to her brest. But oure tender mother Jhesu, he may homely lede us into his blissed brest by his swet, open side, and shewe us therin perty of the godhed and the joyes of heven, with gostely sekernesse of endlesse blisse. (60:25–28, 33–36)

In her first comparison of Jesus with an earthly mother in this passage, Julian describes how his food is that of the Eucharistic sacrament, the source of life. While an earthly mother may feed her child with her own milk, Jesus feeds us with his very flesh. In her second comparison, she goes even further in speaking of Christ's wounds at his side as the opening to the mysteries of the Godhead and to mystical union with him. Entrance to the feminized breasts of Christ is through his wounds. For Julian, male and female are both expressed in the Godhead and since women are imaged in God, God can also be imaged in the female: "as verely as God is oure fader, as verely is God oure moder" (59:10). In her redefinitions of the roles of male and female and in her use of theological terminology and male discourse, Julian resists conventional attitudes to women while speaking within orthodox tradition. She cuts through exclusive language and imagery for God.

Julian's Inclusive Terminology

Another important indication of Julian's awareness of her place as a woman writing in a male-dominated society is in her silencing between the two versions of her visions, possibly written several years apart.[28] In the first text she apologizes for being an uneducated female: "Botte God forbede that ye schulde saye or take it so that I am a techere. For I meene nought soo, no I mente nevere so. For I am a woman, lewed, febille, and freylle" (*Vision* 6:35–37). However, by the time she writes her second, longer version, she has omitted this phrase. This suggests that she has reevaluated her position. In her second version, she makes no apology for writing with the authority of a mature and obviously educated woman who speaks because she *knows* from attested experience.

As an anchorite and a woman with a position in the religious world, Julian occupied a liminal space somewhere between the clergy and laity. Her language and terminology throughout is equalizing and inclusive of all "even Cristene." According to Christian mystical tradition, originating with Pseudo-Dionysius,

28. For the debate on dating, see n. 2 above.

the Christian journey was a process of conversion and conformity to God's will in three progressive stages with the final goal as union with God in loving contemplation of him. All Christians could attain the first two stages of purgation and illumination, but the third stage of union with God was reserved for the religious elite. Both Bernard and Anselm believed that the higher levels of mystical contemplation on the wounds of Christ were only attainable by the monks and ordained clergy. By the mid-late fourteenth century, however, hierarchical structures had begun to break down, especially as increasing numbers of laypeople and women were being educated and actively choosing to participate in the structures of the Church. This shift in perspective is reflected in the fourteenth-century English mystical writers. Rolle, Langland, and Hilton all value the mixed life of contemplation and action, or, as Julian termed it, "wo and wele." Rolle states that it is the most difficult form of living. Langland explains the threefold method as "dowel," "dobet," and "dobest," with the suggestion that even the laity can aim to "dobest." Julian makes no distinction between the various modes of living, whether active, contemplative, or both. She writes her book for all "even Cristene," who are faithfully leading the Christian life. Indeed, she goes to great lengths to explain that all "that shal be saved" are caught up in a process of being joined to the Godhead by the bonds of love.

Julian's Relevance for Contemporary Christians

Julian's manuscripts had gone out of circulation at some point after the Reformation, but they were rediscovered in the late nineteenth and early twentieth centuries with the publication of two updated editions of the longer text.[29] T. S. Eliot, for instance, paraphrased the words spoken to her in the fourteenth revelation by Christ as "And all shall be well and / All manner of thing shall be well," incorporating it into *The Four Quartets* (1942).[30] In the mid-twentieth century, many theologians focused on her depictions of God as Mother. More recently, Julian's revelations have been meditated upon by "Praying with Julian" groups, readily lending themselves to such varied forms of exploration.

In her first book, Julian succinctly and poetically describes the properties of a hazelnut to explain the essence of Christianity.[31] Its delicate formation is proof

---

29. Henry Collins, ed. and trans., *Revelations of Divine Love, Shewed to a Devout Anchoress, by Name Mother Julian of Norwich* (London: Thomas Richardson and Sons, 1877); Grace Warrack, ed., *Revelations of Divine Love, Recorded by Julian, Anchoress at Norwich, Anno Domini 1373: A Version from the MS. in the British Museum* (London: Methuen and Co., 1901).

30. Books 3 and 5 of *Little Gidding*.

31. *Vision* 4:7–20.

that God made it, God loves it, and God keeps it. Such deep appreciation of the tiniest products of God's creation, such as the hazelnut, is steeped in a theology of love, inspired by Anselm, Bernard, Rolle, and others. In their meditations, they employed the *lectio divina* method, not only for the Scriptures, but also for the church fathers, such as Augustine. When reading Julian, we could also adopt a form of the *lectio divina*, internally digesting the words and tasting their sweetness. Hence we may be able to savor something of Julian's ability to integrate her visions of the crucifixion with an intense *sapiencia* or tasting of the love of God for each and every one of his creatures.

Chapter 22

Dante: The Path of the Pilgrim

JANET MARTIN SOSKICE

To stand in Florence's sun-drenched Piazza del Duomo is to find oneself among one of the most gracious ensembles of buildings in Europe and indeed the world. Executed in alternating panels of white and green marble, the constellation of domed cathedral, baptistery, and bell tower (this last designed by Dante's friend Giotto di Bondone) are a hymn to civic and religious life—the *beau ideal* of harmonious dwelling of "man with man." The piazza is, and has been, the civic center of Florence (with various changes of buildings through the ages) for over 1600 years, but it is at the same time the religious center—like all medieval cathedrals, the complex was built to be the city on the hill, the new Jerusalem, and a place where God will dwell with the people and be their God (Rev 21:1–3).

Being Someplace: Dante in Exile

It was the Baptistery of St. John (San Giovanni) that had pride of place for Dante. The present structure was completed in his lifetime to replace a fifth-century baptistery that had served Florentines on the same site already for some hundreds of years. Like its predecessor, the medieval baptistery is an octagonal building separate from the cathedral itself (for the proselytes were not yet ready to enter that sacred space), whose eight sides represented the seven days of creation and the eighth day of new creation into which the baptized would now enter. To be baptized here was to receive new birth and become a new creation. It was also to become a Florentine. Dante's love of Florence was lifelong and unabated, and its symbolic focus was the baptistery ("my own beloved Saint John's" (*Inferno* 19.17). One of its vivid apse mosaics, that of Satan devouring the damned, is thought to have inspired Dante's own Lucifer.

But famously Dante was not to walk in this piazza, or to witness the ongoing construction of the new cathedral (begun in 1296), because he was exiled from his city in 1302 on what he, and posterity, believe were trumped-up charges. He was just thirty-six. Refusing any offer of amnesty and return that involved apologizing for misdeeds he insisted he had not committed, Dante remained an exile until his death in 1321. The result is the poem we call the *Commedia*, the *Divine Comedy*, a work suffused by memories of Florence, but surprisingly a work of hope and faith, of exile turned into pilgrimage.

Being Someone: Christian Life "In Particular"

Some bridle at the alacrity with which, in the poem, Dante dispatches his contemporaries variously to heaven or hell, but this is to misunderstand the genre. It is fiction, but fiction that depends on real places and persons, as well as biblical, mythological, and fictional ones, for its efficacy. In any case, Dante puts his enemies (and he had real enemies) in heaven and purgatory as well as hell. It is this attention to the particular, including particular persons, times and places, that make the *Commedia*, like Augustine's *Confessions*, so fine a study in Christian living. It is in the unfolding of real lives that we come to know what it is to love God, to love our neighbor and—not to be neglected—properly to love ourselves for, as Augustine insisted, loving your neighbor as yourself depends on rightly ordered love of self.

Theological tomes on Christian anthropology (what used to be called "the doctrine of man") frequently make dull reading. It is the anchoring of this great poem in real if fictionalized lives that enables it to have a grip on us even today—for different though Dante's fourteenth-century liars, cheats, braggarts, and gluttons were, we see reflected in them our contemporaries and, more pointedly, ourselves. In that sense Dante's poem is a guide to us today and has been reverenced as such by many Christian writers who have drawn upon it directly—among them T. S. Eliot, Dorothy Sayers, and C. S. Lewis—or those who have done so subliminally.

Dante began his work around 1307, some five years after his exile, but sets the story in 1300, two years before exile and very specifically on Good Friday. The three cantica see Dante, the pilgrim author, traverse Inferno, Purgatory, and Paradise while still himself alive, guided through Inferno and much of Purgatory by the Latin poet Virgil.

The opening scene of the work, *Inferno* 1, is chaotic, dystopic—in a dark wood. Dante, full of sleep, doesn't know where he is or how he came to be there.

He doesn't know, one could add, who he is.[1] The opening lines, which seem equally memorable in all the languages into which they are translated, bring us immediately there with him:

> Nel mezzo del cammin di nostra vita,
> >   mi ritrovai per una selva oscura,
> ché la diritta via era smarrita. (*Inferno* 1.1–2)

> At one point midway on our path in life,
> I came around and found myself now searching,
> through a dark wood, the right way blurred and lost.[2]

In the middle of the path of "our life" Dante finds or "refinds" himself searching through a dark wood. It is his life, he tells us, but it is also the path of "our life"—any of our lives. We see already the overlaying of interpretive layers characteristic of the *Commedia*. Is the reference to his condition as political exile, or his condition as morally and spiritually lost, or our own parallel state? Very likely all three. Dante has, in some underexplained fashion, returned to his senses. This is a *metanoia*—a conversion whose nature is as yet unexplained and unfulfilled. Dante sees the brightening dawn on the hill before him, the springtime stars that rose with creation, but he is stalked by animals—a leopard, a lion, a ravening she-wolf, gorged with prey but still hungry. What these beasts (apparently drawn from Jeremiah 5:6, for Dante has a very considerable knowledge of the Bible) represent is not made clear—lust, pride, avarice, sins not just of Dante but also of the corrupted city of Florence. Dante rushes into the dark wilderness, terrified, and there sees a figure. Not knowing whether this is a "shadow or truly man," he cries out "save me!" or more specifically, "*Miserere* di me." This tossed-out prayer/plea (anticipating the *Miserere* of the psalms and liturgy) meets a response of grace. The shadowy figure turns out to be, oddly enough, Virgil. Virgil, for Dante the greatest Latin poet, lived before the birth of Christ and in the poem does not "know" the name of Christ, and it seems odd that Dante should be guided through hell and much of purgatory by a figure who is, in Dante's poem, outside the fullness of salvation and a resident

---

1. That is to say, Dante, the pilgrim, is represented as having from the outset a pretty strong, if not altogether healthy, sense of self, but he does not know who he is in the eyes of God. This will become apparent in the *Purgatorio*.

2. All text and translations are from that of Robin Kirkpatrick (London: Penguin, 2006, 2007, 2007). I'm indebted further to Robin Kirkpatrick's notes, which I think are the finest for theological consideration, and also to his personal comments over several years teaching these texts together at Cambridge.

of a not unpleasant but somewhat featureless limbo. However, Virgil, we soon discover, is not acting on his own account but as an agent of grace.

Virgil, if ignorant of the name of Christ, has some sense of the grace of the created order and of God. He sees the bright and lovely hill that Dante longs to climb but through fear cannot. He is an astute and clear-eyed judge of men's follies and represents, for Dante, not only a hero of poetry but of civic virtue and humane wisdom. Yet pagan virtue alone could not lead Dante on the journey he now undertakes.

Virgil tells Dante that he cannot directly ascend the hill but must take a longer route. This will involve seeing those who mourn ancient pain and long for death to come again (*Inferno*), and those souls content to hope for their time to come (*Purgatorio*), until they meet a soul "far worthier," Virgil says, than he. Dante accepts this guidance from a shade unable to enter the realms of the blessed and who does not know the name of Dante's God, that is, Christ (*Inferno* 1.130–31).

Love and Grace

Yet as we enter Canto 2, Dante is filled with self-doubt: "am I in spirit strong enough . . ." (*Inferno* 2.10). "Why me?" I am not Aeneas or St. Paul. "No one— not me!—could think I'm fit for this" (*Inferno* 2.31–33). The poet-pilgrim Dante, still alive in the narrative, is terrified of the prospect of journeying through the realms of the dead. Virgil points out sharply that his fear is ignominious—just the kind of fear that puts people off a good course. To calm Dante he explains how he came to be on his mission. Apparently, while Virgil knew independently of Dante's plight, his present undertaking began when he was addressed by a blessed and beautiful lady who beseeched him to come to the aid of a man dear to her, now "entrammelled on the lonely hill" and turning "all terror, from the way" (*Inferno* 2.61–62).[3] She has told Virgil she is from heaven and added

> For me you'll go, since I am Beatrice.
> And I have come from where I long to be.
> Love is my mover, source of all I say. (*Inferno* 2.70–73)

3. We might note that the modesty of Dante's earlier "why me?" is absent in his suggestion that even in Limbo, the great Virgil would know of his living Florentine copractitioner, Dante! Dante, the author, it emerges, is quite self-conscious of the dangers of artistic vanity. It is always somewhat taxing to know how to distinguish Dante, the author of the work, from "Dante," the character in the story. I will sometimes refer to the latter as the "pilgrim-poet" but in general leave it to the reader's judgment to sort this.

Virgil, for his part is delighted to obey but questions that Beatrice should be so unafraid to come down to this "dead middle point." She answers,

> Since you desire to know so inwardly, then briefly . . . I'll tell you why I feel no dread at entering down here.

> We dread an object when (but only when) that object has the power to do some harm. Nothing can otherwise occasion fear. (*Inferno* 2.85–90)

Perfect love casts out fear, and Beatrice in the *Commedia* is perfect—or better, "perfected" love. "I was created by the grace of God," she says (*Inferno* 2.91), and speaks of a court of saintly women who have been alarmed on Dante's account—the Virgin Mary, (Saint) Lucy, and also the Old Testament Rachel. All these in concert, by contrast with the lonely masculine isolation of Dante in his dark wood, have pleaded with Beatrice to make haste to help him on the grounds that

> He loves you, and, loving you, he left the common herd . . . (*Inferno* 2.104–5)

This is an astonishing sequence, and it introduces us to the picture of humanity and grace that is almost uniquely Dante's: the pagan Virgil is a just and good man but he can promise to lead Dante towards "utmost good" (*Inferno* 2.126) only because he is in turn directed by three ladies in Paradise. They in turn have sent Beatrice, pleading Dante's love for her. And this love, though human and in many ways flawed, as we shall see, is also godly. It is Dante's love for another mortal, it seems, that has called forth their aid, but when Beatrice tells Virgil that "Love is my mover, source of all I say" (*Inferno* 2.105), it is the love of God of which she speaks. It is this love, "the love that moves the sun and other stars," that frees the frozen Dante and sets him on his way.[4]

Choosing Hell

The Inferno is naturally the *Cantica* that most attracts when first we read Dante. Comic and tragic by measure, its famous *contrapasso* devices—punishments that fit the crimes—have fortune tellers doomed to walk round a trench with their heads on backwards, in a parody of their deceptive claims to be able to

---

4. The final lines of the poem speak of God as "the love that moves the sun and other stars" (*Paradiso* 33.145).

predict the future when alive (*Inferno* 20), flatterers plodding through a pit of human excrement (*Inferno* 18), and a Simoniac pope buried upside down, his feet licked by flames in a reversal of the tongues of fire that came down on the heads of apostles at Pentecost.[5] It can all seem the work of a vindictive God but, as C. S. Lewis sketches with grim humor in *The Great Divorce*, these figures are in hell because they want to be, so eternally wedded to their own vain and delusive self-understandings that they cannot answer to grace. In Paul Ricoeur's memorable term, they are all wedded to "self-positing." If hell has a theme tune if would be a rousing and unrepentant singing of "I Did It My Way."

The figures in hell are, from the outset, self-isolating and self-justifying. Even the sympathetically portrayed Francesca, one of the carnal lovers blown on the winds of hell like flocks of starlings in Canto 5, speaks only to Dante, not to her wind-tossed companion in love, Paolo. Guided in life by instinctual bent, not reason, they are now condemned to be blown about like flocking birds as though to underscore the point that a collectivity brought together by instinct is not a community. Francesca's transgression cannot simply be the all-too-humanly-understandable adultery she has committed, for there are worse sexual sinners in Dante's *Purgatorio* and even in *Paradiso*. It is rather her inability to see the wider repercussions of her betrayal that leaves her driven on the infernal winds like a flocking bird.

Dante is impressed by what is good, and what is for the common good. The deepest circles of hell are reserved for those who betray the common good as traitors. The deeper Virgil and Dante go in hell the less able those they meet are able to communicate, for communication, the shared word, depends on trust, and in the end lies, deceit, betrayals, robbery, and treachery destroy trust, and thus any possibility of shared "good" life. Even in the upper circles of hell, the circlings of those condemned for carnal sin, including Cleopatra, Paris, and Semiramis, are accompanied by meaningless keening. But in the depths, the communicative word by which humans—even sinful humans—image the creative and self-communicative Word that is Christ is completely silenced.[6] Dante's hell is frozen over. The giants of Canto 31, appropriately including Nimrod, the builder of Babel, can only babble incoherently. In deepest hell the souls are frozen like straws in ice—some flat, some vertical, "another like a bow, bent face to feet" (*Inferno* 34.14–15)—presided over by a gigantic Lucifer, frozen to his waist in a lake of ice. As Robin Kirkpatrick observes, while many authors

5. See Robin Kirkpatrick's note on this canto.

6. For an elegant essay on the relationship of language and love in the *Commedia* see Vittorio Montemaggi, "In Unknowability as in Love: The Theology of Dante's *Commedia*," in *Dante's Commedia: Theology as Poetry*, ed. V. Montemaggi and Matthew Traherne (Notre Dame: University of Notre Dame Press, 2010).

give the devil the best lines (consider Milton and Blake) Dante's Lucifer is pure negation, failing even at being the emperor of his dark realm.[7] Instead Dante gives us an unthinking machine, "a mere refrigerator whose flapping wings cool the ice of lower Hell, and a grinding mill."[8] Each of Satan's three mouths is busy devouring a traitor—Judas, Brutus, and Cassius—and stuffed mouths cannot speak.

Climbing down Satan's hairy frame, Virgil and Dante move through a crevice and find the world inverted. Satan in his fall has punched through a cone of earth that has become the Mountain of Purgatory in the southern hemisphere, its crown topped with the earthly, Edenic paradise so that, even out of this great evil, the possibility of renewal is given. Dante and Virgil crawl from a dark crevice to glimpse the stars that shone over Adam and Eve at the first creation.

Learning to Love Our Neighbor and Trust in God

The doctrine of purgatory was a late articulation of Christian thought—the Venerable Bede is thought to give one of the first full theological treatments, and Dante's *Purgatorio* is far from being the place of punishment it became in later writers. Despite the apparent hardships the souls here endure, purgatory is a place of learning, growth and, above all, movement, in contrast to the frozen wastes of hell. The icy winds fanned by Satan's wings that produce only paralyzing cold are, at the entrance to purgatory, replaced by the wings of an angelic boatman who fans the winds that blew over the waters at the first creation. Deepest hell's eternally isolated souls, frozen like straws in ice, are succeeded by the boatman's chorusing passengers, a hundred or more,

> "*In exitu Israel de Aegypto*":
> they sang this all together in one voice,
> with all the psalm that's written after this.
>
> (*Purgatorio* 2.46–48, citing Psalm 114)

While the *Inferno* exercises ghoulish fascination, the *Purgatorio* is the cantica most rich in Christian guidance for our own earthly pilgrimage. Dante has no desire to prognosticate about life after death but does want to tell us what is involved in living the good life now. His souls in purgatory, whatever their past (and they include seducers, cheats, and murderers), are now seeking the good

---

7. Robin Kirkpatrick, Introduction to Dante's *Inferno* (lxxxiv).
8. Kirkpatrick, notes to *Inferno* 34, p. 445.

with their salvation, effected by grace, now secure. But conversion is not the end of Christian life but its beginning, the beginning of a walk with God that will demand we discard many self-delusions. And just so also Dante.

Only as they enter purgatory do we learn how near to death, both physical and spiritual, Dante had come. Virgil explains to Cato, the gatekeeper, that Dante has not "escaped" from hell by the back door because he is not yet dead:

> This man has yet to see his final night,
> But through his own stupidity was close,
> And scarcely had the time in which to turn. (*Purgatorio* 1.58–60)

Had then Dante been close to suicide, or perditious despair? Does this represent a kind of conversion on Dante's part—certainly he describes himself in the initial lines of the poem as variously "coming to" or returning to himself. It is grace, he tells us, flowing down through the ladies in heaven and executed by his pagan guide, Virgil, that takes him on a different path.

Dante journeyed through hell because he had to—there was no other way to go—but even where he is touched and appalled by what he sees, he is almost always an observer.

In purgatory this changes. He is no longer merely a transient witness as was the case in hell; he is now himself a pilgrim. He is not the same as the sojourning souls he goes amongst (they are astonished to see he casts a shadow and thus is still alive), but nonetheless, he will be riven to the core and forced to face his own sins of selfishness, pride, envy, and arrogance. It will hurt.

This pain, in Dante's *Purgatorio*, is not punishment but healing and reforming, difficult though this may be to be believed in some cases. So the envious in *Purgatorio* 13 have their eyelids stitched together and rest their heads on each other's backs as they proceed. The image is cruel, and causes Dante to weep, but the allusion is to the training of hunting sparrow hawks, and the violently envious in life now, weeping in repentance, learn that they depend on one another. Dante addresses them as those who are sure of salvation—confident "to see the Light Supreme" (*Purgatorio* 13.86), and they in turn reply collectively, "We are, dear brother, now all citizens of one true place." Those who have sinned against the common good now patiently learn that they need one another to live a blessed life.

Purgatory is as much a place of love and desire as pain, indeed the "pain" is only a form of this thirsting love, as Dante's friend and former poetic sparring partner, Forese, explains to Dante on the Terrace of Gluttony, Purgatory's sixth terrace. Gluttony does not seem too severe a transgression—we find on this terrace popes who have consumed too many eels and too much Vernaccia wine, and others who drank as if they would never have their fill. Yet these are souls who have sought satisfaction in mere satiety—in the end impossible for they are seeking satisfaction in what cannot satisfy, a constant theme of St. Augustine's.[9] Their desire is not in itself wrong, nor is good wine or food, but filling your gullet "past all norms" shows a disordered life, the extreme template for which is Lucifer in the deepest pit of hell, eternally gnawing but never satisfied.

The glutton eats beyond hunger out of—what?—a fear that he will miss something, a lack that can never be met by pouring food or drink into a no-longer hungry or thirsty body. Forese says he and all souls of this terrace are

> weeping as they sing,
> because their gullets led them past all norms,
> are here remade as holy, thirsting, hungering. . . .
> I call it pain. Rightly I should say solace.
> For that same yearning leads us to the tree
> That led Christ, in his joy, to say "Eli,"
> when through his open veins he made us free. (*Purgatorio* 23.64–74)

The food for which these raked, skeletal souls hunger is from the tree which is the cross, and the drink they thirst for is water from the living rock, that is to say, Christ (*Purgatorio* 22.136ff.). The pain is equally solace and preparation. A pen being prepared for use, Forese explains to Dante, is sharpened and pared. He whom he loves, he prunes.

The Limits of Pagan Wisdom: Virtue Ethics in Dante's *Commedia*

T. S. Eliot points it out as one of the great achievements of the *Commedia* that Dante effortlessly populates it with those then living and recently dead, famous contemporaries, saints from heaven, figures from the classical past, and even, like Ulysses, from fiction and mythology.[10] A striking role is given the pagan Virgil as his guide, and even to pagan Cato, who somehow becomes the doorman of purgatory. Virgil, though not a denizen of *Inferno*, knows his way around it and even here in purgatory, where he appears to be finding his way as much as Dante, is a wise guide. Though sometimes puzzled by the workings

---

9. It remains a puzzle why Dante makes so little overt reference to Augustine when the poem seems so theologically indebted to him. Much of the "Augustinianism" may come through his debt to Aquinas, which is clearly evidenced.

10. T. S. Eliot, *Dante* (London: Faber and Faber, 1929).

of grace, it is Virgil who voices a strongly Augustinian understanding of rightly
ordered love:

> The natural love can never go astray.
> The other, though, may err when wrongly aimed,
> Or else through too much vigour or the lack.
> Where mind-love sets itself on primal good
> and keeps, in secondaries, a due control,
> it cannot be the cause of false delight.
> But when it wrongly twists towards the ill,
> or runs towards the good too fast or slow,
> what's made then works against its maker's plan.
>   Hence of necessity, you'll understand
> That love must be the seed of all good powers, as, too, of penalties your
>   deeds deserve. (*Purgatorio* 17.94–105)

Dante credits this natural theology to Virgil: it should be evident to all that
the world is made for and guided towards the Good, and that all right ordered
things, all life, moves towards this. But here we should point to the influence of
a teaching that would not be within the historical Virgil's gift—the Christian
doctrine of creation. All things come from God and have their being only
as God holds them continuously in being. We all are made by Primal Good
(in Virgil's term) and long for the Primal Good. All our desiring actions are
inflections of this life force within which is part of our animal—or better in
Christian terms—our *creaturely* nature. We desire the Good, although reasoning creatures like human beings can mistake lesser, shabby simulacrums
for this good.[11]

Yet as Dante and Virgil reach the earthly, Edenic paradise that surmounts
the Mountain of Purgatory, Dante grows more confident and Virgil less so,

---

11. It is not a position wholly dependent on Christian conviction—there are Platonic and
Aristotelian variants, a famous modern one being Iris Murdoch's essay, *The Sovereignty of Good*
(London: Routledge & Kegan Paul, 1970), but it is a position that is only fully coherent, in my view,
if one posits a loving Creator God and an attendant theology of participation. It is a view largely
lost to our modern popular culture and in need of recovery. On the ethics of the *Purgatorio*, Robin
Kirkpatrick, who highlights this speech of Virgil's in his introduction, says that "Rules certainly
matter to Dante—or did in the first *cantica* of the *Commedia*. Now, though, in the *Purgatorio*,
ethical principle ceases to be a form of control and becomes instead (as it did for Aristotle and, recently, for neo-Aristotelians such as Alistair McIntyre and Martha Nussbaum) an encouragement
in the 'flourishing' of our natures in the full spectrum of their powers" (Kirkpatrick, Introduction
to *Purgatorio*, xix).

saying to Dante that "you're in a place where I, through my own powers, can tell no more" (*Purgatorio* 27.128–29). Indeed, Virgil will say no more in the poem. As they proceed through the holy forest, Dante, filled with "radiant wonder," turns to "honest" Virgil to be met not with his usual wise words but "with looks no less weighed down by heavy awe" (*Purgatorio* 29.56–57).

A highly allegorical procession appears, representing as in a continuous present, the unfolding of divine revelation across the span of created time: twenty-four elders, representing the books of the Old Testament (according to Jerome's numbering); four winged creatures, signifying the evangelists, who surround a chariot pulled by a Gryphon; three dancing ladies representing faith, hope, and charity (the theological virtues); and another four representing the moral virtues. Then comes St. Luke, the physician, St. Paul, signified with a sword, four men with "humble looks" signifying James, Peter, John, and Jude, and finally the sleeping but alert prophet of the book of Revelation. The whole is too rich in interlocking symbolism to summarize and indeed is probably intended to keep us from too easy a reading. What is clear is that the truth of these highest realms is revealed truth.

Virgil has, thus far in their journey, signified poetic virtue and humane wisdom, but there is a higher Wisdom to which Dante must now turn. This is of course Christ, who is represented in the allegorical procession by the Gryphon in its twin natures, but figured forth here in the figure of one of the blessed. This is the soul "far worthier than me," which Virgil had promised would come and meet Dante in the realm of souls who live in fire and in hope (*Inferno* 1.118–22).

Beatrice as a Perfected Christian Believer

It is a startling fact, and one that should go part way to countering many centuries of male theological condescension, that Dante should make a woman his emblematic perfected Christian, the *imago Dei* imaging the one who is the true image of the invisible God, Christ. Through a drift of petals scattered by angels Dante sees a woman riding in the chariot. Although he apparently still sees her through a veil, he trembles, "sensing the ancient power of what love was," and turns, as a frightened child "to its mum," to Virgil (*Purgatorio* 30.44–45). But Virgil is gone and a sharp voice addresses him:

> Dante, that Virgil is no longer here,
> do not yet weep, do not yet weep for that.
> A different sword cut, first, must make you weep. (*Purgatorio* 30.54–56)

Dante is startled to hear his own Christian name being used (the first time it has been used in the *Commedia*), and indeed used in harsh reprimand by the woman he now realizes is Beatrice.

The poet-pilgrim and we, the readers, might have expected Beatrice would welcome Dante warmly at this juncture, having made such efforts to get him this far, but not so. She is stern and addresses him with ferocity:

> Look. I am, truly, I am Beatrice [*Ben son, ben son Beatrice*].
> What right had you to venture to this mount?
> Did you not know that all are happy here? (*Purgatorio* 30.73-74)

The Higher Repentance

While a number of Dante scholars discuss this as a "recognition" narrative, it seems as much a "summons" narrative parallel to that of Moses at the burning bush and, of course, St. Paul in Acts 9:4, who similarly is addressed by name—"Saul, Saul, why are you persecuting me?"[12] Beatrice's "I am, truly I am" heightens the Mosaic resonances. The veiled Beatrice is one who, like Moses having to veil his face before the Israelites, has been in the presence of the living God. She "truly is" and "truly is" Beatrice because wholly constituted as what she is by the grace of the One who alone truly is (Exod 3:16). Dante, by contrast, is shamed and silent. Although he has repented much, he has further to go. We are at the brink of heaven, but there remains a hint of hell. The frozen wastes of the *Inferno* find an echo in the ice stretched around Dante's core, ice finally melted in tears of sorrow.

> The ice, so tightly stretched around my core,
> turned now to breath and water, issuing,
> at mouth and eye, in spasms from my heart. (*Purgatorio* 30.95-98)

The proud poet is reduced to the speechlessness of infancy by Beatrice's account of his vanity and the error of his ways. Over many verses she speaks of his natural blessings, his missed opportunities to seek the good, his trifling pursuit of what could never satisfy, sins of omission and commission. Dante stands like a little boy, "dumb with shame." The great orator can barely mumble his words, yet like Augustine at his moment of conversion, his tax of penitence

---

12. Recognition narratives can also, in the Bible, be call narratives; see for instance Mary Magdalene, who recognizes the risen Lord only when he calls her by name.

"pours out flowing tears" (*Purgatorio* 30.144–45). We have come to the point of baptism and new birth. Dante the pilgrim, fully penitent, has now to die symbolically as all Christians do by baptism and is submerged in the stream of the Lethe. When he emerges he looks to the now unveiled face of Beatrice, but she looks, not to him, but to the Gryphon, whose double-natured reflection Dante sees in her eyes. His eyes must now look where hers do.

This is not the end of the *Commedia*, for we have still all the *Paradiso* before us, but this meeting of Dante with Beatrice is a culmination of that story which began with Dante lost in the dark woods, not knowing where or who he is, and meeting a guide sent by a "blessed and beautiful lady" (*Inferno* 2). It is also the fullest statement, not of his doctrine of God, which, while subtending the whole, comes to a climax in the *Paradiso*, but of his theological anthropology: his doctrine of the human being made in the image of God.

Let's return to the dramatic double-naming that opens the encounter of Dante and Beatrice in *Purgatorio* 30. Dante, stirred by the appearance of a veiled woman whom he does not yet seem to recognize, turns to Virgil to comment but abruptly and without explanation, faithful Virgil is gone. Instead the woman addresses Dante by name,

"Dante," says the lady, "that Virgil is no longer here."

Dante, startled to hear his own name spoken, turns to see the woman, still veiled, fixing her eyes upon him. She then names herself, disclosing to Dante what he has not yet fully seen, her true nature,

"Look, I am, truly, I am Beatrice." (*Purgatorio* 30.73)

Being More Truly What One Truly Is: Our Life in Christ

Beatrice is a symbolic figure—not just here but throughout the *Commedia* and his earlier *Vita Nuova*—but it is important for the theology of the poem that she is also a real person who lived in Florence and who knew Dante.[13] She calls Dante by name, as God called Moses by name from the burning bush, and discloses herself to him as "I am Beatrice," with all the echoes of the "I AM WHO I AM" of God's self-disclosure at the burning bush. Beatrice is not God, but one who, like Moses, has come fully into the divine presence. She has become not

---

13. The historical Beatrice died at twenty-four years of age, already a married woman. Dante probably only met her twice.

less, but more than she was when alive on earth (*Purgatorio* 31.82–84): "I am, truly, I am Beatrice." She is not then a sugary stand-in for the "ideal woman" or even the ideal Christian, like a woman in a 1950s advertisement for cleaning products. She is wholly, truly, fully, and distinctively herself, and it is as such that she chronicles the many failings of Dante, who has yet to see who truly, fully he is in the eyes of God.

But which Dante? Here, as in the dark wood with which the poem began, we see a fusion of Dante, the man in exile, and Dante the pilgrim-poet of his own narrative. Both are summoned up by Beatrice's invocation of his real name. Dante, the exile, will never return to his beloved Florence and the Baptistery of St. John. But Dante the pilgrim, symbolically rebaptized in the Lethe, knows that the city and the citizenship he must seek is that of the City of God.

PART FIVE

Identity in the Age of Reformation

Chapter 23

Thomas More: For Our Season

Robert Bork

The continuing contemporary interest in Thomas More (1478–1535) is hardly to be accounted for by popular fascination with sixteenth-century English politics or even by admiration for a martyr to a religious cause no longer universally popular.[1] It is more likely that More's memory remains fresh after almost half a millennium because his life casts light on our time. More lived, as we live today, in a time of rapid social and cultural unraveling. The meaning of his life, at least for us, is not so much his worldly success and religious piety, extraordinary as both of these were, but rather the courage and consistency with which he opposed the forces of disintegration.

The culture war of the early sixteenth century was fought over the breaking apart of Christianity, its loss of central authority, and the consequent fragmentation of European civilization. Our war rages about the collapse of traditional virtues across all of the West and the rise of moral indifference and cheerful nihilism. Many parallels between the two eras could be drawn, but a crucial similarity lies in the central role played by law in each. Though More was a profoundly religious man, it should not be forgotten that he was also a preeminent lawyer and judge. The law, quite as much as Catholicism, is crucial to an understanding of the man and the martyr. Law and its institutions were, of course, major forces of cohesion in More's age, and are perhaps the primary symbols in ours of stability and continuity as well as justice. When moral consensus fades, as it did in More's time and does in ours, we turn to law; when law falters, as it must when morality is no longer widely shared, society and culture teeter on the brink of chaos.

1. This essay is reprinted with permission from Robert Bork, *A Time to Speak: Selected Writings and Arguments* (Wilmington, DE: ISI Publications, 2008).

That is another way of saying that law cannot be divorced from morality—and, there is reason to think, morality, at least in the long run, cannot be divorced from religion. Law and religion are alike, therefore, as reinforcements of social order. It is a subject for speculation at least, whether either can long remain healthy and self-confident without the other. Each imposes obligations, but each is subject to the therapeutic heresy, softening those obligations to accommodate individual desires. It is a sign of our distemper that Thomas More is today so often regarded as a hero of civil disobedience, a man who refused to obey law with which he was in profound moral disagreement. That is a considerable distortion of the truth, and it was not More's understanding of his motives. For him, in a very real sense, law was morality. It is equally true that for More morality was superior to law and was the standard by which law must be judged. If that seems a paradox, I do not think it truly is one.

More, as his biographers make clear, had the utmost respect for authority, hierarchy, and social discipline. He was born into an age when schooling stressed these virtues. Early education, including the study of musical harmony, as Peter Ackroyd informs us, emphasized the paramount importance of order and hierarchy. Then came the study of rhetoric, memorization of simple syllogisms and verbal formulas, by which young students were "made aware of the presence of external authority while at the same time becoming familiarized with the implicit demands of order and stability. . . . Beyond all this, too, was the image of God."[2] These tendencies were confirmed in More's study of the law. "The central and important point," Ackroyd writes, "is that both [religion and law] were conceived to be visible aspects of the same spiritual reality. . . . The attitude More adopted towards the primacy and authority of law governed all his subsequent actions."[3]

Contrast this with today's anarchic popular music and primary education, embodied at their extremes in rap and the self-esteem movement, which cater to and encourage the natural indiscipline of the young. It should not be surprising that similar manifestations of the disorder appear in adult fields of endeavor, including law and religion. These tendencies were present in More's age as well, as Ackroyd makes clear:

It is of the greatest significance in understanding his [More's] behavior . . . to realize that he wrote about the law in precisely the same way he

2. Peter Ackroyd, *The Life of Thomas More* (New York: Anchor Books, 1999), 27. All subsequent citations from Ackroyd are to this edition.
3. Ackroyd, *Life of Thomas More*, 62.

described the Church. There was, for him, no essential or necessary difference. That is why he understood at once the nature of Martin Luther's heresy, when the German monk spoke of judgment "according to love . . . without any law books." When Luther emphasized the importance of the "free mind," as opposed to the tenets of "the law books and jurists," More recognized instinctively that he was mounting an attack upon the whole medieval polity as constituted by the Catholic Church; when Luther argued that law was written within the heart of man, and that judges should ignore matters of precedent and tradition, he was assaulting the principles by which More's life and career were guided.[4]

Thomas More and the Law

More saw Luther's advocacy of lawless law to be at the heart of their culture war. Luther spoke for the individual conscience and so necessarily attacked the authority of precedent and tradition in the law. More's view of law and the duty of judges was quite different. More's son-in-law quotes More as saying: "If the parties will at my hands call for justice, then, all were it my father stood on the one side, and the devil on the other, his cause being good, the devil should have right."[5] Luther and many modern jurists would reinterpret the law to do the devil down, and the moderns, at least, would reserve to themselves authority to decide which is the father and which the devil.

Robert Bolt's *A Man for All Seasons* got More remarkably right. In one scene, More, then the Lord Chancellor, argues with family members who are urging him to arrest Richard Rich, the man who was later to betray him. More's daughter, Margaret, says, "Father, that man's bad." More answers, "There is no law against that." William Roper: "There is! God's law!" More: "Then God can arrest him. . . . The law, Roper, the law. I know what's legal, not what's right. And I'll stick to what's legal. . . . I'm not God. The currents and eddies of right and wrong, which you find such plain sailing, I can't navigate. I'm no voyager. But in the thickets of the law, oh, there I'm a forester."[6]

Bolt, in a familiar passage, has More say when assailed by his son-in-law with the charge that he would give the devil the benefit of law:

4. Ackroyd, *Life of Thomas More*, 63.

5. William Roper, *The Mirror of Vertue in Worldly Greatness or The Life of Sir Thomas More* (Oxford: Oxford University Press, 2007), 27.

6. Robert Bolt, *A Man for All Seasons: A Play in Two Acts* (New York: Vintage, 1990), 65.

MORE: Yes. What would you do? Cut a great road through the law to get after the devil?

ROPER: I'd cut down every law in England to do that!

MORE: Oh? . . . And when the last law was down, and the Devil turned round on you—where would you hide, Roper, the laws all being flat? . . . This country's planted thick with laws from coast to coast—man's laws, not God's—and if you cut them down . . . d'you really think you could stand upright in the winds that would blow then? . . . Yes, I'd give the Devil the benefit of law, for my own safety's sake.[7]

To understand More, then, it is equally important to realize his absolute commitment to law and his recognition of the fallibility of human moral reasoning. To be ruled by each individual's moral beliefs is to invite, indeed to guarantee, social tumult and disorder. The law alone is uniform, a composite or compromise of varying moral assessments, to be applied to all alike, regardless of personal attitudes about the persons involved: father or devil, it makes no difference. If an acceptable mix of freedom and order is to be maintained, obedience to law must be accepted as a primary moral duty.

Thomas More and Constituted Authority

The veneration More gave to law, he also gave, and for the same reason, to constituted authority. More served Henry VIII, a sovereign whose policies he often believed to be immoral or profoundly unwise. He was under no illusions about his king, even as we should be under no illusions about our governors or even the democratic will. When Roper rejoiced at how friendly Henry was to More, he replied, "I have no cause to be proud thereof, for if my head could win him a castle in France it should not fail to go." Yet he did not disobey; he might give contrary advice, but, the policy or the law once decided upon, he complied. He disapproved of Henry's ruinous war with France, but, as Speaker, he asked Parliament for extraordinary and unpopular taxes to support that war. Later, when More was Lord Chancellor, and it was proposed to put Parliament in control of the Church, Richard Marius tells us, "More was sick at heart at the prospect. . . [but] he could not control events. Worse, he was a respectable figurehead, kept by the government to lend it whatever authority his reputation

7. Bolt, *A Man for All Seasons*, 66.

gave him, serving by his very presence in the post of Lord Chancellor a cause which was to him abominable." He wanted to resign. "Yet he could not resign, for to do so would have been to run the risk of making his opposition to the king public."[8]

Henry commanded More to speak in the House of Lords to say that the king was pursuing his divorce from Catherine as a matter of religious scruple and not for love of any other woman. In doing so, More pointed out that various universities agreed the first marriage had been unlawful. Someone asked More's opinion and he replied that he had given it to the king and said no more. As Chambers put it, "Respect for authority . . . was the foundation of [More's] political thinking."[9] He presented the king's case, but would not go an inch further.

Why, then, this obedience to constituted authority and to law, even when he regarded them as immoral? It may have been partly ambition; it was surely, in large part, fear of the alternative to law. An Elizabethan play, probably written by Shakespeare, has More attempt to quell rioters against aliens in London:

> Grant them removed, and grant that this your noise Hath chid down all the majesty of England. Imagine . . . Authority quite silenced by your brawl. . . . What had you got? I'll tell you. You had taught How insolence and strong hand should prevail, How order should be quelled; and by this pattern Not one of you should live an aged man; For other ruffians, as their fancies wrought With self same hand, self reasons and self right Would shark on you; and men like ravenous fishes Would feed on one another.[10]

It may be counted unfortunate that More's speech was followed immediately by a riot. He was no more successful than were a few professors in the sixties extolling the virtues of prudence and order to rampaging students.

The Fallibility of Human Minds

But there is more than the fear of lawlessness and tumult. There is the thought that he is not sure about morality, that he may be wrong. When Roper says to him, "The law's your god," More replies, "Oh, Roper you're a fool, God's my

8. Richard Marius, *Thomas More: A Biography* (Cambridge: Harvard University Press, 1999), 382.

9. See R. W. Chambers, *Thomas More* (London: Peregrine, 1963).

10. *Sir Thomas More: A Play by Anthony Munday and Others,* ed. Vittorio Gabrieli and Giorgio Melchiori (Manchester: Manchester University Press, 1990), 100.

god. . . . But I find Him rather too subtle . . . I don't know where He is nor what He wants."[11]

Again he says: "God made the angels to show Him splendor—as He made animals for innocence and plants for their simplicity. But man He made to serve Him wittily, in the tangle of his mind."[12] Not in the pride and certainty of the individual conscience, but in the tangle of his mind. It was because More recognized the fallibility of individual minds that he obeyed authority but saw no need or virtue in doing more than authority required when his mind told him that what was ordered was wrong. The recalcitrance that brought More to the headsman was his refusal to take the oath that Henry was the Supreme Head of the Church in England and endorse a series of acts ending the supremacy of the Pope. The source of More's devotion to papal supremacy illuminates the man. The point was not that the Pope's authority had been instituted immediately by God (indeed Christianity was several centuries old before papal authority as it would come to be understood was clearly established), but that the Pope's power rested upon the inherited traditions and beliefs and the general councils of the Church. The councils, of course, and the evolution of the Church were believed to be guided by God. Here again, More's faith and his view of law became almost indistinguishable.

His recalcitrance may be seen, as it often is, as More's one great act of disobedience. Bolt writes that More seemed to him "a man with an adamantine sense of his own self. . . . He knew where he began and left off, what areas of himself he could yield to the encroachments of his enemies, and what to the encroachments to those he loved. . . . But at length he was asked to retreat from that final area where he located his self. And there this supple, humorous, unassuming, and sophisticated person set like metal, was overtaken by an absolutely primitive rigor, and could no more be budged than a cliff."[13] It is this behavior that causes Bolt to refer to More as a "hero of selfhood."[14] Indeed it was extraordinary behavior: More was the only person not a member of the clergy who died rather than take the oath.

11. Bolt, *A Man for All Seasons,* 42.
12. Bolt, *A Man for All Seasons,* 74.
13. Bolt, *A Man for All Seasons,* xv.
14. Bolt, *A Man for All Seasons,* xvii.

Submitting to a Higher Law

Yet it seems wrong, or at least potentially misleading, to attribute More's be-havior to "selfhood." It is a symptom of our disorder that we glorify, practically deify, the individual conscience. It was not always so. It must have been well into this century before "civil disobedience" and "heresy" became terms of praise. To the contrary, More's behavior may be seen as submission to external authority, a conscious and difficult denial of self.

The refusal to take the oath should not, of course, be viewed as disobedi-ence at all. There was a law higher than Henry's and Parliament's, and More knew that the oath violated that law. There were few other occasions on which that could be said with certainty. More, an exemplary courtier, servant, and confidante of the king, did not suppose that God's will was clear enough to re-quire refusal to serve the king even when his purposes seemed to More unjust; he even assisted the king in temporal struggles against the pope, as, given his understanding of his respective duties, he should have. God's law is not often clear to the tangled mind of man, but there was a central fact about which More could have no doubt: Christ did not leave behind a book but a Church, and that Church must not be divided. As to this ultimate thing, he, at last, knew where God was and what he wanted. More was caught between two authorities, and the question for him, the commands of both being clear, was which authority was superior. At this extremity, God was no longer too subtle for him, and More obeyed God's law and went to his death. This was not disobedience but obedience, a thought he expressed in his last words as he placed his head on the block: "I die the king's good servant, but God's first."[15]

Individualism in the law, as in matters of faith, produces the substitution of private morality for public law and duty. This is precisely what More thought Luther was encouraging in his own day, and it is even more prominent in ours. That may be seen in the growth of legal nullification, the refusal to be bound by external rules, that is not only widespread among the American people but, more ominously, in the basic institutions of the law. More applied his injunction as much to the judge on the bench as to rioters in the street. We all recognize rioters as civil disobedients, but we are less likely to recognize that the judge who ignores law or who creates constitutional law out of his own conscience is equally civilly disobedient. In 1975 Alexander Bickel, in *The Morality of Consent*, recounted the then-recent American experience with disrupters in the streets, but added: "The assault upon the legal order by moral imperatives was not only

---

15. See *The King's Good Servant, But God First: The Life and Writings of Sir Thomas More* (San Francisco: Ignatius Press, 1997).

or perhaps even most effectively an assault from the outside." It came as well from a Court that cut through law to do what it considered "right" and "good." Our law schools now construct theoretical justifications for that particularly corrosive form of civil disobedience, explaining that judges should create, and enforce as constitutional law, individual rights that are nowhere to be found in the Constitution.

Refusing to Be Bound by Law or Evidence

Against the backdrop of Justices disregarding the law, it is not surprising that jurors are refusing to be bound by either law or evidence if the results do not fit their personal views. Our representatives enact the laws but juries scattered across the country vote on them again, often overturning the democratic choice. This pernicious practice occurs not only *sub silentio* but is coming into the open. There is even a national organization, the "Fully Informed Jury Association," to justify and encourage jury lawlessness. Some nullification occurs because black jurors think the law is arrayed against them or out of racial solidarity (the O. J. Simpson verdict), but other defiances reflect libertarian attitudes and personal disapproval of the law (the Jack Kevorkian acquittals). According to the *Washington Post*, a poll shows that three out of four Americans say they would disregard the judge's instructions if the law contravened their own ideas of right and wrong.

Now we have seen Senate nullification of the law of impeachment. The evidence left no doubt that the President had deliberately and repeatedly committed perjury, tampered with witnesses, and obstructed justice. Felonies, all of them. Nor is there any doubt, based on the Framers' understanding and prior Senate precedent, that these offenses constituted "high crimes and misdemeanors" requiring removal from office. Yet the Senate felt free to prefer partisan interests to law, and refused to convict.

These are manifestations in the law of the absorption with self and the disrespect for inconvenient rules that permeate our culture. This absorption, variously called radical individualism or autonomy, is taken to justify even institutional lawlessness. As Bickel noted, civil disobedience, no matter by whom or in what cause, is always "a decision in favor of self, in favor of the idea of self." That is why, in the law, it encourages moral relativism, which is a leading feature of modern constitutional adjudication as well as jury verdicts and legislatures sitting as courts of impeachment.

A Struggle over the Uniformity and Stability of Law

To all this Thomas More provides the sharpest contrast. As Chambers notes, "From [his book] *Utopia* to the scaffold, More stands for the common cause, as against the private commodity of the single man." If obedience to constituted authority and to established law was at the center of More's morality in the reign of Henry VIII, how much more would it have been his guiding principle when law and policy owe their legitimacy to being democratically made, when they are, in the most real sense they can be, the will of the community?

For More, morality was superior to both human law and the will of the sovereign in that it could be used to shape or to alter that law and that will, though not to justify disobedience to it. This clearly appears in *Utopia*, where he argued that it was a man's duty to enter public life despite the evil necessarily entailed, saying, "That which you cannot turn to good, so to order it that it be not very bad."[16] In a word, try to make law as moral as you can, More constantly argued, but when it is made, whatever it commands, morality lies in obedience. If disobedience is ever justified, it is only when the issue is of transcendent importance and when you are absolutely sure of the right and wrong of the matter. In a democratic polity there can be such occasions, but they will be extremely rare.

These are issues of law and morality internal to the United States, but they arise internationally as well. What we call international law is, of course, in many respects not yet law in any real sense. It is in a formative stage, the stage at which More would have felt free to infuse morality. This raises the increasingly important question whether we should try to build an international law, or pretend there is one, about the use of armed force between nations. In the present condition of the world—a condition that looks permanent or at least likely to be of indefinite duration—I think More would say no. It must be "no" because such law cannot be moral, since, to be called international, rules about armed force must necessarily express a "morality" acceptable to immoral regimes.

Go back to the debate over the legality of the United States' invasion of Grenada in October 1983. At the time, a number of people denounced the invasion as illegal, while others defended its legality. In a discussion with an international law expert, I pointed to three factors that most people deemed relevant to the American action in Grenada. First, the Grenadan government had been formed by a minority that seized power by violence and maintained it by terror. Second, it was a Marxist-Leninist regime and so represented a further advance in this hemisphere of a power that threatened freedom and democracy throughout

16. See Thomas More, *Utopia* (New York: Penguin, 2003).

the world. Third, the people of Grenada were ecstatic at being relieved of that tyrannical government on its present course.

If some find the obedience More taught too austere for comfort, they ought at least reflect on the question of how much glorification of the individual conscience any legal order can tolerate and remain a legal order. They ought also to ask how much privatization of morality the moral order can withstand and remain a moral order. In the culture war of the sixteenth century, More was an active combatant for the binding force of law and the uniformity of religion under the Catholic Church. Our culture war is more confusing and diffuse, but at its center it too is a struggle over the uniformity and stability of law. What is true of law is true of other social restraints, not only of morality, ethics, and manners, but also of respect for craftsmanship, which requires, at its highest, the sublimation of self-will to external standards. Hence, as one might expect from the progress of radical autonomy in the law, we observe formless music, meaningless and offensive art, adolescent entertainment, subjective journalism, and an enthusiasm for genetic technology that may soon threaten the essence of what it is to be human. One important segment of a culture does not collapse and leave the adjacent structures intact.

Law both reflects the state of our culture and actively alters it. The divisions between areas of culture are only membranes, and permeable ones at that.

More's life reminds us that the struggle between order and disorder, between authority and the urges of self, is a permanent feature of our condition. Liberty of conscience is a concept easily blurred, or indeed born blurry, and, misunderstood, it can be a force for social fragmentation. Liberty of conscience, insofar as it means the freedom of the individual to construct his own norms, moves from religion to morality, from morality to law, and hence to religious, moral, and legal anarchy. As Ackroyd said: "More embodied the old order of hierarchy and authority at the very moment when it began to collapse all around him." He died for the sake of that order.

More lost, and so may we, but he has much to teach us, nonetheless, about steadfastness as a minority, even perhaps as a permanent and dwindling minority. He may even teach us that sometimes staunch minorities are remembered well.

Chapter 24

Martin Luther: The Self-less Christian

RONALD K. RITTGERS

Martin Luther has traditionally been seen as an icon of modern Western individualism.[1] Many have interpreted his defiant "Here I stand" speech at the Diet of Worms (1521) as a watershed moment in the development of modern selfhood.[2] Luther the courageous individual stood against religious tyranny and stood for religious liberty and self-determination.[3] He followed the inner dictates of his conscience and defied the external commands of reigning authorities. He interpreted Scripture for himself and openly broke with received tradition. For these reasons and others, Luther has been viewed as the first modern man and the Protestant Reformation as the first modern revolution. On this interpretation, modern selfhood, with its emphasis on interiority, individuality, and liberty is simply a secularized version of Luther's early modern Protestant self.[4]

The great irony is that Luther did not even think he had a self, certainly not the kind of self that is assumed in the Luther-as-first-modern-man inter-

---

1. See A. G. Dickens and John M. Tonkin, *The Reformation in Historical Thought* (Cambridge: Harvard University Press, 1985), 130, 164, 198, 250–52, 317. For an especially critical treatment of Luther's role in the emergence of modern individualism, see Jacques Maritain, *Three Reformers: Luther, Descartes, Rousseau* (London: Sheed & Ward, 1928).

2. For a brief discussion of this interpretive tradition, see Merry E. Wiesner, *Early Modern Europe, 1450–1789*, 2nd ed. (Cambridge: Cambridge University Press, 2013), 164. Luther's speech at the Diet of Worms may be found in WA 7:814–857; *LW* 32:101–31. WA = *D. Martin Luthers Werke, Kritische Gesamtausgabe, Schriften*, 73 vols. (Weimar: Böhlau Verlag, 1883–); *LW = Luther's Works, American Edition*, ed. J. Pelikan and H. T. Lehmann, 55 vols. (Minneapolis: Fortress, 1955–).

3. The 2003 film *Luther* is a good example of this view in popular culture.

4. See Steven Bruce, *Religion in the Modern World: From Cathedrals to Cults* (New York: Oxford University Press, 1996), 3; and Craig M. Gay, *The Way of the (Modern) World; Or, Why It's Tempting to Live as If God Doesn't Exist* (Grand Rapids: Eerdmans, 1998), 256.

pretation of his life. While many of the seeds of modern selfhood were sown in the late medieval and early modern periods,[5] with Luther playing an important but largely unintended part,[6] the Wittenberg reformer was actually a prophet of radical self-less-ness that was intensely anti-modern in its guiding assumptions. We must not forget that at the Diet of Worms Luther declared his conscience to be captive to the Word of God,[7] implying that this captor compelled him to take the stand he did. Luther claimed that the Word was the agent of his protest, not his own will, conscience, or intellect. Luther's sense of agency—his sense of who or what enables and moves a person to think, speak, and act—was decidedly anti-modern. This anti-modern sense of agency provides important counterpoint and correction to the modern notions of selfhood that predominate in much of Western Christianity today. But important questions have also been raised of late about Luther's understanding of human personhood—that is, his theological anthropology[8]—and these questions must also be faced as we consider how Luther's thought may benefit the development of Christian identity in the present.

The Adam-Self[9]

The radical nature of Luther's theological anthropology may be seen already in his earliest lectures on the Psalms (1513–1515), which took place several years before his appearance at the Diet of Worms. Humility is a central theme in these lectures, so much so that some Luther scholars have described his early theology as Humility Theology.[10] According to Luther, in order to be justified, human beings have to "justify God,"[11] that is, they have to agree with the Word's verdict on them and come to see themselves as "vile and nothing, abominable

5. See Charles Taylor, *Sources of the Self: The Making of the Modern Identity* (Cambridge: Harvard University Press, 1989), esp. part 2.

6. See Brad S. Gregory, *The Unintended Reformation: How a Religious Society Secularized Society* (Cambridge: The Belknap Press of Harvard University Press, 2012).

7. WA 7:838.7; *LW* 32:112.

8. For a recent treatment of Luther's theological anthropology, see Notger Slenczka, "Luther's Anthropology," in *The Oxford Handbook of Martin Luther's Theology*, ed. Robert Kolb, Irene Dingel, and L'ubomír Batka (New York: Oxford University Press, 2014), 212–32.

9. Portions of this section draw on Ronald K. Rittgers, *The Reformation of Suffering: Pastoral Theology and Lay Piety in Late Medieval and Early Modern Germany* (New York and Oxford: Oxford University Press, 2012), 87–102.

10. See Martin Brecht, *Martin Luther: His Road to Reformation, 1483–1521*, trans. James L. Schaaf (Philadelphia: Fortress, 1985), 198, 221.

11. WA 55/2:24.7–8; *LW* 10:27. See also WA 55/2:272.105; *LW* 10:238.

and damnable" before the righteous God, the mark of true humility.[12] Luther speaks of the sinner's need to judge and condemn himself (*accusatio sui*), that is, to become truly contrite. When commenting on this self-judgment or contrition, Luther asserts,

> Therefore as long as we do not condemn, excommunicate, and loathe ourselves before God, so long we do not "rise" [cf. Ps 1:5] and are justified . . . There will not be, nor arise in us, the righteousness of God, unless our own righteousness falls and perishes utterly. We do not rise unless we who are standing badly have first fallen. Thus altogether the being, holiness, truth, goodness, life of God, etc., are not in us, unless in the presence of God we first become nothing, profane, lying, evil, dead. Otherwise the righteousness of God would be mocked, and Christ would have died in vain.[13]

Eschewing the more optimistic theological anthropology of much late medieval soteriology, Luther argued throughout these early Psalms lectures that human beings, owing to their utter sinfulness, could contribute nothing to their salvation, save humility.[14] He also maintained in these lectures that the goal of human existence is to be inhabited by God—to have God at the center of one's being. The purpose of humility and contrition is to prepare the way for forgiveness and divine indwelling.

Luther again sounded the message of humility in his *Lectures on Romans* (1515–1516). "The chief purpose of this letter," Luther writes, "is to break down, to pluck up, and to destroy all wisdom and righteousness of the flesh."[15] Elsewhere in these lectures he asserts that "the whole task of the apostle and his Lord is to humiliate the proud and to bring them to a realization of this condition, and teach them that they need grace, to destroy their own righteousness so that in humility they will seek Christ and confess that they are sinners and thus receive grace and be saved."[16] Faith, which emerges as a dominant concern in

12. WA 55/2:438.133–35; *LW* 10:404.

13. WA 55/2:36.17–22; *LW* 10:33–34.

14. There has been an enormous debate about the salvific value of humility in Luther's early theology. Some have seen the emphasis on humility as a Catholic holdover that the mature Luther eventually rejected, while others have seen it as a consistent emphasis throughout Luther's career. Humility does seem to be salvific in Luther's early lectures, that is, it does seem that a human being is able and obliged to produce humility in response to the Word in order to prepare the way for salvific grace. In Luther's later works, humility is more the result of grace, although it remains very important. For a recent discussion of the place of humility in Luther's soteriology, see Rittgers, *Reformation of Suffering*, chaps. 3 and 4.

15. WA 56:157.1–2; *LW* 25:135.

16. WA 56:207.7–11; *LW* 25:191–92.

these lectures, is not simply trust in God; it is also a confession and acceptance of one's utter nothingness before God. Faith entails the death of the sinful self and of its endless attempts at self-justification.[17]

It is important to understand that in these early lectures Luther was not simply saying that human beings must acknowledge that they are sinners and realize that they cannot save themselves through their own efforts—every late medieval theologian said this; Luther was saying much more. As the defining features of his new evangelical theology gradually emerged, it soon became clear that his theological anthropology was far more radical than any such theology that preceded it. We must avoid viewing Luther as a complete theological maverick, for he was shaped in significant ways by the medieval tradition, but there is still something new and revolutionary about his theology of human beings. This fact became especially clear at the Heidelberg Disputation (1518).

In the theses that Luther prepared for this meeting of the Augustinian general chapter, he claimed that the will of fallen human beings is completely enslaved to sin and therefore unable to contribute anything to salvation, save rebellion against God, something the late Augustine had also said.[18] But Luther went beyond Augustine when he asserted that even the prelapsarian human will had only a "passive capacity" (subiectiva potentia) to do good.[19] Even in Eden the human will had to be acted upon by God if it was to choose the good. According to Luther, human beings have never had free will, in the sense of being able to choose freely and of our own accord between good and evil. Human beings have a will, but it has never been free, not even in Eden; it has always been moved and enabled to act by an external force, God or Satan. Luther argues that pride prevents fallen human beings from acknowledging both humanity's original dependence on God along with humanity's original sin and its dire effects. Therefore, God has taken extreme measures to crush human pride, revealing himself in the last place fallen human beings would expect to find him: the cross. At the Heidelberg Disputation, Luther insisted that human beings must be annihilated through the cross,[20] that is, human beings must be persuaded ever afresh of their utter intellectual and moral impotence in spiritual matters. This annihilation, which takes place through suffering and the condemnation of the law, enables human beings to become "Christ's action and instrument" (Christi operatio seu instrumentum).[21]

17. WA 56:419.11–420.26; LW 25:411.
18. See theses 12–18, WA 1:354.3–16; StA 1:214.23–215.9; LW 31:40. StA = Hans Ulrich Delius, ed., Martin Luther Studienausgabe, 6 vols. (Berlin: Evangelische Verlagsanstalt, 1979–c.1999).
19. See thesis 15, WA 1:360.13–23; StA 1:206.1–11; LW 31:49–50.
20. WA 1:363.34; StA 1:210.15; LW 31:55.
21. WA 1:364.15–16; StA 1:211.4; LW 31:56.

Here it is important to stress the influence of medieval German mysticism on Luther's theological anthropology.[22] In 1518, the same year he participated in the Heidelberg Disputation, Luther published an edition of *A German Theology* (*Eyn Deutsch Theologia*), a fourteenth-century anonymous work of mysticism that he saw as a summary of the theology of Johannes Tauler, a mystic who had a strong influence on him.[23] As Luther states in his preface to the work, "To boast with my old fool [i.e., the apostle Paul], no book except the Bible and St. Augustine has come to my attention from which I have learned more about God, Christ, man, and all things."[24] The subtitle he appended to *A German Theology* indicates what Luther found so valuable in the work: "The Right Understanding as to What Adam and Christ Mean and How Adam Must Die Within Us and Christ Rise."[25] Luther was drawn to the work's theological anthropology.

The author of *A German Theology* argues throughout that the only way to reach union with God is by putting to death the self, the old Adam, with all of its egotism, self-preoccupation, and unholy external attachments: "Man must put aside all 'self-dom' [*selbheit*] and concern with the 'Self' (*icheit*) so that he does not look out for himself at all, indeed as though he did not exist."[26] Only then will Christ take up residence within him. Christ himself is the model of this complete purging of all self-referentiality and of utter surrender to God: "Christ's humanity stood wholly free from the self, more than with any other human. Christ's humanity was nothing but a house or a habitation for God [*ein hauß oder eyn wonung gottes*]."[27] In Christ there was no "self-dom" or "I-dom," that is, he laid no claim to anything he was or had or did as his own; everything was God's and God was everything. Thus, there was no separation between Christ's humanity and God. As the author of *A German Theology* puts it, in a divinized person "God Himself becomes the person in such a fashion that there is nothing that is not God or things of God and also so that there is nothing left in man of which he considers himself to be the proprietor."[28] At the end of

22. For a recent treatment of Luther's complicated relationship with medieval mysticism, see Rittgers, *Reformation of Suffering*, 97–100.

23. Ibid., Luther had already published an incomplete edition of the work in 1516. The title, *A German Theology*, is Luther's. Tauler was not the author of the work.

24. WA 1:378.21–23; *LW* 31:75.

25. Hermann Mandel, ed., *Theologia Deutsch* (Leipzig: A. Deichtert'sche Verlagsbuchh. Nachf.—Georg Böhme, 1908), pt. 2; Bengt Hoffman, trans., *The Theologia Germanica of Martin Luther* (Mahwah, NJ: Paulist Press, 1980), 43.

26. Mandel, *Theologia Deutsch*, 31; Hoffman, *Theologia Germanica of Martin Luther*, 76.

27. Mandel, *Theologia Deutsch*, 32; Hoffman, *Theologia Germanica of Martin Luther*, 77.

28. Mandel, *Theologia Deutsch*, 100–101; Hoffman, *Theologia Germanica of Martin Luther*, 147.

the work the author summarizes, "If you can come to the point where you are to God what your hand is to you, be content."[29]

Luther did not approve of everything in *A German Theology*, especially its Neoplatonism, but he was clearly sympathetic to its theological anthropology. We have seen him use the language of *A German Theology* when he calls for the annihilation of the self and when he says that the goal for the Christian is to become a habitation and instrument of God. Luther would continue to promote this self-less theological anthropology after the Diet of Worms. In a 1522 sermon on Luke 2, he refers to the humanity of Christ as "an instrument or house of divinity" (*eyn handgetzeug und hauß der gottheyt*).[30] In *The Bondage of the Will* (1525), Luther asserts that the whole purpose of human existence is to be "a vessel for [God's] honor and glory."[31] God created human beings apart from all human help so "that He might work in us and we might cooperate with Him." Luther says the same is true of God's intention in re-creating human beings through Christ.[32] Here, as in *A German Theology*, cooperation simply means coworking with God in the sense that a tool "works with" the hand of the human being who wields it.[33] Ultimate agency is attributed to God in both temporal and spiritual matters. While late medieval German mystics such as Tauler and the author of *A German Theology* stressed human passivity, they still allowed for minimal human agency in preparing the way for union with God, and they also believed that there was a higher or deeper part of the soul—the *grunt*—that was ontologically connected to God and that therefore longed for return to God. Luther rejected all of this.[34] (He also rejected medieval Habitus theology, which assumes the presence of a human subject into whom habits of virtue can be divinely infused as gifts of grace.)

Luther's unprecedented emphasis on human nothingness was motivated not only by his deep sense of human sinfulness but also by his view of God. In *The Seven Penitential Psalms* (1517), when commenting on Vulgate Psalm 37:22 [38:21]—"Do not forsake me, O Lord! O my God, be not far from me!"—Luther writes, "It is God's nature to make something out of nothing; hence one who is not yet nothing [*darumb wer noch nit nichts ist*], out of him God cannot make anything." The consistent emphasis in Luther's early works on the need for human beings to become nothing before God was directly informed by

---

29. Mandel, *Theologia Deutsch*, 102; Hoffman, *Theologia Germanica of Martin Luther*, 149.

30. WA 10/I/1:447.11–15.

31. WA 18:787.14; *LW* 33:295.

32. WA 18:54.1–17; *LW* 33:242–43.

33. See *Archiv zur Weimarer Ausgabe der Werke Martin Luthers, Operationes in Psalmos, 1519–1521*, pt. 2, ed. Gerhard Hammer und Manfred Biersack (Cologne: Böhlau, 1981), 2:320.25–321.5.

34. See Rittgers, *Reformation of Suffering*, 99.

this conviction about the nature of God as a Being who always creates (and re-creates) *ex nihilo*. Luther continues, "Therefore God accepts only the forsaken, cures only the sick, gives sight only to the blind, restores life only to the dead, sanctifies only the sinners, gives wisdom only to the unwise. In short, He has mercy only on those who are wretched, and gives grace only to those who are not in grace." According to Luther, the only way to become God's "material" (*materien*) is to become *nichts*.[35]

The reason Luther advocated this self-annihilation is related to another essential characteristic of deity that he had already mentioned in his early lectures on the Psalms: divine self-sufficiency. As Luther explained in his lecture on Vulgate Psalm 117 [118],

> To every judgment of reason it is characteristic of divinity and fitting to be self-sufficient, to need nothing, and to impart benefits to others *gratis*. Therefore He also confounded and reproved all our righteousness, all good-ness, all our wisdom altogether, and He wants us to acknowledge Him to be the true God and to confess ourselves to be unrighteous, evil, and foolish in everything that we did not receive from and [or] do not acknowledge having received from Him.[36]

Thus, God's action of reducing sinners to nothing flowed logically and necessarily from his very nature as God, the self-sufficient divine Giver. It did not flow from some misanthropic impulse; on this point Luther is emphatic, both in the early Psalm lectures and in *The Seven Penitential Psalms*. Luther went on in the former work to address this issue squarely.

> Is He, then, good and fair in that He confounds and reproves and tramples upon all that is ours and offers and establishes only His own? He is the very best, indeed, because, as I have said, in this He proves Himself to be the true God, who wants to give His gifts to us and to be our God, to impart benefits to us, to want us for Himself, and not to take what is ours, not to have us as His benefactors and as gods, and not to have need of us. To impart benefits to another is divine. But He cannot be our God and give His goods to us unless He first teaches that He does not want our things and that our things are nothing before Him, as Isa 1:11ff. tells us, so that, thus humbled, we might become capable and desirous of what is His. . . . If He would take anything of ours and not utterly repudiate it, then He would not be the true God nor

---

35. WA 1:183.30–184.10; *LW* 14:163.
36. WA 55/2:888.15–889.21; *LW* 11:410.

good alone, because we, too, would contend with Him in benefits. But now He wants us to do nothing but receive and Himself to do nothing but give and thus be the true God.[37]

For Luther, human beings had to learn that to seek to contribute anything to their salvation was fundamentally to fail to understand who God was, the Creator, and who human beings were, creatures.[38] The central sin of the Adam-self was to reject this distinction and to seek to be the Creator to itself and others. The Adam-self was not free; it was in complete bondage to sin, a position that sits rather awkwardly with the assumptions and assertions of personal autonomy and agency that are so crucial to many modern notions of selfhood, to say the least.[39]

The Christ-Self

As we have seen, the putting to death of the Adam-self is only part of Luther's theological anthropology; there is also the rising of the Christ-self. Already in the early Psalm lectures Luther refers to the "new man" who is a "man of grace."[40] In *Two Kinds of Righteousness* (1519), he speaks of a "spiritual man, whose very existence depends on faith in Christ,"[41] something he also says in *The Freedom of the Christian* (1520).[42] While the law and suffering annihilate the old man, faith creates and receives the new man as a gift of grace. According to Luther, there is a new anthropological entity in a Christian. Who is this new person?

In *Against Latomus* (1521), Luther writes the following with respect to the "I" in Romans 7:17 who longs to do the good but who commits evil owing to the strength of the sinful nature:

> Who is this "I" [*ego*] who now does not do what it has just been said to do? It is the "I" [*ego*] which I spiritually am, because according to this "I" [*ego*], I am now looked at in terms of the grace which does not allow me to be looked at

37. WA 55/2:889.24–31 and 33–36; *LW* 11:410–11.

38. See WA 55/2:889.39–40; *LW* 11:411.

39. There are certainly modern understandings of selfhood that do not stress human autonomy. Such understandings emphasize instead human bondage to psychological, societal, or genetic forces and thus question how free modern human beings truly are. I am aware of these alternative modern anthropologies but do not deal with them in this short essay.

40. WA 3:182.24–25; *LW* 10:154.

41. WA 2:147.8–9; *LW* 31:300.

42. WA 7:50.14–15, 51.32; *LW* 31:344, 347.

in terms of the sin which makes me carnal. Everything is washed away, and now there is a self [*ego*] different from the one before grace, for that one was evaluated in terms of sin as wholly carnal.[43]

Based on this passage alone, it is tempting to conclude that for Luther the new person exists only in the mind or eyes of God: there is nothing new in the sinner, only in God's view or evaluation of him. But we should resist this reading.

In the *Lectures on Galatians* (1531/1535), when commenting on Galatians 2:20—"Nevertheless, I live; yet not I, but Christ lives in me"—Luther further elaborates on the new self:

> When he says: "Nevertheless, I live," this sounds rather personal, as though Paul were speaking of his own person. Therefore he quickly corrects it and says: "Yet not I." That is, "I do not live in my own person now, but Christ lives in me." The person does indeed live, but not in itself or for its own person. But who is this "I" [*ego*] of whom he says: "Yet not I"? It is the one that has the Law and is obliged to do works, the one that is a person separate from Christ. This "I" [*ego*] Paul rejects; for "I" [*ego*], as a person distinct from Christ, belongs to death and hell. This is why he says: "Not I, but Christ lives in me." Christ is my "form," which adorns my faith as color or light adorns a wall. (This fact has to be expounded in this crude way, for there is no spiritual way for us to grasp the idea that Christ clings and dwells in us as closely and intimately as light or whiteness clings to a wall.) "Christ," he says, "is fixed and cemented to me and abides in me. The life that I now live, He lives in me. Indeed, Christ Himself is the life that I now live. In this way, therefore, Christ and I are one."[44]

There is a new spiritual "I" here, but it has no existence apart from its vital union with the living Christ, who, as Luther makes clear a little earlier in these lectures, is himself the Christian's indwelling righteousness.[45] Thus, the Christian has two "I's" or two selves, a flesh-I and a Christ-I, but the Christ-I is the Christian's truest or best self.

It is striking how reluctant Luther is to speak of the new self apart from Christ; in fact, he refuses to do so. Again, the new self has no existence apart from union with Christ; it is a Christ-I or a Christ-self. Luther drives this point home when he imagines a malicious interlocutor challenging Paul's statement

43. WA 8:120.36–42; *LW* 32:248.
44. WA 40/1:283b.19–32; *LW* 26:167.
45. WA 40/1:282b.16–18; *LW* 26:166.

that he is dead and no longer lives, for Paul clearly is alive and able to write and speak. Luther has Paul reply, "I do indeed live; and yet not I live, but Christ lives in me. There is a double life [*duplex vita*]:[46] my own, which is natural or animate; and an alien [*aliena*] life, that of Christ in me. So far as my animate life is concerned, I am dead and am now living an alien life. I am not living as Paul now, for Paul is dead." "Who then is living?" the interlocutor asks. "The Christian [*Christianus*]," Paul responds. Luther continues, "Paul, living in himself, is utterly dead through the Law but living in Christ, or rather with Christ living in him, he lives an alien life. Christ is speaking, acting, and performing all actions in him; these belong not to the Paul-life, but to the Christ-life."[47] As we have seen, the Christian is to function as a tool or instrument that God can use to accomplish his purposes through Christ in the world; the Christian is a channel or vessel through which divine grace flows to others. As the flesh-I was in bondage to sin and Satan, the Christ-I is joyfully enslaved to grace and Christ; it is He who provides its very animation and direction. Luther can even claim that the teaching and preaching he undertakes in the flesh do not arise from the flesh but "are given and revealed directly from heaven."[48]

Thus, even with respect to the new man (or woman) in Christ, there is very little human agency in Luther's theological anthropology, and because such agency is so central to many modern notions of selfhood, one must also say that there is very little sense of a modern self, certainly not in the spiritual realm.[49] The Christian is not a mere puppet, for he is alive and endowed with all human faculties, including a will. But Christ is the one who animates and moves these faculties. In *The Freedom of the Christian*, Luther uses the language of intoxication to express how the soul of the Christian is completely possessed by Christ and the divine promises of salvation in his name.[50] Luther also uses marital imagery in both *The Freedom of the Christian* and the *Lectures on Galatians* to convey how close the union is between Christ and the Christian and how complete the exchange of possessions is between them.[51]

46. In his *Lectures on Genesis* (1535–1545), Luther asserts that already in Eden Adam had a double life, but the spiritual one was not yet fully revealed (WA 42:43b.7; *LW* 1:57). Thus, it seems that one effect of justification is to restore or fully reveal the spiritual life that Adam had in potential form but lost through sin and therefore never enjoyed.

47. WA 40/I:287b.24; *LW* 26:170.

48. WA 40/I:289b.26–27; *LW* 26:171.

49. Luther does seem to allow for limited human agency in the temporal realm. Even fallen human beings possess a certain volitional capacity that they employ in purely mundane matters that are not related to salvation, although Luther would say that God is still the ultimate agent in these mundane decisions. See WA 18:648.4–11; *LW* 33:70.

50. WA 7:53.18; *LW* 31:349.

51. *LW* 26:168–69; WA 7:54.31–55.6; *LW* 31:351.

Here it is important to observe that Luther interpreted Christ's self-emptying (Phil 2:5–11) not as a pre-incarnate occurrence within the Godhead but as a daily self-emptying undertaken by the incarnate Christ for the good of the world.[52] The Christian, animated and enabled by the indwelling Christ, was to do the same. The Christian life was to be a kenotic life of continual self-emptying for others.[53] The focus of the Christian life was always to be upward to God by faith and outward to the neighbor in love; it was never to be inward in self-scrutiny or self-preoccupation.[54] One cannot imagine a more anti-modern anthropology than Luther's, whatever the long-term, unintended consequences of his stand against Roman Christianity might have been for the development of modern selfhood.

Too Self-less?

Luther's radically kenotic theological anthropology has the great virtue of taking the apostle Paul's own kenotic language very seriously (and literally). The Wittenberg reformer thus offers an important and refreshing corrective to modern notions of selfhood that place such great emphasis on human agency, individuality, and autonomy, and which have a very shallow sense of human sin and self-centeredness. Luther is surely correct in his assertion that the highest form of human selfhood is to be realized through union with Christ, and that this union, which is a gift of pure grace from our generous God, entails the death of the sinful self and the birth and growth of the Christ-self at the center of a human being. Luther is surely right in his insistence that the desire to be and have a self apart from such union with God is deeply sinful. One can also admire his emphasis on the Christ-self as a conduit of divine grace for the neighbor and the healthy decentering of self that it can entail. All of this is of great value for considerations of Christian identity today.

But we should note that a number of important questions have been raised about Luther's theological anthropology, most of which stem from the concern that it is too self-less and therefore too problematic for use in the development of Christian identity in the present. One source of such questions has been the scholarship on Luther's Christology.[55] Owing to the Wittenberg reform-

---

52. See Paul Althaus, *The Theology of Martin Luther*, trans. Robert C. Schultz (Philadelphia: Fortress, 1966), 194.

53. See WA 7:64.38–66.5; *LW* 31:365–67.

54. WA 7:69.12–18; *LW* 31:371.

55. For a recent treatment of Luther's Christology, see Matthieu Arnold, "Luther on Christ's Person and Work," in *The Oxford Handbook of Martin Luther's Theology*, ed. Robert Kolb, Irene Dingel, and L'ubomír Batka (New York: Oxford University Press, 2014), 274–93.

er's emphasis on the *Alleinwirksamheit Gottes* (i.e., the all-sufficiency and sole agency of God the Father) in all things, including Christ's work on the cross, the Catholic theologian Yves Congar once opined, "In our view, the development of his thought scarcely seems to allow of a positive role proper to the humanity of Christ." According to Congar, Luther taught that Christ's humanity was simply the "theatre" for the soteriological drama in which God the Father was the sole Actor; Christ's humanity was utterly passive in this drama and thus seems to have been something less than fully human.[56] Lutheran theologians have expressed additional concerns. Bernhard Lohse has worried that Luther "might have been in danger of abbreviating Christ's human nature," because of his allegedly radical reading of the *enhypostasis* doctrine, which in Luther's hands came to mean that Christ's human nature had no viability of its own apart from its union with the divine.[57]

Such concerns about Luther's Christology, especially his treatment of Christ's humanity and the consequences of this view for his understanding of human personhood as such, arise from the fear that his theology is not fully Chalcedonian. The Definition of Chalcedon asserts that Christ was "perfect in human-ness" and also "truly human." Although Luther did affirm the full and complete humanity of Christ,[58] his theology has still seemed to some to fall short of the Chalcedonian mark—his Christ has seemed to lack something that is vital to human nature. There have been attempts to allay or refute such concerns,[59] and Congar has even retracted much of his criticism,[60] but the debate about the orthodoxy of Luther's Christology and its implications for his theological anthropology continues today.

The other key source of questions about Luther's theological anthropology has been modern feminism. Theologian Daphne Hampson has charged Luther with denying any real sense of selfhood to human beings because of his insistence that the self is constituted through ongoing dependence on God, which in her mind necessarily leads to the disempowerment of self. Hampson

56. Yves Congar, "Considerations and Reflections on the Christology of Luther," in *Dialogue between Christians: Catholic Contributions to Ecumenism*, trans. Philip Loretz (Westminster, MD: Newman Press, 1966), 382–84 (quotation on 382).

57. Bernhard Lohse, *Martin Luther's Theology: Its Historical and Systematic Development*, trans. and ed. Roy A. Harrisville (Minneapolis: Fortress, 1999), 229.

58. See WA 39/2:93.2; *LW* 37:362.

59. See Marc Lienhard, *Luther: Witness to Jesus Christ: Stages and Themes of the Reformer's Christology*, trans. Edwin H. Robertson (Minneapolis: Augsburg, 1982).

60. See Yves Congar, "Nouveaux regards sur la christologie de Luther," *Revue des Sciences philosophiques et théologiques* 62 (1982): 180–97. See the brief discussion of this article in Franz Posset, *Luther's Catholic Christology according to His Johannine Lectures of 1527* (Milwaukee, WI: Northwestern Publishing House, 1988), 18.

wants a self that is secure in itself, having its center in itself, that can grow in relationship with other selves. She is especially critical of Luther's call for self-annihilation, which she finds to be utterly antifeminist. According to Hampson, patriarchal society has denied women selfhood for centuries; therefore Luther's message of self-abnegation is diametrically opposed to the feminist interest in empowerment of women's selves. Hampson believes that Christianity, owing to its inherent patriarchalism, is incompatible with feminism, and she asserts that Lutheranism is an especially pernicious expression of this misogynist religion.[61]

Other feminists have sought to redeem Luther for modern feminist usage. Mary Gaebler has argued that from the early 1520s on Luther allowed for human agency both in the temporal sphere and in the process of sanctification, a process that she maintains was far more important to his theology than most scholars have appreciated. God is still the ground of the self and the sole agent in justification, according to Gaebler, and God even wills in, with, and under the human will, but she insists that the self exercises real agency as it cooperates with the Holy Spirit in the life of regeneration, which includes appropriate self-love and myriad real decisions to follow the way of Christ (or not).[62] There are problems with Gaebler's work, for it is difficult to find the kind of human agency in Luther's theology that she posits, but her scholarship demonstrates that the debate about the "orthodoxy" of Luther's theological anthropology from the feminist point of view also continues today.

As is true of so much in Luther, the incisive, radical, and, in many cases, salutary critiques and correctives that he offers the Christian tradition can create new problems and challenges that require their own critiques and correctives. Of course, Luther would not have conceded the need for any revision to his theology, for he was convinced that God had revealed it to him via the Word, therefore it was pure and sound. But it seems clear enough that there was more of the man Martin Luther in this theology than he was either willing or able to see. His theological anthropology did not really allow or require such self-awareness, for it excludes the possibility of a human contribution to the discernment or development of theological truth, just as his soteriology excludes the possibility of a human contribution to salvation. Luther, the antimodern, was a monergist in both his anthropology and his soteriology.[63]

---

61. Daphne Hampson, "Luther on the Self: A Feminist Critique," *Word and World* 8, no. 4 (1988): 334–42.

62. Mary Gaebler, *The Courage of Faith: Martin Luther and the Theonomous Self* (Minneapolis: Fortress, 2013).

63. I wish to thank David Luy of Trinity Evangelical Divinity School for commenting on an earlier draft of this chapter.

Chapter 25

John Calvin: Knowing the Self in God's Presence

Julie Canlis

If Luther was a man caught "between God and the devil,"[1] then Calvin was a man caught between God and a world on fire. As a second-generation reformer, Calvin was not hammering out a personal theology of justification—of the God *pro me*—to ease the scrupled consciences of those around him. Calvin was born into a *Europa afflicta*[2] where fear was palpable at every turn. "We have seen battles for such a long time. There is no end to them . . . they are killing an infinite number of people. . . . One sees poor people dead among the bushes, and others who are left have to endure hunger and thirst, heat and cold."[3] Calvin's task was to hammer out a theology of the God *pro nobis* for those whom God appeared to have abandoned. They had followed God into a promised land that flowed, not with milk and honey, but with plague, war, persecution, displacement, and terror. When Calvin preached, he was articulating the fears of many in his congregation, "Why should I continue believing? What is there left for which I may still hope? Where can I still flee?"[4]

When one hears Calvin's answer to this rhetorical question, we must not envision him tucked safely away in his study on the *rue de Chanoines*, but on the deck of the *Titanic*. Calvin felt himself to be daily, hourly on the *Titanic*.

---

1. This is a reference to Heiko Oberman's landmark intellectual biography of Luther: *Luther: Man between God and the Devil* (New Haven: Yale University Press, 1989).

2. "Europe is a mess!" (translation by Heiko Oberman), quotation taken from Calvin's *Commentary* on Isaiah 9:10. See Oberman's "*Europa Afflicta*," in *John Calvin and the Reformation of the Refugees* [hereafter: *Refugees*] (Geneva: Droz, 2009), 187.

3. Calvin's sermon on 2 Samuel 2, as quoted in Bruce Gordon, *Calvin* (New Haven: Yale University Press, 2009), 292.

4. Calvin's sermon on Psalm 116:11, as quoted in Herman Selderhuis, *Calvin's Theology of the Psalms* (Grand Rapids: Baker Academic, 2007), 259.

Reading Calvin, therefore, has made some seasick. One minute one is in the trough of the wave; the next one has been tossed to its crest. One minute the comfort of providence; the next the abyss of despondency. Perhaps this is why the Psalms were such a comfort for Calvin, for their realism reflected Calvin's own storms. Identifying with Psalm 30, he wrote, "Our condition in this world, I confess, involves us in such wretchedness, and we are harassed by such a variety of afflictions, that scarcely a day passes without some trouble or grief. Moreover amid so many uncertain events, we cannot be otherwise than full of daily anxiety and fear. Whithersoever men turn themselves, a labyrinth of evils surrounds them."[5] The theology of this Reformer cannot be lifted off of the decks of his Titanic—personal or otherwise. His pulpit was his mast, enabling him to give direction and comfort to a troubled congregation in even more troubled times. From this height, Calvin preached to the refugees in his congregation who more than doubled the population of Geneva during Calvin's stay. But perhaps most of all, Calvin preached to one French refugee in particular: himself.

Why was this particular man, who confessed to being "awkward and shy," heard throughout Europe? In the midst of crisis, Calvin, a refugee himself, became a father to refugees: "Yet for the children of God, who know that they are the heirs of this world, it is not so difficult to be banished. It is in fact even good for them, so that through such an experience they can train themselves in being strangers on this earth."[6] He heeded the literal call of Abraham to "leave your country." He heeded the call of Moses to "lead my people" out of oppression. And finally, over the rest of his life, he followed that other famous biblical refugee—David—through his own interior shadowlands. For biographers, Calvin has proved elusive over the years—*De me non libenter loquor*[7]—but this too is a part of understanding him and his "oblique modes of communication."[8] In this skeletal biography of Calvin, we will follow Calvin the fugitive through his exodus out from the innocence of Eden, out from the security of Rome, and finally out from the confessional. Through this interior and exterior exodus, Calvin's existential and societal fear is transformed into a deepened fear of the Lord.

5. Calvin's *Commentary* on Psalm 30:5. Unless otherwise noted, I have used the 1846 Calvin Translation Society edition for *Calvin's Commentaries,* 46 vols. (reprint; Grand Rapids: Baker, 1974).

6. 1554 Letter to the English refugees in Zurich, as translated by Herman Selderhuis, *A Pilgrim's Life* (Downers Grove, IL: InterVarsity Press, 2009), 83.

7. "I am unwilling to speak of myself," wrote Calvin in his 1539 Letter to Cardinal Sadoleto. See John C. Olin, ed., *A Reformation Debate: Sadoleto's Letter to the Genevans and Calvin's Reply* (New York: Harper, 1966), 59.

8. William Bouwsma, *John Calvin: A Sixteenth-Century Portrait* (New York: Oxford University Press, 1988), 5.

Youth

Calvin's childhood lacks the normal signs of stability and love that give children confidence.[9] His mother died when he was six, long enough for him to have absorbed some of her genuine piety and devotion, but not long enough to protect him from expecting disappointment of life. Calvin seems well aware of this tendency in children, remarking that "those who have been accustomed to suffering from their childhood become insensible to it . . . so that we cease to think of it, or to regard it as anything unusual."[10] One wonders whether Calvin is speaking from experience here, for even as an adult his tendency was to protect himself from too much joy.[11] Calvin's image-conscious father seems to have little interest in Calvin himself, but in what he could make *of* Calvin (which may have been alright with Calvin, who perhaps by this time had decided that what he wanted didn't matter much). Maneuvering his church connections to procure religious incomes for his son, he sent a fourteen-year-old Calvin off to Paris to become a priest. When Calvin had nearly finished his studies, his father did an about-face and decided law to be the more lucrative profession. He uprooted Calvin from Paris and sent him to Orleans. Within a year, Calvin's father was excommunicated, perhaps giving us a glimpse of the instability of the man who had raised him. Regardless, when Calvin's father died a few years later, Calvin had very little to say about it.[12] His letter to a friend mentions the death of his sole surviving parent in passing, but for the most part, the letter is preoccupied with Calvin's big news—his new book. This brings us to Calvin and youthful ambition.

9. The three biographies that I have followed have been that of Herman Selderhuis (2009), Bruce Gordon (2009), and William Bouwsma (1988). While Bouwsma's might be seen as too radical, I follow Oberman in my appreciation of it as a "significant new departure in the search for the person behind the system, recovering the man of flesh and blood, exposed to a complex bundle of contradictory psychological impulses" (Oberman, *Refugees*, 51). Gordon brings us the best of contemporary scholarship in the wake of Bouwsma; Selderhuis provides an equally compelling companion, and draws solely upon Calvin's letters for a retelling of the story.

10. Calvin's *Commentary* on Psalm 42:4.

11. Selderhuis draws our attention to a letter from Calvin to Farel. Becoming gravely ill within a fortnight of marriage, Calvin "immediately attributed this to God ensuring that no one would take too much delight in something as beautiful as marriage" (Selderhuis, *Pilgrim*, 169). Calvin's theology of marriage was remarkably positive and profound—revealing that his theology and his emotional life were not always in synch.

12. For Calvin's letter to Nicolas Duchemin, see Bruce Gordon's comments (*Calvin*, 31). Gordon notes that Calvin would need the Psalms to learn a vocabulary for his rich emotional life.

Although Calvin refers to himself at that awkward period of life as "timid,"[13] an observant school teacher today might diagnose "low self-esteem." And how do smart boys with low self-esteem get noticed? In grade school they might play the role of tattletale (as at the Collège de Montaigu, where Calvin was known as *accusativus*—not exactly a term of endearment). Then their tactics move underground and they make it their goal to become noticed as the smart boy—the smart boy not afraid to have all the answers, perhaps even willing to challenge the reigning humanist giants, for the sake of a dual over a gnat.[14] Such was Calvin's commentary on the great stoic Seneca at the age of 22, which won him no friends, influenced no people, and put him into debt.

Calvin's failed attempt to make it into the humanist inner circle of Paris coincides roughly with the time of his conversion (1532). And perhaps this is no accident. The gravitational pull of Seneca reflects both societal and personal anxiety in Calvin. It is reflective of a law student living in turbulent times and his desire to clarify issues of legitimate power. It is also reflective of a youth's naïve attempt to deal with the "abyss" that he sensed deep within.[15] Although many have looked to Seneca as proof of stoic *apatheia* in Calvin's emotional life, this is a misstep. It more likely points to its *absence*. But the problem is that *apatheia* proved to be a child's toy against Calvin's deep angst.

After his "unexpected" conversion around the age of twenty-three, Calvin becomes a man on the run. Finding himself on the side of the reform, he discovered himself to be on the wrong side of the king. Calvin's teenage years in Paris had taught him that torture and death by burning were the lot of those who defied the Sorbonne.[16] Even at the end of his life, Calvin can still tap into the strength of this anxiety: "I wanted to die to be rid of those fears."[17] And so, Calvin fled east. This experience of becoming a refugee was so definitive that even when he finally received citizenship many years later, he still would see himself as a permanent sojourner—*peregrinus*.[18]

Calvin's early anxiety must be seen as both a personal and a public phe-

---

13. Calvin's "Preface," in the *Commentary* on Psalms (French edition: *un peu sauvage et honteux*).

14. For Calvin's habit of scoring exegetical points against his elders, see Selderhuis, *Pilgrim*, 23.

15. Bouwsma is the first to see this in Calvin and trace Calvin's language of the abyss, though Oberman develops it with a more even-handed and biblical-historical treatment (Oberman, *"Initia Calvini,"* in *Refugees*, 107–13).

16. The *Affair des Placards* can only be understood when it is seen as nearing the high point of a crescendo of persecution that began in 1525, when the Sorbonne's Faculty of Theology pressured Parlement to mount a campaign against "lutheranism."

17. Oberman draws our attention to Calvin's sermon on July 1, 1562, where, dealing with 2 Samuel 5:12-17, Calvin reflects back on this season of terror: "j'ay este en ces déstresses là, que i'eusse voulu ester quasi mort, pour oster ces angoisses." See Oberman, *"Initia Calvini,"* 113 n. 84.

18. Selderhuis, *Pilgrim*, 146.

nomenon shared by many. His letters and sermons are rife with references to daily life's reign of terror—"our very birth is an entrance into a thousand deaths"[19]—not to mention the Sorbonne's literal reign of terror during Calvin's impressionable teenage years.[20] Calvin has left us with three accounts of his conversion, all of which make reference to anxiety. The first account is sketched in shadowy form in *Psychopannychia* (1534),[21] the second in his Letter to Cardinal Sadoleto (1539), and the third at the end of his life, in his Preface to the Psalms (1557). As we ourselves sojourn through these conversion narratives, we are able to individuate Calvin out of his ideology, for the Calvin of the first edition of the *Institutes* is hardly the Calvin of the last edition twenty-three years later.

Conversion Account I (1534): *Exodus from Eden*

Calvin rarely spoke of his personal narrative, preferring to speak of God and to give God the glory.[22] He opted to stay hidden, tucked away behind the generalities of common experience or of the royal "we." Yet the search is not in vain, for, as Ganoczy remarks, "I am persuaded that the 'I' of Calvin is inseparably tied to his doctrine."[23] Written less than two years after his conversion, Calvin's own portrayal of life without God in his first Christian treatise is spinetingling—not for its graphic horrors of hell or judgment but for its psychology.[24] Terms such as *confounded, crushed,* and *desperate* are part of Calvin's litany of *terrors*[25] that very much reflects the anguish of alienation. Oberman notes that

19. Calvin's *Commentary* on Psalm 71:6.

20. For this, see James Farge, *Orthodoxy and Reform in Early Reformation France* (Leiden: Brill: 1985), 255–68.

21. This has not traditionally been considered a conversion narrative, though I feel the textual clues point to autobiography. *Psychopannychia* means "soul sleep" and was a treatise against those who believed that the soul slept without awareness (of either heaven or hell) after death. I am using the Henry Beveridge version in *Tracts & Treatises in Defense of the Reformed Faith* III (Grand Rapids: Eerdmans, 1958).

22. "For it is not very sound theology to confine a man's thoughts so much to himself, and not set before him, as the prime motive of his existence, zeal to illustrate the glory of God. For we were born first of all for God, and not for ourselves. As all things flowed from him, and subsist in him, so, says Paul (*Rom 11:36*), they ought to be referred to him" (Calvin's Letter to Sadoleto, in *A Reformation Debate*, 58).

23. Alexandre Ganoczy, *The Young Calvin* (Philadelphia: Westminster, 1987), 242.

24. Oberman refers to Calvin's treatment of the *imago* as nothing short of a paradigm shift "from ontology to psychology" ("Pursuit of Happiness," in *Refugees*, 161).

25. Calvin's *Psychopannychia*, 454.

in Calvin's new portrayal of the soul and hell, "we are here far removed from the ontological language of the medieval tradition."[26] Could it be that Calvin's early experience of elemental mistrust enabled him to reinterpret hell as abandonment? Calvin writes,

> Would you know what the death of the soul is?
> It is to be without God—to be abandoned by God, and left to itself.[27]

This, for Calvin, is excruciating judgment. This is God's wrath: it is to be left alone; to experience nothingness; to disappear. This is not gentle oblivion, as theorized by those who believed in "soul sleep." This is the horror of not being known, not being recognized, of disappearing from the sight of the one by whom we most want to be known. Calvin likens this to Adam hearing God's question *Adam, where art thou?* and says that "it is easier to imagine it than to express it—though imagination must fall far short of reality."[28] For those who know this existential experience of "dreadful anger," Calvin says that there are no words, only shared memory and experience of this "death."

Being cast out of Eden is a descent into terror and spiritual alienation.[29] It is a loneliness so profound it is inexpressible. This is in direct contrast to how Calvin portrays existence in the garden—not as a static existence but one of communion and participation.[30] The fall is not just the rupture of relationship, but it is a rupture of *being* and, in particular, being connected. Calvin's earliest version of the *Institutes* (1536), penned just two years later, reflects this profound sense of disintegration. Adam has become "a complete stranger," losing the gifts that "could be held only in God."[31] One sees echoes of this in the way Calvin portrays Adam and Eve, who no longer "experience God as Father," but instead of trust, experience elemental mistrust.[32] We now misinterpret those very things "by which he would draw us to himself."[33] This is the grand inversion.

26. Oberman, "Pursuit of Happiness," in *Refugees*, 162.

27. *Psychopannychia*, 454, my emphasis.

28. Ibid.

29. See chapter 2 of my *Calvin's Ladder* (Grand Rapids: Eerdmans, 2010).

30. "Direct communication with God was the source of life to Adam" (Calvin's *Commentary* on Genesis 3:22). "Man was blessed, not because of his own good actions, but by participation in God" (*Institutes* II.2.1). Unless otherwise noted, all references to Calvin's *Institutes of the Christian Religion* are to the 1559 edition (ed. John T. McNeill, trans. Ford Lewis Battles, 2 vols., LCC 20–21 [Philadelphia: Westminster, 1960]).

31. 1536 *Institutes* I.2.

32. Calvin corrects Augustine's view of sin-as-concupiscence and reorients it toward communion: "Unfaithfulness, then, was the root of the Fall" (*Institutes* II.1.4).

33. Calvin's *Commentary* on Genesis 28:12.

"But who might reach to him? Any one of Adam's children? No, like their father, all of them were terrified at the sight of God."[34] This is the reign of terror—not God's, but our own newly developed terror of God.

Conversion Account II (1539): *Exodus from Rome*

Calvin's first conversion narrative functions as an assessment of humanity's existential fear and alienation since the exodus from Eden. Calvin's second conversion narrative recounts his own journey through these sixteenth-century badlands, and particularly how the church extended—rather than mitigated—this reign of terror. In his letter to Cardinal Sadoleto, Calvin recounts his exodus from the "tyranny" endured in his youth to "safety," and proposes that this is not his unique journey alone:

> I, O Lord, as I had been educated from a boy, always professed the Christian faith . . . but I stumbled at the threshold. I believed [in your redemption] but the redemption I thought of was one whose virtue could never reach me. I anticipated a future resurrection, but hated to think of it, as being an event most dreadful. And this feeling not only had dominion over me in private, but was derived from the doctrine which was then uniformly delivered to all people by their Christian teachers.[35]

Calvin lists the fear-mongering tactics of the priests who portrayed God as a "stern judge and strict avenger of iniquity," whose presence must indeed be "dreadful." Having followed the usual methods for making satisfaction, Calvin reported that he "was still far off from true peace of conscience." Worse, whenever he thought about himself ("descended into myself") or about God ("raised my mind to thee"), "*extreme terror seized me—terror which no expiations nor satisfactions could cure. And the more closely I examined myself, the sharper the stings . . . so that my only solace was to delude myself by obliviousness.*"[36] Next, Calvin reports something very interesting. As the "light broke in upon

---

34. *Institutes* II.12.1.

35. Calvin's Letter to Sadoleto, in *A Reformation Debate*, 81. Calvin uses Sadoleto's literary device against him, by placing these words in the mouth of a "plebeian" who is before the tribunal of the Lord. Sadoleto is an interesting historical figure, in that he candidly admitted the corruption of the church, but called Geneva back to the safety of her "mother." In one of those grand ironies that was not lost on Calvin, the Genevan Senate asked Calvin, whom they had recently banished, to reply on their behalf!

36. Calvin's Letter to Sadoleto, in *A Reformation Debate*, 82.

me," Calvin experiences even deeper terror. "Being exceedingly alarmed at the misery into which I had fallen, and much more at that which threatened me in the view of eternal death, I, as in duty bound, made it my first business to betake myself to thy way, condemning my past life, not without groans and tears."[37] For Calvin, the first step to God was confronting fear. It was owning it as an objective and subjective reality.

Calvin's is not the straightforward journey from fear to faith, nor from terror to tranquility. It is from nameless anxiety to sanctified fear: the *fear of the Lord*. This is not Adam's "terror at the sight of God," but the trembling that "comes from the reverence that comes from his majesty."[38] Calvin never was able to fully shake his fear, but through the tutelage of Scripture and the Holy Spirit, he was able to tame it into proper fear and teach others to do the same. It is doubtful that Calvin desired a fear-free existence, as he felt that fear was indispensable to proper reverence.[39] In fact, Calvin does not believe that a believer would ever be free from fear, for "experience teaches that hope can only truly reign where fear also keeps part of the heart occupied."[40] Oberman points out that Calvin "before and after conversion knew fear in all the grada-tions which the Latin language suggests on the escalating line from *metus* and *timiditas* via *timor* to *anxietas* and *terror*."[41] Calvin took great comfort from the fact that both David and Jesus felt genuine fear.[42] It is not fear but despair that is the real enemy.[43]

If terror is indeed our common inheritance, due to Adam and Eve, then Calvin felt that the job of the church was to "lead docile souls, placidly, by the hand"[44] into a proper fear of the Lord. "Our hearts are frightened, and they falter, because there is nothing more difficult for us than to come to realize that God is gracious."[45] This is precisely what Rome had not done:

37. Ibid.

38. Calvin, *Institutes of the Christian Religion, 1541 French Edition*, trans. Elsie Anne McKee (Grand Rapids: Eerdmans, 2009), 28.

39. Historian Philip Schaff writes in his Preface to *Modern Christianity: The Swiss Refor-mation*, vol. 8 of *History of the Christian Church* (New York: Charles Scribner's Sons, 1910) that "Calvinism breeds manly, independent, and earnest characters who fear God and nothing else, and favors religious and political freedom." This is an interesting remark, reflecting Calvinism as it moved onto North American soil, but not its roots.

40. Calvin's *Commentary* on Psalm 56:4 as translated by Selderhuis, *Psalms*, 263.

41. Oberman, "*Subita Conversio*," in *Refugees*, 143.

42. See Calvin's *Commentary* on Psalm 22, with the phrase "My God, My God, Why have you forsaken me?"

43. Calvin's *Commentary* on Psalm 32:1.

44. Calvin's Letter to Sadoleto, in *A Reformation Debate*, 47.

45. Calvin's *Commentary* on Psalm 103:8, as translated by Selderhuis, *Psalms*, 258.

> Sure, they have long sermons about the fear of God, but, because they keep miserable souls trapped in their doubts, they may be building but without the foundation.[46]

And what is this foundation? Calvin explores 1 John 4:18: "there is no fear in love." This has nothing to do with our love of God, as most of Calvin's contemporaries would claim, but with *his love of us*—"the love of God, really known, tranquilizes the heart."[47] If Calvin's conversion was from terror to fear of the Lord, he made it his business to "lay the foundation" for others to follow.

Calvin's first catechism (1538) reveals this to already be a pastoral goal of his, written the year after his first edition of the *Institutes*. He writes, "True godliness does not consist in a fear which willingly flees God's judgment. . . . True godliness consists rather in a sincere feeling which loves God as Father as much as it fears and reverences him as Lord."[48] This is Calvin's great breakthrough: God as both Lord *and* Father. This is not so much a conversion of the thoughts (though it certainly is that) as it is a conversion *of the emotions*. "It is not sufficient that we are loved by God unless the experience of love also gets through to us."[49] Great fear and great love best summarize Calvin's newfound emotional and theological state, so much so that Calvin summarizes the gospel as "our salvation consists in having God as our Father."[50] This is no small thing for a man who lost his mother at a young age and could not grieve the death of his undemonstrative father. Calvin, who readily identified with orphans, at last knew what it was to be included in a family.[51]

There is no space in this paper to follow this theme, but many of Calvin's theological metaphors revolve precisely around family. At every possible juncture, Calvin paints the Christian life in familial terms, as children with their loving Father. Prayer, for example, reveals to us the reality of being God's children—"we do not pray aright unless we are persuaded that he is our Father."[52]

46. Calvin's *Commentary* on Psalm 130:4, as translated by Selderhuis, *Psalms*, 270.
47. Calvin's *Commentary* on 1 John 4:18.
48. Section II of Calvin's First Catechism. See the Ford Lewis Battles translation, as found in John Hesselink's *Calvin's First Catechism: A Commentary* (Louisville: Westminster John Knox, 1998), 9.
49. Calvin's *Commentary* on Psalm 4:7, as translated by Selderhuis, *Psalms*, 255.
50. Calvin's *Commentary* on Romans 8:17.
51. For a more robust development see Julie Canlis, "The Fatherhood of God and Union with Christ in Calvin," in *'In Christ' in Paul*, ed. Kevin Vanhoozer (Tübingen: Mohr Siebeck, 2014), 399–424.
52. Calvin, *Commentary* on Romans 8:16.

Baptism is our adoption into a family.[53] The Lord's Supper is the way a benevolent Father feeds his household.[54]

> Therefore God both calls himself our Father and would have us so address him. By the great sweetness of this name he frees us from all distrust, since no greater feeling of love can be found elsewhere than in the Father. Therefore he could not attest his own boundless love toward us with any surer proof than the fact that we are called "children of God."[55]

Even more far-reaching, Calvin argues that these are not metaphors but the essence of God's very life into which we have been included through union with Christ.[56] It is only through union with Christ that Jesus's father becomes *our* Father and that we in turn become children, entering the family dynamic. It is the Spirit's unique work to make God's fatherhood concrete: "We are the sons of God, because we have received the same Spirit as his only Son."[57] Even in wrath "yet he ceases not to be a father."[58]

What is unique to Calvin is this profound sensitivity to the horror of alienation, loneliness, and abandonment. Calvin employs all the traditional medieval (and scriptural) imagery of offended honor and recompense, of guilt and retribution, of sacrifice and propitiation. Calvin's innovation is his psychological sensitivity, or as Oberman writes, "both his teaching and preaching are programmatically directed at awareness and mental health."[59] His early experience of anxiety, combined with his horror of being awakened to his own separation and alienation, were prime ingredients in his developing theology of participation. And if indeed "no more terrible abyss can be conceived than to feel yourself forsaken and estranged from God,"[60] then Calvin's theology is the thread out of the labyrinth to the Fatherhood of God.

53. Calvin, *Institutes* IV.17.31.
54. Calvin, *Institutes* IV.18.19.
55. Calvin, *Institutes* III.20.37.
56. Calvin, *Institutes* II.14.5.
57. Calvin, *Commentary* on Galatians 4:6. Also, "the Spirit testifies to us that we are children of God," in Calvin, *Commentary* on Romans 8:16.
58. Calvin, *Commentary* on Psalm 74:9.
59. Oberman, "*Subita Conversio*," 133.
60. Calvin, *Institutes* II.16.12.

Conversion Account III (1557)

Between Calvin's second and third conversion narratives nearly twenty years elapsed in which Calvin proved the worth of his words that "I am unwilling to speak about myself."[61] This was due to Calvin's desire for God's glory, as well as his deep desire to stay hidden. Yet even as Calvin kept his cards close to his chest, he kept Scripture there as well, particularly the Psalms. The book of Psalms was the only book that Calvin preached through every week in Geneva. And while Calvin's ever-growing *Commentaries* and *Institutes* generated interest, it was his commissioning of a Psalmody that became a publishing sensation. Few refugees that passed through Geneva left without a Psalmbook set to Calvin's metrics and Clément Marot's melodies. This was not just an innovation but a shakedown in the churches that had been silent until Calvin's arrival. Selderhuis muses that "Luther sang to stand firm against the temptations of Satan; Calvin sang to warm himself against the coldness of the human heart."[62]

As the Psalms grew more central to Calvin's public ministry, they also accumulated weight in his writings. In his first edition of the *Institutes* (1536), they are his least-quoted book of Scripture. In the final edition (1559), they are the single most quoted book after Romans.[63] In the Psalms, Calvin left behind the detachment of the *Institutes* and entered into the Scriptures as a history of his own soul. The Psalms reflected Calvin's theology as it lived in his heart:

> There is no other book in which there is to be found more express and magnificent commendations, both of the unparalleled liberality of God towards his Church, and of all his works; there is no other book in which there are recorded so many deliverances nor so many evidences and experiences of the fatherly providence and solicitude which God exercises towards us.[64]

And this was no small thing for someone dealing with not only personal anxiety, but societal anxiety on a European scale. The refugee crisis was escalating in Geneva, alongside the anti-immigrant sentiment of the locals. The magistrates had given Calvin approval to reform the city with their right hand, but with their left took it away. So Calvin, himself a refugee, taught and sang the exile

---

61. Calvin's Letter to Sadoleto, in *A Reformation Debate*, 47.

62. Selderhuis, *Pilgrim*, 135.

63. Selderhuis summarizes the role that the Psalms played in Calvin's Geneva, in his first chapter of *Calvin's Theology of the Psalms*.

64. Calvin's extended reflection on the Psalms is in his "Preface" to the *Commentary*. All quotations, unless otherwise noted, come from here.

songs with those in crisis, songs which reminded them of the fatherhood of God who promised providential protection through all the storms.

For one who did not like to talk about himself, Calvin found it much easier to lift his personal narrative up into those of the great biblical heroes to better understand himself. Various biblical leaders were not just heroes—they became patterns of Calvin's own story.[65] But of all these heroes, David—the refugee, the nobody-called-to-be-somebody—was Calvin's greatest mentor who "suffered the same or similar things from the domestic enemies of the Church. For although I follow David at a great distance, . . . I have no hesitation in comparing myself with him."[66] For Calvin to write an autobiography would have been unthinkable. But to discover himself in the pages of the Psalms was a great gift. In them, he "did not wander in an unknown region"[67] but one he knew all too well. Calvin makes no attempt at pretense: "My readers, too, if I mistake not, will observe, that in unfolding the internal affections both of David and of others I discourse upon them as matters of which I have familiar experience."[68]

In the Scripture, Calvin found his biography. In the Psalms, he discovered his anatomy. Five years before Calvin started preaching on the Psalms, a book on human anatomy was published at Basel, taking the region by storm.[69] Two-hundred and forty-seven precise woodcuts revealed what had never been seen with such accuracy or precision: the mysterious inner workings of the human body. In the Psalms, Calvin felt he was looking at his insides. "For there is not an emotion of which anyone can be conscious that is not here represented as in a mirror." He had to hand his own private anatomy—with 150 illustrations—accurately portraying his own mysterious inner life. "The Holy Spirit has drawn a living portrait of all the pain, depression, fear, doubt, hope, worries, anxieties,

---

65. The only problem with this is that reading the Bible as one's own biography does not allow for subtlety: are we Israel? Who are the Philistines? Calvin's anxiety seemed to guide these interpretations, which often rendered his identification in black-and-white terms. He lost a long-time friend, Roussel, who was trying to reform Catholicism from "within," because for Calvin, there was no middle ground. Selderhuis writes of a general tendency here among those who follow in Calvin's footsteps: "Reformed people give their all. When they do something, they do it well, and others who do not follow in certain choices are unfortunately kept at a distance and declared outsiders." See Selderhuis, *Pilgrim*, 48–50.

66. Calvin's "Preface," in the *Commentary* on Psalms.

67. Calvin's "Preface," in the *Commentary* on Psalms.

68. Calvin's "Preface," in the *Commentary* on Psalms.

69. Andreas Vesalius published *On the Fabric of the Human Body* in 1543. Vesalius proved Galen—the reigning "anatomist" for over a millennium—wrong, illustration by illustration. Never before had a doctor actually opened up the body himself (this was left to the barber) nor had the illustrators been in the room.

confusion—in short, all the feelings that swing man's inner being to and fro."[70] For this reason, Calvin nicknamed the Psalms, "An Anatomy of All the Parts of the Soul." In David, Calvin finds no stoic self-mastery (though at one point in his life, stoic *apatheia* could well have been a desirable commodity). For it was not Seneca but the Psalter that helped Calvin process his grief when he lost his son and wife. Unlike his reticence over his father, he was able to lament after his wife's death, "I am no more than half a man."[71]

It is no surprise that Calvin's third conversion narrative tumbles out of his *Preface* to the Psalms, almost unbidden. Calvin finds himself in an unusual situation—at a loss for words to express how meaningful this "treasury" is. In light of the book that is like a "living portrait" of his soul, Calvin comes under the spell of the Psalms and launches into its proper genre: the holy ground of spiritual autobiography.

> When I was as yet a very little boy, my father had destined me for the study of theology. But afterwards when he considered that the legal profession commonly raised those who followed it to wealth this prospect induced him suddenly to change his purpose. Thus it came to pass, that I was withdrawn from the study of philosophy, and was put to the study of law. To this pursuit I endeavored faithfully to apply myself in obedience to the will of my father; but God, by the secret guidance of his providence, at length gave a different direction to my course. And first, since I was too obstinately devoted to the superstitions of Popery to be easily extricated from so profound an abyss of mire, God by a sudden [*subita*—"unexpected"] conversion subdued and brought my mind to a teachable frame.[72]

Gone is the angst of his first account (1534) where one senses the lingering taste of terror in his mouth. Gone are the maturing reflection on the sources of that terror (1539) and Calvin's growing call to help remove this terror from others.[73]

---

70. Calvin's "Preface," in the *Commentary* on Psalms, my translation, "le sainct Esprit a yci *pourtrait au vif* toutes les douleurs, tristesses."

71. This does not mean that Calvin had no feelings for his father—this we cannot know. But it does reflect the inability (or undesirability) to communicate them. To another man, Calvin writes much later, "What a terrible injury, what a pain the death of your wife has caused you, and I speak from my own experience. For even now, I know how fully difficult it was, seven years ago now, to deal with such grief" (Selderhuis, *Pilgrim*, 172).

72. Calvin's "Preface," in the *Commentary* on Psalms.

73. In his second account, he plainly admits that "had I wished to consult my own interest, I would never have left [Rome]. . . . I never desired it" (Calvin, *Psychopannychia*, 465), while in this third account, his mature sense of calling trumps any earlier memory of hesitation.

In this final account, Calvin hardly differentiates between his conversion and his calling, beholding in the biblical David a mirror both of "the beginning of my calling, and the further course of my function."[74]

Calvin makes an interesting connection of his calling with God's fatherhood—although for Calvin, this "calling" was experienced more as a disagreeable draft. Likening himself with others who found themselves similarly drafted (including the suffering servant, Isaiah/Jesus),[75] Calvin lays out their calling in terms that could summarize his own life: called to the delivery of doctrine[76] for the glory of God. Twice Calvin gives hints as to the relational reality surrounding his own experience of this call. To explain his calling to aid in the glorification of God, Calvin places it into the Father-Son intimacy, "Father, glorify thy Son, that thy Son may glorify thee" (John 17:1). Second, Calvin says that the significance of the Servant's being "formed" in the womb is "clearer than noonday"—it has less to do with physical forming than being formed by the Father for "discharging one's office," which is to help gather the flock into Christ, the only "bond of union."[77] Calvin's particular calling goes beyond job-description to the sphere in which he experienced the particularizing fatherhood of God.

As Calvin meditated upon the Psalms, he came to see them as both anatomy and assignment.

> Here the prophets themselves, seeing they are speaking to God and laying open all their inmost thoughts and affections, *draw each of us to the examination of himself* in particular in order that none of the many infirmities to which we are subject, and of the many vices with which we abound, may remain concealed.[78]

---

74. This is no eighteenth-century revivalist account of conversion. This is a slow, studied process in which conversion is not as important as a sense of vocation and call. Calvin finds in David a colleague and friend with some remarkable life-parallels. "But as he was taken from the sheepfold, and elevated to the rank of supreme authority; so God having taken me from my originally obscure and humble condition, has reckoned me worthy of being invested with the honorable office of a preacher and minister of the gospel" (Calvin's "Preface," in the *Commentary* on Psalms).

75. Calvin immediately connects Isaiah's sense of call to Paul's (mentioning Gal 1:15) and then Jeremiah's (Jer 1:5) and even Christ's (Heb 5:4-5).

76. *Commentary* on Isaiah 49:2: "he hath placed my mouth as a sharp sword." Calvin's explanation is that "Christ hath therefore been appointed by the Father not to rule after the manner of princes . . . but his whole authority consists in doctrine, in the preaching of which he wishes to be sought."

77. "In the world there is miserable dispersion, but in Christ there is *anakephalaiosis*, 'a gathering together' of all (Eph 1:10) as the Apostle speaks; for there can be no other bond of union" (*Commentary* on Isaiah 49:5).

78. Calvin's "Preface," in the *Commentary* on Psalms, my emphasis.

This is shown by the way that, in this particular commentary alone, Calvin forthrightly drops all argumentation, all unnecessary detours, and presents only that which will help his readers in their own task of self-examination in the presence of God. For this book is like none other, says Calvin. "The other parts of Scripture contain the commandments" while this one is a "mirror" for the emotions. Although Calvin's final conversion account occurs only in the *Preface*, Calvin himself offers the entire book of the Psalms as a mirror for the understanding of him, and of ourselves.[79]

In so doing, the Psalms became Calvin's portable confessional, replacing a key psychological element of medieval spirituality.[80] Who of us can understand the psychological loss of this practice for the sixteenth-century refugee? Much had changed since the 1215 Fourth Lateran Council, seen as progressive for its time, in which all Christians were charged to confess their sins annually. By Calvin's time, the call to frequent confession was heard across Europe[81] and played into the mass phenomenon of the sin-anguished conscience in the West.[82] Calvin found the Psalms to be more than ample to play the role of both penitent and priest.[83] In them, "we have permission and freedom granted us to lay open before him our infirmities which we would be ashamed to confess before men."[84] And following this shameful confession, "there is no other book in which there is to be found . . . the unparalleled liberality of God . . . and his fatherly providence."[85] Although the Psalms have spoken to believers across cultures and generations for millennia, their implementation by Calvin's refugee

79. Here we see Calvin in line with the reforms of the *devotio moderna*, which brought the psychological insights from the monastery into lay consciousness and spirituality (Oberman, "*Via Calvini*," in *Refugees*, 33).

80. "Calvin knew [what it was to live without the comfort of priestly protection] and described it in vivid terms. In searching for the reasons of the impact of Calvin it is therefore important to note that no religious thinker of the sixteenth century dealt so squarely and head-on with this new situation as did John Calvin, who exposes in every sermon and prayer the direct confrontation with the holiness of God" (Oberman, "The Mystery of Calvin's Impact," in *Refugees*, 63).

81. This was informed by Jean Gerson's vernacular handbook on the subject, *Opus Tripartium*. Gerson is particularly liked by Calvin, though Calvin would take pains to emphasize confession in the context of God's good favor. Despite Luther's passionate crusade against indulgences, he still believed in the "medicinal" value of confession for the Christian (see his 1526 sermon, "The Sacrament of the Body and Blood of Christ—Against the Fanatics," in vol. 36 of *Luther's Works*, ed. H. J. Grimm [Philadelphia: Fortress, 1959], 359).

82. See James McCue, "*Simul Justus et peccator* in Augustine, Aquinas, and Luther: Towards Putting the Debate in Context," *Journal of the American Academy of Religion* 48 (1980): 90.

83. As Calvin continued to be challenged by the problems of pastoral oversight of a city-state, he instituted the pastoral home visit as a replacement to the Confessional (Selderhuis, *Pilgrim*, 88).

84. Calvin's "Preface," in the *Commentary* on Psalms.

85. Calvin's "Preface," in the *Commentary* on Psalms.

congregations (some of which still, to this day, chant the Psalms as a part of their Sunday liturgy) must be seen in the light of the exodus from the confessional.

This is why Selderhuis reclassifies the Psalms as the "pastoral variation"[86] of the *Institutes*, which opens with the importance of the double-knowledge: knowing God and knowing ourselves.[87] The answer to the double-knowledge is not theological propositions, but action: a "laying open" (*descouvrent*) of the heart. As Oberman emphasizes,

> the *cognitio nostri* [knowledge of ourselves] of the opening chapter of the *Institutes* I.1.1 does not refer primarily to a series of doctrinal "truths" about the fallen state of man, but stands for the emotionally complex self-analysis which lifts the lid or cover of the soul, allowing for the discovery of the underlying abyss of drives and frustrated longings. The *cognition dei* [knowledge of God] is not merely the intellectual attainment of revealed truth about God, but the awakening of longings (*affectus*) which enable the thoughts and meditations to soar high to get a taste (*gustus*) of the mysteries of God.[88]

While the *Institutes* guide us in the truth about ourselves and God, the Psalms turn that double-knowledge into prayer. Rome taught a despairing double-knowledge, as recounted in Calvin's second conversion narrative: "for, whenever I descended into myself, or raised my mind to thee, extreme terror seized me."[89] Surprising to some, Calvin never prized mere knowledge—even correct knowledge—above the heart. ("The knowledge of faith consists in assurance rather than comprehension."[90]) God and the self cannot be known in isolation, either through introspection or abstraction, but only as they are *in relation* to one another. This is the secret of Calvin's strict emphasis on only knowing God through his economy. While the Psalms make room for feelings of despair, they teach the faithful to channel their despair into prayer. In the

86. Selderhuis, *Psalms*, 284.

87. "Our wisdom, in so far as it ought to be deemed true and solid Wisdom, consists almost entirely of two parts: the knowledge of God and of ourselves. But as these are connected together by many ties, it is not easy to determine which of the two precedes and gives birth to the other" (Calvin, *Institutes* I.1.1). Here Calvin self-consciously stands in the line of the philosophers, starting with the Delphic Oracle ("With good reason the ancient proverb strongly recommended knowledge of self to man," *Institutes* II.1.1) through the church fathers, who also emphasized the importance of self-knowledge in the light of God. See James M. Houston, "The 'Double Knowledge' as the Way of Wisdom," in *The Way of Wisdom: Essays in Honor of Bruce K. Waltke*, ed. J. I. Packer (Grand Rapids: Zondervan, 2000), 308–26.

88. Oberman, "*Subita Conversio*," 133.

89. Calvin's Letter to Sadoleto, in *A Reformation Debate*, 82.

90. Calvin, *Institutes* III.2.14.

Psalms, "men will be most effectually awakened to a sense of their maladies, and, at the same time, instructed in seeking remedies for their cure."[91] This is not therapeutic introspection,[92] but knowing the self *in God's presence*. There is no knowing one without the other.

Self-examination to what end? Calvin's increasing self-knowledge was in order to place more and more of his heart in the hands of his loving Father, as portrayed in his seal. Calvin's seal was of a heart being offered up by a willing hand. Were it not for the inscription, *My heart, Lord, I offer you, promptly and sincerely*, we would have cause to wonder: is this Calvin offering his heart to the Lord? Or are these hands the Lord's, tenderly caring for Calvin's heart? In regard to the seal, we know it to be the former, but the latter is also true: as Calvin experienced more of his own inner abyss, he knew the "abyss" of the Father's mercy.[93] The more Calvin knew the depths and love of God in his innermost places, the more he could testify to this God's loving character. In a sense, as Calvin offered his own heart to the Lord through the Psalms, he was able to place more and more of the Father's heart into believers' hands.

If the Psalms are a mirror, they are also a battlefield against anxiety. Each Psalm represents an existential crisis familiar to every believer, but particularly to those who lived in Calvin's turbulent age. Calvin writes in the *Preface*: "In many places [in the Psalms] we may perceive the exercise of the servants of God in prayer so fluctuating, that they are almost overwhelmed by the alternate hope of success and apprehension of failure."[94] In and through the emotional honesty of the Psalms, faith is able to confess its emotions and to simultaneously "renounce the guidance of our own affections and submit ourselves entirely to God."[95] This submission is based on the twin doctrines that function as Calvin's ramparts against anxiety: providence and predestination. Providence assured refugees that, evidence to the contrary,[96] God was indeed their providential provider. Yet we are to "have ever before our eyes the providence of God, to whom it belongs to settle the affairs of the world,

---

91. Calvin's "Preface," in the *Commentary* on Psalms.

92. Krister Stendahl charges the Augustinian position on the fall as leading to "the introspective conscience of the West" (reprinted in *Paul among Jews and Gentiles* [London: SCM, 1976], 78).

93. Muller points to Calvin's paraphrase of Luke 18:13: "May the abyss of thy mercy swallow up this abyss of sin" (Richard Muller, *Unaccommodated Calvin* [Oxford: Oxford University Press, 2001], 88).

94. Calvin's "Preface," in the *Commentary* on Psalms.

95. Calvin's "Preface," in the *Commentary* on Psalms.

96. "According to all outward appearance, the servants of God may derive no advantage from their uprightness," Calvin admits in Psalm 1, setting the pastoral tenor for his commentary as a book in which to deal with grief, disappointment, loss, and to turn it into praise.

and to bring order out of confusion."[97] Predestination assured refugees that their safety was not in any home, but in God's own choosing of them—and that God would indeed be their dwelling place. "He chose for himself from amongst the lost race of Adam a small portion to whom he might show himself to be a father."[98] Although Calvin's colleagues in other city-states thought his stance on predestination too extreme, Calvin was unwilling to reconsider any other option, for to do so was to open the door to Satan and his tyranny of fear again. Having already lived under a tyranny of fear, Calvin preferred the tyranny of a loving father to that of Rome any day.

Being "In Christ" Trumps All Social Bonds

John Calvin's biblical heroes were always on the run. Fittingly, Calvin's lasting influence was not on those who already had a home, but those who had no home.[99] As news of repeated persecutions would reach his ears, he would be taken ill and unable to work.[100] Calvin was the pastor of the outpost, the shepherd of the "safe haven." His unique message was for those who had lost everything, who knew the agony of daily fear, and who struggled to make sense of it all. For those who had left their fatherland, Calvin offered them a Father who would guide them home. For those who had lost the safety of city-walls, Calvin offered the fortified security of predestination. For those who had been scattered and had lost all that gives connection, Calvin offered a new adoptive family gathered into Christ, their brothers-in-suffering. For those who knew daily fear, Calvin offers not stoic *tranquilitas* but terror and alienation converted into the *fear of the Lord*. Calvin never moved fully from fear to peace, but rather experienced God in the very human battle between the two.

Only a suffering church can understand Calvin's message, and particularly the comfort given by the doctrine of predestination. As those who feared above all recanting under persecution, Calvin's message of election gave them hope that they would not fail their Lord. Predestination was a fortress against anxiety and a lasting message of comfort to those who seemed *unelect* by society. When all around them seemed lost, they were to look to Christ—himself

97. Calvin's "Preface," in the *Commentary* on Psalms.

98. Calvin's *Commentary* on Psalm 105:3.

99. "A life in exile is the worst that one can encounter" (Calvin, *Commentary* on Psalm 126:2, translated by Selderhuis, *Psalms*, 35).

100. Selderhuis, *Pilgrim*, 187. It is telling that the only part of Calvin's *Institutes* that remained constant through all the editions was his Prefatory Address to King Francis, in which he begged for clemency for the persecuted believers in France.

a "fugitive"[101]—for evidence of their election, as they traveled through their own desert of displacement. And Christ's God becomes a *Father* guiding them into a new fatherland, a new kingdom. In many ways, predestination gave Calvinism its mobility and its wings. Yet when these refugee communities, flung abroad, became established and no longer hung on election as their sure hope of deliverance, this doctrine became "emptied of all relation to existential life experience and distorted beyond recognition."[102] The wings of Icarus melted not upon escaping, but upon settling.

But it was not an abstract doctrine that was a fortress against Calvin's existential and societal angst; predestination functioned to secure Calvin in the arms of his true father. "Should affection be wholly extinguished," writes Calvin, God "fulfills the duty of both father and mother to his people."[103] Identifying with orphans, Calvin moved from a solitary childhood toward a theology of participation, where his identity *in Christ* trumped all previous social bonds. For this reason he shows extreme exegetical sensitivity to passages where the self-in-Christ is compromised.[104] Calvin could no longer separate his identity from being "in Christ" or, indeed, from those who formed Christ's body. His pastoral sense of calling was to unite what had been alienated and abandoned. Identifying with Isaiah's call "from the womb," Calvin articulates his own sense of call: "to gather the scattered flock, that under Christ we may all be united in the same body. In the world, there is miserable dispersion, but in Christ there is 'a gathering together' of all."[105] Through the Psalms, Calvin discovered that he did not know God unless he knew himself; and he could not know himself unless he knew God. Calvin's sense of "self" became profoundly marked by the presence of another. While this is far removed from the modern therapeutic quest, it is not far from Augustine's *Noverim te, noverim me!—let me know Thee, O God; let me know myself!*

---

101. Oberman notes that Calvin is the first to portray Christ as leading the Israelites through the wilderness, a "fugitive" himself ("*Via Calvini*," in *Refugees*, 47).

102. Oberman, "*Via Calvini*," in *Refugees*, 33.

103. See his *Commentary* on Psalm 27:10.

104. He is particularly irked by Erasmus who, though a normally excellent translator, misses the import of the Greek preposition "in" (*en*) consistently. See Canlis, "In Christ," 414.

105. "In the world there is miserable dispersion, but in Christ there is *anakephalaiosis*, 'a gathering together' of all (Eph 1:10) as the Apostle speaks; for there can be no other bond of union" (*Commentary* on Isaiah 49:5).

Chapter 26

Thomas Becon: Popular Devotional Writer

Jonathan Reimer

There are several respects in which an account of the life and writings of Thomas Becon (1512–1567) may appear out of place in this volume. A second-tier English clergyman, polemicist, and best-selling devotional author, he was not one of the most consequential reformers of his day. Neither was he one of the great theologians of that era. Furthermore, during his lifetime, the majority of his countrymen, those who remained faithful to the traditional Catholic teaching in which they had been raised, believed his writing to be heretical, or what they pejoratively termed "new learning."[1] Notwithstanding these factors, from the 1540s to the 1630s, Becon was both an exceedingly popular and a strikingly populist devotional writer.

At least 128 early modern editions of his writing were printed. Throughout the sixteenth century, his output was only surpassed in the English-speaking world by Thomas More, John Fisher, William Tyndale, and John Calvin.[2] His works did not discuss abstract theology "farre remoued from the common sense and capacitie of the people," but rather "such matters, as might edifye

---

1. During the 1980s and 1990s, so-called "revisionist" historians, such as Christopher Haigh, J. J. Scarisbrick, and Eamon Duffy, succeeded in demonstrating both the vitality of the late medieval English church and the protracted character of religious change in England. This effectively dismantled the previous paradigm of the English Reformation, most fully articulated by A. G. Dickens, which saw religious change as the result of an alliance between a disaffected and anti-clerical laity and the Crown and argued that Protestantism had developed a widespread following by the middle of the sixteenth century. Peter Marshall, "(Re)defining the English Reformation," *Journal of British Studies* 48 (2004): 564–86. For a description of the use of the phrase "new learning" see Richard Rex, "The New Learning," *Journal of Ecclesiastical History* 44 (1993): 26–44.

2. These statistics are based on the Universal Short Title Catalogue, hosted by the University of St. Andrews at www.ustc.ac.uk.

brethren."[3] These texts, as well as wills and inventories, reveal that, while Becon's writings were owned by a wide variety of English readers, they held particular importance to poorer owners and women. While for wealthy owners, such as the Norfolk MP Sir Richard Townshend and the Vice-Chancellor of the University of Cambridge Dr. Andrew Perne, a book by Becon was one edition within a substantial library; for poorer owners, such as the yeomen Richard Rix and Richard Humphrey, a volume by Becon was the only text they owned besides the English Bible.[4] Likewise, when the Suffolk draper Thomas Fella made his will, he left to his grandson his Bible and all his books, except his copies of Latimer's *Sermons* and Becon's dialogue *The Sycke Mans Salue*, which he bequeathed to his granddaughter along with her grandmother's "mortor and spice boxes and a cupboard full of household stuffe."[5] That Becon's books were thought suitable for uneducated men and women is unsurprising: he calls the readership of one work "simple and unlearned Christians," and his contemporary John Bale notes that he had written "for the instruction of the common people."[6]

As a wildly popular writer, whose books sought to popularize the teachings of the English Reformation, Becon's life and writings offer a unique perspective from which to assess early modern Christian identity and make sense of the various fractured identities that have followed in its wake. Because he wrote across the diverse reigns of Henry VIII, Edward VI, Mary Tudor, and Elizabeth I, his biography and compositions bear witness to both the historical circumstances and theological convictions by which popular Christian identity was reformed, ruptured, and revolutionized in early modern England.

3. Thomas Becon, *The worckes of Thomas Becon whiche he hath hitherto made and published, with diverse other newe bookes added to the same* (London: John Day, 1564), vol. I, sig. Cvr.

4. R. J. Fehrenbach and E. S. Leedham-Green, eds., *Private Libraries in Renaissance England: A Collection of Tudor and Stuart Book-lists* (New York: Medieval and Renaissance Texts and Studies, 1992), 3.1–3.286, 191.1–191.2, 199.1–199.2; E. S. Leedham-Green, *Books in Cambridge Inventories: Book Lists from Vice-Chancellor's Court Probate Inventories in Tudor and Stuart Periods* (Cambridge: Cambridge University Press, 1989), 419–81.

5. Suffolk Record Office, Ipswich Branch, Shelfmark: IC/AA1/76/54.

6. Becon, *The gouernaunce of vertue teaching al faithfull Christians, howe they oughte dayly to leade their lyfe, and fruitefully to spend their tyme vnto the glorye of God and the health of their owne soules* (London: John Day, 1560), sig. Aviiir; John Bale, *Illustrium Moiris Brittanniae scriptorium* (Wesel: Derick van der Straten, 1548), fol. 236r.

A Man Mightily Tossed About

Becon was born in Norfolk in 1512. There he was taught the beliefs, pieties, and practices of traditional English Catholicism, which he would remember (perhaps unfairly) in markedly Pelagian terms. Reflecting upon this period in one of his later sermons, Becon recalled that before "this opening of the Gospell at oure tyme, I thought that God had no regard of me, and that the gouernance of my saluation consisted in my self."[7] Around the age of sixteen he matriculated into the University of Cambridge, likely in Michaelmas Term 1527. Though he completed the Arts course in four years, graduating in 1531, Becon did not distinguish himself. In the *ordo senioritatis* of Grace Book B, which lists graduands to some extent in order of their academic achievement, Becon is recorded thirty-sixth out of the thirty-eight names.[8]

Despite his lack of scholarly accomplishment, Cambridge played a transformative role in Becon's life, for it was here that he was converted to evangelical belief by the preaching of Hugh Latimer and the lectures of George Stafford.[9] Recalling this period of his life some twenty years later, Becon described Latimer as the person "to whom nexte to God I am specially bounde to gyue moste hertye thankes for the knowledge, if any I haue, of God and hys moste blessed worde."[10] Becon attended Latimer's famous Card Sermons, which provoked heated controversy in the university, and as a "pore scholar" may have been the recipient of Latimer's charity.[11] Also significant to Becon's conversion were the lectures of George Stafford on the New Testament. Calling to mind Stafford's humanist exegesis, undoubtedly tinged with evangelical doctrine, Becon remembered how he had "beutified the letters of the blessed Paul wyth hys godlye exposicions" and "learnedlye setforth in hys lectures the natiue sense and true understandynge of the fore Euangelistes, uiuely restoryng unto us the

---

7. Becon, *A new Postil Conteinyng most Godly and learned sermons upon all the Sonday Gospelles, that be redde in the Church thorowout the yeare* (London: Thomas Marsh, 1566), fol. 46v.

8. Mary Bateson, ed., *Grace Book B: Containing the Accounts of the Proctors of the University of Cambridge, 1511–1544* (Cambridge: University of Cambridge Press, 1905), 164.

9. For much of the sixteenth century, the term "Protestant" was used in England to refer to those continental princes and reformers who protested against Charles V, rather than to reformers in England. Thus, to avoid the anachronism of referring to early English reformers as Protestants, many scholars have suggested calling these proto-Protestants "evangelicals": the usage I have adopted throughout this chapter. For more on this debate, see Diarmaid MacCulloch, "Henry VIII and the Reform of the Church," in *The Reign of Henry VIII: Politics, Policy and Piety* (Basingstoke: Palgrave, 1988), 168–69; and Peter Marshall, "The Naming of Protestant England," *Past and Present* 214 (2012): 91–92.

10. Becon, *The Jewel of joye*, sigs. Diiiv–Diiiir.

11. Becon, *The Jewel of joye*, sigs. Diiiir–Dviv.

Apostls mynde and the mynd of those holye wryters, whyche so manye yeares before hadde lien unknowen and obscured thorowe the darknes and mistes of the Pharises and Papistes."[12] Both Latimer and Stafford profoundly influenced Becon, and he left Cambridge a changed man.

In light of his poor academic showing, Becon did not proceed to a master's degree but returned home to Norfolk, where he was ordained and took a post instructing boys at the College of St. John the Evangelist in Rushford. His evangelical faith percolated and, in November 1538, Thomas Lord Wentworth of Nettlestead wrote to Thomas Cromwell that Becon was a "discret onest [honest] pryst and well lernyd of whom I haue knowledge to be not only a trew precher of the worde of god but also agrett setter fourthe to the pepull of the kynges most iust and lawfull tytell of supremacy a prouyd [approved] by gods worde."[13] This evangelical preaching soon got Becon into trouble. During the summer of 1540, after the conservative Act of Six Articles had come into effect, Becon was made to recant "in opyn sermons" the doctrine he had been preaching.[14]

After this recantation, Becon relocated to Kent, where he wrote a series of twelve best-selling devotional works. By April 1543, his texts were circulating in at least twenty-five editions, including two Dutch translations.[15] The popularity of his books made him a prime target for religious conservatives during the Prebendaries' Plot of 1543 that sought to oust Archbishop Cranmer and purge evangelical preachers in Kent. On Relic Sunday (July 8), he was forced to recant his beliefs at Paul's Cross in London.[16] Having abjured, Becon spent the rest of Henry VIII's reign at his family home in Norfolk and traveling in the Midlands, where local reformers, such as John Olde, housed him. During his travels Becon surreptitiously began to write and translate; even daring to publish an anonymous collection of biblical quotations in flagrant disregard for the Act for the Advancement of True Religion, which limited Bible reading to gentlewomen and men above the rank of yeoman.[17]

Upon Edward VI's accession in 1547, Becon's circumstances were transformed radically. Not only was he presented with the London parish of St.

---

12. Becon, *The Jewel of joye*, sig. Dviiir.

13. British Library, Cotton Vespasian MS F/XIII, fol. 211r.

14. London Metropolitan Archives, Shelfmark: DL/A/A/006/MS09531/012/001, fol. 43r. Recantation was a formal act by which one publically renounced heterodox beliefs after prosecution for heresy.

15. Jonathan Reimer, "Thomas Becon's Henrician Writings: Composition and County Patronage, 1541–1543," *Reformation* 21, no. 1 (2016): 8–24.

16. William Douglas Hamilton, ed., *A Chronicle of England during the Reigns of the Tudors, from AD 1485–1559, by Charles Wriothesley, Windsor Herald* (London: Camden Society, 1875), 142.

17. Becon, *The Jewel of joye*, sigs. Bviv–Eiiir; *The gouernaunce of vertue*, sig. Aviiir.

Stephen's Walbrook, he was appointed as chaplain to both Edward Seymour, Lord Protector of England, and to Archbishop Thomas Cranmer. In these roles he made important contributions to the 1547 *Book of Homilies,* the 1549 *Book of Common Prayer,* and the 1553 *Primer.*[18] Becon also reestablished himself as a best-selling devotional writer.[19] From the outset of Edward's reign, his books were published chiefly by John Day, the foremost English printer during the second half of the sixteenth century. Furthermore, these works were dedicated to the most elite members of English society, including the future Queen Elizabeth; Anne of Cleaves, the fourth wife of Henry VIII; Anne Stanhope, Duchess of Somerset; and Becon's patron, Archbishop Cranmer.

The premature death of Edward VI during the summer of 1553 resulted in another reversal of fortune for Becon. Arrested as a "seditious preacher" on 16 August along with several other evangelical leaders, he was imprisoned in the Tower of London for just over seven months.[20] Released on 22 March 1554, he rapidly fled to the continent. Though he resided for a time in Strasbourg, perhaps as part of a group dedicated to the production of anti-Marian propaganda, by November 1554 he had moved to Frankfurt, where he played a part in the "troubles" that erupted between two factions of exiles over the extent to which the Edwardian prayer book might be further reformed. In 1556, he made his way to Marburg, where he became a client to Philip, Landgrave of Hesse.[21] His experience of imprisonment and exile greatly emboldened his style and his writings began to include vituperative attacks on his confessional adversaries. At the same time, he also began to compose for continental rather than English readers: for the first time he wrote in Latin and one work was even translated into French.

The accession of Elizabeth in late 1558 pulled Becon back to his native land. In January 1559 he returned to London to have his son Basil baptized at his former parish of St. Stephen's Walbrook.[22] As Brett Usher has shown, during this period William Cecil, the secretary of state, considered him for episcopal

18. For descriptions of Becon's contributions to these texts, see Diarmaid MacCulloch, *Thomas Cranmer: A Life* (New Haven: Yale University Press, 1996); and D. S. Bailey, *Thomas Becon and the Reformation of the Church in England* (Edinburgh: Oliver and Boyd, 1952), 55.

19. A. G. Dickens, *The English Reformation* (University Park: Pennsylvania State University Press, 1989), 251–52.

20. The National Archives, State Papers, 11/13, fol. 119v; Becon, *A confortable Epistle / too Goddes faythful people in England* (Wesel: Joos Lambrecht, 1554), sig. vv.

21. Rudolf Jung, *Die englische Flüchtlings-Gemeinde in Frankfurt am Main, 1554–1559* (Frankfurt: Joseph Baer, 1910), 26–44; Christina Garrett, *Marian Exiles: A Study of the Origins of Elizabethan Puritanism* (Cambridge: Cambridge University Press, 84–85; Bailey, *Thomas Becon,* 77–91.

22. W. Bruce Bannerman and Major W. Bruce Bannerman, eds., *The Registers of St. Stephen's, Walbrook and of St. Benet Sherehog, London* (London: Harleian Society, 1919), 1.

preferment.[23] Though not elevated to a bishopric, he was the recipient of several significant benefices, including a prebend at Canterbury Cathedral; the city parish of Christ Church Newgate, presented by the Mayor and Common Council; and the rectory of St. Dionis Backchurch, bestowed by the Dean and Chapter of Canterbury.[24] Throughout the first decade of Elizabeth's reign, Becon was an extremely popular preacher, routinely giving sermons at elite funerals, weddings, and other occasions.[25] During this same period, his writing rose to new prominence. Not only were his Edwardian writings reprinted, his dialogue *The Sycke Mans Salue* became a runaway best-seller. In 1564, John Day published a three-volume folio edition of his *Worckes*, which recast texts previously consumed as cheap octavos and sextodecimos into a new luxury format. In 1566, Becon was among the London clergy suspended for their refusal to wear a surplice during public prayer.[26]

Both his literary and pastoral activities were cut short during the summer of 1567. An undated letter to Archbishop Matthew Parker complains of "certayne infirmities and diseases, wherewythe I haue bene troubled more then thys half yeare at certayne tymes unto the greate losse of my time and hyndrauns [hindrance] of my studies."[27] On 29 June, Becon made a nuncupative will, declaring his "lyuely faythe in Jhesus Christe and continewall [continual] medytation of goddes most holly woord to the great comfort and consolacion of his soul healthe."[28] He died the following day. Though nothing is known of his funeral, many of his contemporaries undoubtedly mourned his passing and he came to be remembered as a "worthy and reverend Clergyman" with "reall experience of changes."[29] The seventeenth-century historian John Strype evocatively summarized the reformer's life by describing him as "a man mightily tossed about."[30]

23. Brett Usher, *William Cecil and Episcopacy, 1559–1577* (Aldershot: Ashgate, 2003), 27–29, 33, 36, 45, 49.

24. Bailey, *Thomas Becon*, 92–93.

25. John Bruce and Thomas Perowne, eds., *Correspondence of Mathew Parker* (Cambridge: Parker Society, 1853), 275; Richard Miller and Collete More, eds., *A London Provisioner's Chronicle, 1550–1563, by Henry Machyn: Manuscript, Transcription and Modernization*, hosted by the University of Michigan at quod.lib.umich.edu/m/machyn. Becon is mentioned in the following entries: 21 October 1559, 16 April 1560, 23 July 1560, 23 December 1560, 14 April 1561, 20 July 1562, [unknown] February 1562 and 3 June 1563.

26. Patrick Collinson, *The Elizabethan Puritan Movement* (London: Trinity Press, 1967), 76.

27. Parker Library, Corpus Christi College, Cambridge, MS 114B, fol. 831.

28. Kent History and Library Center, PRC 32/30, fol. 459.

29. Jacob Verheiden, *The History of the Modern Protestant Divines* (London: John Okes, 1637), 331.

30. John Strype, *Memorials of the Most Reverend Father in God Thomas Cranmer* (Oxford: Clarendon, 1812), 1:608.

Gospel as Text, Christian Obedience, and Dying Well

Having described the vicissitudes of fortune that characterized Becon's life, it is possible to consider several themes that can be traced throughout his writing. While these themes reflect the specific circumstances in which he found himself, they also illuminate broader movements of thought in early modern England. As Becon wrote from the epicenter of a religious paradigm shift, his writings display the contours of two competing, yet overlapping Christian worldviews. Though other themes can be found in his works, the following three were both foundational to his thought and indicative of the realignment of Christian belief and practice taking place during his lifetime.

At the core of the English Reformation was an abiding preoccupation with the text of the Bible, believed to have been restored to its pristine meaning through the insights of humanist exegesis and made accessible to expanded segments of the population through new vernacular translations. Though Christianity had always been a religion of the book, the advent of the printing press in the mid-fifteenth century profoundly changed what this meant. When Becon began to write, sixty-five years after William Caxton had introduced printing technology into England, Henry VIII had authorized the English Bible and it was cheaper than ever before (between 2s 2d and 12s).[31] Thus, it could be read more easily in extra ecclesial settings and interpreted by a wider section of the literate population (10 percent among men and 1 percent among women).[32] From his earliest writings, the provision of the Bible in English was significant to Becon, and it definitively influenced his understanding of the Christian message. For example, in his first book, *Newes out of Heauen* (1542) he offers a fascinatingly novel account of the purpose of the incarnation:

> seyng that the world is without all knowledge of god, corrupte with Idolatrye, poysoned with theyr owne ymaginacions, drowened with Ipocrisy [hypocrisy], and altogyther set on wickednes (the head Prestes, Bisshops, lawers, Scribes and Pharisees corruptyng the holy scriptures on such a maner with theyr pestilent gloses) it is necessary that Christe the wisdom of the father come downe, and redresse theise great absurdities, reducyng and bringynge the deuyne Scriptures agayne to theyr true sence, that men maye forsake all Idolatrye, all ungodly doctryne, all wicked customes, and lerne to knowe the true God.[33]

31. Brad Pardue, *Printing, Power, and Piety: Appeals to the Public during the Early Years of the English Reformation* (Leiden: Brill, 2012), 82; Tatiana String, "Henry VIII's Illuminated Great Bible," *Journal of the Warburg and Courtauld Institutes* 59 (1996): 315.

32. Pardue, *Printing, Power, and Piety*, 19.

33. Becon, *Newes out of heauen* (London: John Mayler for John Gough, 1542), sig. Fiiiv.

As James Simpson has recently noted, in this passage Becon conceives of the incarnation primarily as a textual event: a world enslaved to ignorance and idolatry through the willful misuse of the text of Scripture is liberated by the coming of a divine exegete, who restores the Bible to its true meaning.[34] Though unusual in how starkly it subordinates the second person of the Trinity to the text of Scripture, Simpson observes that the primacy of place that this passage gives to the Bible as "a single, textual source of irrefragable authority" was a crucial element of evangelical culture in England.[35] The new availability of the text of Scripture combined with a firm belief in its perspicuity allowed evangelical writers such as Becon to circumvent traditional interpretations of the Bible in line with patristic, conciliar, and magisterial teaching.[36]

For Becon and many of his coreligionists, the written or printed word offered the only certain source of revelation, over against an unholy trinity of human invention, false authority, and inherent idolatry. Because of the technological innovation of the printing press, the Bible could be disembedded from the corporate worship of the church and seen in contradistinction to many aspects of traditional English worship and belief, which now seemed irredeemably untrustworthy. In an evocative image from one of his homilies (1566), Becon contrasts the assimilation of doctrine through church architecture, in particular the rood and the depiction of the last judgment behind it, with the teaching found in the text of Scripture:

> The Pope preacheth of Christe, that he is a seuere Iudge, and that we must healpe before hym by our good woorkes, and that the Intercession of the saintes are to be hadde, yf any man wyll be sure from damnation. For so hath he putte it foorthe in picture, howe Christe commeth in iudgement, and howe he holdeth a swoorde and a rodde in his mouthe, whiche bothe are signes of wroth. And where as Mary and Iohn standeth on bothe sydes, it shewethe, that prayers and intercessions of them, and other suche good Sainctes, must be soughte for and trusted in. . . . But in this Gospel he teacheth us otherwyse, that is, that he shall not come to iudge and condemne us, but deliuer and redeme us, and that he will graunt in dede that that we praied for, and bring us to his kingdom.[37]

34. James Simpson, *Burning to Read: English Fundamentalism and Its Reformation Opponents* (Cambridge: Belknap Press, 2007), 271–72.

35. Simpson, *Burning to Read*, 272.

36. Becon, *A newe pathway unto praier* (London: John Mayler for John Gough, 1542), sigs. Cviir–Cviiv.

37. Becon, *A new Postil*, fol. 11v.

Just as the Bible had been liberated from false interpretations, so Becon believed that it could free Christians from beliefs and practices that could not be proved *sola scriptura*, or in Becon's preferred idiom, according to the "pure uayne of the holye scriptures."[38]

Despite this new juxtaposition of the text of the Bible with received tradition and some of the ecclesiastical establishment, evangelical teaching did not abnegate but rather augmented political authority in England. Central to the mainstream reformations across Europe was a strategic and theological alliance between religious reformers and secular authorities. In the realm of England this alliance was both instantiated and accentuated by the doctrine royal of supremacy embraced by Henry VIII and his evangelical successors.[39] Based on the proof texts of Romans 12:1, 1 Peter 2:14, and Matthew 22:21, and defined in contradistinction to perceived Anabaptist theology, Becon's understanding of the significance of obedience to the Christian life highlights the inherent conservatism of evangelicals on the matter of political submission.[40]

Though Becon treats the subject of obedience numerous times throughout his works, the most forthright account is found in his dialogue *A Pleasaunt Newe Nosegaye* (1542), which presents the five virtues of humility, innocence, charity, assistance of the poor, and obedience. The centrality of obedience to Becon's thought is highlighted by the fact that, while he allots thirty-nine pages to humility, twenty-six to innocence, twelve to charity, nineteen to the assistance of the poor, he dedicates sixty-one pages to obedience. In fact, he goes so far as to claim that learning "to do our duties both toward God, our kynge, and our christen brothers" is "the uery whole summe of christianitie."[41] While Becon's usage of this triad of God, king, neighbor (a regular feature of Henrician rhetoric) was an effort to align his teaching with royal policy, his placement of obedience at the heart of the gospel was entirely orthodox among early English evangelicals.[42]

In another of Becon's dialogues, his mouthpiece character shows his neighbors two tables on his wall: the first displaying the Ten Commandments, "whiche teachethe us what we oughte to do, and what to eschew," and the second disclosing "the offyces of al degrees and estates," that "teacheth us whatte

---

38. Becon, *Newes out of heauen*, sig. Ciiiir.

39. Richard Rex, "The Crisis of Obedience: God's Word and Henry's Reformation," *Historical Journal* 39 (1996): 863–894; Ryrie, *The Gospel and Henry VIII: Evangelicals in the Early English Reformation* (Cambridge: Cambridge University Press, 2003), 58–89.

40. Becon, *A Pleasaunt newe Nosegaye* (London: John Mayler for John Gough, 1542), sigs. Gvv–Liiv.

41. Becon, *A Pleasaunt newe Nosegaye*, sig. Ciiir.

42. Ryan Reeves, *English Evangelicals and Tudor Obedience, c. 1527–1570* (Leiden: Brill, 2014), 80.

we owe to oure mooste noble Prince, to our parents, and to al superioures."[43] This interrelation of Christian piety to secular obligation runs throughout Becon's writing. Many of his prayers detail the specific duties of certain states and vocations: subjects, masters, servants, husbands, wives, single men, maids, and householders.[44] Likewise, his Elizabethan tome, A Newe Catechisme (1564), recounts in exhaustive detail the duties incumbent on magistrates, ministers, schoolmasters, mothers, fathers, children, widows, the young, and the elderly.[45] For Becon and his fellow English evangelicals, to explicate the Christian faith was to speak about the political order and the obligations it demanded.

Though writers such as John Knox, John Ponet, and Christopher Goodman began to articulate resistance theory during the reign of Mary, this was not the default position for the majority of English evangelicals.[46] While Becon highlights the problem of female rule and fulminates against the idolatry and misrule taking place in Marian England, his works are careful not to advocate treason. This was not simply a dogged conservatism. Rather, such views were the product of an intensely held biblical belief that the monarch's heart was in God's hands (Prov 21:1).[47] Since the writing of William Tyndale, evangelical biblical theology has esteemed political obedience as a foundational virtue.[48] Thus, Becon could encourage his readers "aboue all thinges" to "be obedient to the kynges graces maieste, yea and that not onlye for feare but much more for conscience sake, in all thynges, as becommeth faythe full subiectes."[49]

If Becon's writings bear witness to a newly textual religion and to the belief that the political order was divinely sanctioned, they also reveal the consistent concern for a good death in early modern England. Throughout the middle ages, it was commonly held that the devil's favorite trick was to assault the dying with the depravity of their sin, tempting them to despair of God's mercy and to die unrepentant and unshriven. During the fifteenth century, a new genre of devotional manuals, collectively called ars moriendi ("the art of dying"), was created to help laypeople to comfort, exhort, question, and pray for the dying.

---

43. Becon, Newes out of heauen, sigs. Biiiiv–Bvr.

44. Becon, The Pomavnder of Prayer (London: John Day, 1561).

45. Becon, The Worckes of Thomas Becon, vol. 3, sigs. QQiiiir–FFfiiiv.

46. Reeves, English Evangelicals and Tudor Obedience, 129–64.

47. Becon, Newes out of heauen, sig. Avv–Avir; Reeves, English Evangelicals and Tudor Obedience, 2.

48. William Tyndale, The obedience of a Christen man and how Christen rulers ought to governe (Antwerp: Hans Luft, 1528); Ryrie, The Gospel and Henry VIII, 58–60.

49. Becon, A Christmas bankette (London: John Mayler for John Gough, 1542), sigs. Biiiiv–Bvr.

These manuals instructed Christians in how to prepare for their own final battle with the devil, how to resist his temptations, and how to navigate between the twin sins of presumption and despair. They offered readers prayers and examinations to be used alongside the deathbed sacraments (unction, penance, and communion) and other sacramentals (the crucifix and holy water). By providing a regimen of prayer and ritual, these handbooks instructed the dying and those near to them how to wage spiritual war through the repentance of sin, the invocation of Mary and the saints, and the remembrance of the Passion of Christ.[50]

Despite having a markedly different worldview, Becon shared with late medieval Catholics and his contemporary theological adversaries the premise that the deathbed was a battleground of temptation.[51] Unlike Luther, who simply rejected *ars moriendi* manuals as having caused "nothing but error" and made people "more downcast," other Protestants believed that this paradigm of deathbed consolation could be transformed by the insights of biblical faith.[52] Thus, in his dialogue *The Sycke Mans Salue* (1553), Becon dramatizes the consolation and exhortation of a dying man by his four friends, deliberately reforming this medieval paradigm of how to die well in light of his evangelical beliefs. He argued that the best way to resist Satan was not "as the supersticious papistes were wont to do, with casting of holy water about your chamber, with laying holy bread in your window, with pinning a Crosse made of halowed Palmes at your beds head, nor with ringing of the hallowed bel, or such other beggarly, superstitious, Popishe, and deuelish ceremonies," but "with faith, with prayer and with the word of God."[53] Becon thus proposed a regimen of scriptural reading and prayers (including several of his own) that would both reassure the dying and catechize the living with the doctrine of justification *sola fide*.[54] His work immanentized the character of a good death, by rejecting the medieval doctrine of purgatory and by describing how one ought to depart from one's household and dispose of worldly goods.[55] This dialogue was Becon's most popular work: it was printed at least twenty-five times over the next century and became part of

50. Eamon Duffy, *The Stripping of the Altars: Traditional Religion in England, 1400–1580* (New Haven: Yale University Press, 2005), 313–27.

51. Becon, *The sycke mans salue* (London: John Day, 1561), sigs. Aaiir–Aaiiv.

52. Austra Reinis, *Reforming the Art of Dying: The Ars Moriendi in the German Reformation, 1519–1527* (Aldershot: Ashgate, 2007), 1; Ronald K. Rittgers, *The Reformation of Suffering: Pastoral Theology and Lay Piety in Late Medieval and Early Modern Germany* (Oxford: Oxford University Press, 2012), 125–62.

53. Becon, *The sycke mans salue*, AAiiiv.

54. Becon, *The sycke mans salue*, LLiv, MMiiiv.

55. Becon, *The sycke mans salue*, Oiiv, Kiiv.

the zeitgeist of early modern England, as can be seen through several references to it in the writings of the Jacobean playwright Ben Jonson.[56]

Though these three themes reveal Becon's early modern world in transition, they also undergird many of the tensions that have characterized modern Western Christianity until the present. Debates over the relationship of the text of Scripture to the community of faith and the celebration of the liturgy have intensified. The entanglement of European churches with national governments in the twentieth century has called into question former models of Christian obedience. Medieval affective piety has continued to be a source of inspiration, even among those churches whose doctrines of justification by faith alone and predestination would seem to invalidate such expressions of faith. By recovering the Christianity of early modern individuals like Becon, historians and theologians are better able to understand contemporary Christian identity.

---

56. Ben Jonson, *Epicoene, or the silent woman* (London: William Stansby, 1620), sig. Kiir; *Eastward hoe* (London: George Eld for William Aspley, 1605), sig. Hiiiir.

Chapter 27

Teresa of Avila: The Christian Mystic

Robyn Wrigley-Carr

"Teresa found and claimed her place under the cross, and there became sure of God and herself."

— Jürgen Moltmann[1]

"Teresa's writings should be the subject of tomorrow's theology, for academic theology has yet to catch up with her profound grasp of the experience of God."

— Harvey Egan[2]

Teresa's *Marrano* Duplicity—A Heightened Complexity

Teresa Sánchez de Cepeda y Ahumada was born in Avila in 1515 and died in 1582. Though she is commonly known by many as the great Spanish saint "Teresa of Avila," the old, walled city of Avila was not always the hometown for Teresa's family. Formerly from Toledo, Teresa's grandfather, Juan Sánchez, her six-year-old father, Alonso, and Teresa's three uncles had previously been publicly humiliated on seven different Fridays, wearing the *sanbenito* [penitential garment]for being *conversos* [Jewish converts].[3] After the Inquisition's public humiliation, the

---

1. Jürgen Moltmann, "Teresa of Avila and Martin Luther: The Turn to the Mysticism of the Cross," *Studies in Religion* 13, no. 3 (1984): 278.

2. Harvey Egan, *Christian Mysticism: The Future of a Tradition* (New York: Pueblo Publishing, 1984), 118.

3. Yirmiyahu Yovel, *The Other Within: The Marranos: Split Identity and Emerging Modernity* (Princeton: Princeton University Press, 2009), 258. Teresa's grandfather used the "'grace period' [when Judaizers could confess without severe punishment] to confess of the Judaizing practices

family took on Teresa's grandmother's Old Christian name, *Cepeda*, purchased *hidalguia* (complete with the titles of *Don* and *Dona*), and moved to Avila where they tried to masquerade as "Old Christians" and escape public shame.[4]

When Teresa was a young child, the "secret" of her family's auto-da-fé "burst into the open with great scandal."[5] So Teresa grew up with an awareness of why they had moved to Avila and were surrounded by male family members trying to hide that Jewish identity and "de-Judaize" themselves in unique ways.[6] These attempts contributed to Teresa's "duality" and confused identity, and acted to heighten her innate complexity. For so many *conversos* "ended in a state of incomplete identity—a mixed or divided self, in which the Other is preserved within the Self and partly constitutes it."[7] In the case of Teresa's grandfather, Juan Sánchez, his Jewishness was so deeply embodied that he couldn't "renounce his residual Jewish feelings" but was careful to make sure "no outward trace" revealed "their existence."[8] Yovel suggests that a "*Marranesque* duality . . . marked his entire life" and that the "message [that] . . . what is truly valuable in religion is unspoken and lies inside the soul" was "inadvertently passed to Teresa."[9]

By contrast, Teresa's father, Alonso de Cepeda, tried to "completely obliterate his Jewish background . . . to merge into the Catholic fold and climb its social ladder."[10] It is suggested that Teresa's father's response influenced Teresa towards "a non-conformist attempt to deepen and reform the Christian experience itself—by penetrating into its hidden spiritual heart, which was veiled

---

that ran in the family from generation to generation. . . . Their *sanbenitos* were hung in the parish church, a family stigma for generations to come" (Yovel, *The Other Within*, 257–58).

4. Yovel, *The Other Within*, 258. Yovel notes that "a new concept penetrated Spanish society—the *Conversos*. Within a quarter century (1391–1415), the Jewish community lost more than one hundred thousand people, and a similar number of New Christians entered Christian society" (Yovel, *The Other Within*, 57). Davies reminds us that "among many Converso families in sixteenth century Spain it was taught that it was a sin to talk openly about one's ancestry, the importance of guarding the secret of being a converso was paramount." Gareth Alba Davies, "St. Teresa and the Jewish Question," in *Teresa de Jesus and Her World*, ed. Margaret A. Rees (Leeds: Trinity and All Saints College, 1981), 50–51.

5. Yovel, *The Other Within*, 258. One of the "tangible advantages" of attaining *hidalguia* was "exemption from the king's taxes." Yovel, *The Other Within*, 67.

6. Yovel, *The Other Within*, 258.

7. Yovel, *The Other Within*, 78.

8. Yovel, *The Other Within*, 258.

9. Yovel, *The Other Within*, 258. The "marranos" (literally "pigs"), "a nickname given the judeoconversos at that time, had to face a world of not always silent hostilities . . . and of social isolation. This created a suffocating atmosphere for them." Teófanes Egido, OCD, "The Historical Setting of St. Teresa's Life," in *Carmelite Studies I: Spiritual Direction*, ed. John Sullivan, OCD (Washington, DC: ICS Publications, 1980), 142.

10. Yovel, *The Other Within*, 258.

from all ordinary Christians, old and new."[11] We eventually see this in Teresa as a writer, spiritual director, and reformer.

A different attitude was displayed by Teresa's uncle, Pedro de Cepeda, who late in life turned his back on fortune and "honor," immersing himself in the writings of the *alumbrados*.[12] Pedro was the one to introduce Teresa to the writings of the *converso* Osuna, who greatly helped her during two decades of spiritual dryness.[13] Teresa affirms its significance: "I was very happy with this book and resolved to follow that path . . . taking the book for my master. For during the twenty years . . . I did not find a . . . confessor, who understood me."[14] Interestingly, Osuna's work is laced with reminders about human self-deception. He recommends retiring into one's heart and being aware of sin,[15] because, Osuna argues, "snow can cover dung, pills are gilded, and bitter almonds can be candied."[16]

So we see that Teresa grew up in an environment of complexity and hidden, dark secrecy. Teresa even states in her autobiography that "all of earthly life is filled with deception and duplicity."[17] Though she never explicitly mentioned her Jewish background in her writings, Teresa's life displays this "split-identity," the complexities and "restlessness" experienced by many *marranos* due to their "social exclusion" and a need to hide "the other within."[18]

Conflict between "Friendship with God" and "Friendship with the World"

Teresa's undaunted spirit and feisty passion were displayed at the tender age of seven when she attempted to run away to be martyred as a missionary. Rescued by her uncle on the outskirts of Avila, she subsequently tried to build a hermit cell from large stones in her garden. When Teresa was twelve, her mother died suddenly in childbirth, leaving her a lonely adolescent. During

---

11. Yovel, *The Other Within*, 258.

12. Yovel, *The Other Within*, 258.

13. Kieran Kavanagh states that Osuna's *The Third Spiritual Alphabet* was among the works leaving the deepest impression on Teresa. Kieran Kavanagh, "Notes," in *The Collected Works of St. Teresa of Avila* (Washington, DC: ICS Publications, 1976), 1:289.

14. Teresa of Avila, *The Book of Her Life*, 4.7 (hereafter referred to as *Life*). All references to Teresa's writings are taking from volumes 1 to 3 of *The Collected Works of St. Teresa of Avila*, ed. Kieran Kavanaugh, (Washington, DC: ICS Publications, 1976).

15. Francisco de Osuna, *The Third Spiritual Alphabet*, ed. Mary E. Giles (Mahwah, NJ: Paulist Press, 1981), 15.6.

16. Osuna, *The Third Spiritual Alphabet*, 5.1.

17. *Life*, 21.1.

18. Yovel, *The Other Within*, xi.

her teens, Teresa was entranced by chivalric novels and had a desperate need to be loved and to love. Teresa was naturally social, lively and vivacious, physically attractive, and had a keen sense of humor. But her insecurity made her flirtatious, vain, and concerned with pleasing others and gaining their affection. Teresa was also being influenced by a cousin, whose friendship "pained" her father and older sister. Teresa herself confesses, "I was strikingly shrewd when it came to mischief";[19] "since I feared so much for my honour, I used every effort to keep my actions secret."[20] Teresa's father, concerned Teresa might lose her virginity, placed her in an Augustinian convent boarding school at the age of sixteen. At the dormitory Teresa was befriended by a nun who influenced her towards an authentic relationship with Christ. Teresa reflects, "the Lord wished to begin to give me *light*."[21] Through the nun's influence, she "strove" to be Jesus's "companion" in Gethsemane.[22] In her autobiography, Teresa writes, "Most nights, for many years before going to bed when I commended myself to God in preparation for sleep, I always pondered for a little while this episode of the prayer in the garden. I did this even before I was a nun."[23]

Thereafter, Teresa struggled with whether to become a nun. Eventually, the letters of St. Jerome, coupled with her fear of marriage and death in childbirth, drove her to take the habit in the Carmelite Convent of the Incarnation at the age of twenty. As her father forbade her to leave, Teresa planned her escape with her younger brother, and on November 2, 1535, she entered the convent. Her vibrant personality reflected in the "bright red dress" she wore as she crossed the threshold.[24] Teresa received the habit on November 2, 1536, and made her profession of vows on November 3, 1537. Teresa tells of her "great happiness" within an hour of receiving the religious habit, which never left her.[25] Her entrance seems to have been an escape and a rebellion, but her profession of vows led to a "new joy" that "amazed" Teresa.[26]

In her first eighteen years as a Carmelite nun, Teresa experienced a "great [spiritual] dryness."[27] She writes, "I tried as hard as I could to keep Jesus Christ

---

19. *Life*, 2.4.
20. *Life*, 2.7.
21. *Life*, 2.10, italics added.
22. *Life*, 9.4.
23. *Life*, 9.4.
24. Dorothy Day, *The Long Loneliness: An Autobiography* (San Francisco: Harper & Row, 1952), 140.
25. *Life*, 4.2.
26. *Life*, 4.2.
27. *Life*, 4.9.

... present within me, and that was my way of prayer."[28] Yet she was largely living a life of religious pretense—gossiping in the parlors, appearing to be prayerful, but often simply concerned with her own personal esteem. The situation at the Convent of the Incarnation at the time mirrored that in society, with a class system and over one hundred nuns (even 180 at one point). Teresa, being of minor nobility (Dona), had an "apartment" with a kitchen. She had her own sister living with her for some time. Other rich nuns had suites of rooms, whereas the poor sisters lived in dormitories and served the well-to-do as domestic servants. Teresa's later reform of the Carmelite Order was a returning to the Primitive Rule and spirit of the origins of the Order in order to help the Church (the Body of Christ) in its predicament with "the Lutherans." Returning to the Order's origins necessarily involved undoing what was happening in the Incarnation because there they were living under the mitigated Rule.[29]

Struggling with an inner, dry, religious life, Teresa spent some of her energies in the convent trying to manipulate her religious life—and God. She writes, "I was deceiving people since exteriorly I kept up such good appearances.... I strove to be held in esteem.... I grieved very much for being held in esteem since I knew what was down deep in my heart."[30] Teresa even states how easy it was to "conceal" bad deeds in her monastery.[31]

Within this long, dry season of duplicity and deceit, Teresa endured periods of sustained, serious illness, including falling into a coma and paralysis for three years, almost to the point of death. She tells of how she woke to find the wax already placed on her eyelids! When her father was dying and asked Teresa for direction in prayer, Teresa recognized she was "more sick in soul than he was in body."[32] Teresa had long "voyaged on this tempestuous sea" and "suffered this battle and conflict between friendship with God and friendship with the world."[33] She reflects,

> On the one hand God was calling me; on the other hand I was following the world.... I desired to harmonise these two contraries—so inimical to one another—such as are the spiritual life and sensory joys, pleasures, and pastimes.[34]

28. *Life*, 4.7.
29. My thanks to Sister Jocelyn Kramer, OCD, of Varroville NSW, Australia, for these insights about life in the Incarnation during Teresa's first two decades as a nun.
30. *Life*, 7.1.
31. *Life*, 7.4.
32. *Life*, 10.7.
33. *Life*, 8.2, 3.
34. *Life*, 7.17.

Teresa states that she was "like one who is blind or in *darkness*."[35]

During a long period of convalescing, we see a shaft of light. Some progress in her soul came from reading her Uncle Pedro's copy of Osuna's *Third Spiritual Alphabet*. Teresa came to follow that path of recollection. But it was not until her spiritual awakening of 1554 that Teresa found her unique source of Christian identity and entered a life of being "in Christ."

Identity Unified around the Person of Christ

An encounter with a statue of the wounded Christ, scourged at the pillar, was central to Teresa's conversion. She suddenly encountered Christ in the grandeur and the mercy of the cross and thereby saw her own poverty and sinfulness. She was "utterly distressed" and suddenly struck by what he had suffered for her and fell to her knees in surrender. She exclaims, "I felt so keenly aware of how poorly I thanked Him for those wounds . . . my heart broke . . . I threw myself down before Him with the greatest outpouring of tears."[36] Not long after this, while reading Augustine's *Confessions*, Teresa reports, "it seemed to me I saw myself in them . . . it was I the Lord called . . . I . . . dissolved in tears."[37] God gave Teresa light to see herself for the first time. She subsequently writes,

> This is another, new book from here on—I mean another, new life. The life dealt with up to this point was *mine*; the one I lived from the point where I began to explain these things about prayer is the one *God lived in me*. . . . May the Lord be praised who freed me from *myself*.[38]

Being *freed from self* was key to Teresa's new identity of being "in Christ." No longer was she only concerned with her honor and personal esteem, now her entire identity was centered around Christ. Thus Teresa was able to confess, "I can say what St. Paul said . . . that I no longer live but that You, my Creator, live in me."[39] The significance of her family's *converso* connection and duplicity faded as she aligned herself deeply with Jesus. So after her conversion, Teresa no longer signed her letters, "Dona Teresa de Ahumada," but as "Teresa de Jesus," and she opened her letters with "Jesus be with you."[40]

35. *Life*, 9.6, italics added.
36. *Life*, 9.1.
37. *Life*, 9.8.
38. *Life*, 23.1, italics added.
39. *Life*, 6.9.
40. The first word of this greeting was often represented by a large IHS, with a stroke running

In 1559, when books on prayer in the vernacular were banned by the *Valdes Index*, Teresa was disheartened, being unable to read Latin. But Jesus told Teresa that he would be to her a "Living Book."[41] Teresa reports,

> I wasn't able to understand why this was said to me for as yet I had received no visions. Afterwards, within only a few days, I understood very clearly because I received so much to think about and such recollection in the presence of what I saw, and the Lord showed so much love for me by teaching me in many ways, that I had very little or almost no need for books. His Majesty had become the true book in which I saw the truths.[42]

Thereafter, Christ revealed himself to Teresa in "supernatural," mystical experiences.[43] In her early visions of Jesus, Teresa doubted whether she had "fancied the vision" or if it was from the devil.[44] She wrote, "Christ appeared. . . . I saw Him with the eyes of my soul more clearly than I could have with the eyes of my body."[45] Looking back on those years, Teresa wished she had known, or had had spiritual confessors who could help her understand, that it is "possible to see in other ways than with the bodily eyes."[46]

For the twenty-eight years after her conversion, Teresa was to become a Christian mystic who had vivid, firsthand, dramatic "favors" from God: visions, divine ecstasies, levitations, and other supernatural experiences. Teresa also experienced "raptures," describing her soul as "completely under the control of another."[47] Alongside visions of Christ, she had visions of the Blessed Trinity: "all three Persons were represented distinctly in my soul and they spoke to me."[48] These intimate encounters she likened to the "experience of two persons here on earth who love each other deeply . . . just by a glance . . . they understand each other."[49] Teresa's experiences of the Trinity were "inexplicitly intertwined" with her experiences of Christ: "She would have us understand that one enters

---

through the H, to form a cross, a reminder of Christ's sacrifice. E. Allison Peers, *The Letters of Saint Teresa of Jesus* (London: Sheed & Ward, 1980), 1:15–16.

41. *Life*, 26.5.

42. *Life*, 27.5.

43. The first two people Teresa consulted about her mystical experiences told her they were from the devil. Teresa eventually came to recognize Jesus's voice and was liberated from a fear of deception.

44. *Life*, 7.7.

45. *Life*, 7.6.

46. *Life*, 7.7.

47. *Life*, 25.4.

48. *Spiritual Testimonies*, 13.

49. *Life*, 27.10.

into the mystery of the Trinity through participation in the mystery of Christ."[50] So we see that Teresa's "mental prayer," her "intimate sharing between friends,"[51] while focused on Christ, also involved all three persons of the Trinity.

Mystical Experiences and the Inquisition

To claim to have had such supernatural experiences of God placed Teresa in a dangerous position with regard to the Spanish Inquisition. Indeed, Teresa's visions of Christ transcended anything known to the Inquisitors. The common piety of Teresa's day was "spoken prayer," which followed the Church's liturgy and was deemed "safe" by the authorities. But within this context, a proliferation of spiritual movements flourished that explored "mental prayer" and other spiritual practices. Yet it was also the scene for rivalry between those influenced by *devotio moderna*, the *espirituales* (spiritual writers), and the *letrados* (theologians). The *letrados* distrusted any knowledge of God that was intuitive or based upon *lived* experience rather than grounded in dogma. By contrast, the *espirituales* exalted knowledge gained through direct experience and prayer.

Within this context, Teresa occupied a unique position. As Prioress of the Convent of the Incarnation, a reformer of the Carmelite Order, and a spiritual director to many (including the King of Spain), Teresa held a position of mediation in the division between *letrados* and *espirituales*. Teresa sought out "learned men" and had a great respect for those who had studied doctrine, but in practice she was a great *espirituale* and mainly read works written by *espirituales*.

However, not all *espirituales* were orthodox. The "Illuminists" were a popular movement of interior prayer, recollection, and penance that ran from the first decade of the sixteenth century until the 1620s. Those in the movement were known as *alumbrados*, "those who are lit," and were divided into *recogidos* and *dejados*. The *recogidos* attached importance to recollection, which consisted of self-knowledge, imitation of Christ, and union with God.[52] But the *dejados* were inclined to false mysticism, semi-quietism, licentious sexuality, and had a passion for ecstatic phenomena such as raptures, visions, and inner voices.[53]

---

50. Anne Hunt, *The Trinity: Insights from the Mystics* (Collegeville, MN: Liturgical Press, 2010), 142.

51. *Life*, 8.5.

52. Kieran Kavanaugh, "Spanish Sixteenth Century: Carmel and Surrounding Movements," in *Christian Spirituality, Post-Reformation and Modern*, ed. Louis Dupré and Don Saliers (London: SCM Press, 1990), 71.

53. This heretical sect viewed union with God as dependent upon passivity. They believed that when a person reached an exalted stage of union with God, nothing they did was sinful.

This group were prone to religious eccentricity and devil-induced states. During Teresa's life, a visionary, Magdalena de la Cruz, a Poor Clare who had a reputation for holiness, confessed to the Inquisition that her mystical experiences were the result of having made a pact with the devil. Teresa's claim of having had direct contact with God placed her in the dangerous position of being mistaken for a *dejado*. For "mental prayer" was increasingly seen as suspicious and the means to an inflated confidence in one's individual religious authority.[54] Inquisitorial anxiety focused upon anything that suggested that God could work directly upon the soul, without any kind of institutional mediation.

This turbulent period of history, like the previous age of chivalry and crusaders, was predominantly male. So in church, as in society, women had little influence on the public sphere, unless of noble birth. The theologian Medina said publicly at the University of Salamanca, "women are good for nothing but to spin, cook and at most say vocal prayer."[55] Melchior Cano, a theologian at the Council of Trent, declared, "We are in a time when one preaches that women should take up their hand work and their rosary, and not worry about more devotion."[56] A deep suspicion of women was rooted in the view that women, as daughters of Eve, were more susceptible to the devil's deceptions. Thus females were viewed as potential heretics and were not permitted to have a secret, inner prayer life. Teresa's place in her milieu as a mystic and, most importantly, as a woman made her extremely vulnerable to accusation by the Spanish Inquisition. Teresa's autobiography, *Life*, ended up in the hands of the Inquisition. Written at the request of her confessors, she sent it to John of Avila in 1568, then in 1570, other confessors read it. Fortunately in 1575, when it was sent to the Inquisition, it fell into the right hands. The Inquisitor in Madrid who assessed her work was sympathetic, having encouraged her to write her autobiography in the first place!

Other works written by Teresa include her *Spiritual Testimonies*, also written for her confessors and discussing the state of her soul between 1560 and 1581. Teresa's *Soliloquies,* written in 1569, contain her intimate prayers after taking the Eucharist. Teresa's nuns asked her to write about prayer, so she wrote *The Way of Perfection* in 1566 and *Meditations on the Song of Songs* in 1567. In 1577, Teresa's spiritual director, Father Gratian, ordered Teresa to "Write another book, but put down the doctrine in a general way without naming the one to whom the

54. The Inquisition's Index of 1559 forbade the publication of all vernacular books on religious themes, especially prayer.

55. Teresa Iglesias, *Saint Teresa of Avila: The Roots of Her Greatness* (Dublin: Dominican Publications, 1970), 28.

56. Otger Steggink, "The Doctorate of Experience," in *Carmelite Studies IV Edith Stein Symposium: Teresian Culture*, ed. John Sullivan (Washington, DC: ICS Publications, 1987), 250.

things you mentioned there happened."[57] *Interior Castle* is the result and is Teresa's most symbolic and mature work. In obedience to another confessor, Teresa wrote her *Foundations* in 1573, an account of the monasteries she founded.[58]

In her writings, Teresa is often deliberately self-deprecating, embracing stereotypes of female ignorance, timidity, or physical weakness, as a subtle defense against being thought of as a seductress or as demon possessed. Alison Weber highlights the way that Teresa employed "self-deprecatory" language as a "rhetorical . . . strategy," taking on "a persona that mimicked the feminine character idealised by her male contemporaries . . . to survive."[59] Here we see a subversive element in Teresa—a play-acting, gender complexity—essential to Teresa's "survival."

Teresa the Mystical Theologian

Teresa herself uses the term "mystical theology" to refer to knowledge of God that is directly *infused* by God.[60] She writes, the "feeling of the presence of God would come upon me unexpectedly so that I could in no way doubt He was within me and I was totally immersed in Him. . . . I believe they call the experience 'mystical theology.'"[61] As such, Teresa's theology is not primarily *rational* but *relational*—an in-dwelled knowing. Where speculative theology sought to know about God through human reasoning, mystical theology is a knowing formed in the soul by prayer, through God's action alone. As such, Teresa, as a mystic is "a rebuke to those who theologise without praying."[62] She believed that knowledge of God, directly given through visions and "favors," is the only theology worth pursuing, telling her nuns:

> avoid tiring yourselves or wasting your thoughts in subtle reasoning . . . when the Lord desires to give understanding, His Majesty does so without our

---

57. Kieran Kavanaugh, Introduction to *The Interior Castle*, in vol. 2 of *The Collected Works of Teresa of Avila* (Washington, DC: ICS Publications, 1980), 263.

58. Teresa's other works include *Constitutions* and *On Making the Visitation*. She also wrote some poetry and hundreds of letters.

59. Alison Weber, *Teresa of Avila and the Rhetoric of Femininity* (Princeton: Princeton University Press, 1990), 169.

60. *Life*, 9.1; 11.5. When writing to her nuns about the Song of Songs, she says, "I shall be able to say only what the Lord teaches me." *Meditations on the Song of Songs*, 1.9.

61. *Life*, 10.1.

62. James M. Houston, "Reflections on Mysticism: How Valid Is Anti-Mysticism?" In *Gott Lieben und Seie Gebote Halten* (Umbshlag: Brunnen Verlag Gieben, 1991), 172.

effort . . . accept with simplicity whatever the Lord gives us, and what He doesn't we shouldn't tire ourselves over . . . let us humble ourselves.[63]

Once again we see *humility* as key in receiving this infused knowledge of God.

Teresa's mystical theology is most clearly expressed in her final work, *Interior Castle*. Here we see Teresa forced to utilize an imaginative, rich language of symbolism to describe her experiences of the mystical journey of the soul to God. Symbolic language enables Teresa to write about her essentially incommunicable experiences of supernatural prayer. As Soskice argues,

> The mystic . . . often feels a crisis of descriptive language because there do not seem to be words and concepts in the common stock adequate to his or her experience. This straining of linguistic resources leads to the catechetical employment of metaphor.[64]

Fifty-three metaphors are used in the *Interior Castle*. The soul is symbolized as a castle composed of seven dwelling places, and the life of prayer is viewed as a journey into the castle, with the ultimate aim of union with God by entering into the seventh dwelling place. And as the journey into the center deepens, the number of symbols increases. A major division occurs in the work between the first three and last four dwelling places. The first three dwelling places can be entered through *our* work in prayer. By contrast, the last four dwelling places are a gift from God and entrance to them is *his* initiative. Teresa argues that self-knowledge and humility are required to enter these latter dwelling places. A byproduct of her mystical experiences in the latter dwelling places is an ever-growing, fervent love for Christ. Teresa, the mystical theologian, is, essentially, Teresa the lover.

Teresa's passionate love for Christ is most vividly expressed in her *Soliloquies*. Here we see Teresa addressing Jesus directly—vulnerable and unselfconscious.[65] The seventeen soliloquies were written on different occasions in 1569 when Teresa had just received the Eucharist. We glimpse Teresa's impassioned heart as she intimately addresses Christ:

> O true Lover, with how much compassion, with how much gentleness, with how much delight, with how much favour and with what extraordinary signs

63. *Meditations on the Song of Songs*, 1.2.

64. Janet Soskice, *Metaphor and Religious Language* (Oxford: Clarendon, 1985), 151.

65. It is likely Teresa was inspired by Augustine's *Soliloquies*, for the styles are remarkably similar.

of love You cure these wounds. . . . O my God and my rest from all pains, how entranced I am![66]

Similarly she declares, "my Christ, how pleasing and delightful Your eyes are to one who loves You . . . one such gentle glance . . . is enough reward for many years of service."[67] And certainly "service" is part of Teresa's mission. However, Teresa's preference would probably have been to simply stay with her Lover in her prayer cell. Indeed, she comes to view people as "like little sticks of dry rosemary" that "break" whenever there is criticism or contradiction. She simply wants to "be attached to the cross," to "the *true* friend."[68] However, Teresa recognizes that she cannot simply stay in her prayer cell but is called to the *mixed* life of contemplative prayer *and* service, as a writer, reformer, and founder of convents.

Teresa the Reformer

We see Teresa's remarkable life of supernatural prayer gave rise to an extraordinarily *active* life: being appointed prioress of the Convent of the Incarnation in 1571, reforming the Carmelite Order, founding new convents throughout Spain, and writing prolifically. Teresa valued the mixed life, as revealed in a letter to Father Gratian: "the most potent and acceptable prayers . . . are followed up by *actions*."[69] For the mature Teresa had congruence between her inner life and her outward actions; her inner life informed her outer life.

In the 1560s and 1570s, Teresa was central to cultural changes of her day through her reform of the Carmelite Order back to the original Rule of Carmel. Worldliness had crept into the Order along with an obsession with "honor." At San Jose, Teresa wanted only a few nuns, a maximum of twelve nuns plus Prioress (like the twelve disciples and Jesus), and for them all to be friends and help each other, to be equal. That is why she was so hard on anyone who tried to flaunt their honor or family background. As she saw it, such an attitude undermined the fundamental gospel precepts of love of God and love of neighbor.[70] So Teresa reformed her own house to strict enclosure and a rhythm of daily routines, including more daily times for mental prayer. Believing solitude to be essential for the practice of contemplative prayer, Teresa's primary goal was to

66. *Soliloquies*, 16.2.
67. *Soliloquies*, 14.1.
68. *Spiritual Testimonies*, 3.1, italics added.
69. *Letters*, 1:316, italics added.
70. I thank Sister Jocelyn Kramer, OCD, of Varroville NSW, Australia, for these insights about Teresa's Reform.

reform the Order around the person of Christ. And the new rule of poverty was the counterpoise to the honor and comfort of the Incarnation. Indeed, Teresa is described as saying that life is a "night spent at an uncomfortable inn."[71] So the new Carmelites became known as "discalced" (literally barefoot, though Teresa wore sandals), as a symbol of simplicity and poverty.

Teresa founded the Convent of San Jose in 1562 and received permission by the Superior General in 1567 to establish other convents. In 1570, she was told by the wounded Christ in an imaginative vision that she

> shouldn't grieve over those wounds, but over many that were now being inflicted upon Him. I asked Him, what could I do as a remedy for this. . . . He told me . . . that I should hurry to establish these houses.[72]

And so Teresa founded another sixteen convents during her remaining fifteen years.[73] A crucial part of her reform was her desire that convents be free from being indebted to benefactors, so Teresa took a strong stand against endowments. Teresa's reform of the Carmelite Order was in its own way a protest against, and rejection of, empty and meaningless social distinctions. Teresa recognized that God's acceptance of us as his friends, regardless of our unworthiness, provides a model for community where all must be friends, irrespective of social standing. And Teresa advised her nuns to have no duplicity, encouraging them to be "truthful" with Christ: "don't say one thing and then act differently."[74]

Though Teresa never referred to her *converso* status, she was well aware of it and we see some fascinating clues in her actions. For example, her original foundation at Toledo (now marked only by a plaque on a wall), where her family came from, was adjacent to the Jewish quarter and former synagogue.[75] Teresa also had business dealings with enormous numbers of people who assisted in various ways with her foundations. Many of these were *conversos*, and it seems Teresa had a natural ease and affinity with that "set."[76]

71. Quoted in Day, *The Long Loneliness*, 140.

72. *Spiritual Testimonies*, 6.

73. Teresa also helped to reform the Carmelite friars with St. John of the Cross. Travelling around Spain in an old cart was often hazardous. One day after her cart overturned and she was thrown into the mud, apparently Teresa felt God say to her, "This is how I treat my friends." Teresa promptly replied, in typical humorous style, "And that is why You have so few of them." Day, *The Long Loneliness*, 140.

74. *Way of Perfection*, 37.4.

75. Even the Incarnation in Avila was, and still is, adjacent to the Jewish cemetery. It is hypothesized that one reason for the choice of location is that after the Jews were expelled from Spain, their land was cheap to purchase.

76. I thank Sister Jocelyn Kramer, OCD, of Varroville NSW, Australia, for these insights.

From Honor to Humility

In Teresa's day, honor was the very soul of social behavior in Castile and exercised a paralyzing hold on many people. It expressed the relation of the individual to society encompassing both public dignity and social standing. Teresa reacted strongly to this obsession with honor rampant in the social system of her day. Her own grandfather had earlier purchased a certificate of nobility to secure both public standing and wealth, and had changed the family name to conceal their Jewish ancestry. Teresa came to despise such widespread pretense and concern with externals. Throughout her writings, she is highly critical of the obsession with what she calls "*Nigra honora*," black honor. Describing honor as a "toxin" that "kills perfection,"[77] Teresa exclaims, "My blood freezes when I write about this . . . I see it as the main evil in monasteries."[78] Teresa perceived that honor subverts the soul's freedom in Christ as we are distracted by tangible, external appearances. Teresa reminds us that true moral worth is an *interior* reality. Rather than being concerned with one's *own* honor, Teresa points her nuns towards honoring *God*.[79] Thus, social honor is replaced by Teresa with what is true and authentic: honoring Christ by *humbling* ourselves.[80]

The accomplished Teresian scholar, E. Allison Peers, writes, "An insistence on humility is the keynote of all her work . . . this humility comes by self-knowledge."[81] Standing in the Augustinian tradition, Teresa recognized the journey to union with God is a progressive emancipation from self-love to the double-knowledge of knowing self in the light of who God is.[82] Unlike many contemporary, self-grounded "techniques of self-examination . . . loosely grounded in psychoanalytic theory,"[83] Teresian self-knowledge is rooted in knowing God. For true self-knowledge strives "to construct the narrative least unfaithful to the divine perspective."[84] The self is defined in the light of who

---

77. *Way of Perfection*, 12.7.

78. *Way of Perfection*, 7.10.

79. *Way of Perfection*, 27.3.

80. This is repeated across her writings. For example, *Way of Perfection* (3.6–7), *Interior Castle* (IV.1.7; VII.3.6), and *Life* (21.1).

81. E. Allison Peers, *Studies of the Spanish Mystics* (London: SPCK, 1951), 1:132.

82. Bernard of Clairvaux, who greatly influenced Teresa, wrote, "In the light of Truth men know themselves and so think less of themselves. . . . They are brought face to face with themselves and blush at what they see." Bernard of Clairvaux, *The Steps of Humility and Pride* (Kalamazoo, MI: Cistercian Publications, 1989), 45.

83. Rowan Williams, "'Know Thyself': What Kind of an Injunction?" in *Philosophy, Religion and the Spiritual Life*, ed. Michael McGhee (Cambridge: Cambridge University Press, 1992), 214.

84. Williams, "'Know Thyself,'" 221.

God is; knowledge of self and of God are conjoined. Teresa's understanding of self-knowledge can be best described in her own words:

> Let's strive to make more progress in self-knowledge. In my opinion we shall never completely know ourselves if we don't strive to know God. By gazing at His grandeur, we get in touch with our own lowliness; by looking at His purity, we shall see our own filth; by pondering His humility, we shall see how far we are from being humble.[85]

As Ruth Burrows remarks, "what surer grounds for fostering true self-knowledge than the consideration of the mystery of sin?"[86] For Teresa, "meditation on the humanity of Jesus . . . is a coming to know ourselves *through* Christ."[87] We "gaze" on him, the "Model and Master" of authentic humility.[88] In fact, "all harm" comes from not keeping our "eyes fixed" on him.[89]

But the humility of Jesus is not simply historical. Teresa teaches her nuns that Jesus continues "humbly . . . teaching you" in the present.[90] In her *Interior Castle*, Teresa emphasizes that the favors given by God in the final four dwelling places of the castle deepen our self-knowledge. Through encountering God in his majesty through supernatural favors, God gives greater insight into his grandeur and infuses us with a richer, deeper, authentic self-knowledge. Self-knowledge is the effect of "supernatural" prayer in these deeper dwelling places. Teresa emphasizes that self-knowledge comes only at God's initiative. He is the one who chooses to reveal himself and provides spiritual favors, with such dramatic effect: "More improvement in self-knowledge is felt from one of these words than would be got from many days of reflection on our wretchedness, for it *engraves* on us an undeniable truth."[91]

Teresa also emphasizes that humility is "indispensable"[92] as it "draws" God to the soul. Using the metaphor of a chess game, Teresa says that the humility of the queen "*draws* the King."[93] Spiritual favors are given by God only if hu-

---

85. *Interior Castle*, I.2.9–10.

86. Ruth Burrows, *Interior Castle Explored* (London: Sheed & Ward, 1981), 15–16.

87. Rowan Williams, *Teresa of Avila* (London: Geoffrey Chapman, 1991), 89.

88. *Way of Perfection*, 36.5. Teresa encourages her nuns to meditate on Jesus's humility in prayer (*Way of Perfection*, 42.5), focus on his sufferings and enduring of unjust accusations in silence (*Way of Perfection*, 18.5; 26.5), and "take the lowest place" and "serve" (*Way of Perfection*, 17.1; 34.5).

89. *Way of Perfection*, 16.11.

90. *Way of Perfection*, 26.1; 33.4,5.

91. *Life*, 38.16, italics added.

92. *Way of Perfection*, 17.1.

93. *Way of Perfection*, 16.2, italics added.

mility is truly present.[94] Teresa exclaims, "There are some persons who demand favours from God as though these were due them in justice. That's a nice kind of humility!"[95] She asserts that "this King . . . delights more in the unpolished manners of a humble shepherd . . . than He does in the talk of very wise and learned men . . . if they don't walk in humility."[96] This authentic humility is gained through being "in Christ."

From "Split-Identity" of *Self*-Focus to a Unified *Christ*-Focus

In Teresa's final and most celebrated work, *Interior Castle*, she symbolizes her soul as a silkworm that dies in a cocoon, which is Christ, then is transformed into a butterfly:

> The silkworm, which is fat and ugly, then dies, and a little white butterfly which is very pretty, comes forth from the cocoon. . . . this house is Christ . . . our life is hidden in Christ . . . weave this little cocoon by getting rid of our self-love . . . let the silkworm die. . . . And you will see how we see God, as well as ourselves placed inside His greatness, as is this little silkworm within its cocoon.[97]

Then, from being "in Christ" in the fifth dwelling place, a second death occurs in the seventh dwelling place: "the butterfly dies with great joy, because its life is now Christ."[98] As Teresa's soul dies *with* and *in* Christ, she enters into the inner-Trinitarian relations of the Trinity. She experiences both "mystical union" with all three divine Persons and comes to know herself from *within* this mystery.[99] Her soul is joined with God to such a degree that it almost ceases to exist apart from him. The effects of this death are "forgetfulness of self"[100] and "a great desire to suffer."[101] She becomes less; Christ becomes greater. Her self-love evaporates and Christ is all.

---

94. *Way of Perfection*, 17.7.
95. *Way of Perfection*, 18.6.
96. *Way of Perfection*, 22.5–7.
97. *Interior Castle*, V.2.2–7.
98. *Interior Castle*, VII.2.5.
99. Hunt, *The Trinity*, 142.
100. *Interior Castle*, VII.2.
101. *Interior Castle*, VII.4.

From Self-Protection to Embracing Suffering

Teresa's ongoing union with Christ leads to an ever-increasing willingness to surrender her will. This increasing desire to embrace the suffering of Christ is revealed in 1572, when Teresa feels her mouth fill with blood during the Eucharist and recognizes she is entering into Christ's sufferings.[102] From being a woman of "impure blood," a *converso*, now she has internalized the pure blood of Christ. Jesus tells Teresa this suffering is an effect of spiritual marriage: "Because of this espousal, whatever I have is yours. So I give you all the trials and sufferings I underwent."[103] To this Teresa responds, "I look very differently upon what the Lord suffered, as something belonging to me."[104] Teresa comes to understand her living as an ongoing death to self and being constantly alive to Christ. She hears Jesus say, "Eat for Me and sleep for Me . . . as though you no longer lived but I."[105] The words of her final testimony, only a year before her death, reveal her soul in its "surrender to the will of God."[106] *His* desire has become fully *her* desire. Her experience of God's presence is "almost continual," and her "surrender" so complete that "the soul wants neither death nor life."[107] She declares, "May He reign, and may I be captive."[108] A "captivated" lover of Christ, Teresa died in 1582.

Coda

So in Teresa we encounter a remarkable woman whose identity became completely surrendered to Christ. She was so "taken over by Christ" that she exhibited "a whole new identity,"[109] a wholeness, a union, from her ongoing encounters with him. She came to be liberated from herself and her concern with her *converso* background. After twenty years of largely masquerading as a nun, she lived an extraordinary life experiencing mystical favors, writing works of mystical theology, providing spiritual direction, reforming the Carmelite Order and founding convents all over Spain. It is hardly surprising that she was can-

102. *Spiritual Testimonies*, 22.
103. *Spiritual Testimonies*, 46.
104. *Spiritual Testimonies*, 46.
105. *Spiritual Testimonies*, 51.
106. *Spiritual Testimonies*, 65.9.
107. *Spiritual Testimonies*, 65.9.
108. *Soliloquies*, 17.3.
109. James M. Houston, *Joyful Exiles: Life in Christ on the Dangerous Edge of Things* (Downers Grove, IL: InterVarsity Press, 2006), 108.

onized in 1622 and was the first woman to be made a Doctor of the Church in 1970. Teresa came to have a massive influence on public, social life through the outworking of her humble, inner private life. And it is Teresa's unique identity as a person-in-Christ that brought about her transformation from a concern with honor to humility, from self-focus to Christ-focus, from self-protection to embracing suffering. Unlike the fake mystics of her day, Teresa was an authentic Christ-centered mystic.

Teresa reminds us that "the self-love that reigns in us is very subtle."[110] We need to get our "professional" identities out of the way and, in Teresa's words, be "oned" with Jesus;[111] for "we are never more our true selves than when we are most 'in' Christ Jesus."[112]

I close with some phrases from a Teresian poem:

Happy the enamored heart,
Thought centred on God alone . . .
Living *forgetful of self*,
In God is all its intention,
Happy and so joyfully it journeys
Through waves of this stormy sea.[113]

110. *Foundations*, 4.2.

111. "On Those Words 'Dilectus Meus Mihi,'" in *Poetry*, in vol. 3 of *The Collected Works of St. Teresa of Avila* (Washington: ICS Publications, 1985), 380 (poem no. 3).

112. Houston, *Joyful Exiles*, 18.

113. Teresa of Avila, "Happy the Enamored Heart," in *Poetry*, 381 (poem no. 5), italics added.

Chapter 28

Fray Luis de León (1527–1591): "The Imprisoned Self"

Colin Thompson

Luis de León, one of the foremost writers of sixteenth-century Spain, was an Augustinian friar who occupied a number of Chairs at Salamanca, most notably the Chair of Bible from 1579 until his death. His prose masterpiece *On the Names of Christ* is an exploration in dialogue form of the names and titles given to the Messiah in a series of prophetic texts from the Old Testament, and combines exposition with a profoundly Christocentric theology of redemption. His choice of the vernacular for such a work was pointed: in the dedication to the first book he states explicitly that it is intended to make up for the fact that lay people are not permitted to read the Scriptures in their own language. He also wrote Latin commentaries on Psalm 26, the Song of Solomon, Obadiah, Romans, Galatians, and 2 Thessalonians.[1] He made numerous verse translations both of classical poets (especially Horace and Virgil) and the Psalms, while his vernacular *Exposition of the Book of Job*, including a translation of each chapter into Spanish tercets, remained unpublished until the eighteenth century. But he is chiefly read today for his small corpus of exquisitely crafted poems, regarded as among the finest in the language.[2]

---

1. From Psalms 10–146 the Vulgate numbering of the Psalms is one behind the Hebrew and subsequent English versions; its 26 is therefore our 27, "The Lord is my light and my salvation."

2. There are many modern editions of his works in Spanish, but few translations into English. For versions of his poems (numbered differently from standard Spanish editions), see Willis Barnstone, *The Unknown Light: The Poems of Fray Luis de León* (Albany: State University of New York, 1979); also Edith Grossman, *Poems of the Spanish Renaissance* (New York: W. W. Norton, 2006), which includes four. For the prose, see Luis de León, *The Names of Christ*, trans. M. Durán and W. Kluback, Classics of Western Spirituality (London: SPCK, 1984).

In the Cells of the Inquisition

The defining moment of his adult life was the period of almost five years that he spent in solitary confinement in the cells of the Spanish Inquisition in Valladolid. The reasons for this long imprisonment are complex. They include his work as a Hebraist and biblical scholar of partly Jewish ancestry in an age of deep anti-Semitism; his vernacular manuscript commentary on the Song of Songs at a time when the Scriptures were available only in Latin; and the deep-seated rivalry between the religious orders at the University of Salamanca. Behind them lay the disputed question of the authority of the Latin Bible (the Vulgate) in relation to the Hebrew and Greek originals from which it had been translated. The Council of Trent's decree on Sacred Scripture at its fourth session (April 1546) had pronounced the Vulgate to be "authentic" for public reading, disputations, preaching, and exposition, but had not defined the meaning of the word or what it implied about the status of the Hebrew and Greek texts. While earlier in the sixteenth century, Spain had embraced the new ideas associated with Erasmus, the rise of Protestantism in the Spanish Netherlands and in the German lands brought about a marked shift in the intellectual climate. In 1559 Spanish students and professors had been recalled from foreign universities (except Naples and Bologna), and that same year the first Spanish Index of Prohibited Books was published. Fray Luis had been part of a group of Salamanca professors in the 1560s formed to consider the revision of the Complutensian Polyglot Bible, published in 1520, a controversial proposal for what would later come to be known as the *Biblia Regia* or Plantin Polyglot. Its members held sharply opposing views, especially in relation to the relative importance of the Latin, Greek, and Hebrew texts. Fray Luis was arrested, as were two of his colleagues, in March 1572, and was released, cleared of all charges, at the end of 1576.[3] Fray Luis conducted his own defense from his prison cell, arguing tirelessly and at length that his views were entirely orthodox and had been misrepresented through a combination of ignorance and malice. The trial documents reveal both the vigor of his scholarship and the sufferings of a man who believed he was the victim of a great injustice.[4] Rather than turning his back on dispassionate enquiry as the best way to ascertain the sense of Scripture, he stood his ground and turned the accusations back against his accusers.

---

3. These were Gaspar de Grajal, Professor of Bible, who died in prison before his case was completed, and Martín Martínez de Cantalapiedra, Professor of Hebrew.

4. See *El proceso inquisitorial de Fray Luis de León*, ed. Ángel Alcalá (Salamanca: Junta de Castilla y León, 1991).

Imprisonment as Metaphor

This direct engagement with those who had denounced him is, however, only a part of the story. Many of his poems adopt a first-person voice and use the metaphor of imprisonment to explore the wider human condition, as a symbol for the ignorance and delusions that prevent people from reaching a true understanding of their origins and destiny, as well as more broadly to contrast the soul's eternal nature with the perishable materiality of the body. Some are addressed to named individuals, who become case studies of the imprisoned self. This first-person voice may sometimes be autobiographical, but more often is representative of anyone yearning to find a freedom hitherto denied them.

This representative nature is clearly present in the twenty-three psalms Fray Luis translated, several of which call on God to vindicate his servant against his enemies or cry for help amidst suffering (Vulgate 4, 11, 12, 17, 26, 38, 41, 87, 129, 136). Only one (24) fits the more conventional pattern of *metanoia*, with its confession of guilt and plea for pardon. The figure of Job as the embodiment of the innocent sufferer also appealed to him, as it did to other neo-Stoical writers of the period who had not experienced long physical confinement, because it provided biblical authority for their interest in the Stoics' doctrine of *ataraxia*, that is, of not allowing external events over which one had no control, however distressing they were, to interfere with one's inner tranquility.

In the past, critics tended to interpret references to imprisonment in the poems as referring to Fray Luis's own ordeal, and dated them accordingly. This is not a tenable position: the metaphor is an ancient one, stretching back into Plato's account of the relationship of the soul to the body in his *Phaedo*, and it was extensively borrowed in Neoplatonic writing in terms of the body and its material desires as the prison of the soul. Some form of stimulus—in Fray Luis's case, contemplation of the night sky or listening to beautiful music—was required to awaken awareness that the spiritual self existed at all (the Platonic theory of *anamnesis*). I shall consider first the imprisoned self of Fray Luis himself; then those poems which are largely neo-Stoical in inspiration, in which the poet seeks to escape from the restless search for power, status, and wealth to the peace and natural beauty of the countryside; and finally those cast in a Neoplatonic mold, in which the soul ascends from the realm of the ephemeral to contemplate eternal verities. In each case the different facets of the prison metaphor function as a means of reflecting on the bondage of the human self and its longing for liberation.

The first work Fray Luis published after his release was a commentary on Psalm 26.[5] In the short dedication he wrote to the Inquisitor General Gaspar

5. *In Psalmum Vigesimum Sextum Explanatio* (Salamanca: Lucas à Iunta, 1580), §§2–3.

de Quiroga, whom he credits with securing his release, he speaks both of the suffering he endured at the hands of his enemies and of the divine ability to turn such experiences into blessings: "I was slanderously summoned on suspicion of harming the faith and was kept isolated not only from the words and company but even from the sight of men, and lay for almost five years in prison and in darkness." Yet "those things held to be the greatest evils I have experienced as full of the sweetest delights" (a view he explicitly contrasts with the Stoics' desire to flee from anything troublesome). While he explains that he drew comfort from his own clear conscience, reading this psalm in prison at a time of great personal distress gave him a strong sense of the power of divine goodness, and he decided to use his enforced leisure fruit-fully by beginning work on a commentary. This rhetoric of self-justification may sit uneasily with the Christian emphasis on sin and repentance, but Fray Luis was not so much defending himself as his integrity as a biblical scholar who was not afraid to argue that the Vulgate had not always translated the Hebrew original accurately, against those who (like modern fundamentalists) believed it to be inerrant.

The Neo-Stoical Self

His shortest poem (XXIII) is a single *décima* (ten-line verse) assumed to have been written shortly after his release:[6]

> Here envy and lies
> held me imprisoned.
> Happy the humble state
> of the wise man who retires
> from this wicked world,
> and with a poor house and table
> in the delights of the countryside
> measures himself only by God,
> and passes his life alone,
> neither envied nor envious.

6. I follow the text and numbering as given in Fray Luis de León, *Poesías completas*, ed. Cristóbal Cuevas (Madrid: Castalia, 1998). All translations are my own. For a useful introduc-tion to Fray Luis's poetry, see Elias L. Rivers, *Fray Luis de León: The Original Poems* (London: Grant & Cutler, 1983); more generally on his life and writing, see Colin P. Thompson, *The Strife of Tongues: Fray Luis de León and the Golden Age of Spain* (Cambridge: Cambridge University Press, 1988).

The emphatic "here," the personified envy and lying, and the metaphor of past confinement express in the tersest form his sense of having been the victim of injustice, in contrast to the classical topos of the *beatus ille*, that evocation of the joys of the peaceful life of the countryside, given a more spiritual sense by the reference to God.[7] The antithesis is worked out more fully in XIV, but this time it begins with an implied confession of the poet's own culpability:

> Oh haven safe at last
> from my persistent error! O longed for
> rest, sweet, happy, tranquil,
> as the certain remedy
> for the grave evil of the past!

The seafaring metaphor, often used by Fray Luis to indicate a disordered life, gives way to an evocation of the haven: the thatched roof where envy and perjury have never dwelt, and the lofty mountain range which rises far above the living death of blind and foolish mortals towards a heavenly peace, and which the poet asks to receive him:

> for persecuted, I flee
> from the erring multitude,
> from labours lost,
> false peace, undeserved evil.

There, in a further change of image, he will be able to recover from the poison he so thoughtlessly drank and gradually unlearn the *proceso* of his past, with its vain joys and misguided direction (*proceso* means both "course" and "trial"). From these heights, "almost divested of this corporeal veil" and passing his life in joy, peace, and uncorrupted light, he will look down with compassion on those still beset by storms and shipwreck. The future tense, however, indicates that the poet is operating in the realm of desire, not achievement, as the final stanza underlines with its wish that he may not fail to reach this haven, and fail instead only in his attachment to blind error. The nature of this error is never specified, and his identity appears split between attachment to the world of change and loss in which he finds himself, and a longing for a place beyond their reach, which, we must assume, can be found only beyond death.

The darkest of these more autobiographical poems, and the most difficult

---

7. The most famous example of the topos is Horace's second Epode, much imitated by Renaissance poets, both in vernacular and neo-Latin verse.

to interpret, is XVII, a series of tercets in which the poet calls on false hopes to be banished from his breast. It has generally been taken to refer to a moment during the trial when Fray Luis's hopes of release had been raised, only to be dashed. Like Cowper's "The Castaway," its tone is one of unrelieved gloom. The poet recalls his public exile from all he held dear to the place of unrelieved darkness and misery where he now finds himself. Everything is the reverse of what it should be: all that is good has conspired against him to harm him; the more he tries to clean his hands, the dirtier they become; peace and friendship are as cruel war to him; he is blameless, yet his punishment endures, the prisoner of the wrongdoing of others. His innocence only binds his chains more tightly; like the bird caught in the net, the more he struggles to be free, the more entangled he becomes. Neo-Stoical *ataraxia* offers no consolation here, nor is there any sign of the more Christian attitude towards suffering found in the commentary on Psalm 26 (27). Even when the closing stanzas imagine the *beatus ille*, it recedes into an unreachable distance. The stanzas describe the happy man untouched by laws, tribunals, cities, and all the harsh ways of the world, the man who lives in innocent solitude and enriches his soul with truth:

> he is accompanied by what is just, and by the radiant
> truth, by simplicity in hearts of gold,
> by faith which is not falsely coloured,
> a beloved choir of rich hopes
> and peace with its ease surround him,
> and joy, from whose eyes weeping flees.

But this vision only increases his torment, because he can see no way to attain it.

If in these poems the circumstances of his own imprisonment are never far from the surface, Fray Luis more often adopts a first-person voice to articulate a more general human dilemma. The most famous of all his poems, his first ode, begins with a contrast between two ways of living and is largely Horatian in inspiration, though with echoes of Matthew 7:13–14:

> How peaceful is the life
> of him who would all worldly clamour shun
> to take the hidden way
> whereon have walked alone
> the few wise men the world has ever known.

The poet develops the contrast in terms of the many who chase after status, wealth, and power, never finding the peace they seek, and the few who follow the hidden path to a place of retreat in which nature ministers to human needs and simplicity and moderation are prized over ambition, flattery, and dangerous voyages of trade in search of wealth. At the heart of this vision of the peaceful life is a garden, "planted by my hand," which may refer to a country retreat belonging to the Augustinian community which Fray Luis visited from time to time. But the garden is also a symbol rooted in both biblical and classical traditions (Genesis, Song of Solomon, Horace, Cicero), watered by a life-giving stream, in which the cares of "gold and sceptre," metonyms for wealth and power, can be forgotten. It is not a prelapsarian vision, since outside the garden storms blow and lives are ruined, and it can seem a selfish one, with its picture of the poet resting in solitary peace and singing in the shade while others are consumed by their insatiable thirst for the dangers of power. But the poet has not been immune from such temptation:

> The ship's almost a wreck;
> to your dear rest I flee
> from ravages of this tempestuous sea.

The subjunctive mood of the closing stanzas makes it clear that the poem expresses an unfulfilled desire rather than an attitude that privileges self-preservation over engagement with others, one that is meant to point both poet and reader to the diagnosis of human ills and the proposed remedy.

An instructive comparison may be drawn with another poem, XI, addressed to his friend the neo-Latin poet Juan de Grial. It begins with a beautiful evocation of autumn, with its dying vegetation, shortening days and migrating cranes, an appropriate time to resume "noble studies," to gain the summit and drink the purest water, in contrast to those thirsty for gold. But there is a violent and unexpected twist at the end. Having called on Grial to take up his pen and write his inspired verse, the poet cannot contain his feelings:

> For I, assailed by a treacherous
> whirlwind, and cast down from the middle of the way
> to the depths, have broken
> my beloved plectrum
> and the wings of my flight.

If in the first ode the poet celebrated the pure waters flowing down from the heights and sang in the shade to the sound of music, insulated against the tempests that beset the ignorant and foolish, now he himself has become their victim and his instrument is silenced. It is easy to interpret these lines as a direct reference to his trial and imprisonment, but they are inspired by the first poem of Ovid's *Tristia*, itself written by the Latin poet in a period of exile, which speaks of the poet as harassed by storms and living in fear of imminent death, a state inimical to writing of verse. Fray Luis's version is more condensed and dramatic, but shares with Ovid the sense that circumstances have made it impossible for him to write: a confession made, ironically, in the form of one of his finest poems.

The ultimately destructive power of the quest for material gain is the theme of several other poems—a warning against the avarice of those who risk every-thing on voyages of trade to the Far East (V), an attack on a greedy judge who perverts justice (XVI; see Mic 3:9–12), and more generally against the lust for riches and sex (XII). But the first-person voice also addresses fictional individ-uals, urging them to turn away from a life of vice and embrace virtue. Odes VI and IX share a similar structure and have a number of images in common. Ode VI is addressed to Elisa, a woman who, it appears, has enjoyed many lovers but is now well past her prime. What begins as a serious poem in the classical *carpe diem* tradition, however, turns at the midpoint into something quite different.[8] As Elisa is encouraged to embrace heavenly beauty and trust to the mercy of divine love, the scene shifts to the house of Simon the Pharisee, where Mary Magdalene bathes Christ's feet with her hair and begs forgiveness of him (Luke 7:36–50). She is offered as the model of the repentant sinner, the fire of sexual passion once burning in her eyes now extinguished by her tears:

> that which sweated in your offence,
> may it now labour to serve you . . .
> may my eyes, two deadly forges,
> become two flowing springs.

In IX the poet addresses Cherinto, who is still addicted to the pursuit of sexual pleasure, despite increasing age and ill health. His rational self will be forfeited if he persists; he will become like the sailors entertained by the sorceress Circe in the *Odyssey*, transformed into a brute beast; or like Solomon, whose wisdom deserted him in his later years; or Samson, betrayed by feminine wiles. Instead he should follow the example of Ulysses as he and his crew approached the rocks where the sirens sang their fatal song: stop up his ears to the tempting sound, and, like Joseph, flee from the grasp of Potiphar's wife. In both poems repentance is urged and classical and biblical models, both negative and posi-tive, are offered. Ode VII retells the legend of Rodrigo, the last Visigothic king

---

8. The phrase, meaning "seize the day," comes from Horace, Ode I.xi.

of Spain, according to which the loss of Christian Spain in 711 to the invading Berber armies was blamed on the king's seduction or rape of a powerful no-bleman's daughter. The poet again directly addresses the offender, contrasting his idle pleasures with the gathering fleet and appealing to him to take swift military action. Readers knew that Rodrigo had been defeated and that Spain had fallen under Moorish domination for nearly eight centuries. In the me-dieval ballad tradition the vanquished Rodrigo flees, finds a hermit, confesses his sin, and is buried alive with a snake. But the appeal in Fray Luis's poem is not answered, and a terrible price has to be paid for the king's sexual sin by the fatherland itself.

The Neoplatonic Self

But sexual temptation and sin as exemplified by Elisa, Cherinto, and Rodrigo are symptoms of a deeper spiritual malaise, which Fray Luis explores in his Neoplatonic poetry. One of his friends at Salamanca was the blind organist and music theorist Francisco de Salinas (1513–1590). In Ode III, as the poet listens to Salinas playing, all grows calm and the air is bathed in unaccustomed beauty and light. The "divine sound" of music playing in time awakens the soul to the buried memory of its eternal nature, enabling it to forget the gold and the "deceptive, fleeting beauty" beloved of "the lowly masses," as it ascends through the music of the heavenly spheres of the Ptolemaic universe to "another kind of music, imperishable, the fount, the first," that of the Creator himself[9] God, under the classical guise of Apollo, is imagined as playing the universe into being and sustaining it with his heavenly music. Here, in this lofty state, the soul rests in a "sea of sweetness," exclaiming in the kind of paradoxical language beloved of the mystics, "Oh happy swoon! Oh death which gives life! Oh sweet forgetfulness!" But the ascent cannot be sustained. The end of the poem reveals it to be at best a fleeting experience, at worst an unfulfilled desire, as the poet prays that the music of Salinas may always sound in his ears so that his senses may be alive only to the "divine good," rather than "this base and lowly sense."

One of his best-loved poems is his hymn to the night sky (VIII). As he contemplates the starry heavens and then looks back to earth "encircled by night, buried in sleep and oblivion," he cries out to this "temple of brightness and beauty" at the ill fortune that condemns the soul, "born for such heights,"

9. These poems of ascent, like so many others of the period, are influenced by the com-mentary of Macrobius on the *Somnium Scipionis* (*The Dream of Scipio*), from the sixth book of Cicero's *Republic*.

to be held "in this low, dark prison." What "mortal folly" condemns it to forget its divine origins and instead seek "the empty shadow, the pretended good"? The human chasing after insubstantial goals is not exposed directly, but imagined variously in terms of night, sleep, oblivion, death, imprisonment, shadow, folly, futility, deception; by contrast, the true destiny of the soul is waking, beauty, truth, and above all, light, which comes to dominate the ascent through the spheres of the moon and the planets to the divine dwelling. How, then, can anyone who contemplates the harmony and light of the night sky not sigh and groan to break the chains of all that keeps the soul in exile from its true home, where peace, contentment, and divine love reign supreme? This is the place of "immense beauty revealed in all its fullness," "the purest, brightest light which never darkens," "eternal spring." The imagery balances the classical (the eternal spring of Ovid's *Metamorphoses* 1.107) with the biblical (the vision of the holy city in Revelation 21), in its depiction of the absolute antithesis to the darkness, ignorance, and ephemeral desires that imprison the earthbound soul. The final stanza dissolves into an exclamatory evocation of a pastoral paradise that owes something to the Elysian Fields, Renaissance pastoral, and biblical metaphor, but this time without the jolt back to earthly realities:

> Oh true fields!
> Oh meadows fresh and lovely with truth!
> Richest mines!
> oh charming hollows!
> valleys adorned and full with countless blessings!

Ode X opens with a plea: "When shall I, free from this prison, be able to fly to heaven?" The prison in question is that of the embodied self; the freedom desired is only possible beyond death, when the soul can return to its homeland in the eternal heavens. The intellectual vision that follows, of being able to understand the mysteries of creation, is expressed emphatically in the future: the poet repeats "Veré," "I shall see," eight times. What he will see relates to the questions the Lord asks of Job out of the whirlwind in chapter 38: I shall see the causes of everything, how the earth and the seas were formed, where storms arise, and above all this, the movement of the spheres, and the One who governs the stars. The soul will finally reach the highest sphere, heaven itself:

> the dwellings
> of joy and contentment,
> built of gold and light,
> inhabited by blessed spirits.

The life of heaven is the subject of another ode (XIII). Here, the focus is a pastoral one influenced less by classical than by biblical tradition (notably Psalm 23, the Song of Solomon, and the Gospel of John), as the Good Shepherd leads his flock to their immortal pastures and their midday rest. As he plays his rebec and the sweet sound passes into the soul, earthly treasures grow dim and the soul, now aflame, rises into a state of ecstasy. But the sense that the heavenly ascent cannot be sustained is even stronger here, as the ending dissolves into conditionality:

> Oh sound! Oh voice! if but the
> merest fragment might descend
> into my sense, and bring my soul to ecstasy,
> and convert it wholly into you, oh Love!

Then, the poet concludes, it would be free from the prison in which it suffers and never stray from the Beloved's flock.

The Self in Process

The historical and poetic selves of Fray Luis encompass the theme of imprisonment at both the personal and the broader human level. They cannot be separated from the contingencies of their time and their speech is mediated through older voices that were an integral part of the culture of the age—some classical, others biblical. But whether the first-person voice alludes to the poet's own traumatic experience in the Inquisitorial cells of Valladolid or more generally to the human capacity for error and delusion, it belongs to a self that is always in process, one constituted by contemplation of the world as it is and of people as they are, and of a desire to be free of the constraints that prevent them from becoming the moral and spiritual beings that is their true created goal. Its voice is directed towards the fundamental questions of how to live as good and peaceful a life as possible in an unstable and sometimes hostile world, and how to break free of the prisons imposed on us by others or our own false priorities, in order to discover the truth about ourselves and creation. As an autobiographical reflection, this voice struggles with depression and despair, sometimes glimpsing the grace that can lift it up, at other times seeing no way out. It does not hide from such things or take refuge in too easy a Christian hope: like Jacob's, it is a self that wrestles in order to progress; like Job's, it is one that is not afraid to protest his innocence when others tell him he has sinned. Adopting a neo-Stoical tone, it urges those trapped in worldly pursuits, such as sexual pleasure, personal enrichment, or the lust for power, to turn their backs on such vanities and find the peace—which constantly eludes them—in a simpler, purer form of living. From a Neoplatonic perspective, it speaks of the human being as a spiritual entity imprisoned in the ephemeral world of matter and needing to be awakened to its true nature and ascend towards the divine. But it does not do so from a superior, detached vantage point, for the poet knows both the literal and the metaphorical prison cell from the inside.

Fray Luis's blending of the pagan, classical world with that of the Bible belongs to a tradition that stretches back through Renaissance humanism to at least the second Christian century, when the Greek Apologists, like Clement of Alexandria, reread their own pagan literature through Christian eyes, rather than reject it, as some had urged. But the lack of overtly Christian statements of faith in the classically inspired poems or in those directly linked to his imprisonment does not represent some kind of existential crisis. His Ode on the Ascension (XVIII) may adopt the perspective of the apostles bereft of the physical presence of the resurrected Christ and wondering how they will manage without it, but his poems addressed to all the saints (XIX), to St. James (XX), especially to the Virgin (XXI) display a deeply felt devotional sensibility that is most fully and eloquently expressed in his dialogues *On the Names of Christ*. Each of his poems is a finely woven fabric, complex and beautiful in the making. Together they reveal a sixteenth-century voice that encompasses the full range of human experience, from the depths of despair to the hope of eternal transformation in divine love, mediated through the cultural prism of his times and his personal experience. He may not waver for a moment in his conviction of his own innocence or in the mendacity of his opponents when it comes to his own protracted ordeal; but he knows himself to be imprisoned, as much as anyone else, by those misdirected desires that drag us down to the level of the beasts and by that clouded vision above which we long to rise into the light.

PART SIX

Christian Identity in the Emergence of the Modern World

Chapter 29

John Amos Comenius:
A Life of Loss, a Theologian of Hope

Howard Louthan

For a seventeenth-century polymath interested in esoteric knowledge, John Amos Comenius (1592–1670) has had a remarkable afterlife. Schools, colleges, and universities across Europe and North America proudly bear his name. Even in China a group of leading universities has dubbed an elite management program "the Comenius course." In his native land, the Czech National Bank has emblazoned his likeness on the two-hundred crown note, while he remains the darling of European bureaucrats who have created a range of Comenius prizes and programs to commemorate his legacy. Perhaps most prominently, the United Nations has honored him through their Comenius medal, a prize that recognizes outstanding achievement in educational research. But if we peel back this legacy and look at the man himself, it is frankly surprising that Comenius, an orphan from a remote corner of rural Moravia and member of a persecuted religious community, ever emerged at all to become such an influential figure. Indeed, if there is any constant to Comenius's life, it is loss. In one of the most difficult periods of Central Europe's past, Comenius's personal story was particularly tragic. He lost his parents early. He buried two wives. He belonged to a church that was not only persecuted but had essentially disappeared by the end of his life. He feared that his native language, Czech, might actually vanish as well. He suffered through the worst war Europe had ever experienced and was sent into exile not once but twice. At an especially low moment he watched as soldiers burned his library and destroyed much of his life's work. Yet despite this series of catastrophes, Comenius is more often associated with hope and promise. He did not succumb to despair and remained optimistic concerning humanity's future.[1]

---

1. See for example Jan Milič Lochman, "Jan Amos Komensky—ein Theologe der Sehnsucht

What accounts for this resiliency? How, despite great personal loss, did Comenius maintain his spiritual equilibrium? Understanding Comenius aright is not an easy task. One of the most frequent metaphors associated with his life is the labyrinth. The image of a maze is an apt picture both of his wanderings across Europe and the remarkable but bewildering range of his intellectual endeavors. This is an individual, after all, who wrote approximately one hundred texts and treatises. It is easy to lose one's way trying to map Comenius's complicated world. There is a thick body of literature on the Moravian, but much of it is highly specialized, ahistorical, or undeniably hagiographical. Even today what remains the best biography of Comenius is at times a confusing jumble of facts and ideas.[2] With these challenges in mind, we will focus on the theme of loss and how it affected Comenius's understanding of self. Towards that end we will limit our study to an examination of three key texts spanning nearly fifty years of his career. These works, autobiographical in nature, belong to a smaller group of his spiritual writings. They help chart his life's course and explain the origin of the hope that undergirded his broader reform agenda for which he is famously known.

The Labyrinth of the World (1623)

According to legend, as the Bohemian Brethren, a small Protestant community, were leaving the Czech lands for an uncertain exile in 1628, they sang a series of songs to commemorate their lost homeland. In the most famous of these melancholy choruses, they praise the city of Prague and the winding Vltava River (Moldau) that rises in the Šumava hills and runs through the meadows and forests of the Bohemian heartland. In the penultimate verse the tone changes. Praise of the landscape gives way to a sad tribute of a heritage and culture under threat. Marching eastward, they stoically sang, "We have taken nothing with us; everything is lost. We have only our Kralice Bible and The Labyrinth of the World."[3] Scholars have singled out the texts praised by the Brethren as the two great landmarks of early modern Czech literature. The Kralice Bible, which took nearly twenty years to complete by a team of accomplished scholars, remains today the most famous translation of Scripture into Czech and represents the

und der Hoffnung," *Unitas Fratrum* 32 (1992): 5–17; Josef Polišenský, *Komenský muž labyrintů a naděje* [Comenius: Man of Labyrinths and Hope] (Prague: Academia, 1996); Josef Smolík, "Comenius: A Man of Hope in a Time of Turmoil," *Christian History* 13 (1987): 15–18.

2. Milada Blekastad, *Comenius* (Oslo: Universitetsforlaget, 1969).

3. S. Souček, *Domnělá píseň pražských vyhanců na slovensko a její Slovenské příbuzenstvo* (Brno: Filosofická fakulta, 1923), 3.

high point of the Brethren's intellectual tradition. *The Labyrinth of the World* was a very different undertaking altogether. Written with remarkable wit and verve, it was a satire and spiritual allegory that, like Erasmus's more famous *Praise of Folly*, took no prisoners. Its author launched a series of attacks on society's great and powerful. He spared no one and nothing as he exposed the hypocrisy and corruption of his day. What may be the most surprising aspect of *The Labyrinth* was the author himself. While *Praise of Folly* was written by a scholar of mature years with a well-established reputation, the author of this learned satire had never completed university training and had only just begun a career as a schoolteacher.

The author of course was the young John Amos Comenius, whose path to celebrity status was anything but conventional. Comenius was the youngest son of an industrious miller from a village in southeast Moravia. The family were members of the Bohemian Brethren (*Unitas Fratrum*), a Protestant sect that traced its origins back to the Hussite movement of the fifteenth century. His parents died early. At first, relatives oversaw his education. He was, however, a precocious child and eventually drew the attention of the Brethren's most important patron in Moravia, Charles the Elder of Žerotín, who served as governor of the region. The original separatist character of the Brethren had weakened over the decades, and by the time of Comenius they were sending their most gifted youth to important Protestant schools in western Europe. Comenius's destination was the Calvinist schools of Herborn and Heidelberg, where he studied for several years. Though he never earned a formal degree, this study trip was a particularly formative period of his life. His interaction with the encyclopedist Johann Heinrich Alsted and the irenicist David Pareus helped shape his distinctive philosophical and religious views. By 1614 he was back in Moravia. He began teaching at a Brethren school. Two years later, his church ordained him priest, and after a further two years he married. The match seemed good. His bride, Magdalena Vizovská, came with some wealth, and children quickly followed. A promising future seemingly lay before him. Fortunes, however, reverse quickly, and for Comenius the coming of war changed his life's course in ways he could have hardly imagined.

The Thirty Years' War, the most devastating conflict Europe had ever known, ravaged the Czech lands. According to some estimates, Central Europe lost thirty percent of its population, while marauding mercenaries displaced countless others through their scorched earth tactics. The war began as a religious struggle. A Protestant coup in Prague triggered a chain of events that eventually brought Spanish soldiers to Comenius's village in Moravia, which they occupied. A delicate confessional balance that had developed across Bohemia and Moravia was replaced by a unilateral Catholic settlement where no dissent was tolerated. With the stroke of a pen in Vienna, the Protestant Comenius lost both his homeland and his profession. Further personal tragedy awaited. Sickness and disease carried off his wife and children. Forced into hiding, Comenius turned inward and sought solace through reflection and writing. The result of this period of confinement was his satirical masterpiece, *The Labyrinth of the World*.

The Labyrinth is the story of a pilgrim who wanders through the world in search of meaning and significance. Accompanying him is a group of rather dubious guides who endeavor to either distract or mislead the pilgrim in his quest for truth. Though the text is not strictly autobiographical, Comenius weaved in significant details from his early life, and not surprisingly, *The Labyrinth* reflects a rather dark view of human existence. In a letter of dedication to Count Žerotín, Comenius noted, "The first part depicts, through a series of scenes, the ludicrous and worthless things of the world . . . and how all things end miserably either in laughter or in grief."[4] The tragic events that surrounded the Thirty Years' War obviously had a significant impact on Comenius. They dispelled whatever illusions he may have had concerning the innate goodness of human nature and destroyed what little confidence he had in the basic building blocks of society, in either the family or the state. In *The Labyrinth* the pilgrim views unhappy marriages where partners are unequally paired. Authorities bind couples together with iron fetters and leave them to batter each other with fists and cudgels. Even the most successful unions bring little joy as husband and wife are harnessed with a string of children who "screamed, shrieked, quarreled, got sick and died."[5] Comenius depicts the state as despotic and corrupt. In a marvelous scene where the pilgrim visits the rulers of the world, initially all appears in good order. He encounters constables and mayors, judges and governors who seem to be discharging their duties equitably. But upon closer examination, he discovers that each one of these individuals is deformed. There are those with no ears to hear the complaints of their subjects, no eyes to see the exploitation of the poor, and in some cases not even a heart to defend the weak and powerless. In short, "town halls and law courts, and offices were as often workshops of injustice as of justice, and those who were called defenders of order were as much (or even more) defenders of disorder."[6]

Though Comenius's critique of both the family and the state are certainly significant, he devoted most of *The Labyrinth* to an examination of the profes-

---

4. J. A. Comenius, *The Labyrinth of the World and the Paradise of the Heart*, trans. and intro. Howard Louthan and Andrea Sterk (Mahwah, NJ: Paulist Press, 1997), 57.

5. Comenius, *The Labyrinth of the World*, 81.

6. Comenius, *The Labyrinth of the World*, 135, 141.

sions. His allegory begins with the pilgrim looking for a job. While the authorities simply assign most citizens of *The Labyrinth* a craft or trade, they give the pilgrim an opportunity to explore for himself a broad array of seventeenth-century occupations. A pattern slowly emerges. The pilgrim's guides direct his attention to a specific profession that at first glance seems quite attractive, but upon further examination, he sadly realizes that what he thought was so promising is actually a fraud. Doctors who boast they can heal the sick have no real understanding of the human body. Lawyers who advertise their skill at adjudicating disputes contribute to yet further conflict. Alchemists who claim they can turn base metal into gold end up scalding or even killing themselves. Comenius reserves his most caustic comments, however, for one of his own callings, that of scholar and teacher. The pilgrim starts his tour by observing young students struggling to learn as they memorize useless facts and endure senseless beatings by their masters. The situation hardly improves if they survive this harrowing experience. They engage in empty activities and despite claims to the contrary seem to care little for the pursuit of truth and knowledge. Instead they spend their time attacking their rivals with a fury that shocks the pilgrim. "I observed here a cruelty unusual elsewhere. They spared neither the wounded nor the dead but mercilessly hacked and lashed at them all the more, each more gladly proving his valor against one who did not defend himself."[7]

How, then, does *The Labyrinth* speak to the specific question of self? What does it tell us about Comenius's understanding of identity? Though the allegory can obviously be read on many different levels, autobiographically it traces a story of loss. It is a tale of a young man whose prospects for the future were seemingly wrecked overnight and who is now coping with the loss of family, homeland, and even profession. These personal tragedies created a fundamental tension that Comenius struggled with his entire life. By nature he was ambitious, energetic, and enterprising, and yet at a relatively young age he was challenged by the apparent meaninglessness of human existence expressed so clearly in *The Labyrinth*. He saw his own situation mirrored in the New Testament story of Mary and Martha. "The world is full of Marthas, hustling and bustling, striving to gather things from all sides, yet never having enough."[8] Catastrophe, though, initiated a process of weighing and sifting priorities and values. In a world of constant movement and endless activity, one must winnow to discover what is most important. These early losses instilled within Comenius a reformer's instinct that seeks the heart of the matter, an ability to cut through the extraneous to expose the essential.

7. Comenius, *The Labyrinth of the World*, 100.
8. Comenius, *The Labyrinth of the World*, 209.

We see this dynamic at a very early stage in his career. After the expulsion of the Brethren from the Czech lands, Comenius joined a group that found refuge in Polish territory and there resumed his work as schoolmaster teaching Latin to his young pupils. Traditional methods, however, frustrated him. A pedagogy based on a complicated system of rules and coupled with rote memorization was, as Comenius argued, inherently problematic. With a reformer's zeal he published a textbook that cut through a thicket of abstract verbiage and revolutionized language learning by placing the emphasis not on words but on objects. That book, *The Gate of Languages Unlocked* (1631), catapulted him to celebrity status. It was translated into nearly a dozen languages, including Persian and Armenian. Comenius followed this success with a string of other "best-sellers," including the first illustrated book for children, the *Orbis pictus* (1658), a language primer that taught Latin through an entertaining game of matching pictures and words.

The Bequest of the Unity of Brethren (1650)

With the expulsion of the Bohemian Brethren from the Czech lands in 1628, Comenius embarked on what became a life of exile. Exile, however, had a rather unexpected effect on Comenius. Though it was a moment of trauma, the experience also reshaped Comenius's own vision of self in a more positive fashion. Had Comenius remained in Moravia, he may have led the simple life of priest and schoolteacher. The coming of war closed this option and forced Comenius to think in more radical terms. It sharpened his pedagogical reforms. At the same time, exile also had a decided impact on his other profession, that of pastor. During the Reformation, exile tended to radicalize religious communities. Many of the Protestants who left England during the reign of Catholic Mary came back after her death as Calvinist zealots. Catholics, too, could return from an involuntary time abroad more convinced in their divine calling and unwilling to compromise with their confessional rivals.[9] Surprisingly, such was not the case with Comenius. The experience of exile, in fact, pushed him in the opposite direction. In this context we turn to a short treatise Comenius wrote towards the middle of his long career, *The Bequest of the Unity of Brethren*.

If *The Labyrinth of the World* reflects Comenius's loss of family and homeland, *The Bequest* is a poignant testimony of a dying religious community. Comenius published the short text in 1650 as a tribute to the *Unitas Fratrum*.

9. For a recent case study on exile and radicalization, see Geert Janssen, *The Dutch Revolt and Catholic Exile in Reformation Europe* (Cambridge: Cambridge University Press, 2014).

Comenius's church had grown out of the Hussite movement of the early fifteenth century. The religious movement launched by the charismatic reformer Jan Hus splintered after his execution at the Council of Constance (1415). There were radicals such as the militant Taborites and Adamites as well as "mainline" Utraquists, the name given to Hus's followers for their practice of receiving the Eucharist in two kinds, *sub utraque*. The Unity of Brethren emerged in the middle of that century as an independent body with a separate priesthood. Initially, they kept aloof from the state in small, tight-knit communities, though over time this orientation slowly changed. They lived a tenuous existence. Though the Utraquists reached an accommodation with the kingdom's Catholic princes, this agreement did not cover the smaller and more vulnerable Brethren communities, which suffered periodic persecution. Their involvement in the Schmalkaldic War (1546–1547) placed them in the crosshairs of the Hapsburgs, who imprisoned their bishop in the dismal castle of Křivoklát, and in the war's aftermath many of the Brethren moved to Moravia while a substantial group looked even further afield for safe haven and immigrated to Polish territory. The low point came with their official expulsion from the Czech lands in 1628. The Brethren scattered across the continent finding refuge on the estates of sympathetic nobles. Comenius joined a community that had settled in the town of Leszno in Greater Poland. During this troubled period, the fate of the church depended on outside powers. Comenius and other Brethren leaders placed their hopes with the Lutheran Swedes. Despite Comenius's relationship with Chancellor Axel Oxenstierna, Sweden, however, did not represent their interests at the negotiating table. After the Peace of Westphalia (1648) Bohemia remained closed to the Brethren.

In the aftermath of this bitter disappointment *The Bequest* has a surprisingly positive tone. Just two years earlier Comenius had written *The History of the Persecutions of the Bohemian Church*. In this sobering account Comenius quickly sped through the church's early struggles with pagan princes to focus most closely on the sufferings of the Brethren and the disastrous events of the seventeenth century for the kingdom's Protestants. For Comenius the book was an opportunity to reach an international audience and publicize the dire situation of his church even as the continent's mightiest Protestant power, the Swedes, were set to solidify their gains through the Peace of Westphalia.[10] *The Bequest*, in contrast, was a quieter reflection and assessment of the Brethren that eschewed the more graphic descriptions of suffering and adversity of his martyrology. It was as the full Czech title implied (*Kšaft umírající matky Jed-*

10. J. A. Comenius, *Historia persecutionum ecclesiae bohemicae* (s.n., 1648); reprinted in Jan Amos Komenský [Comenius], *Opera Omnia* (Prague: Academia, 1989), 9.1:199–329.

noty bratrské) a final will or testament a dying mother desired to pass on to her children. Once more the prospect of loss helped clarify Comenius's vision, for it appeared likely that the Brethren would not survive as an independent body after the war's end. Comenius was in fact the last bishop of the *Unitas Fratrum*, and *The Bequest* was the final word he gave to his church.

The text begins with a call to repentance. Adopting the tone of an Old Testament prophet, Comenius cries out against the church's leaders who had "allowed strange fire in the sanctuary of the Unity." He reminds them that when foreign armies defeated Israel in the time of the Judges, the nation turned to God collectively and sought his forgiveness. Politically, the Brethren had suffered near total defeat and, like the Israelites, must now come before God in humility and contrition. Comenius was certainly implicating himself, for as he explained, alongside the sins of vanity, pride, and pomp, strange fire also included the trappings of "worldly wisdom."[11] What was Comenius implying? Was he repudiating his work as a teacher and champion of pedagogical reform? Was he calling his church to withdraw fully from society and return to its original separatist orientation? His message was not that simple. He clearly saw the importance of his reforming activities and after 1650 continued them unabated. But as events twenty-five years earlier had forced Comenius to turn inwards and reevaluate his personal and professional goals, this time events were compelling him to return once more to essentials and reflect on the character of his church specifically and the nature of Christian identity more generally.

Though the Brethren as a body had not recommended a voluntary disbanding of their church in the wake of Westphalia, Comenius did not entirely agree with this decision and wrote *The Bequest* at least in part as a practical guide to its members in a time of great uncertainty. The text for him became an exercise in distillation. What were the key elements of his faith tradition? What lessons must be passed on to the next generation? How should his church's orphaned members interact with other Christian communities? He was particularly concerned with his own group, the Brethren who had settled in Poland. The original refugees who had arrived in the middle of the sixteenth century had found favor with many of the Polish nobility and had prospered. With that prosperity, however, came the danger of conformity, of following "foreign customs" and losing those key distinctives of their spiritual tradition.[12] Comenius was also concerned with the health of other Protestant churches. He saw the Lutherans as heirs of an incomplete Reformation, a church "having begun in the spirit

11. J. A. Comenius, *The Bequest of the Unity of Brethren*, trans. Matthew Spinka (Chicago: National Union of Czechoslovak Protestants in America, 1940), 16–17.

12. Comenius, *The Bequest*, 19–22.

now continuing in the flesh." His assessment of the Reformed, though more positive, included a word of warning: Their penchant for theological speculation was dangerous, "ever searching for novelties and never obtaining stable convictions."[13] In contrast, he argued that the great legacy of the Brethren was their simplicity. His community rested on a solid foundation that consisted of three basic elements: devotion to Scripture, commitment to discipline, and desire for unity.[14]

This period around 1650, then, a time when Comenius was reaching the height of his career, helped clarify his thinking on his own spiritual identity and that of the *Unitas Fratrum*. After the Peace of Westphalia, Comenius understood what he had hoped was temporary exile was now likely permanent, that his scattered church would never return to the Czech lands. This sobering realization pushed him to evaluate the legacy of the Brethren and his place within a broader Christian community. Once more, loss sharpened his vision and reordered his priorities. As he outlined in *The Bequest*, his was a practical Christianity that refused to become "befuddled with speculations" but instead embraced "the simplicity of Christ."[15] Though he had pursued theological studies at Herborn and was a prolific author, Comenius, in fact, wrote surprisingly little theology.[16] Westphalia reminded him that his priorities were elsewhere. From Comenius's perspective, theology often created unnecessary divisions between otherwise likeminded communities. As Comenius argued in *The Bequest*, the spiritual orientation of the Brethren was different. Theirs was a tradition that, though committed to thorough reform, sought to mitigate doctrinal difference.

The *Unitas Fratrum* had a long history of seeking compromise. Well before the Germans had reached their own confessional settlement with the Peace of Augsburg (1555), the Bohemians had negotiated a religious truce between the kingdom's Utraquists and Catholics in 1485. For the Brethren, the high point of their ecumenical activity came in 1575 with the adoption of the Bohemian Confession, a theological statement accepted by all the Protestant churches of the Czech lands. Comenius's irenic character, which was such a key aspect of his spiritual identity, grew out of this tradition. It was evident as early as *The Labyrinth*. During his travels, Comenius's pilgrim examines the Christian religion, only to be disillusioned by the petty differences that divided its adherents into

---

13. Comenius, *The Bequest*, 27, 29.
14. Comenius, *The Bequest*, 33–36.
15. Comenius, *The Bequest*, 21.
16. Emidio Campi, "John Amos Comenius and the Protestant Theology of His Time," in *Shifting Patterns of Reformed Tradition* (Göttingen: Vandenhoeck & Ruprecht, 2014), 259–83.

warring factions.[17] When in 1632 his church ordained him as bishop, Comenius returned to this theme in *Haggaeus redivivus*, a text that outlined a plan for the restoration of a unified Protestant church in Bohemia. As prospects in the Czech lands worsened, Comenius turned his attention to broader questions of Christian unity. He undertook his most significant work in the years immediately prior to the publication of *The Bequest*. In an unpublished treatise of 1643, he laid out an ambitious plan to reunite not only Catholics and Protestants but also the Eastern churches.[18] Two years later he followed up his theoretical work with his involvement in the *Colloquium Charitativum*. This conference, sponsored by the king of Poland, was an attempt to reunite the various churches of this divided state. Though the discussions stalled and ultimately failed due to partisan bickering, Comenius was actually one of the few delegates who was critical of both Catholics for their aggression towards other churches and Protestants for their willingness to countenance schism.[19]

Unum necessarium (1668)

The experience of loss, then, helped shaped Comenius's intellectual and spiritual outlook in profound ways. It was a painful and difficult process that pared and reduced. It honed his approach to pedagogy and clarified his vision of the church. As an orphan, widower, and exile, Comenius learned to identify that which was most essential. *The Bequest* is an eloquent testimony of those difficult lessons, lessons that continued in the latter portion of his life. In the trying days of 1648 when the *Unitas Fratrum* was excluded from the discussions at Westphalia, Comenius also buried his second wife. The song he composed for her funeral reflected both his anguish and feelings of rootlessness as a religious refugee in Poland.[20] Comenius's personal situation reached a new low in 1656. Troops burned Leszno to the ground, destroying his precious library and driving him into a new exile. The destruction of the town, which sheltered the Brethren for so many years, sealed the fate of this church in Poland. They would not survive another generation. This disaster in fact pushed Comenius out of central Europe altogether. He moved on to the Low Countries, where he

17. Comenius, *The Labyrinth of the World*, chap. 18, 125–34.

18. *De dissidentium in rebus fidei christianorum reconciliatione hypomnemata* (1643); manuscript copy in Göttingen university library.

19. Blekastad, *Comenius*, 399–407; Matthew Spinka, *John Amos Comenius: That Incomparable Moravian* (Chicago: University of Chicago Press, 1943), 100–106.

20. "A song concerning the sorrow of the earthly wanderings of all people." See Blekastad, *Comenius*, 450.

continued with his many publishing projects. He died in Amsterdam in November 1670. Friends and family transported his body to its final resting place, a peaceful cemetery in the village of Naarden just outside the city.

Two years before his death Comenius published one of his most personal reflections on the spiritual life, *Unum necessarium*. While he wrote *The Labyrinth* in the shadow of exile and composed *The Bequest* as his church was dying, Comenius in *Unum necessarium* faced that final loss, one's own mortality. Knowing that his end was not far, he assembled his thoughts "now as the grave is before me."[21] In *Unum necessarium* Comenius returned to a series of questions he had wrestled with his entire career. What matters most in our short human existence? How do we balance the active life with the contemplative? Do all our efforts to change and improve the world around us amount to anything at all? Comenius began *Unum necessarium* with three metaphors or images that vividly capture these tensions he so keenly felt. The first was the labyrinth. God, as Comenius maintained, created the world as a showplace or theater of his wisdom. There were no secrets, no hidden knowledge. All was open to humanity. With the fall came confusion and chaos. The clear and orderly theater became a confounding labyrinth where wisdom lay concealed and obscured. Comenius developed his second metaphor, Sisyphus, for those like himself who had great plans to change and remake the world around them. For Comenius, who had watched his life's work literally go up in smoke as soldiers burned his unfinished manuscripts, his efforts at times must surely have seemed an exercise in futility. Like Sisyphus, he, too, had struggled repeatedly to reach the crest of a hill only to see his hard work come crashing down behind him. Finally, there was Tantalus and his cruel punishment in the underworld. Could the quest for knowledge ever bring peace and contentment in the first place? Or, as Comenius questioned, are we like wretched Tantalus whose hand never quite reached that desired object, always tempted but never satisfied?[22]

Comenius had long struggled with these questions, but as his life was drawing to an end, they assumed a new sense of urgency. A visionary reformer, he was convinced his projects could make a difference in his society. In the last chapter of *Unum necessarium* he reviewed his long career and highlighted those undertakings that had meant so much to him. He discussed both his educational reforms and his ecumenical efforts. He noted that his critics often did not see the connection between these two undertakings. Some accused him of devoting too much energy to activities that distracted him from the church,

21. J. A. Comenius, *Unum necessarium*, reprinted in Jan Amos Komenský, *Opera Omnia* (Prague: Academia, 1974), 18:125.

22. Comenius, *Unum necessarium*, 78–79.

while others of promoting intellectual schemes that unnecessarily incorporated religion. But as Comenius argued, his greatest calling was a third endeavor that combined these individual strands into a single program of universal reform. This grand experiment was Comenius's ambitious program of pansophism.[23]

Comenius as a youth had studied with Johann Heinrich Alsted, whose overarching intellectual project was to unite all knowledge in a scheme known as encyclopedism. Alsted's influence was lasting, as Comenius was a lifelong critic of specialization. He constantly complained of those who knew very little outside their one small branch of knowledge.

> Metaphysicians sing to themselves alone, natural philosophers chant their own praises, astronomers dance by themselves, ethical thinkers make their laws for themselves, politicians lay their own foundations, mathematicians rejoice over their own triumphs, and theologians rule for their own benefit.[24]

What use were these specialists if they could not help others, especially students, see and appreciate truth as a whole? Comenius devoted his entire career to unite all branches of knowledge, but taking a step beyond the encyclopedists, he sought a practical program that would put this great learning in the service of humanity in specific and concrete ways. In the 1640s he began work on this project of universal reform, his seven-volume *A General Consultation on the Improvement of Human Affairs*. Though it remained incomplete, the outline of Comenius's pansophic vision is clear. His religious and educational proposals were not isolated reforms. He harnessed them to a political program as well, "so that the whole body of human society is maintained in true peace."[25] Without a genuine renewal and a lasting *renovatio* of these three critical areas of activity, society would never flourish and prosper.

Although many today salute Comenius's foresight and anticipation of institutions such as the United Nations, his work at the time generated substantial controversy. Within his church, the Polish noble Jerome Broniewski argued that he confused divine and human wisdom and infected young minds with pagan learning. He encountered the opposite critique from René Descartes, who was suspicious of his attempts to combine the study of the natural world with that of the heavenly. His greatest criticism, however, came from himself. In *Unum necessarium* Comenius questioned the relevance of his own work. Concerning

---

23. For a brief summary of pansophism see Craig Atwood, *The Theology of the Czech Brethren from Hus to Comenius* (University Park: Pennsylvania State University Press, 2009), 366–71.

24. Cited in Spinka, *Incomparable Moravian*, 66.

25. J. A. Comenius, *Panorthosia*, trans. A. M. O. Dobbie (Sheffield: Sheffield Academic Press, 1995), 172.

his irenic activities, he lamented the "savage irreconcilability" of many Christians and wondered if his efforts would have any impact.[26] Was true reform even possible? What hope did his programs and proposals have in such a disordered world? In short, Comenius realized that despite his good intentions he was actually trapped in the same labyrinth that he had vainly hoped he was helping others escape. All human endeavor, both for good and for ill, seemed to end in futility. Thus, he finally came to the heart of the matter in *Unum necessarium*. Comenius did not seek a complicated theological resolution to the quandary of the labyrinth. For him there was only one exit, and that was the route of spiritual simplicity. While he certainly never repudiated his reforms, he ceased questioning their ultimate utility and laid them aside. "Is there a cure or remedy at all?" he queried. "There is only one thing necessary, to return to Christ."[27]

Hold Tightly to That Which Is Necessary

John Comenius offers a very different model and approach to the issue of spiritual formation than other well-known figures of the early modern period. In comparison to Martin Luther, Ignatius Loyola, and Blaise Pascal, there was for Comenius no great turning point or moment of conversion that led to startling new insights. Instead, his course was one of deepening, of returning to familiar struggles and grappling with old questions at various stages of life, as he matured in his understanding of Christian identity. Few in this period could match his personal story of loss, and it was precisely this experience that had such a profound effect, sharpening his spiritual focus. He underwent a protracted and painful process where he learned to discard that which was superfluous and hold tightly to that which was necessary. This dynamic affected him professionally, honing his program of pedagogical reform, but more importantly, it shaped his understanding of himself. In an age when doctrinal distinctives were becoming increasingly significant, Comenius was moving in the opposite direction as he sought commonalities between Christians. He offered a brief summation of his beliefs in *Unum necessarium*.

> If someone should investigate my theology, I would take hold of the Bible (with the dying Aquinas, for I am also about to die) and would say openly

---

26. Comenius, *Unum necessarium*, 124. Concerning the criticism he received from Broniewski and Descartes, see his own account in his 1669 treatise, *Continuatio admonitionis fraternae*, reprinted in R. F. Young, *Comenius in England* (London: Oxford University Press, 1932), 37.

27. Comenius, *Unum necessarium*, 120.

with my whole heart, "I believe everything that is written in this book!" If someone should ask more pressingly for my confession of faith, I would point to the Apostles' Creed, for there is nothing shorter, simpler and more succinct. . . . If someone will inquire about my rules of life, I will produce the Ten Commandments, for I am sure that no one can better express what is pleasing to God than God himself.[28]

This was a capacious piety. Unlike Luther or Loyola who seized on a specific spiritual insight and developed it into a sophisticated reform program, Comenius actually had a broader appreciation of the Christian tradition and could embrace ideals that seemingly ran counter to each other. His understanding of Christian identity was broad enough to incorporate that tradition of activism so evident with his reform program alongside the simpler and even mystical piety that came to characterize groups such as the Moravians in the next century.

28. Comenius, *Unum necessarium*, 127.

Chapter 30

Anna Maria van Schurman and Madame Jeanne Guyon: The Oblation of Self

Bo Karen Lee

Self-denial can ruin a person. Women in particular have been harmed by tragic manipulations of Christian theology, and it seems obvious that a stronger sense of self is needed, especially to bolster the defenses of female victims of abuse.[1] Yet strangely, women mystics throughout the history of the Christian church have taught that the pouring out of self to God strengthens the self, rather than diminishing it. The soul that loves God is enlarged precisely by being offered up, or "surrendered" to God.[2] Understandably, the modern reader may find the writings of these mystics bewildering.

Madame Jeanne Guyon's spiritual writings from the seventeenth century, for example, seem to contain an unhealthy preoccupation with the notion of self-annihilation, and her extreme language seems to confirm misgivings about the church's teaching on self-denial. As one reads more deeply, however, an unexpected beauty emerges. Guyon herself drew power from her theology; indeed, it enabled her to overcome cruel hardships, including persecution from the church and royal court, and inhumane imprisonments. Her theo-

---

1. Numerous accounts of women abused in the name of Christianity fill our theology bookshelves. Annie Imbens's book *Christianity and Incest* is especially poignant, as it describes how fathers, appealing to Jesus's self-denial as a model for "good Christians," forced their daughters into unspeakable acts. Her case studies come from the Dutch Reformed Church but can extend to other contexts, including our own (a friend of mine from the midwestern United States was a victim of incest at the hands of her father, a prominent church elder who forced her into submission with all the weight of the church's teachings). Much of this essay comes directly from Bo Karen Lee, *Sacrifice and Delight in the Mystical Theologies of Anna Maria van Schurman and Madame Jeanne Guyon* (South Bend, IN: University of Notre Dame Press, 2014). The author and editors gratefully acknowledge the University of Notre Dame Press for their permission to use this material.

2. For distinctions between "self" and "soul" in Guyon, see Lee, *Sacrifice and Delight*, 209 n. 9.

logical and spiritual framework provided resources with which she could confront the ecclesial and political structures of her day. Guyon's writings have inspired many notable thinkers across multiple continents, and her enduring influence is astonishing given that she was a condemned figure in the Catholic Church.

A similar pattern interestingly marks the Reformed theology of "the Star of Utrecht," Anna Maria van Schurman, in seventeenth-century Holland. Her reflections on self-denial promise a deep inner strength, peace, and even joy. According to van Schurman, self-denial, when understood and practiced properly, empowers rather than weakens the individual. Indeed, we see a gradual transformation of tone in van Schurman's own writings—from that of acquiescent female to self-possessed leader in her circle and beyond.

These women and their texts, oddly enough, resonate with a growing movement within feminism today. This newer generation of scholars promotes a feminism that does not seek to mimic that which it resists. In other words, this brand of feminism does not seek power as the primary good, necessary to redress previous imbalances of power. Rather, it embraces counterintuitive avenues by which an individual might be strengthened and made whole.[3]

In many ways, these two women of seventeenth-century Europe promoted a similarly counterintuitive journey. But they were even more radical in their formulation of how one may find true freedom. They argued that self-denial or, more appropriately, self-surrender toward God, was not only the path to finding one's true self, but also the secret to the deepest enjoyment possible in God. This coupling of self-denial with enjoyment is surprising and deserves to be explicated. Both van Schurman and Guyon claim that they experienced self-denial as the source of an "unspeakable joy, which the world does not know."[4] Their bold writings, theologies, and lives have shaped many people and movements, making them significant figures in the history of the church. They have become so precisely through this curious theology—a theology that promotes the deepest enjoyment of God, even through sacrificial surrender.

---

3. Sarah Coakley's *Powers and Submissions: Spirituality, Philosophy and Gender* (Malden, MA: Blackwell, 2002), for example, sparked many conversations. See also Anna Mercedes, *Power For: Feminism and Christ's Self-Giving* (London: T&T Clark, 2011); and Carolyn Chau, "'What Could Possibly Be Given?' Towards an Explanation of *Kenosis* as Forgiveness—Continuing the Conversation between Coakley, Hampson, and Papanikolaou," *Modern Theology* 28 (January 2012): 1–24.

4. Anna Maria van Schurman, *Euklēria seu Melioris Partis Electio. Tractatus Brevem Vitae ejus Delineationem exhibens. Luc 10:41,42. Unum necessarium. Maria optimam partem elegit.* (Altona, 1673), chap. 9.IV, 187.

Brief Biographical Sketches

Anna Maria van Schurman (1607–1678) was arguably the most remarkable female scholar of her generation. She rose to prominence among the leaders of the Dutch Reformed Church, and her fame reached far beyond the Reformed world. Lauded as the "tenth muse," the "brightest star" among the educated women of Europe, van Schurman was the pride of royalty, theologians, and poets alike.[5] She became the first woman admitted to study at the University of Utrecht (albeit hidden behind a screen in the corner of the lecture hall) and received the special honor of commemorating the university's opening in 1636 with her own Latin composition. (It was not until 1872 that another woman would be allowed to study at the university level in all of the Netherlands.)[6]

Aspiring to become a sophisticated biblical exegete, van Schurman mastered over twelve languages and compiled the first Ethiopic grammar.[7] She exercised an uncanny command of Hebrew, Greek, Arabic, Aramaic, and Syriac and wrote treatises in Latin and French; she also composed poems in her native Dutch tongue.[8] Her appetite for knowledge was unbounded and her reputation crossed geographic lines. Van Schurman's renown became more widespread with the publication in 1641 of her *Dissertatio de Ingenio Muliebris ad Doctrinam, et meliores Litteras aptitudine* ("A treatise regarding the fitness of the female mind for the study of the arts and sciences"), and of her elaborate praise poems continued to be written by the elite in admiration of this "marvel of nature." Indeed, to "have been in Utrecht without having seen Mademoiselle de Schurman was like having been to Paris without having seen the king."[9]

5. Queen Christine of Sweden was among her many devotees, for example. Van Schurman's fame and influence are further explored in chapter 2 of Lee, *Sacrifice and Delight*, and in Anne Larsen, "'The Star of Utrecht' Anna Maria van Schurman: The Educational Vision and Transnational Reception of a Savante" (unpublished manuscript).

6. See Pieta van Beek, *First Female University Student: Anna Maria van Schurman (1636)* (Utrecht: Igitur, 2010), 7 and 249. The next female to study at a Dutch university would be Aletta Jacobs over two centuries later.

7. Larsen's "Star of Utrecht" lists fifteen languages mastered by van Schurman. The introduction to this new volume provides an in-depth overview of van Schurman's educational background and scholarly reputation, as well as the historical context of female erudites in early modern Europe in general.

8. See, for example, van Schurman, *Opuscula Hebraea, Graeca, Latina, Gallica: Prosaica & Metrica* (Lugduni Batavororum, 1648). See also Cornelia Niekus Moore, "Anna Maria van Schurman," in *Women Writing in Dutch*, ed. K. Aercke (New York: Garland, 1994), 191.

9. Joyce Irwin, "Anna Maria van Schurman: The Star of Utrecht," in *Female Scholars: A Tradition of Learned Women before 1800*, ed. J. R. Brink (Montreal: Eden Press Women's Publications, 1980), 68, quoting and translating from a work by Pierre Yvon, van Schurman's earliest biographer, entitled "Abrégé sincère de la vie et de la conduite et des vrais sentiments de feu Mr.

However, upon joining a controversial new Pietist movement in the 1660s, van Schurman quickly fell out of favor. Devoting herself to a new spirituality, van Schurman integrated themes from mystical literature.[10] She taught a more extreme form of self-denial than her contemporaries, requiring full surrender to God at the start of the Christian journey. At the same time, her theology promised a deep enjoyment of God in this life, making "union with God" the supreme goal of theology. Though she retained her theological commitments to Calvinism, van Schurman expanded her categories, embracing the thought and spirituality of both nascent Pietism and Catholic mysticism.[11] Self-denial became her central theme,[12] and her life motto, "My love has been crucified," found consistent expression throughout her theological writings in various ways.[13]

Guyon's reception among her contemporaries followed a similar trajectory, although she boasts coming from an uneducated background.[14] Madame Jeanne Guyon (1648–1717) rose to prominence in the courts of Madame de Maintenon, the second wife of King Louis XIV. Serving as her spiritual counselor, Guyon won the respect of nobles and clerics of the court. She also became François Fénelon's trusted friend and inspired his thought throughout his career as royal tutor and eventual archbishop of Cambrai. Nonetheless, her "unconventional" teachings on the interior life, first found in her *Short and Very Easy*

De Labadie," included in its entirety in Gottfried Arnold, *Unparteyische Kirchen- und Ketzerhistorie* (Frankfurt, 1715).

10. While Labadism was primarily a Pietistic movement, a strong mystical bent also characterized its doctrine, as well as its way of life. (For the definition of mysticism I am employing for this essay, see n. 27 below.) Significantly, Pietism incorporated much of Catholic mystical thought into its own; Gottfried Arnold, one of its key leaders, for example, borrowed directly from Fénelon's writings—and Fénelon considered himself a disciple of Madame Guyon; see, for example, Peter C. Erb, ed., *Pietists: Selected Writings* (New York: Paulist Press, 1983). Of course, Labadie was himself a former Jesuit. See Trevor J. Saxby, *The Quest for the New Jerusalem: Jean de Labadie and the Labadists* (Dordrecht: Martinus Nijhoff, 1987), as well as Michel de Certeau, *The Mystic Fable: The Sixteenth and Seventeenth Centuries*, trans. Michael B. Smith (Chicago: University of Chicago Press, 1992), 271–93.

11. On her continuing commitment to Calvinism, see, for example, Joyce Irwin, "Anna Maria van Schurman and Antoinette Bourignon: Contrasting Examples of Seventeenth-Century Pietism," *Church History* 60 (September 1991): 301–15.

12. See, for example, Una Birch, *Anna van Schurman: Artist, Scholar, Saint* (London: Longmans, Green, 1909), 110.

13. Van Beek, *First Female University Student*, 38–39.

14. Such boasts made one's claim to illumination by God (i.e., direct inspiration from the Holy Spirit) more believable, as Guyon argues in her *Moyen Court*. See *Le Moyen court et autres écrits spirituels: Une simplicité subversive, 1685*, ed. Marie-Louise Gondal (Grenoble: Jérôme Millon, 1995).

Method of Prayer, elicited suspicion, even hostility. Chief among her critics was the indomitable Bossuet.[15]

Religious authorities were on the alert against novelty, and Guyon became a prime target. After harsh interrogations in 1694, Guyon was locked away in Vincennes by Louis XIV in 1695, then imprisoned in the Bastille until 1703, and finally kept under house arrest in Blois until her death in 1717.[16] Guyon continued to minister to many even under these constraints, and loyal Protestants, who carefully preserved and published her works, surrounded her at her deathbed.[17]

A Radical Surrender: Enjoyment's Shadow Side

In the midst of heightened theological controversy between Protestants and Catholics of the seventeenth century, both van Schurman and Madame Guyon held on to a theme whose prominence had waned throughout different seasons and sectors of the church: *fruitio Deo* (enjoyment of God). Van Schurman

15. See Marie-Florie Bruneau, *Women Mystics Confront the Modern World* (Albany: SUNY Press, 1988); and Michael de la Bedoyere, *The Archbishop and the Lady: The Story of Fénelon and Madame Guyon* (London: Collins, 1956).

16. Even Madame Maintenon turned against Guyon, who had previously been her spiritual guide. The political machinations involved in this betrayal are described in Bruneau, *Women Mystics*. Guyon experienced multiple stages of trial before the authorities. Her second interrogation of 1694 led to her arrest in 1695, though without clear charges or a fair trial. This began her imprisonment, which lasted approximately eight years, first in Vincennes and then in the infamous Bastille.

17. Guyon's influence extended far beyond her lifetime as well: John Wesley and Watchman Nee are among the numerous onlookers who appropriated her work in significant ways. Guyon's influence on the early Methodists in England, as well as the American holiness movement, for example, has been widely documented. Her thought has also wielded power in the thought of important figures such as Søren Kierkegaard and Arthur Schopenhauer, i.e., those whose reflections often focus on the perplexities of grave suffering. Schopenhauer said of her: "To become acquainted with that great and beautiful soul, whose remembrance always fills me with reverence, and to do justice to the excellence of her disposition while making allowances for the superstition of her faculty of reason, must be gratifying to every person of the better sort, just as with common thinkers, in other words the majority, that book [*Autobiography*] will always stand in bad repute." Arthur Schopenhauer, *The World as Will and Representation*, ed. Judith Norman, Alistair Welchman, and Christopher Janaway (Cambridge: Cambridge University Press, 2010), 384. Less well known, however, is her current popularity among various movements in America, as well as in Europe and Asia. Her books litter bookshelves in the most unexpected of places (e.g., in the heartland of China) and are often the main textbooks at conferences on prayer and spirituality; her *Song of Songs Commentary* alone has gone through multiple English translations and reprints, via a number of different publishers, and there continues to be a clamoring for her work and ideas. A simple web search alone reveals the breadth and popularity of this phenomenon.

and Guyon both argued that the "chief end of humanity" was to "enjoy God" both "in this life" and forever. This enjoyment, however, came at great cost. If the highest call was to find one's pleasure in the *summum bonum* (the greatest good), they argued together with Augustine that one consequently had to forsake "lesser" pleasures as an end in themselves. Inferior joys offered a mere façade and proved a barrier to the purest pleasure available in God. Ridding oneself of false joys required self-abnegation.

But van Schurman and Guyon went further. Departing from Augustine, they argued that union with God was possible on this earth through this process of purification. The trouble with this claim was not that they extended a strong form of *fruitio Deo* to the temporal; the mystics of the medieval period had already introduced that idea. Rather, it was that they regarded union with God as impossible apart from self-sacrifice. A thoroughgoing denial or annihilation of the self was required for the greatest pleasure in God to be experienced. Put another way, the uprooting of inferior joys required deep, painful purgation. The accent in their writings fell uncomfortably on the arduous nature of the path that leads toward union, even as they purported to celebrate the goal.

An emphasis on self-denial, of course, already had a long history in Christian theology and spirituality.[18] What makes van Schurman and Guyon unique is the way in which they coupled self-denial with pleasure. They intensified the denial as well as the pleasure.[19] Though van Schurman and Guyon described

---

18. The traditional itinerary of *purgatio, illuminatio, uniona* is well known in the history of Christian mysticism and dates back to Pseudo-Dionysius. See, for example, Andrew Louth, *The Origins of the Christian Mystical Tradition: From Plato to Denys* (1981; repr., Oxford: Clarendon, 1999), 63. Van Schurman and Guyon, however, intensify the use of these themes in their writing through their extreme, totalizing rhetoric.

19. Although there is growing scholarship on the violence of love in mystical theology (see, for example, Bernard McGinn, "The Abyss of Love: The Language of Mystical Union among Medieval Women," in *The Joy of Learning and the Love of God: Studies in Honor of Jean LeClerq*, ed. E. Rozanne Elder [Kalamazoo, MI: Cistercian Publications, 1995], 95–120), as well as the nature of finding pleasure *in* various forms of pain, some of the literature (e.g., Julie B. Miller, "Mystical Masochism and the Spiritual Status Quo: The Limitations of Appropriation," in *The Eclectic Edition*, ed. Phil Lampe and Julie B. Miller [San Antonio, TX: University of the Incarnate Word, 2004]) likens this (wrongly in my estimation) to masochism. On the other hand, feminist theologians have offered important correctives to and qualifications of the imagery of submission to violence within Christian theology. See, for example, Joanne Brown and Carol R. Bohn, "For God So Loved the World?" in *Christianity, Patriarchy, and Abuse: A Feminist Critique*, ed. Joanne Brown and Carol R. Bohn (Cleveland: Pilgrim Press, 1989), 1–30; Marie M. Fortune, "The Transformation of Suffering: A Biblical and Theological Perspective," in *Violence against Women and Children: A Christian Theological Sourcebook*, ed. Carol J. Adams and Marie M. Fortune (New York: Continuum, 1995), 85–90; Beverly Wildung Harrison and Carter Heyward, "Pain and Pleasure: Avoiding the Confusions of Christian Tradition in Feminist Theory," in *Sexuality and the Sacred: Sources for*

this journey toward God in painstaking detail, they were careful to affirm that the drive toward self-denial (for van Schurman) or self-annihilation (for Guyon) is an innate longing of the soul to become more intimate with the object of desire. In other words, the soul's desire—its delight—is what motivates and sustains self-denial. Just as union with God is impossible apart from self-denial, the theme of self-abandonment becomes unintelligible apart from the desire for God. Desire (or enjoyment) and denial are thus mutually illuminating.

From this perspective, the "sacrifice" of the self becomes an oblation of love, a self-giving that is voluntary and delightful. This yearning for God becomes the driving pulse behind a radical loss of self, as dying to self leaves more room for God to "fill" the whole of self. Only then can the soul come to know and enjoy God in intimate union. Self-denial therefore becomes the secret to a more profound joy.[20] In this manner, Guyon and van Schurman's understanding of desire and delight provides a key insight into their theology of sacrifice. Self-denial—as opposed to self-hatred or self-effacement—is for them ultimately life-giving.

"I Wish to Be Nothing": Self-Denial in Anna Maria van Schurman's *Euklēria*

> "Then Jesus told his disciples, 'If any want to become my follow-ers, let them deny themselves and take up their cross and follow me.'"
> — Matthew 16:24 (NRSV)

Throughout the history of Christianity, the call of Christ to deny the self has inspired his disciples to acts of great sacrifice—from martyrdoms to rigorous forms of asceticism. The power of this appeal to self-denial is especially evident

---

Theological Reflection, ed. James Nelson and Sandra P. Longfellow (Louisville: Westminster John Knox, 1994), 131–48; Sheila A. Redmond, "Christian 'Virtues' and Recovery from Child Sexual Abuse," in *Christianity, Patriarchy, and Abuse*, 70–88; Annie Imbens, *Christianity and Incest*, trans. Patricia McVey (Minneapolis: Fortress, 1992); Rita Brock, *Journeys by Heart: A Christology of Erotic Power* (New York: Crossroad, 1988); Rita Brock, "Losing Your Innocence but Not Your Hope," in *Reconstructing the Christ Symbol*, ed. Maryanne Stevens (Mahwah, NJ: Paulist Press, 1993), 30–53; and Julie B. Miller, "Eroticized Violence in Medieval Women's Mystical Literature: A Call for a Feminist Critique," *Journal of Feminist Studies in Religion* 15, no. 2 (1999): 25–49.

20. The Quietist doctrine of "pure love" forbade the explicit desire for such "self-fulfillment." Love for God, *for God's own sake* (and with no regard for self-benefit) was central. Self-fulfillment, however, was an inevitable result in both van Schurman's and Guyon's thought, because God's goodness and radical commitment to the individual were never to be doubted. This dynamic is further explored in chapters 5 and 6 of Lee, *Sacrifice and Delight*.

in the writings of Anna Maria van Schurman, who went so far as to identify self-denial as the lifespring of Christianity, without which true Christianity cannot exist "except one that is counterfeit [*fucatus*]."[21] According to van Schurman, self-denial was not a *goal* or destination for mature believers alone, as others were wont to claim. Rather, it was a *prerequisite* for all who desired even to begin the Christian journey. While self-denial was not by any means a novel concept, the priority that she attached to it was surprising to her contemporaries.

For van Schurman, the final purpose of self-denial was union with Christ. This goal would be unattainable without self-denial, through which one was emptied of the self and thus made ready for union with Christ. Even before the goal was to be reached, however, van Schurman yearned for a kind of knowledge that she would label "the one thing necessary." This *unum necessarium* was an "intimate" or "inmost" knowledge of God (*intima notitia Dei*) and this too was inaccessible apart from a radical renunciation of the self. Self-denial, then, would be the engine behind an intimate knowledge of God that would, in turn, lead ultimately to union with Christ.

While self-emptying was supremely desirable, it proved impossible for van Schurman. Self-denial, she discovered, would not be achieved by sheer effort; rather, it would be the byproduct of another process. Only a greater, more pleasurable gain would provide the impetus to motivate (and ultimately enable) her to surrender herself, as if by sheer coincidence. Faithful to the creeds of the Reformed Church, van Schurman held that "the chief end of [humanity] is to ... enjoy [God] forever."[22] As she describes in the closing pages of her mature treatise, the *Euklēria*, this enjoyment of God would become the secret to self-denial; it would also lead the seeker, ultimately, toward union with Christ. In fact, when *fruitio Dei* became the individual's supreme desire, self-denial would inevitably occur. Likewise, greater self-repudiation resulted in sweeter enjoyment of God. Rather than debilitate the soul, self-denial granted deep pleasure and delight to the soul that had learned to relinquish itself *for the sake of* a greater good. It found both its source and its fruit, its impetus and its reward, in the greater enjoyment of God.

Other theologians in the Dutch Reformed Church of van Schurman's time took issue with her emphasis on self-abnegation. They argued that it was a "mark of perfection" for mature Christians and feared that its primacy in her

21. Anna Maria van Schurman to Johann Jakob Schütz, letter 2, 12/22 August 1674, MS G2.II.33, fols. 2r–3v, University of Basel Library Archives, 3. Thanks to Joyce Irwin for providing information on these unpublished letters.

22. See the Westminster Shorter Catechism of 1647 and the Heidelberg Catechism; see also Lee, *Sacrifice and Delight*, 3, 180 n. 17.

writings might oppress or discourage the everyday Christian.[23] Against their doubts, van Schurman contended that self-denial need not be a daunting or restrictive imperative. Rather, it had the power to enlarge and enrich every individual. Indeed, this was the case in van Schurman's own experience. Although the established elite in both the academy and the church would abandon her for her choices, as she also had to abandon her former loves, van Schurman held to her convictions and found her theological voice. A stronger sense of self emerged, by the very *means* of her self-denial. She became a key spokesperson for the Labadists, a newly emerging Pietistic movement of her day led by Jean de Labadie. She was also a forerunner of German Pietism, as her writings arguably shaped this important movement from its outset.[24] At the end of the day, van Schurman emerged as a poised and confident leader. Her emphasis on self-renunciation served not to weaken but to liberate and strengthen her.

To understand van Schurman's argument, one needs to uncover the development in her thought. A dramatic shift marks her theological pursuits and indicates the contours of, and the reasoning behind, her spiritual trajectory. We examine that shift by exploring the argument in her *Euklēria*, published in 1673, and contrasting it with her *Dissertatio*, published in 1641. This turn in van Schurman's thought, finalized in the 1660s, was coupled with her decision to join the Labadist movement, a decision that led to the overthrow of her fame throughout Europe. In 1669, van Schurman made the controversial decision to leave the life of intellectual pursuits in order to devote herself to a life of piety within the Labadist community. This repudiation of her elite past created upheaval among those who had been her most loyal supporters. It also marked an upheaval in her own thinking about what theology and the reading of Scripture were ultimately to attain.

As one reads the *Euklēria*, it appears that a series of disenchantments had set her up for her introduction to Jean de Labadie in 1666. She explains that she had become increasingly aware of the spiritual impotence of her former ways of doing theology. In addition to the lack of change within her own heart (i.e., a lack of love for those she served in works of charity), she began noticing the ineffectiveness of the theology that surrounded her. As a result, she fled from

---

23. See, for example, van Schurman's correspondence with Johann Jakob Schütz. The dialogue between Schütz and van Schurman around this issue is further explored in chapter 3 of Lee, *Sacrifice and Delight*.

24. Wallmann argues persuasively in *Philipp Jakob Spener* that van Schurman influenced the genesis and development of Lutheran Pietism in nearby Germany (290–306), particularly through her influence on Schütz and Philipp Jakob Spener. Notably, Spener's *Pia desideria* was published in 1675, two years after van Schurman's *Euklēria*. Her correspondence with leading figures like Johann Jakob Schütz serves as another link to this important movement.

the company of those whom she calls "worldly theologians . . . not only because they contained not a whit of solid learning or genuine eloquence, but primarily because they did not savor or give off the scent of even a drop of that oil that the Spirit of Christ pours into the hearts of his own."[25]

Throughout the *Euklēria* (translated as "choosing the better part"),[26] van Schurman attributes the break with her past to her newfound pursuit of the "one thing" that was "necessary" (Luke 10:41–42). The reader is invited to discern from the whole of her writing, as well as from the scriptural context itself, that this "one thing" involves an intimate knowledge of God (*intima notitia Dei*) or an experience of "being taught by the Master directly."[27] Van Schurman also contrasts inmost knowledge with that which it is *not*: merely formal or external knowledge (*scientia*).

As van Schurman defends her choice to join the Labadists, she refers to her *Dissertatio de Ingenio Muliebris ad Doctrinam, et meliores Litteras aptitudine*, published thirty-two years earlier. This treatise was a vigorous defense of the education of women and had contributed to her rise as "the star of Utrecht." Yet now she could only "blush" to think of its contents, as she describes her former writings as "redolent of such superficiality of mind, or an empty and worldly spirit."[28] Upon closer examination of her *Dissertatio*, however, it becomes almost impossible to detect anything objectionable or potentially embarrassing to a religiously sensitive conscience. Indeed, it had won the praise of eminent theologians, including André Rivet and Gisbertus Voetius, precisely because she had declared in the *Dissertatio* that it is "fitting for women to study sciences instrumental to theology, since these lead to greater love of God."[29] In this treatise,

25. Van Schurman, *Euklēria*, chap. 2.XI, 26 (Irwin, 88). It is not clear from the context if she includes Voetius and Rivet among the "worldly theologians."

26. Inscribed on the cover page of her treatise, one finds: "Luc. 10:41, 42: *Unum Necessarium. Maria meliorem partem elegit*" ("One thing is necessary: Mary has chosen the better part"). Van Schurman also provides for her reader the Latin equivalent of the title on that same page: "*Euklēria: Seu Melioris Partis Electio.*" Hence, one can render her usage of *Euklēria* as "choosing the better part."

27. Van Schurman, *Euklēria*, chap. 2.XV, 32 (Irwin, 91). The theme of "direct" revelation was astir in seventeenth-century Europe in other writers such as George Fox in England; a desire for direct contact with the Divine (i.e., Bernard McGinn's definition of *mysticism*, the "immediate and direct consciousness of the presence of God"; *The Foundations of Mysticism;* vol. 1 of *The Presence of God: A History of Western Christian Mysticism* [New York: Crossroad, 1991], xvi–xvii, 262) was made explicit in their thought. Van Schurman is one representative of this growing trend of her time.

28. Mirjam de Baar, "'Now as for the Faint Rumours of Fame Attached to My Name . . .': The *Euklēria* as Autobiography," in *Choosing the Better Part: Anna Maria van Schurman, 1607–1678*, ed. Mirjam de Baar et al., trans. Lynne Richards (Dordrecht: Kluwer Academic Publishers, 1996), 87.

29. Eileen O'Neill, "Schurman, Anna Maria," in *Routledge Encyclopedia of Philosophy* (London: Routledge, 1998), 8:557.

she regarded theology as the supreme "science." Furthermore, the goal of study was to promote the glory of God, salvation, virtue, and magnanimity of spirit. What could be more noble or lofty? Wherein lay its "superficiality" or "empty, worldly spirit"? Van Schurman's previous call for the education of women had been precisely theological, not secular, in nature. Her "conversion" was not from a secular to a religious worldview; rather, she experienced a dramatic shift within her theological worldview. She now regarded her former ways of doing theology as sorely insufficient and devoid of true or lasting meaning.

According to van Schurman, theology's proper aim was "union with the Highest Good," namely, God; this union was characterized by deep enjoyment of God, the soul's truest happiness. The "one thing" necessary for attaining that goal was an "inmost knowledge" (*intima notitia*) of God, as opposed to complicated theological reflection *about* God. This allowed for a deeply felt *experiential* knowledge of God that would penetrate inwardly, while the latter left the individual detached or distant from God, even after complex considerations about the nature of God, the world, and self.

In van Schurman's view, erudite theological reflections functioned primarily in the realm of externals; God would remain outside the individual, and the individual outside God. Arid doctrine, marked by artificial systems and syntheses, prevailed within this mode, and the things of God would fail to reach the soul at a deeper level. Theological propositions might be placed in their proper order, but they would not be placed within the soul. "Inmost" knowledge of God, however, was marked by true change of heart and life. It implied *direct* communication with God and *intimacy* with the object of one's knowledge. One could attain union with God, in which God was not only "comprehended" but radically enjoyed as the soul's highest good and truest happiness.[30] Furthermore, this intimate (*intima*) connection with God alone had the power to effect a transformation of inward disposition and consequently to deepen one's love of God and neighbor. But how could one arrive at this "inmost knowledge"? Van Schurman notes her own failure to achieve *intima notitia* when she relays her failure to love her aunts, as well as others she was called to serve upon her mother's death. Even after all of her theological investigations, she had found herself spiritually bankrupt.

In the *Euklēria*, van Schurman contrasts *scientia* (a "knowledge so dry and superficial regarding divine matters") with *notitia* ("true, innermost, and salu-

---

30. Van Schurman juxtaposes this "excessive desire to learn" (*nimii sciendi desiderii, multiplicatarum scientiarum comprehensione*) against "*simplici & pura cognitione Christi crucifixi*" (*Euklēria*, chap. 9.XXIV, 204). Christ, then, is not to be "comprehended" (a term that in the Latin also connotes a grasping, seizing, or arrest) but rather "known" in the most inward parts, "simply and purely."

tary knowledge of God and his glory").[31] While *scientia* connotes knowledge, skill, and expertise of a more formal and academic sort, *notitia* (from *nosco*) is consistently qualified by van Schurman as true, health-giving, and *intima* (intimate or innermost). *Scientia* might leave the knower detached and outside the object of investigation, but *notitia* had the power to effect something—to create internal change. Doctrine could no longer remain outside the individual but would have to be incorporated into the very heart of one's life. She explains further that the object of *scientia* has nothing within it that "attracts our spirits to the contemplation and *innermost knowledge*" of God (*quod animos nostros ad ejus contemplationem intimamque cognitionem alliciat*) "unless its every essence be contemplated in a holy fashion." How, then, should God, the "end" of "true knowledge," be contemplated?

According to van Schurman, an inflow of grace was required to contemplate God "in a holy fashion." Grace would not be given apart from the reading of Scripture, however. As one meditated upon the sacred page, divine love would be imparted—a love that would, in turn, become the key to unlocking Scripture's inmost meaning. As van Schurman puts it, one had to be "instructed, not with philosophical modes of reasoning, or with human reason, but with the light of grace and scripture" as one is "truly imbued with divine love."[32] This kind of heartfelt instruction would overcome the superficiality and aridity of *scientia*. In fact, even the "slightest sense of God's love would provide a much more reliable and deeper understanding of the scriptures than the most extensive knowledge of biblical languages."[33]

Had van Schurman stopped at this point, she would have sounded no different from the burgeoning Pietists of her day. She makes a striking turn, however. While love for God is the necessary handmaid of a "truer and deeper understanding of the sacred page," an unqualified love, in the end, will be deemed insufficient. *Caritas* is powerless in the absence of one vital element, namely, a *radical overthrow of the self*. One can never arrive at the "one thing needful" (*intima notitia Dei*) without it. In other words, a love that is not accompanied by self-denial is rendered inadequate.[34]

In explicating this condition, van Schurman makes a threefold distinction among different forms of comprehension: "And yet, as in other things, the sub-

31. *Euklēria*, chap. 3.V, 39. Van Schurman contrasts "tam arida ac superficialis de rebus divinis scientia" with "veram, intimam, ac salutarem Dei notitiam."

32. Van Schurman, *Euklēria*, chap. 3.XII, 46.

33. Van Schurman, *Euklēria*, chap. 2.XVI, 32, trans. Desmond Clarke, "Anna Maria van Schurman and the 'Unum Necessarium,'" unpublished paper (August 18, 1999), 23.

34. This love is rendered inadequate for it has not yet been made "pure." See the discussion of "pure love" in n. 36 below.

stance and the conception often differ greatly; thus also, I am learning daily that there is a great difference between those truths comprehended by the intellect, as if pictured in the mind, and even received by a certain love in the heart, and between a total overthrow, conversion, and emendation of mind and heart."[35] Three types of knowing or "comprehension" thus emerge: (1) the knowing of the mind, that is, "truths comprehended by the intellect"; (2) knowledge received even "by a certain love in the heart"; and (3) the kind of knowledge that can come only from a life radically changed in both mind *and* heart, that is, "a total overthrow, conversion, and emendation of mind and heart." In other words, if love is not attended by a complete "overthrow" (*eversio*) of the mind and heart, it too will be insufficient in granting the individual *intima notitia*, "inmost knowledge" of God.[36] This overthrow involves the entirety of the individual and cannot occur simply in one faculty. Loving devotion and direct illumination from the Holy Spirit therefore must be complemented by a radical overthrow, even "destruction," of the whole self. This is what van Schurman calls self-denial, and this she regards as the final cure for a mind and heart that are turned in upon themselves and hence unable to receive the fullness of *intima notitia*.

It is important to note that self-denial, for van Schurman, meant a surrender of the will to God, along with all of one's loves and possessions, rather than concrete practices of asceticism, per se. She does not specify particular activities, but rather attitudes. This entailed a willingness to let go of personal ambition and desires, for example, and a focusing of love upon God, instead of promotion of self or of any created being. *Eversio* ("overthrow" or "destruction"), furthermore, made way for a genuine "conversion and emendation" of life.

Freedom and contentment are also impossible for van Schurman without the individual first renouncing finite desires. When the self and its creaturely attachments are relinquished, or destroyed, the individual is able to achieve union with God. According to this understanding, undivided affection, desire,

---

35. Van Schurman, *Euklēria*, chap. 4.I, 53: "Atqui, ut in caeteris rebus, res, et conceptus plurimum saepe differunt; ita que inter illas intellectu comprehensas veritates, in mente quasi deppictas, atque etiam amore quodam in corde receptas; et inter totalem mentis & cordis eversionem, conversionem & emendationem multum interesse quotidie addisco."

36. In distinguishing different types of comprehension, van Schurman thus separates two kinds of love. "Pure" love stands apart from a love for God that is mixed in with other loves. Only when the latter is accompanied by a radical "overthrow . . . of mind and heart" does it gain power; only then is it distilled into its essential purity. For a further discussion of "pure love," see van Schurman to Schütz, letter 4, December 22, 1674, MS G2.II.33, fols. 9r–12r, University of Basel Library Archives (hereafter "letter 4"), 6–7. Van Schurman follows a long tradition, beginning with Augustine, that argues for the perfection of love through distillation or simplicity.

and attention are prerequisites for attaining the supreme good. And this is the precise purpose of self-denial. One is to deny oneself in order to attach oneself to that which is supremely good and that which truly satisfies. The soul is thereby freed from the distractions and cares that keep the individual away from her one "good," and she becomes free to enjoy all else *in* that highest good.[37]

Van Schurman further explains that union with God, which she describes in various places as the happy "immersion" into the "infinite ocean of divinity," is inextricably linked with an awareness of one's own nothingness.[38] She says: "Altogether other is the mind of the Christian man and the limit of his felicity, who considers his very self and all his own as nothing, or as if, gazing upon a tiny drop of the ocean, only then judges himself blessed, when immersed in the measureless ocean of divinity, enveloped, penetrated, and filled, by that goodness and happiness."[39]

---

37. See Erica Scheenstra, "On Anna Maria van Schurman's 'Right Choice,'" in *Choosing the Better Part: Anna Maria van Schurman, 1607–1678*, ed. Mirjam de Baar et al., trans. Lynne Richards (Dordrecht: Kluwer Academic Publishers, 1996), 125. This state of abandonment also enables the individual to *return* to the finite world, with an appropriate love of self, others, and all creation *in God*.

38. As van Schurman states in letter 4, "Finally God himself becomes all things, [and] they themselves truly become nothing" (7). In the end, union with God, for van Schurman, involves an immersion into something that is infinite—a measureless ocean of divinity—and an awareness of one's own "nothingness" in light of God's magnitude. The way beyond finitude is to embrace one's nothingness. This recognition—that is, the "overthrow" (*eversio*) of self—is the necessary condition for immersion. One must either renounce oneself *entirely* or be left in the world of partial goods. One cannot have it both ways. This repudiation of the self coheres with a vision of God as infinite and measureless: because God is all encompassing, the soul can enter that vastness only when it has lost sight of itself and become nothing. God becomes all consuming, leaving room for nothing else. (At the same time, the love of creature [including the love of self] is retrieved in the end, through a purified love. This dynamic is further discussed in chapters 3 and 6 of Lee, *Sacrifice and Delight*.) As the soul is lost in God's fullness, it can finally be surrounded and filled by divinity.

39. Van Schurman, *Euklēria*, chap. 3.XII, 46–47. See also 55: "But therefore, to this extent, it is necessary that the Spirit of Christ be in us, that it may pray in us and for us and cause us to pray, and may *unite our mind and heart to God, and immerse [them] in his infinite ocean of divinity*" (italics mine) (*At ideo necesse est Spiritum Christi esse in nobis, ut in nobis & per nos precetur, & nos precari faciat; mentemque & cor nostrum Deo uniat, iusque infinito Divinitatis Oceano immergat.*) For more on the image of the "ocean of divinity" prevalent within mystical literature, see McGinn, "Abyss of Love."

Although van Schurman employs the language of *becoming* nothing, she does not go so far as to say that the self is annihilated. The context of her words is essential. As she explains in the *Euklēria*, "I wish to be nothing, to own nothing or to do nothing *other than* that which he always shows through his workings to be his will" (translated and quoted in Baar, "'Now as for the Faint Rumours,'" 94; italics mine).

Furthermore, the individual is to "*consider* his very self . . . as nothing"—not to become nothing in actuality. The key here is one of perspective. When one regards the self as something, then God becomes less than everything to the individual. Once God becomes all, and the self is

The individual then rejoices to rest in God alone. In "resting" (*acquiescere*), one can be said to "become quiet," or even, in this particular construction, to "die."[40] Significantly, the term *acquiescere* also suggests an element of pleasure and delight. One might therefore say that there is a certain pleasure in dying to the self. The individual finally comes to quiet, rest, and peace, finding delight in the singular object of her desire. According to this schema, the surrender, or oblation, of the self leads to a profound peace and enjoyment.

From this perspective, self-denial is the source of "unspeakable joy, which the world does not know." The self is abandoned and "destroyed" in order to create space, ultimately, for a greater joy. An alternate form of pleasure-seeking is thus spiritually validated,[41] and paradoxically, self-denial is the precise means through which the greatest pleasure is achieved. In a letter to Johann Jakob Schütz in December 1674, van Schurman further explains:

> Just as we are able to conquer all things, through him who loved us, and therefore especially our very selves, who were by nature the enemies of God, *that practice does not weary or weaken us, but strengthens [us] in a wonderful manner*, in the way of life. Even more, we believe that no Christian can enjoy perfect and constant inward peace, except after he has snatched away his very self and all his possessions, temporal and eternal, with his own hands and cares, through the denial of self and the transfer of all things into the hand and will of God.[42] (italics mine)

Though self-denial may seem like a difficult teaching to the novice Christian, van Schurman emphasizes that it is the key to great gain. It un-

---

regarded as nothing, the individual finds himself "enveloped, penetrated, and filled" by that infinite "goodness and happiness." Again, van Schurman thinks in spatial terms, arguing implicitly that competing loyalties cannot occupy the same space in the heart, or in one's purview.

Throughout her writing, van Schurman attempts to qualify her emphasis on the soul's "nothingness" before God in order to preserve the integrity of the individual. Potential dangers remain in her language, however, especially when her theology is misconstrued or misapplied. There are limits to retrieving her thought today, and one needs to apply her thought with wisdom. Potentially healthful retrieval of her thought is further explored in chapter 6 of Lee, *Sacrifice and Delight*.

40. *Euklēria,* chap. 3.XIII, 48.

41. Admittedly, "pleasure-seeking" is often seen as the antithesis of self-denial. Van Schurman's theology, however, presents the contrary. For a helpful discussion of *eudaimonism* in the Christian tradition, see Frederick Simmons, "Eudaimonism and Christian Ethics," in *Love and Christian Ethics: Tradition, Theory, and Society,* ed. Frederick V. Simmons (Washington, DC: Georgetown University Press, 2016). See also n. 20 above for the complexities of seeking fulfillment in God.

42. Letter 4, p. 13 (see Appendix B of Lee, *Sacrifice and Delight,* for the original letter in Latin and its English translation).

locks an inner strength and ushers in perfect peace. Once finite attachments are removed, the individual is free to enjoy her supreme good. The self is abandoned only that it may fasten itself anew to a greater object. Again, self-denial here does not necessitate an ascetic lifestyle; rather, it entails radical trust and the surrender, or "transfer," of all things into the care of God. And trust is possible because the soul comes to discover that God is supremely good.

The Impossibility of Self-Denial

Despite van Schurman's insistence that each Christian learn to deny herself, van Schurman ironically concludes that self-denial is an impossible task even for the most determined. It is made possible only by a larger vision, a "new affection,"[43] granted by the "embrace" of the "vastness of God's own infinite Majesty."[44] In van Schurman's own life, she was *unable* to "refuse" (*abnego*) or "forget" herself until she had the experience of being enfolded in God's presence. Self-denial in effect happened to her, rather than van Schurman being the agent of her own self-forgetfulness. In the final analysis, self-denial became contingent upon the divine "embrace." This embrace enabled her to "surrender [herself] entire, all [her] desires, all [her] good and evil circumstances" and to become "profoundly forgetful of [her]self" as a secondary consequence.[45] This profound lack of concern with herself became the source of freedom, and self-forgetfulness would not be a goal towards which to strive but an inevitable byproduct of being consumed in the presence of God.

According to van Schurman, self-denial (or synonymously in this instance, self-forgetfulness[46]) thus becomes impossible without a fuller revelation of God.

---

43. I borrow here from the words of Thomas Chalmers, "The Expulsive Power of a New Affection," in *Sermons and Discourses* (New York: Thomas Carter, 1844), 2:271–78.

44. *Euklēria*, 207; see Lee, *Sacrifice and Delight*, Appendix C, for my translation as well as the original Latin.

45. *Euklēria*, 207.

46. To understand the priority of self-denial in van Schurman's and Guyon's theologies, it is important to note that self-denial for them becomes equivalent to self-forgetfulness in light of God's overwhelming love. One does not seek to deny or forget oneself; it happens as one becomes lost in God's care. Likewise, one does not strive to protect or preserve the self, because one becomes secure in God's wisdom, provision, and strength, having experienced the shelter of God's wings. This self-forgetfulness leads to a deeper freedom, so that one is no longer anxious about oneself or about how one is perceived. Rooted in divine grace, one need not examine how effective one's labors have been. In fact, there is freedom to fail, and this failure results in a profound recognition of one's finitude, which further transforms self-reliance into a dependence upon God's infinite

That which leads to a deeper knowledge of God (i.e., self-denial) is rendered ineffective on its own merit, but it is granted, in fuller measure, by an intimate encounter with the object of one's desire. The goal becomes the impetus that again leads to a deeper appreciation of the goal—namely, the direct experience and enjoyment of the presence of God. Rather than looking at self-denial as the simple prerequisite to union with God in van Schurman's theology, one can conclude that deeper levels of *intima notitia* are made possible by deeper levels of self-denial, and self-denial is born out of a realization of the grace and majesty of God. This pattern leads, finally, to union with God. The goal and the means become interchanged in circular fashion, each leading to a more profound knowledge of God. As van Schurman put it, "the grace of Jesus Christ, reigning in the faithful, is the universal foundation of the denial of all things which are not God; whose general unfolding and, as it were, continuous series stretches out through all steps and intervals of life."[47]

Similarly, Guyon offered a spiritual itinerary by which the soul might become united to God. Hers was a more striking trajectory, however, requiring death, or "annihilation," of the self. In her *Commentary on the Song of Songs*, Guyon elucidates the journey of the soul toward this painful, yet life-giving, end.

Madame Jeanne Guyon's Song of Death

"The marriage takes place when the soul falls dead and senseless into the arms of the Bridegroom, who, seeing her more fit for it, receives her into union."[48]

---

resources. This dependence, in turn, leads to a greater release of divine resources because one's prior self-reliance no longer limits God's free activity in the individual's life.

When surrounded by this expansive vision of God's love, one also becomes freed from self-interest, for all one's deepest interests are held safely by God's goodness. In other words, God, as the highest good, seeks also the greatest good of the individual, which frees him or her to love others. Freed from anxious striving, the "pernicious I" no longer operates willfully but relaxes into a trusting posture. And self-love is redeemed as one learns to love self, among all other creatures, under the umbrella of God's care.

47. Letter 4, p. 7 (see Appendix B of Lee, *Sacrifice and Delight*): "Porro certissimum est gratiam J[esus] C[hristi] regnantem in fidelibus esse fundum universalem abnegationis rerum omnium, quae non sunt Deus; cuius explication generalis et veluti series continua sese extendit per omnes gradus ac intervalla vitae." Van Schurman also writes that "the universal foundation of his grace is in the faithful, which unfolds itself through the whole course of their lives" (12).

48. Jeanne Guyon, *Commentaire au Cantique des cantiques de Salomon*, in *Les torrents et Commentaire au Cantique des cantiques de Salomon, 1683–1684*, ed. Claude Moralie (Grenoble:

The Song of Songs has held wide appeal in the rich history of the Christian mystical tradition. Well-loved authors, such as Bernard of Clairvaux and St. John of the Cross, among others, have taken its most intimate images and transformed them into tender accounts of the union that takes place between Christ and his bride.[49] The Song undeniably contains vivid imagery that earns it the right to be called *the* song of love—whether it be the love shared between a man and his bride, God and Israel, or Christ and his beloved.[50]

At the turn of the eighteenth century, however, the Song quickly became a song of death. Under the pen of Madame Jeanne Guyon, the vision of a "dead bride" rose to the fore with ever-increasing urgency.[51] Her piling up of violent images evokes discomfort, as she details the union of the "annihilated bride" with her "bloody bridegroom," who is to her a "bridegroom of death."[52] Might

Jérôme Millon, 1992), comment on Song 6:4. "The marriage takes place when the soul falls dead and senseless [*morte et expirée*]."

49. While the tradition of interpreting the Song of Songs as the celebration of the individual's union with God emerged as early as Origen in the third century (see his *Commentary* and two *Homilies* on the Song), the medieval period experienced a boom in this approach. For detailed studies on medieval exegesis of the Song, see Denys Turner, *Eros and Allegory: Medieval Exegesis of the Song of Songs* (Kalamazoo, MI: Cistercian Publications, 1995); E. Ann Matter, *The Voice of My Beloved: The Song of Songs in Western Medieval Christianity* (Philadelphia: University of Pennsylvania Press, 1990); Ann W. Astell, *The Song of Songs in the Middle Ages* (Ithaca, NY: Cornell University Press, 1995); and George Louis Scheper, "The Spiritual Marriage: The Exegetic History and Literary Impact of the Song of Songs in the Middle Ages" (PhD diss., Princeton University, 1971). For an overview of its wider trajectory (beginning with the patristics), see Richard A. Norris Jr., ed. and trans., *The Song of Songs: Interpreted by Early Christian and Medieval Commentators*, The Church's Bible (Grand Rapids: Eerdmans, 2003). A helpful compilation of patristic commentaries can also be found in J. Robert Wright and Thomas Oden, eds., *Proverbs, Ecclesiastes, Song of Solomon*, Ancient Christian Commentary on Scripture 9 (Downers Grove, IL: InterVarsity Press, 2005). See also J. Paul Tanner, "The History of Interpretation of the Song of Songs," *Bibliotheca Sacra* 154, no. 613 (1997): 23–46. Certainly, this tradition continues well beyond the medieval period to authors such as Teresa of Avila, St. John of the Cross, and Madame Guyon.

50. The bride, according to Bernard of Clairvaux's *Commentary on the Song of Songs*, can refer to the church, as well as to the individual believer, a view that originated from Origen's work. In St. John of the Cross's account, more attention is given to the union of the individual soul with Christ. As we shall see, Guyon focuses more upon the individual nature of the union, as well; she concedes, however, that what is true of the individual is true of the church as a whole (cf. Guyon, *Commentaire au Cantique*, 170, comment on 6:9).

51. While St. John of the Cross also emphasizes annihilation in his *Canticles*, as does St. Francis de Sales in his *Treatise on the Love of God* (and most immediately to Guyon, Pierre de Bérulle in the French school of spirituality), they do so with less intensity; the depictions with which they paint the bride are not as stark or "bloody" as Guyon's. To help support her work, Guyon cites St. John of the Cross and Francis de Sales directly in her *Les justifications de Madame J. M. B. de la Mothe Guyon*, 3 vols. (Paris: Dutoit, 1791).

52. He is also a "bloody husband, and crucified lover." See Jeanne Guyon, *Commentary on*

these vivid pictures somehow border on the morbid and macabre, or open Guyon to charges of spiritual necrophilia? Her interpretation shocked the religious authorities of her day, who expediently banned her work.[53] While her writings continued to offend some readers,[54] they nonetheless gained an extraordinary audience in many quarters, both during her time and beyond.[55]

Why was the image of a dead bride so attractive to Guyon? In other words, why was it that only an annihilated soul could be received into the bridal chambers of the bridegroom? Guyon writes that "all the graces of the Christian spring from [this] death of self."[56] She also argues that the full enjoyment of God in this life can be attained only on the other side of an excruciating spiritual death. Her goal, from the outset, is blissful union with God. From a human perspective, one would suppose that a dead spouse is the last thing a lover would desire. As in the case of all analogies, however, serious differences exist; and in Guyon's commentary, a dead bride is the *first* thing that the *divine* lover desires.

Annihilation (*anéantissement*) is a term that Guyon repeatedly employs as she traces for her reader the mystical path to union with Christ. While an English translation may render her French simply as "death," "destruction," or "annihilation," her descriptions include rich expressions that help to elucidate the semantic contours of *anéantissement*. A simple listing of Guyon's terminology reveals verbal constructions as vivid as *détruite* (destroyed), *abattre* (to demolish, pull down, slaughter, or overthrow), *terasser* (to knock down), and *arracher* (to dig up, uproot, tear out, or snatch). In addition to these images that

---

the *Song of Songs,* trans. as *Song of the Bride* (New Kensington, PA: Whitaker House, 2002), 46. Among Guyon's lost works (the biblical commentaries, in particular), one is left to wonder if she commented on Exodus 4:25–26. Many of her works are unfortunately missing, her books having been placed on the Index. During her lifetime, only her *Moyen Court* and *Commentaire* were published. A loyal Protestant follower, Pierre Poiret, did much to preserve and publish her writings, most of which occurred posthumously. See Marjolaine Chevallier, "Madame Guyon et Pierre Poiret," in *Madame Guyon,* ed. Joseph Beaude et al. (Grenoble: Jérôme Millon, 1997), 35–49.

53. While it may be difficult to trace the exact source of offense, we know that both her *Moyen Court* and *Commentaire* elicited controversy and, ultimately, condemnation.

54. For a number of reasons (which may or may not include her *Commentary on the Song of Songs,* in particular), interpreters such as Ronald Knox have relegated Guyon to the realm of the egomaniacal; they find in her writings evidence of derangement, regarding her mental state as off-kilter. Guyon was charged as a "madwoman" in her time as well as in subsequent eras; she was also relegated to the realms of oblivion within the Catholic Church until recent decades, when interest has been renewed among Catholic scholars. After centuries of neglect, she has been reclaimed as a valid voice meriting careful attention. See especially Marie-Louise Gondal, *Madame Guyon, 1648–1717: Un Nouveau Visage* (Paris: Éditions Beauchesne, 1989), for a definitive biography of Guyon.

55. See n. 17 above.

56. *Madame Guyon's Spiritual Letters* (Augusta, ME: Christian Books Publishing House, 1982), 54.

evoke the violent action of divine love, Guyon makes lavish use of other phrases to describe the soul, both during and after its annihilation: the soul is said to be "stripped" by this process (*dénuée*), and "skinned" or "pillaged" (*dépouillée*). On a softer note, the soul finds itself "lost" (*perdue*), "melted" (*fondue*), and "sunk" or "submerged" (*abîmée*) into the "ocean of divinity."[57]

As Guyon begins to explain the process by which the self is annihilated, she writes that the first thing that needs to die is the *perception* of one's self. One ceases to "discern" or recognize anything but God. Annihilation of the self is, first and foremost, an annihilation of one's *self-awareness*. From the start, it is an *action* of the self that is being destroyed, regardless of how one defines the self's essence. The soul moves beyond its fixation with self and loses itself in the "abyss of God," no longer aware of anything but God alone.[58] Significantly, it is not that the *self* has been lost, but that the "feeling," "knowledge," and "discernment" of itself is lost.[59]

In order to advance in her journey, an additional turn is required. Even as the bride ceases to see herself, she must also lose her awareness of the very act of perceiving. In other words, she becomes oblivious of her gaze, or the redirection of her gaze, having become utterly enrapt in the other. Self-reflection is thus annihilated to a second degree. If in the initial stages the soul could no longer say, "I see myself," at this more advanced state it no longer says, "I see that I see." The soul has become steadfast in her focus upon her beloved, but is incognizant of her faithfulness.

Finally, the bride needs to cease her habit of self-praise, or the attribution to self of divine qualities, such as wisdom, righteousness, and power. But this

---

57. See, for example, her commentary on 3:8; 4:9; 6:4; and 7:13. Chapters 3, 5, and 6 of Lee, *Sacrifice and Delight*, discuss the question of *who* performs the stripping action: God, the self, or both? In other words, who is the primary agent?

58. Guyon, *Commentaire au Cantique*, 233: *et que, ne s'apercevant plus en elle, elle ne se trouve plus qu'en lui.* "The coming forth is far other than the one before alluded to [1:7], and much farther advanced; for the first was but a leaving of natural gratifications, that she might please her Well-beloved, but this is a departure from the possession of self, that she may be possessed by God only, and that, perceiving herself no more in self, she may be found in Him alone. It is a transportation of the creature into its original, as will be shown by and by" (Guyon, *Song of the Bride*, 54, comment on 2:10).

For more on the "abyss of God," see McGinn, "Abyss of Love." See also the language of van Schurman along these lines (finding oneself lost in the "measureless ocean of divinity"), in notes 38–39 above.

59. Guyon employs various terms to describe the lure of self-perception. The soul "sees" itself, has "regard" for itself, and pays "attention" to itself. The key issue here is that of *attending to* self. Self-attention prevents the soul from *attending to* God and focusing one's mind and affections upon him. Simone Weil develops this theme further in her writings on the spiritual life.

process is difficult, even impossible, for the soul. Toward this end, she is invited to make a decisive "sacrifice" of herself upon the "painful bed of the cross." She finds, however, that she is unable to, for she remains attached to self-regard and self-commendation. Only the divine bridegroom can educe this sacrifice, as he carefully places the soul in "the field of combat, labor, and suffering."[60]

Feeble in the face of love's crucifying demands, the soul is keenly aware that those "who will not consent to this crucifying process must be content to remain all their lifetime in self and imperfection."[61] The bride therefore despairs of herself, for she clings yet to self.[62] In ironic fashion, "holy despair" becomes the very key to the fulfillment of the soul's longing. Once she has despaired of her*self,* a window opens by which she may breathe anew. Personal dejection leads her to make the "final sacrifice," as she throws herself upon the mercy of God; she learns finally to offer nothing of her own righteousness and strength to him. Stripped of her pride, the bride undergoes one last annihilation, that which Guyon calls the "final renunciation." Once she has experienced this, however, an unexpected source of power is released.[63] As Guyon explains, "the more we despair of self, the more we trust in God." And trusting in God creates space for the power of God to infuse the soul anew.

When the soul is thus annihilated, the bride is finally ready for the consummation of her marriage. By this strange twist of providence, the "stripping" of the "veil of her own righteousness" allows the soul to "flow sweetly into her Original."[64] The bride brings nothing of her own righteousness to this union, thereby receiving all of God's righteousness.[65] She has become nothing; God has become all. And the bride enters into her apostolic vocation, exponentially more fruitful and active in her service than before.[66]

Despite the excesses in Guyon's language, her overall message might yet be applicable to a church that has resigned itself to a complacent, self-centered faith. Perhaps the constant preoccupation with self, and with one's own ac-

---

60. Guyon, *Song of the Bride*, 52.

61. Ibid., 122.

62. Ibid., 87.

63. Bruneau even argues that such spiritual exercises (prayer and self-surrender) were the key to Guyon's mental strength, amidst the horrific circumstances that she was forced to endure. She posits that others, in similar straits, would not have survived emotionally or mentally (*Women Mystics Confront the Modern World*).

64. Guyon, *Song of the Bride*, 88, 90. Guyon's use of Neoplatonic imagery is striking, inherited most probably from Augustine's *Confessions*. For a further discussion of Platonic imagery within commentaries on the Song of Songs, see Turner, *Eros and Allegory*.

65. Guyon, *Song of the Bride*, 90.

66. For more on the annihilated soul as apostolic bride, see chaps. 4 and 5 of Lee, *Sacrifice and Delight*.

complishments and successes, is one of the impediments that the soul faces in experiencing deeper union with the divine. The self has become small, rather than expanding into a generous, hospitable space for God and the other. Guyon challenges her reader to focus on Another, and to see all of one's strengths as flowing from the divine.

This, in the end, is what "annihilation" means for Guyon. It is the cessation of human striving, for the sake of radical receptivity to the grace, power, and wisdom of God. "Annihilation" is not so much the violent destruction of the human component; it is rather a complete surrender, or submission, such that it comes under a new guidance and control. This may appear very much like death, and Guyon certainly calls it so: all things human need to be "slain" so that they can be resurrected. However, death and "radical receptivity" amount to nearly the same thing, in the final analysis of Guyon's writing. Once human faculties are decisively redirected, or "annihilated," Guyon teaches that multiplied facility flows from the divine source. In her words, "the all-powerful voice of God" has summoned the bride "from the tomb of death to the spiritual resurrection,"[67] and her faculties become "a source of every blessing," poured out as a healing balm for others.[68]

A Shared Vision of the *Summum Bonum*

Despite the differences in Guyon's and van Schurman's theological contexts, a rather unexpected point of convergence is evident.[69] In their writings, self-denial emerges as a core element of the Christian gospel, significant both for Catholic and Calvinist thought of the seventeenth century. Self-denial and sacrifice, however, are never to serve their own end. Through the process of self-denial, a new self is formed: a God-made self, rather than a "self-made" self.[70] The best version of self that one can create is, in their eyes, a long shot away from the freshly empowered, fruitful, and "resurrected" self that they

67. Ibid., 120.
68. Guyon, *Song of the Bride*, comment on Song 7:4.
69. Perhaps we ought not be terribly surprised, however. In Calvin's *Institutes,* for example (particularly in Book III, on the Christian life), the theme of self-denial and "picking up one's cross" becomes prominent, sounding remarkably similar to Guyon's own rhetoric. One of the tasks of Lee, in *Sacrifice and Delight,* is to discern whether or not "self-denial" means the same thing, in both Quietist and Pietist (Labadist) thought, as specifically evidenced by Guyon's and van Schurman's writings. Interesting differences emerge, and one needs to be careful not to make too much of apparent similarities.
70. Thanks go to my colleague Gerald L. Sittser for this particular distinction and terminology.

envision. Yet, resurrection comes only on the other side of a dark and painful death. Put another way, new wine cannot be poured into "old" wineskins, and old wineskins are not repaired by being stretched or stitched: they are tossed out and replaced by something completely new.

The goal for van Schurman and Guyon is the attainment of a more profound level of joy in the Supreme Good. This joy, though reached at a steep cost, ushers the individual into an intimate knowledge of God that surpasses all sense of "sacrifice."[71] They argue that the way of self-sacrifice, that is, self-surrender, is the path to the deepest enjoyment of the greatest good. Where preoccupations with the self are removed, whether it be in a sense of self-importance, or even self-protectiveness, room is created for the *summum bonum* to fill and satisfy. Even today, in a context where individualism and convenience are held in special esteem, the call to deny oneself for another and to consider again the cost of discipleship just might result in a revitalization of Christian theology and practice.

Van Schurman and Guyon offer unique insights by vividly integrating a theology of sacrifice with a theology of desire and delight. Self-sacrifice, or the oblation of oneself, is, in the end, the door to a profoundly satisfied self. Both writers claim that in "losing" their lives, they have "found" life to the fullest. In essence, they have created space for the divine to dwell, becoming radically hospitable to God's presence. From this perspective, self-denial might be called "self-giving"—the offering in love of the self to another.

In fact, self-denial is made possible only because of *God's self-giving* toward the individual. The offering of the self to God is simply a response to God's tremendous sacrifice on behalf of humanity. In her *Commentary*, Guyon keeps her eye on this crucified lover, steeped in blood, because this self-pouring death was the highest expression of God's love for humanity. Van Schurman, likewise, focused on this theme. Her life motto, "My love has been crucified," had double meaning for her in that, as Christ's life had been poured out for her, so too lesser loves in her life would be crucified for Christ, her single love.[72]

---

71. This may be what the apostle Paul had in mind when he wrote, "I want to know Christ and the power of his resurrection and the fellowship of sharing in his sufferings, by becoming like him in his death, and so, somehow, to attain to the resurrection from the dead" (Phil 3:10). Keeping his eye on the prize, and impelled by a desire for *intima notitia*, Paul writes that power and resurrection are indeed reached—after one has passed through death.

72. Van Beek, *First Female University Student*, 38–39. Van Beek explains that van Schurman wrote a poem (in German) on this motto of hers, possibly after receiving a marriage proposal that she declined as part of her promise of chastity. Van Schurman wrote this poem in Gothic lettering over a paper-cutting labyrinth composed of hearts and crosses, an image of which is on the front cover of Lee, *Sacrifice and Delight*.

Through this radical hospitality to the divine Other, the individual is enlarged, finding more resources to be self-giving also to neighbor. Indeed, the reverse of self-denial is not healthy self-affirmation, but rather a destructive form of self-interested egotism. This kind of egotism is closed off, unable to love or give freely. It may be argued, then, that a self-interested posture (i.e., the opposite of self-denial) is that which precisely *destroys* life and deeply loving relationships.

When a love of comfort and consumerism mark our culture, and even our faith, it appears that the timeless call of the gospel to "deny oneself" can be all too easily neglected. Much will remain lost if we fail to retrieve these core and indispensable gospel themes—albeit with careful attention to their excesses and abuses—for contemporary theology.[73] "Following after Jesus," for van Schurman and Guyon, necessarily entails "picking up [one's] cross" and "denying [oneself]"[74] for the sake of an Other. The reader must keep in mind, however, that denying oneself never entails the repression of one's gifts; rather, van Schurman and Guyon demonstrate confidence that an unreserved outpouring of the self to God offers deep spiritual nourishment and strength, resulting, ultimately, in a greater enjoyment of humanity's *summum bonum*.[75]

73. This emphasis on a total self-denial, or self-annihilation, remains troubling to many contemporary readers. Important corrections have indeed been made by feminist theologians in recent decades—corrections that rightly challenge the abuse of such themes; and yet it becomes easy to then neglect altogether the call of Christ to "deny oneself" joyfully and "pick up one's cross." (For the corrections by feminist theologians, see notes 1 and 19 above.)

One needs to keep in mind that the object of van Schurman's and Guyon's final pursuit is God, the source of all pleasure. They seek a deeper joy, though it comes at great cost. Even Kristeva, who searches for the pathological in Guyon's mysticism, acknowledges that the mystics, in general, pursued some "good" (Julia Kristeva, *Tales of Love*, trans. Leon S. Roudiez [New York: Columbia University Press, 1987], 185; see also 297–317). Indeed, van Schurman and Guyon argue that self-sacrifice or self-surrender is the path to the deepest enjoyment of the greatest good. When preoccupations with the self are removed, whether in attitude, a sense of self-importance, or even self-protectiveness, space is created for the *summum bonum* to fill and satisfy the soul. This too was Augustine's struggle and his ultimate yearning; and it may be a universal cry in every age: "The house of my soul is too small for you to come to it. May it be enlarged by you. It is in ruins: restore it" (*Confessions* 1.5.6, trans. Henry Chadwick [Oxford: Oxford University Press, 1991], 6). For van Schurman and Guyon, the denial, or annihilation, of the self paradoxically serves this purpose; it leads to the expansion of the soul, to be newly filled by the infinite.

74. Matt 16:24; Mark 8:34–37; Luke 9:23–24.

75. What does this theology look like in practice? Might the reader of van Schurman's and Guyon's texts find something life-giving in their approach to the theological task and also in their coupling of self-denial with the joyful pursuit of God? The purpose of self-denial or self-annihilation for van Schurman and Guyon is to create more room for God's presence in one's life. Letting go of one's own agenda opens up space for God's Spirit to work, to lead, and to create the individual anew. This surrender is at times painful, as one clutches to the things that one cherishes.

In this place of surrender, van Schurman and Guyon claim that the soul comes to find the deepest enjoyment of God possible on this earth. A series of difficult "renunciations" precedes this delight, but with the apostle Paul they count these losses as nothing, for they are in pursuit of "the better thing" (*Euklēria*). Guyon writes of this immeasurable gain: "Oh, unutterable happiness! Who could have ever thought that a soul, which seemed to be in the utmost misery, should ever find a happiness equal to this? *Oh, happy poverty, happy loss, happy nothingness, which gives nothing less than God himself in his own immensity. . . . Oh, happy dying of the grain of wheat*, which makes it produce a hundred-fold! (John 12:24)."[76] Van Schurman and Guyon exclaim that they have found an inexpressible happiness, and they invite their readers to risk, to trust, and to offer themselves with abandon for the sake of this greater joy.

Releasing one's loves, however, only allows the Divine Lover to offer new graces in the place of lesser loves previously grasped.

In surrendering herself, the bride of Christ waits upon her bridegroom. As she waits for God's leading, strength, and wisdom, she is also an active worshipper who places her life upon the altar. Certainly, courage is necessary for such a surrender. The offering of oneself to God and God's purposes does not come easily. Apart from a deep trust in God's beauty, good designs, and trustworthiness (as seen in the case of the bride in Guyon's *Commentary*, as well as in van Schurman's own experience at the close of her *Euklēria*), the courage to release one's hopes and ambitions would elude the individual.

Van Schurman's understanding of *intima notitia* is instructive here. Just as she argued that self-denial is the doorway to a deeper knowledge of God, she also demonstrated that the surrender of oneself occurs only after one experiences the tenderness and compassion of God. An inmost knowledge of God as kind, generous, and gracious is thus necessary for the individual to place her trust in God. At the same time, when one makes the offering, or "sacrifice," of oneself, one comes to experience the beneficence of God again and again.

76. Guyon, *Autobiography of Madame Guyon, in Two Parts* (Chicago: Moody Press, 1988), 147.

Chapter 31

John Bunyan: The Bible and the
Individual Life Narrative in *Pilgrim's Progress*

STEPHEN NEY

> "I have sometimes seen more in a line of the Bible then I could well tell
> how to stand under, and yet at another time the whole Bible hath been
> to me as drie as a stick, or rather, my heart hath been so dead and drie
> unto it, that I could not conceive the least dram of refreshment, though
> I have lookt it all over."
>
> — *Grace Abounding to the Chief of Sinners*, 102

John Bunyan, the seventeenth-century tinker who is better remembered today
as an allegorist, preacher, and prisoner of conscience, believed that the depth
of a Christian's engagement with the Bible is indicative of their spiritual health.
Looking back at his long and agonizing religious conversion in his twenties and
the subsequent years of intense Christian service, he views his own life as an
unending oscillation between a healthy affection and a sick disaffection for the
Scriptures. Yet though his passion for the Bible may have been inconstant, all
his sixty published writings, whether autobiographical, sermonic, or allegorical, are infused with the Bible's language and themes. This essay will describe
what Bunyan took to be a life infused with and refreshed by the Scriptures, and
how by exhibiting such lives in his published writings he sought to help others
develop such a life.

Born in 1628 into a poor Bedfordshire family, Bunyan received only an
elementary education. By his sixteenth birthday, just after the deaths of both
his mother and younger sister, he had joined a local Parliamentary army. When
he describes these early years in his spiritual autobiography, *Grace Abounding
to the Chief of Sinners,* he emphasizes the poverty but especially the unremitting dishonesty and blasphemy that eventually generated some of the guilt and
contrition that led him toward repentance and assurance of salvation. The po-

litical and religious conflicts associated with nonconformity and the English Civil War deeply marked his development and provided the debates into which his preaching and writings intervened. After the Restoration in 1660, he spent about a dozen years in prison because of his refusal to give up "unlicensed" preaching and because of his commitment to the dissenting congregation in Bedford. But the unending doctrinal disputes reflected in his writings—disputes on themes such as acceptable worship, millennialism, baptism, sanctification, and biblical hermeneutics—were not only with the Anglicans, who enjoyed political favor after 1660, but also with many other stripes of Puritans or nonconformists.

To understand what is innovative in Bunyan's formulation of a biblically grounded Christian identity and the legacy that he left in the Christian tradition, it must be considered that he lived during the period of a dramatic increase in literacy—England's literacy rate probably passed fifty percent during his lifetime[1]—and in the availability of Bibles. Gutenberg, Tyndale, Luther, and the Authorized Version came before him, and during Bunyan's lifetime the intense biblical and theological agitation and innovation these innovators and innovations prompted continued in England. These were precisely the years in which the vernacular Bible was beginning to find its way into the hands and onto the tongues of laypeople, and in which laypeople sought to know how to put their Bibles to use.[2]

Bunyan's writings, particularly his allegory *The Pilgrim's Progress from This World to That Which Is to Come,* can be helpfully understood as pastoral responses to the rapid rise in biblical literacy. Bunyan felt passionately that his listeners and readers, though already familiar with biblical passages, needed help in the first place to adjudicate among competing interpretations and in the second place to apply the passages experientially. The epigraph above thus describes an unresponsiveness to the Bible that he assumed was familiar to his readers, and that called for heroic struggle. Though his evangelical and Calvinist beliefs convinced him that the Holy Spirit must create an inner transformation to put an end to the dryness and deadness, divine sovereignty did not warrant a passive attitude on the part of an unresponsive Bible reader. This essay will argue that, on the contrary, Bunyan's writings, especially *The Pilgrim's Progress,* are his attempts to guide Bible-readers in making the book alive and fertile for them. For three hundred years, their influence was immense upon Christians

1. J. A. Sharpe, *Early Modern England: A Social History, 1550–1760* (London: Edward Arnold, 1987), 277.

2. W. R. Owens, "John Bunyan and the Bible," in *The Cambridge Companion to Bunyan,* ed. Anne Dunan-Page (Cambridge: Cambridge University Press, 2010), 40.

seeking to be guided by the Scriptures towards total transformation in the image of Christ. The first part of *The Pilgrim's Progress* is the second best selling book of all time, and it is the Bible, of course, that has always surpassed it in sales.[3]

Biblical Interpretations at War in the Human Heart

Correctly interpreting and applying biblical passages could not have had more personal urgency than it did for Bunyan. Compared with many of his contemporaries, Bunyan was particularly skillful at apprehending specific passages from the Bible at moments when they had remarkable personal relevance. It was almost as though they forced themselves upon him from without, and then he would proceed to meditate intensely upon them in order to situate himself in relation to them. Not what we would call a narrative or a literary theologian, Bunyan approaches the Bible as though it were a collection of timeless, divine utterances. Apart from the distinction between the Old and New Testaments (the former of which refers typologically to the latter), he applies essentially the same hermeneutic to the entire Bible. It is not to be viewed primarily as one large, time-bound narrative, or even a collection of narratives corresponding to biblical books or characters' lives. Rather, it is a vast reservoir of insight to be skillfully applied to the narrative of a reader's life. In other words, the narrative character of the Bible consists primarily in its ability to structure the life narrative of its reader.

As author, Bunyan's primary concern is always for the individual interpreter, which is to say the individual Christian, and his burden is to help the individual make sense of one's own time-bound narrative.[4] *Grace Abounding* at many points gives the impression that interpreting biblical verses and interpreting a life are equivalent tasks, and when a biblical verse apprehends him, nothing could be more urgent to him than fitting it into his life. The complete hermeneutical task involves cross-referencing with other verses—for Bunyan believes firmly that as a whole the Bible provides its own interpretive keys—and prayerful submission to God's testimonies. Thus the assumptions of biblical per-

3. Andrew Bradstock, "John Bunyan," in *The Blackwell Companion to the English Bible*, ed. Rebecca Lemon et al. (Oxford: Blackwell, 2009), 287; cf. Jonathan Rose, *The Intellectual Life of the British Working Classes* (New Haven: Yale University Press, 2001), 85.

4. The anti-hierarchical implications of Bunyan's theological individualism explain why his works have found approbation from democrats and anticolonialists around the world. See Stuart Sim and David Walker, *Bunyan and Authority: The Rhetoric of Dissent and the Legitimation Crisis in Seventeenth-Century England* (Bern: Peter Lang, 2000).

spicuity, inspiration, authority, and contemporary relevance are fundamental to all his oeuvre.

One well-known episode in his journey towards assurance of salvation occurred when Bunyan, in his twenties, was overcome by despair and exasperation in his seemingly unending pursuit of God's favor and briefly entertained the thought of abandoning Christ. Immediately one particular "Scripture did seize upon my Soul," Hebrews 12:16–17, which tells of the patriarch Esau whom God rejected permanently, despite his attempts to repent, for the sinful folly of selling his birthright.[5] Bunyan became convinced he was in exactly the same situation as Esau, and at that moment "I felt myself shut up unto the Judgment to come; nothing now for two years together would abide with me, but damnation, and an expectation of damnation" (*GA* 43, 44).

This long period coincided with Bunyan's longest and deepest episode of the depression that profoundly marked his understanding of the Christian life.[6] He describes that period as an inner battle among many conflicting biblical passages. A promise of God's gracious acceptance of sinners would apprehend him and raise his spirits, but not for long, for "still that saying about *Esau* would be set at my heart, even like a flaming sword, to keep the way of the tree of Life, lest I should take thereof, and live. O who knows how hard a thing I found it to come to God in prayer?" (*GA* 55). Despite the force of the hopeful passages, Bunyan could never consider ignoring the passage on Esau. The only hope lay in a reinterpretation of both himself and the text. Finally, at the end of this period of agonizing soul-searching and isolation, the pronouncement of Esau's final condemnation and the biblical assurances of pardon

> boulted both upon me at a time, and did work and struggle strangly in me for a while; at last, that about Esaus birthright began to wax weak, and withdraw, and vanish; and this about the sufficiency of Grace prevailed, with peace and joy. And as I was in a muse about this thing, that Scripture came home upon me, *Mercy rejoyceth against Judgment*. Jas 2:13. (*GA* 67)

This respite, however, was only temporary. The quote from James seems to have produced a victory on the affective level but to have failed to resolve all the intellectual concerns about the text in Hebrews, which prevented Bunyan from believing he could be forgiven. A larger step towards hope and healing

---

5. John Bunyan, *Grace Abounding to the Chief of Sinners*, ed. Roger Sharrock (Oxford: Oxford University Press, 1963). Hereafter referred to in parenthetical citations as *GA*.

6. Richard Greaves, *Glimpses of Glory: John Bunyan and English Dissent* (Stanford: Stanford University Press, 2002), 35.

came shortly thereafter when Bunyan identified three reasons why Esau's sin was of a higher order than his, and two reasons why Esau's repentance was less effective than his; as he describes them in *Grace Abounding* they give the clear impression of a sermon.

Bunyan's method was not simply to "personalize" the Scriptures by identifying himself imaginatively with one or more biblical characters. He emphasized the rational and theological, not the narrative, coherence of the Bible as God's unique testimony and felt that truths of spiritual and of practical relevance could be drawn from it, assuming always that one verse was read in light of other parts of the Bible. Concluding the story of his struggle against Esau's story, he uses one of his characteristically memorable analogies:

> And now remained only the hinder part of the Tempest, for the thunder was gone beyond me, onely some drops did still remain, that now and then would fall upon me: but because my former frights and anguish were very sore and deep, therefore it did oft befal me still as it befalleth those that have been scared with fire. (*GA* 72)

This is a good example of how Bunyan's poetic originality has enabled his experience and his reflection on Scripture to become a guide and an encouragement for millions of readers.

As his twelve years in prison would indicate, Bunyan was very involved in the political conflicts of his time, which were, of course, profoundly religious. His understanding of those conflicts and his interventions into them dealt centrally with biblical interpretation, beginning with his first published work, *Some Gospel-Truths Opened According to the Scriptures*, which is a refutation of Quaker doctrine and a response to some public debates organized by Quakers in the spring of 1656. Bunyan's book endeavors to refute Quaker teachings, including that the individual's inner light can lead them to the kingdom of God. He begins by admonishing his readers, who he supposes are not yet saved, to "examine thine own heart by the rule of the word of God."[7] He is concerned throughout the work to show that the Holy Spirit speaks through the Bible, and never apart from the Bible, as the Quakers with their emphasis on personal revelation imagine.

In contrast, Bunyan's polemic moves in an opposite direction in his ultimately unsuccessful plea of innocence at the Bedford court in 1661, after his arrest for unlawful preaching and for participating in a dissenting congregation.

7. John Bunyan, *Some Gospel-Truths Opened*, in vol. 1 of *The Miscellaneous Works of John Bunyan*, ed. T. L. Underwood (Oxford: Oxford University Press, 1980), 23.

Here his main point is that all worship must be according to the inner prompt-ings of the Spirit and not to any humanly devised plan. His target is of course the Book of Common Prayer. His aim is to show that the Bible insists upon the Spirit's direct communication to each praying believer, thus disallowing worship according to the prayer book, and his method, as always, is scriptural interpretation. The crucial text for his argument is 1 Corinthians 14:15 on pray-ing with the Spirit and the understanding.

As the two examples above indicate, Bunyan's biblical hermeneutic was deeply self-implicating even while it could be applied homiletically to all read-ers, and it steered a middle course between subjectivistic and rationalistic ex-tremes. The Bible is able to interpret its interpreter. This was Bunyan's personal experience when he returned, after having received consolation and hope that his sin was not unforgivable like Esau's, to the very passages that had trauma-tized him: "I found their visage changed; for they looked not so grimly as before I thought they did" (*GA* 70). That he could reinterpret them as grace-bearing was both a cause and a consequence of the grace he received.

Biblical Authority and Catechesis in *The Pilgrim's Progress*

Bunyan must have been aware that not all of his parishioners shared his "special talent"[8] for leading his own life with constant reference to a vast number of biblical texts. His fictional writing functions as a mediating step between the individual's life and the scriptural text, effectively providing training-wheels.

He almost certainly wrote the bulk of *The Pilgrim's Progress* while in close confinement during a crackdown on dissenters, when many dissenting leaders and publishers of dissenting literature were imprisoned.[9] The allegory, full of implicit criticism of the Church of England, was bound to be controversial, and so he prefaced his work with a poetic apology that claims he had sought widely for advice before consenting to publish it. The apology also draws upon biblical precedent in a witty defense of his decision to propound Christian doctrine through fiction rather than proposition. Anticipating criticism from his primarily Puritan reading audience for having eschewed the "plain" style, Bunyan points out that "The prophets used much by Metaphors / To set forth

---

8. Brainerd P. Stranahan, "Bunyan's Special Talent: Biblical Texts as 'Events' in *Grace Abound-ing* and *The Pilgrim's Progress*," *English Literary Renaissance* 11, no. 3 (1981): 330.

9. Robert G. Collmer, "John Bunyan," in *The Oxford Handbook of English Literature and Theology*, ed. Andrew Hass, David Jasper, and Elisabeth Jay (Oxford: Oxford University Press, 2009), 577.

Truth."[10] And just as the book's literary form is sanctioned by the Bible, its content, he insists, is borrowed from the Bible:

> This Book is writ in such a Dialect
> As may the minds of listless men affect:
> It seems a Novelty, and yet contains
> Nothing but sound and honest Gospel-strains. (*PP* 7)

As has been noted, Bunyan did not typically approach the Bible as a metanarrative. The brilliance of *The Pilgrim's Progress* is partly that its framework of an individual's difficult journey through life worked so effectively as a narrative in which key gospel teachings could be inserted.[11] This framework itself reflects biblical influence too, particularly Hebrews 11, which identifies a vast array of Old Testament characters as "strangers and pilgrims" who left their country of origin for a better, heavenly country; and 1 Corinthians 9, which exhorts its audience to follow Paul's grueling example of evangelistic commitment to a race in which only "one receiveth the prize. So run, that ye may obtain."

Bunyan felt that running the race, and eventually obtaining the prize, were partly a matter of interpreting and applying the Bible. Hundreds of references to individual verses from the Authorized Version, sometimes half a dozen references in a single sentence, were included in Bunyan's text. For example, Hebrews 11:15–16 is cited when the protagonist, Christian, explains to an acquaintance his decision to set out on pilgrimage, "now I desire a better Countrey; that is, an Heavenly" (*PP* 49). In some cases the narrative of Christian and his fellow pilgrims seems to provide the key for interpreting the scriptural reference rather than vice-versa.[12]

These self-interpreting narratives often resemble moments from Bunyan's autobiography, such as the passage at the allegory's conclusion as Christian is struggling to swim across the river that represents death, overwhelmed by the memory of all his sins, much as Bunyan was before he found assurance of salvation. All of a sudden, the words of Isaiah 43:2 burst from Christian's lips, "When thou passest through the waters, I will be with thee" (*PP* 158), and instantly he found solid ground under his feet, allowing him to cross to the side of the Ce-

10. John Bunyan, *The Pilgrim's Progress: From This World to That Which Is to Come*, ed. James Blanton Wharey and Roger Sharrock, 2nd ed. (Oxford: Oxford University Press, 1967), 10. Hereafter referred to in parenthetical citations as *PP*.

11. Matthew Arnold deemed *The Pilgrim's Progress* to be "a complete reflection of scripture" (Bradstock, "John Bunyan," 286).

12. Kathleen M. Swaim, *Pilgrim's Progress, Puritan Progress: Discourses and Contexts* (Urbana-Champaign: University of Illinois Press, 1993), 81.

lestial City. All at the same time, the Bible is lending its authority to the author's story, and that story is suggesting an interpretation for the poetic biblical text (that is, Isaiah's waters refer typologically to death)—an interpretation that in turn allows readers to find themselves in the twinned Bible-Bunyan story. Christian is of course an everyman figure, and so readers can find in Christian's story hope for deliverance when they are called to cross the river of death.

At times, the narrative of *The Pilgrim's Progress* proposes the Bible as its antecedent action, which is the closest Bunyan gets to a narrative approach to the Bible. Thus Christian and his companion Hopeful come upon the pillar of salt into which Lot's wife was transformed: it is a warning for them against unbelief. Thus in the town of Vanity Fair Christian and his companion Faithful are dragged before a judge and jury consciously standing in the legal tradition of godless rulers Pharaoh, Nebuchadnezzar, and Darius. As this implies, Bunyan is audacious to propose his work as the Bible's successor—not, of course, to supplant it, but to train readers in reading and living biblically.

Like the apostle Paul, Bunyan's incarceration did not stop him from active involvement as a pastor to his Bedford congregants. *The Pilgrim's Progress* was written with the central intent of exhorting women and men whom Bunyan knew and loved to persevere in their faith:

> This book will make a traveller of thee,
> If by its counsel thou wilt ruled be;
> It will direct thee to the Holy Land,
> If thou wilt its Directions understand. (*PP* 6)[13]

Scholars in the past half-century have given close attention to the ways that the allegory works to transform its readers and guide them in becoming Christian "pilgrims." Arguably the story's allegorical method, rather than being opaque and potentially misleading, as Bunyan's imagined critics fear, is the simplest way of teaching readers to see a deeper, spiritual layer in their everyday experience.[14] Each reader is carried by a process of vicarious transposition into and

---

13. The second part of *The Pilgrim's Progress*, describing the journey of Christian's wife and sons along the same road he traveled, was written after his release, but by then Bunyan had developed an international audience. So the second part became, like the first, a way of disseminating Bunyan's biblical teaching to many whom he would never be able to meet and exhort in person.
> Go then, my little Book and shew to all
> That entertain, and bid thee welcome shall
> [and] make them chuse to be
> Pilgrims, better by far, then thee or me. (*PP* 172)

14. Barbara A. Johnson, "Falling into Allegory: The Apology to *The Pilgrim's Progress* and

through the Bible's story of human salvation.[15] In particular, by demonstrating how characters heading towards eternal life and characters heading towards damnation act and how they read themselves into the biblical intertexts, the allegory provides its readers with opportunity to evaluate whether they are among the elect. But Bunyan's Calvinistic commitments are not the whole story: he practices what his biographer Richard L. Greaves calls a "pastoral Arminianism"[16] that warmly and determinedly holds out hope of salvation for each reader who is willing to think and act according to faith. However, since the pilgrims continue to experience the failures of doubt and disobedience even as they approach the Celestial City, the careful reader is forced to realize that spatial and spiritual progress are far from equivalent, and thus the reader gains practice in rejecting carnal forms of knowledge in favor of the spiritual knowledge that consists of trust in God's promises.[17]

Biblical catechesis concisely indicates the pedagogical intent and method of *The Pilgrim's Progress*, for catechesis is typically a process that aims at personal transformation by means of repeating and meditating upon words not of one's own composition.[18] This is a helpful designation because it allows that neither a character's failure fully to act out the implications of their professed faith nor a reader's failure fully to identify with the faith of a character is necessarily a failure of catechesis. Like the biblical verses that burst into Bunyan's mind, the descriptions of Christian faith that Bunyan composes are *invitations* for the reader's faith, but the invitation may not be understood and accepted for a time. Like all catechetical statements these descriptions have the potential to function as performative speech acts, to create or catalyze the reality they describe.

Unceasing Interpretation and Creativity:
The Burden and Opportunity of a Secular Age

In some senses this time lag is as long as a human life. Bunyan allows the possibility that the reader, like his protagonist, Christian, who nearly drowns at the

Bunyan's Scriptural Methodology," in *Bunyan in Our Time*, ed. Robert G. Collmer (Kent, OH: Kent State University Press, 1989), 136.

15. David Lyle Jeffrey, *Houses of the Interpreter: Reading Scripture, Reading Culture* (Waco, TX: Baylor University Press, 2010), 10.

16. Greaves, *Glimpses of Glory*, 106.

17. Stanley Fish, "Progress in *The Pilgrim's Progress*," *English Literary Renaissance* 1, no. 3 (1971): 277.

18. Dennis Danielson, "Catechism, *The Pilgrim's Progress*, and the Pilgrim's Progress," *Journal of English and Germanic Philology* 9, no. 1 (1995): 53.

last stage of his journey as he considers that his sins may finally exclude him from salvation, will never fully internalize the hopeful and faith-filled interpretation of their life narratives that he depicts in *The Pilgrim's Progress*. Greaves's biography shows that Bunyan struggled with melancholy through much of his life, including major depressive episodes lasting as long as several years (in the 1650s) but recurring even into the 1680s.[19] Though Bunyan tends to divide his life into the periods before and after he received God's grace, even in the latter he found himself constantly reverting into a state where "the whole Bible hath been to me as drie as a stick." This is precisely the sense in which literary critic Stanley Fish famously contends that the Pilgrim makes no progress.[20] The ability to trust obediently in God's promises rather than in his own senses or rationality is the only kind of progress affirmed by the allegory, yet there is no linear relationship between it and the distance Christian has covered along the road towards the Celestial City. Doubt and disobedience are plot elements in each chapter of the Christian life.

Robert Bell draws an instructive comparison between the hermeneutics of conversion in Bunyan and Augustine that also indicates the challenges of Christian living in the wake of the Enlightenment. In Augustine's *Confessions*, there is an absolute distinction between the fallen perspective of the biography's subject—the young, unruly Augustine—and the reborn perspective of the narrator.[21] Augustine the narrator can now see unambiguously what the theft of the pears means—his unregenerate sinfulness—and the value of the theft is purely as a step on the road to grace. There is no alternative interpretation to consider. In contrast, as Bunyan's wrestling with the Esau story reveals, for him an event and its spiritual meaning are always separated by a gap that the interpreter must cross. Sometimes the interpreter must recross it many more times, which is why Bunyan's faith-filled characters, including Christian, Faithful, and Hopeful, tell and retell their stories of faith as they walk along the road. That the author assume the burden of authority in guiding the reader, and that the reader come to terms with that authority, cannot be avoided.

Puritan preachers characteristically take this burden as an invitation to determine and declare the "uses" of the text. Bunyan accepts this burden, and his primary strategy of response, which defines his approach to composition, is the similitude (metaphor). He declares this on his title page—"Delivered under the similitude of a dream"—as well as in the introduction to the Second Part:

19. Greaves, *Glimpses of Glory*, 57, 399.
20. Fish, "Progress in *The Pilgrim's Progress*."
21. Robert Bell, "Metamorphoses of Spiritual Autobiography," *English Literary History* 44, no. 1 (1971): 110.

> I also know, a dark Similitude
> Will on the Fancie more it self intrude,
> And will stick faster in the Heart and Head,
> Then things from Similies not borrowed. (*PP* 171)

Thus creative interpretation is simultaneously unavoidable and rhetorically strategic.

The comparison with Augustine indicates that Bunyan's age was well along the path towards our secular age. In our age an individual is charged with the burden of identifying and even achieving meaning in one's own life, and a literary author, perhaps assisting the individual towards that end, has new opportunity and new authority not just to state nature's similitudes but also to create their own.[22] However, the poetic introduction to *The Pilgrim's Progress* shows Bunyan's anxiety to defend himself against charges that his creative license was a usurpation of God's unique authority as Creator. Bunyan's art, he insists, is displaying, not creating, truth: "Some men by feigning words as dark as mine, / Make truth to spangle, and its rayes to shine" (*PP* 4). This is a fine balance, and whereas Bunyan's Puritan readers may have felt he went too far in the direction of autonomous creativity, contemporary readers may feel he was not "original" enough.

If we set aside considerations of theology and literary creativity to consider instead the dissemination of *The Pilgrim's Progress*, we will conclude that he found the perfect balance. Translated into more than 200 languages, it was in many African languages the first book published apart from the Bible and was promoted widely by European missionaries.[23] It seems to leave just enough imaginative freedom to allow readers to make sense of it in geographies, climates, and cultures very different from Bedford: a man clothed in rags, a great burden on his back, setting out from his hometown, a book in his hand. Christian could almost as easily be, say, Yoruba as English.

Yoruba Anglican catechist Robert Scott Oyebode explained in an autobiographical letter that his first "religious impressions" began in 1865 when a British missionary "gave me an English copy of Bunyan's *Pilgrims Progress* with a small English Dictionary to help me to read it to understanding, my knowledge of the English language being very poor. I am glad to say that I went through the book with great benefit to my soul; it first gave me an enlightenment as to

22. Peter Harrison, *The Bible, Protestantism, and the Rise of Natural Science* (Cambridge: Cambridge University Press, 1998), 193; cf. Charles Taylor, *A Secular Age* (Cambridge: Harvard University Press, 2007), 35.

23. Isabel Hofmeyr, *The Portable Bunyan: A Transnational History of* The Pilgrim's Progress (Princeton: Princeton University Press, 2004).

what a true christian life is, and from that time I can date my conversion."[24] The book was enough to make a traveller of Oyebode, and then to prompt him to begin telling and retelling the story of how he got to where he was.[25] All this corresponds to Bunyan's hopes for his writings, though perhaps less so than if Oyebode had reported that Bunyan's book gave him an enlightenment as to what *the Bible says* a true Christian life is. Bunyan's aim was for his book to be the second, not the first, book on the Christian's shelf.

24. Church Missionary Society, G3 A2 O 1893, Section IV, Africa Missions, Part 1–9 (Marlborough, UK: Adam Matthew Publications, 1998–99).

25. The following year, David and Anna Hinderer, the missionaries with the Church Missionary Society who mentored Oyebode, finished their Yoruba translation of *The Pilgrim's Progress*, entitled *Ilọ-Siwaju Èro-Mimọ` lati Aiye Yi si Eyi ti Mbọ*, which in the twentieth century became a key literary influence upon the earliest Yoruba novelists (see Bernd Lindfors, "Amos Tutuola and D. O. Fagunwa," *Journal of Commonwealth Literature* 9 [1970]: 57–65).

Chapter 32

Jonathan Edwards:
From Him, Through Him, and To Him

Jonathan Sing-cheung Li

Jonathan Edwards (1703–1758) was a multidimensional figure: a theologian-pastor, a preacher, a revivalist, a missionary, a psychologist of religious consciousness, an ethicist, an apologist, and a philosopher. Though rooted in a small-town New England setting, his reach was broad. He wrote tracts for the transatlantic evangelical revival, the missionary movement in Great Britain, as well as treatises engaging with contemporary Enlightenment philosophers. A number of his works were translated into Welsh, Dutch, and German, during and soon after his lifetime. And indeed, he still speaks to us today through his threefold vision of God, humankind, and the world—an all-encompassing ontology based upon a Trinitarian metaphysics—together with a metanarrative of human history that stretches from pretemporal eternity, throughout time and space, and to an eschatological eternity. Humanity is situated *in medias res*, as a being that only reaches fulfillment in eternity. Edwards's threefold vision and all-encompassing metanarrative offers a profound sense of unity in the various disciplines of human life and knowledge. This worldview propelled Edwards himself along the Christian pilgrimage, sustaining him and his family through many trials and tribulations—including the deaths of his own children and students, the controversies over the Great Awakening, his dismissal from his own Northampton church, and his missionary work at Stockbridge.

The threefold vision and grand metanarrative had their impetus in Edwards's dramatic conversion experiences in the spring of 1721, during which he was given "a new sense" of God and his immanent presence to all things. According to his *Personal Narrative* (1740), he underwent ecstatic experiences with the Spirit that lasted on and off from 1721 to 1724—before he took up his tutorship at Yale College. These events, and Edwards's reflection on them, became pivotal for shaping the rest of Edwards's life, forming the very basis of his identity as a Christian, and providing the seedbed for the ingenious and creative theological and philosophical themes for which he would become so well known.[1]

This essay will explore in three parts the question of how Edwards contributes to our understanding of Christian identity. First, I will look at how his sense of identity was formed during his prolonged conversion, especially in light of his New England Puritan culture and his familial context.[2] In the second part, I will show how the insights to which Edwards came in these ecstatic conversion experiences shaped his professional identity as a theologian-pastor. Finally, in the last part I will show how these ideas also forged his identity as an apologist for Christianity in the age of Enlightenment, contending with the likes of Locke and Newton for a full-orbed Christian ontology. For Edwards, and for us today, human identity is shaped by a God whose supremacy and excellence transcend the created world but are immanently present to it, sustaining it and holding it together at every moment. It is a life, to paraphrase St. Paul, from him, through him, and to him (Rom 11:36).

Earthly and Heavenly Fathers:
The Formation of Edwards's Personal Identity

To a certain extent, each person's life is shaped by the familial structures in which he or she grows up. But for Edwards this was especially the case. His father, Timothy Edwards, was a famous pastor, preacher, and revivalist, who would also become a teacher and mentor to his son. Marsden describes Timothy as "an intensely disciplined perfectionist, a worrier about details, a firm

---

1. A number of Edwardsean scholars, William S. Morris (*The Young Jonathan Edwards: A Reconstruction* [New York: Carlson, 1991]), Avihu Zakai (*Jonathan Edwards's Philosophy of History: The Re-enchantment of the World in the Age of Enlightenment* [Princeton: Princeton University Press, 2003]), and George M. Marsden (*Jonathan Edwards: A Life* [New Haven: Yale University Press, 2003]), have pointed out the significance of Edwards's conversion experiences in the forging of the entire system of his thought, as well as the function of his *Resolutions* and *Diary* in this process. Marsden comments, e.g.: "without an appreciation of the intensity of these life-transforming experiences and their monumental implications for all else he did, it is impossible to make sense of Edwards" (*Jonathan Edwards: A Life*, 44).

2. The texts I am using are mainly personal writings: *Personal Narrative* (abbreviated as PN), *Resolutions*, *Diary*, and early writings around the time of his conversion, such as *Scientific and Philosophical Writings*, *Miscellanies a–500*, *Sermons & Discourses, 1720–1723*, reading them together to get a better picture of his extended conversion experiences. I will be using the critical Yale edition of *The Works of Jonathan Edwards* (ed. Harry S. Stout, 26 vols. [New Haven: Yale University Press, 1957–2003]), hereafter cited as Y.

authoritarian who was nonetheless capable of good humor and warm affections towards his family."[3] Most scholars take note of the role that Timothy played in Jonathan's early education—he trained young Jonathan in classical languages, liberal arts, and the spirituality and theology of the Puritan divines. Jonathan's mother, Esther, the daughter of the famous New England preacher Solomon Stoddard, was also highly educated, intelligent, and well acquainted with the Scriptures. She "held a tall, dignified, and commanding appearance," yet was "affable and gentle in her manners."[4] Between his father, mother, and grandfather, the young Edwards had exemplary mentors who stimulated his love for the Scriptures and for doctrine.[5] For better and for worse, Edwards accumulated the traits of his family—a mixture of devotional piety, intellectual acuity, and a moral and intellectual perfectionism.[6]

Jonathan Edwards was the only son among ten daughters, and so naturally his parents held out high hopes for his success. The family was remarkably affectionate—a fact that can be observed by the warm correspondence exchanged between Jonathan and his father and sister Mary.[7] His affection for his family could also lead the emotionally sensitive Edwards to depressive episodes and serious bouts of homesickness when he travelled off to school.[8]

However, after his unique conversion experiences in the early 1720s, he began to feel the growing tension between the traditional Puritan upbringing of his parents and his "new sense" of God. He remarked in his diary entry on May 18, 1723: "I have great reason to believe, that their counsel and education

3. Marsden, *Jonathan Edwards*, 22.

4. Sereno E. Dwight, *The Life of President Edwards* (New York: C. & C. & H. Carvill, 1830), 16, 18. Five biographies of Edwards's life are useful for different purposes. Dwight's is good for source materials. Ola Winslow's *Jonathan Edwards, 1703–1758* (1940) places Edwards in his social setting. Perry Miller's *Jonathan Edwards* (1949) is a brilliant though often misleading interpretation of Edwards's intellectual life. Iain Murray's *Jonathan Edwards: A New Biography* (1987) is a well-documented updating of biographies in the tradition of uncritical admirers. Marsden's *Jonathan Edwards: A Life* is a magisterial synthesis of Edwards's life and the range of ideas, well contextualized in his social-historical setting of New England.

5. Wilson H. Kimnach, ed., *Sermons and Discourses, 1720–1723*, vol. 10 (New Haven: Yale University Press, 1992), 3–15. Also Peter J. Thuesen, *Catalogues of Books* (2008), Y 26:5–8.

6. Taking Erik Erikson's reductionist approach, Richard L. Bushman has done an interesting psychoanalysis of the three generations of Edwards's genealogy: Richard, Timothy, and Jonathan, and particularly Timothy's ambivalent mixture of high demands, intense love, and fear of destruction that may be linked to his mother's mental illness. Richard L. Bushman, "Jonathan Edwards as Great Man: Identity, Conversion, and Leadership in the Great Awakening," in *Critical Essays on Jonathan Edwards*, ed. William Scheick (Boston: G. K. Hall, 1980), 41–64.

7. *Letters and Personal Writings*, ed. George S. Claghorn (Y 16:29–40).

8. Edwards suffered pleurisy in his last year of college in New Haven. He had to convalesce at home for four months in 1725 because of an illness when he was a tutor at Yale College.

have been *my making*; notwithstanding, in time of it, it seemed to do me *so little good* . . . that their prayers for me have been in many things very powerful and prevalent; that God has in many things, taken me under his care and guidance, provision and direction, in answer to their prayers for me."[9] One can detect the depth of anxiety and tension in these lines, and how it was explicitly linked to his conversion. His conversion—as recorded in *Personal Narrative*—did not conform to the typical Puritan "morphology of conversion."[10] This was un-settling to his parents, and their expressed disapproval challenged the sense of self that was emerging and being shaped by his experiences with God. To be sure, Edwards's conversion was not entirely unconventional—he records that he went through a stage of "legalistic humiliation" (though not quite the "terror" that Puritans often talked about).[11] More important, however, was the way in which he grappled with the doctrine of God's sovereignty. What once was an obstacle he now saw as an exercise of God's immediate omnipotence in the natural world,[12] leading him to understand God's sovereignty in election

---

9. Y 16:770, my emphasis.

10. Edwards's father, Timothy, was an expert on the science of conversion. There were three steps in the typical Puritan narrative of conversion: (1) an awakening sense of one's sad state with reference to eternity and the attempts to be saved by one's own resources to do God's will; (2) a time of "legalistic humiliation" in which one comes to realize by "terror" both God's righteousness and one's own moral and spiritual bankruptcy in earning it; and (3) the evangelical conversion in which there is the infusion of grace and one's habitual dependence on the Holy Spirit for the rest of one's life. See Marsden, *Jonathan Edwards: A Life*, 26–28.

11. Edwards began his *Personal Narrative* with his "awakening" to seek salvation and "the self-righteous pleasures" in trying to find "delight" in religious activities in a self-deceptive way but kept backsliding into "ways of sin" (para. 1, Y 16:791). It was while he was troubled by "many uneasy thoughts about the state of my soul" that God was "pleased" to seize him with a pleurisy, that brought him over "the pit of hell" (para. 2). This encounter with death woke him up to battle with "wicked inclinations" and with "repeated resolutions and bonds" such as vows to God. His inward struggles forced him to make "seeking my salvation the main business of my life," and as a result, he writes, "I felt my spirit to part with all things in the world for an interest in Christ," though "it never seemed to be proper to express my concern that I had, by the name of terror" (para. 2, Y 16:791).

12. See *Of Atoms* (written September 1720 and March 1721) and *Long Series* 1–8 (end of 1720) (hereafter *LS*). In *Of Being* and *Long Series* 9–20 (January 1721), one can see Edwards's evolving views: (1) God's sovereignty operating in the natural world as the immediate exercise of his om-nipotence, giving being to all existence and sustaining their beings by the laws of nature, and that God, as pure spirit, is the only true "substance" and *ens entium* (the Being of beings) (*Of Atoms*, prop. 2, corol. 11–17; Y 6:214–16). (2) God as pure spirit is "the Space," that is, "the necessary, eter-nal, infinite, and omnipresent being," which contains all existences within his consciousness—this will form the basis of Edwards's "objective idealism," on which see below, the section on Vocational Identity (*Of Being*, first 3 paragraphs; Y 6:202–3). (3) God's absolute wisdom and omniscience of all things in temporal sequences; Edwards sees the effects of God's presence in history "according

as the gift of God himself in the Holy Spirit, who works in a "more immediate, arbitrary and divine" way in the supernatural realm.[13]

When Edwards began to see God's sovereignty in a new light, he experienced what he called "a wonderful alternation" of mind. As he read of "the King eternal, immortal, invisible, the only wise God" (1 Tim 1:17), he experienced the movement of the Spirit as "that sort of inward, sweet delight in God and divine things," endowing him with "a new sense" that enabled him to see in the Scriptures the glory of God and the excellence of his being. He came to regard his heavenly Father "with a new sort of affection," qualitatively different from the self-fabricated affections of religious duty that characterized his childhood. However, since this "new sense" did not occur from meditating on the suffering Christ—as was the typical Puritan pattern—Edwards doubted whether there was "anything spiritual, or [of] a saving nature in this."[14] When he felt "an inward sweetness" of "the lovely way of salvation, by free grace in Christ," these "pleasant views and contemplations" were not of the redemptive work of Christ but of "the beauty and excellency of his person," a beauty akin to the "rose of Sharon, the lily of the valleys" (Song 2:1). As he continued reflecting on the book of Canticles, his meditations tended less towards God's forgiveness of the terrible sinner and more towards "a calm, sweet abstraction of soul from all concerns of this world," being alone in nature "sweetly conversing with Christ," stirring up "a sweet burning" in his heart and "an ardour" in his soul.[15]

Soon after, he went to give an account of his conversion to his father, but the elder Edwards expressed doubts about its authenticity.[16] Ironically, after receiving his father's disapproval, Edwards was given yet another "sweet sense of the glorious majesty and grace of God," which he describe as a "sweet conjunction . . . [of] majesty and meekness," "an awful sweetness; a high and great

---

to strict rules of justice and harmony," from pre-temporal eternity to post-temporal eternity (*LS*, nos. 9, 14–17, 19; Y 6:230–32).

13. This is what Edwards meant by "I have oftentimes since that first conviction, had quite *another kind* of sense of God's sovereignty, . . . not only a conviction but a *delightful* conviction."

14. *PN*, para. 5 (Y 16:792–93).

15. *PN*, para. 6 (Y 16:793).

16. Kimnach suggests two scenarios for the interview between Edwards and his father: in the first, Jonathan feels affirmed in his conversion by Timothy's warmth and reassurance that "he found [an] anthropomorphic correlative in nature"; in the second, Edwards is fleeing into the pasture to "gaze skyward with tear-streaked face, projecting into the heavens the vision of a parent who could be both a wise mentor and a maternal comforter." Kimnach thinks it was the second scenario (Y 10:275), while Zakai takes the first (*Philosophy of History*, 65–66). I agree with Kimnach here (as does George Claghorn and George Marsden), because of the way in which for the next four years Jonathan was repeatedly haunted by the unfitness of his conversion with the Puritan paradigm.

and holy gentleness." He further describes this experience as a comingling and interpenetration of opposite divine attributes, as if they were God's consolations and confirmation. After this, his sense of divine things elevated even higher, and he experienced even more contemplations of "the Creator and Redeemer." He saw in a new way God's immanent presence in all aspects of nature: in the sun, moon, and stars; in thunder and lightning, which had once terrorized him as a child; and in world history, particularly in what he saw as "the advancement of Christ's kingdom" throughout history.[17]

Edwards's conversion continued, deepening in spiritual experience and widening in mental perception of the mystery of God. He continued to experience "vehement longings of [the] soul"—longings for Christ and for holiness—with "his mind greatly fixed on divine things," his heart so "full and ready to break" into prayers and soliloquy. Away from home at his first pastorate in New York (August 1722–April 1723), his yearnings for "God and holiness" and "the sense of divine things" increased further. He responded to this inflow of grace by recording his experiences in *Resolutions* and his *Diary*. These works comprise Edwards's efforts to maintain an openness and receptivity to the Spirit.[18] The result was a near constant outpouring of creative theological and philosophical meditations. The works that followed this period—e.g., *Miscellanies (a–zz)*, *Things to be Considered and Written fully about* (*Long Series* 21–44)—were innovative understandings of classical ideas, ideas that stimulated his later thinking both in the pastoral and theological writings, such as *Miscellanies* (1384 entries, 1722–1757), *Notes on Apocalypse* (1723–1758), and *Notes on the Scripture* (1724–1754); and in his philosophical thinking, such as *The Mind* (1723–1748).

---

17. *PN*, paras. 7 and 8 (Y 16:793–94): "God's Excellency, his wisdom, his purity and love, seemed to appear in everything"; and paras. 19, 33 (Y 797, 800): "I used to be earnest to read public news-letters, mainly for that end" of longing and praying for "the advancement of Christ's kingdom in the world" (797). Zakai compares the conversion narrative of Edwards with those of Augustine, Luther, and Calvin and notices that Edwards's is essentially "an entranced vision of God's glory," more of *theologia gloriae* of God than a *theologia crucis* of Christ (*Philosophy of History*, 66–74). I think Edwards's entranced vision of God's glory in nature and Christ's beauty and excellency in salvation is more compatible when we look at it in the context of God's sovereignty over both creation and redemption. Edwards saw salvation on a cosmic scale, especially in his reading of such passages as Prov 8:30–31; John 17:21–24; Col 1:15–20; Eph 3:9–11. See *Misc.* 104 {End of Creation}, 702 {Work of Creation, Providence, Redemption} in which Edwards constructs something of his theology of history.

18. *PN*, para. 11, "It was my continual strife day and night, and constant inquiry, how I should be more holy, and live more holily, and more becoming a child of God and disciple of Christ. I sought an increase of grace and holiness, and that I might live a holy life, with vastly more earnestness than ever I sought before" (Y 16:795).

After the "interview" with his father at age seventeen, Edwards was for the next four years intermittently disturbed over the authenticity of his conversion and hence whether or not he was saved. His first diary entry is telling in this regard, and sets the tone of his spiritual and personal struggles. One sees Edwards here in the throes of self-doubt, questioning the tutelage of his parents, and even of the Puritan divines themselves, especially in regard to their teaching on the "steps of regeneration." On the whole he found himself at odds with New England culture expressed in his parents.[19] And yet, in the midst of it, a clearer and more focused Christian identity was being formed—one received more immediately from his ecstatic experiences with God.

The most basic question he faced at this juncture in his life was this: Which voice would he follow—the voice of his parents and the Puritan tradition, or the God-given experiences that had so powerfully stirred within him? Edwards was driven to resolve the issue by August 12, 1723, first coming to grips with the Puritan teaching on the steps to conversion. He resolved first to "search . . . till I have satisfyingly found out the very bottom and foundation, the real reason, why [the Puritan divines] used to be converted in those steps." Then he set out to be so "thoroughly acquainted with the Scriptures" that on controversial issues, "I can proceed with abundantly more confidence; can see upon what footing and foundation I stand." For Edwards, a secure Christian identity needed to be rooted, not in the Puritan traditions, but in the Word of God.[20] This became the foundation for every work of theology and philosophy henceforth. He was, at the core of his Christian identity, a biblical Christian.[21] Edwards settled his internal struggles with his parents' culture by resolving to be thoroughly open to the Holy Spirit's leading. The preceding four years had convinced him that

19. See the entries on December 18, 1722 (Y 16:759); May 25, 1723 (ibid., 771); July 4, 1724 (ibid., 773), August 12, 1724 (ibid., 779), November 6, 1724; with his parents, May 18, 1723 (Y 16:770).

20. Y 16:779. This was the approach he took to the Puritan "morphology of conversion": he concluded from Scripture and his conversion experience that the true penitent's thoughts do not "always run exactly this order" but "they are of a nature and a principle." In other words, "the Holy Spirit leads and guides, and he is governed by a vital principle of true holiness . . . [evangelical humiliation is] not always to the same degree; but it is always of the same nature" (Sermon, "True Repentance Required" [1723], Y 10:514–15). In the same vein, he asserted that true conversion is not a one-time thing but a deepening conversion throughout the Christian life: "let those that are true Christians yet change their lives, for the lives of the best need an alternation, and true converts themselves need to be converted" to be more Christ-like (Sermon, "Living to Christ" [1723], Y 10:575), which later became the seventh sign in *Religious Affections* (Y 2:340–44).

21. His student Samuel Hopkins comments: "He took his religious principles from the Bible, and not from any human system or body of divinity. Though his principles were Calvinist, yet he called no man, father. He thought and judged for himself, and was truly very much of an original" (*The Life and Character of the Late Reverend Mr. Jonathan Edwards* [Boston, 1765], 41).

indeed the Spirit was indwelling him as the abiding principle of a transformed life and a self-authenticating source of "the new sense" of God and divine realities as he saw in the outflow of his productivity and creativity.[22]

Professional Identity: A Theologian-Pastor

Out of this new sense of personal identity Edwards began to perceive anew his vocation as a pastor-theologian. In the pastorate he would see the outworkings of the conversion experiences of the early 1720s into a more developed vision of God, humanity, and the world, mapped onto a grand metanarrative of creation-history-redemption, all of which enables human beings to understand their purpose and identity. In his New York pastorate (August 1722–April 1723) he aspired to be a preacher who was "very conversant with the Scriptures," "much in seeking God, and conversant with him in prayers, who is the fountain of light and love," so that in his own ministry he might become "both a burning and a shining light."[23] During this period, as his entries in his *Resolutions, Diary,* and *Personal Narrative* show, Edwards took very seriously the task of praying the Scriptures, for he knew that they were the source of living waters for himself and his parishioners.[24] Edwards came to read Scripture with a Trinitarian and cosmic perspective in order to speak to the "the reasonable creatures" of his day.

22. *Diary*, May 28, 1725, "It seems to me, that whether I am now converted or not, I am so settled in the state that I am in, that I shall go on in it all my life . . . yet I will continue to pray to God, not to suffer me to be deceived about it, . . . and ever and anon, will call into question and try myself, using for helps, some of our old divines, that God may have opportunities to answer my prayers, and the Spirit of God to show me my errors, if I am in one." During those four years he gradually knew with certitude that he had made strides in his spiritual experiences and theological reflections on most fundamental elements of the Christian faith, as witnessed in *Miscellanies* entries and the recollections in *PN*.

23. "The True Excellency of a Minister of the Gospel" (1744), as cited by Kimnach, *Sermons and Discourses* (Y 10:25).

24. Three sequential *Resolutions* entries are revealing: "Resolved to study the Scriptures so steadily, constantly and frequently" (#28), "Resolved never to count that a prayer, . . . that I cannot hope that God will answer it" (#29); "Resolved to strive to my utmost every week to be brought higher in religion, and to a higher exercise of grace" (#30) (Y 16:755). His self-examinations often record either his relish with the Scriptures or his negligence in attending to them (*Diary* entries: in 1723: January 5, 12, 14; March 2; May 12; July 19, 20, 23; August 13, 28; December 27; in 1724: January 10; February 23; and January 22, 1734). He summed up the indispensable place of the Scriptures for his life in *PN*: "I had then, at other times, the greatest delight in the holy Scriptures, of any book whatsoever. . . . every word seemed to touch my heart. . . . I seemed often to see so much light, exhibited by every sentence, and such a refreshing ravishing food communicated, that I could not get along reading" (para. 21, Y 16:797).

Edwards's habit, as can be seen in his early sermons, was to juxtapose spiritual and secular values, as in the case of the doctrine of creation.[25] The created world became his point of contact with the age of science, enabling him to teach his congregation how to grapple with the claims of the Enlightenment, while also remaining faithful to the Scriptures.

His early spiritual conversion experiences shaped his thinking about science, philosophy, and theology, configuring them into a unified system of thought. He saw the unity of reason and revelation,[26] began to elaborate a Trinitarian metaphysics of the natural world,[27] and sought to reclaim a typological narration of salvation history and world history.[28] All disciplines of knowledge, for Edwards, were illumined by the biblical revelation and an understanding

25. E.g., "Way of Holiness" (Y 10:471, 466); "Christ, the Light of the World" (Y 10:535–46).

26. He experienced this unity as a "wonderful alternation" in his mind over "the justice and reasonableness" of the doctrine of God's sovereignty in election, followed by God's self-revelation. Just like the Mosaic Law is to prepare man for the revelation of the gospel of grace to work faith in us, so revelation is to unfold its rationality and reasonableness and to bring transcendent fulfillment to human reasoning for his glory (PN, paras. 4 and 5). Such unity is also seen in the structure of his sermons in building his arguments and proofs by "the light of nature" and "the light of Scriptures."

27. Upon the tradition that God the Father created the universe through his agent and designer the Son by the Holy Spirit as the executor and perfecter, Edwards's logic of Trinitarian metaphysics runs as follows: (1) "occasionalism": God (the Father) is the only substance that gave the forms of being to all existences by the laws of nature as "the stated methods and stated conditions of alteration of his acting" (through the Word) and sustains them by his moment-to-moment omnipotence (by the Spirit) (Of Atoms, Y 6:213–16); therefore, (2) "objective theo-centric idealism": all existences exist only as relatively permanent beings in God the Father's consciousness, perceived and known by his Idea (the Word), and willed and loved by his Spirit (Of Being, Y 6:202–7); (3) all existences are positioned in the hierarchy of the great chain of beings—triune God as the pure spirit, next the angels, then the composite being of man in spirit and body, then animals, then plants and vegetation, and lastly all kinds of inanimate matter—the more spiritual and closer to God, the more real and substantial the being is (Misc. tt, 42, 1263); (4) all these existences are hanging together in various "magnitude, greatness" (being) and in various "proportion, harmony, and excellence" (different degrees of being increased by the consent of each being to Being and decreased by its contradiction to Being) (Mind 1, Y 6:332–38); (5) God's excellence consists in his being the triune God—Father, Son, and Spirit—in absolute loving communion with one another, the supreme harmony of all. That excellence particularly falls on the Holy Spirit within the Godhead (Mind 45, §9).

28. Edwards extends biblical typology (OT types as antitypes of those in the NT) to an "ontological" typology—including natural types (in the physical world), historical types (e.g., the Sabbath celebrating the old creation, a type of the Lord's Day celebrated in the new creation). See Misc. 28, 64, 119. In Mind 40, he writes, "there has been in times past [pre-temporal eternity] such a course and succession [in history] of existences that these things must be supposed to make the series complete, according to divine appointment of the order of things" in the foreknowledge by the divine mind (Y 6:356–59).

of the triune God's purpose for creation, deliberated in pretemporal eternity.[29] Furthermore, he saw God's sovereign rule and divine enchantment over the world as "the theatre of his glory in creation," and he saw world history as the stage on which was played out the drama of God's redemptive love.[30] One can only perceive such a vision, Edwards claimed, by the Holy Spirit, who sustains the world and brings history towards its eschatological consummation. The Spirit, who inspires the biblical revelation, continues to speak today to those who read the Scriptures by the illumination of the same Spirit. Such a unique configuration of theological metaphysics "greatly influenced his selection and interpretation of key biblical passages and affected his thinking on almost every topic."[31]

Edwards's eschatological vision of humankind was forged out of the kind of personal eschatological experiences that he described in *Resolutions* and *Diary*.[32] In *Resolution* #1, Edwards describes the goal of his life: "I will do whatever I think to be most to God's glory, and my own good, profit and pleasure," and "most for the good and advantage of mankind in general"—a sentiment eloquently elaborated in his treatises *End of Creation* and *True Nature of Virtues*. This assertion together with #43 ("no other end but religion shall have any influence at all on any of my actions") and #63 (to be "properly a complete Christian in all respects of a right stamp, having Christianity always shining in its true lustre"), make up the framework of his professional identity. The eschatological shape of life stands out sharply.[33] He was resolved to lead, like the

---

29. *The End of Creation* (1755) spells out the whole purpose of creation-for-redemption, beginning in pre-temporal eternity with God's self-communication of divine knowledge (Christ) and divine love and holiness (the Holy Spirit) for glorifying himself, as salvation being enacted in history through the *felix culpa* (happy fault) of the fall, which occasioned the glorification of man (becoming Christ-like through deification) in post-temporal eternity.

30. *History of the Work of Redemption* (1739) is Edwards's attempt to open our eyes to see the various levels of the Spirit's shaping salvation history in the order of saving grace, interlacing, intersecting, and interweaving with world history in the order of common grace.

31. An insightful observation of Thomas A. Shafer, a scholar who knows Edwards well (Y 13:40).

32. Dwight (*Life of President Edwards*) makes two observations about *Resolutions*: they formed "the basis of conduct and character, the plan by which he governed the secret as well as the public actions of his life" (qtd. in Edward Hickman, *The Works of Jonathan Edwards* [Edinburgh: Banner of Truth, 1974], 1:xx), and were regarded by Jonathan "in succeeding years . . . containing the great principles of spiritual life," exhibiting "a deep and extensive knowledge of the heart," "holy consistency of character" in longing for "the holy perfection of heavenly, . . . awake with Divine likeness" (ibid., xxii–xxiii).

33. See #1 (living in light of eternity); #5 (the maximum use of time for the maximum spiritual profit); #6 (to live with all my might); #7 (abstinence from anything); #9 (to meditate on my own death); #10 (to meditate on pains of martyrdom and of hell); #17 (to live as I shall wish I had done when I come to die with no sins of omission, negligence and regret); #18 (to live for

monks of old, a life of *ascesis*, which had as its aim the eschatological fulfillment of his personhood.

Out of his "eschatological lifestyle," Edwards's productivity proliferated. He was well aware of the originality of his own thinking, understanding himself to be making innovations of classical ideas.[34] He began to hold in high esteem, after the Bible, his own biblical, theological, and philosophical notebooks, which he found more beneficial to his soul than reading many religious books![35]

By now we can begin to appreciate his sense of professional identity as a theologian-pastor. Edwards saw himself "called of God and sent by Christ," to be a "teacher of men in Christianity." Edwards understood the identity of the pastor to be one called by Christ to care for his church, and one whom Christ had set apart from others—"either by [his knowledge of the] Scripture, or reason without Scripture"![36] When he considered the authority with which a minister was to operate, he was thinking in terms of the apostolic office, because the minister, like the apostles, was required to be "instructed in the mind of Christ" and "under the *infallible* guidance of Christ." Only then could a minister have "the power to teach the world the will of Christ" so that Christians and non-Christians "would be obliged to hear me."[37]

---

the gospel & the other world); #22 and #48 (constant conversion towards God and certainty of the state of soul before death); #50 (to act so as to be best and most prudent in light of future life); #51 (not to be damned at last breath); #52 (no regret when become old); #55 (happiness of heaven, torments of hell).

34. See, e.g., *Misc. a* {holiness} (experienced as a divine beauty of God in his relations with all creatures); *Misc. o* {irresistible grace} (experienced as irresistible fitness to the original nature of human will before the Fall); *Misc. p* {infused grace} (as compatibilism, i.e., divine *initiative* of efficacious grace and human *active response* of faith that every good deed of the Christian is one-hundred percent God's work and one-hundred percent human work).

35. In his *Dairy*, Edwards repeated this new estimation of his own works—"the fruits of my study in divinity"—that he sometimes used to evangelize people. For instance, his August 28, 1723, entry reads, "When I want books to read; yea, when I have not very good books, not to spend time in reading them, but in reading the Scriptures, in perusing *Resolutions, Reflections* [*Miscellanies*], etc., in writing on *types of the Scriptures* [*Notes on Scripture*]. . . . Remember as soon as I can, to get a piece of slate, or something, whereon I can make short memorandums while traveling" (perhaps referring to his lifelong habit of pinning thoughts written on papers on his clothes while travelling) (Y 16:780). See also entries on May 12, June 8, July 25 of 1723; October 5, 1724.

36. *Misc. mm* {Minister} (Y 13:187).

37. *Misc. 40* {Minister} (Y 13:222); the expression "under the *infallible* guidance of Christ" appears three times.

Vocational Identity: Christian Apologist in the Age of Enlightenment

From the midst of his pastorate, Edwards began to sense a further calling—to be a writer on an international stage. This impetus gradually worked itself out as a calling to speak directly to the Enlightenment thinkers of his day. As he was laying out the plan for his *Notes on Natural Philosophy*, he sketched something of the method by which he hoped to speak to the "learned men" of his day: he knew his words were "exceedingly beside the ordinary way of thinking," and so he must show "a superabundance of modesty"—even to the point of hiding his being "conversant with books or the learned world."[38] He knew that his natural philosophy would sound "very strange to many learned divines and philosophers"—especially those of a Newtonian ontology and Lockean episte-mology—because his was a theological metaphysics rooted in the Scriptures, one "that the world will judge but frivolous for proofs." Yet he was confident of the power of the Divine Mind's rationality and the reasonableness of the biblical revelation. The Christian faith, he believed, unfolds its own reasoning that transcends yet perfects human reason.[39]

Edwards's plan for the *Treatise on Mind* came from interacting especially with the works of Newton and Locke when he was a student and tutor at Yale College. He was especially concerned to address the implicit deism and au-tonomous reason that characterized these thinkers, a mode of thought that he would contest for the rest of his life.[40] He was interested in the latest and best writing in Europe, and his *Catalogues of Books*, begun in 1722, is one attempt to remain current with Enlightenment writings.

He was especially interested in reading Enlightenment works in "Republic of Letters" so that he could re-present Calvinist doctrines in a setting immersed in

38. Cover-leaf *Memoranda*, side 2, [5] (Fall of 1723), [6] (October 1723), his confidence was boosted after sending his letter and article "On Spider" to the Royal Society of London, [9] (1724) (Y 6:193). The treatise would properly refer to "Mind," which most likely also includes his writings on natural philosophy.

39. Cover-leaf *Memoranda*, side 2, [18]–[20] (Y 6:194–95). His final goal was to get published in London, but he should "play at small games" in New England first with this treatise. His father once doodled, "Jonathan. London. Corruption" on the edge of his sermon back in 1722 already, when Jonathan may have broached the subject of going to London (Marsden, *Jonathan Edwards*, 60).

40. Edwards may have been taught by Samuel Johnson about Newton's *Principia* and *Optics*. Locke's *An Essay Concerning Human Understanding* came from Jeremiah Dummer's collection as a gift to Yale College in 1718. Edwards likely read through these works during his years as a tutor (1724–1726); see Y 6:15–16; 24–26. Though he put the plan aside or may have tried to alter it into other projects, such as in "A Rational Account of the Main Doctrines of the Christian Religion" (1729/30), he never stopped thinking about reforming the Enlightenment mindset (Y 6:128).

this culture.[41] At the same time, he aimed to remain anchored in the "theocentric objective idealism" forged in his early conversions.[42] By "theocentric objective idealism" I mean that Edwards conceived of God as the only Substance or Entity, who, as the Being of beings and the center of all created entities, has endowed existence to created things by perceiving and willing them as ideas in his mind. Created things, for Edwards, are *derived* entities, relatively objective and of a quasi-permanent substance. They are immediately sustained by God's power and operations moment-by-moment (occasionalism), and can be expressed by the laws of nature. These laws are governed by the order of ideas, by which God communicates to other created minds in order that they can come to know the nature of each entity and their relationships to other entities and to God.[43] All such "laws" of creation (whether pertaining to angels, men, or the natural world) are expressions of God's "excellency" (Edwards's favorite term for his ontology, axiology, ethics, and aesthetics)—the marvelous, astounding, and mysterious harmony of relations between God and creation and among created things.[44] The excellency of excellencies is God's triune self—the supreme harmony of all.[45] This is the basis for Edwards's belief that God's universe is both *relational* and *real*.[46]

41. The term was a metaphor used to describe a community of scholarly exchange during the seventeenth and eighteenth centuries. It was first used in Pierre Bayle's journal *Nouvelles de la République des Lettres* (1648–1718), which tried to avoid religious decisiveness and rally its readers behind a common pursuit of knowledge. Edwards formed his own evangelical republic of letters to promote revivals of religion through his transatlantic network, namely, with George Whitefield, James Robe, John MacLaurin, William McCulloch, and John Erskine. See the Introduction to *Catalogues of Books* by Peter J. Thuesen, who observes that "the fruitful tension between Enlightenment 'latitude' [freedom and tolerance] and Reformed traditionalism animated Edwards's entire career, immersing him in a culture that was increasingly dispassionate towards old orthodoxies even as he remained firmly rooted in a religious system that presupposed the existence of only one truth" (Y 26:3).

42. I coin this expression by combining "objective idealism" of Sang-hyun Lee (*The Philosophical Theology of Jonathan Edwards*, 1988) and "theocentric metaphysics" of Michael McClymond (*Encounters with God: An Approach to the Theology of Jonathan Edwards*, 1998). To distinguish it from George Berkeley's idealism, this expression captures the dual emphases of Edwards's idealism: (1) the universe has a relatively permanent reality in the mind of God, and (2) this God is, first and foremost, the only substance, the Being of beings.

43. *Of Atoms; Of Being; Things to be Considered and fully Written about*; especially *LS*, nos. 14–17, 22–23, 27 (occasionalism), 44; *Mind* 10, 15, on knowledge of truth as aligning human ideas with God's ideas of all things; *Mind* 13, 27, 34, 40, about God's series of ideas as his determinations for all things and events expressed by the laws of nature (God's divine stable ideas and will) in Y 6.

44. For example, *Mind* 1, 62, 64 (on ontology and axiology); 14 (on axiology), 39 (on conscience); *Misc.* 42, 44, 27b (on ontology and axiology of all things); *Misc. tt*, 178 (on the role of the Holy Spirit in sustaining the ontology of all things).

45. *Mind* 45; *Misc.* 117, 182.

46. Edwards had foreseen the phenomenon that is today called "the butterfly effect": "the

Edwards understood his idealism in reference to the epistemological challenges of the Enlightenment program's attempt at the "naturalization, rationalization and humanization of the gospel."[47] Here I will focus on Newtonian ontology and Lockean epistemology. Locke's metaphysical dualism aimed to naturalize and rationalize the universe. Newton's metaphysical dualism attempts to separate the "divine being," conceived as the "absolute, real" space-time, and "relative" space as a physical reality—an eternal, infinite isotropic continuum in which all things in the universe are contained in rigid positions and spatial relations in Euclidean geometry. In other words, they are independent of time and affixed by the law of universal gravitation in the fashion of mechanistic determinism. In such a conception, the natural world acquires an autonomous ontological status, independent of the immediate operations of God, who exists only by inference as a theoretical construct and as a final cause for the contrivance of the universe.[48]

The epistemological implication of such an ontology is significant in the construction of Locke's empiricism, as well as the Kantian split between *noumenon* and *phenomenon*, in which man cannot know the essence of things that are beyond senses and rational reflections.[49] Edwards took issue especially with the idea of an autonomous universe. Space and time were not, for Edwards, something that could be granted an independent status; rather, they held an ideal existence in his "theocentric objective idealism."[50] The world in space and time, objective and real as it is, is constantly an immediate exertion of God's power. God and all things can be known in themselves because the substance

---

motion, rest and direction of the least atom has an influence on the motion, rest and direction of every body in the universe" (Y 6:231).

47. Josh Moody, *Jonathan Edwards and the Enlightenment: Knowing the Presence of God* (Lanham, MD: University Press of America, 2005), 17. Edwards also combats the modern notion of free will as a contingent self-determination, sovereign of the will itself, in *Freedom of Will*. In *End of Creation* he attacks the self-glorification of the modern man and shows God's self-glorification in communicating himself to be the happiness and glorification of man.

48. In *Optics*, Query 28, Newton writes, "does it not appear from phenomena that there is a being incorporeal, living, intelligent, omnipresent, who in infinite space, as it were his sensorium, sees things intimately, . . . and comprehends them wholly by their immediate presence to himself?" (Y 6:58 n. 5).

49. "In bodies, we see only outward figures and colors, we hear only sounds, we can touch surfaces, we can smell only the smells and taste the savors; but their inward substances are not to be known by our senses, or by reflex act of our minds: much less, then, have we any idea of the substance of God. We know him only by his most wise and excellent contrivances of things, and final causes" (*Principia, General Scholium*, quoted in Y 6:61).

50. At one point Edwards had followed the notion of space put forth by Henry More (hence Newton in *Of Being* [Y 6:203]), but he reduced it to an ideal existence in the same manner as any external thing because all existence is mental in God's infinite mind (*Mind* 9, 13; Y 6:341, 343–44).

of each entity is conceived not individually as a substratum hidden inside and holding it together, but relationally as a particular law that governs the order of those ideas concerning it in relation with other entities to be communicated to the human mind by God.[51]

Edwards's epistemology and concept of substance reject or consciously modify those of Locke, making Locke's notion of "sense/idea" stand on its head. Locke's empiricism splits the sensory data of an object and its unknowable substratum while holding the traditional notion of substance as the internal particular arrangement of corpuscles—something hidden—that upholds its properties and causes its continuance. The sensory data of a thing and the ideas they correspondingly cause in the mind are not its real properties, but only representational knowledge. The human being, "a thinking substance," does not have innate ideas but is a *tabula rasa* whose mental faculties possess capacities for knowledge. "Knowledge" is the perception by reason of the agreement or disagreement of any of our ideas, either by intuitive perception or indirect demonstration. Locke's turn to subjectivity in his notion of "abstract ideas" as "creatures of the mind" formed by reason's ability of reflection and the free will's selective attention, highlights humans as free and active agents who are able to form "beliefs, assents and opinions," which are not "knowledge" and may not be real or demonstrable. Therefore, religion and morality are just "beliefs," not innate principles or something acquirable by reason, but rather something derived from the reasonable postulate of the existence of "a God."[52] Revelation is *above* reason; it is "purely a matter of faith, with which reason has directly nothing to do"—thus it does not have access to the same kind of certainty as the senses or reason, and thus cannot be proved.[53] Yet no alleged revelation can ever be accepted against the clear evidence of reason, which is "to judge of the truth of its being a revelation."[54]

Edwards contests Locke's epistemology by his defense of the supremacy of revelation and reason's subservience to it. Human powers of reason and volition

---

51. For Edwards's concept of substance, see *Mind* 25b, 27, 61.

52. See *Essay concerning Human Understanding*, I.iv.8, for the idea that God is not innate; II.xxiii.33–34 on the mind conceptualizing the idea of God; IV.x.1, 3, 6 on the inference of the existence of "a God" from the existence of all things; IV.x.4–5, 7–8 on the deduction of God's eternity. On the fallacy of Locke's "proof" and contradiction with empiricism, see D. J. O'Conner, *John Locke* (Hammondshire: Penguin, 1952), 180–82.

53. *Essay concerning Human Understanding*, IV.xviii.7, 4.

54. Ibid., IV.xviii.5 and IV. xviii.8. One can see Locke's confidence in the ability of the senses and reason, and also his ambivalence towards reason's arbitration on biblical revelation when reason decides that it is *above* reason (fallen angels losing their first happy state, the dead will be resurrected) or *contrary to* reason. In this he is an instigator of the historical critical study of the Scriptures.

do not entail the mind's absolute governance over its thoughts and judgments. Casual inferences, perceptual judgments, formations of memories, and abstract ideas are all determined by a number of "laws": laws of the associations of ideas; of mental principles of resemblance, habits, and inclinations; and of natural dispositions in us (innate or from previous experience). Above all, it is difficult to discover "laws of nature" that govern our mental acts.[55] However, innate ideas do exist and so substantiate the claim for the existence of a God, the natural inclination of the soul for excellence (harmony) and order of things (e.g., injustice demands to be redressed by a superior being), and the habit of the mind to argue causes from effects.[56] The mind, argues Edwards, is not a *tabula rasa*. He points to "the exceeding imperfection of human understanding" by noting two facts: (1) the difference between God's understanding, in which God has "a direct ideal view" of himself and all other things "by actual and immediate presence of an idea of the thing understood," and the inability of man's mind to have actual ideas of things like God's, hence to be forced to resort to the use of signs for "representatives of things" and (2) the noetic depravity resulting from the fall—"the alienation of the inclinations and natural *dispositions* of our soul" from divine things, and "the sinking of our *intellectual powers*, and the great subjection of the soul in its fallen state to *external senses*."[57] Noetic depravity is just one aspect of original sin, which is man's "*innate* sinful depravity of heart," or a "natural tendency or propensity" of the will to sin.[58] It is "a wild fancy" for "Mr. Locke" to say that divine revelation is not necessary and that reason is "the only way" to teach us true religion, for history shows that "men in this state" for many generations considered "the things of the world in lower views," and that true religion began with revelation, not reason; therefore reason *before* revelation is bound to go "very wrong."[59] Without revelation the world would forever be uncertain about the being of a God, the first cause of all things—whether as a principle exerting itself by natural necessity or an intelligent and voluntary agent. There would be myriads of confusing views on the purpose of humanity's existence, and how persons should relate to one another.

Revelation is a necessity for the basic functioning of human life, for it gives us knowledge of first principles as the basis for "a most rational account

55. Subjects to be handled in the *Treatise on Mind*, no. 43; *Mind* 69.

56. *Misc.* 268 {God's Existence. Innate Ideas}; also *Mind* 54 on causal reasoning depending on an innate principle (Y 6:370).

57. *Misc.* 782 {Ideas. Sense of the Heart. Spiritual Knowledge or Conviction. Faith} (my emphasis, Y 18:457–58, 461–62). In this entry Edwards engaged in a head-on attack of Locke, whose name is mentioned.

58. *Original Sin* (Y 3:107, 120, 398).

59. *Misc.* 986 {Revealed Religion} (Y 20:309–11).

of religion and morality, highest philosophy." Consequently, it gives us a basis for knowledge concerning the world, human nature, spirits, providence, time, and eternity.[60] Scriptural revelation, immediately inspired by the Spirit of God, provides truths of "an absolute sort of certainty,"[61] and faith, though not "of absolute certainty," nonetheless has a very high degree of certainty. This certainty is "infinitely strong," much stronger than reason by argumentation or demonstration, because "certainty of faith" is given by the testimony of the Holy Spirit. At the same time, "such a belief is agreeable to reason, agreeable to the exact rules of philosophy."[62] The truth of things, divine and natural, "may be defined after the most strict and metaphysical manner": "the consistency and agreement of our ideas with the ideas of God . . . according to God's stated order and law."[63] Knowledge, therefore, is not what Locke understands it to be—the perception of agreement or disagreement of ideas about the sensory and rational world. Rather, it is the recognition of the mind's ability to perceive the objective relations of ideas fixed by God, including truths of mysteries of faith—in other words, to discern "that they are united," "that they belong to one another, though we may not know the manner how they are tied together."[64] Edwards has a high regard for human reason,[65] but it must be a "reasoning *after* revelation," a "reasoning *according to* revelation." Reason is a good handmaid but a bad master. Edwards deploys Locke's "sense and reason" in the empirical epistemology for his spiritual epistemology. When God gives a person a "sense of heart" that enables him or her to grasp the truth of scriptural revelation, then and only then can reason be a means to explore the mysteries of faith and convince others of their rationality and reasonableness.

The Eschatological Shape of Living

In a diary entry on February 12, 1725, Edwards seemed to have written a mission statement for his life: "The very thing I now want, to give me a clearer

---

60. *Misc.* 350 {Christian Religion} (Y 13:421–26). Edwards firmly believes that only scriptural revelation can offer a unified vision of how, in all arts and sciences, "the more they are perfected, the more they issue in divinity, and coincide with it, and appear to be parts of it" (*Outline of a Rational Account of Christian Religion*, Y 6:396).

61. *Mind* 20, "Inspiration" (Y 6:346).

62. *Mind* 5, "Certainty" (Y 6:339–40); *Misc. aa*, "Faith" (Y 13:177–78).

63. *Mind* 10, "Truth" (Y 6:341–42).

64. *Mind* 71, "Knowledge" (Y 6:385).

65. Edwards even thinks that it is "within the reach of naked reason" to perceive the truth of the Trinity after accepting this scriptural doctrine, *Misc.* 94 (Y 13:257).

and more immediate view of the perfections and glory of God, is as clear a knowledge of the manner of God's exerting himself with respects to spirits and mind, as I have of his operations concerning matter and bodies." Looking back over Edwards's life one sees how his early conversion experiences gave birth to particular perceptions of biblical truth. Consequently, his understandings of theology, spirituality, science, ontology, epistemology, ethics, and aesthetics were welded together into a unified vision of all things, natural and divine, from pre-temporal eternity to post-temporal eternity. The eschatological shape of living—as witnessed especially in his *Resolutions, Diary,* and *Personal Narrative*—extended to the rest of his life, and primed Edwards towards an openness to the movements of the Holy Spirit. This gave him the profound Christian identity that voiced the Scriptures from the pulpit and engaged with the brightest Enlightenment minds of his day in philosophical treatises. It is especially rare to see a life so committed as Edwards's. He sought to understand divine and natural realities with a biblical cast of mind, to articulate these perceptions to ordinary Christians and to contemporary scientists and philosophers, and to apply them to both personal and public life. Such a legacy bears laudable testimony to Edwards's entire life, a life that is lived "from him, through him, and to him" in all things (Rom 11:36). To him be the glory.

Chapter 33

Charles Wesley: Christian Identity in the Enlightenment

BRUCE HINDMARSH

> Till we cast our crowns before thee,
> Lost in wonder, love, and praise.

Charles Wesley's famous hymn, "Love Divine, All Loves Excelling," ends on a note of ecstasy and prayer, anticipating the day when, changed from glory into glory, we "cast our crowns before thee, / Lost in wonder, love, and praise." This is the conclusion of a great parabolic movement in the hymn that begins in its opening lines with the descent of the Son of God in the incarnation as the "Joy of heaven, to earth come down," and aspires in prayer to the full salvation of the finished new creation wrought by Christ himself, until transformed in him we finally "take our place" in heaven. The climactic phrase, "lost in wonder, love, and praise," is an exemplary sentiment that Wesley has put in the mouths of Christian singers of all denominations since the eighteenth century, since this hymn quickly became established in common use in Christian worship. The only proper response to the "great salvation" achieved by Christ is for the believer to be lost in an apophasis of wondering love.[1]

Lay Methodists would have been regularly singing this hymn by the time Charles Wesley's brother John published his "compendium" of the natural philosophy of the period, *A Survey of the Wisdom of God in the Creation* (1763). This was a composite work, characteristic of John as an editor and abridger, in which he drew upon a number of authors to present a simple account ("in the plain-

---

1. John Wesley, *A Collection of Hymns for the Use of the People Called Methodists*, ed. Franz Hildebrandt and Oliver A. Beckerlegge, vol. 7 of the *Bicentennial Edition of the Works of John Wesley* (Nashville: Abingdon, 1983), 545-47 (hymn #374). First published in 1747, and then republished during the perfectionist revivals in 1761.

est dress, simply and nakedly expressed") of the latest findings of eighteenth-century science in the post-Newtonian period. He confessed that he thought it best to drop all the mathematics as he aimed not to present a theoretical account but a descriptive one. Wesley continued to revise and add to the work, and by the fourth edition his simple compendium ranged over five volumes. The conclusion of his preface, however, takes us full circle to the close of Charles's earlier hymn. John hoped that his account would display the "amazing power, wisdom, and goodness of the great Creator," and that it would serve to "warm our hearts, and to fill our mouths with wonder, love and praise!"[2] The heart "strangely warmed" by God in redemption was now likewise to be warmed in contemplation of creation.

On the cusp of the modern period, then, and in the midst of the Enlightenment, as the Scientific Revolution of the preceding century was beginning to reshape society in profound and lasting ways, the Wesley brothers bore their witness to what it meant to identify as a Christian. In this essay, I will focus particularly on Charles Wesley and his hymnody. At a time when many leading thinkers were widening the distance between God and the world, and between God and human nature, the poetry of Charles Wesley pressed in the opposite direction, and it did so in both form and content. His hymnody was a literature of prayer and devotion that remains one of the most lasting contributions of the evangelical revival to the wider church, and in it we see a deeply personal sense of Christian identity that responded to God's immediate presence in the modern world as creator and redeemer with wonder, love, and praise. For Charles Wesley, the contemplation of God's work in creation and redemption expanded one's horizons from the mundane to the transcendental.

Charles Wesley (1707–1788)

The first eight years of Charles Wesley's life were spent in the rectory at Epworth in rural Lincolnshire where his father was the parish minister.[3] These were years

2. John Wesley, *A Survey of the Wisdom of God in the Creation; or, A Compendium of Natural Philosophy* (Bristol, 1763), 1:iv. The preface to the 4th edition also appears in *The Works of John Wesley*, ed. Thomas Jackson (1872; repr. Grand Rapids: Baker Book House, 1984), 14:300–303.

3. For Charles Wesley's biography, one may consult several new studies inspired by the tercentenary of his birth in 2007. See, e.g., Gareth Lloyd, *Charles Wesley and the Struggle for Methodist Identity* (Oxford: Oxford University Press, 2007); G. M. Best, *Charles Wesley: A Biography* (London: Epworth, 2007); John Tyson, *Assist Me to Proclaim: The Life and Hymns of Charles Wesley* (Grand Rapids: Eerdmans, 2007); and Kenneth Newport and Ted A. Campbell, eds., *Charles Wesley: Life, Literature and Legacy* (London: Epworth, 2007). Much work has also been done to prepare

of disciplined training under the firm hand of his mother, Susannah, and he witnessed the dedicated devotion of both his mother and father. He probably inherited an emotional temperament more like his volatile father, Samuel, but he certainly also retained a good measure of his mother's strength of mind too. His schooling continued at Westminster school in London, where he lived with his elder brother Samuel Jr., and where he was confirmed in the principles of a Tory High Churchman, principles that would stay with him for the rest of his life. This is also where the foundation was laid for his felicity as a poet in his classical education. But when he went on to Oxford he grew somewhat more relaxed in his seriousness about religion and complained once to his brother, "What? would you have me to be a saint at once?"

The turning point came in 1729 when, like his brother John, he returned to the high ideals of devotion he had been raised to appreciate, and he renewed his dedication to "purity of intention" after the pattern of Caroline High Church Anglican piety. "A man made for friendship," as one of his Oxford friends described him, Charles soon gathered others around him in his disciplined pursuit of the highest Christian ideals. The young George Whitefield was one of those recruited into this movement by Charles. During these years the two brothers Wesley were the center of a devotional movement often described as "Oxford Methodism" to distinguish it from the later evangelical period of Methodist revival. Their piety followed the pattern of the serious Anglican ascetical devotion of Jeremy Taylor and William Law.

A second turning point in Charles's life occurred between 1736 and 1739. It was during these years that he passed through a profound crisis of insufficiency, experienced a climactic evangelical conversion, and found his voice as an evangelist and poet. A year as a failed missionary in Georgia in 1736 was traumatic, with its interpersonal conflict, serious life-threatening illness and debility, and social estrangement, culminating in a sense of spiritual malaise and inadequacy. Together, these experiences provoked an assurance quest for the sort of direct experience of God's mercy to which the Moravian Brethren testified. And so it proved on May 21, 1738, back in London, in one of the most liturgically well-timed conversion experiences in history. On the Day of Pentecost, bed-ridden with pleurisy, Charles experienced that "strange palpitation of heart" that was parallel to John's "strangely warmed heart" three days later, and he knew person-

---

critical editions of Charles Wesley texts, including *The Unpublished Poetry of Charles Wesley*, ed. S. T. Kimbrough Jr. and Oliver A. Beckerlegge, 3 vols. (Nashville: Kingswood Books, 1988–1992); *The Sermons of Charles Wesley*, ed. Kenneth Newport (Oxford: Oxford University Press, 2001); *The Manuscript Journal of the Reverend Charles Wesley, M. A.*, ed. S. T. Kimbrough Jr. and Kenneth G. C. Newport, 2 vols. (Nashville: Kingswood Books, 2008); and *The Letters of Charles Wesley*, ed. Kenneth Newport and Gareth Lloyd, vol. 1, *1728–1756* (Oxford: Oxford University Press, 2013).

ally that his sins were forgiven. It truly was, as John Tyson says, "Pentecost made personal," and Charles moved on from this experience to a new confidence as an evangelist and Christian poet. He wrote a hymn to mark the occasion, and it was possibly the one entitled "Free Grace," published the following year. The sense of wonder that God's great salvation could be experienced personally is communicated in the opening five interrogatives of the hymn, its central exclamation ("Amazing love!"), and its thrice repeated "for me":

> And can it be, that I should gain
> > An interest in the Saviour's blood?
> Died he for me, who caused his pain?
> > For me? Who him to death pursued?
> Amazing love! How can it be
> That thou, my God, shouldst die for me?[4]

The surest proof that this conversion was a turning point was the new fluency he found in every sphere. He began to preach extempore for the first time and found himself buoyed up by the ease and facility he discovered in preaching and the reception he was given. His sermon texts from this period show a new boldness in proclaiming God's grace and the work of the Holy Spirit. He also began to preach outdoors in 1739. And it was in 1739 too that he began to publish with his brother a remarkable corpus of evangelical hymns that he would add to for the rest of his life.[5] The classic body of Methodist hymnody appeared in some 500 hymns published jointly with John between 1739 and 1746. Thereafter Charles would publish under his own name. According to the calculation of the late Frank Baker, the Methodist scholar who laid the foundation for the present renaissance in Charles Wesley studies, Charles produced some 9,000 hymns or poems by the time he died—roughly 27,000 stanzas or 180,000 lines. That is three times the output of Wordsworth.

---

4. John Wesley, *Collection of Hymns*, 322 (hymn #193). This hymn was first published in 1739.

5. On Wesley's literary art, see the treatment in J. R. Watson, ed., *An Annotated Anthology of Hymns* (Oxford: Oxford University Press, 2002), and J. R. Watson, *The English Hymn* (Oxford: Oxford University Press, 1999). See also Donald Davie, *The Eighteenth-Century Hymn in England* (Cambridge: Cambridge University Press, 1993), 57–70, and Donald Davie, "The Classicism of Charles Wesley," in *Purity of Diction in English Verse* (London: Chatto and Windus, 1952), 70–81. The starting point for studies in Charles Wesley's hymns remains Frank Baker, *Charles Wesley's Verse: An Introduction* (London: Epworth Press, 1964). For online editions of Charles Wesley's published and unpublished verse, and related resources, see "Wesley Texts," *Center for Studies in the Wesleyan Tradition, Duke Divinity School*, https://divinity.duke.edu/initiatives-centers/cswt/wesley-texts (accessed December 1, 2015).

Thus far, Charles's formation and experience was running along tracks parallel to those of his brother John. This was true of both the conversion to seriousness in 1729, and also the evangelical conversion in 1738. For both Wesleys there had been a period of great religious earnestness, and then an arc from travail, through evangelical conversion, to evangelical fluency. For the next decade, while Charles Wesley was in his thirties, he was in partnership with his brother John as a young and single Methodist itinerant in the heady days of evangelical revival when everyone seemed to walk in a cloud of wonders. And there is good evidence (much of it from lay testimony) that Charles was actually regarded during these years as the more effective and powerful preacher of the two brothers. Certainly, when you read the few sermon manuscripts that are extant from this period, you sense the fire in his bones, and he pulled no punches in preaching either the law or the gospel. He might have been more critical than John of some of the ecstatic phenomena of revival that were observed during these years, but he was certainly front and center as a cofounder of Methodism in London and Bristol, and then regions beyond, as Methodism began to spread.

In his forties, however, Charles began to mark out a course of life very different from his brother. During the period of 1747 to 1749, he met, courted, and married Sarah Gwynne and commenced a happy season of life as a husband, father, and householder. When it seemed that John was approaching a similar turning point in his own life as he began to form a close affectionate bond with the lowborn Grace Murray, who had nursed him in an illness and subsequently travelled with him for a time, Charles intervened dramatically to crush the prospect. Historians still disagree in how they interpret this episode. Did Charles act rightly to end a scandal that threatened Methodism at its roots? Or did he act impulsively and recklessly? However one evaluates this episode, the brothers would from this point on move through life on different paths. When John Wesley did marry, he did so without informing Charles, and the marriage was a disaster.

For the next seven years or so, Charles would struggle with divided loyalties, torn between his allegiance to his wife, to his brother and Methodism, to the Church of England, and above all, to his own conscience. But from 1749 forward, we must place the model offered in Charles Wesley of a Methodist evangelist as a happily married man with a family, alongside that of his brother John as the singular itinerant whose unsuccessful marriage seemed only an interference to his travelling ministry.

It was a matter of some significance, then, when Charles withdrew from active, regular itinerancy in 1756, as he settled down as a local Methodist minister in Bristol, and then, after 1771, in London. John would continue his superhuman travelling ministry as an almost mendicant figure, but Charles would maintain a respectable household and remain an anchor for Methodism in its heartland.

He was by no means inactive, though, and he was very much at the center of the main developments in Methodism, such as the perfectionist revivals in the early 1760s. Here again, Charles was much more critical than his brother of the extravagant claims to perfection and the apocalyptic prophecies that emerged in this revival. This was a matter both of discipline and doctrine. Charles formed a higher view of the ideal of Christian perfection than John and therefore was less willing to accredit it among those of their followers who made claim to it. He considered perfection scarcely attainable before death.

It is important to emphasize what a long phase of Charles's life this period as a settled Methodist was—some thirty-two years. It was during these years that Charles became, as Gareth Lloyd has shown, the voice of those Methodists who wished to remain firmly in the Church of England. Partly because of his resistance to Methodism becoming its own denomination, Charles Wesley became a much-diminished figure in Methodist historiography by the mid-nineteenth century. It is only in more recent scholarship that Charles Wesley has come to be seen as a significant figure in his own terms, distinct from his brother, in eighteenth-century religion and literature. We are now able to see him more clearly and to appreciate his contribution to Christian self-identity in the period of the Enlightenment, especially as a hymn writer.

Charles Wesley and the Enlightenment

What were the social and intellectual conditions under which Charles Wesley came to maturity and bore his own personal witness to what it means to identify as a Christian? It is important to bear in mind that the evangelical devotion that he did so much to inspire emerged at a key transitional point in the history of Western society as more recognizably modern patterns of thought and practice were taking root in many spheres. Contemporaries often spoke of their period as "a more enlightened age" when compared with the past. This was true at many levels, not least politically. The ideal of Christendom that had long stirred the medieval imagination and that still inspired serious legislative programs to sustain the uniformity of the confessional state well into the late seventeenth century was arguably in recession in the eighteenth century. So it was on the trailing edge of this Christendom ideal and the leading edge of modernity that Charles Wesley and other evangelical leaders established a spiritual movement concerned to spread "real Christianity" among a populace that still thought of itself as Christian even as social change was devolving more weight upon individual agency in spheres such as commerce, the press, and politics. As the ancien régime was superseded by the modern world with its constitutional guarantees of freedom of religion, its democratic ideals and commercial free-doms, its industry and technology, its enlarged print and other public media, and its efficient and long-distance communication and trade, evangelicals like Wesley would increasingly appeal to women and men as personal agents and connect them in intimate small groups and larger associations that were vol-untary, rather than mandated by corporate hierarchies or social custom. Just as Charles Wesley had experienced his own "personal Pentecost," so also the wider evangelical revival would be concerned to establish a deeply personal sense of Christian identity among its adherents.

As profound changes were taking place on the ground in the practices of politics, commerce, communication, transportation, and other spheres, there were parallel changes happening in the world of ideas among leading Enlighten-ment thinkers in Britain and throughout Europe. Here too there was a sense that the eighteenth century was "a more enlightened age." Many of these intellectual developments were, however, more troubling to evangelicals such as Charles Wesley. The bent of natural and moral philosophy in the period was toward giv-ing an account of nature and human nature in terms that marginalized religious belief. A fundamentally religious account of the natural world was replaced by a more mechanical philosophy and materialist science. And a religious an-thropology was supplanted by a moral philosophy that separated religion and ethics.[6] It was in the eighteenth century that the question of being good without God came center stage for the first time through philosophers such as the Third Earl of Shaftesbury or David Hume. In many ways, the poetry of Charles Wesley can, at least in these terms, be read as "counter-Enlightenment."

The enormous scholarship of the last generation bearing on the Enlight-enment makes it dangerous to offer generalizations, however, since almost ev-ery narrative of the Enlightenment has been qualified, nuanced (sometimes overturned), and contextualized in important ways.[7] Above all, perhaps, the place of religion in relation to natural and moral philosophy ("science and eth-ics") is complex, and in England particularly it has been shown that Lockean and Newtonian ideas were debated and assimilated widely by churchmen with deeply religious concerns.[8] This was true also of ethics.[9] Yet, as John Hedley

6. This is the narrative given of moral philosophy in J. B. Schneewind, *The Invention of Au-tonomy* (Cambridge: Cambridge University Press, 1998).

7. See, e.g., Roy Porter, introduction to *Eighteenth-Century Science*, ed. Roy Porter, vol. 4 of *The Cambridge History of Science*, ed. David C. Lindberg and Ronald L. Numbers (Cambridge: Cambridge University Press, 2003).

8. See B. W. Young, *Religion and Enlightenment in Eighteenth-Century England: Theological Debate from Locke to Burke* (Oxford: Clarendon, 1998).

9. See Isabel Rivers, *Reason, Grace, and Sentiment: A Study of the Language of Reli-*

Brooke argues, "Although the extension of naturalistic explanation often went hand-in-glove with natural theology, a certain distancing of the Creator from the creation could easily result," and he contrasts the attitudes of the early and later eighteenth century in this regard.[10] Where proponents of the physico-theology of the early eighteenth century seemed to win the battle in their apologetic argument with Deism, in the long run they lost the war by conceding too much to the capacity of reason to deduce from impersonal forces the nature and personality of God.

Charles Wesley and "the God of Nature and of Grace"

Here is where Charles Wesley followed a different trajectory in both form and content as he bore personal witness to God as creator and redeemer. We will turn below to examine his response to the natural world in the context of Enlightenment thought, but we should note at the outset that his greatest theme was "Love's redeeming work." This phrase is from the resurrection hymn, "Christ the Lord is ris'n today," with its repeated Easter Alleluias. Wesley declares triumphantly that with Christ's rising from the dead, "Love's redeeming work is done." But the response of poet and singer to this event in salvation history is personal, since the believer is united to Christ: "*Ours* the cross, the grave, the skies." This is altogether characteristic of Wesley's response to the biblical narrative of salvation.

In another of Charles Wesley's great festival hymns, his response to the economy of salvation is likewise personal. In one of the original verses of "Hark! the herald angels sing" he does not simply describe the nativity but rises to the language of prayer and invocation, "Come, Desire of Nations, come, / Fix in Us thy humble Home." The language of personal entreaty intensifies as the hymn continues, contemplating in the nativity the fall and restoration of humankind in fulfillment of ancient prophecy:

> Rise, the Woman's Conqu'ring Seed,
> Bruise in Us the Serpent's Head.
> Now display thy saving Pow'r,
> Ruin'd Nature now restore,

---

gion and Ethics in England, 1660–1780, 2 vols. (Cambridge: Cambridge University Press, 1991, 2000).

10. John Hedley Brooke, "Science and Religion," in *Eighteenth-Century Science*, ed. Roy Porter, vol. 4 of *The Cambridge History of Science*, ed. David C. Lindberg and Ronald L. Numbers (Cambridge: Cambridge University Press, 2003), 751.

And, finally, the stanza climaxes with a cry for our nature to be wholly incorporate in the Christ seen at Bethlehem: "Now in Mystic Union join / Thine to Ours, and Ours to Thine."[11] This is a clue to Wesley's very personal sense of Christian identity. It is not simply that he wanted to give his testimony (though he did), but that he understood salvation itself to derive from a real union with Christ. His language is therefore personal without becoming sentimental; it is robustly doctrinal and didactic, without becoming abstract.

His great festival hymns for Christmas, Easter, Whitsuntide, and other occasions responded to the biblical story of redemption in intimate, but never private, terms. Indeed the whole economy of salvation could be illustrated from single lines of Wesley's devotional verse. Or, again, each doctrinal article of the ecumenical creeds could be reconstructed from lines of his poetry. The doctrine of the incarnation is, for example, described in appropriately concise language in the imperatival sentence, "Veil'd in flesh, the Godhead see!"[12] The personal invitation to "see" is marked, as so often, with an exclamation point. Or, again, the mystery of the kenosis appears in the line, "Emptied himself of all but love."[13] There is a self-limitation in the spareness of this language that matches the doctrine. On the atonement Wesley's language is, if anything, even more dense in marking the mystery of divine impassibility and the death of Christ in two striking paradoxes of great simplicity: "Impassive, he suffers; immortal, he dies."[14] In other hands, diction this stripped of all ornament would appear simplistic or descend into bathos, but not for Wesley. His poetry reflects deep personal attention and intellectual engagement with the mysteries of God's saving work.

It would be possible to continue tracing the events of salvation history and the language of personal devotion in Charles Wesley's hymns since his poetry was so comprehensively biblical. Indeed, his scriptural imagination provides the foundation of all his art. As Frank Baker says, "His verse is an enormous sponge filled to saturation with Bible words, Bible similes, Bible metaphors, Bible stories, Bible ideas." So, for example, the last verse of "And can it be" is an unbroken catena of biblical allusions. Here is the stanza, as set out in the original in 1739:

---

11. Stanzas 7 and 8 of "Hymn for Christmas Day," in John and Charles Wesley, *Hymns and Sacred Poems* (London, 1739), 207.

12. Ibid. (from stanza 4).

13. From the third stanza of "And can it be," in John Wesley, *Collection of Hymns*, 323 (hymn #193).

14. From the third stanza of "On the crucifixion," in Charles Wesley, *Hymns on the Great Festivals* (London, 1746), 9 (hymn #4).

No condemnation now *I* dread;
Jesus, and all in Him, is *mine*;
Alive in Him, *my* living Head,
And clothed in righteousness divine,
Bold *I* approach th'eternal throne,
And claim the crown, through Christ *my* own.[15]

"No condemnation now I dread" is the peak statement of St. Paul in the first verse of Romans 8 that there is therefore now no condemnation for those that are in Christ. "Jesus and all in him is mine" is the climax of Paul's argument in 1 Corinthians 3:22 that all things are yours in Christ. "Alive in him, my living Head" is the new Adam Christology in 1 Corinthians 15. "And clothed in righteousness divine" alludes to Philippians 3:9, where Paul wants to be found in Christ having a righteousness not his own. "Bold I approach the eternal throne" is the turning point in Hebrews 10, the declaration that we have confidence to enter the Holy Place through the blood of Jesus. "And claim the crown through Christ my own" is 2 Timothy 4:7–8, where Paul talks of finishing the race and the crown of righteousness to be awarded him by the Lord, and to all who have longed for his appearing. All of these biblical allusions are precise, and most of them pick up on climactic or summary statements in Paul. The entire stanza is built of them, and yet they are pressed into service not as allusions per se, but as words to be sung through in a bold confession of first-person devotion (the italicized pronouns are original) and as the climax of a hymn celebrating "love's redeeming work."

In 1745 and 1746 Charles Wesley published a number of hymnbooks related to liturgical themes and the liturgical calendar. The full title of his *Whitsundtide* or *Pentecost* hymnbook was *Hymns of Petition and Thanksgiving for the Promise of the Father* (1746), hymns, that is, to the promised Holy Spirit. Most of the hymns invoke the Spirit to make personal the work of Christ for the believer, in terms similar to what we have observed already. Hymn 28, however, takes a wider view of the work of the Spirit in creation and re-creation. This hymn helps us most clearly to see the way in which Charles Wesley pressed in the opposite direction of those who were increasingly separating nature and grace into isomorphic spheres in the eighteenth century. For Wesley, nature too was part of "Love's redeeming work." This is evident right from the outset of hymn 28, since the first stanza describes the Spirit as the author of every work divine, who shines with a transfiguring light through *both* the original creation and the redeemed creation.

---

15. Originally published under the title "Free Grace," in John and Charles Wesley, *Hymns and Sacred Poems*, 117–19, and reprinted in John Wesley, *Collection of Hymns*, 323 (hymn #193, stanza 5).

1 AUTHOR of every work Divine,
    Who dost through both creations shine,
        The God of nature and of grace,
    Thy glorious steps in all we see,
    And wisdom attribute to Thee,
        And power, and majesty, and praise.[16]

The Holy Spirit is here the same God of nature and of grace without division
for Wesley. Not only does the Spirit irradiate or transfigure the old and new
creation, as the disciples witnessed on Mount Tabor, but the Spirit also leaves
traces of his work—glorious footsteps that we may see in all his works, and
so the one who discerns the Spirit in the history of the universe, as in the
history of redemption, attributes to the Spirit the fourfold characteristics of
wisdom, power, majesty, and praise. Wesley was nothing if not biblical, and
these attributes were by no means random. *Sophia, dunamis, doxa*—these are
throughout the New Testament the words most associated with the Spirit.
Wesley seemed to understand this instinctively, and he hymns the Spirit accordingly as the one whose presence he witnesses in natural history and the
history of redemption.

In a dense second stanza, Wesley compresses the account of the original
creation in Genesis, as the Spirit broods over the chaos and creates *ex nihilo*:

2 Thou didst Thy mighty wings outspread,
    And brooding o'er the chaos, shed
        Thy life into the impregn'd abyss,
    The vital principle infuse,
    And out of nothing's womb produce
        The earth and heaven, and all that is.

The language of pregnancy and womb here are combined with the traditional *ex
nihilo* doctrine in a daring way. This is no fertility myth or doctrine of emanation, and Charles distinguishes clearly between the created and the uncreated,
but nonetheless he communicates the intimate bond of love between the creator
and the creation. That the hovering Spirit "shed" his life into the impregn'd abyss
suggests already a kind of suffering maternal love. And the language of "vital
principle" recalls a Paracelsian sense of the immanence of the divine life as the
animating center of the material world. The word "vital" does not, of course,

16. John and Charles Wesley, *Hymns of Petition and Thanksgiving for the Promise of the Father*
(Bristol, 1746), 31–32 (hymn #28).

as in our own everyday usage simply mean important, but is the adjective for the Latin *vita*, or life. The Holy Spirit thus animates the world as an infused, principial life force.

Reginald Ward argues that in the German evangelical tradition this appreciation of the universe as animated by divine life was all but universal. When Pietists sought to renew religious vitality in their churches, they understood this as in direct continuity with the cosmic principle of life that they saw in the Paracelsian, alchemical outlook. The life within and the life without were the same; this was simply another aspect of microcosm and macrocosm. The *same* Holy Spirit was at work in people as in the world, just as we see in Wesley's hymn. Indeed, Ward makes "vitalism" one of the hallmarks of the whole German evangelical tradition as it emerges in the late seventeenth and early eighteenth centuries. "The vitalism that characterized the whole alchemical tradition," he writes, "was a clear attraction to men like Arndt and the Pietists of a later generation who were seeking to recover religious vitality."[17] In this hymn by Charles Wesley it is clear, however, that this cosmological vital principle was equated not with cabbalistic, hermetic Neoplatonism, but with the biblical Holy Spirit.

The following stanza extends this sense of the Holy Spirit of God as the life of the world under the image of inspiration:

3 That all-informing breath Thou art
  Who dost continued life impart,
    And bidd'st the world persist to be:

The Spirit is thus critical not just to the original creation at the beginning of time but also to the sustaining of the world at every moment since then. The continuing action of the Holy Spirit to will the persistence of the world echoes the doctrine of continuous creation in Jonathan Edwards, for whom God every moment creates the world anew. In Wesley's hymn, the image of the Spirit as the interior life of the world is balanced in the last half of this stanza by the picture of the transcendent Spirit holding the stars and planets in place, suspending them by golden filaments.

  Garnish'd by Thee yon azure sky,
  And all those beauteous orbs on high
    Depend in golden chains from Thee.

17. W. R. Ward, *Early Evangelicalism: A Global Intellectual History, 1670–1789* (Cambridge: Cambridge University Press, 2006), 11.

The "golden chains" which hold the universe in suspension, like the divine breath that gives life to the world, describe a reality that is not in any way autonomous, reduced to the operation of abstract law or to material properties and mechanical operations. His use of the verb "depend" is well considered, expressing not only contingency in the abstract but also the notion of hanging, like one might hang a picture. The "beauteous orbs on high" thus depend utterly and entirely upon the Spirit for their moment-by-moment existence. The universe is suspended from an Archimedean point in God himself: it is not an independent sphere. Thus, although the Spirit is the immanent life of the world, he also transcends it.

The theme of continuous creation is sustained in the fourth stanza, where nature is described not as blind and mute but as responsive to the Spirit of God, perceiving the Spirit's motions and acknowledging the Spirit's governance:

> 4 Thou dost create the earth anew,
>   (Its Maker and Preserver too,)
>   By Thine almighty arm sustain:
>   Nature perceives Thy secret force,
>   And still holds on her even course,
>   And owns Thy providential reign.

The conceit, if it is a conceit, that nature perceives the Spirit's motions and responds consciously to obey and acknowledge his lordship suggests a dynamic view of nature as capable of answering in some way to God, just as the psalmist describes the heavens "declaring" the glory of God. Wesley allows nature an agential response to the Spirit, as it perceives, holds, and owns the Spirit's providential work. Even the rocks cry out.

Boldly, Wesley draws on the language of Plotinus and Neoplatonism but without a hint of a demiurgic doctrine of emanation, when he continues, addressing the Spirit in the next stanza:

> 5 Thou art the Universal Soul,
>   The plastic power that fills the whole,
>   And governs earth, air, sea, and sky:

What Wesley writes here echoes Alexander Pope, who said similarly, "All are but parts of one stupendous Whole, / Whose body Nature is, and God the soul."[18]

---

18. Alexander Pope, *Essay on Man* (London, 1763), 24.

But Wesley's view was both more personal and biblical in hymning the Spirit. Thus he returns to the central image of divine breath:

> The creatures all Thy breath receive,
> And who by Thy inspiring live,
>   Without Thy inspiration die.

Far from reflecting an uncritical Platonism in his reference to the "Universal Soul," Wesley here echoes the Psalter's language about creaturely dependence upon the breath of God. The whole poem could be seen as a commentary on Psalm 104, and here especially the verses, "When thou takest away their breath they die, and are turned again to dust. When thou lettest thy breath go forth they are made; and thou renewest the face of the earth" (Ps 104:30–31 BCP).

Clearly, Charles Wesley believed that the being of the natural world was utterly dependent at every moment and in every place upon its divine author. The world is distinct from God, but its being derives wholly from God, who remains as closely knit to the creation as soul to body. The Spirit is the "vital principle" of all created beings, without whom they cease to be. The creation thus participates in God while remaining distinct from God.

Finally, in the last stanza, Charles Wesley returns to his more usual theme of the work of the Spirit of God in the redemption of humankind. It is this same immense God, this eternal *nous*, who works to save the lost and redeem the world.

> 6 Spirit immense, eternal Mind,
>   Thou on the souls of lost mankind
>   Dost with benignest influence move,
>   Pleased to restore the ruin'd race,
>   And new-create a world of grace
>   In all the image of Thy love.

The conclusion of this poem here could not be more clear in describing the work of salvation, in terms that go back to Irenaeus, as a work to "restore" or recapitulate the original creation. The restoration of the human race involves a new creation of a world of grace, or, as it is put in Romans 8, a sharing of the creation in the liberty and glory of the children of God. To be thus remade in the image of God is to be remade also in the image of the Spirit of God as the eternal and incessant love that binds the Father and the Son. It is, as this hymn concludes, to be created anew in all the image of thy Love.

One might worry that the emphasis of this poem could blur the distinction between God and the world, but it is clear from other poems that Wesley affirmed just as robustly the infinite dissimilarity between the creation and the creator. The being of the world was neither equivocal nor univocal when compared to God's own being; it was analogical. Although human persons were made for a divine end, and the new-created world with them, this divine end surpassed all human comprehension. And so, in another hymn to the Spirit, Wesley invokes the Spirit to come and dwell within his own soul, to prepare and consecrate his soul as a temple, as the apostle Paul described it:

> 1 Come, Holy Ghost, all-quick'ning fire,
>   Come, and in me delight to rest!
>   Drawn by the lure of strong desire,
>   O come, and consecrate my breast:
>   The temple of my soul prepare,
>   And fix thy sacred presence there![19]

The "Universal Soul" that in the first hymn fills the whole of earth, air, sea, and sky, here is invoked to fill the human heart. The "vital principle" that in the first poem was cosmological is here the "principle divine" that properly animates the Christian soul and excites its desire to be united with the Godhead in love.

> 3 Eager for thee I ask and pant,
>   So strong the principle divine
>   Carries me out with sweet constraint,
>   Till all my hallowed soul be thine:
>   Plunged in the Godhead's deepest sea,
>   And lost in thy immensity.

There is often in Charles Wesley this recognition of God's immensity and our corresponding experience of vertigo, which he typically signals, as he does here, with the word "lost." The believer recognizes his own finitude and the infinitude of God for which he is made. It is the very deepest of seas, and even as one enters in, one is lost. One is disoriented by the vastness of the divine life and the greatness of divine love. It is thus that Wesley's poetry always rises, in the end, to leave the singer "lost in wonder, love, and praise," whether he is contemplating nature or grace.

Modern forms of thought and practice treated more and more of the pro-

---

19. John Wesley, *Collection of Hymns*, 532 (hymn #363). The hymn is titled "Hymn to the Holy Ghost."

cesses of the natural world as autonomous, and although most leading thinkers of the period would still have acknowledged the divine origin of the world, natural philosophy increasingly explained the world without invoking supernatural agency, just as moral philosophy did likewise with human nature. There are therefore three important affirmations in Charles Wesley's poetry that run counter to the expectations we might have of a devotion shaped by its context in the early modern period of Enlightenment. First, created being was contingent upon its divine author, not autonomous. Second, created being was oriented toward final causes beyond itself, destined as it was for a divine end. Yet, third, divine being was infinite, far surpassing comparison to created being, and beyond the power of human telling. As Charles Wesley wrote elsewhere in adoration of the Holy Trinity:

> Beyond our utmost thought,
>   And reason's proudest flight,
> We comprehend Him not,
>   Nor grasp the Infinite,
> But worship in the Mystic Three
> One God to all eternity.[20]

Jason Vickers makes the important point that Charles Wesley approached the mystery of the Godhead not by way of speculation, as with so much of the natural theology of the period, but by way of ontological affirmation in worship. Early in the eighteenth century, as fierce theological battles were fought between the orthodox party in the Church of England and the Deists over the nature of God, the orthodox sought to provide a rational account of personhood in God that would not entail a belief in three distinct gods. In this debate, the orthodox apologists gained some victories, but in the process theology became sterile in losing touch with its sources in doxology. Or, as Vickers puts it in contemporary terms, all the focus was upon providing a rational defense of the immanent Trinity, without reference to the economic Trinity. Vickers writes, "Charles's doctrine of the Trinity is primarily, if not exclusively, concerned with the divine economy, i.e., with the Holy Spirit's coming to dwell in us so that we might become 'partakers of the divine nature', and not with demonstrating that a doctrine of the immanent Trinity was compatible with or confirmable by unaided human reason."[21] I think something similar could be said about how

20. Charles Wesley, *Hymns on the Trinity* (Bristol, 1767), 123–24 (hymn #41).
21. Jason E. Vickers, "Charles Wesley and the Revival of the Doctrine of the Trinity: A Methodist Contribution to Modern Theology," in Newport and Campbell, eds., *Charles Wesley*, 288.

Wesley approached the mystery of creation itself as sustained by the life of God. He approached this cosmological mystery by way of doxology.

The Form of Charles Wesley's Witness

In his hymns Charles Wesley was not directly entering into late medieval debates about universals or the analogy of being, but the language of worship and devotion that he employed still did a kind of metaphysical work. Charles, like his brother, rejoiced in what some have called the moderate Enlightenment, marveling at the order of the natural world revealed by experimental science and mathematics as confirmation of the truths of revelation. Yet he believed that divine revelation went far beyond what natural reason could infer from natural phenomena. The form of Charles Wesley's witness was therefore important. One of the leading thinkers of the Enlightenment in France, a co-editor of the *Encylopédie*, Jean d'Alembert, described the mathematical basis of all science as "the art of reducing." This was the true "systematic spirit," or what one of d'Alembert's contemporaries called "*l'esprit géometrique*" or "the quantifying spirit." The secretary of the Paris Academy of Sciences, Bernard le Bovier de Fontenelle, argued that mathematics could improve whatsoever it touched: "A work on ethics, politics, criticism, and, perhaps, even rhetoric will be better, other things being equal, if done by a geometer."[22] Wesley was no geometer. The form of Wesley's response to creation and redemption was, in contrast, nonreductionist and personal. Although he could appreciate, like his brother, advances in scientific discovery and mechanical invention, and, no doubt, mathematics, he wrote not in a "quantifying spirit," but in a spirit of poetry and prayer. This was the only proper response to a world in which the divine person of the Holy Spirit was present.

Poetry is perhaps the most nonreductionist form of language possible. Wesley was a master of a large number of meters and poetical devices, and his diction was exact, even as he explored theological paradoxes and mysteries that took him to the edge of language. Indeed, several literary critics acknowledge the power of his poetics and the extent of his achievement as an Augustan poet in his own right. For example, Donald Davie, an English poet and critic, writes about Wesley's art, impressed by the strength of diction and a kind of pleasing austerity that chastens even as it delights. "It is obvious that Wesley's

---

22. Quoted in J. L. Heilbron, "Introductory Essay," in *The Quantifying Spirit in the 18th Century*, ed. Tore Frängsmyr, J. L. Heilbron, and Robin E. Rider (Berkeley: University of California Press, 1990), 1.

verse exhibits these virtues because it is throughout doctrinal, that is, didactic." His hymns are not, like most later hymns, geysers of warm "feeling." And yet, heaven knows, the "feeling is there."[23] This combination of doctrine and feeling is something Davie admires. With regard to the "feeling" in Wesley's hymns, he says, "We respect its integrity and we take its force just because it is not offered in isolation but together with its occasion, an occasion grasped and presented with keen and sinewy intelligence."[24] Moreover, this intelligence is not artificial or extrinsic to the poetry. "Intelligence comes into the poetry of this period not as contraband, smuggled into a conceit as 'ingenuity,' or intangibly as ironical tone, but straightforward and didactic. And the intellectual strength does not desiccate the emotions but gives to them validity and force."[25] Wesley's response to the reductions of the Enlightenment was not therefore simply romantic or emotional. It was, instead, to cultivate the response of the whole person, intellectually and emotionally, to the God of the Scriptures who remained present in the natural world as its creator and redeemer, "who doth through both creations shine, / the God of nature and of grace."[26]

If poetry is nonreductionist, so also is prayer. Throughout his poem "Author of every work divine," Wesley does not simply describe the Spirit's work, but he addresses the Spirit personally in an encomium of praise. Like the philosophical work that Augustine did in Book X of the *Confessions*, the metaphysical affirmations that Charles Wesley made in the hymn "Author of every work divine" were made, altogether typically, in the form of prayer in a direct address to the third person of the Trinity. Just as Augustine looked around at all he could see, and everything seemed to speak to him, announcing its own contingency, saying, "We did not make ourselves, but he who abides forever made us," so also the prayerful disposition of Charles Wesley, hymning the Holy Spirit, does the same.

Again, Reginald Ward has described the ways in which something similar could be observed among the continental Pietists. John Wesley published one of Gerhard Tersteegen's hymns that began, "Lo, God is here! Let us adore, / And own how dreadful is this place!" This simple invocation of God's presence was replete with metaphysical implications. As Ward says with characteristic terseness, "It perfectly encapsulates Tersteegen's reply to both the early Enlightenment which seemed to be exiling God from his universe, and the physico-

---

23. Davie, "Classicism of Wesley," 79.
24. Ibid.
25. Ibid.
26. Charles Wesley, *Hymns of Petition and Thanksgiving for the Promise of the Father* (London, 1746), 31–32 (hymn #28).

theologians who could only bring Him back at the end of a long argument."[27] A simple hymn turns out to have great intellectual significance in its cultural moment. It is like the devout poet George Herbert praying, "Teach me, my God and King, in all things thee to see." The pure in heart do not simply see God; they see God in everything. Thus, Charles Wesley saw planets and stars "depending" in golden chains from the Spirit. Piety clearly had metaphysical implications for him, as for Tersteegen and Herbert. It was thus that he bore his witness and proclaimed these implications in poetry and prayer during the period of Europe's Enlightenment as familiar modern forms of thought and practice were emerging. His Christian identity was not reductionist; it was hymnic. Everything, when viewed aright, was to rise to "wonder, love, and praise."

27. Ward, *Early Evangelicalism*, 59.

Chapter 34

Christina Rossetti: Identity in the Communion of Saints

Elizabeth Ludlow

Surveying the earliest narratives of Christian martyrdom, Rowan Williams emphasizes the extent to which the language of the "church" was problematic for an imperial system that claimed "to be the ultimate source of holy and legitimate power." Against this system, he writes, "the story of the Christian tried and executed by the imperial power is the most dramatic but also the simplest possible demonstration of what 'church' means—and so of what holy power looks like and what is involved in claiming a different sort of citizenship."[1] In what follows, I discuss Christina Rossetti's engagement with narratives of Christian citizenship and suggest how she foregrounds martyrdom as a revelation of God's church on earth. I argue that, at a time when the martyrs of the ancient and medieval world were an object of religious and literary scrutiny, Rossetti's recognition that "one who cannot be martyr in deed may yet be martyr in will" forms the root of her understanding of the foundation of Christian identity.[2] Registering how her writing is inextricable from worship practices, I consider how her poetry conveys an appreciation of the Eucharist as the place where Christian identity is expressed most visibly. Moreover, my discussion reveals her ongoing concern with expressing the identity of Christians as "strangers and pilgrims" (1 Pet 2:11) who, joining with the saints gone before, maintain a claim to a different—heavenly—citizenship.

1. Rowan Williams, *Why Study the Past? The Quest for the Historical Church* (Grand Rapids: Eerdmans, 2005), 34.

2. Christina Rossetti, *The Face of the Deep: A Devotional Commentary on the Apocalypse* (London: SPCK, 1893), 465.

Christina Rossetti and Tractarian Worship

Christina Rossetti (1830–1894) was the author of hundreds of poems, six volumes of devotional prose, and a number of short stories. Born in London as the youngest of four siblings in a literary family of Italian origin, she grew up immersed in conversations about art and aesthetics. In 1848, when she was eighteen, her brothers, Dante Gabriel and William Michael were involved in founding the Pre-Raphaelite Brotherhood, a movement that sought to reform aesthetic sensibility. While the Brotherhood wanted to distance themselves from "the particular movements in the religious world," the female members of the Rossetti household remained devout Anglicans.[3] Rossetti began attending the newly established Christ-Church in Albany Street as a twelve-year-old with her mother and her sister Maria, who would eventually join an Anglican Sisterhood. Situated at the heart of the Oxford Movement in London, it witnessed the changes that accompanied the most turbulent years of Tractarianism. William Dodsworth, the perpetual curate from 1837 until his secession to Roman Catholicism in 1850, was among the first of the clergy to promote full adherence to the doctrines set out by Tractarian leaders John Henry Newman, John Keble, and Edward Pusey. In an account of the church in its early days, Henry W. Burrows describes William Dodsworth's "zealous earnestness" and outlines the changes that he initiated; many involved introducing aspects of ritualism that were countercultural, if not controversial, to an early Victorian audience.[4] These included a concern with liturgical symbolism, a fuller appreciation of the Real Presence, and a reorientation towards the communion table.

In his book, *Victorian Devotional Poetry: The Tractarian Mode*, G. B. Tennyson highlights the central place of poetry for the Tractarians and suggests how the verse of the leaders was "as much [a] cause and symptom" of the Oxford Movement as a result.[5] Of the many Tractarian anthologies and collections that were published during the first phase of the Oxford Movement's activity, John Keble's *The Christian Year* (1827) was the most widely read. Edward Pusey records that one hundred and nine editions were in existence by the

3. William Michael Rossetti, "Preface," in *The Germ: Thoughts Towards Nature in Poetry, Literature and Art. Being a Facsimile Reprint of the Literary Organ of the Pre-Raphaelite Brotherhood, published in 1850* (London: Elliot Stock, 1895), 1:134. For more on the connection between the Pre-Raphaelites and religious concerns, see my chapter, "Christina Rossetti and the Pre-Raphaelites," in *The Oxford Handbook to the Oxford Movement*, ed. Jonathan Baker, Peter Nockles, and James Pereiro (Oxford: Oxford University Press, 2015).

4. Henry W. Burrows, *The Half-Century of Christ Church* (London: Skeffington & Son, 1887), 14.

5. G. B. Tennyson, *Victorian Devotional Poetry: The Tractarian Mode* (Cambridge: Harvard University Press, 1981), 8.

end of 1867, the year following Keble's death.[6] Commenting on its status as a "runaway bestseller," F. Elizabeth Gray draws attention to the fact that, "as the nineteenth-century—and the literary influence of Tractarianism—progressed, Keble himself became a poetic Father for countless women poets, a guarantor of the moral correctness of that poetry fashioned closely after his."[7] Rossetti was able to move a step further than many of Keble's other poetic daughters by virtue of the fact she could draw from the medieval breviaries upon which the Prayer Book was based and which many, including her sister Maria, were translating. Through this practice, she extends rather than imitates Keble's emphasis on disciplined pilgrimage and encourages a renewed understanding of what it means to belong to the Communion of Saints.

Though, as Linda K. Hughes writes, "Rossetti could not directly influence public worship as Keble did, she separated 'Devotional Pieces' from other poems in her 1862 and 1866 volumes, cordoning off poetic space to which readers could bring a worshipful orientation."[8] Rossetti remained acutely aware of the responsibility of guiding readers in their worship and, in her letters and devotional prose, she expresses a concern with responding to her divinely ordained "duty."[9] Recognizing that true worship involves a willingness to become a "martyr in will," she increasingly sought to bring readers to a "worshipful orientation" by illuminating the connection between holy aspiration, vocation, and renunciation. Drawing on the figures of liturgy and song, her poetry emphasizes the vitality of the Communion of the Saints through the past, present, and future. Repeatedly, she envisages the interface between the harmonious worship of the redeemed through eternity and the chanting of the psalms on earth.

Rossetti wrote "Martyrs' Song" in March 1863. It was first published two years later by the Tractarian writer and anthologist Orpy Shiply in *Lyra Mystica: Hymns and Verses on Sacred Subjects, Ancient and Modern* (1865) and was subsequently incorporated into the devotional sequence that concludes Rossetti's second volume, *The Prince's Progress and Other Poems* (1866). The poem offers a neat example of how Rossetti contributed to the Tractarian sacramental vision and encouraged worshippers, as "strangers and pilgrims," to push beyond the boundaries of lived experience. The first stanza, which echoes biblical promises, has the martyrs of Christ as its collective speakers:

6. Edward Pusey, ed., "Introduction," in *Occasional Papers and Reviews by John Keble, MA* (Oxford and London: James Parker & Co, 1877), v–xxii (viii).

7. F. Elizabeth Gray, "'Syren Strains': Victorian Women's Devotional Poetry and John Keble's *The Christian Year*," *Victorian Poetry* 44, no. 1 (2006): 61–76 (63).

8. Linda Hughes, *The Cambridge Introduction to Victorian Poetry* (Cambridge: Cambridge University Press, 2010), 150.

9. For example, see Christina Rossetti, *Time Flies: A Reading Diary* (London: SPCK, 1885), 22.

We meet in joy, tho' we part in sorrow;
We part tonight, but we meet tomorrow.
Be it flood or blood the path that's trod,
All the same it leads home to God:
Be it furnace fire voluminous,
One like God's Son will walk with us.[10] (1–6)

Enacting the comforting hope of reunion by bracketing the "sorrow" of martyrdom within a chiasmic framework, the first two lines contain the pain of parting through death. It is not, however, until the end of the entire poem, when this focus has been redirected *away* from a profane desire to restore earthly relationships and *towards* an expression of holy aspiration, that this pain is fully overcome.

Towards the end of "Martyrs' Song," the image of finding "safety within the Veil and the Ark" provides a reconception of personhood (52). This reconception enacts the movement from observation to participation: from the old understanding of the redeemed as "these that glow from afar" (7), to a new recognition of one's own part in the Communion of Saints. Through the poem, Rossetti draws on the invitation in Hebrews for believers to "draw near" to God in recognition of the "new and living way" that Jesus "hath consecrated for us, through the veil, that is to say, his flesh" (Heb 10:22, 20). By focusing on the ultimate promise of "safety within . . . the Ark" (53), Rossetti forges an understanding of the self as both a part of the Ark of the new Covenant *and* a part of the typologically realized Noah's ark. Incorporating into the poem references to the "flood" (4, 58), the "bar" (8), and the "Red Sea" (46), she recalls the protection offered by Noah. In line with her concern to define personhood within the Communion of Saints, she extends the traditional typological association between Noah and Christ and insistently links the dove of Genesis 8 with the Christian. In the final verse, God's hold of the faltering dove-like pilgrim is imagined and an appropriate response of adoration and praise is articulated:

God the Father we will adore,
In Jesus' Name, now and evermore:
God the Son we will love and thank
In this flood and on the further bank:
God the Holy Ghost we will praise,

10. *Christina Rossetti: The Complete Poems*, ed. Rebecca W. Crump, with notes and introduction by Betty S. Flowers (London: Penguin, 2001), 176–78. All subsequent references will be given parenthetically in the text as *CP*, followed by page number.

In Jesus' Name thro' endless days:
God Almighty, God Three in One,
God Almighty, God alone. (55–62)

This concluding declaration expresses the movement that the poem makes towards participation with the worshipping multitudes we read of in Revelation 6 and 7, who wait for the coming of the kingdom. The thrice repeated "we will" (55, 57, 59) not only implies participation with them in the Trinity but also echoes the prayer-book response, the "I will," of the baptismal candidate. The fact that "Martyrs' Song," with this final declaration of praise, was incorporated into several key anthologies and devotional manuals points to the part Rossetti played in informing and disseminating Anglo-Catholic theology and in forging among devotional readers a renewed understanding of their identity as worshippers among the larger body of Christ.

The Un-Selfing of the Martyr

For Christians, to belong to the Communion of Saints means to conform oneself to the model of Christ crucified. In this sense, martyrdom is not an isolated episode but comes, as Rowan Williams writes, "as the natural culmination of a far more prosaic process of un-selfing."[11] It nonetheless remains "a climax . . . the final stamping upon the human coinage of the likeness of God in Christ."[12] In his discussion of Ignatius of Antioch, who lived and died in conformity to Jesus crucified, Williams comments on how the "the cross of Jesus and the martyr's identification with it are both revelation and actualization of the truth."[13] From her earliest collections, by incorporating poems about early church martyrs among poems about fictional and historical women, Rossetti foregrounds the revelation that the martyrdom brings in attesting to the values of a radically different kingdom.

In "The Martyr," a poem that she includes towards the end of her 1847 collection *Verses*—the booklet of poetry that her maternal grandfather arranged to have printed with a private press—Rossetti traces the emotion of a "young and tender" believer moments before death (*CP*, 639–41: 3). The moment of her death is couched in the language of espousal:

---

11. Rowan Williams, *The Wound of Knowledge: Christian Spirituality from the New Testament to St John of the Cross*, 2nd rev. ed. (London: Darton, Longman & Todd, 1990), 27.

12. Ibid.

13. Ibid., 28.

> Quickened with a fire
> Of sublime desire,
> She looked up to Heaven, and she cried aloud,
> "Death, I do entreat thee,
> Come! I go to meet thee;
> Wrap me in the whiteness of a virgin shroud." (31–36)

The fire that brings the martyr's earthly life to a close recalls the biblical associations of fire with God's blessing (e.g., Ps 104:4; Isa 10:17; Acts 2:3). Situated towards the end of the collection, the poem extends Rossetti's other explorations of female subjectivity. In addition to poems focused on the Greek poet Sappho and various women from late eighteenth- and early nineteenth-century fiction, the booklet contains a memorial poem for Lady Isabella Howard, the young noblewoman who had been a pupil of Rossetti's maternal aunt. Rossetti's refusal to idealize ancient and medieval martyrs as figures far removed from the lived experience of contemporary individuals continues through her subsequent volumes of poetry. Her recognition is that all are joined in the a-temporal space of the Communion of Saints, which stands apart from chronological history.

In the sense that martyrdom witnesses to the tensions between the historical and temporal age and "the [eternal] age to come," Williams comments on the process through which, under a baptized emperor, monasticism came to be understood as "a kind of substitute for martyrdom."[14] In "The Convent Threshold," a narrative poem she includes in her first published volume, *Goblin Market and Other Poems* (1862), Rossetti forges a link between the blood martyr and the monastic. Rather than recount the activity of the newly established Anglo-Catholic convents with which she was familiar, Rossetti repeatedly explores the death-in-life experience of women who choose the immured and contemplative life. As Diane D'Amico explains, this choice is indicative of her concern with articulating the spiritual struggles that occur in "looking forward beyond this life and beyond the end of time."[15]

Through "The Convent Threshold," Rossetti has the speaker address her lover and persuade him to look beyond the fleetingness of the world. While his "eyes look earthward," hers "look up" (*CP*, 55–59: 17). What she sees is the place where the "righteous" eat, rest, and worship with the angels. After contemplating the blessing they enjoy, she turns to the pain of their martyrdom:

14. Ibid., 103.

15. Diane D'Amico, *Christina Rossetti: Faith, Gender and Time* (Baton Rouge: Louisiana State University Press, 1999), 52.

> They bore the Cross, they drained the cup,
> Racked, roasted, crushed, wrenched limb from limb,
> They the offscouring of the world:
> The heaven of starry heavens unfurled,
> The sun before their face is dim. (25–29)

In these lines, Rossetti combines a number of Bible references with an unflinching acknowledgement of execution methods faced by the early church martyrs. In the gospel accounts of the passion, Jesus is described "bearing his cross" to Golgotha (John 19:17) and drinking from the "cup" of suffering that, according to Isaiah, represents God's wrath and "fury" (Matt 26:42; Isa 51:17). Before his crucifixion, he had warned his disciples that they could expect to drink from this same cup (Matt 20:23; Mark 10:39). In his letter to the Corinthian church, Paul attests to the reality of their ongoing suffering and describes how they must suffer persecution and endure the humiliation of being "made as the filth of the world [and] the offscouring of all things" (1 Cor 4:13). By associating herself with those who, after the pattern of the first Christian martyr, St. Stephen, are strengthened in their moment of anguish by a vision of "the heaven of starry heavens," the speaker of "The Convent Threshold" draws on the long history of connecting the immured religious life with martyrdom. Situating herself in a place of death-in-life, she tells her lover that her face is "gone before; It tarries veiled in paradise" (139–40). The disparity that she establishes between herself and her lover is heightened by the juxtaposition between the different temporalities of earth and heaven.

In "From House to Home," which Rossetti wrote five months after "The Convent Threshold," the choice to bear the cross and drain the cup of suffering is explored through the narrative of a female speaker who moves away from the worldly pleasures that she had once relied upon and towards incorporation into the Communion of Saints. As she comments at the end of the poem, her experiences have left her determined to "pluck down" the house of lies in which she once trusted and to rebuild a true castle "in a distant place" (*CP*, 76–82: 207–8).

After describing her luxurious "pleasure place," the poem's speaker recounts how, when she refused to follow her divine companion, her joy turned to despair. Swooning in agony after the failure of her search, she experienced a death-trance where she was surrounded by "spheres and spirits" (106) who discuss her fate. Recognizing her as a "sister" (107), they eventually prepare her to "live again" (111) and, as means of strengthening, offer her a vision of her spiritual double. Sustained in her sorrow by a "chain of living links" that is "anchored fast in heaven" (138–40), this woman demonstrates the possibility of holding firm while undergoing intense suffering.

> She bled and wept, yet did not shrink; her strength
> > Was strung up until daybreak of delight:
> She measured measureless sorrow toward its length,
> > And breadth, and depth, and height. (133–36)

This vision of the suffering woman reveals the possibility of drawing on Christ's strength and of moving from intense suffering through to glory. It recalls two episodes in John Henry Newman's novel *Callista: A Tale of the Third Century* (1855).[16] The first is when the eponymous heroine, a Greek image-maker living in Sicca, North Africa, in AD 250, tells her suitor, Agellius, about a dream a Christian slave of hers, Chione, had before she died. In this dream, Chione is taken by a company of "bright shades" to the Virgin Mary, who gives her flowers to symbolize love, chastity, death, and resurrection.[17] At the end of the novel, another dream—this time Callista's own—makes sense of this first. In this dream, she sees a "well-known face, only glorified."

> And when she had come close to this gracious figure, there was a fresh change. The face, the features were the same; but the light of Divinity now seemed to beam through them . . . there was a crown of another fashion than the Lady's round about it, made of what looked like thorns. And the palms of the hands were spread out . . . and there were marks of wounds in them.[18]

By drawing towards the wounds, Callista begins her journey into the company of heavenly saints: a journey that would find its completion in her identification with Christ's passion through martyrdom. In "From House to Home," Rossetti's speaker steps toward the subject of her dream vision in a similar move of identification when she consents to tread on thorns and drink from the cup of suffering that is made "sweet" (209–10)—in other words, when she claims citizenship among the Communion of Saints.

As Callista's dream and the vision of "From House to Home" reveals, renouncing the world for citizenship in heaven involves a repudiation of bounded individuality. As a constitutive part of Christian spirituality in the 1850s, the discourse of martyrdom throws a question mark over what personhood means. The broadly Catholic recognition of the vital presence of the martyrs of the early

---

16. For a discussion of the connection between Rossetti and Newman, see Elizabeth Ludlow, *Christina Rossetti and the Bible: Waiting with the Saints* (London: Bloomsbury Academic, 2014), 28–30.

17. John Henry Newman, *Callista: A Tale of the Third Century* (London: Longman, Green & Co., 1904), 126.

18. Ibid., 356.

church reveals the tension between the temporal and the eternal and under-lines the message that, while they might not have the opportunity of becoming a blood martyr, every Christian is called to be a "martyr in will" and to find their identity in the crucified body of Christ. Thus, in her unpublished poem, "A Martyr" (1856), which recounts an early martyrdom, Rossetti can pose the direct challenge, "Will you follow the track that she trod, / Will you tread in her footsteps, my friend?" (*CP*, 782–83: 19–20). As the paragraphs below explain, Rossetti perceived that one way of following in the footsteps of the martyrs, and of joining with them in worship, is through participation in the Eucharist.

Participating in the Eucharist

Rossetti participated in Holy Communion twice a week. Considering that this meant she was engaged with the liturgy of the service upward of three thousand times in her life, Karen Dieleman suggests the inevitable effect on her religious imagination. Describing the dynamics of the liturgy outlined in the prayer book, she stresses how the "threefold movement [from Word to Sacrament] of the historic liturgy . . . lent itself to the possibility of viewing Communion as the chief end of the service, the point toward which all other elements led."[19] Extending the discussion of Rossetti's engagement with the doctrine of the Real Presence that I offer in *Christina Rossetti and the Bible*, I suggest here how her vision of the Eucharist points to an awareness of what it means to conform to the pattern of Christ crucified and to find one's place in the Communion of Saints.[20]

For the church from its earliest days to the present, the Eucharist is the site where fellowship with Christ and with the church, as the "body of Christ," is expressed most visibly. In his hugely popular novel *Fabiola, Or The Church of the Catacombs* (1854), Cardinal Nicholas Wiseman writes of the active communion with the saints that the Eucharist brings.[21]

> We need not remind our readers that the office then performed was essen-tially, and in many details the same as they daily witness at the Catholic altar.

19. Karen Dieleman, *Religious Imaginaries: The Liturgical and Poetic Practices of Elizabeth Barrett Browning, Christina Rossetti and Adelaide Proctor* (Athens, OH: Ohio University Press, 2012), 103.

20. Ludlow, *Christina Rossetti*, 41–44.

21. For more on the popularity and readership of *Fabiola* see Margaret Maison, *Search Your Soul, Eustace: A Survey of the Religious Novel in the Victorian Age* (London: Sheed & Ward, 1961), 157.

> Not only was it considered, as now, to be the Sacrifice of Our Lord's Body and Blood, not only were the oblation, the consecration, the communion alike, but many of the prayers were identical.[22]

By participating in the feast, Wiseman implies, readers are keeping the martyr's protest alive and identifying with the circularity of the liturgical calendar rather than with the secular model of history as progression. As an Anglo-Catholic, Rossetti shared the broadly Catholic concern with the individual joining her prayers to the worship of the saints who had gone before. As such, her poems repeatedly recall the "cloud of witnesses," which the writer of the letter to the Hebrews speaks of as surrounding and encouraging the believer (Heb 12:1).

Remembering the Old Testament saints who refused "deliverance; that they might obtain a better resurrection," the writer of the book of Hebrews affirms the importance of godly obedience (Heb 11:35). In her poem "A Better Resurrection," which she wrote in 1857 and included among the "devotional pieces" in *Goblin Market and Other Poems*, Rossetti reflects on what it means to suffer with and for Christ. After expressing the complete alienation of finding that her life is empty, "like a faded leaf" (*CP*, 62: 9), she finds hope in the possibility of being reconstituted by and in Christ:

> My life is like a broken bowl,
> A broken bowl that cannot hold
> One drop of water for my soul
> Or cordial in the searching cold;
> Cast in the fire the perished thing,
> Melt and remould it, till it be
> A royal cup for Him my King:
> O Jesus, drink of me. (17–24)

The speaker's recognition of her own brokenness and alienation can best be understood in the context of the economy of martyrdom. After having described her life through the imagery of purgation: a "faded leaf" (9), "a husk" (10), and "a frozen thing" (12), she conveys the radical nature of being consumed by Christ and points to the rejection that this will involve. Karl Rahner defines martyrdom as "Christian death in acceptance of the death of Christ" and writes of how it "places man completely at the disposal of God, radically unifying an act of love with the act of being taken from oneself in confrontation with man's

---

22. Nicholas Wiseman, *Fabiola, Or the Church of the Catacombs* (New York: Benziger Brothers, 1886), 336.

incomprehensible, but very powerful denial of the love revealed by God."[23] In terms of these definitions, the voluntary blindness and alienation of Rossetti's speaker can be understood as indicative of the vindication of another citizenship: one that is incomprehensible from a worldly perspective. By emphasizing how Christ surpasses and completely overrides the speaker's strength, Rossetti reveals the possibility of finding one's identity in the nexus where God's power meets human weakness. As the imagery of the communion chalice in the final verse indicates, this nexus is best understood in terms of the Eucharist.

To conclude, I wish to reinforce the connection that Rossetti forges between poetry and worship. "It may be," she writes in her sonnet sequence *Later Life: A Double Sonnet of Sonnets,* that if we could "look with seeing eyes"—or with sacramental vision—we would perceive that the "spot we stand on is a Paradise" (*CP*, 346–58: Sonnet 10, 2–3):

> Where dead have come to life and lost been found,
> Where Faith has triumphed, Martyrdom been crowned,
>   Where fools have foiled the wisdom of the wise;
>   From this same spot the dust of saints may rise,
> And the King's prisoners come to light unbound. (4–8)

Through the witness of the martyrs who have renounced earthly citizenship for heaven, a different temporality comes into view: one where death does not exist and all identity is centered around and in Christ. In capturing the glimpse of the eternal that becomes visible through their lives and deaths, and through the worship of believers around the Communion table, Rossetti's poetry offers a challenge that carries a particular resonance at a time when individuality is prioritized over community.

23. Karl Rahner, ed., *Encyclopedia of Theology: A Concise Sacramentum Mundi* (London: Burns & Oates, 1975), 938.

Chapter 35

Blaise Pascal: Perpetual Contemporary

RICHARD V. HORNER

"Quelquefois difficile, toujours actuel."[1]

A month after Pascal's death, the Jansenist theologian Pierre Nicole lamented the fact that Blaise Pascal would be little known to posterity. Thankfully, Nicole proved to be wrong. Not only do we know Pascal today, but his fame has grown with the passing decades and centuries. Nicole's comment, however, should give us pause. Why do we know Pascal? Nicole was probably not wrong to think that Pascal's reputation would not endure. Dying at age thirty-nine, Pascal passed away all too young, and while he had published some significant contributions in the fields of science, mathematics, and criticism, there was no reason to think those contributions would last. Science would march on, leaving Pascal's contributions as footnotes to the work of the more famous scientists who came before and after, and the story to which Pascal's *Provincial Letters* contributed did not turn out well for anyone. At the time of his death, moreover, Pascal's most mature and potentially enduring work remained in disarray—a collection of unpublished scribblings. Why, then, do we know him today? Why has Pascal endured, and how is it that he remains *toujours actuel*, perpetually contemporary?

One answer to this question lies in the happy fact that his friends and family did not allow his disorganized scribblings to remain unpublished. Though

1. These words conclude Michel Le Guern's introduction to Pascal's *Oeuvres complètes*: "*La rencontre du lecteur avec ses écrits établit un véritable dialogue, quelquefois difficile, toujours actuel.*" "The encounter of the reader with [Pascal's] writings establishes a genuine dialogue, sometimes difficult, always current." Michel Le Guern, "Introduction," Blaise Pascal, *Oeuvres complètes* (Paris: Gallimard, 1998), xxxii.

it took several years, and though the initial publication did not capture the full richness of Pascal's thoughts, his family and friends did make it possible for posterity to learn what Pascal was thinking in the final years of his life. Published under the title of *Les Pensées de M. Pascal*—the sort of nondescript title that should have guaranteed failure—Pascal's thoughts caught the attention of his own generation and of those that followed. One of those rare books whose title is almost never translated, we know it simply as the *Pensées*, and it has everything to do with why we know their author today. Pascal's *Pensées* continues to stand as one of the most thought-provoking books the modern era has produced. While the rediscovery of the manuscript in the middle of the nineteenth century has led to more complete, better-organized versions of the *Pensées*, they have never lost their aphoristic, unfinished character. The *Pensées* do not come with a beginning or an ending, nor do they reveal an obvious flow of ideas. For the most part, they give us Pascal's thoughts as they came to him. As a result, the overall argument remains puzzling and open to interpretation, and so do many individual thoughts. Far from being a liability, however, the unfinished character of the book and its thoughts only draws the reader in all the more powerfully. The style itself invites conversation. "I will write down my thoughts here as they come and in a perhaps not aimless confusion," Pascal admits. "This is the true order and it will always show my aim by its very disorder. I should be honouring my subject too much if I treated it in order, since I am trying to show that it is incapable of it" (532).[2] Little wonder that such unedited honesty would draw readers into a conversation that is sometimes difficult but always intriguing.

While the aphoristic style and the unfinished character of Pascal's thoughts have played a role in drawing attention to the *Pensées*, the enduring power of the book lies not in its style but in its author and in the substance of his thoughts. It is the thinker behind the thoughts who fascinates us, and when the *Pensées* are placed alongside Pascal's works on math and science, his *Provincial Letters*, his personal letters, his theological works, his design for the arithmetical machine, and his plans for the public carriage service, they reveal an intriguing individual. His writings reveal Pascal to be many things: student, mathematician, scientist, inventor, theologian, biblical scholar, philosopher, amateur psychologist, public servant, critic, essayist, conversationalist, and poet, while also being a dutiful Catholic, loving son, and devoted brother and friend. Those who have studied him have struggled to capture his identity or sum him up. The results

---

2. References to Pascal's *Pensées* will be inserted in the text in parentheses according to the numbering of Lafuma and as they appear in Pascal, *Pensées*, trans. A. J. Krailsheimer (New York: Penguin Classics, 1966).

have varied widely. His sister exalted him as a saint, Paul Valéry described him as a "French Jansenist Hamlet," and William Barrett concluded emphatically, "Pascal *is* an existentialist." Harold Bloom belittles him as a polemicist and "ironic quietist," while Jean Mesnard admires him as a mathematician and scientist but most centrally as a poet. Most have captured him in conflicted or contradictory ways. Voltaire famously identified him as a "sublime misanthrope"; Chateaubriand called him "a slanderer who had genius"; Victor Cousin complained that Pascal combined "boundless skepticism with convulsive piety"; and T. S. Eliot portrayed him as "a man of the world among ascetics and an ascetic among men of the world."

As if this mix of roles and reputations were not enough to intrigue us, Pascal fascinates still further by hiding behind several pseudonyms. Most famously, he wrote as Louis de Montalte, author of the *Provincial Letters*. Less famously, when submitting the winning entry in a mathematical contest of his own making, he hid behind the name of Amos Dettonville, and much more quietly, Pascal wrote under the name of Salomon de Tultie, a pseudonym that appears in the background of the *Pensées*. The fact that each is an anagram of the others affirms Pascal's cleverness, but these false identities reveal yet another reason why he has always fascinated his readers. His writings both expose and hide him. As Ben Rogers notes, "We know little about Pascal. We also know a great deal about Pascal. We know little [because] Pascal never wrote about himself or his life in any detail." And yet, "We know a great deal about him" because his writings "tell us much about his own view of the world."[3] Nowhere is this truer than in the *Pensées*. Their raw, unedited character provides a genuine window into the man while also leaving endless, unanswered questions as to just who Pascal was or what he was thinking. We will never stop wondering what Pascal might have meant, or what he might have said, if only he had been able to finish his thought. It is not only Pascal's God that remains both accessible and hidden in Pascal's writings.

Mysterious polymath though he may be, Pascal's most central identity lies finally in Jesus Christ. Blaise Pascal was born a Christian and remained one throughout his life. Though he lost his mother at age three, Blaise grew up in the Church and under the tutelage of a father who carefully orchestrated his children's education, giving priority to the Bible and the writings of the Church Fathers. The doctrines of grace and the call to a life devoted to Christ were present from the beginning, but Blaise's faith does seem to have sprung to life personally after he moved with his father and sisters from Paris to Rouen in Normandy in

3. Ben Rogers, "Pascal's Life and Times," in *The Cambridge Companion to Pascal*, ed. Nicholas Hammond (Cambridge: Cambridge University Press, 2003), 4.

his late teens. There, while still in his early twenties, he responded to the Jansenist call to total devotion, and in the words of his sister, Pascal's "respect for the religion in which he had been raised as a child was changed into an ardent and tender love for all the truths of the faith."[4] This episode is often described as his first conversion, but a second, better-known conversion followed nearly a decade later and took him to a much deeper place in his Christian identity. A two-year period of worldliness, during which he admitted to a dryness of soul and dissatisfaction and in which he gave himself to the world of Parisian salons and high society more than his sisters found acceptable, came to an end when the "night of fire" brought him out of his malaise.

> From about half past ten in the evening until half past midnight.
>> Fire
> "God of Abraham, God of Isaac, God of Jacob," not of philosophers and
>> scholars.
> Certainty, certainty, heartfelt, joy, peace.
> God of Jesus Christ.
> God of Jesus Christ.
> *My God and your God.*
> [...]
> "And this is life eternal, that they might know thee, the only true God, and
>> Jesus Christ
> whom thou hast sent."
> Jesus Christ.
> Jesus Christ [...]

Dated Monday, November 23, 1654, these words appear in Pascal's "Memorial" to the moment that confirmed his most central identity and took him deeper into that identity than ever before.

While it would be wrong to think of this episode as Pascal's conversion to Christ, it would also be wrong to underestimate its significance in shaping Pascal's life and thought in the final eight years of his life. The night of fire brought a deepened sense of the reality of the living Christ and fueled Pascal's work. As a result, he wrote prolifically in the final eight years of his life in ways that drew on all his identities: student of life, experimental scientist, rigorous mathematician, amateur psychologist, biblical scholar, theologian, philosopher, critic, inventor, public servant, poet, conversationalist, and most centrally, Christian. While the night of fire was one of great emotion that set his heart ablaze, it clearly set his

---

4. Gilberte Périer, *La Vie de Monsieur Pascal* (Paris: La Table Ronde, 1994), 41.

mind on fire as well and brought his observational powers as an experimental scientist and his careful reasoning as a mathematician together with the depth of his theological reflections. The fruit ranged from the *Provincial Letters* to his writings on grace and from his excursions into the foundations of the calculus to his harmony of the Gospels. Most significantly, this period yielded eight years of disorganized thoughts that have secured Pascal's place in the philosophical discourse of modernity, and while the style may capture our attention, the depth of his *Pensées* are what have made him our perpetual contemporary for the past three-and-a-half centuries.

In his *Pensées* Pascal demonstrated a remarkable ability to anticipate the philosophical discourse of modernity. With uncanny prescience he recognized at modernity's dawn what late-modern critics would come to recognize only much later in the day. This prescience has allowed him not only to stay current but to become all the more relevant as centuries have passed and the modern quest for certainty has played out. Pascal predicted the failure of Cartesianism and recognized the limits of the Enlightenment before it happened. As John Diggins notes, "The criticism of the Enlightenment leveled by contemporary post-structuralists had its predecessor in . . . the religious writers who voiced their doubts at the dawn of the 'Age of Reason.'"[5] Diggins cites Pascal specifically. "It should be remembered that religious thinkers like Pascal pronounced modern philosophy dead before it came to life." They anticipated the "revolt against Cartesian rationalism" and the "'hermeneutics of suspicion' that late-modern critics share."[6] Pascal stands as a contemporary of Nietzsche and Freud, of nineteenth-century pragmatists and twentieth-century existentialists, of poststructuralists, neo-pragmatists, and other late-modern critics of the Enlightenment. This prescience has allowed him not only to stay current but to become all the more relevant as centuries have passed and the modern quest for certainty has played out.

Although the *Philosophes* criticized him for what they considered to be his pessimism, not even they could ignore him, and the deeper we have traveled into the modern story the more his voice has resonated. Whether discussed by French Catholics and Romantics over two hundred years ago, engaged by Friedrich Nietzsche and William James over a century ago, or appropriated by Pierre Bourdieu, John Diggins, or Leszek Kolakowski more recently, Pascal has always had the ability to remain a contemporary in the philosophical discourse of modernity.

5. John Patrick Diggins, *The Promise of Pragmatism: Modernism and the Crisis of Knowledge and Authority* (Chicago: University of Chicago Press, 1994), 437.

6. Diggins, *Promise of Pragmatism*, 475.

As one browses the *Pensées* Pascal's voice immediately resonates with the late-modern thinkers who followed him over two centuries later. "The will is one of the chief organs of belief," Pascal observes, "not because it creates belief but because things are true or false according to the aspect by which we judge them." He continues:

> When the will likes one aspect more than another, it deflects the mind from considering the qualities of the one it does not care to see. Thus the mind, keeping in step with the will, remains looking at the aspect preferred by the will and so judges by what it sees there. (539)

The words belong to Pascal, but they could just as easily have come from the pen of Nietzsche, and the similarities between these two intellectuals do not stop here. Nietzsche's description of his own work as "an escapade into the idle hours of a psychologist" could apply as readily to Pascal's *Pensées* as to Nietzsche's *Twilight of the Idols.* So could Nietzsche's comment that "this little book is a *grand declaration of war,*" and a "sounding out of idols."[7] The resonance continues with Nietzsche's principal interpreters. Heidegger cites Pascal; Sartre cites him; and students of existentialism have repeatedly observed Pascal lurking in the background. Pascal agonizes over "the terrifying spaces of the universe" that fill him with dread. He also agonizes over the encounter with the self that is lost in that cosmos—"that part of me which thinks what I am saying, which reflects about everything and about itself, and does not know itself any better than it knows anything else" (427).

Pascal's critique of reason also echoes in our late modern world. "We attempt to question afresh the limits of thought, and to renew contact in this way with the project for a general critique of reason," writes Michel Foucault.[8] "What is this Reason that we use? What are its historical effects? What are its limits, and what are its dangers?"[9] Here the words belong to Foucault, but they express the agenda and raise the questions that Pascal had asked three centuries before. Pascal is a master at exposing reason as a mask behind which "the other of reason" does its work. Observing that it is imagination, not reason, that dominates our understanding of truth, he notes that imagination is "master of

7. Friedrich Nietzsche, *Twilight of the Idols or How to Philosophize with a Hammer*, trans. R. J. Hollingdale (New York: Penguin Books, 1968), 32.

8. Michel Foucault, *The Order of Things: An Archeology of the Human Sciences* (New York: Vintage Books, 1973), 342.

9. Michel Foucault, "Space, Knowledge, and Power: An Interview with Michel Foucault," quoted in the "Introduction," in *The Foucault Reader*, ed. Paul Rabinow (New York: Pantheon Books, 1984), 14.

error and falsehood," and "all the more deceptive for not being invariably so." It is "imagination [that] decides everything: it creates beauty, justice, and happiness" (44). Indeed, it is among the wisest of individuals that "imagination is best entitled to persuade. Reason may object in vain, it cannot fix the price of things." Reason is "the sport of every wind," Pascal laments, and "at its wisest adopts those principles which human imagination has rashly introduced at every turn" (44). Similarly, custom and habit lead the mind along unconsciously and fix our beliefs. We are automatons governed far more by custom and habit than by reason. "Custom is our nature" (419), but "how many natures lie in human nature?" (129) he asks. "Habit is a second nature that destroys the first. But what is nature? Why is habit not natural? I am very much afraid that nature itself is only a first habit, just as habit is a second nature" (126).

In similar ways Pascal reflects on the power of feeling, fancy, and passion and probes the ways in which human interests, agendas, and perspectives shape not only our beliefs but even our vocabularies. "I have never judged anything in exactly the same way," Pascal admits. "I cannot judge a work while doing it. I must do as painters do and stand back, but not too far. How far then? Guess" (558). In a way that resonates with the late-modern linguistic turn, Pascal observes, "Different arrangements of words make different meanings, and different arrangements of meanings produce different effects" (784). Continuing along this line of thought he notes, "The same meaning changes according to the words expressing it. Meanings are given dignity by words instead of conferring it upon them" (789). So, then, we are right to choose among alternative true descriptions according to the agenda at hand. "Mask and disguise nature," Pascal writes. "No more king, pope, bishop, but August monarchy, etc. . . . Not Paris, but capital of the realm. There are places where Paris must be called Paris, and others where it must be called capital of the realm" (509). Most profoundly, and again in keeping with the late modern prophets of suspicion, Pascal recognizes that "power rules the world" (554), and so reason and knowledge are in the service of power. Power, in turn, is subject to a "corrupt nature" (491) that hides behind it and is never more dangerous than when it hides behind the mask of reason. "When wickedness has reason on its side," Pascal warns, "it becomes pleased with itself and displays reason in all its lustre" (537).

As trenchant as his critique of reason may be, Pascal still wants to make the most out of our ability to think. However corrupted and proud our reason may be, "all our dignity lies in thought," he asserts, and so his *Pensées* take the form of an apology. Although he recognizes three orders of knowledge and acknowledges an inner vacuum that only God can fill, in the end, Pascal wants to win an argument. He wants to persuade us not through the art of persuasion, an art that belongs rightfully to God alone, but through an appeal to reason and reasons. The fame of "Pascal's wager" has sadly led people to think of him as a fideist who advocates a leap of faith, but this fails to recognize the nature and force of his argument.

Here again his approach to inquiry and argument resonates with important voices in the philosophical discourse of modernity. Most fundamentally, his method reflects the experimental approach to which he was committed in his scientific research. Pascal resists the theological and philosophical assumptions of his day and moves by way of observation, reflection, and testing. He also anticipates the pragmatists who would follow him two centuries later. He does not begin with abstract questions that descend from ethereal realms. He begins with common experience. He observes, reflects, and allows experience to identify questions worth bothering over. Before he is anything else he is a student of life, and when he has identified questions worth bothering over, he continues to follow the ways of the scientists and the pragmatists by trying on alternative hypotheses for how we might best answer these questions. In doing so, he neither seeks certainty nor allows doubt to paralyze the conversation. Instead, he weighs alternatives against each other on the basis of the best reasons we can give. Unwilling to bear the Cartesian burden of doubt that would dissolve over the course of modernity into an unbearable burden of lightness, Pascal recognizes that while our settled beliefs aren't "necessarily so," they may still be true—and we may hold them for good reasons.

Having built on the practices of the experimental sciences and having anticipated William James in his method, Pascal anticipates Sigmund Freud in his musings on the nature of human experience. Both of these students of human experience focus on what Pascal called "contradiction." Freud found the contradiction in the "struggle between Eros and Death or between the instinct of life and the instinct of destruction."[10] Pascal found the contradiction in the striking difference between the greatness (*grandeur*) and the wretchedness (*misère*) that characterize human experience. The theme of "contradiction" dominates his thinking. "Man is naturally credulous, incredulous, timid, bold" (124), he remarks. Caught between the extremes of "*infinity—nothing*" (418), we find ourselves "always torn by inner division and contradictions" (621). There is something profoundly noble about human beings, Pascal observes, and there is also something tragically amiss. "*Greatness and wretchedness,*" he muses. "One has followed the other in an endless circle, for it is certain that as man's insight increases so he finds both wretchedness and greatness within himself. In a word man knows he is wretched. Thus he is wretched because he is so, but he is truly

10. Sigmund Freud, *Civilization and Its Discontents*, trans. James Strachey, (New York: W. W. Norton & Company, 1961), 82.

great because he knows it" (122). For Freud, the struggle is primordial; it was present from the beginning. For Pascal, it is historical; it developed in human history. For Freud, it is an instinctual conflict. For Pascal, it is an existential contradiction.

The parallels between the two thinkers continue with Freud's exploration of the pleasure principle and the reality principle. What do people demand of life? Freud asks. "The answer to this can hardly be in doubt. They strive after happiness; they want to become happy and to remain so," but this pleasure principle "is at loggerheads with the whole world." As a result, "The programme of becoming happy, which the pleasure principle imposes on us, cannot be fulfilled; yet we must not—indeed, we cannot—give up our efforts to bring it nearer to fulfillment by some means or other."[11] We find ourselves not simply unhappy but burdened by boredom, discontent, a *malaise* or *unbehangen* that weighs heavily. Two hundred and fifty years earlier, without the aid of psycho-analysis, Pascal made similar observations when he wrote:

> All men seek happiness. There are no exceptions. However different the means they may employ, they all strive towards this goal. The reason why some go to war and some do not is the same desire in both, but interpreted in two different ways. The will never takes the least step except to that end.
>
> Yet . . . [a]ll men complain. . . . So, while the present never satisfies us, experience deceives us, and leads us on from one misfortune to another until death comes as the ultimate and eternal climax. (148)

Caught in this conundrum and plagued by boredom, people seek diversion, finding ways to keep themselves from thinking about the unhappiness to which the quest for happiness so often leads. The pleasure principle, the reality prin-ciple, and the problem of boredom and *malaise* all appear in Pascal two-and-a-half centuries before they appear in Freud. Harold Bloom has suggested that "a Christian polemicist in our time ought to find his true antagonist in Freud, but nearly all do not."[12] Curiously, Pascal did, although he anticipated Freud by two-and-a-half centuries.

What Pascal saw in others he apparently found in himself as well, and he struggled with what he found there. Late in life, well after the night of fire and even after the onset of illness had further reordered his priorities, Pascal helped organize a contest to see who could solve a mathematical puzzle that he knew

---

11. Freud, *Civilization and Its Discontents*, 25 and 34.

12. Harold Bloom, "Introduction," in *Modern Critical Views: Blaise Pascal*, ed. Harold Bloom (New York: Chelsea House Publishers, 1989), 1.

he alone had succeeded in solving at the time. In other words, the contest would largely have served to show Pascal's own brilliance. In recording this episode Jean Mesnard notes that Pascal "showed himself ready to glory in his own superiority, skillful in claiming his due, pitiless towards opponents, and without indulgence for their weaknesses."[13] Perhaps Mesnard is being harsher in his criticism than Pascal deserves, but the episode does suggest that when Pascal writes that "The vilest feature of man is the quest for glory, but it is just this that most clearly shows his excellence" (470), he may have had himself in mind. Pascal's early demonstrations of genius, his pride in his arithmetical machine, his delight in his growing fame as a young adult, and his engagement in the mathematical contest later in life all suggest that Pascal was quite familiar with the quest for glory. His deep reflections on the subject of diversion also give the reader the sense that Pascal often had himself in mind in his *Pensées*. Not only does he sometimes write in the first-person plural, he writes specifically about those who "sweat away in their studies to prove to scholars that they have solved some hitherto insoluble problem in algebra" and then adds the even more self-deprecating comment that "there are others who exhaust themselves observing all these things, not in order to become wiser, but just to show they know them, and these are the biggest fools of the lot" (136). Whether Pascal penned these thoughts before or after the famous contest, both the thoughts and the contest betray the contradictions that Pascal found in himself as well as in his peers.

The contest, together with Pascal's comments, leads Mesnard to suggest that Pascal backed away from a wholehearted devotion to science and math not because he doubted the value of such enterprises or because he thought them to be worldly in themselves, but because they tempted him to pride—a temptation that hounded Pascal throughout his life. The comments also lead Michel Le Guern to conclude that Amos Dettonville, in whose name Pascal represented himself in matters surrounding the contest, represents more than just a pseudonym. This alternate identity offers Pascal a way of dealing with the contradiction that he finds within himself. Dettonville, the proud scientist, Le Guern argues, does not so much write for Pascal as Pascal for Dettonville. Whether or not these scholars are right in their assessments, Pascal appears to see in himself the same contradictions that he sees everywhere. Even after his night of fire and a further reorienting of his priorities, he struggled to reconcile the greatness of genius and the wretchedness of pride. Gilberte sweetly asserts that her brother "never had a passion for reputation,"[14] but we know otherwise.

---

13. Jean Mesnard, *Pascal: His Life and Works* (New York: Philosophical Library, 1952), 116.
14. Périer, *La Vie*, 31.

He took great pride in his accomplishments and found pleasure in his growing fame. He had an engaging but imperious personality, and we have every reason to believe that the contradictions that captured his attention ran as deeply in Pascal as they do in any of us.

As Pascal tries on alternative hypotheses for how we might best understand our contradictory human ways, he looks briefly to the philosophers but concludes that the philosophers fail us here. Typically, they point us toward either one side or the other of the contradiction that we find within. Either they recognize human greatness and tempt us to think of ourselves as Gods, or they view our brokenness as the "truth of man" and give us over to corrupted passions to drag us where they will. In the jargon of the seventeenth century, they give us up to our concupiscence. In the language of the twenty-first century, they give us up to a notion of individual freedom that leaves our will captive to our passions. "Do the philosophers, who offer us nothing else for our good but the good that is within us," Pascal asks, make sense of the contradiction that we find within? "Is it curing man's presumption to set him up as God's equal?" On the other hand, he wonders, "Have those who put us on the level of the beasts" done any better? Having seen the pretentiousness of thinking that we are like God, they have "cast you into the other abyss, by giving you to understand that your nature was like that of the beasts, and they induce you to seek your good in concupiscence" (149). They encourage you to give yourself up to your passions and to follow where they lead. Pascal doubts, however, that the passions are to be trusted, and so he warns his readers against philosophers who "give free rein to concupiscence and check scruples [but] ought to do the opposite" (363).

Disappointed by the philosophers, Pascal tries on a Christian understanding of experience and finds it both existentially and intellectually compelling. Not only does it offer a great principle of greatness and a great principle of wretchedness, but it also helps us understand that wretchedness more fully. Human greatness reflects the image of God in us. Human wretchedness betrays our resistance to him. The glory of the image never goes away, and yet it never finds full expression. Both a greatness and a wretchedness remain, and so we live in a place of tension or contradiction. Christian doctrine also helps us understand the nature of our discontent. Our wretchedness, Pascal argues, is that of a dispossessed monarch. We experience a sense of loss and longing that is like the feeling a prince would have who was born for the throne but whose family was dispossessed and exiled and who never ascended to the throne for which he was born. Following Augustine, Pascal argues that we are not only made in God's image, we are also made for God. He is both the source and the object of our deepest longings, but here too our wretchedness enters in and confuses us. Because a trace of greatness and a memory of our deepest happiness remain, we seek after God, and yet, because of the corruption and blindness that afflict us, we settle for surrogates in the place of God. Because these idols are typically God's good gifts, we do find a degree of satisfaction in them and often convince ourselves that they are what we've been longing for all along, but the longing remains. As Pascal observes:

> God alone is man's true good, and since man abandoned him it is a strange fact that nothing in nature has been found to take his place. . . . Since losing his true good, man is capable of seeing it in anything, even his own destruction, although it is so contrary at once to God, to reason and to nature. (148)

This "is the state in which men are today. They retain some feeble instinct from the happiness of their first nature, and are plunged into the wretchedness of their blindness and concupiscence, which has become their second nature" (149). Pascal reminds us, however, that a glory remains in each one of us that cannot be eradicated. "Now observe all the impulses of greatness and of glory which the experience of so many miseries cannot stifle" (149). The greatness of the image of the Creator remains, and even the awareness of our own wretchedness reveals it to us. There are both excellence and abasement in all of us, and Pascal maintains that once we see this contradiction between the greatness of the ineradicable *Imago Dei* and the equally constant wretchedness of our corruption, we will see it everywhere.

One hundred fifty years after Darwin, our sophisticated, highly scientized culture finds it difficult to take Pascal's appeal to ancient Christian doctrine seriously, but Darwin or his popularizers need not mute Pascal's voice today any more than Copernicus or Galileo did in his own day. Here again, Pascal saw clearly and spoke prophetically. Challenging both the philosophical and theological authorities of his day, Pascal argued that scientific questions should be answered by science. He also concurred with Nietzsche in arguing that science should not have the final word in answering our deepest questions. Pascal knew the difference between the methodological naturalism that he practiced and endorsed and the metaphysical naturalism that he foresaw and feared. Recognizing both the atheism implicit in Descartes's ontotheological argument for a philosophically necessary God—and also the cracks in the foundations on which Descartes hoped to erect that idol—Pascal rejected rationalism in the name of reason. Convinced that reason does not take us very far if it does not show us its own limits, Pascal rejected the quest for certainty and argued for a more modest approach to inquiry and argument that compares alternative hypotheses against each other on the basis of the best reasons available. Sadly, in the decades after his death, Pascal lost and Descartes won. Over time the reductionistic tendencies of modern rationalism gradually drove Pascal's deeper understanding of the human condition into the margins, and Descartes's God died. Now that the modern story has played out, however, and we have experienced the burden of lightness to which the burden of proof has led, Pascal's ways of thinking can once again open the conversation for the reconsideration of deeper understandings that were unfairly driven to the margins. Having benefitted from both his critique and his method, we can reconsider his conclusions as well.

Pascal continues to attract our attention and remains current, then, not only because of his aphoristic style, his enigmatic character, and his prescience in anticipating the modern story, but finally because of the depth of his contributions to the larger, enduring human conversation about human identity. By granting us entry into the depths of his own soul, we not only come to know the author behind the thoughts, we come to know the man, and in coming to know the man, we come to know ourselves as well. In the style of Albert Camus's *Jean Baptiste*, Pascal draws his readers in and begins to speak for us before we realize what has happened. In doing so, he humbles us. He makes us uncomfortable. "What sort of freak then is man!" he declares. "How novel, how monstrous, how chaotic, how paradoxical, how prodigious! Judge of all things, feeble earthworm, repository of truth, sink of doubt and error, glory and refuse of the universe!" (131). We do not like being told that we are the refuse of the universe, and so we admit with Le Guern that the conversation Pascal creates is *quelquefois difficile*. Perhaps, however, the greater difficulty lies not in Pascal's pessimism but in his optimism. We are, after all, bearers of the *imago Dei*. We are the glory of the universe. "Man transcends man," asserts Pascal; and again, "man infinitely transcends man" (131). Herein lies the greater difficulty, and herein lies Pascal's greater contribution to the human conversation. Given our late-modern context, in which we have reaped the harvest of modern rationalism and breathed the air of its reductionism far more deeply than we realize, we hardly know how to think with Pascal at such depths. If we will allow him, however, he may not only free us from the burden of doubt, he may also take us deeper into our shared human experience than we would ever have gone on our own. He may be able to lead us "beyond dogmatism and skepticism, beyond all human philosophy" to a place where we can reconsider truth that "lies beyond our scope" and is known most fully through "the uncreated and incarnate truth" (131). Herein lies his deepest and most lasting contribution. Herein lies the reason why he is both *quelquefois difficile* but also *toujours actuel*.

PART SEVEN

Christian Identity in the Upheavals of the Twentieth Century

Chapter 36

Søren Kierkegaard: Becoming a Self

MURRAY RAE

The opening paragraph of Søren Kierkegaard's work *The Sickness Unto Death* presents the reader with one of the most enigmatic sentences in all of Kierkegaard's authorship: "What is the self?" Kierkegaard asks. More exactly, the question is asked by Anti-Climacus, one of the many pseudonyms under whose names Kierkegaard presented about half of his published works. Anti-Climacus is said by Kierkegaard to be a Christian "to an extraordinary degree."[1] Kierkegaard would make no such claim for himself. As is evident through notes made in his *Journals*, Kierkegaard was acutely conscious of his own shortcomings, and he strenuously resisted any suggestion that readers should consider him to be a model for the authentic Christian life that he so passionately presents.

But let us return to the question posed at the outset of *The Sickness Unto Death*: "What is the self?" Anti-Climacus poses the question, and then responds: "The self is a relation that relates itself to itself or is the relation's relating itself to itself in the relation; the self is not the relation but is the relation's relating itself to itself."[2] Read in isolation from Kierkegaard's subsequent explanations, this definition of what the self consists in is virtually incomprehensible. Yet from this puzzling beginning Kierkegaard develops a profoundly Christian account of our human situation in which the project of becoming a self is conceived as

---

1. See *Kierkegaard's Journals and Notebooks*, vol. 6, NB 11:209, ed. Bruce Kirmmse et al. (Princeton: Princeton University Press, 2012), 127. Although it is often important to note a distinction between Kierkegaard's own views and those of his pseudonyms, I will in this case presume Kierkegaard's agreement with the account of human selfhood presented by Anti-Climacus and so refer to Kierkegaard as the author of *The Sickness Unto Death*. In the same note referred to above Kierkegaard claims that Anti-Climacus's "portrayal of the ideal might be entirely true, and on that matter, I'll yield."

2. Søren Kierkegaard, *The Sickness Unto Death*, ed. and trans. Howard V. Hong and Edna H. Hong (Princeton: Princeton University Press, 1980), 13.

a task that is undertaken before God and brought to fulfillment only in Christ. Before tracing this development, however, let us consider the historical and intellectual context in which Kierkegaard found himself and the influences upon his own thinking.

An Age of Self-Assertion

In the first half of the nineteenth century during which, from 1813 to 1855, Kierkegaard lived out his short life, we see the beginnings of what might be described as an age of self-assertion. The intellectual currents generated by the Enlightenment had given rise to the conviction that human beings were to be masters of all that they surveyed. We find within ourselves, furthermore, the criterion of all truth and the means to live a truly human life. Accepting the serpent's promise that "we will be like gods" (Gen 2:5), the assumption of human mastery found expression in various forms among the intellectual giants of Kierkegaard's age. Immanuel Kant had died less than a decade before Kierkegaard was born, leaving a legacy of confidence that the moral law was generated by rational deliberation and could be adhered to simply enough by allowing reason to dominate and subdue desire. The rational deliberations of the self, which Kant mistakenly presumed would yield agreement among all those endowed with reason, became the authority to which all claims to truth and understanding must be subjected. Iris Murdoch captures the mood and notes its continuing influence:

> How recognizable, how familiar to us is the man so beautifully portrayed in the *Grundlegung*, who confronted even with Christ turns away to consider the judgement of his own conscience and to hear the voice of his own reason. Stripped of the exiguous metaphysical background which Kant was prepared to allow him, this man is with us still, free, independent, lonely, powerful, rational, responsible, brave, the hero of so many novels and books of moral philosophy.[3]

While Kant himself acknowledged some limits to reason's prowess, no such limitation was admitted by G. W. F. Hegel, who set about developing a single

---

3. Iris Murdoch, *The Sovereignty of Good* (London: Routledge, 1970), 80; cited in Charles Taylor, *Sources of the Self: The Making of Modern Identity* (Cambridge: Harvard University Press, 1989), 84. *Grundlegung* is of course a reference to Kant's *Grundlegung zur Metaphysik der Sitten* published in 1785.

comprehensive system that would account for and explain the totality of existence, from human freedom and subjectivity to the vast expanse of world history, and indeed to all the operations of the cosmos. He aimed to do this through reason alone. In 1831, the year of Hegel's death, Kierkegaard was a student at the University of Copenhagen where Hegel's system, including within it Hegel's account of Christian faith, was being enthusiastically promoted by Kierkegaard's teachers. Kierkegaard, however, was unpersuaded by Hegel's view of reality and especially by Hegel's conception of Christ as a mere exemplar and of reconciliation as a work of human intellect. The root of the problem, in Kierkegaard's view, was Hegel's forgetfulness of what it is to exist as a human being, subject to finitude and caught up in the bondage of sin.

While Kierkegaard continued his studies at the university, D. F. Strauss was working away on a manuscript soon to be published as *Das Leben Jesu kritisch bearbeitet* (The Life of Jesus Critically Examined). Adapting slightly Murdoch's description of Kant above, it may be said of Strauss too that he turned away from the Christ presented to us in the Gospels to consider the judgment of his own historical reasoning in light of which he declared that the Gospels present us with mythical portrayals of Jesus behind which lies a faint historical figure to whom we have almost no access at all. It is, again, our own rational judgments that determine the boundaries of what is true, and anything that falls outside the bounds of historical reasoning must be regarded as mythical embellishment. According to Strauss, however, the myths are not worthless. In their ascription of divinity to the human Jesus, they convey a truth about humanity as a whole. Strauss contends, following Hegel, that humanity itself is a synthesis of the human and the divine. Thus begins a trajectory that leads Strauss eventually to abandon the idea that our true humanity is realized through an obedient response to God's call upon us to live in communion with him. In his 1872 work, *The Old Faith and the New*, Strauss contends that Jesus can no longer be decisive for us. We are left with a humanistic ethic, the content of which is to be determined by our own rational deliberations.

Another contemporary of Kierkegaard's was Ludwig Feuerbach, whose influential work, *The Essence of Christianity*, was published in 1841. Its second edition was read by Kierkegaard in 1843 as Kierkegaard himself was writing *Philosophical Fragments*. Feuerbach alleged that religion was merely a human construction. We human beings are not creatures of a transcendent and sovereign God, but are ourselves responsible for the creation of "God." The idea of God is a product of our own imaginations, a projection and personification of our own highest ideals. Religion, therefore "can be nothing else than the consciousness which man has of his own . . . infinite nature."[4] Human beings in Feuerbach's scheme are again made the center and measure of all things.

Finally, in this brief survey of the intellectual currents of the time, we must mention Friedrich Schleiermacher, who rivaled Hegel as the presiding genius of the intellectual milieu within which Kierkegaard received his university education. Schleiermacher appears at first to be an exception to the general mood of self-assertion, insisting as he does upon humanity's absolute dependence upon God. But the welcome note of humility in Schleiermacher's approach does not preclude him from proposing a capacity of our own as the cornerstone upon which the edifice of Christian theology is to be built. It is our own imagination, in Schleiermacher's early work, and then, later, our own "feeling" that is said to be the starting point and criterion of all religion.[5] It is on the basis of this "emotional a priori," as Geoffrey Bromiley has described it,[6] that the essence of Christianity is defined—well in advance of any attention being paid to Jesus Christ. When in his major work, *The Christian Faith*, Schleiermacher does turn his attention to Christology, the theological and the anthropological categories within which Jesus is to be understood have already been established. Schleiermacher's Christology is made to fit within a conceptual framework already determined by his analysis of what it is to be a human being.[7] Although less inclined than others of his age to assert that the self is sovereign over all and the criterion of truth, Schleiermacher nevertheless proceeds under the assumption that awareness of self, rather than the fear of the Lord, is the beginning of wisdom.

The preceding paragraphs convey something of the cultural and intellectual milieu within which Kierkegaard found himself when he embarked upon the study of philosophy and theology at the University of Copenhagen. In accord with the theological training offered by the universities, the "gospel" commonly proclaimed from Denmark's pulpits was a gospel adapted to the spirit of the age. The Christian identity of all upright citizens was taken for granted, while

4. Ludwig Feuerbach, *The Essence of Christianity*, trans. George Eliot (New York: Harper, 1957), 2.

5. In his 1799 work, *On Religion: Speeches to Its Cultured Despisers*, trans. Richard Crouter (New York: Cambridge University Press, 1988), Schleiermacher attributes his theological claims to the work of the imagination, which he describes as "the highest and most original element in us" (138). In *The Christian Faith*, however, Schleiermacher portrays religion as founded upon "a modification of Feeling, or of immediate self-consciousness." See *The Christian Faith*, ed. H. R. Mackintosh and J. S. Stewart (Edinburgh: T&T Clark, 1989), 5.

6. G. W. Bromiley, *Historical Theology: An Introduction* (Edinburgh: T&T Clark, 1978), 362.

7. A fuller discussion of Schleiermacher's theological program and Kierkegaard's critique of it can be found in Murray Rae, *Kierkegaard's Vision of the Incarnation* (Oxford: Clarendon, 1997), 42–46.

the costly demands of following Christ crucified were hardly given a second thought. The intellectuals of the day, meanwhile, had important work to be getting on with, namely, the work of establishing a sure epistemological foundation for our scientific and moral advancement, an advancement that would ensure the overcoming of ignorance and remove all obstacles to the perfection of humankind. This thoroughly humanistic soteriology required that attention be given to divine revelation, if at all, only to confirm God's approval of humanity's prodigious achievement.

Within the household and in conversations around the dining table of Kierkegaard's family home, however, another mood prevailed. Kierkegaard's father, Michael Kierkegaard, was an intense, melancholy man who believed that as a child he had committed an unforgiveable sin, in consequence of which a curse now lay over his family. The premature deaths of his first wife and of five of his seven children confirmed, in Michael's mind, the conviction that he was being justly punished by God. In material terms, Michael had worked his way out of the misery of his childhood to become a successful and wealthy merchant in Copenhagen. He undoubtedly valued his hard-won status as a respected member of Danish society, counted Bishop Jacob Mynster among his friends, and participated, as was expected, in the observances of the established Lutheran Church. Prompted in part, no doubt, by the sense of guilt that burdened him, Michael was not content with conventional, established religion; he was attracted as well to the Moravian tradition that, in opposition to the theological rationalism of the day, emphasized disciplined, personal piety, concrete obedience to the way of Christ, and the heartfelt love of God. Having attended the Lutheran service on Sunday mornings, the Kierkegaard family went in the afternoon to meetings of the Moravian Congregation of Brethren. In further expression of his dissatisfaction with a Christian faith that made few existential demands on its adherents, Michael Kierkegaard spent many hours in conversation with N. F. S. Grundtvig, the Danish pastor, Romantic poet, and teacher who criticized the prevailing rationalism of Danish theology and the reduction of Christianity to a philosophical idea.

In place of the carefree and innocent pleasures of childhood, the young Søren Kierkegaard became entwined instead in his father's pursuit of consolation and in the relentless earnestness of his theological enquiries. The child sat for hours listening to his father's conversations, not only with Grundtvig, but also with other leading figures in Danish society. Denied the opportunity to make friends or to engage in play with other children, Søren later claimed that he had been robbed of his childhood.[8] Yet Kierkegaard could also see benefit

8. See Søren Kierkegaard, "The Point of View of My Work as an Author," in *The Point of*

in this rigorous upbringing. Alongside the melancholic temperament passed on to him by his father, Kierkegaard also inherited his father's powerful imagination, his gift for storytelling, a passion for understanding, and a prodigious intellect. Among the stories his father would tell, Søren was impressed above all by the fearful story of Jesus's crucifixion. How could it be, Kierkegaard wondered, that the crowd could turn against the most compassionate man that ever lived? The fickleness of the crowd became an enduring theme in Kierkegaard's later writings, a fickleness that Kierkegaard saw replicated in Christendom's abandonment of Christ. While the citizens of his age wished to inherit Christ's good name, they largely declined the invitation to follow Christ in suffering and costly obedience.

Unmasking the Errors of the Age

Unlike Schleiermacher, Kierkegaard did not suppose that the greatest challenge to Christian faith originated with "religion's cultured despisers." In Kierkegaard's view, the greatest threat to Christian faith came from those who supposed themselves already to be Christian simply in virtue of their having been born in Denmark, a so-called Christian country. For Denmark, of course, we may substitute any nation that regards itself as Christian and in which the baptism or "christening" of infants is routinely undertaken merely in fulfillment of a social convention. In such a context, Kierkegaard complained, becoming a Christian had become as easy as pulling on one's socks, and being a Christian required nothing more than going along with the crowd. The notion that discipleship might bring one into conflict with the surrounding culture or that faith might involve a sacrifice did not enter anyone's head. Given this assumption, combined as it was with the view briefly considered above that we ourselves are the fount of all truth and knowledge, Kierkegaard determined that it was impossible to communicate directly with his age. Errors such as these cannot be confronted directly but must be surreptitiously unmasked. Kierkegaard thus adopted a strategy of indirect communication. The pseudonyms were a key feature of this strategy; purporting to conduct a rational enquiry into some aspect of the human condition, Kierkegaard through his pseudonyms played along with the assumptions of his age, only to show that those assumptions led in a direction quite foreign to the biblical account of what Christian faith consists in.

In *Philosophical Fragments*, for instance, Kierkegaard ponders (pseudon-

View, ed. and trans. Howard V. Hong and Edna H. Hong (Princeton: Princeton University Press, 1998), 82.

ymously again) the age-old question of how one learns the truth.[9] He presents first the Socratic view, which is founded upon the assumption that we already possess the truth and, through the exercise of reason, need merely to recollect it.[10] It turns out that this Socratic view corresponds in all essential respects to the view of Christianity touted by Kierkegaard's contemporaries, especially by theological professors and clergy. According to this scheme, Christ is merely a midwife bringing to birth the divine knowledge that lies within us all. Call this our own latent spirituality if you will. Salvation, according to this conception of ourselves, comes through the realization that we are destined to be god-like ourselves.

In contrast with this view of our human situation, Kierkegaard proposes an alternative, the opposite in each essential respect to the Socratic view already surveyed. So, for instance, where the Socratic view begins with the assumption that we are all in possession of the truth, the alternative proposed is that we are bereft of truth. And where the Socratic view supposes that we have the condition (our rational capacity) to recollect the truth, Kierkegaard's alternative account assumes that we have no such condition. Where the Socratic view supposes that the truth can be learned with no substantive change to the self, Kierkegaard's alternative includes the suggestion that if we are to learn the truth then something like a new birth, or a transformation of the self, will be required. And so on . . . It becomes increasingly plain that the "Truth" with which Kierkegaard is most concerned is the truth made known in Jesus Christ. Is that truth contained already within the self, or does it come to us through revelation, through the transformative gift of God's self-communicative presence? Kierkegaard does not offer a verdict on this matter. He merely presents his account as an alternative to the view held by many of his contemporaries.

Pursuing further his alternative to the Socratic account, Kierkegaard suggests that our existence in untruth should properly be called sin, for we are responsible for our own alienation from the truth. Furthermore, because we are incapable of escaping from our bondage to sin, we stand in need of one who can give us not only the truth but also the condition for understanding the truth. This one we should properly call Savior and Redeemer, Kierkegaard explains, for he rescues us from our existence in untruth and overcomes the sin that held us there. Kierkegaard then proposes that "conversion" would be an apt name for this process of learning the truth, and suggests that it ought to

---

9. See *Philosophical Fragments* and *Johannes Climacus*, ed. and trans. Howard V. Hong and Edna H. Hong (Princeton: Princeton University Press, 1985), esp. chap. 1.

10. This is the view that Socrates sets out in his dialogue with Meno. See Plato, "The Meno," in *Protagoras and Meno*, trans. W. K. C. Guthrie (Harmondsworth: Penguin, 1956).

be accompanied by repentance. Having undertaken this "thought experiment" in which two opposing views are set side by side, Kierkegaard leaves the reader to decide which view is to be preferred. He does admit, however, to having plagiarized his alternative account, and he expects his readers also to recognize that his alternative closely resembles the portrayal of salvation that is found in the New Testament.

Those of Kierkegaard's readers who had happily assumed that Christianity could easily be accommodated within the Socratic view ought by now to be feeling distinctly uncomfortable. It turns out that the New Testament account of where and how the Truth is made known contrasts markedly with the Socratic (and modern) assumption that "sin" is mere ignorance and can be overcome through the exercise of our own truth-telling capacities, whether they be conceived in rationalistic or romantic terms. Kierkegaard's alternative, drawn as it is from the New Testament, entails that our existence in untruth may be overcome only through the work of a "Teacher" who gives not only the truth, but also the condition for understanding it. This condition is later identified as faith, and its reception by the learner involves conversion, repentance, and new life. The person who recognizes in the New Testament the origin of this soteriology is now obliged to choose between the New Testament view and the counterfeit gospel that is widely proclaimed in Christendom.

What Is the Self?

With this introduction, first to Kierkegaard's communicative strategies, and second, to his efforts to present faithfully what is given to us through revelation, we are now in a position to return to the question with which we began, and to Kierkegaard's response. What is it to be a self? "The self is a relation that relates itself to itself." This initially puzzling claim rests on the contention that human beings are a synthesis—a synthesis of the finite and the infinite, of the temporal and the eternal, of possibility and necessity. Put in more familiar biblical terms, we are formed from the dust, from finite matter, and are subject, therefore, to the conditions of creaturely existence. And yet, we are made in the image of God. As the psalmist puts it, we insignificant specks of matter in a vast universe have been made a little lower than God and have been crowned with glory and honor (Ps 8:5). We who are made from dust and will return to dust are called into covenant relationship with God. The self, however, is not merely a static relation between these two aspects of human being. The self does not exist simply in virtue of our being a synthesis of matter and spirit. The self is to be understood rather as a project. It comes into being only through our active realization, day by day, of the possibilities latent in the synthesis. Putting the matter once more in biblical terms, the self may be understood as the lived response we offer to God's call. It is our active engagement in the possibilities established through the divine declaration, "I will be your God and you will be my people" (see Exod 6:7; Jer 30:22).

"The self is a relation that relates itself to itself," we have learned. That is to say, it is a project in which the possibilities latent in the synthesis of the finite and the infinite, the temporal and the eternal, possibility and necessity,[11] are realized day by day just in so far as we live our lives in response to God's call upon us. God is not mentioned explicitly to begin with, but we do learn that when the self is truly realized it "rests transparently in *the power that established it.*" That power, of course, is that of our Creator. An echo may be heard here of Augustine's renowned confession: "For Thou [Lord] has formed us for Thyself, and our hearts are restless till they find rest in Thee."[12]

There are numerous ways in which we may fail in this project of becoming a self, but Kierkegaard classifies them all according to two basic types, each of which he describes as a form of despair. To be in despair does not mean, necessarily, that one will feel miserable. One can be blissfully unaware of being in despair, just as one can be blissfully unaware of being a sinner. As it turns out, being in despair is a place-holder for what Kierkegaard will later call sin. Despair is the state of alienation from one's true calling to become a self before God. As noted, such despair has two forms: "In despair not to will to be oneself," and "in despair to will to be oneself." Again, this seems puzzling, if not contradictory, but let me explain.

This failure to will to be oneself is the failure to will to be the selves that God has created us to be. It is to prefer some other self than the self created in God's image and called to live in relation with him. Such despair may be exercised in weakness or in defiance. In the first case, the failure to take up one's divine vocation may result from ignorance, from a lack of awareness of the conditions under which human life is to be lived, or from preoccupation with merely finite goods. Despair, in this case, arises from the failure to recognize both God's call upon us, and the possibilities and limitations presented through our being a synthesis of the finite and the infinite. Despair in defiance, on the other hand, is that form of despair in which, having heard the call of God, we actively resist it. Christians will know this form of despair in their own failures, failures that

---

11. I will from now on refer simply to "the synthesis of the finite and the infinite" and take this phrase as representative of the various ways in which our dual constitution as matter and spirit may be described.

12. Augustine, *Confessions* 1.1, trans. J. G. Pilkington (*NPNF1*, 1:45).

arise not from ignorance of God's call, but rather from a reluctance to trust ourselves wholly to the Lordship of Christ and to the guidance of his Spirit.

The second form of despair—"to will to be oneself"—is simply the other side of the same coin. Here we will to be a self on our own terms rather than on the terms given by God. This is the sin of *self*-assertion. We seek to be free of God, to be self-made men or women who are answerable to no one. The freedom that is God's good gift to us is here misconstrued as the prerogative to do as we like, without constraint or obligation. A person guilty of such despair, Kierkegaard explains, "wants to begin a little earlier than do other men, not at and with the beginning, but 'in the beginning'; he does not want to put on his own self, does not want to see his given self as his task—he himself wants to compose his self by means of being the infinite form."[13] The allusion here is to Genesis 1. Such a person wants to go back before the creation of humankind in God's image; he does not want to see himself as one created by God and given a vocation by God. He wants to start "in the beginning," with a blank slate, as it were. He wants to realize the autonomy and supposed lack of constraint represented in the serpent's promise, "you shall be like gods."

Kierkegaard's diagnosis of these two forms of despair is accompanied by an analysis of the symptoms, each of which manifests as a misrelation in the individual between the finite and the infinite, between the temporal and the eternal, or between freedom and necessity. Let us consider some examples of such despair. Working successively through each pair of categories that constitute the conditions of human life, Kierkegaard explains first that "infinitude's despair is to lack finitude."[14] A misrelation of the finite and the infinite appears, for instance, whenever one's ideals are not properly aligned with the concrete realities of one's everyday existence. Consider the Christian who claims to be concerned for the poor and the outcast and talks passionately of the church as a place where the outcasts of society are welcome, but then, when a smelly, homeless person seeks refuge in the church, the person professing the high ideals is repelled. One is reminded of Charles Schulz's famous "Peanuts" cartoon in which Linus protests, "I love humankind; it's people I can't stand!" The person's awareness of infinitude represented in the high ideals is not properly aligned with the concrete reality within which those ideals need to be lived out. Such a person lacks finitude, lacks commitment to and perhaps awareness of how the high ideals are to be worked out within the constraints of everyday existence. The problem does not lie with the ideals. The person does not need less infinitude. He needs more finitude, a better realization of his high ideals within the constraints of daily life.

13. Kierkegaard, *The Sickness Unto Death*, 68.
14. Kierkegaard, *The Sickness Unto Death*, 30.

Alternately, "finitude's despair is to lack infinitude." Here we might think of the person who has no sense of or defies any higher calling. Such a person invests her whole life in the pursuit of finite goods. A professor of theology, for instance, may believe that her worth as a human being depends on the acclaim she receives from her scholarly peers. The professor strives for public acclaim by devoting herself to the task of scholarship. She publishes regularly and receives numerous invitations to speak at academic conferences, in consequence of which her self-esteem is immeasurably enhanced. Such a person does not lack finitude; she may be enormously diligent in the cultivation of finite goods. But she lacks infinitude. She is devoted to an ideal that falls far short of God's call upon her. In attributing infinite worth to her reputation among her peers, she has made an idol of something that has merely finite worth and has lost sight of the theologian's true calling, which is to bear witness through prayerful study to the summons and the love of God.

Kierkegaard proceeds to further discussion of the ways in which the elements of our humanity may be improperly related. One such misrelation is particularly worthy of attention. "Necessity's despair," Kierkegaard explains, "is to lack possibility."[15] Necessity refers to the conditions of everyday existence to which we must be responsible. I have an obligation, though not absolute, to obey the laws of the land and to observe particular social conventions that contribute to the well-being of the community. I am also constrained by "laws of nature" that set limits to what I can accomplish. Respect for such "necessities" is an important aspect of responsible human being. But we are not completely caged in by such necessities. Our lives are characterized as well by a degree of freedom and possibility. It is a form of despair, therefore, to suppose oneself to be utterly constrained by one's present circumstances. Fatalism is an instance of such despair. So is a sense of hopelessness in the face of apparently insurmountable challenges like poverty, war, climate change, and the like. Any view of the world in which it is imagined that things must always be as they are now is a form of despair arising from a lack of possibility. This applies at a global level and at a personal level. Consider, for example, a person who despairs of the forgiveness of sins. Such a person may be tortured by a sense of guilt and shame, and while she may recognize the possibility of salvation for others, she considers herself to be unworthy of forgiveness. She is held captive by sin, and can see no release. Kierkegaard again echoes Augustine who, in *On Christian Doctrine*, writes, "A person who does not believe that his sins can be forgiven is made worse by despair, feeling that nothing better awaits him than to be wicked, since he has no faith in the

---

15. Kierkegaard, *The Sickness Unto Death*, 37.

results of being converted."[16] Luther's despair at ever being able to fulfill the demands of a righteous God is an example of such captivity. It was not until Luther discovered that the righteous God was a God of mercy and grace that he was set free from his bondage and new possibilities were opened up. So it is for everyone who discovers God's forgiveness. Release from despair, release from sin, requires faith, Kierkegaard reminds us. It requires faith that with God all things are possible.[17]

In the second part of *The Sickness Unto Death*, Kierkegaard employs theological categories much more explicitly than in the first. Consistent with the observation made above with respect to Kierkegaard's account in *Philosophical Fragments* of how we learn the truth, so also in *The Sickness Unto Death* Kierkegaard eventually declares that a true understanding of the matter can only be revealed to us. We cannot discover the true nature of sin for ourselves. It is only before God that we learn that sin is, at root, a refusal to be the selves that God calls us to be. Thus in part 2 Kierkegaard adds a qualification to his earlier definition of despair, a qualification crucial to the recognition that what he has been speaking of all along is best understood as sin. "Therefore the definition of sin given in the previous section still needs to be completed as follows: sin is—after being taught by a revelation from God what sin is—*before God* in despair not to will to be oneself or in despair to will to be oneself."[18] More simply, and according to the scriptural definition, sin is disobedience.[19]

Having made it explicit now that the self is a project given us by God and to be undertaken in responsive relation to God, Kierkegaard then explains that God is not only the one who calls us to be a self, God is also the criterion and the goal. We will come soon to discover the christological root of this claim, but first Kierkegaard takes us on a little excursion by which he demonstrates how absurd it is to imagine having any other criterion.

> A cattleman who (if this were possible) is a self directly before his cattle is a very low self, and, similarly, a master who is a self directly before his slaves is actually no self—for in both cases a criterion is lacking. The child who previously had only his parents as a criterion becomes a self as an adult by getting the state as a criterion, but what an infinite accent falls on the self by having God as the criterion![20]

16. Augustine, *On Christian Doctrine* 1.15, ed. and trans. R. P. H. Green (Oxford: Clarendon, 1995), 28–29.

17. Kierkegaard, *The Sickness Unto Death*, 38.

18. Kierkegaard, *The Sickness Unto Death*, 96; my emphasis.

19. Kierkegaard, *The Sickness Unto Death*, 81.

20. Kierkegaard, *The Sickness Unto Death*, 79.

Let us imagine a cattleman who spends his life tending his cattle and has very little exposure to life beyond his cattle ranch. He prides himself on being quite smart; after all, he is smarter than his cows! We recognize immediately the absurdity of his claim. His cows are no criterion against which to estimate his own worth. But before we laugh too loudly, consider the criteria that *we* commonly use to estimate our worth. The temptation to associate worth with wealth is everywhere present in contemporary society. Or we imagine that our worth depends on success in our field of employment, or on being better educated than others. Or we might suppose that our religious observance makes us superior. How often our self-esteem, our sense of worth, is based on comparison with others. Whenever we employ such criteria, however, we do no better than the Pharisee who stood in the temple to pray and thanked God that he was not like other people (Luke 8:9–14). We may scoff at the cattleman who, in comparison with his cows, thinks of himself as rather smart, but the comparative judgments we often make for ourselves are equally absurd. That is true whether we judge ourselves to be better than others, or, as is equally common, whether we suppose ourselves to be much less worthy than others. Kierkegaard insists that the criterion is wrong.

The true criterion is God. We are made in God's image; we are called to live in covenant relationship with him; God is mindful of us, and our worth as human beings depends entirely on that fact. Humanity's true worth depends entirely on the fact that we are created and loved by God, and called to live in relationship with him. The refusal to accept this, and the commonly indulged preference to find a criterion of worth elsewhere, is just one more manifestation of sin. It is in this light that Kierkegaard insists that the opposite of sin is not virtue, but faith.[21] "In relating itself to itself and in willing to be itself, the self rests transparently in the power that established it. This formula," Kierkegaard explains, "is the definition of faith."[22] To put this more plainly, faith involves acceptance of the self that God has called us to be, and active engagement in the realization of that self. It is by such means, by trusting ourselves wholly to the purposes of God, that we rest transparently in the power of God.

Moving successively further away from the fashionable assumption that we human beings are the measure and goal of all things, Kierkegaard now makes explicit the basis upon which his conception of the self has been developed.

A self directly before Christ is a self-intensified by the inordinate concession from God, intensified by the inordinate accent that falls upon it because God

---

21. Kierkegaard, *The Sickness Unto Death*, 82.
22. Kierkegaard, *The Sickness Unto Death*, 131.

allowed himself to be born, become man, suffer, and die also for the sake of this self. . . . Qualitatively a self is what its criterion is. That Christ is the criterion is the expression, attested by God, for the staggering reality that a self has, for only in Christ is it true that God is man's goal and criterion, or the criterion and goal.[23]

Kierkegaard's recognition of "the staggering reality that a self has" places him in the company of those who confess, on the basis of revelation, that of all the creatures, only human beings are made in God's image (Gen 1:27); it places him alongside the psalmist who is filled with wonder and awe that God should be mindful of us (Ps 8:4); it puts him in the company of Paul who saw that human beings have been predestined to be conformed to the image of God's Son (Rom 8:29). Christ, says Kierkegaard, is humanity's true criterion and goal. It is in him that we see what our true humanity consists in, and it is through him that our true humanity is secured and redeemed. For this reason, Kierkegaard explains, "'What do you think of Christ?' is actually the most crucial of all questions."[24]

Alone before God

In contrast with the widespread assumption in modern Western culture that we are to be self-made men and women, that we are ourselves the measure of all truth, that we are ourselves responsible for the determination of what is right and wrong, and that we are ourselves capable of living the good life, Kierkegaard presents us with a picture of human life that is realized in its fullness only before God in faithful obedience. Such obedience involves the recognition that "to need God is a human being's highest perfection."[25] Defiance of that relationship with God in and for which we were made is the original temptation put before humankind. In answer to the serpent's promise, we aspire to be like gods, obedient to a word of our own making, and masters of our own destiny. But this sinful determination, expressed with infinite variety, leads only to despair.

God's gift of salvation, of forgiveness, of reconciliation, confounds the assumption that we are to be self-made men and women. Although we ought properly to recognize that we are responsible for sin, it is a mistake to imagine that we must also be responsible for overcoming it. "Your sins are forgiven," we

23. Kierkegaard, *The Sickness Unto Death*, 113–14.
24. Kierkegaard, *The Sickness Unto Death*, 131.
25. Such is the title of one of Kierkegaard's *Eighteen Upbuilding Discourses*, ed. and trans. Howard V. Hong and Edna H. Hong (Princeton: Princeton University Press, 1990), 297–326.

hear; but then we are inclined to respond: No, wait! I want to save myself—by being a good person, by developing my own spirituality, by amassing a fortune. Similar temptations beset us in the political realm: we imagine that salvation can be secured through economic growth, through military might, or through scientific and technological progress. These are common delusions in an age of self-assertion, but, in Kierkegaard's view, they are simply forms of despair. By way of an antidote to this sickness, Kierkegaard directs our attention to the place where the Creator of all things has himself established the criterion and the goal for truly human life. He directs our attention to Christ in whom we see that obedience rather than self-assertion, humility rather than mastery, faith rather than sinful defiance—these are the means by which a truly human life may be lived.

To what extent did Kierkegaard himself manage to live the life that he commends? There is abundant evidence in his *Journals* of his intent and of his striving. He writes, for example:

> What use would it be to be able to propound the meaning of Christianity, to explain many separate facts, if it had no deeper meaning for *myself* and *my life*? . . . What use would it be if truth were to stand there before me, cold and naked, not caring whether I acknowledged it or not, inducing an anxious shiver rather than trusting devotion? Certainly I won't deny that I still accept an *imperative of knowledge*, and that through it one can also influence people, but *then it must be taken up alive in me*, and *this* is what I now see as the main point. It is this my soul thirsts for as the African deserts thirst for water.[26]

We may thus acknowledge and respect Kierkegaard's own efforts to be a self before God, but we utterly miss the point and violate Kierkegaard's own wishes if our conclusions after reading Kierkegaard concern the content of *his* life. Kierkegaard's intention through the course of his authorship is not to draw attention to himself, but to leave his readers alone before God. It is *our* task, enabled by the Spirit, to grow into the likeness of Christ and so respond to God's call to live a truly human life.

---

26. *Journals and Notebooks*, 1:19–20, AA: 12, 24 (June 1, 1835), ed. Niels Jørgen Cappelørn et al. (Princeton: Princeton University Press, 2007), 127.

Chapter 37

Karl Barth: Human Identity and the Freedom of God in Christ

Ross Hastings

> "The ontological determination of humanity is grounded in the fact that one man among all others is the man Jesus."
>
> — *CD* III/2, 132

Legend has it that a student once fell asleep in one of Karl Barth's seminars. He was awoken by the sound of his professor's voice saying, "please answer the question for us." Without missing a beat the student responded, "Jesus Christ." Barth's response was, "Exactly right!" True or not, this story points to the taproot of Barth's theology. Adam Neder, in whose book this story is told, goes on to say that this taproot is

> the confession that God's gracious action toward the world is concentrated "in Christ," who is both the saviour of the world and its salvation, the giver of grace and grace itself. Not since the apostle Paul has one phrase so dominated a theologian's work. According to Barth, revelation, election, creation, reconciliation, and redemption all take place "in Christ," and their meaning and content may be rightly apprehended only in him. In fact, the very being of humanity itself is objectively included in the being of Jesus Christ, and is likewise subjectively (i.e., by individual people) realized in him. In these acts of inclusion and realization, the creature is incorporated into a depth of fellowship that is nothing less than participation in the being of God. Statements such as these are at the heart of Barth's theology. Yet they cry out for explanation.[1]

---

1. Adam Neder, *Participation in Christ: An Entry into Karl Barth's Church Dogmatics* (Louisville: Westminster John Knox, 2009), xi.

Thus, in Karl Barth's opinion, if we want to discover specifically who the human being is, as well as our personal identity, we do not in the *first* place look at or into ourselves, our personal history, nor even to the empirical sciences. We must learn all we can from these sources, but these are not, as Barth interpreter Wolf Krotke says, appropriate for "*establishing theologically* what it is that constitutes the essential character of the human."[2] For that we do not observe human beings in general, or human beings in history, but we turn first to the very inner being of the triune God, and in particular to his *freedom to love*. In freedom the triune God eternally elected the Son to become human, and in the Son therefore, he elected freely to be *for* the humanity he would create, such that in Christ, humanity is the covenant partner of God. Barth goes so far as to say that "Jesus is the divine disposition which precedes all history, indeed the creation of the world."[3] From the beginning God is not undisposed, or "neutral,"[4] towards his creation and humanity, for he exists eternally in his covenanting will, which is his will to be incarnate in Jesus. As such, the divine disposition is to create and redeem creation and human persons to live in a freedom derived from him, through the Son.

It is important to realize that election in Barth's understanding is *not* a secret decree in the hiddenness of God by which he selects some humans for himself while passing over others, thus passively electing some to perdition, in a manner that is abstracted from Christ. Barth's well-known, radical christological renovation of this doctrine was motivated by his perceived concern that the classical Reformed doctrine of election, which includes the arbitrariness of the *deus absconditus*, cannot provide assurance. Edward T. Oakes relates how Barth actually transformed Calvin's (and Augustine's) version of predestination by grounding election in Christ.[5] Oakes comments, "He alone is the primal object of the Father's election. It is in him that the family of man is summoned to election. And the individual is summoned to his own personal and private relationship with God only as a part of this family."[6] Thus, in Barth, election is

2. Wolf Krotke, "Karl Barth's Anthropology," in *The Cambridge Companion to Karl Barth*, ed. John Webster (Cambridge: Cambridge University Press, 2000), 159.

3. Karl Barth, *Church Dogmatics*, vol. IV, pt. 3, pt. 1, ed. G. W. Bromiley and T. F. Torrance, 2nd ed. (Edinburgh: T&T Clark, 1975), 230 [hereafter all volumes (1956–1972) are referred to as *CD* vol./pt.: e.g. *CD* IV/3/1].

4. *CD* IV/1, 42.

5. Edward T. Oakes, "Predestination in America," *Nova et Vetera* (IJT) 8, no. 3 (Summer 2010): 683–702. For more on Barth's critique of Calvin's doctrine of predestination, see John E. Cowell, *Actuality and Provisionality: Eternity and Election in the Theology of Karl Barth* (Edinburgh: Rutherford House, 1989).

6. Hans Urs von Balthasar, *The Theology of Karl Barth: Exposition and Interpretation,* trans. Edward T. Oakes (San Francisco: Ignatius Press, 1992), 175.

the very best news of the gospel. God has in his freedom, in the very act of the eternal generation of the Son that defines the immanent Trinity (some Barth scholars would say), and at least in the eternal covenant of God, chosen the Son to become human,[7] to become Jesus, the one Man who defines humanity in its freedom, the one Man in whom God has chosen all humanity. This primal decision in God from all eternity thus made Jesus of Nazareth the prototypical human, after whose image we have been created. By his participation in humanity as an entity, in the Son, God imparts that intended identity-in-freedom to humanity, at least by design.

In the freedom of God's act of election, the Son is both the *electing God*, a free agent in his nature as a person within the Trinity, and also the *elect man*, receiving freedom vicariously for humanity. As Robert Osborn has stated, this ensures both that Jesus as the electing God is the "beginning of all God's ways," and that as the elected man he is "the goal and fulfillment of God's eternal will . . . the event in which God's eternal will is actualized. The creation comes from Christ, and it is fulfilled in him."[8] Osborn clarifies by saying that, as "Jesus is at the beginning and in the middle, he is also at the end. . . . Whatever comes to man in the freedom of God and in the fulfillment of his eternal will comes first of all to Jesus as *the* elected man."[9] This is the very heart of the gospel for Barth. He is, in his christological expression of election, defending it against "all non-Christological interpretations of divine and human freedom in orthodox Calvinism and Lutheranism, and in philosophical versions of the same in mod-

---

7. What exactly this means for the essence of the triune God is a hotly debated topic among Barth scholars, and principally, Bruce McCormack and George Hunsinger. For an able summation of the controversy, see Phillip Cary, "Barth Wars: A Review of *Reading Barth with Charity*," *First Things* (April 2015) (all quotes in this footnote come from this article). The issue is not just that Barth is saying that this one human being is present at the beginning and foundation of all things, but that, on McCormack's "hyper-Protestant" account, the divine act of electing this incarnate human being in which the Son participates as electing God, actualizes the immanent Trinity. This radical understanding is termed "Barth-revisionism" by Hunsinger. As Cary says, "Even after he worked out his mature doctrine of election, Barth kept talking as if the Trinity could be conceived independently of Jesus Christ." Instead, Hunsinger "asks us to read Barth 'with charity,' seeking to discern the fundamental coherence of his thinking," and his conscious debt to the tradition, not modernity. Hunsinger appeals to "the 'doctrine of antecedence,' according to which all that God does in the world finds its ground in what God is antecedently in himself, prior to the work of creation and redemption. God's grace toward the world in Christ corresponds to, but is not identical with, what he is in himself as the triune God. In this context, there is a place for the notion of a logos *asarkos* or unincarnate Word, not as a principle of rationality to which we have access apart from Christ, but as a necessary concept in the doctrine of the immanent Trinity."

8. Robert T. Osborn, "Karl Barth: Freedom in Christ," chap. 4 in *Freedom in Modern Theology* (Philadelphia: Westminster Press, 1967), 118.

9. Ibid.

ern Protestantism. . . . he is endeavoring to correct deterministic constructions of God's freedom on the one hand and existentialistic, indeterminate constructions of human freedom on the other hand."[10]

But what does this communicate about our human identity? What we are elected for in Christ, is *freedom*. I venture to say that this is the most crucial descriptor of identity in Barth's anthropology. It is *derivative*, a freedom *received*, received from the freedom of God to be God, his freedom to love, his freedom to elect Jesus and all humanity in him. Yet it is *real*, for the end goal of that election is the creature living in freedom. This is not freedom of a modern kind that says "I can do or be whatever I want." The free creatures live into their identity-in-freedom, paradoxically, by being bound to the freedom of God in Christ, and are never more themselves than by being ever in union with him.

In the quaint expression of Barth, the freedom of elect humanity is summarized as a "freedom *for*" and a "freedom *from*" and a "freedom *for freedom*."

> **Freedom *for*:** The doctrine of the eternal election of Jesus (and humanity in him) means that the beginning and the end, the ground and the goal of humanity's freedom is Jesus. This freedom *for* Jesus means four things: *free for an eternal will* (the divine eternal purpose and covenant), *free for an actual fact* (the historical reality of Jesus), *free for a present word* (being spoken now), and *free for a living Spirit* (which saves now and to the end). This fourfold freedom *for* is expressed again in this way: freedom for and in an eternal word spoken from the beginning; freedom for a word made flesh spoken "once upon a time" in history; freedom for apostolic words spoken in the church (a duty to confess in mission); and freedom for a creative word spoken by the Christian through the Spirit to the world (spirituality). These latter two are where Christology finally arrives at anthropology in Barth, that is, at human duty, including prayer, responsibility for the cosmos, and spirituality.

> **Freedom *from*:** There is a correspondence in each to the freedoms *for*. The first is *freedom from the devil* (*Das Nichtige*, nothingness, anti-creation). The revelation of Christ as God's eternal will sets us free from this negation to be for God, for our fellow-humanity and for the creation. The second is *freedom from pride and sloth*. These two features of the life of nothingness are overcome in the death and resurrection of Christ, his humility as a priest and his victory as king, and the participation of the believer in both. The third is the *freedom from falsehood*. The person who denies the reality of election rejects

10. Ibid.

Christ and the truth, manifests a false freedom, the "impossible freedom that binds man to nothingness and the vanity of the world, a powerless freedom, a powerless power that binds him in service to the law and his own lost self."[11] It is from this bondage to damnation that Jesus as Word and prophet sets the Christian free. The fourth is the *freedom from silence*. Corresponding to the fourth freedom *for*, which is "freedom for the world through creative unity with the Spirit," this is the freedom from "the uncreative silence of a spirit subject to the stifling and confuting sounds of the world."[12] By the Spirit, reconciled and redeemed humanity ceases to be silent and can fulfill its destiny to bring the creation to its destiny as the creation of God in the full liberty of the sons and daughters of God.

Freedom *for freedom*: Barth then integrates freedom *for* and freedom *from* with *freedom for freedom*. There "is a unity of freedom which is the very essence of Barth's view of freedom," which gives to freedom a spontaneous joy, so that "when I do *what Christ* gives me to do, there is no contradiction, but the occurrence of the original, the possible, the most joyful; there is freedom. . . . To be free in, for, and through Jesus is to be free indeed. In a word, Jesus is both the goal and ground of freedom, subject and object, alpha and omega."[13] This freedom for freedom given us in Christ sets us free to be participants in the prophetic office of Christ, as witnesses to Christ in the world by the preaching of the Word of God.

In this chapter, we can consider only the first two (of four) and most foundational aspects of "freedom *for*," in the hope that this may stimulate the reader's interest in reading the rest of this section in the *Church Dogmatics* (III/2, *The Real Man*). Let us examine these two great concepts in ways that drive us deeply into the life of God in our search for identity.

Freedom For an Eternal Will (The Divine Eternal Covenant): For and In an Eternal Word

First then, the freedom that brings human identity is an echo of divine freedom in the eternal Godhead, which is, in turn, evident in the eternal nature of the Son as being in his very being, bound for humanity. The doctrine of eternal

---

11. Ibid., 170.
12. Ibid., 172.
13. Ibid., 173. This reflects *CD* IV/3, 49–52.

election in Barth means that God is eternally a covenanting God, a gracious God, and humanity through Jesus is from the beginning God's covenant partner. God exists in his free and gracious decision in which he binds himself by electing for himself another (his Son, Jesus Christ) to become the limit of his freedom and the very context of his eternal existence. He binds himself by the act of election to the eternal Son who will become Jesus, and in Jesus, he therefore binds himself to all humanity.[14] Barth justified his belief in the eternal orientation of the Son towards incarnation (*incarnandus*) and the eternal purpose and identity of God around this biblically from John's Prologue and especially 1:1 and 1:15, which radically identify the eternal Word (the *Logos*, who is as Word eternally engaged towards revelation) with Jesus of Nazareth, and also from Colossians 1, in which Paul speaks of Jesus as the One who "is before all things, and in him all things hold together" (v. 17).

Our identity as humans on this account is thus first our freedom for God's eternal Word in Jesus. That is, the freedom in which God creates is the freedom of Christ, and so "God in Jesus is the only possibility, the only content of man's created and true freedom."[15] As such, he is man's "ontological determination."[16] Barth speaks of this as *original freedom*. In our original created nature, humanity is both "from God" and "toward God," and as such, the freedom of the human person is the freedom found in being loved. *Each human person is beloved of God.* Each enjoys a natural and spontaneous freedom in her original createdness by God, for she is bonded in Christ to the inner freedom of God. And this has nothing to do with her—for she is elected by God before she is created. This is, of course, only true because in the eternal counsels of God, she and all humanity are bound up in the humanity of the Son who God in freedom elected to become human and to represent humanity. In other words, as Osborn states in summary of this section in the *Dogmatics* on the *Real Man* (III/2, 126–94), "the only humanity which God's eternal word presupposes is

---

14. What this says about the freedom of God has led some Protestant theologians to question whether the freedom of *God* gets compromised by this (e.g., Peter Brunner and Robert Jenson, who claim that, in this construct of divine freedom and election, Barth "denies to God the freedom of his wrath [*Alpha and Omega*, 160]." Osborn, "Freedom in Christ," 123 n. 24). On the other hand, the freedom of the *human*, in Barth's schema, is also questioned by Catholics (e.g., Hans Küng, von Balthasar, who understood freedom as immanent to humanity, and a prerequisite condition to salvation). Balthasar objects that "the priority of Christ in no wise demands [as Barth tends to insist] that the whole work of creation must necessarily be pressed painfully into a Christological scheme" (*Theology of Karl Barth*, 253). In response, it must be noted that Barth's thorough theological method ensured that this imbalance did not persist. There are evidences in our exposition below that his anthropology was indeed robust.

15. Osborn, "Freedom in Christ," 126.

16. *CD* III/2, 132–36.

that of Jesus Christ; Christ precedes Adam."[17] All other humans are included in his real humanity, and thus at the very core of human identity is this great reality that we are loved by God from all eternity, and that it is a secure reality. As Osborn boldly states, "Like a drowning man in the arms of his rescuer he is not constrained to ask about his own potentialities."[18]

Irrespective of whether universal election means that every human person will be saved, we can say that, according to Barth, the prior love of God is true for all humanity and energizes the sharing of good news that God is, in his design and desire, *for* humanity in general, and every human in particular. Suffice it also to say that, for Barth, believing people, who accept this verdict of themselves, that is, who have accepted their *calling* by God to acknowledge and obey the gospel, knowing that they have already been elected from eternity, are able to enter into that real reality about themselves. This beloved-ness is the core of human identity. The justification in Christ that is acknowledged by the believer is not a product of something inside of the believer, endemic to human nature. It is sheer grace, sheer eternal electing grace, given to us *ex nihilo*, not through natural theology or "points of contact."

How does the human person enter into this freedom *for* the freedom of the triune God expressed in the election of the Son to become human and to justify humanity and creation? Barth speaks here of *answering or responding freedom*. This is *not* an innate potentiality for response in human persons, as if such potentialities had some prior existence. Rather, response is all grace, all gift, and it is intrinsic to the Word as it is received. God does not merely give us the gift of election and justification in Christ, but he gives us also the capacity for response in the Word of the gospel, in the living Word Christ, who has already responded for us. His faith or faithfulness is the great reality in which all our responses are made. He is both the gift and the means of its receiving.

This does not destroy the identity of the human person, but rather establishes it, for our identity is in his. This is perhaps best expressed as an *asymmetric compatibility*, in which God's actions in Christ and our actions can coinhere, and in which his actions have priority (just as in Barth's Cyrilline Christology, the divine nature is coexistent with the human nature, but the divine nature has precedence, for it is the divine nature that takes in the human nature), and yet our actions have absolute integrity. In fact, they secure our identity. Barth outlines three aspects of freedom for the eternal Word, a "joyful movement toward the grace of God which alone is in the beginning." These are termed "response-abilities." The *first* is the freedom of knowledge, or a freedom to

17. Osborn, "Freedom in Christ," 127.
18. Ibid.

understand and accept God's eternal electing love in Christ, that is created by grace. Barth indicates that this includes a *self*-knowing, and knowledge of oneself as actual and true only in the response to grace by grace. This is the basic act of reason given in the response to grace, and it is the basis for all other human knowledge. It is a rejection in Barth of the Cartesian *cogito ergo sum* (I think, therefore I am), and a replacement of it with the concrete "*Christus est ergo sum*" (Christ is and therefore I am). Barth makes the point that this is "the truth, the universal truth which creates all truth." The first and ultimate truth about all reality and life, he insists, is "not an objective or abstract knowing, but a subjective self-knowledge, it is 'living knowledge' (*Dogmatics in Outline*, 25)."[19]

The second grace-enabled response-ability is a volitional one, in response to the knowledge. Acknowledgement of our existence within the electing love of God in Christ leads to an active response of the free will. It "established existence as obedience. Life is thus not only a gift (*Gabe*), as signified by the Sabbath and the gift of the knowledge of God; it is also a task (*Aufgabe*)." This is not insignificant to identity, but definitive of it, giving the lie to the popularly held, super-spiritual concept of "being without doing." As Osborn states, "The decision of will thus called forth is not one among others behind which the true ego neutrally resides; no, the decision for God's Word is one of 'to be or not to be' (*KD* III/2, 216)—a decision so radical and comprehensive 'that no question remains regarding the way back, that the willing individual already exists in his decision and thus no longer knows or possesses himself in any sort of neutrality' (*KD*, III/2, 217)."[20] The way in which this most concretely manifests itself in the life of the Christian is in the *confession* before God and humans of the grace that has been received. The freedom before God is the freedom to confess before humanity.

The third response-ability is that of invocation, or prayer. Hearing the word of grace that establishes his existence in the electing love of God in Christ, and which leads to the response of obedience in mind, will, and deed, is expressed through invocation. The believer who has received the word of grace and is obedient to it is always conscious that all of it is grace. She can never be self-confident and complacent. The existence of the believer is, in fact, defined by thanksgiving. Prayer is primary to Christian existence and it is primarily in the form of a petition, the "utterance of a lack and need" and "the expression of the certainty that the thing needed . . . is to be found in God" (*CD* III/4, 99). The essence of prayer and its basis is in fact the "freedom of man before God,"

19. Ibid., 131, *KD* refers to the German edition of the *Church Dogmatics*: *Die Kirkliche Dogmatik* (Zurich: TVZ Verlag, 1932–1967).

20. Osborn, "Freedom in Christ," 131.

and this response to the majestic and superior will of the gracious God is man's "ground, his permission, his necessity" (*CD* III/4, 102).

These grace responses, which describe the freedom of the human person in their hearing of the Word of his eternal election, are summarized by Barth as the *real history* of new creatures. By history, Barth did not mean history as a result of an evolution or adjustment of the human person. Rather, he meant history of the creature as having experienced something new, something beyond his own sinful nature. But this history (*Geschichte*) of the human person is not to be thought of as merely a state or condition. Rather, it is something radically new, in that it occurs in the encounter and decision between the human person and God. The history of the human person is therefore *Heilgeschichte*, a meeting within the history of God. Our story is only a story in light of God's eternal story of electing in grace to send his Son to assume humanity and grace it in him.

If defining human freedom for God in this first category, in addition to *original freedom*, and *responding freedom*, and its response-abilities, Barth spoke also of *freedom in* creation.

Suffice it to say that Barth, like Calvin, depicts the first Adam even pre-fall as living in a freedom as response to grace. The givenness of the created order as expressed in the garden of Eden in Genesis 2 stakes out the realm of grace for humanity in participation with God in a good creation. The tree of the knowledge of good and evil speaks to Adam and Eve that their lives and righteousness are God's decision for them, and they are offered the privilege and necessity of accepting God's election and life. They were not to eat of it for it was not theirs to know good and evil and decide for themselves what freedom and life is. Their existence could be sustained only by grace, in hearing God's word and in acceptance of God's decision. God's demand was the promise of grace. That humanity was only free within the limits of God's eternal will helps us to understand how Barth viewed the law of God throughout his work. It is the form in which the eternal will of God confronts humanity, and it is as such the form of *grace*. It tells the human person who she really is by the eternal decision of God and it establishes the person in this decision of God. God's law as grace tells the human person who she is and also invites the person into this decision. As Krotke states, summarizing Barth, "The invitation claims man because it is the call of man's true self. As such it actually grants man the permission to be himself." Barth states, "We must learn . . . what God wants with us and from us only from what he has done for us" (*KD* II/2, 621), and Osborn adds, "Because God's law speaks of what he has done *for* us it lays so radical a claim *upon* us. *It is the claim of our critical selfhood*."[21]

21. Ibid., 135, emphasis added.

By contrast with the cherished Lutheran notion that the law follows the gospel and is the subsequent expression of it, for Barth the law or command of God is the word of a decision that both reveals and imparts the gospel of humanity's new humanity in God's elect-man Jesus. The gospel is the context, the sphere in which the law demands and claims for the human an obedient decision. And this graced decision is all-important for human identity. This in fact establishes freedom, "the granting of a very definite freedom" (*KD* II/2, 650), allowing the human "to be, by his own decision, what he is by God's decision—elect from the beginning in Jesus."[22] Identity as God's elect person, to summarize, is lived out in the freedom of obedience to God's command.

But this freedom for an eternal will, for and in an eternal word spoken from the beginning, is conveyed by Barth finally as *freedom for the fellow human*. The logic is this: Jesus is the man elected by and for God, on behalf of all humanity. He is therefore "for the other man." Therefore the human person who lives for and from Christ will also be radically for the other person. The human person will be "radically with his fellowman . . . basically, essentially and necessarily 'togetherness with fellowman' (*Mitmenschlichkeit*) (*KD* III/2, 296)."[23] That is, the human person is by identity, *both personal and relational*, in an I-Thou relationship, not able to say "I" without both relating to and distinguishing from "Thou" (*CD* III/2, 256). This becomes evident by way of a profound dependence of the "I" on the "Thou," the human other, and the divine Other. As surely as the free person is with God, through God's eternal Word spoken in Jesus, the free person is with her fellow human. For Barth, my spontaneous and joyful existence with my fellow human person is the only possibility I have as a creature of the triune God's eternal will. The I-Thou relationship is thus an essential dimension of our identity in freedom. Another way to say this is that as God has become a neighbor to humanity in the person of Jesus, and as Jesus, who was eternally the brother of all humanity, the Man for all humanity, we too, if we live into our free identity in God, in Christ, will *be* also, as we are *for the other*. We will have a radical freedom for the other. There will be space for the other, entered into with spontaneity and joy (*CD* III/2, 319). This includes both the near neighbor and the distant neighbor (*CD* III/4, 116), as Barth put it. That is, the person in our home and neighborhood, and the person across the seas in poverty and hunger. We are less than our selves when we do not act in love for the fellow human that we can help.

22. Ibid., 136.
23. Ibid.

Freedom for an Actual Fact (The Historical Reality of Jesus):
For a Word Made Flesh

To understand human identity, we must turn, secondly, to the concrete human person of Jesus Christ, the one in whom God actualized his gracious will, and in whom "God bound himself and entered into human history."[24] What Barth wishes to emphasize is that there can be no discussion of humanity without dealing with the reality of God the Creator, the electing God, who from eternity past elected to be for humanity and to become human for humanity. Barth states that the "free man is an actuality in Jesus of Nazareth."[25] This actualizing of God's gospel orientation towards humanity in the incarnate Son has two dimensions that relate to freedom. The first has to do with freedom from sin, that is, forensics. It relates to justification. The second has to do with the freedom to be image-bearers through Christ.

Freedom from Sin

The reality of the humanity to which the Word came was its sinfulness. Expounding Barth, Osborn states, "the existing man, the man whom Christ calls brother, is the man who crucifies Christ—the man who exists, therefore, in a freedom, if it may be called that, which is quite other than that which Jesus actualized."[26] This true freedom that Jesus actualized and offers to humanity gives humanity freedom over the powers of sin, and in Christ, "man is restored to the freedom he possesses as the creature of God—a freedom to be *from* and *for* God—and he is also given a freedom to be *with* God in fulfillment of the covenant and to share with God victory over the devil, sin, and death." In the one new man for humanity, Jesus, the human is both sinner (*peccator*) and justified (*iustus*) (*KD* IV/1, 649). As justified persons, we are free persons. Humanity's freedom is first of all the freedom of the man Jesus. Barth speaks of the justification of humanity as "the liberation of man" (*KD* IV/1, 634–40). In this new humanity, humanity is free. This is in one sense, for Barth, true of all humanity. Justification in Christ was a consequence first of the participation of the Son in humanity, that is, the prior participation of God in humanity, in Christ, the Son of God. This for Barth implies the *de jure* participation and justification of all humans, though he distinguishes this from the *de facto* par-

---

24. Krotke, "Barth's Anthropology," 159.
25. Osborn, "Freedom in Christ," 138.
26. Ibid.

ticipation of believing people in Christ by the Spirit.[27] The intent and design of God for humanity in the one new human, Jesus, is justification pronounced over our heads. We had nothing to do with it.

For the person who has believed and for whom justification is *de facto*, Barth speaks of three aspects of their identity defined by concrete freedom from sin in Christ. First he speaks of the *freedom of humility*, and second of a *living freedom*, and third of *new freedom*. The *freedom of humility* is the freedom of faith, a "free, human act" (*KD* IV/1, 846), the freedom given to existing humans "by virtue of the fact that his essential humanity and true freedom exist first of all in Jesus of Nazareth, in his humanity and his freedom."[28] This faith is principally justifying faith that humbly admits that justification is in Jesus alone, more centered on his faith and faithfulness than on our own. For Barth, justification is more emphatically "by Christ" than "through faith," and it is emphatically "through faith," not "by faith." It "is altogether faith *in*; it is absolutely determined by its object, Jesus, who does for man what he cannot do for himself."[29] The *sola fide* is simply a weak yet necessary echo of the *solus Christus* in Barth's theology. It is therefore not meritorious. It is faith as radical humility. It is described as a "confident despair," the despair that the old humanity cannot suffice, and a confidence gained in the new humanity of Christ. It is faith that acknowledges that freedom is received; received from the freedom of the triune God; received from the freedom of the triune God in the real man, Jesus. In this sense, faith, for Barth, is first of all a cognitive event rather than a creative one, an acknowledgement involving recognition (a knowledge of its object), cognition (a knowledge about its object gained from within the church and the holy Scriptures), and confession (taking public responsibility for one's faith, standing for Jesus). If the cognitive aspect of faith seems dominant, the knowledge of Christ assumed here turns out to be knowledge as an act of the whole self. Thus the knower in the act of knowing God, knows herself also. The knower is not therefore left unmoved. The last aspect, confession, is spoken of by Barth as faith's freedom *for* confession and as freedom *from* fear.[30]

But if faith is first of all an act of humility involving cognition, not creativity, there is, as a result of faith and associated with it, something profoundly new, something indeed that is truly creative. Freedom is a *living freedom*. The human situation is altered, and "individual Christian subjects"[31] are confirmed as such,

27. These nuances of Barth's doctrine of participation are referenced by Adam Neder in his *Participation in Christ*, 82–85.
28. Osborn, "Freedom in Christ," 140.
29. Ibid.
30. Ibid., 143–44.
31. *CD* IV/1, 752.

and these subjects exist in a likeness to Christ, in death and resurrection, that is, in mortification and vivification. Identity is thus an identity with Christ in death and resurrection, lived out in overcoming pride and sloth. And it is, as such, *new freedom*. Their newly gained sense of identity as new creatures in Christ is lived out in likeness to Christ. This is the truth of rebirth or regeneration. Thus, Barth sees humble, justifying faith as that which receives the freedom for God's *eternal will* in Jesus, and creative, regenerating faith as that which enables freedom for *Jesus* as God's eternal will. Space precludes a full consideration of human participation in Christ, and the consequent justification, sanctification, and vocation of the reconciled human (Barth's *triplex gratia*) so crucial to human identity. A second aspect of freedom in the new Man, Jesus, one that relates to our being rather than our standing before God, is that of image bearing.

Freedom to Be Image-bearers

Barth does not go first to Genesis 1 to discover what the image of God means, but to the last Adam, the substance of whom the first Adam is but a shadow. For Barth, creation could not be understood as a sphere independent to the premundane decision of God to elect to be for humanity. Krotke states, "Creation was called into existence by God as a space for the realization of this electing decision."[32] The covenant of God in eternity past with and for humanity, in Christ, was therefore the basis for the creation. This close relationship between creation and covenant was expressed by Barth's adage that "covenant is the internal basis of creation," and creation is the "external basis of the covenant" (*CD* III/1, 94–96). When Barth does speak of Genesis, he speaks of creation (Gen 1) as the arena for the working out of the covenant (Gen 2). This is immediately reflected in the fact that God creates the human being in such a way that being a real partner with God is possible. Humanity is created in a way that is analogous to God's own relational, triune being. But Genesis 1 and 2 are eschatological for Barth. The image is not a reality without its being recapitulated in Christ. The similarity or analogy of humanity to God's own being is only fully found "in the concrete man Jesus in whom God has elected the whole of humanity and in whom true human existence intended by God is realized."[33] For as Barth said, "the humanity of Jesus is . . . the repetition and reflection of God Himself, no more and no less. It is the image of God, the *imago Dei*" (*CD* II/2, 219). It is only through Christ that humanity "is created in the image of God" (*CD* II/2, 324).

32. Krotke, "Barth's Anthropology," 167.
33. Ibid.

This is in keeping with Paul's designation of Christ as the image of the invisible God (Col 1:15). Lest there be confusion, this did not mean that Barth had a poor view of all humans other than Christ. In fact, in the design and desire of God, in Christ, all humanity takes on the image of God, including those humans who lived before the time of Christ for whom this is true retrospectively. There is no higher basis for human rights and dignity than the fact that in Christ all humanity is his elect people, and they are cohumanity with Christ and to each other.[34] Barth's novel grounding of the image of God in humanity as being in Christ is termed the *analogia fidei*. It involves an analogy or similarity between human existence and divine existence that is grounded in Christ, over against a similarity to God of the human being itself. Barth spoke in pejorative terms of the latter as it is expressed in the *analogia entis* of Roman Catholic theology.[35] Such an analogy that does not need Christ was suspect for him. Rather,

34. For a discussion of how Barth and Brunner disagreed over the basis for human rights and the meaning of the image of God, see Joan Lockwood O'Donovan, "Man in the Image of God: The Disagreement Between Barth and Brunner Reconsidered," *Scottish Journal of Theology* 39, no. 4 (1986): 456. Barth's major concern with any view of the image based on capacities immanent to the human being ("immanent-structural"), as opposed to his transcendent, Trinitarian, relational view grounded in God's election of all humans in Christ, was that they permitted Nazism's culling of "useless mouths."

35. The Catholic *analogia entis* ("of the same substance as God," developed by Polish Jesuit Erich Pryzwara, with its "orders of creation") stands over against the Bonhoefferian-Barthian-Reformed *analogia relationis* or *analogia fidei*. As Bruce McCormack of Princeton has noted in his review of Barth's *The Holy Spirit and the Christian Life: The Theological Basis of Ethics* (trans. R. Birch Hoyle [Louisville: Westminster John Knox, 1993]), in *The Princeton Seminary Bulletin*, 1994, Book Reviews, 312–14), Barth, as a Reformed theologian, being against the *analogia entis*, might have used the language of *entis* as corrected or "rightly ordered" (312) by the *analogia relationis* and *fidei*, but chose to avoid the use of *entis* all together. In fact, to avoid all misunderstanding, as McCormack notes, "In the 1929 essay, . . . against Pryzwara's view, Barth held that human beings can know a great deal of themselves, but they cannot know that they are creatures in the strict theological sense of the term" (312). McCormack states in light of the stress Barth places on the Creator "in his relation" to the creature, that this "means that the true *analogia entis* must be understood to be the consequence of a dynamic relation of God to the creature, a relation that is never simply a given (a *datum*) but is always, in every moment, to be given (a *dandum*)" (313). Thus, Barth's actualistic account of faith is the end of all synergism. This will undoubtedly strike some readers as stern stuff, "but the drift of contemporary theology into the abyss of self-deification shows just how needed such a word is today" (313). For a state-of-the-art, full-orbed discussion of the *analogia fidei* and surrounding issues, see Archie J. Spencer, *The Analogy of Faith: The Quest for God's Speakability* (Downers Grove, IL: IVP Academic, 2015). See also Spencer's work on Barth's ethics in light of the freedom of God (*Clearing a Space for Human Action: Ethical Ontology in the Theology of Karl Barth* (New York: Peter Lang, 2003), as well as the work of John Webster, *Barth's Ethics of Reconciliation* (Cambridge: Cambridge University Press, 1995); John Webster, *Barth's Moral Theology: Human Action in Barth's Thought* (Edinburgh: T&T Clark,

the analogy was something "that only discloses itself in faith in the God who affirms all human beings in the man Jesus."[36]

This essence of humanity as defined by correspondence to God reflected in the image of God in Christ, and the *analogia fidei*, has three main constitutive aspects.

The Person in Relation

The first is the relationality of God and therefore of humanity—that is, Barth reemphasizes humanity understood as cohumanity. The human creature lives structurally in relation, which is an external expression of the fact that the triune God exists as Father, Son, and Holy Spirit in relations, the relation of love (*CD* II/2, 220–30). But it is in Jesus as a man that we have seen this. It is the humanity of Jesus, "His fellow-humanity, his being for man and the direct correlative of his being for God," which "indicates, attests and reveals this correspondence and similarity" between him and God (*CD* III/2, 220). But humanity in general participates in this correspondence and similarity in such a way that the human person is human only in relation to fellow human beings.[37]

This reemphasizes that relationality with the other is crucial to human identity. Identity-in-freedom is identity-in-relation to God as covenant partner in Christ, and to the fellow human to whom I am bonded because s/he too is also bonded to Christ as cohuman. This profound relationality is worked out in family relations, and especially in the church. As such, whether in singleness or marriage, in human relationality, the male and female binary plays an important role. Humanity functions as cohumanity in its being male and female together, and by humans being male or female individually. Human relationality structured in this sexual binary manner has correspondence to God and his covenant partner. Barth gleaned this from the primal passage on the image of God in Genesis 1:26–27. Barth sees God creating man and woman, even apart from marriage in Genesis 1 (marriage is not mentioned until Genesis 2), "because he is not solitary in himself, and therefore does not will to be so *ad extra*" (*CD* III/2, 324). Krotke comments that "This is because what is manifest in the irrevocable differentiation and relatedness of man and woman is that in order 'to be God's partner in this covenant man himself requires a partner' (*CD*

1998); and that of Joseph L. Mangina, *Karl Barth on the Christian Life: The Practical Knowledge of God*, Issues in Systematic Theology 8 (New York: Peter Lang, 2001).

36. Krotke, "Barth's Anthropology," 167.

37. Ibid., 168.

III/1, 290), and cannot be understood as God's creature without this partner."[38] The relation of man and woman, as sexually differentiated, within society, and in marriage, as an *ordered relation*, is a concept much ignored in contemporary evangelical anthropology, and has obvious ramifications for the same-sex marriage debate. This, in turn, influences all human relations to be based on partnership as nearness with differentiation. Without the "I and Thou" of human encounter, man is not human (*CD* III/2, 289).

The relational nature of identity as Barth presents it creates a powerful dynamic for personal and social ethics. The power is the gospel orientation behind it, that is, the fact that God has chosen freely in Christ to be our covenant partner. This shapes the ethics thus to be evangelical and not legal. That is, they are a living out of freedom in Christ. This notion of the interpersonal self is also a significant insight for human psychology, and it is not surprising to see that this is a primary concept in Fairbairn's object relations theory[39] and Bowlby's attachment theory.[40]

The Human Person as the Soul of the Body

The precedence and subsequence that is implicit within the definite order in which the human person exists relationally is used in describing the being of the individual human person. Barth speaks of the human person as "the soul of his body" (*CD* III/2, 325), in that in its unity with the body the soul is given priority in the structuring of individual life. The man Jesus is pointed to as the "whole man" in whom "the interconnection of the soul and body and Word and act of Jesus" is "of lasting significance . . . from within" because "it is not a chaos but a cosmos, a formed and ordered totality" (*CD* III/2, 332). In the person of Christ as divinity that has assumed humanity, in an asymmetric way, is illustrated the correspondence of the relation between God and humanity. His life as soul and body, yet soul over body, is one he has full authority over (*CD*

---

38. Ibid.

39. See Daniel J. Price, *Karl Barth's Anthropology in Light of Modern Thought* (Grand Rapids: Eerdmans, 2002). Price has demonstrated a very interesting link between Karl Barth's analogy of relations and the object relations theory of human development developed by Scottish psychologist R. D. W. Fairbairn, which challenges Freud's individualistic determinism with respect to the psychological understanding of humanity with the determinative impact of key human interactions with others in the development of the person.

40. See Melissa Kelley, *Grief: Contemporary Theory and the Practice of Ministry* (Minneapolis: Fortress, 2010), 54ff. for a brief but good summary of attachment theory and its chief proponents and those who have integrated it with Christian theology.

III/2, 332). Correspondingly, all human beings also are required "to fashion, to take responsibility for, and to risk their own lives in the life-giving presence of God's Spirit."[41] In this section Barth guides the reader away from both abstract materialism (the human person is only a body) and abstract spiritualism (the Greek doctrine of the immortality of the soul) (*CD* III/2, 382–84) towards a biblical view of the human person as an ensouled body and an embodied soul. The body requires the soul for the person to be a "subject"; and the human being needs a body in order to be an "object" (*CD* III/2, 378). But the soul has precedence within equality, in that it is "the formative centre which makes human life into an 'independent life' (CD/2, 397) over against God and other human beings."[42]

Thus, along with his great emphasis on the relationality of human person-hood, Barth in III/2 emphasizes the independence of the human person, indeed the irreducible identity of each. Identity is robust in Barth's human person as expressed in the "individual's own perceiving, thinking, willing, desiring, and active existence."[43] Each human person is to be considered "distinctive" and "unsubstitutable" in the eyes of God and other people, who is "never merely one among many, and may never be degraded into a mere object."[44] This led Barth to emphasize that, in light of Christ, every human person has the freedom by grace to encounter God, to hear him, to make decisions, to obey him and to be active in the public square. That is, pertinent to our theme of freedom, the human person as made in the image of God, christologically framed, "is claimed by God *in the freedom of ethical responsibility*."[45] Krotke thus concludes that "it is no accident that the theologically explicit character of Barth's ethical and political discourse made him one of the most listened to and seriously received theologians of his day, at least in the German-speaking world."[46] Barth did not need the *analogia entis* for this but the christological participation of God in humanity, as in the *analogia fidei*. He could assume that in Christ all humanity had been graced, thus enabling all to participate in the public square and especially the Christian.

41. Krotke, "Barth's Anthropology," 169.
42. Ibid., 170.
43. Ibid.
44. Ibid.
45. Ibid., emphasis mine.
46. Ibid., 171.

The Human Person in Limited Time

All decisions made by the individual person spoken of above are of course subject to limits—those of the fellow human person whose dignity and rights must be considered, and those that arise from the embodied nature of human existence. Krotke aptly states that the "humanness of the human person would be lost if he or she were to be regarded—as possible by means of modern technology—as a creature without limits, whose threatened and vulnerable character need not be taken into account in a fundamental way."[47] Cohumanity, soul-body structure, and temporal/spatial limitation were thus the three crucial dimensions of human identity in Barth (*CD* III/2, 325–587). This temporal and spatial limitation was not viewed by Barth as in any way fallen or evil, but intrinsically *human*, as seen paradigmatically in the life of Jesus himself (*CD* III/2, 537–51). The time allotted to us is our unique opportunity to serve, just as it was for Jesus in the uniqueness of his saving life and death, in time and space. This involves acceptance of the "shadow side" of a good creation, that is, its suffering, pain, and the experience of meaninglessness, with a view to bringing what relief we can, and with a view to aggressive resistance of the real evil behind it. Even the end of this temporal life should be received not as a tragedy but as the temporal completion of our work. Barth's anthropology was thus one of great realism. Krotke summarizes its sentiments well:

> But the goal of human action can never be to negate the boundaries of human existence and to lead human beings to believe in the illusion of a life without inescapable limitations, without old age, sickness, and death. Only idols, and not God make such promises. For this reason, human life is to be a matter of singing the praise of the creatureliness of the human being precisely in the face of this "shadow side."[48]

In a footnote, Krotke adds that according to Barth, "Mozart can stand as an outstanding example of how the praise of the creation can be sung in the face of the creation's shadow side."[49] The goal of humanity in Christ is clearly for humans to be truly human, and fully alive. This is the great freedom that being free for an actual fact, the actual fact of the God-man, Jesus, brings.

In sum, misunderstandings around the realness of the human person in Barth's theological approach to human identity arise because his approach is

47. Ibid.
48. Ibid., 173.
49. Ibid., 175 n. 14.

so counter the culture of modernity in its self-obsession, and even the culture of Christian theology in our time in its obsession with psychological salvation. They arise above all because Barth's understanding of humanity emerges from the primacy of the revelation of God in the living Word and the written Scriptures, and the great conciliar tradition of the faith. This leads Barth to speak of humanity as derivative. But having done so, and crafted within this properly theanthropological manner, humanity actually takes on its richest and most dignified and most real reality. In fact, once human persons accept the freedom that comes not from within, but from the freedom of God in Christ, that is, as they become analogies of Christ, they become most truly themselves.[50]

50. With reference to this statement by Barth at the beginning of his account of the "Creature," in *CD* III/1, "As the Man Jesus is Himself the revealing Word of God, He is the source of our knowledge of the nature of man as created by God," John Webster comments that this "announces the reversal of an entire tradition of theology in which the self-reflective human subject and agent is considered to be axiomatic." However, Webster quickly adds, "Yet the reversal does not, despite much misinterpretation of Barth at this point—entail the repudiation of a robust sense of the human person as subject and agent, but rather the reintegration of anthropology into a teleological account of God and God's creatures in which to be human is to act out of gratitude for grace." John Webster, *Karl Barth*, 2nd ed. (London: Continuum, 2004), 95.

Chapter 38

C. S. Lewis: From Self-Obsession to *Plerosis*

Sharon Jebb Smith

C. S. Lewis addressed the topic of identity so often that one critic, James Como, has said that Lewis should have written a book on the self because he talked about little else. While I cannot agree that Lewis talked about little else—he talked about an incredible amount else—I will argue in this essay that Lewis had a lifelong interest in the self and that his understanding was one developed throughout his life. This chapter will set out the development in his thinking on the self and, in particular, will pay attention to what he wrote in the somewhat overlooked *Till We Have Faces*, a late book that is essentially about personhood and the nature of the self. Reference will also be made to another late book, *Prayer: Letters to Malcolm*, as well as the crucible in which Lewis explored identity: his own life.

From Self-Obsession to Self-Negation

Even as a teenager, Lewis was interested in the topic of the self. His thoughts on identity were probably influenced by his reading of Hegel, whereby self is understood through self-reflection, and through the awareness of others' perceptions about oneself. While his tutor Kirkpatrick ensured that he engaged with philosophical ideas and not just imaginative worlds, it is clear from his letters and writings that he was somewhat introspective, even self-obsessed. As he later wrote in a long letter to his lifelong friend Arthur Greeves, "One out of every three is a thought of self-admiration."[1] Living an isolated life, without any

1. C. S. Lewis, letter to Arthur Greeves, January 30, 1930, *The Collected Letters of C. S. Lewis*, vol. 1, ed. Walter Hooper (San Francisco: HarperSanFrancisco, 2007), 878.

603

duty and few relationships, allowed him to live in a world of ideas and dreams. Kirkpatrick wrote that in his late teens, Lewis had

> singularly little desire to mingle with mankind, or study human nature. His interests lie in a totally different direction—in the past, in the realm of creative imagination, in a world which the common mind would call unreal but which is to him the only real one.[2]

Although Lewis was still an atheist in his teens and twenties, the poems he was writing suggest that he yearned to be freed from his self-interest and to find the transcendence that he was reading about in the mystics (as was so fashionable in the early twentieth century). In *Tu Ne Quaesieris* (pub. 1918) we find him articulating the limitations of his introspective approach to date:

> Yet what were endless lives to me
> If still my narrow self I be
> And hope and fail and struggle still,
> And break my will against God's will,
> To play for stakes of pleasure and pain
> And hope and fail and hope again,
> Deluded, thwarted, striving elf,
> That through the window of myself
> As through a dark glass scarce can see
> A warped and masked reality?[3]

In his twenties, Lewis concluded that he needed to relinquish the will, "which as everyone has told us is the only thing to do."[4] And increasingly he realized that he must reject his habitual introspection: "The only healthy or happy or eternal life is to look so steadily on the World that the representation 'me' fades away. Its appearance at all in the field of consciousness is a mark of inferiority in the state where it appears. Its claiming a central position is disease."[5]

But while Lewis recognized that he needed to eliminate desire for public praise and all other means by which he might seek to buoy up his sense of self, at this stage he was still unsure what the "cure" was to be "except for the sort of vio-

---

2. K. James Gilchrist, "2nd Lieutenant Lewis," *Seven: An Anglo-American Literary Review* 17 (2000): 77.

3. C. S. Lewis, *Poems*, ed. Walter Hooper (London: Harper Collins, 1994), 220.

4. Lewis, letter to Arthur Greeves, January 30, 1930, *The Collected Letters*, 879.

5. Lewis, letter to Greeves, August 18, 1930, *The Collected Letters*, 930. The words were actually written in Lewis's diary in March 1926, but he cited them to Greeves on this date in 1930.

lent, surgical cure which Reality itself may be preparing for me."[6] Philosophy had been a significant aspect of Lewis's journey to this stance. His reading of Samuel Alexander's *Space, Time and Deity* forced him to conclude that attempting to discern truth through introspection leads only to a falsification of consciousness, a conclusion that played into his rejection of stream of consciousness works by modernist writers. For philosophy was not just a study of ideologies for Lewis. His philosophical studies and companions had led him to see philosophy as a way of life that involved action. Lewis conveys this in *Till We Have Faces* when he has Orual say, "But if I practiced true philosophy, as Socrates meant it, I should change my ugly soul into a fair one. And this, the gods helping me, I would do."[7]

It was inevitable, then, that Lewis's conversion to theism and then to Christianity at the age of thirty-three or so was going to be accompanied by changes in his life. He had reached his philosophical basis for living, and he knew that it would have practical implications.[8] Interestingly, Lewis's thoughts continued to hold to the path of self-abnegation, albeit with some adjustments. He continued to develop his philosophy that attention to himself was an obstacle to his spiritual growth, although he now saw this as being in line with Christian teachings. In one sense, his thinking in this respect had indeed moved much closer to a New Testament understanding of the self, whereby the old self must be put off in order for a new and transformed self to be put on (Col 3:9–10). But his ideas had a particular emphasis that was subtly different. It is possible that his ideas were heavily influenced by George MacDonald, who had played a significant role in his conversion, and whom he considered his "master." The importance to Lewis can be seen in his anthology of quotations from the work of MacDonald. One sixth of them are about the self, with many emphasizing the need to *deny* the self. For example:

> The self is given to us that we may sacrifice it: it is ours, that we, like Christ, may have somewhat to offer—not that we should torment it, but that we should deny it; not that we should cross it, but that we should abandon it utterly: then it can no more be vexed. "What can this mean?—we are not to thwart, but to abandon? . . ." It means this:—we must refuse, abandon, deny self altogether as a ruling, or determining, or originating element in us. It is to be no longer the regent of our action. We are no more to think "What should I like to do?" but "What would the Living One have me do?"[9]

6. Ibid., 930.
7. C. S. Lewis, *Till We Have Faces* (London: Fount Paperbacks, 1998), 213.
8. C. S. Lewis, *Surprised by Joy* (London: Fount Paperbacks, 1955), 175.
9. C. S. Lewis, ed., *George MacDonald: An Anthology* (London: Fount Paperbacks, 1983), 104.

Although he stops short of saying that we should utterly put to death the self, MacDonald speaks of abandoning it and refusing it. He stresses the need to watch out for the cunning and deceitful self, prone primarily to self-worship and self-regard.[10] "Self! I deny you, and will do my best every day to leave you behind."[11] Lewis similarly seemed to see the self as set in opposition to God. "From the moment a creature becomes aware of God as God and of itself as self, the terrible alternative of choosing God or self is opened to it."[12] He summarizes Augustine by portraying this opposition as pride, "the movement whereby a creature (that is an essentially dependent being whose principle of existence lies not in itself but in another) tries to set up on its own, to exist for itself."[13] In "Two Ways with the Self," Lewis sets out his basic thesis:

> Now the self can be regarded in two ways. On the one hand, it is God's creature, an occasion of love and rejoicing; now, indeed, hateful in condition, but to be pitied and healed. On the other hand, it is that one self of all others which is called *I* and *me,* and which on that ground puts forward an irrational claim to preference. This claim is to be not only hated, but simply killed; "never," as George MacDonald says, "to be allowed a moment's respite from eternal death." The Christian must wage endless war against the clamor of the *ego* as *ego*; but he loves and approves selves as such, though not their sins. The very self-love which he has to reject is to him a specimen of how he ought to feel to all selves; and he may hope that when he has truly learned (which will hardly be in this life) to love his neighbour as himself, he may then be able to love himself as his neighbour: that is with charity instead of partiality.[14]

For MacDonald and Lewis, the self came second; love of God and neighbor came first. Throughout his thirties Lewis worked diligently at this; we see this very clearly in his letters of that time. For example, in a letter that he wrote to Arthur Greeves in August 1930, he speaks very clearly about needing to relinquish the desire to have literary success. Writing from his own experience, he urged Greeves to regard his inability to find a publisher as an opportunity to learn to die to the self; "the only thing for you to do is absolutely *kill* the part

---

10. Ibid., 106.

11. Ibid.

12. C. S. Lewis, *The Problem of Pain* (London: Fount Paperbacks, 1977), 60.

13. Ibid., 59. Lewis considered pride to be his besetting sin.

14. C. S. Lewis, "Two Ways with the Self," in *The Grand Miracle*, ed. Walter Hooper (New York: Ballantine Books, 1986), 120.

of you that wants success."[15] But, he says, "such disappointments, if *accepted* as death, and therefore the beginning of new life, are infinitely valuable."

As a theist, Lewis found that this inattention to the self was easier than it had been as an atheist as he had the help of God in doing so: "one of the first results of my Theistic conversion was a marked decrease of the fussy attentiveness which I had so long paid to the progress of my own opinions and the states of my mind . . . to believe and to pray were the beginning of extroversion. I had been, as they say, 'taken out of myself.'"[16] So for the newly converted Lewis, God cooperates in enabling the forgetting of the self. Indeed, God may do more than cooperate; Lewis felt that, one way or another, God may be actively involved in an almost surgical procedure and will cauterize the inflated ego of the Christian. In *Till We Have Faces* we find that the gods perform surgery on Orual in stripping away the masks behind which she has hidden. And in *Mere Christianity* we are told that Christ will come and interfere with our self, killing the old natural self and replacing it with the kind of self he has.[17]

His emphasis upon such self-denial was an extreme position but it was shaped by a number of factors besides MacDonald: recognition of his own need to counteract his tendency to self-absorption; an awareness that self-aggrandizement or self-centeredness is not in line with the teachings of Christ; and a reaction against the modernist turn to interiority (although Lewis disliked the use of such "isms" and certainly did not fit neatly into any single category). For these reasons perhaps, an emphasis upon self-denial remained in his work for the next twenty years or so, alongside a strong sense that identity can only be found in God. The human cannot achieve any selfhood by his own efforts; the Existentialists, he later said, feel *Angst* because of their belief in solitary self-creation.[18] One's soul is not one's own, he believed. In writing about Adam and Eve, Lewis says: "They wanted, as we say, to 'call their souls their own.' But that means to live a lie, for our souls are not, in fact, our own."[19]

For mid-life Lewis, identity is something given and not made; human freedom is responsive first and foremost. To refuse to receive is to turn back in towards oneself.[20] One becomes a self through a life constantly given back to God, and Lewis argued for a determined self-discipline: "Some tendencies in each natural man may have to be simply rejected. Our Lord speaks of eyes

15. Lewis, letter to Greeves, August 18, 1930, *The Collected Letters,* 927.

16. Lewis, *Surprised by Joy,* 181.

17. C. S. Lewis, *Mere Christianity* (New York: Macmillan, 1952), 191.

18. C. S. Lewis, *English Literature in the Sixteenth Century Excluding Drama* (Oxford: Clarendon, 1954), 380.

19. Lewis, *The Problem of Pain,* 63–64.

20. Lewis deals with this in *The Problem of Pain,* chap. 5.

being plucked out and hands lopped off—a frankly Procrustean method of adaptation."[21] To fail to seek God first in this respect is to fail to become a person. Mark Belbury in *That Hideous Strength* is in danger of losing any sense of personal identity at all because he has let others mold and manipulate him and his desires. He has not learned to die to the standards of the fallen world.

Deemphasizing the Subject

Academically, Lewis argued for this in a literary debate with E. M. W. Tillyard, in a series of articles collected and known as *The Personal Heresy*. There he argued against the contemporary emphasis in literary criticism upon the personality or character of a writer. A writer (or poet, to use the old term as Lewis used it) should not focus on the personal, but on the public, the impersonal and the common; the reader is to look with the poet's eyes, not at him. To do otherwise, he argued, is to pervert the role of the poet into a kind of Poetolatry. Tillyard was unable to shift him from this stance in the exchange that followed, even when Tillyard argued that in the process of self-surrender, the poet may end up being all the more unmistakably him or herself.

Lewis continued to be a determined apologist for the importance of objectivity, as opposed to subjectivism. He perceived around him an ongoing transfer of emphasis from the external "object" to the "subject," and targeted this, not least in *The Abolition of Man* (the book that he considered the most important and enduring out of all he had written, alongside *Till We Have Faces*).[22] In *The Discarded Image,* he spoke of "that great movement of internalisation, and that consequent aggrandisement of man and dessication of the outer universe."[23] He believed that this emphasis would paradoxically but inevitably lead to the emptying of the person:

> In this great change something has been won and something lost. I take it to be part and parcel of the same great process of Internalisation which has turned genius from an attendant *daemon* into a quality of the mind. Always, century by century, item after item is transferred from the object's side of the account to the subject's. And now, in some extreme forms of Behaviourism the subject himself is discounted as merely subjective; we only think that we

21. C. S. Lewis, "Membership," in *The Weight of Glory and Other Addresses* (New York: Touchstone, 1996), 130.

22. As told to James Houston when he asked what Lewis thought was his most important work.

23. C. S. Lewis, *The Discarded Image* (Cambridge: Cambridge University Press, 1964), 42.

think. Having eaten up everything else, he eats himself up too. And where we "go from that" is a dark question.[24]

Lewis's high value of the objective tradition led to an emphasis upon objectivity in his own writing; books from this mid-life period include *The Problem of Pain* (1940), *Mere Christianity* (written throughout the 1940s), *The Abolition of Man* (1943). These books emphasize the value of orthodox Christianity and the value of common morals; they exclude that which is individualistic or idiosyncratic or subjective.

This deemphasizing of the subject and inattention to the "I" was also seen in Lewis's life to an extreme degree. He lived sacrificially, both with his energies and with his money. He replied to all letters, neglected his appearance and allowed himself to be endlessly interrupted when working at the home he had made with Janie Moore, his dead friend's mother. But even beyond that, he seems to have determined to focus on the objective to such an extent that there was little room for any personal attention to the self, not even with others. Strikingly, those who knew him testify that his manner was impersonal. Even his friends felt that they knew very little about him personally, and some spoke of his having a persona. His good friend Owen Barfield put it this way:

> What I think is true is that at a certain stage in his life he deliberately ceased to take any interest in himself except as a kind of spiritual alumnus taking his moral finals. . . . I suggest that what had begun as a deliberate choice became at length (as he had no doubt always intended it should) an ingrained and effortless habit of the soul. Self-knowledge, for him, had come to mean recognition of his own weaknesses and shortcomings and nothing more. Anything beyond that he sharply suspected, both in himself and in others, as a symptom of spiritual megalomania. At best, there was so much else in letters and in life, that he found much more interesting![25]

As Stephen Medcalf has pointed out, Lewis set aside the persona of his early life, that of the introspective writer, in order to adopt a mid-life persona of spokesperson for mainstream Christianity.[26] But that mid-life persona too

24. Ibid., 214-15.
25. Owen Barfield, "Introduction" to *Light on C. S. Lewis*, ed. Jocelyn Gibb (London: Geoffrey Bles, 1965), xvi.
26. Stephen Medcalf, "Language and Self-Consciousness: The Making and Breaking of C. S. Lewis's Personae," in *Word and Story in C. S. Lewis: Language and Narrative in Theory and Practice*, ed. Peter J. Schakel and Charles A. Huttar (Columbia: University of Missouri Press, 1991), 109-44.

came to be set aside as Lewis approached his fifties, and rethought some of his emphases upon the self.

Unveiling a Sense of Self

This reenvisioning of the self appears in rather veiled forms in his later work; he made no overt statement that would have flagged up his changing attitude, nor did he explicitly restate his theses on identity. But it seems as if Lewis came to realize that his attack on encroaching subjectivism was such that he was in danger of eliminating the subject. For one thing, we find that he begins to allow for a lot more of himself to come into his writings; no longer is he striving so much for objectivity. An overview of his works is one key to this. From the late 1940s onwards, we find that Lewis is no longer writing the objective books that he wrote in the 1930s and 1940s. In *Mere Christianity*, Lewis had articulated that human souls who are taken into God will be very much more themselves than they were before.[27] But it is only in the later books that we begin to see that trajectory playing out in Lewis's own work, as his work became both more creative and more obviously personal. His later books are still strong statements of his faith, but they are either fictional presentations of his beliefs, or they are personal, rather than written with any attempt to be objective. *A Grief Observed* (1961) was so personal that he had to publish it under a pseudonym. *Prayer: Letters to Malcolm* (1964) seems to consist entirely of material drawn straight from his own life.

But in my opinion, it is in *Till We Have Faces* (1956) that we find the most complete, albeit hidden, statement of the changes that had taken place in him. The novel is a tale of a soul that buries itself in duty and in stoic functionalism to the detriment of its spiritual growth, all the while being very productive and efficient.

It stands in very clear contrast to the cosmic sweep of Lewis's earlier fiction, both the science fiction trilogy and the Narnia stories. And it points towards a more nuanced understanding of Christian identity than can be found in his previous work. It was a story that Lewis had been composing for decades. Since an undergraduate, he had been fascinated by *Metamorphoses*, the myth of Cupid and Psyche, as told by Apuleius. The story itself developed in his mind, he said, until the themes suddenly interlocked in his fifties, turning a pagan myth into one with profound Christian reverberations. The plot details are as follows. A king in an ancient country has three daughters: Orual, Psyche, and Redival.

27. Lewis, *Mere Christianity*, 161.

Psyche's beauty is such that she is sacrificed to appease the gods. Out of jealousy that Psyche is content to have been translated to become the bride of a god, her older sister, Orual, denies the gods' existence, despite the clear testimony of her sister Psyche and her own glimpse of their palace. Thereafter, she chooses to veil herself, in an act that suggests a disconnection from the rest of the world. In the following years, as a veiled queen, she builds up the country to a state of success and efficiency, but at great cost to those around her, and to herself. Desensitized by jealousy and hurtful to those who are most loyal to her, she is also limited in her own growth, becoming "the queen." She effectively locks up inside herself the person that she used to be. But she becomes more and more troubled by her own trapped and diminished self, and eventually provoked to action by a series of events, she takes a complaint to the gods. In response, she finds that they take her on a journey into a long and complex process of deconstruction. Dreams, conversations, stories, and events all combine to force her to see the truth that she has for so long been denying to herself. For the truth is that she has veiled herself because she does not want to face the gods, and that in doing so, she has been living not only in denial of her own behavior, but in isolation from the relationships (with the gods and with others) which would have drawn her out of her long interior exile. Her stoic outlook is portrayed with striking clarity:

> I did and I did and I did . . . and does it matter what I did? I cared for all these things only as a man cares for a hunt or a game, which fills the mind and seems of some moment while it lasts, but then the beast's killed or the king's mated, and now who cares? It was so with me almost every evening of my life; one little stairway led me from feast or council, all the bustle and skill and glory of queenship, to my own chamber, to be alone with myself; that is, with a nothingness.[28]

Orual's materialistic and self-enclosed approach has diminished her greatly. Her act of willful rejection of the divine, caused by jealousy of her sister, has contributed to a concomitant lack of self-knowledge. She has not acknowledged the reasons why she has adopted the veil, nor the consequences of her behavior, and this long trajectory has led her to a place where she ultimately has no personhood—she is a gap, she says.[29] And yet, despite all of this, Orual must still learn to die to herself. The gods tell her to "Die before you die."[30] But she has

---

28. Lewis, *Till We Have Faces*, 177.
29. Ibid., 202.
30. Ibid., 212.

not succeeded. "It was as if I were dead already, but not as the god, or Socrates, bade me die."[31] If she had truly died to herself, she would have had a better sense of self; Lewis remained resolute on this point. But his understanding of that paradox was no longer the same.

It takes a complex series of actions to bring Orual to a point of *metanoia*, and to enable her to see her failings. In the end, she is able to speak to those around her directly and truthfully *because* she learns to accept the divine truths and submit to them. Orual is probably drawn from many sources, but in certain respects, she seems to be drawn directly from Lewis's own experience. In his determined rejection of attention to the self, he had, on some levels, forced himself into the same position as Orual. He had confused introspection with self-knowledge and in doing so, had diminished his ability to know himself, and for others to know him. But as Calvin and so many others in the Christian spiritual tradition point out, knowledge of self is tied to knowledge of God. As Orual puts it: "How can the gods meet us face to face till we have faces?"

Only a deep level of honesty with oneself can call forth a response from the divine. In one sense, Lewis still adhered to his emphasis upon setting aside oneself in order to submit to God. He continued to believe that this was essential to the spiritual life. But he came to understand in his own life that this should not negate the particularity of his soul. He, like Orual, came to see that he could only address the divine with his own particular voice.

Lewis did explain this in a letter to one correspondent—perhaps the closest he got to really indicating what *Till We Have Faces* is about. "The idea was that a human being must become real . . . must be speaking with its own voice (not one of its borrowed voices), expressing its actual desires (not what it imagines it desires), being for good or ill itself, not any mask, veil or *persona*."[32] The image of unveiling obviously struck a chord with Lewis—so much so that he chose to use it again in *Prayer: Letters to Malcolm*. As he put it there, when we assent with our will to be known by God, we have unveiled: "Instead of merely being known, we show, we tell, we offer ourselves to view. . . . By unveiling . . . we assume the high rank of persons before Him. And He, descending, becomes a Person to us."[33] The inability to be open and vulnerable limits spiritual progress. "God is in some measure to a man as that man is to God."[34] To assume "the high rank of persons" involves a willingness to allow God to engage with the particular person he has made.

31. Ibid., 216.
32. C. S. Lewis, letter to Dorothea Conybeare, in *Letters to a Sister from Rose Macaulay*, ed. Constance Babington Smith (London: Collins, 1964), 261.
33. C. S. Lewis, *Prayer: Letters to Malcolm* (London: Fount Paperbacks, 1998), 18–19.
34. Ibid., 19.

By the end of the book, Orual has no will, no pride, and no jealousy left in her. She is "unmade." And yet it is then that she catches a glimpse of herself as beautiful. Her refusal to face the truth about herself has taken her on a long and unnecessary journey. In contrast, her sister Psyche (whom Lewis referred to as an *anima naturaliter Christiana,* or natural Christian soul) has unerringly followed the promptings of her pure soul, having always longed for heaven and the presence of the gods. Human longing, or "Joy" as Lewis called it, is rooted in God's longing for humans, and Psyche instinctively understands this and follows it. The theme of self-denial is found in the life of Psyche, but the basis of it is love. There is no stoical self-abnegation. Rather, the emphasis is upon going beyond the self for love of others and love of the divine. As she puts it: "to leave your home . . . to lose one's maidenhead—to bear a child—they are all deaths." But they are also actions that bring new life. Orual comes to resemble Psyche because she learns that self-abandonment (true *ekstasis*) is relational, and that following Psyche's way of self-sacrifice is a way that leads to freedom and fulfillment; Psyche becomes "a thousand times more her very self than she had been before the Offering."[35]

Prayer, Love, and *Plerosis*

We get another glimpse of this gentler approach in Lewis's last book, *Prayer: Letters to Malcolm* (published posthumously in 1964). The (unnamed) letter writer, markedly like Lewis himself in a host of ways, articulates something of his mature thinking on the topic of the self. And now prayer has become a vital aspect of his sense of self. Prayer is presented to us as the hinge between God and the self, a way of moving towards a union of the human will with the divine will. Because God is the ground of our being, and the source of all human agency and identity, as we engage with him through prayer, we gain a deep sense of self. "The deeper the level within us from which our prayer, or any other act, wells up, the more it is His, but not at all the less ours. Rather most ours when most His."[36] The revealing of oneself to God, and being vulnerable—unveiling—is an important element of this. "Only God can let the bucket down to the depths of us," Lewis believed.[37] But first we must ask God for his

---

35. Lewis, *Till We Have Faces*, 232.

36. Lewis, *Prayer: Letters to Malcolm*, 66–67. "When one is among Pantheists one must emphasise the distinctness, and relative independence of the creatures. Among Deists . . . one must emphasise the divine presence in my neighbor, my dog, my cabbage patch" (71).

37. Ibid., 79.

help. We should pray before all other prayers, "May it be the real I who speaks. May it be the real Thou that I speak to."

There are limitations to this. For Lewis, the earthly life of prayer is also the means by which one is reminded that in this life we can easily make the mistake of falling into the belief that the "I" as I perceive myself is an ultimate reality. Most of us, Lewis says, hide behind veils, living with what he called a "phantasmal self," a façade that he likened to being an actor in a play. Psychologists such as Freud, he believed, have introduced us to a sense of the depth of the soul, but they have still underestimated the real depth and variety. To a large extent, we cannot understand the soul in this life—just as God too will remain in large part an unknown, even a "bright blur."[38] Just as even in prayer the real "I" struggles to address the real God. So self-knowledge here and now will only ever be partial, and Lewis presumed that we should not try to seek total self-knowledge in this life. "I sometimes pray not for self-knowledge in general but for just so much self-knowledge at the moment as I can bear and use at the moment; the little daily dose. . . . have we any reason to suppose that total self-knowledge, if it were given us, would be for our good?"[39] In this life there is no possible sense of completion. There will always be more.

Although pre-glory transformation can also be seen in his earlier fiction (especially *Perelandra* and *That Hideous Strength*), *Till We Have Faces* portrays the two extremes of Christian transformation by contrasting the two sisters. The correct understanding of longing and love that marked Psyche's soul on earth draws her straight towards that glorious fulfillment, in contrast to the roundabout and anguished humiliation which Orual must endure before she eventually finds herself reaching the same understanding. Psyche, like Ransom in the cosmic trilogy, exhibits traits of the Christian saint—sacrificial, joyous, seer-like, and capable of coexisting in both the earthly and the heavenly sphere concurrently. The novel points us towards this high rank, the utmost "fullness of being," or *plerosis*, as something to be lived *towards*, only partially experienced in this life.

This fullness is not, in Lewis's world, something that happens in isolation. Just as Ransom is in the community of St. Anne's, so too Orual is connected to others at the end, if in a mystical fashion. By the conclusion of *Till We Have Faces*, Orual is Psyche, we are told; she too has become a Christian soul. Psyche has in part taken some of her suffering, such is the interconnectedness of people in the great divine economy. As the Fox puts it, "We're all limbs and part of one Whole. Hence, of each other. Men, and gods, flow in and out and mingle."[40] The

---

38. See Lewis, *Prayer: Letters to Malcolm*, chap. 15.
39. Ibid., 32.
40. Lewis, *Till We Have Faces*, 228.

self participates not only in the life of God (see his essay "Transpositions") but also in the lives of other Christians.

These thoroughly supernatural dimensions of the self—or the soul—had been central to Lewis's thinking all his life. The self/soul—Lewis nowhere differentiates between the two words—will always remain a created being, but by divine grace, humans can become what God is by nature. These long-held ideas of Lewis's are very close to a full doctrine of deification—the theosis of the church fathers. For example, in *Mere Christianity* Lewis expresses confidence in the idea that humans could become "gods":

> [God] said [in the Bible] that we were "gods" and He is going to make good His words. If we let Him—for we can prevent Him, if we choose—He will make the feeblest and filthiest of us into a god or goddess, a dazzling, radiant, immortal creature, pulsating all through with such energy and joy and wisdom and love as we cannot now imagine.[41]

When Orual sees Psyche after her sacrificial death, she says of her, "I had never seen a real woman before."[42] At the end of *Till We Have Faces*, Orual too realizes that, like Psyche, she has come to the utmost fullness of being that the human soul can contain. But unlike Psyche, her journey has been long and arduous because she did not understand the true nature of sacrifice. Whereas Psyche's sacrifice has been carried out for love, Orual has also put herself to death but out of fear and jealousy and the inability to see things as they are. In the end she must accept that she has put herself to death, in the wrong way—in a way that has left her locked up inside. It is only by the end of the trial when the divine perspective has helped her to see with the eyes of love for Psyche and for herself, that she finds that in giving up her own desires—in practicing *kenosis*—she has found herself filled: *plerosis*. It is very much in line with the teaching of Gregory of Nyssa, "For the participation in the divine good is such that it makes anyone into whom it enters greater and more receptive. As it is taken up it increases the power and magnitude of the recipient, so that the person who is nourished always grows and never ceases from growth."[43] In contrast, Orual's stoic self-denial was not participation in the divine good. Whereas Psyche is marked by love, joy, and peace from the outset, so Orual learns it all in a rush at the end of her life—love for the gods, love for others, love for self.

41. Lewis, *Mere Christianity*, 206.

42. Lewis, *Till We Have Faces*, 232.

43. Gregory of Nyssa, *St. Gregory of Nyssa: On the Soul and the Resurrection*, 87. The resonances with Orthodox theology may have come from Lewis's connection with Nicholas Zernov as well as his wide reading in medieval literature.

Like Orual, it seems that Lewis came late to a personal grasp of the extent to which transformation is rooted in love rather than personal asceticism, and in a willing engagement with the triune God so that each person can become that "dazzling, radiant, immortal creature," pulsating with "energy and joy and wisdom and love." Where Lewis had rigorously set himself aside out of love for God, he came to love himself for God's sake, as Bernard of Clairvaux would have us learn. In the later works we see Lewis's mature understanding of self-transcendence as motivated by love, rather than a stoical self-denial. It would seem that he was at last able to grasp the biblical emphasis of putting away the old self in order to take up the new self, rather than the determined emphasis upon denying the self absolutely. Comments in *Letters to Malcolm* indicate this. For example, Lewis points out that Alexander Whyte advocated permanent horror at one's own inner corruption and that the Christian should daily scrutinize this filth, in order to be repulsed by it. But Lewis rejects this.

> Can he be right? It sounds so very unlike the New Testament fruits of the spirit—love, joy, peace. And very unlike the Pauline programme; "forgetting those things which are behind and reaching forth unto those things which are before." And very unlike St Francois de Sales' green, dewy chapter on *la douceur* towards one's self.

There may be a time to be repulsed, Lewis ponders, but a "regular diet of emetics" is not the way to spiritual health either.

The Pauline verses that inform the primary image of *Till We Have Faces* in 2 Corinthians 3:18 suggest only one side of the picture, "And we, who with unveiled faces all reflect the Lord's glory, are being transformed into his likeness with ever increasing glory, which comes from the Lord, who is the Spirit." There are other Pauline verses that echo the connectedness between love and fullness of self that can be heard in Lewis's later work, and they reflect many of Lewis's themes:

> Out of [*the Father's*] infinite glory, may he give you the power through his Spirit for your hidden self to grow strong, so that Christ may live in your hearts through faith, and then, planted in love and built on love, you will with all the saints have the strength to grasp the breadth and the length, the height and the depth; until, knowing the love of Christ, which is beyond all knowledge [*gnōseōs*], you are filled with the utter fullness of God [*plērōma tou theou*].[44]

44. Eph 3:16–19, taken from Bernard McGinn, *Foundations of Mysticism* (New York: Crossroad, 2002), 73. I inserted "the Father" in order to show fully the triune emphasis of the verses.

Here in Ephesians we find that God's glory is a strong self, rooted in Christ and planted in the love that is beyond all knowledge. And so, holding both emphases together, Lewis's mature thought shows that identity is to be found in engaging with the triune God but in a participatory way. Such engagement is not only about humans reflecting back the divine face (rather than seeking to gain one that is solely their own), but it is also about God reflecting back to humans the selves that they present to him.

Orual, like Lewis, learns the nature of a love that does not self-seek, but does not self-efface. Of Psyche, she realizes, "I loved her as I would once have thought it impossible to love; would have died any death for her. And yet, it was not, not now, she that really counted. Or if she counted (and oh, gloriously she did) it was for another's sake. The earth and stars and sun, all that was or will be, existed for his sake."[45] *Till We Have Faces*, in combination with *Letters to Malcolm*, strongly suggests that Lewis was beginning to grasp, not just intellectually, but also emotionally and spiritually, that the triune God's upbuilding of the self is rooted in a love that not only calls the human person out of their narrow limitations, towards a spiritual fullness that is beyond human reasoning. His journey from self-obsessed teenager was far from complete—the eschaton still beckoned—but his life-long journey was one that had been profoundly shifted away from obsession and self-denial towards a hidden self made strong and full with divine fullness.

45. Lewis, *Till We Have Faces*, 233.

Chapter 39

Flannery O'Connor: Novelist and Believer

Jay Langdale

A Catholic writer in a predominately Protestant region of America, Flannery O'Connor (1925–1964) is commonly regarded as a central figure in the twentieth-century Southern Literary Renaissance. Born in Savannah, Georgia, she was the only child of devout Catholic parents Edward Francis O'Connor and Regina Cline. The deepening Great Depression forced her father, a real estate agent, to move the family to Atlanta and eventually compelled Flannery and her mother, neither of whom liked the city, to relocate to Milledgeville, Georgia, where the Clines were socially prominent land owners. Compounding the family's difficulties, her father was diagnosed with the autoimmune disease lupus in 1937 and, four years later, died at the age of forty-five. His death was both a shattering moment for Flannery at age fifteen and an ominous foreshadowing of what would subsequently become her own acquaintance with this incurable debilitating disease. From this point forward, the specter of suffering and the shadow of death would transform her art and her faith.

The Making of a Catholic Artist in the Protestant South

In 1941, O'Connor enrolled in Georgia State College for Women. Shortly after graduating in 1945, she left middle Georgia to accept a scholarship at the University of Iowa's graduate writing program. While in residence, she read modernists such as James Joyce, T. S. Eliot, and William Faulkner. She also was exposed to the ascendant New Literary Criticism, which esteemed art for art's sake, encouraged questions of faith, and revered the ability of language to deepen understanding of life's complexity. In the spirit of these high modernist writers, O'Connor, much as Joyce turned to his native Ireland and Faulkner embraced rural northern Mississippi, determined to plumb the depths of middle Georgia as a means to, she maintained, "ground" the "supernatural in the "concrete."[1] She frequently described this errand in sacramental terms. "The best American fiction," she observed, "has always been regional," and though "the ascendency passed roughly from New England to the Midwest to the South; it has passed to and stayed longest wherever there has been a shared past, a sense of alikeness, and the possibility of reading a small history in a universal light." Southerners, she continued, "have had our Fall" and "have gone into the modern world with an inburnt knowledge of human limitations and with a sense of mystery which could not have developed in our first state of innocence—as it has not sufficiently developed in the rest of our country."[2]

Despite this observation, it is fair to say that O'Connor, like many of her Southern literary contemporaries, did not intend to pursue her art from her native region. While a student in Iowa, she kept a prayer journal that, while it seldom mentions the South, deals poignantly and intimately with her devotion to God and her artistic vision. In an April 1947 entry, she wrote:

> I must write down that I am to be an artist. Not in the sense of aesthetic frippery but in the sense of aesthetic craftsmanship; otherwise I will feel my loneliness continually—like this today. The word craftsmanship takes care of the work angle and the word aesthetic is the truth angle. Angle. It will be a life struggle with no consummation. When something is finished, it cannot be possessed. Nothing can be possessed but the struggle. All our lives are consumed in possessing struggle but only when the struggle is cherished and directed to a final consummation outside of this life is it of any value. I want to be the best artist it is possible for me to be, under God.[3]

After completing her MFA in 1947, O'Connor spent time first at the Yaddo artists' colony near Saratoga, New York, and then in New York City. In the spring of 1949, she took up residence at the Ridgefield, Connecticut, farm of her friends and fellow Catholic writers Robert and Sally Fitzgerald. However, this plan was interrupted in 1951 when O'Connor was herself diagnosed with lupus. In recognition of the inevitable worsening of her condition and her refusal to burden the Fitzgeralds with her care, she returned to live permanently with her overprotective, unintellectual mother Regina at Andalusia, the Cline family's 500-acre

---

1. Flannery O'Connor, "The Church and the Fiction Writer," in *Mystery and Manners* (New York: Farrar, Straus & Giroux), 148.
2. Flannery O'Connor, "The Regional Writer," in *Mystery and Manners*, 58–59.
3. Flannery O'Connor, *A Prayer Journal* (New York: Farrar, Straus & Giroux, 2013), 29.

dairy farm outside Milledgeville. Though it was a return home, her sense of physical and intellectual dislocation as well as her loss of independence made it seem, at least initially, more like a state of exile. O'Connor was transformed by this move, but not necessarily in the sense she envisioned. Sally Fitzgerald later described Flannery's acceptance of her fate as "graceful" and noted that she derived strength from Teilhard de Chardin's notion of "passive diminishment"— the serene acceptance of suffering beyond our ability to change.[4] O'Connor, in a letter to a friend, described such attenuations as "those afflictions that you can't get rid of and have to bear." In testimony to the authenticity of her graceful acceptance of her condition, O'Connor, redolent of her prayer journal, went on to relate that she had been to Lourdes for healing baths where she "prayed there for the novel I was working on, not for my bones which I care about less, but I guess my prayers were answered about the novel inasmuch as I finished it."[5]

To better understand O'Connor's vision of art and faith, it is useful to consider the historical and cultural context in which she wrote. Twentieth-century writers in the Western world labored in the shadow of both the Enlightenment and Romanticism. In 1911, writer George Santayana captured the temperament of the age when he noted that "the civilization characteristic of Christendom has not disappeared yet another Civilization has begun to take its place."[6] This circumstance informs the writings of a host of early twentieth-century writers like Santayana, James Joyce, and T. S. Eliot. These artists and their contemporaries labored in a culture that, Charles Taylor writes, esteemed literature as a "work of art" that "brings us into the presence of something which is otherwise inaccessible, and which is of the highest moral or spiritual significance." At its highest expression, modernist poetry, Taylor writes, "shifted the locus of epiphany to within the work itself."[7] In numerous regards, the modernist literary aesthetic endeavored to make literature and literary criticism a surrogate for religious faith. This, though, had its limits and was rooted in a moment when a shared culture and assumptions could be taken for granted. O'Connor, though writing only three decades removed from Eliot's epic poem *The Waste Land* (1922), could not make these assumptions. Indicative of this, she, with a mixture of regret and astonishment, noted in a 1956 book review that an author somehow seemed "able to assume an audience which has not lost its belief in Christian

4. Sally Fitzgerald, ed., *The Habit of Being: The Letters of Flannery O'Connor* (New York: Farrar, Straus & Giroux, 1979), 53.

5. O'Connor to Janet McKane, February 25, 1963, in *The Habit of Being*, 509.

6. George Santayana, "The Intellectual Temper of the Times," in *Winds of Doctrine* (New York: Charles Scribner's Sons, 1912), 1.

7. Charles Taylor, *Sources of the Self: The Making of the Modern Identity* (Cambridge: Harvard University Press, 1989), 419–20.

doctrine."[8] Accordingly, O'Connor's writing was perpetually and purposefully distant from the modernist literary aesthetic of art for art's sake. In an essay titled "The Fiction Writer and His Country," she observed:

> The novelist with Christian concerns will find in modern life distortions which are repugnant to him, and his problem will be to make these appear as distortions to an audience which is used to seeing them as natural; and he may well be forced to take ever more violent means to get his vision across to this hostile audience. When you can assume that your audience holds the same beliefs you do, you can relax a little and use more normal means of talking to it; when you have to assume that it does not, then you have to make your vision apparent by shock; to the hard of hearing you shout, and for the almost-blind you draw large and startling figures.[9]

Unlike the preceding generation of modernist writers, O'Connor labored under the realization that she could not afford these presumptions. In O'Connor's shadow, Walker Percy, a Catholic writer in the post-World War II South, poignantly wondered how the artist functions "when the holy has disappeared."[10] Among other things, modernity entailed an interminable shift from religion to science in support of human progress and welfare. Consequently, many modern artists and intellectuals, Charles Taylor notes, "cherished the notion that facing the Godless universe liberated reserves of benevolence in us." The climate O'Connor faced was, perhaps, typified by Samuel Putnam, who proclaimed that once "one loses confidence in God or immortality in the universe," one becomes "more self-reliant, more courageous and more solicitous of aid where only human aid is possible." Putnam and like-minded progressive intellectuals aimed at nothing less than to free mankind from violence, suffering, and death. Taylor points out that, had the most important moral questions remained "surrounded by mystery," these moral calls would have been easily "undercut."[11] They, of course, were not and, as a consequence of the loss of mystery and of the ascent of "non-theistic universal concern," Taylor proclaims, "something else has to play the role of grace."[12]

---

8. Flannery O'Connor, "Humble Powers," *The Bulletin of the Catholic Layman's Association of Georgia*, June 6, 1956.

9. Flannery O'Connor, "The Fiction Writer and His Country," in *Mystery and Manners*, 33–34.

10. Walker Percy to Caroline Gordon, April 6, 1962, quoted in Jay Tolson, *Pilgrim in the Ruins: A Life of Walker Percy* (Chapel Hill: University of North Carolina Press, 1992), 300.

11. Taylor, *Sources of the Self*, 405.

12. Taylor, *Sources of the Self*, 410.

In her letters, fiction, and essays, the reader witnesses O'Connor's acceptance of grace in the face of a succession of passive diminishments including a forced return to Georgia, an inability to return to life with the Fitzgeralds, and her gradual acceptance of the finality of her illness. This transformation is palpable in her personal correspondence, which, Sally Fitzgerald notes, amounts to nothing less than a "self portrait in letters."[13] Indeed, in her correspondence, one witnesses her evolving Christ-like acceptance of her fate and the concomitant deepening of her spiritual character, which was formed far more by what she endured and lost than by her achievements. As the years in Milledgeville passed, her letters reflect a perpetual and intensifying acceptance of her affliction. In April 1956, O'Connor, faced with crippling side effects of her treatment for lupus, announced that "It's crutches for me from now on."[14] In a succession of letters during the summer of 1956, O'Connor confessed that "I have never been anywhere but sick. In a sense sickness is a place, more instructive than a long trip to Europe, and it's always a place where there's no company, where nobody else can follow."[15] Along these same lines, she observed that "Sickness before death is a very appropriate thing and I think those who don't have it miss one of God's mercies." The following year, O'Connor characterized her "bone trouble" and resulting immobility as a "blessing in disguise" which left her nothing to do "but write."[16] "Lord," she confessed during the summer of 1957, "I am glad I am a hermit novelist."[17]

Much as she once outlined it in her prayer journal, O'Connor's artistic vision remained consistently marked by humility. She routinely professed to be "only a storyteller."[18] Addressing her sense of vocation, she described her "subject in fiction" as "the action of grace in territory held largely by the devil" and described her "audience" as one "which puts little stock in either grace or the devil."[19] O'Connor was a splendid storyteller and her fiction can be uncovered on a number of levels. On her readers, O'Connor once noted that her native region, in a certain sense, furnished an ideal audience because Southerners remained capable of recognizing "freaks." She further explained:

> To be able to recognize a freak, you have to have some conception of the whole man, and in the South the general conception of man is still, in the

---

13. Fitzgerald, ed., *The Habit of Being*, xi.

14. O'Connor to "A," March 24, 1956, in Fitzgerald, ed., *The Habit of Being*, 151.

15. O'Connor to "A," June 28, 1956, in Fitzgerald, ed., *The Habit of Being*, 163.

16. O'Connor to Cecil Dawkins, August 4, 1957, Fitzgerald, ed., *The Habit of Being*, 233.

17. O'Connor to Marayat Lee, June 28, 1957, in Fitzgerald, ed., *The Habit of Being*, 227.

18. O'Connor to "A," August 2, 1955, in Fitzgerald, ed., *The Habit of Being*, 94.

19. Flannery O'Connor, "On Her Own Work," in *Mystery and Manners*, 118.

main, theological. . . . But approaching the subject from the standpoint of a writer, I think it is safe to say that while the South is hardly Christ-centered it is most certainly Christ-haunted.[20]

Though it is fair to say that she was initially dismayed by her 1951 return to Milledgeville, O'Connor, by the late fifties, saw things quite differently. "I stayed away" from the South, she wrote to a friend, "from the time I was 20 until I was 25 with the notion that the life of my writing depended on my staying away. I would certainly have persisted in that delusion had I not got very ill and had to come home. The best of my writing has been done here."[21] By the late fifties, O'Connor had become the "Christ-haunted" region's "Hillbilly Thomist" who, much as Jacob wrestled the Angel, grappled with the South's complexity until she "extracted a blessing."[22] Within the South, she discovered a setting for her predicamental stories populated with an array of outcasts ranging from preachers and serial killers to armless carpenters and philosophers. Though a diverse lot, O'Connor noted that, in the end, all her stories were "about the action of grace on a character who is not very willing to support it."[23]

Hulga Was "Like Me": O'Connor's Short Story *Good Country People*

This was, perhaps, nowhere more the case than with her 1955 short-story "Good Country People," which concerns Hulga, a thirty-two-year-old unemployed philosophy PhD who lives with her overbearing mother. Hulga, who purposefully changed her name from Joy, had lost a leg at age ten in a hunting accident and prides herself on being a nihilist. She, O'Connor notes, had "the look of someone who has achieved blindness by an act of the will and means to keep it."[24] In her infirmity, Hulga had never had any "normal good times," and she wastes no opportunity to let others know that "if it had not been for [a weak heart], she would be far from these red hills and good country people."[25] Soon,

---

20. Flannery O'Connor, "The Grotesque in Southern Fiction," in *Mystery and Manners*, 44.

21. O'Connor to Cecil Dawkins, July 16, 1957, in Fitzgerald, ed., *The Habit of Being*, 230.

22. O'Connor to Robie Macauley, May 18, 1955, in Fitzgerald, ed., *The Habit of Being*, 81. Flannery O'Connor, "The Catholic Novelist in the Protestant South," in *Mystery and Manners*, 209.

23. O'Connor to "A," April 4, 1958, in Fitzgerald, ed., *The Habit of Being*, 275.

24. Flannery O'Connor, "Good Country People," in *Flannery O'Connor: The Complete Stories* (New York: Farrar, Straus & Giroux, 1971), 273.

25. O'Connor, "Good Country People," 276.

Hulga encounters Manley Pointer, a young Bible salesman, whom she determines to seduce for the purpose of humiliating him. Alone in a barn loft, Hulga
informs him that she "is one of those people who sees *through* to nothing" and
that "we are all damned, but some of us have taken off our blindfolds and see
that there is nothing to see. It's a kind of salvation."[26] When Hulga informs him
that she "has a number of degrees," Manley rebuffs her by requesting that she
"prove" her love for him by showing "where your wooden leg joins on."[27] Convinced that his appeal represented the "face of real innocence," she complies,
but discovers, shortly thereafter, that his valise contained two "hollow" Bibles,
which concealed a flask of whiskey, a pack of playing cards, and some condoms.
Manley, far from "good country people" or a "fine Christian," descends from the
loft with her leg in hand, but pauses just long enough to let her know that "one
time I got a woman's glass eye this way. And you needn't to think you'll catch
me because Pointer ain't really my name. I use a different name at every house
I call at and don't stay nowhere long. And I'll tell you another thing, Hulga," he
said using the name as if he didn't think much of it, "you ain't so smart. I been
believing in nothing since I was born."[28]

O'Connor, who well understood the passive diminishment of physical dis-
ability, the temptations of intellectual pride, and the burden of living with an
unintellectual mother, confessed that Hulga was "like me" and described the
story as a "rare occasion" in which writing "came easy for me."[29] O'Connor, at
the moment of the story's publication, was roughly the same age as Hulga and,
around this time, had analogously begun to walk with a cane. On a serious
level, "Good Country People" exemplified O'Connor's conviction that "violence is strangely capable of returning my characters to reality and preparing
them to accept their moment of grace."[30] In this regard, the story closely ap-
proximates Charles Taylor's concern that "when the commitment to universal
concerns takes on a non-theistic definition, something else has to play the role
of grace."[31] Yet, while the story and its autobiographical undertones deserve
to be taken seriously, the humorous elements of the story cannot and should
not be ignored. O'Connor's friend Thomas Gossett, who described her humor
as "uproarious and sometimes inward and ironic," recalls the occasion that
she invited the students in his Southern Literature class to Andalusia. At the

26. O'Connor, "Good Country People," 287–88.

27. O'Connor, "Good Country People," 288.

28. O'Connor, "Good Country People," 291.

29. O'Connor to "A," August 24, 1956, and September 7, 1957, in Fitzgerald, ed., *The Habit of Being*, 170, 241.

30. O'Connor, "On Her Own Work," 112.

31. Taylor, *Sources of the Self*, 410.

students' request, O'Connor read "Good Country People." As she reached the story's climax, Gossett recalled being surprised at "how deeply the humor of it affected her." When she came to the seduction scene, Flannery, he noted, was laughing so hard that she dropped the book on the floor. Asked about the source of her humor, Gossett simply replied that it proceeded from her "faith in the Christian religion."[32]

O'Connor's Introduction to *A Memoir of Mary Ann* and the Aesthetic of Revelation

In many respects the essence of O'Connor's Christian realism lay in her appreciation of the inextricable link between joy and sorrow. Yet there were occasions where even she herself could, in the words of C. S. Lewis, be "surprised by joy." Such was the case with events leading to her "Introduction to *A Memoir of Mary Ann*." Mary Ann Long was a child cared for by nuns at an orphanage in southwest Atlanta. She had come to live with them in 1949 at the age of three and they cared for her until her death from a lifelong deforming facial cancer nine years later. In the spring of 1960, the nuns, inspired by Mary Ann's spirit, wrote to Flannery requesting that she write a story about her. Flannery demurred, but charitably suggested that the nuns compile their memories of the child and that she would edit them and compose an introduction. Of the young girl and those who cared for her deeply, O'Connor wrote:

> She and the sisters who had taught her had fashioned from her unfinished face the material of her death. The creative action of the Christian's life is to prepare his death in Christ. It is a continuous action in which this world's goods are utilized to the fullest, both positive gifts and what Père Teilhard de Chardin calls "passive diminishments." Mary Ann's diminishment was extreme, but she was equipped by natural intelligence and by a suitable education, not simply to endure it, but to build upon it. She was an extraordinarily rich little girl.[33]

O'Connor went on to relate the manner in which a nun's questioning as to "why the grotesque (of all things) was [her] vocation" unexpectedly and won-

---

32. Thomas Gossett, "Flannery O'Connor's Humor with a Serious Purpose," *Studies in American Humor* 3, no. 3 (January 1977): 178.

33. Flannery O'Connor, "Introduction to *A Memoir of Mary Ann*," in *Mystery and Manners*, 223.

drously deepened her perspective on both her sense of self and her art. O'Connor responded that, though most of us are seldom shocked by evil in the world, the larger dilemma is that we had failed to ponder the good long enough to accept that its "face too is grotesque, that in us the good is something under construction." Yet, when we ponder the nature of goodness, she noted, "we are liable to see a face like Mary Ann's, full of promise." O'Connor, turning to the source of our blindness to this truth, continued that "in the absence of faith now, we govern by tenderness" and this tenderness "wrapped in theory" leads to "forced labor camps and in the fumes of the gas chamber."[34] O'Connor's pithy rebuke of what Charles Taylor terms the modern "heroism of unbelief" and the related "demand of benevolence" was, if possible, even more profound than the one rendered in the climax of "Good Country People."[35] Flannery's introduction to the nun's memories of the young girl stands among her most insightful meditations on the nature of human suffering. In one of her final and sternest rebukes to the modernist notion of art for art's sake, Flannery, reflecting on *A Memoir of Mary Ann*, wrote that "the human comes before art" and, thus, "you do not write the best you can for the sake of art but for the sake of returning your talent increased to the invisible God to use or not use as he sees fit."[36]

During the fall of 1955, O'Connor, by now quite debilitated by lupus, travelled to Nashville, Tennessee, to meet Russell Kirk. O'Connor highly admired Kirk's work *The Conservative Mind* (1953) and subsequently described him as a "voice of an intelligent and vigorous conservative thought." For his part, Kirk, who initially thought O'Connor suffered from a "broken leg," came away an admirer of her as well and would later say that she "understood truths at thirty" that he did not comprehend until the "age of sixty."[37] In one of the best concise statements on her achievement as a literary artist, Kirk wrote that her writing proclaimed "salvation through grace in death" and that "without preaching and without explaining her symbols, Flannery O'Connor became the great philosophical and theological novelist" of "this dissolving twentieth century."[38] Perhaps, of even greater note, Kirk's friend T. S. Eliot did not share his enthusiasm. In reply to a 1957 letter from Kirk expressing his excitement over her fiction, Eliot wrote that he found himself "quite horrified" by her stories and that his

34. O'Connor, "Introduction to *A Memoir of Mary Ann*," 226–27.

35. Taylor, *Sources of the Self*, 404–5.

36. O'Connor to "A," November 26, 1960, in Fitzgerald, ed., *The Habit of Being*, 419.

37. Bradley Birzer, *Russell Kirk: American Conservative* (Lexington: University of Kentucky Press, 2015), 202–3.

38. Russell Kirk, "Flannery O'Connor and the Grotesque Face of God," *The World and I* (January 1987): 429–33.

"nerves" were "just not strong enough to take much of such disturbances."[39] Like Eliot, O'Connor had, early in life, aspired to be an artist "not in the sense of aesthetic frippery but in the sense of aesthetic craftsmanship." Yet, by the middle of the twentieth century, Eliot's high modernist aesthetic of memory and art for art's sake was, as Kirk later understood, yielding to what might be aptly described as O'Connor's "Hillbilly Thomist" aesthetic of revelation.

39. Birzer, *Russell Kirk*, 203.

Chapter 40

Dietrich Bonhoeffer: The Question of Christian Identity

Jens Zimmermann

In his prison cell in Berlin (Tegel), sometime in 1944, Bonhoeffer penned the poem "Who am I?" Like the rest of his prison poetry, these verses express unflinchingly the questions and yearnings of a distressed individual who possessed uncommon self-discipline, a theologically trained, deeply reflective mind, and keen observational power. Bonhoeffer wrestles with this question about his identity during a time he describes as an "extreme case" or "borderline situation" (*Grenzfall*) that exposed and called into question the various elements that make up human identity.[1] Bonhoeffer's life as conspirator and his incarceration stripped away the common social and relational contexts that normally ground human identity, rendering uncertain the established character traits by which we routinely identify others and ourselves as the same person in changing circumstances. In this famous prison poem, he eventually turns to God as the only remaining, stable source of identity: "You know me, Oh God, I am thine."[2] What does Bonhoeffer's supplication to God for securing his identity indicate for the meaning of selfhood? Is Bonhoeffer's appeal to God the desperate cry of a disillusioned man, groping irrationally for a lifeline in a time of duress? Or does this appeal to a transcendent, personal other arise from a deeply Christian and theologically reflective consciousness? What does Bonhoeffer's poem teach us about the structure of identity common to every human being?

In this chapter, I want to show that Bonhoeffer's reflections on identity are indeed deeply rooted in his theology and represent the struggles of a Christian

---

1. *DBW* 8:188. Quotations from the original German are from *Dietrich Bonhoeffer Werke* [*DBW*], ed. Eberhard Bethge et al., 17 vols. (Munich and Gütersloh: Chr. Kaiser-Gütersloher Verlagshaus, 1986–1999). English translations are from *Dietrich Bonhoeffer Works* [*DBWE*], ed. Wayne Whitson Floyd (Minneapolis: Fortress, 1996–2015).

2. *DBW* 8:533.

self fully conscious of its union with God through Christ. Moreover, with the help of Paul Ricoeur's philosophy of selfhood, we will discover that Bonhoeffer's probing of Christian identity illustrates, but also goes beyond Ricoeur's hermeneutics of the self. To arrive at these goals, we will first outline Ricoeur's view of selfhood and apply his principal categories of *idem* and *ipse* identity to Bonhoeffer's struggle with authentic selfhood. Second, continuing to draw on Ricoeur's hermeneutics of selfhood, we will look at the important role Bonhoeffer's understanding of Christian identity plays in his account of ethical agency. As our analysis will show, Bonhoeffer's conviction that Christian identity rests in God, rather than in ourselves, enables an ethics based on a hermeneutical theology of discernment aimed at wisdom, rather than on moral principle. As it turns out, identity plays a central role in Bonhoeffer's theology, connecting personal identity with responsible ethical agency.

Oneself as Another: Ricoeur's Hermeneutics of the Self

In his Gifford lectures *Oneself as Another*, Paul Ricoeur sets out to find a more adequate model of selfhood than the Cartesian one bequeathed to modern philosophy. Descartes's foundationalist quest for certain knowledge based on a rational mind severed from the vagaries of the world, social relations, the body, and time was all too easily deconstructed by Nietzsche, leaving only the shattered cogito in his wake. While Descartes skipped over the world to postulate a self-founding subject of immediate, timeless self-reflection, Nietzsche only had to reintroduce the world to dissolve the self into language and history. Philosophy thus offers us first the exalted self of modernity, which is then replaced with the humiliated, or even dissolved self of postmodernity. Ricoeur charts a path beyond these extremes, by avoiding Descartes's mistake of evading the world in search of selfhood. For Ricoeur, an adequate understanding of the self has to begin from a detailed analysis of our life world, that is, of language and human experience. Thus, his own hermeneutics of the self takes "the detour of reflection by way of analysis" of language use and action, by examining the relation of selfhood to sameness, and, finally, by describing the dialectical relation between selfhood and otherness.[3] For our own application of Ricoeur's analysis to Bonhoeffer, we will only make use of the second and third aspects (the dialectics of same-other and self-other) of Ricoeur's findings.

While Ricoeur makes ample use of analytic philosophy for anchoring

3. Paul Ricoeur, *Oneself as Another*, trans. Kathleen Blamey (Chicago: University of Chicago Press, 1992), 16.

identity in language use and action theory, his approach is more profoundly indebted to the German and French phenomenological traditions, which demonstrate the crucial role of the body and emotions—in short, of the practical relations determining our being-in-the-world—for human perception. From this tradition, Ricoeur also takes a particular conception of truth that is more commensurate with the complexity of human self-understanding than the notion of truth operative in analytic philosophy. While Ricoeur appreciates analytic philosophy's methodical rigor, he fears that it remains too enthralled by a model of truth derived from the natural sciences. This scientific objectivism, with its aspiration to self-evident truth and impersonal description, cannot do justice to the complexity of the relational components that make up so much of our human environment.[4] In contrast to the certainty that science aims at with verification (a knowledge wrongly demanded by Descartes for philosophy), Ricoeur advocates *attestation*, truth as reasonable belief. *Attestation* is not contrasted with verification, but it is a verification of a different kind, for example, how an attorney gathers evidence into a credible narrative, or how someone's testimony convinces us because her narrative lends coherent sense to the details and is backed up by her own life or character. Ricoeur's model of truth recognizes that human knowledge is based not on certainties but on what the scientist John Polkinghorne calls "well-motivated beliefs,"[5] which are never self-evident but rest on reasonable evidence within an intelligible interpretive framework. Such knowledge is conveyed by attestation. Attestation, says Ricoeur, is "the speech of the one giving testimony that one believes."[6] Attestation conveys truth of a complexity scientific reasoning cannot capture, beholden as it is to the metaphor of sight. Sight requires the presentation and description of an object, "expressed in propositions held to be true or false."[7] Instead of propositional verification, attestation aims at veracity rather than measurable truth. Ricoeur's notion of *attestation* shows that belief and trust are essential to human knowing. As we shall see in our analysis of Bonhoeffer's identity poem, acknowledging this relational aspect of truth allows us to recognize responsibility as the ultimate structure of selfhood. The question "who am I?" can only be answered by way of attestation.

Ricoeur's first important insight is that identity consists of two major, interconnected aspects. The first aspect is the kind of sameness that allows us to

4. "It is perhaps due to the very style of analytic philosophy and to its almost exclusive preoccupation with description, as well as with the truth appropriate to description, that it ignores the problems pertaining to attestation" (Ricoeur, *Oneself as Another*, 72).

5. J. C. Polkinghorne, *Science and Religion in Quest of Truth* (London: SPCK, 2011), 11.

6. Ibid., 21.

7. Ibid., 73.

identify an object or set of characteristics as being the same thing or person in various places and times. Ricoeur employs the Latin term *idem* (same) to describe this permanence over time. Not only inherited physical characteristics but also customs and developed character traits make up our *idem* identity. This *idem* aspect cannot be reduced to physical qualities, as if sameness belonged to bodies and true selfhood to some inner, psychological dimension.[8] Ricoeur rightly includes inherited, indeed even developed, beliefs and attitudes as identifiable character traits that allow us to identify someone as the same. "Character," Ricoeur writes, "designates the set of lasting dispositions by which a person is recognized."[9]

Yet, as we all know, character can also change according to a person's development. In fact, as Ricoeur notes, "there is a sense of anxiety that goes with the sense of losing one's identity, understood as losing one's sameness."[10] It is at this fissure of anxiety, this failure of sameness, that selfhood as such emerges. What emerges when the *idem* identity breaks up? We move from the "what" question (*what* kind of person am I) to selfhood proper, or the "who" question. Ricoeur labels this the "*ipse*" aspect of identity. This aspect of "pure selfhood" reveals itself in times of anxiety, when true sameness is disrupted or breaks apart. Philosophers have tried to shore up self-permanence in time by postulating enduring substances such as a memory, or an identifiable sequence of events, or even an abstract transcendental subject. Yet Ricoeur shows that these solutions either fall apart under empiricist scrutiny or fail to do justice to the *personal* nature of selfhood.[11] The problem is that philosophers have hitherto tried to construct permanence in terms of an impersonal substance, such as memory or mind. Instead, Ricoeur turns to the more personal, ethical register and suggests that the *ipse* aspect of identity is best captured by the self-constancy expressed when I keep my word. Here we move decisively from the "what?" to the "who?" question: "Keeping one's word expresses a *self-constancy* which cannot be inscribed, as character was, within the dimension of something in general but solely within the dimension of 'who?'"[12] The permanence conveyed by this self-constancy is not a property or whatness of any kind, but the personal ethical responsibility and reliability of accountability: "counting on someone is both relying on the stability of a character and expecting that the other will keep his

8. Ibid., 128.
9. Ibid., 121.
10. Paul Ricoeur, "Pastoral Praxeology, Hermeneutics, and Identity," in *Figuring the Sacred: Religion, Narrative, and Imagination*, ed. Mark I. Wallace, trans. David Pellauer (Minneapolis: Fortress, 1995), 307.
11. Ibid., 306-7.
12. Ricoeur, *Oneself as Another*, 123.

or her word, regardless of the changes that may affect the lasting dispositions by which that person is recognized."[13] Thus, for Ricoeur, true selfhood rests on a self-constancy beyond the sameness of character or other traits and is defined ethically as responsibility: "Self-constancy is for each person that manner of conducting himself or herself so that others *count* on that person. Because someone is counting on me, I am *accountable for* my actions before another. The term 'responsibility' unites both meanings."[14] When another who needs me asks, "where are you?" and I respond "Here I am," my response is a statement of self-constancy, marking my identity as a person. This promise and effort of ethical reliability constitutes the truly personal *ipse* aspect that shares in, but goes beyond, the *idem* elements of physical, mental, and habitual characteristics.[15] It is this personal element that not only makes a body, character traits, beliefs, or even events permanent in time, but also anchors this permanence in a "who," and therefore in the ethical realm of personhood.

Two more elements round out Ricoeur's account of selfhood: the role of narrative and of the other for the subsistence of personal identity. Already in his earlier work *Time and Narrative,* Ricoeur had argued that personal history requires the narrative elements we similarly employ in the writing of fiction in order to form an identity. The answer to the question "who did this?" is "to tell the story of a life."[16] Narrative unifies events and character into a coherent story centered on a protagonist we can identify. This "narrative unity of life" presents us with "the unity of an actor and the objects/subjects of his or her intervention."[17] Thus narrative identity is the catalyst for self-constancy, for the narratively constructed self can escape the dilemma of breaking up into subjective illusions or fragmenting into infinite impressions "to the extent that its identity rests on a temporal structure that conforms to the model of dynamic identity arising from the poetic composition of a narrative text. Unlike the abstract identity of the Same, this narrative identity, constitutive of self-constancy, can include change, mutability, within the cohesion of a life-time."[18] Ricoeur concludes that narrative identity is the all-important link between the

---

13. Ibid., 148.

14. Ibid., 165.

15. Ricoeur assumes that the *Idem* and *Ipse* aspects of identity stand in dialectical relation to one another. Selfhood-identity (i.e., *ipse*) covers "a spectrum of meaning, from the pole where it overlaps with sameness to the opposite pole, where it is entirely distinct from the latter." The first pole is "character" and the second "the ethical notion of self-constancy" as being counted on and accountable for (*Oneself as Another*, 165).

16. Paul Ricoeur, *Time and Narrative* (Chicago: University of Chicago Press, 1984), 3:246.

17. Ricoeur, "Pastoral Praxeology," 308.

18. Ibid.

poles of *idem* and *ipse* identity, between the sameness conveyed by character and personal selfhood rooted in ethical responsibility. The narrative identity of a life story gives the main character his or her recognizable features within changing events. "Narrative identity," he explains, "makes the two ends of the chain link up with one another: the permanence in time of character and that of self-constancy."[19]

However, on very rare occasions, even narrative coherence can fail. Under extreme circumstances, *idem* and *ipse* separate so that "the passage from 'Who am I?' to 'What am I' has lost all pertinence."[20] When does this happen? The *ipse* identity becomes isolated when a person's narrative is being reconfigured against his will, when all life details seem no longer to add up, and when the subject, deprived of all sameness, becomes "confronted with the hypothesis of its own nothingness."[21] Ricoeur's own examples for such an identity crisis are taken from literature, and he also mentions "conversion narratives" as instances when one's whole life story requires rearrangement around a new orientation or within a new narrative framework. More to the point, this critical moment of the self described by Ricoeur fits precisely the situation Bonhoeffer faced in prison. Bonhoeffer finds himself indeed "in the crucible of this nothingness of identity," in which the question "who am I?" does not completely negate the self but completely lays bare the question of *who* is left after all known identity markers have been stripped away, and he is no longer the author of his own narrative.[22] How is it, Ricoeur, asks, that we can still say, "here I am"? Ricoeur's answer is that this minimal assertion of identity is a response to another. Within an interpersonal context, the ethical identity of accountability is here established by the question: "Who am I, so inconstant, that *notwithstanding* you count on me?"[23] In the final analysis, true selfhood is founded on the ethical relation of responsibility to a personal reality external to myself.

Ricoeur argues that this ethical dimension is intrinsic to selfhood, because, contrary to a common modern misconception, the self is not an autonomous free-floating bubble of consciousness but has otherness built into itself. Otherness is "not added on to selfhood from the outside" as an afterthought to avoid solipsism, but "belongs instead to the tenor of meaning and to the ontological constitution of selfhood."[24] One is oneself only, as the title of Ricoeur's major work on identity suggests, "as another."

19. Ricoeur, *Oneself as Another*, 166.
20. Ibid., 167.
21. Ibid., 166.
22. Ibid., 167.
23. Ibid., 168.
24. Ibid., 317.

Ricoeur runs through the various aspects of otherness that determine the self. First, there is the self as flesh, the body as sensing, enduring, and suffering primordial mediator of self and world.[25] Second, there are other people who limit my ego and impose a moral claim on me.[26] Finally, and of greatest interest for our analysis of Bonhoeffer, is the third kind of otherness, namely "the conscience." Beyond my body and beyond the moral injunction of other people, the self is addressed by another, transcendent dimension of indebtedness. Ricoeur argues for "the original and originary character of . . . the third modality of otherness, namely *being enjoined as the structure of selfhood*."[27] We commonly speak of "the voice of conscience," and Ricoeur rehearses a number of philosophical speculations on what constitutes this voice. For Freud, conscience as the "superego," that is, the unconsciously stored moral traditions of ancestors and parents, functioned as a kind of moral censor. Nietzsche and Heidegger, by contrast, tried to demoralize conscience; Nietzsche by suspecting every such notion as man-made, fateful invention, and Heidegger by immanentizing conscience as self's silent call to self-authenticity.

For Heidegger, conscience has no essential moral dimension.[28] Ricoeur rejects such "authoritarian foreclosures" on the nature of conscience,[29] and claims that one has to keep open the basic ethical structure of the self as moral injunction. In the final analysis, the *ipse* or true selfhood that persists when all other aspects of identity fall away consists in the address from beyond itself by another to which the self responds, "here am I."[30] Ricoeur, is careful, however, not to repeat Levinas's mistake of unilateral responsibility, as if the ethical injunction was a one-sided imposition. Ideally, accountability to an-

25. Ibid., 318.

26. Ibid., 339–40. Ricoeur rejects Levinas's radical opposition of self and other because (a) this asymmetry cannot account for the self to receive the word of the other. Reception requires a capacity of reception based on common reflexive structures, and (b) because Levinas only knows of one "other," namely the master who teaches; what if the other turns out to be "the master who requires a slave," or the "executioner"? Levinas, in short, leaves no room for critical discernment (ibid., 339).

27. Ibid., 354.

28. Ibid., 358.

29. "The ultimate equivocalness with respect to the status of conscience is perhaps what needs to be preserved in the final analysis" (ibid., 353).

30. We cannot do justice in this short overview to the rich and nuanced analysis Ricoeur provides. He essentially proposes three interrelated dialectical relationships that demonstrate by way of attestation rather than scientific evidence that a universal structure of selfhood exists: the dialectic of reflexive thought and action, the dialectic between *idem* (sameness) and *ipse* (selfhood) aspects of identity, and the dialectic of selfhood (*ipse*) and otherness. Each dialectic unveils, in order of increasing philosophical depth, ways of identifying the "who" in our speaking, acting, storytelling, and, finally, moral responsibility.

other is reciprocated by my dependability on him, an ideal best captured by true friendship.[31] Having thus laid bare the universal structure of selfhood as ethical demand, Ricoeur does not proceed to specify the source of this injunction. Ricoeur refuses to identify the injunction that calls to and grounds the "I" as permanent in time. The limits of philosophy forbid such identification. The methodological agnosticism of philosophy forbids Ricoeur from saying "whether this Other, the source of the [ethical] injunction, is another person whom I can look in the face or who can stare at me, or my ancestors for whom there is no representation, to so great an extent does my debt to them constitute my very self, or [whether this Other] is God—living God, absent God—or empty place."[32]

"Who Am I?": Bonhoeffer's Christian Identity

Philosophy may indeed have reached the limit of its competency at this point, but Christian theology does not; and indeed, theology may well say that it makes a big difference whether "my very self" is constituted by a wholly transcendent God who has demonstrated his unconditional love for us in becoming human and dying for the life of the world, or by faceless ancestors, or by some undefined law whose origin is lost in the beginning of time. To illustrate this difference, we will now apply Ricoeur's findings to Bonhoeffer's Christian identity and to his ethics.

Bonhoeffer's identity was strongly shaped by his family in two ways. On the one hand, his family was for him "the center of life to which he always returned."[33] As an upper-class, bourgeois family, the Bonhoeffers could boast a pedigree of remarkably successful ancestors and relations, which they carried, however, without any pretentiousness. Fully aware of their social status, deriving not least from Bonhoeffer's father's position as one of Germany's most reputable psychiatrist-neurologists, the family, who employed five servants, nonetheless disdained flaunting their superiority. From his earliest years, the expectations and attitudes of this "prodigiously talented humanist" family formed

31. Ricoeur, *Oneself as Another*, 330.

32. Ibid., 355. At the same time, however, Ricoeur insists that the ethical injunction at the heart of selfhood cannot be reduced to other people (for this would repeat Levinas's problem of making subjectivity dependent on the tyrant or killer as "other") nor ontologized as a general existential state of indebtedness (for this would buy into Heidegger's depersonalizing of the self). See ibid., 354.

33. Ferdinand Schlingensiepen, *Dietrich Bonhoeffer, 1906–1945: Eine Biographie* (Munich: Beck, 2005), 21.

Bonhoeffer's intellectual and cultural aspirations.[34] They provided him with a sure sense of who he was, which explains the confidence of his judgments. Along with this inheritance came also a strong sense of responsibility, an indebtedness and obligation to this humanist tradition.[35] On the other hand, the effort to assert himself against his accomplished brothers—Karl-Friedrich, Walter, and Klaus—all of whom shared their father's scientific interests, and vie for his father's attention, likely made Bonhoeffer more self-reflective of his own identity than were other family members. One biographer suspects that in Bonhoeffer, the scientific detachment and rather stoic demeanor of his father resulted in a life-long struggle "to compensate for the psychological make up he inherited from his mother [i.e., religiosity, musicality], and to control it by means of the norms taken over from his father."[36] And indeed, Bonhoeffer could appear stern, cold, and distanced.[37] His friends, however, were aware of how much enjoyment he derived from good food, clothing, music, art, and literature, and we may similarly recognize in his prison poems a passionate thirst for life. Nevertheless, Bonhoeffer was conditioned not to bother others with his personal discomfort, and to subordinate personal suffering to whatever task required his attention.

All these various characteristics—these *idem* aspects of his identity—were, however, severely tested in what Bonhoeffer himself called the "extreme case" (*Grenzfall*) of his conspiracy and imprisonment. As conspirator, he no longer had the freedom to explain his actions, and thus appeared suspect to friends, fellow pastors, and political authorities. As his biographer and friend Bethge put it, "with this step into this kind of conspiracy, he gave up the comforting support of command, approbation, and general opinion."[38]

How anguishing it must have been not to share his innermost thoughts with those he loved. Perhaps the most moving testimony of this self-concealment is Bonhoeffer's prison letter to Bethge in which he laments the need to project a certain image of himself to his young fiancé, Maria von Wedemeyer, whom he loved intensely. Mostly because of the Gestapo censorship (even their first kiss occurred under surveillance), but also to shield Maria from any possible suspicion from the Nazi authorities, Bonhoeffer

34. Charles Marsh, *Strange Glory: A Life of Dietrich Bonhoeffer* (New York: Knopf, 2014), 4.

35. Renate Wind, *A Spoke in the Wheel* (Grand Rapids: Eerdmans, 1992), 11.

36. Ibid., 8.

37. Wolf-Dieter Zimmermann, *Wir nannten ihn Bruder Bonhoeffer: Einblicke in ein hoffnungsvolles Leben* (Berlin: Wichern-Verlag, 2004), 36. Bonhoeffer reacted to students drawing attention to this side of him with the curt remark: "can't you accept a person the way he is?"

38. Eberhard Bethge, *Dietrich Bonhoeffer: Theologe-Christ-Zeitgenosse: Eine Biographie*, rev. ed. (Gütersloh: Gütersloher Verlagshaus, 2004), 894.

projected what he felt to be a false image of himself: "Maria considers me a paragon of virtue and a model of Christian behavior, and in order to reassure her, I am obliged to write her letters like an ancient martyr, and thus her image of me becomes ever more distorted."[39] In other words, Bonhoeffer longs to share with Maria his *real* self, the full range of his character, his dreams and insecurities.

Yet in the same letter, Bonhoeffer wonders about the nature of just this real selfhood. He shares with Bethge that, contrary to the reassuring letters he had written to his parents and relations, he does suffer from the psychological stress of imprisonment. While able to cope with physical deprivation, Bonhoeffer confesses that "one never becomes accustomed to the psychic pressure, quite the contrary. I have the feeling that what I am seeing and hearing makes me years older, and the world often feels for me like a nauseating burden."[40] Bonhoeffer concludes these observations with the doubts about his identity that eventually gave birth to his poem "Who am I?" He relates to Bethge, "I often ask myself who I actually am. Am I the one who, always cringing under these horrible experiences, becomes completely paralyzed by this affliction,[41] or am I the one who whips himself into shape, who on the outside (and even to himself) appears calm, cheerful, serene, superior, and allows himself to be admired for this theatrical[42] effort—or is it real? . . . [I]n short, one is less familiar with oneself than ever."[43]

If we interpret Bonhoeffer's description of himself in terms of Ricoeur's categories of selfhood, we witness here the breakdown of the *idem-ipse* dialectic. The perduring sameness granted by one's personal life story and character traits no longer links up with the *ipse* or true selfhood. The problem is not, as the earlier citations and the following lines from his poem make clear, that the struggle is simply between an inner "true" self and a false outward projection. The interjection "or is it real"—i.e., am I only acting this self-disciplined, brave version of myself—indicates Bonhoeffer's awareness that the "acted self" is part of his family training,[44] part of his real *idem* self, and thus part of who he is. As his poem makes clear, his question goes deeper:

39. *DBW* 8:237.

40. Ibid.

41. Amending "going to pieces" for "das heulende Elend kriegen," in *DBWE* 8:221, to capture the passivity in the German expression.

42. Amending "charade," in ibid. to capture the serious effort at playacting (*Theaterleistung*), which "charade" does not convey.

43. *DBW* 8:235.

44. In a subsequent letter to his parents, he refers to this "poise" (Haltung), the stiff upper lip, as "spiritual inheritance from you" (*Weil diese Haltung nur ein geistiges Erbstück von Euch ist*).

Who am I? This one or the other?
Am I this one today and tomorrow another?
Am I both at once? Before others a hypocrite
and in my own eyes a pitiful, whimpering weakling?
Or is what remains in me like a defeated army,
Fleeing in disarray from victory already won?[45]

As Bonhoeffer himself states, he could very well embody "both [identities] at once." What Bonhoeffer's question drives at is thus exactly the same element Ricoeur isolates as *ipse* identity or selfhood: "is there a form of permanence in time that is a reply to the question 'who am I?'"[46]

Bonhoeffer's response also concords with Ricoeur's definition of true selfhood as responsibility, in the sense of both response and accountability. Bonhoeffer writes, "Who am I? They mock me, these lonely questions of mine / Whoever I am, thou knowest me; O God, I am thine!" This well-known translation, unfortunately, does not convey the German very well, which emphasizes Bonhoeffer's isolation. The issue is not "lonely questions" but the "*solitary* questioning" that is "having its mocking way with me."[47] Being stripped of his family and intimate friends like Eberhard who could affirm his identity, self-questioning becomes a vicious cycle of doubt because it is cut off from the personal other(s) who alone can ultimately attest to his personal self. Yet Bonhoeffer *does* know another personal self who is present even in a place no one else can follow.

By anchoring his true identity in God, Bonhoeffer confirms a great deal of Ricoeur's analysis, but he also moves beyond the latter's philosophical reticence in a significant way.

Bonhoeffer affirms that identity lies beyond the ideal of certainty that Cartesian philosophy has deeply embedded in our modern understanding of selfhood. The Cartesian subject, as self-contained, certain starting point in the foundationalist quest for certain knowledge, condemns the modern mind to staking self-certainty on what can be known by an autonomous ego. Bonhoeffer has long realized the futility of this endeavor. Indeed, all of his early theological work is dedicated to unmasking the Cartesian self as the sinful self, curved in on itself and thus never attaining to true self-knowledge.[48] Though we cannot

45. *DBWE* 8:460.
46. Ricoeur, *Oneself as Another*, 118.
47. "Einsames Fragen treibt mit mir Spott." In other words, the problem is not, as the poetic license taken in the English translation suggests, "lonely questions," but that the isolated, solitary context wherein these questions are posed has its own dangerous dynamic, mockingly undermining *idem* identity (*DBW* 8:514).
48. See Christiane Tietz-Steiding, *Bonhoeffers Kritik der Verkrümmten Vernunft: Eine Er-*

know who we are, we are still, as Bonhoeffer puts it, ultimately *known*. And it is only this *being known* by something greater than ourselves that allows *ipse* or "who" to perdure beyond any disruption of sameness that marks the identity of objects. It is in this sense, as Ricoeur rightly points out, that "one has to lose one's self in order to find it."[49] Ricoeur finds affinities with this renunciation of certain guarantees of selfhood in Buddhism, but it is precisely at this point that Bonhoeffer's Augustinian "You know me, O God" shows the clear difference between Christian identity and Buddhist self-surrender. For the Christian, self-renunciation occurs only in the context of personal communion with the Divine other, an actual personal other *who* knows me.

Moreover, this personal other is the God who created and sustains the cosmos, and who himself became human in Christ, summing up in himself all of humanity, and thus also entering *my* narrative in order to transform it.[50] Bonhoeffer beautifully expresses this divine recapitulation of the self when he reflects, in another prison letter, on the idea of restoration as explicated in Irenaeus's *recapitulatio*: "Nothing is lost; in Christ all things are taken up, preserved, albeit in transfigured form. . . . The doctrine, originating in Eph. 1:10 of the restoration of all things . . . is a magnificent and exceedingly consoling thought."[51] These reflections are prompted by the hymns of the German Lutheran theologian and hymn writer Paul Gerhard (1607–1676); it is surely no accident that one of these hymns depicts the writer's self as being enthralled by and taken up into the vision of Jesus.[52] Bonhoeffer comments that hardly anything depicts the meaning of "I and Christ" better than this hymn.[53] Clearly, Bonhoeffer derives considerable comfort in knowing that his identity rests with Christ, who made and sustains reality, and who came into the world to inaugurate the new creation and restore all things. *Idem* and *ipse* realities are unified in Christ, who is the author not merely of Bonhoeffer's faith, but also of his life's narrative. Insofar as he holds its true meaning in his hands, nothing will be lost!

---

kenntnistheoretische Untersuchung, Beiträge zur Historischen Theologie (Tübingen: Mohr Siebeck, 1999); also see Clifford J. Green, *Bonhoeffer: A Theology of Sociality* (Grand Rapids: Eerdmans, 1999).

49. Ricoeur, "Pastoral Praxeology," 313.

50. With this qualification, Christian identity differs from Muslim self-surrender, which is not framed by God's incarnation.

51. *DBW* 8:246; see also *DBW* 4:64–65.

52. These lines in "Ich steh an deiner Krippe hier" convey the writer's desire to grasp or possess his savior, who instead draws the worshipper into himself.

53. *DBW* 8:246.

Christian Identity and Ethics

Being held by this divine other, Bonhoeffer is able to turn away from endless psychological introspection or what he calls fruitless "analysis of the soul." After all, he concludes, "there are more important things than self-knowledge."[54] This forward-looking stance that ultimately surrenders the quest for identity to recognition of one's being in Christ profoundly shapes Bonhoeffer's understanding of ethics as responsible action. Bonhoeffer defines ethics, we recall, as participation in the reality of God as revealed in the God-man Jesus Christ, in whom God has reconciled the world to himself by becoming human.[55] Ethics is thus not about observance of preset rules or moral principles but is rather, as Bonhoeffer already stated in his earlier book *Discipleship*, about the response to Christ's call for living out the reconciliation of God and world in every sphere of life,[56] which requires a hermeneutic effort and the difficult exercise of wisdom rather than adherence to a set of rules. "Christ," writes Bonhoeffer, "does not teach an abstract ethics that has to be implemented no matter what the cost. Christ was not essentially a lawgiver but a real human being like ourselves. . . . [What Christ cares about] is not whether the 'maxim of an action could become a universal moral law' but whether my action at this moment helps my neighbor to be a human being before God."[57]

Bonhoeffer's approach to ethics thus shares with Paul Ricoeur's philosophy a distinction between ethics and morality. Ethics, Ricoeur argues, is the encompassing ground on which morality functions. Why do we need this distinction? The point is not to oppose moral principles to ethics. Both Bonhoeffer and Ricoeur affirm the need for moral guidelines. Yet they also realize that no set of commandments or moral principles can do justice to the complexity of life, wherein ethical conflicts are inevitable. What is needed, therefore, is a basic ethical framework, expressed, perhaps, *as* moral norms, but moral norms that must be applied, or sometimes even changed, in light of the underlying ethical ground: "only a recourse to the ethical ground against which morality stands out can give rise to the wisdom of judgment in [any given] situation. . . . This will be the maxim that can shelter moral conviction from the ruinous alternatives of univocity or arbitrariness."[58] Without a greater ethical framework that

54. *DBW* 8:235 (*Selbsterkenntnis* could also be rendered "self-understanding").
55. *DBW* 6:40.
56. "Der Ort der Verantwortung," in *Die Geschichte und das Gute [Zweite Fassung]*, in *DBW* 6:293–94.
57. *DBW* 6:86. To avoid misunderstanding, we note that this statement about Christ's humanity must be seen within the context of Bonhoeffer's high Christology.
58. Ricoeur, *Oneself as Another*, 249.

grounds any positive moral law, the complexity of life situations will drive the moralist toward rigid legalism or open the door to relativism and its flip side, the arbitrary imposition of moral norms.

Bonhoeffer experienced firsthand the failure of traditional morality when it was not grounded in a deeper ethical vision. Beginning on March 14, 1933, the Nazis ruled Germany under an emergency law (*Ermächtigungsgesetz*) that suspended the rights and freedoms normally accorded citizens. This situation enabled the arbitrary imposition of Hitler's totalitarian, racist blood-and-soil ideology, plunging Germany into "the crisis of all ethics."[59] This crisis began, however, with Hitler's enthusiastic endorsement by numerous citizens (many of them Christians) who saw in Hitler a revival of the German society, the solution to social ills, and the return of national power and pride. "Evil," as Bonhoeffer noted, "came masquerading as an angel of light, disguised as benefit, as historical fate, and as the promise of social justice."[60] In this confusing situation, traditional moral frameworks failed. Bonhoeffer runs through a catalogue of traditional humanistic ethics to show their breakdown. The reasonable person fails to comprehend the fundamental ethical shift that has occurred, and, trying to do justice to all sides, effects no change and withdraws frustrated into his shell. The person committed to unbending moral principle soon finds that evil outmaneuvers him because, like a fighting bull, he can only focus on one issue at a time. The solitary warrior of conscience will be equally confused by the sheer scope of conflicts that confronts him; moreover, the many honorable and seductive masks in which evil approaches him will disorient his conscience, so that he will finally have to lie to himself in order not to despair. The person beholden to ethics of duty falls down because the ethical crisis may well require abandoning one's duty in an initiative of free responsibility. Incapable of such risk and the ensuing uncertainty, the man of duty will do his duty even by the devil.[61]

Bonhoeffer asks, "Who can stand firm" in this crisis of ethics? Not those seeking their identity as people of principle, conscience, or duty as the final measure, but only those pursuing wisdom deriving from a unified ethical ground that allows one to do what each concrete situation requires. Paradoxically, to stand firm requires interpretive fluidity, and this occurs only within an ethical framework that transcends morality in the direction of wisdom, or what Bonhoeffer calls "realistic responsibility" or "reality based action."[62] The

59. Bethge, *Dietrich Bonhoeffer*, 931.
60. "Nach zehn Jahren," in *DBW* 8:20.
61. Ibid., 21–22 (for all examples).
62. *DBW* 6:280.

label "realistic," in this phrase, refers to reality as determined by God's creation of, and love for, the world. For Bonhoeffer, as we explained above, this unifying ground is "participation in the reality of God and the world in Christ Jesus" in whom God reconciled the world to himself and inaugurated a new humanity and a new creation.[63] Bonhoeffer contrasts Christian realistic action and inflexible morality by contradicting Kant's suggestion that love of truth should prompt me to acknowledge the presence of my friend to his enemy who is at my door in murderous pursuit of him. In his little essay "What It Means to Tell the Truth," Bonhoeffer argues to the contrary that truth is contextual, depending on concrete historical, social, linguistic, and political circumstances. To tell the truth, "means something different depending on one's situation."[64] The same is true for ethics in general, although Bonhoeffer adds that each concrete life context is in turn to be interpreted within God's redemptive work. For example, in the context of the murderer at my door asking for my friend, God's command to love my neighbor legitimizes my lying in order to protect another human being.[65] Bonhoeffer does not, however, deny in the least that this action *violates* a moral injunction. The point is that an ethics of responsible action will require transgressing legitimate moral principles for the sake of ethical wisdom. Becoming guilty for the sake of right action does not, therefore, *rationalize* or *legitimize* one's lying in an ultimate sense so that a new principle, "lie when under pressure," could be entered into the moral rulebook.

And yet, the ethically responsible Christian *can* live with this tension because of his participation in Christ. At this point, Bonhoeffer's view of responsible action reconnects ethical agency with our main question of identity. We recall how Bonhoeffer moved beyond the contradictory, conflicting impressions of his *idem* identity by turning away from *idem* to the divine other in response to whom and by whose acknowledgement Bonhoeffer's *ipse* or selfhood actually exists. Thus in losing his *idem,* so to speak, he gained his selfhood. The same basic movement away from the self toward God is required for responsible ethical action. Thus, the real problem with morality divorced from the christological ethical ground Bonhoeffer advocates is that moralists pursue an *idem* identity apart from God. The person who would reveal his friend to a killer in the name of truth and the person who would ultimately justify his lying for the sake of a greater cause are *both* more concerned with maintaining a clear

---

63. *DBW* 6:40. See also "Because in Jesus Christ, the real one, all of reality has been taken up and summed up, because reality has him as origin, essence, and goal, therefore only in him and from him as starting point is realistic action possible" (*DBW* 6:262).

64. *DBW* 16:620.

65. *DBW* 6:280.

conscience based on a logically ordered moral world.[66] In short, they are too preoccupied with maintaining their *idem* selves to risk doing what the situation really requires for the sake of another.

The Christian, by contrast, is freed for responsible action because his identity is ultimately in Christ. This does not mean, of course, that the Christian skips happily along the green meadows of ethical clarity, but that he is able to live with the tension created between ethics and morality because he can surrender the ultimate verdict on his decisions to the merciful judgment of God. In short, the Christian's identity is not fissured because he does not need to maintain it; his identity is unified in Christ, in whom reality is also unified. It is not the moral law that grounds my actions, but the reality of Christ, who is greater than any law, who fulfills every moral law, and who is Lord of my conscience. Bonhoeffer explains:

> Since the law is no longer the final arbiter but Jesus Christ, the free decision for Christ has to determine the conflict between conscience and concrete responsibility. That means not an eternal conflict, but obtaining ultimate unity; because the foundation, essence, and goal of concrete responsibility is the same Jesus Christ, who is also Lord of conscience. Thus responsibility is bound by conscience but conscience is free on account of responsibility.[67]

In this way, the person whose identity rests in Christ is freed for responsible action. Yet in no way is this freedom a license for moral relativism in the name of God. For one, because of the incarnation, reality itself is shaped by God's philanthropy, and participation in this reality should motivate all Christian actions for the service of others. Moreover, the ethical agent remains solely responsible for his actions before God. Necessity may justify his actions before others, but before God, "he hopes only for mercy."[68]

This freedom for ethical action requires a self whose unity is found in God. The importance of this unity for Bonhoeffer is shown by his analysis of conscience. With Heidegger, Bonhoeffer believes that conscience is not a *moral* voice but the yearning for self-unity: "Conscience is the call of human existence for unity with itself, voiced from a deep wellspring beyond one's own will and reason. It manifests itself as the indictment of lost unity and as the warning against losing one's self. Its primary focus is not a specific act, but a specific way

---

66. In this particular case, "every attempt to interpret away the fact that one lied stems only from the legalistic, self-righteous conscience" (*DBW* 6:280).

67. *DBW* 6:283.

68. *DBW* 6:283.

of being. It protests against activity that threatens this being in unity with one's own self."[69] Paul Ricoeur had similarly recognized the importance of Heidegger's existential interpretation of conscience for this attestation of the self. Yet Ricoeur also criticizes Heidegger for stripping conscience of any ethical dimension. In Heidegger, conscience calls *Dasein* away from its superficial life guided by public opinion (*das Man*) into authenticity through realizing and resolutely accepting one's ontological state of guilt or indebtedness (*Schuld*). For Heidegger, however, this indebtedness is strictly ontological and thus impersonal, lacking any ethical dimension toward other people. Without such an ethical imposition from outside the self, the self becomes depersonalized and "self-attestation [is] stripped of any moral ethical significance."[70] Bonhoeffer's theological criticism of Heidegger's conscience goes much further than Ricoeur's. For Bonhoeffer, conscience is a reminder of the self's disunity resulting from the fall, when, deceived by Satan's alluring promise to become *sicut deus*, like God knowing good and evil, mankind lost its original union with God on which true selfhood depends. Bonhoeffer claims that "there was no conscience before the fall. . . . Conscience is not the voice of God in sinful man but, on the contrary, it is the defense against this voice; and yet as defense, conscience, contrary to our knowing or willing, points to the voice of God."[71]

In his interpretation of the biblical creation account, Bonhoeffer shows that human beings were created in the image of the Trinitarian God as relational beings, whose freedom and authentic selfhood are ethically understood as being-with and -for others. Freedom, as Bonhoeffer put it tersely, "is a relation and nothing else."[72] It is only after falling out of communion with God and others that conscience arises and now defiantly reinforces the self's autonomy in an act of self-preservation: "Thus the call of conscience has its origin and goal in the autonomy of one's ego."[73] Once again, in seeking to preserve itself by withdrawing into an isolated fortress of selfhood, the self loses itself. *Ipse* identity is regained only by reestablishing the self's structure of responsibility, its ethical relation to another: "the great change occurs in the moment in which autonomy no longer constitutes the unity of human existence but—through the miracle of faith—is found, beyond one's own ego and its law, in Jesus Christ."[74] In fact, Bonhoeffer argues, Jesus *becomes* my conscience.[75] Consequently, since

69. *DBW* 6:277.
70. Ricoeur, *Oneself as Another*, 355.
71. *DBW* 5:120.
72. *DBW* 5:58.
73. *DBW* 6:278.
74. *DBW* 6:278.
75. *DBW* 6:279: "Jesus Christus ist mein Gewissen geworden."

all of humanity is summed up in Christ, obtaining a unified self through "the surrender (*Hingabe*) of my self to God" includes my surrender to others. Thus obtaining one's true selfhood through surrendering the self to God becomes the foundation for Bonhoeffer's notion of ethics as nonmoralistic responsibility: "Not any law but the living God and the living human being, as I encounter him in Jesus Christ, is origin and goal of my conscience."[76]

Identity thus emerges as a central concept for Bonhoeffer's understanding of a Christian ethics of realistic responsibility: "The responsible person surrenders himself and his deed to God."[77] Thus Bonhoeffer's response to the dilemma of identity, "You know me, Oh God, I am Thine," also forms the ground of responsible action. My action, of course, involves the kind of dialectic between the *idem* and *ipse* parts of my identity (my personal narrative, character traits, inhabited tradition, etc.) that Ricoeur describes in his work. However, my true selfhood or *ipse* identity is not ultimately dependent on these elements, nor is my identity defined by faithful adherence to moral laws. Rather, as Ricoeur intimates and as Bonhoeffer explains in a more profoundly Christian way, my true self is *ethically determined* by my ethical responsibility before God and *therefore* also intrinsically by my responsibility for the flourishing of others.

As with his entire theology, Christology grounds this view of ethics as realistic responsibility. The Christ in whom the Christian participates and whose indwelling presence shapes the follower into Christ-likeness is the living pattern for ethical action. Christ embodied the obedience and freedom that should guide the Christian's life. Knowing the will of the Father, he obeys, but he obeys not as slave but in the freedom of a disciple who has appropriated this will for himself, and thus "with open eyes and joyous heart he, as it were, re-creates God's will out of himself." Obedience, Bonhoeffer continues, "knows what is good and does it. Freedom dares to act and entrusts the judgment about good and evil to God."[78]

The obedience Bonhoeffer envisions is not that of one who fulfills a duty but of one who has entered into an enterprise, carrying out his mission intelligently with passionate conviction. Participation in Christ thus draws the follower into the Christ-reality of "vicarious representative responsibility."[79] In Christ, God became human, gathering up all of humanity in this one man in order to redeem it. Like Adam, Christ is our vicarious representation: Christ

76. *DBW* 6:279.
77. *DBW* 6:289.
78. *DBW* 6:288.
79. These kinds of expressions make it clear that Bonhoeffer is not a "liberal" theologian, insofar as he does not talk about spiritual or moral patterns established by Christ for personal edification, but about *sharing in* the reality of Christ's priestly, mediating work.

became human and thus bore vicarious responsibility for human beings. Without becoming guilty himself, Christ bore the guilt of human beings, and still does so. As the sinless one, "Christ takes upon himself the guilt of his brothers." According to Bonhoeffer, "all vicarious representative responsible action has its origin in this sinlessly guilty Jesus Christ."[80] Thus every Christian has a similar priestly function, albeit not in the redeeming fashion only Christ the God-man has. Nevertheless, participating in him, "I stand at the same time in Christ's stead for human beings and in people's stead before Christ."[81] If Christ did not shy away from becoming guilty for our sake, Christ followers will not withdraw from the community of human guilt. Bonhoeffer concludes provocatively, "Because Jesus took the guilt of all human beings upon himself, everyone who acts responsibly becomes guilty."[82] Some commentators have found this idea of sharing in the sinless guilt of Christ theologically questionable and misleading. Has not Christ finished the work of redemption? Does not Bonhoeffer invite Christians into the illusion of coredemption and also encourage a kind of victim syndrome of becoming guilty for others' sake?[83] I do think that Bonhoeffer's formulations lack precision at this point, but his overall meaning seems fairly clear: just as Christ in doing God's will for our sake entered into guilt and shame, so the Christian in living out the new humanity in service of other human beings should not prefer righteous appearance to acting in the spirit of Christ.

Our Friendship with God

Bonhoeffer offers us an understanding of Christian identity formed by a deeply reflective theological mind and tested in the crucible of extraordinary life experience. The power of Bonhoeffer's insights, however, goes well beyond mere personal circumstances to theological insights of abiding relevance. This relevance is attested not least by the congruence of Bonhoeffer's hermeneutics of the self with Ricoeur's penetrating and elaborate analysis of selfhood. Whether we seek to establish and maintain our identity in extreme circumstances or within the many complexities of life, Bonhoeffer insists that it is only through surrendering oneself (and thus one's self) to God that one finds authentic selfhood—a deep

80. *DBW* 6:276.
81. *DBW* 6:255.
82. *DBW* 6:275.
83. Klaus Kodalle speaks of Bonhoeffer's "victim mania" (*Opferwahn*) in Klaus-Michael Kodalle, *Dietrich Bonhoeffer: Zur Kritik seiner Theologie* (Gütersloh: Gütersloher Verlagshaus G. Mohn, 1991), 104.

truth Christians should embrace. Self-surrender, however, is willing oneself into a state of submission. The whole direction of Bonhoeffer's thinking prohibits such a conclusion. Rather, one surrenders to an actual personal reality outside of oneself. Already in his early theological writings, Bonhoeffer insists that "in God's recognition [*erkennen*] of human beings, they know God. To be known [*erkannt sein*] by God, however, means to become a new human being."[84] In his prison cell, Bonhoeffer learned the existential truth of his earlier theology. Stripped of his free movements and gripped by doubts to his innermost identity, what matters is that *God knows me*.

Not merely the history of philosophy, but also of psychology and sociology, shows us how central the topic of identity, the question "who am I," is for human existence. Ricoeur suggests that this question cannot be reduced to any biological, physical, or even mental aspect of being. Selfhood transcends neuro-pathways, DNA coding, character traits, or any other substance-oriented notions of sameness. Even if all these are part of our *idem* identity, true selfhood is ethical, consisting in our relations to others as accountability. We are true selves when we freely enact this responsibility. Bonhoeffer showed us in turn that the unified self from which true freedom and ethical agency flow is found only when this other is the living God, who gave his own self for the life of others and the redemption of the world. For Ricoeur, friendship is the true figure of selfhood as mutual accountability; for Bonhoeffer this also holds true, and he experienced this relation in his deep friendship with Eberhard Bethge. Yet Bonhoeffer also knew that ultimately his self rested in what patristic theologians called the mystery of our "friendship with God."[85]

84. *DBW* 2:133.

85. Gregory of Nyssa, *The Life of Moses*, trans. Abraham J. Malherbe and Everett Ferguson, Classics of Western Spirituality (New York: Paulist, 1978), 137.

Chapter 41

Jacques Ellul: Christian Identity in the Technological Society

Craig M. Gay

One of the more provocative voices in defense of a distinctively Christian identity over the course of the last half-century was the French sociologist and lay theologian Jacques Ellul. A strikingly original and deeply insightful, if controversial, thinker, Ellul died in 1994 at the age of eighty-two, having witnessed, participated in, and commented extensively in writing upon the extraordinary social and political turbulence of twentieth-century Europe. The only child of an atheist father and a devout, yet reticent mother, Ellul was a keen student and an early (if largely independent) reader of an unusual combination of Karl Marx and the Bible, both of which would leave lasting marks upon his life and thought. Commencing with a profound experience of the divine presence in his late teens, Ellul was reluctantly if inexorably converted to Protestant Christianity over a period of some years. In the intervening time, he trained in law at Bordeaux University, married his wife, Yvette, in 1937, and took up a junior teaching post at Strasbourg University in 1938. Dismissed from his position by the Vichy government in 1940, Ellul fled the city for the countryside where he joined the French Resistance and pastored a small Protestant congregation. Determined to enter government following the Liberation, Ellul was quickly disillusioned by the constraints of ordinary politics and turned instead to a life of scholarship and writing. He accepted a position on the Faculty of Law at Bordeaux University in 1944 and remained there until his retirement in 1980. Author of more than forty books on subjects ranging from law, politics, revolution, mass media, social fragmentation, art, language, and theology, all of Ellul's remarkable oeuvre are aspects of his detailed and multifaceted analysis of the technological milieu; and he is well known for his contention that the intrinsic logic of technology—something he sought to capture in the term "*la Technique*"—has become the single most determinative influence in the modern world.[1] Yet Ellul's further contention that the technological society provides a unique opportunity for Christian witness is at least as, if not more, important for the Christian reader to grasp. Christians are called, Ellul believed, to remind a watching world that *free* and *genuinely personal* action is, even in the face of the impetus and impersonality of "*la Technique,*" *still* possible. The following essay is intended to elucidate Ellul's analysis of the threat modern technology poses to the formation of human persons and, in so doing, to model Ellul's understanding of Christian intellectual identity.

The Christian, Ellul contended, echoing Jesus's high priestly prayer in John 17, is to be "in" this world but not "of" it. By implication, he stressed that Christians needed to make a concerted effort to understand their social and cultural circumstances for the sake of trying to discern where, within these circumstances, the possibilities of genuinely redemptive individual and social action actually lie. "We must seek the deepest possible sociological understanding of the world we live in," Ellul contended in *The Presence of the Kingdom* (1967), "in order to find out, as precisely as may be, where we are and what we are doing, and also what lines of action are open to us."[2] Insofar as such lines of action are concerned, Ellul believed that Christians are called to be *present*—which is to say, to bear witness to the possibilities of *grace* and *freedom*—at precisely those points of maximum tension between a sinful world at enmity with God—a world that is, in effect, bent on *suicide*—and God's redemptive purposes for the world. "Our concern," he stressed, "should be to place ourselves at the very point where this suicidal desire is most active, in the actual form it adopts, and to see how God's will of preservation can act in this given situation."[3] Of course, in this connection Ellul believed that technology had become the most fateful and suicidal force within the modern world. Yet he insisted that the Christian task should not on that account be construed as one of repudiating modern technology, nor even of seeking somehow to reform it. Rather, Christians are called to bear witness to the possibility of freely transcending technological determinism. "How is this to be done?" Ellul asks at the beginning of *The Technological Society* (1964), and confesses: "I do not yet know. That is why this book is an appeal to the individual's sense of responsibility. The first step in the quest, the first act of freedom, is to become aware of the necessity."[4]

1. Jacques Ellul, *The Technological Society*, trans. John Wilkinson (New York: Vintage, 1964).

2. Jacques Ellul, *The Presence of the Kingdom* (1967; 2nd ed., Colorado Springs: Helmers & Howard, 1989), 19; originally from "Mirror of These Ten Years," *The Christian Century* 87.7 (February 18, 1970), 201.

3. Ibid.

4. Ellul, *Technological Society*, xxxiii.

Attempting today to respond to Ellul's appeal for individual responsibility brings us face to face with a perplexing problem, however. For the maximum point of tension between our technologically subjugated world and God's redemptive purposes for our world is precisely that point from which individual and responsible action must necessarily arise, *viz.*, human personhood itself. Not only does modern technology seek to annul the threat human persons pose to its process by relentlessly reducing persons to functionaries and/or standardized units of one kind or another, but the technological process tends toward the elimination of the only context within which personal agency is possible, namely, that described by *time* and *place*. Modern machine technology's relentless compression of time and its progressive "flattening" of place would render even the possibility of genuinely personal action moot. For bereft of any particular place within which to move and deprived of the time necessary for careful and prayerful deliberation, it must become impossible for human beings to act freely, responsibly, and meaningfully. To become conscious of the threat that modern technology poses to personal agency, and particularly to become aware of the threat that machine technology poses to time and place, is clearly one of the first steps we must take if we would transcend "*la Technique.*"

Individual and Responsible Personal Agency

To say "I," even to ourselves and however dimly we may be aware of its significance, is to *perform as*—and hence *to be*—a uniquely individual *person*. In relation to the "You's" to whom we most commonly say "I," furthermore, we experience ourselves as unique and, for lack of a better word, *unsubstitutable* personal agents. We experience the others to whom we say "I" as unique and unsubstitutable as well. This is most obviously the case in our relationships with those we love. We don't simply desire to have "friends," but *our* friends; one doesn't simply want to have a "spouse," but *my* husband or wife; and we expect—or at least we hope and deeply long—to be loved and valued in return by those closest to us as *ourselves*. William Poteat put this somewhat formally in a collection of essays entitled *The Primacy of Persons*:

> [F]or me to exist personally means that I am the agent of concrete intentions, directed toward particular ends or persons, through concrete acts in particular moments of time; and that we know one another and even ourselves as persons *par excellence* through these actions and express intentions. For it is here that my intentions, expressed in this particular act directed upon this

particular objective, encounter yours, and what is most deeply personal in us meets.[5]

Of course, Western modernity has long placed an emphasis upon individual rational *autonomy*, as Kant put it so memorably at the end of the eighteenth century, on "daring to use one's *own* understanding." Similarly, but in its Romantic variant, Western modernity has placed a high value upon "authenticity" and upon "being oneself," most recently emphasizing the importance of "*self esteem*." Along this line, in his magisterial study of the sources of modern identity, Charles Taylor notes that the originally classical object of "self-control," requiring one to master the passions for the sake of realizing the human telos, has for modern Western men and women become one of "*self*-construction,"[6] a project within which we are encouraged to assemble from among a range of possible options our own unique identities. The value and importance of individual—and at least *apparently* personal—agency continues, in other words, to resonate even within modern technological society.

The emphasis that Western modernity continues to place upon individual agency is, of course, very largely the legacy of Christian theological convictions. The Christian doctrine of creation, for example, insists that because existence was and continues moment-by-moment to be an act of sheer generosity, the diversity and particularity so evident in creation is not a defect, but rather reflects divine delight and beneficence. As no single creature could possibly reflect the entirety of God's goodness, so he has created a great many creatures, each reflecting him in some small, perhaps, but nevertheless unrepeatable fashion. Each and every individual creature exists, so the Christian doctrine of creation stresses, because *God desires that it should exist*. The fourteenth-century Christian mystic Julian of Norwich captured this quite wonderfully in the following justly celebrated passage:

> The Lord showed me something small, no bigger than a hazelnut, lying in the palm of my hand, as it seemed to me, and it was round as a ball. I looked at it with the eyes of my understanding and thought: What can this be? I was amazed that it could last, for I thought that because of its littleness it would suddenly have fallen into nothing. And I was answered in my understanding: It lasts and always will, because God loves it; and thus everything has being

---

5. William Poteat, "Faith and Existence," in *The Primacy of Persons and the Language of Culture: Essays by William H. Poteat* (Columbia: University of Missouri Press, 1993), 119.

6. See Charles Taylor, *Sources of the Self: The Making of the Modern Identity* (Cambridge: Harvard University Press, 1989).

through the love of God. In this little thing I saw three properties. The first is that God made it; the second is that God loves it; the third is that God preserves it. But what did I see in it? It is that God is the Creator and the protector and the lover.[7]

That God made, loves, and preserves each and every individual created thing is, of course, especially true of those creatures made after his own image and likeness. "Are not five sparrows sold for two pennies?" Jesus reassured the anxious crowd. "Yet not one of them is forgotten by God. Indeed, the very hairs of your head are all numbered. Don't be afraid; you are worth more than many sparrows" (Luke 12:6–7 NIV).

Christian ecclesiology further stresses the irreplaceable importance of each of the various and sundry members of Christ's body, the church. "If the foot were to say, 'Because I am not a hand, I do not belong to the body,' it would not for that reason stop being part of the body," the apostle Paul writes to the Corinthian church. On the contrary, he insists: "while there are many parts, there is but one body" (1 Cor 12:1). Elaborating on the apostolic teaching, Ian McFarland writes:

> Difference is central to life before God because God calls each human being to a different place within the body of Christ. Human beings are therefore equal in that they are all called by God to be persons in Christ (so that their equality is grounded extrinsically in God rather than in any intrinsic attribute or property they possess); but they differ in that they are called to enact that personhood in distinct and unsubstitutable ways. All are called to live under Christ, the one head, but no two people occupy the same place in the body.[8]

Christianly understood, in short, individual, responsible, and personal agency before God and neighbor is both the ground of human dignity as well as the highest human calling. It confers a very high value upon each and every single one of us while also making very serious claims. Even secular Western values continue to reflect—however dimly and ironically—these originally Christian theological convictions. For this reason, as William Barrett once observed, even modern Western men and women continue in large part to be de facto Judeo Christians.[9]

7. Julian of Norwich, cited in Ian McFarland, *From Nothing: A Theology of Creation* (Louisville: Westminster John Knox, 2014), 60.

8. McFarland, *From Nothing*, ix.

9. William Barrett, cited in William Poteat, *Polanyian Meditations: In Search of a Post-Critical Logic* (Durham, NC: Duke University Press, 1985), 127.

In addition to highlighting the unique and unsubstitutable part that each of us plays in the divine economy, it is also crucial to stress that genuinely personal agency presupposes a context, a kind of "arena," within which responsible agency becomes both possible and—possibly—meaningful. This is why Christian theology speaks not just of a creation per se, but of created "order," and it is in the sense of created *order* that theology affirms that the creation is *complete*.[10] Ordered by the Divine Wisdom, and comprised of space, time, matter, spirit, and the possibilities of movements ordered at the physical level to what modern science calls "laws" and "constant values," the created order delineates a framework—physical, moral, and spiritual—within which the varied and sundry creatures can "be" and in which they are enabled to live and move and thrive. This is why the Genesis narrative describes the creation of *places* before detailing the several categories of creatures that will live in them, i.e., describing "habitats" ordered to the life and flourishing of "inhabi*tants*." The separation of "light" from "darkness," of the "waters above" from the "waters below," of the "sea" from the "dry land," all of these separations prepare places where the various creatures can *be* and where things can actually happen—the fish in the seas, the animals on the dry land, the birds in the air, and for the creatures created after the "image and likeness of God," the entire earth.[11]

"Place" thus describes a basic condition for the possibility of created things to "be" and to be present to one another.[12] It makes it possible for creatures to affect and to be affected by other creatures. For the purposes of the present essay, it is important to see that personal agency inevitably "takes place" in and necessarily only makes sense in terms of particular *places*; for a *place* is the "where" of my particular body; it is where I *am* and delineates the possibilities of where and how I can move. A *place*, furthermore, is where it is possible for me to feel "at home." In fact, the colloquial synonym for home is "my place." As William Poteat observes: "a place is full of objects and of relations upon which I have left my very personal stamp, expressed my own idiosyncrasy, part of my unique history. It is a domicile for the love that issues from the very center of my person."[13] This is why it is so disorienting to be deprived of our places as when, for example, the home we grew up in is torn down and redeveloped, even if we had not lived there for many years. We survive the loss for the most part because we have long since found other *places* that we know and in which

10. Oliver O'Donovan, *Resurrection and Moral Order: An Outline for Evangelical Ethics* (Grand Rapids: Eerdmans, 1986), 60.
11. See John Walton, *The Lost World of Genesis One: Ancient Cosmology and the Origins Debate* (Downers Grove, IL: IVP Academic, 2009).
12. McFarland, *From Nothing*, 65.
13. Poteat, *Primacy of Persons*, 34.

we are known. Were we to have no *place*, we would be lost. Indeed, to have no place, Poteat observes in this connection, is to lack the very ground of becoming a person; it is to lack the minimum conditions for remaining a person.[14]

Time, of course, is the other basic condition of all creaturely existence. While place may well describe the "where" of our bodies, only time will tell just "who" we are and who and/or what we are to become. Responsible personal agency, in short, is historical; it must unfold *in time*. In this connection, Christian theology stresses that all creaturely existence, being finite and in itself incomplete, moves inexorably toward the perfection that is God, and that all of God's creatures do this *in time*. Here again, this is not a defect, but simply reflects God's manifest desire that everything should not all happen at once.[15] The importance of time within the created order is emphasized in the Genesis narrative by the reprise of "mornings" and "evenings" and in the succession of the "days" of creation. In biblical understanding there is, as the writer of Ecclesiastes so memorably put it: "a time for everything, and a season for every activity under the heavens" (Eccl 3:1 NIV).

Place and time together condition the possibility *of* and possibilities *for* creaturely life. They comprise the stage upon which the drama of life is lived out. As O'Donovan notes:

> Creation is the given totality of order which forms the presupposition of historical existence. "Created order" is that which is not negotiable within the course of history, that which neither the terrors of chance nor the ingenuity of art can overthrow. It defines the scope of our freedom and the limits of our fears.[16]

Threats to Personal Agency

Individual, responsible, and personal agency is always at risk, for it is difficult. We often find (Do we not?) that uniqueness and unsubstitutability are heavy burdens that we would rather not bear. Indeed, we often find that we do not actually *want* to be ourselves and that we would rather try to evade freedom and personal "response-ability" than own up to them. One of Ellul's key influences, Søren Kierkegaard, termed this sorry—if typical—condition *despair* and

14. Ibid.
15. Colin E. Gunton, *The One, the Three and the Many: God, Creation and the Culture of Modernity* (Cambridge: Cambridge University Press, 1993), 94.
16. O'Donovan, *Resurrection*, 60.

suggested that it is a basic aspect of the human condition *in sin*. "Surrounded by hordes of men," Kierkegaard observes,

> absorbed in all sorts of secular matters, more and more shrewd about the ways of the world—[the despairing] person forgets himself, forgets his name divinely understood, does not dare to believe in himself, finds it too hazardous to be himself and far easier and safer to be like the others, to become a copy, a number, a mass man.[17]

The essence of the modern secular mentality, Kierkegaard continues, is precisely and by way of mortgaging oneself to the world of human affairs to seek to evade becoming an individual. Such people, he writes, "use their capacities, amass money, carry on secular enterprises, calculate shrewdly, etc., perhaps make a name in history, but themselves they are not; spiritually speaking, they have no self, no self for whose sake they could venture everything, no self before God—however self-seeking they are otherwise."[18] The world of human affairs, for its part, does not take much notice of this ploy, for it finds the acknowledgement of individuality burdensome and would much rather lump us together as members of various "classes" in which we are substitutable by definition, e.g., as "workers," "voters," "citizens," "consumers," and so forth. In this connection, Ellul believed that the submersion of persons within "groups" and/or "classes" had become nearly absolute in the technological society.

"La Technique"

Ellul uses the term "technique" to refer to any standardized set of procedures and/or means designed to attain a predetermined result.[19] Techniques thus include what are ordinarily considered technologies (computers, television, aircraft, etc.), but also any number of other features of modern societies not typically deemed technological (e.g., the pervasive use of money and organizational and/or administrative strategies like bureaucracy). "*La Technique*," Ellul argues, is the sum total of all of these procedures and/or means and their impact upon society and culture. It is, as he put it, "the totality of methods rationally arrived at and having absolute efficiency (for a given stage of development) in

17. Søren Kierkegaard, *The Sickness Unto Death: A Christian Psychological Exposition for Awakening and Upbuilding*, trans. Howard V. and Edna H. Hong (Princeton: Princeton University Press, 1980), 33–34.

18. Ibid., 35.

19. See Robert K. Merton, "Introduction," in Ellul, *The Technological Society*, v-viii.

every field of human activity."[20] "The Technological Society" is basically one in which so many features of social life have been surrendered to standardized means that virtually every aspect of the civilization now reflects the requirements of technical efficiency.

The essential features of *modern* technology over and against premodern technologies, Ellul stressed, are its "rationality" and "artificiality."[21] Rationality refers to the peculiarly modern determination always to select "the one best means" for achieving the desired result. Under modern conditions, the push to identify "the one best means" is often ultimately driven by monetary considerations, that is, the prescribed procedures, best practices, and/or recommended means are quite often the most cost effective. As Lewis Mumford also observed in *The Myth of the Machine*:

> To discuss the proliferation of inventions during the last two centuries, the mass production of commodities, and the spread of all the technological factors that are polluting and destroying the living environment, without reference to this immense pecuniary pressure constantly exerted in every technological area, is to ignore the most essential clue to the seemingly automatic and uncontrollable dynamism of the whole system.[22]

The connection between modern technological "rationalization" and the elimination of human individuality has long been observed and lamented, for the modern workplace has typically been carefully designed and engineered such that tasks are routine and repetitive and workers are readily replaceable. As Peter Berger and colleagues observe in a study entitled *The Homeless Mind: Modernization and Consciousness*,[23] workers in the modern workplace are encouraged to think of themselves and of each other as potentially reproducible components within the production process. Because modern systems have been expressly designed such that no individual and no action are unique, any worker with comparable training can substitute for any other worker within the factory system.[24] An employee's contribution to the work process can, furthermore, be precisely measured and thereby "objectively" evaluated.[25] Workers are

20. Ellul, *The Technological Society*, 25.

21. Ibid., 78–79.

22. Lewis Mumford, *The Myth of the Machine: The Pentagon of Power* (New York: Harcourt, Brace & Jovanovich, 1964), 169.

23. Peter L. Berger, Brigitte Berger, and Hansfried Kellner, *The Homeless Mind: Modernization and Consciousness* (New York: Vintage, 1974).

24. Ibid., 26.

25. Ibid.

thus encouraged to think of the production process, no matter how concrete the actual products of the process may well be, in largely abstract terms—as a system analyzable into its constituent steps, procedures, and components, of which they themselves may be listed.[26] Technological production tends for just these reasons to encourage anonymous social relations. Indeed, as Berger et al. note, the process actually encourages a kind of "self-anonymization."[27]

Yet as machinelike as people have managed to become in order to adapt to the systems and machinery that pervade the modern workplace, they may not ultimately be able to compete with the machines. The machines are stronger, faster, tireless, more precise, more reliable, and significantly less expensive than human beings. Business and industry have, not surprisingly, therefore, been replacing human labor with capital machinery at an ever-increasing rate over the past century and a half. In this connection, John Maynard Keynes coined the term "technological unemployment" nearly a century ago to describe the large-scale displacement of people by machinery.[28] And, while it has long been the case that those displaced by machinery have been able—eventually—to find productive and satisfying work, economists are beginning to wonder how long this trend can continue as machines become increasingly capable of more and more kinds of work.[29] As Brynjolfsson and McAfee report in a work entitled *The Second Machine Age: Work, Progress, and Prosperity in a Time of Brilliant Technologies*, sustained exponential improvement in the speed and capacity of computers, the digitization of extraordinarily large amounts of data, and the use of increasingly sophisticated algorithms to "mine" this data, are yielding technological breakthroughs that will almost certainly make the stuff of yesterday's science fiction actually possible within the coming years.[30] As this happens, the displacement of human by machine labor must inevitably move from the realm of blue-collar employment to the world of the white-collar profession. And while it may once have been assumed that automation would free people up to pursue science, philosophy, art, travel, and so on, it is beginning to look

26. Ibid., 27.

27. Ibid., 33.

28. John Maynard Keynes, "Economic Possibilities for our Grandchildren," 3, http://www.econ.yale.edu/smith/econ116a/keynes1.pdf, accessed June 17, 2016.

29. See Nicholas Carr, *The Big Switch: Rewiring the World from Edison to Google* (New York: Norton, 2013), 136.

30. Erik Brynjolfsson and Andrew McAfee, *The Second Machine Age: Work, Progress, and Prosperity in a Time of Brilliant Technologies* (New York: Norton, 2014), 90; see also Stanley Aronowitz and William DiFazio, *The Jobless Future*, 2nd ed. (Minneapolis: University of Minnesota Press, 2010); also Jeremy Rifkin, *The End of Work: The Decline of the Global Labor Force and the Dawn of the Post-Market Era* (New York: Penguin, 1995).

like this privilege may only actually accrue to the few who own and/or manage the machinery. Ellul put this presciently, if bluntly, in 1964: "Man must have nothing decisive to perform in the course of technical operations; after all, he is the source of error."[31]

In addition to its rationality, Ellul stressed that modern technology is characterized by its "artificiality," by which he meant its propensity both to require as well as to give rise to more and more standardized procedures, methods, and technical means, until the natural—and human—environment is completely submerged beneath technical artifice. Technique, Ellul wrote in this connection:

> destroys, eliminates, or subordinates the natural world, and does not allow this world to restore itself or even to enter into a symbiotic relation with [technique]. The two worlds obey different imperatives, different directives, and different laws which have nothing in common. . . . We are rapidly approaching the time when there will be no longer any natural environment at all.[32]

Hyperbole aside, Ellul's comments contain an important insight, for it is indeed modern technology's penchant for artifice that poses the most elemental threat to human identity. As we will see, the technological process tends toward the elimination of the only context within which personal agency is possible: that described by *time* and *place*. If this process is allowed to continue unchecked, the possibility of genuinely personal action must be rendered moot.

The Technological Obliteration of Place and Time

The technological society has progressively and relentlessly transformed concrete and particular "places" into standardized and more-or-less uniform "spaces," largely for the sake of facilitating commerce, but often also by virtue of simple technical requirements. The engineering of air transport, for example, all but insures that modern airports will both function and have the same "look and feel" the world over. The rationalization of production and distribution of consumer goods, furthermore, as well as the careful design of the "retail experience," means that the shopping mall will be more-or-less identical in Dallas and Shanghai. The machine production and transport of food means that what used to be farmland has increasingly become the site of intensively

31. Ellul, *The Technological Society*, 136.
32. Ibid., 79.

managed industrial "agribusiness" and that our cities are increasingly populated with retail grocery and fast-food "outlets." Indeed, cities are themselves now threatened with redundancy. As O'Donovan observes:

> Traditionally cities acted as a powerful localizing force, drawing us together by virtue of our need to communicate the resources of our culture, industrial, mercantile, educational, and artistic. But with computer terminals and good roads we can pursue cultural intercourse centrifugally. The loss of a sense of place has come to expression in a technology of placeless culture, mapped on the design of the worldwide web.[33]

In sum, concrete and localized *places* have, under the influence of commerce and networked digital technologies, progressively been reduced to mere "spaces," spaces that seem destined to exist only in "the cloud" of so-called cyberspace. Yet as astonishing and as convenient as the worldwide web may well be, its virtual reality must be a poor substitute for the reality requisite for the formation of persons. Again, as Poteat has noted: "When the notion of place is assimilated into that of space . . . or when place is preempted by space, in this sense the concept of a person falls into grave jeopardy."[34]

Time also has become increasingly alien and inhuman within the technological society. This is particularly true given exponential improvements in computing capacity coupled with digital networks that operate at nearly the speed of light. Time, Poor Richard is supposed to have said, *is* money. Yet the real money is tied to transactional velocity as well as to slight time advantages in the possession of information, insights that have been recently exploited and augmented using networked digital computing technologies. As a result, the fluidity and rapidity with which money now circulates the planet, as well as the volume of this circulation, defies human understanding—much less human control. How can human beings possibly be expected, as is so often suggested in contemporary business literature, to adapt to technological change that is accelerating at an exponential rate? And what would the point of adaptation be if efficiency and "through put" are the only "ends" or purposes the technological system is able to value? As Albert Borgmann points out in an insightful piece entitled "Pointless Perfection and Blessed Burdens," technological perfection must inevitably dissolve into indeterminacy.[35] For, he reasons, when

33. Oliver O'Donovan, "The Loss of a Sense of Place," in Oliver O'Donovan and Joan Lockwood O'Donovan, *Bonds of Imperfection: Christian Politics Past and Present* (Grand Rapids: Eerdmans, 2004), 297.

34. Poteat, *Primacy of Persons*, 30.

35. Albert Borgmann, "Pointless Perfection and Blessed Burdens," *Crux* 47, no. 4 (2011): 20–28.

in the disembodied world of machine intelligence the numbers and kinds of artificial experiences become limitless, then nothing in particular will stand out anymore. There will no longer be a "before" and an "after," a "now" and a "then," a "better" and a "worse." The diversity, particularity, and time-bound quality of actual experience, in other words, when transmuted into "information" that is infinite and always and everywhere instantaneously available must make all such narrative and qualitative distinctions meaningless. The old and humane adage "all's well that ends well" can have no meaning within a system that cannot distinguish ends from beginnings, and neither can the notion of personal identity. For just as place is necessary for the formation of personal identity, so also does personal formation require time, often long periods of it. In a world operating at speeds that—from an embodied human point of view—approach simultaneity and in which sequential time is therefore no longer humanly recognizable, the formation of personal identity must be rendered all but impossible.

Theological Interpretation

Yet the questions immediately arise: Why have we allowed all of this to happen? Why are we doing this to ourselves? Here Ellul offers a blunt theological interpretation of the modern predicament. While modern technology does develop out of modern science's understanding of given nature, and particularly out of its understanding of natural forces, human beings deploy this knowledge and these forces in the distinctly un-natural directions of homogeneity and uniformity, and all for the sake of the efficient accumulation of such things as money and power. Why? Because, Ellul reminds us, we are sinners at enmity with the divine purpose. Thus, whereas created nature is profligate, extravagant, apparently wasteful, but full of *life*, we are stingy and miserly, hemmed in by death, scarcity, necessity, greed, covetousness, and the environments we create are very often lifeless. Yet rather than repent of our hubris, we attempt instead to refashion the created order. "Technique," Ellul observes along this line, "advocates the entire remaking of life and its framework because they have been so badly made."[36] Indeed, the whole of modern technological development since Descartes might be described as one assault after another upon the perceived limitations of *place*, *time*, and *persons* by the rationalizing intellect.[37]

36. Ellul, *Technological Society*, 142–43.
37. Poteat, *Primacy of Persons*, 39.

The spiritual impulse behind modern technological development would seem, therefore, to be a distinctly modern form of ancient *gnosticism*, that hoary amalgamation of religious convictions and practices whose adherents shunned the lower realm of materiality and physicality and sought release into an upper, purely spiritual realm by means of initiation into special religious insight or knowledge ("*gnosis*"). While modern technological "gnostics" might not go as far as to say that matter per se is evil (though some do argue that organic matter is unnecessarily fragile) they do chafe at the traditional theological notion that created nature ought to shape and delimit human aspirations. On the contrary, "nature"—which includes the human body—is simply something to be mastered by the human *spirit* and re-mastered if necessary for the sake of purposes that human beings have *willed*. Of course, gnostic themes have hitherto been mostly implicit within the modern technological ethos, but they have tended to surface explicitly and with increasing frequency at the forefront of contemporary technological research and development. Gnostic aspirations would seem, for example, to be very much at the heart of the so-called cybernetic revolution, that view of the world that believes that it is possible to reduce all of material reality to bits of underlying information, information that can then be infinitely manipulated and reconfigured. Given such a view of the world, Brent Waters observes, in a study disturbingly entitled *From Human to Posthuman*, the only thing standing in the way of the radical transformation of "nature"—including human nature—is inadequate technology, a problem that can be remedied, at least in principle, by way of research and development.[38] "There is no real boundary separating nature and artifice," Waters writes describing the cybernetic outlook, "only patterns or lines of information that can be erased and redrawn; no real limit that cannot be eventually overcome."[39]

Responding Christianly

Stung by accusations of pessimism, Ellul was at pains to stress that his critique of modern technology should not be taken to mean that Christians must somehow repudiate it. On the contrary, he insisted, those bearing witness to Christian hope must rather *transcend* modern technology. Along this line,

---

38. Brent Waters, *From Human to Posthuman: Christian Theology and Technology in a Postmodern World*, ed. Roger Trigg and J. Wentzel van Huyssteen, Ashgate Science & Religion Series (Aldershot: Ashgate, 2006).

39. Ibid., x.

the Christian vocation in the technological milieu is to try to discern modern technology's peculiar logic—its essence and impact upon modern society and culture—so as to detect the avenues of free and redemptive action that remain open. There is always, Ellul insisted, room for movement. Even when things are technologically conditioned, structured, planned, and so forth, there are always what he termed "lacunae" within which free and redemptive action remains possible.[40] The necessities of our technological culture are not (yet) such as to have eliminated the possibility of freedom. The Christian, therefore, is the one who brings as much "free play" as possible into government, into bureaucracy, into business, in short, into any social sphere that would otherwise be totally determined by the logic of technology.[41]

Of course, Ellul was quick to remind his readers that the point of free Christian action is not to reform the social order, an order that would, reform notwithstanding, remain subject to sin and death. Rather, the point of Christian action is simply to bear witness to the possibility—and *source!*—of the Christian hope. Christians bear witness to hope, furthermore, simply by refusing to surrender to the logic and requirements of the modern technological system. It is in the exercise of freedom, Ellul stressed, that we overcome "*la Technique*." "If we see technology as nothing but objects that can be useful," Ellul wrote, "and if we stop believing in technology for its own sake or that of society; and if we stop fearing technology, and treat it as one thing among many others, then we destroy the basis for the power technology has over humanity."[42]

Given the threat "*la Technique*" poses to the formation of personality, it is clearly also incumbent upon Christians to protect the possibility of genuinely *personal* agency. Here, beyond heeding Ellul's advice to take care to understand the specific nature of the threat, Christians must also endeavor to *re*-member the basic contours of Christian theology. For not only does the church's theology of creation, for example, begin by emphasizing the goodness, value, and importance of each and every individual and particular thing that God has made, but it further emphasizes that the human vocation within the created order is to mediate the divine essence—*love*—and the divine intention—*fruition*—both *to* and *for the sake of* all of God's creatures. The human rule over creation is—or ought to be—a rule that, as O'Donovan notes, "liberates other beings to be, to be in themselves, to be for others, and to be for God." Liberating other *persons* to be in themselves, for others,

40. Jacques Ellul, *Perspectives on Our Age: Jacques Ellul Speaks on His Life and Work*, ed. William H. Vanderburg (Concord, ON: Anansi, 1997), 110.

41. Ibid.

42. Ibid., 108-9.

and for God must mean respecting—indeed, *celebrating*!—their individuality and unsubstitutable "otherness." It must also mean defending the particular *places* within which they can exercise genuinely personal agency and the *time* necessary for them to become uniquely themselves. This will almost certainly come at the cost of efficiency and effectiveness, but it will just as certainly bear the fruit of *joy*!

Chapter 42

African Christian or Christian African?
Identity Relations in African Christianity

Victor I. Ezigbo

This essay explores the question: How do Christian communities in the continent of Africa understand their Christian identities—who they are or expect to be, both in the private and public spheres, as the people who bear the name "Christian"? As many theologians and historians have shown, contexts condition the contents and forms of expression of the Christian faith.[1] Therefore, the differences in African traditional worldviews, gender relations, ethnic backgrounds, economic powers, political experiences, language structures, and religious landscapes should caution against the notion that "African Christianity" constitutes a monolithic entity. Therefore, when discussing African Christian identity, it is important to attend to the similarities and differences of African Christian communities. To explore the multifaceted African Christian identities, I will draw information from both published works on African Christianity and my research on Nigerian Christianity.[2] I have divided the essay into

---

1. Historians such as Andrew F. Walls, Lamin Sanneh, and Ogbu Kalu have pointed out that African Christianity is shaped by Africans' vernaculars, history, worldviews, and experiences. See Ogbu U. Kalu, "Introduction: The Shape and Flow of African Church Historiography," in *African Christianity: An African Story*, ed. Ogbu U. Kalu (Trenton, NJ: African World Press, 2007), 3–22; Lamin Sanneh, *Disciples of All Nations: Pillars of World Christianity* (New York: Oxford University Press, 2008); Andrew F. Walls, *The Cross-Cultural Process in Christian History* (Maryknoll, NY: Orbis, 2002). For discussions on contextual theological discourse, see Stephen B. Bevans, *Models of Contextual Theology*, rev. and expanded ed. (Maryknoll, NY: Orbis, 2002); Victor I. Ezigbo, "Imagining Mutual Christian Theological Identity: From Apologia to Dialogic Theologizing," *Journal of Ecumenical Studies* 50, no. 3 (2015): 452–72; Angie Pears, *Doing Contextual Theology* (London: Routledge, 2010).

2. Some of the findings of the research have been published. See Victor I. Ezigbo, *Re-Imagining African Christologies: Conversing with the Interpretations and Appropriations of Jesus in Contemporary African Christianity* (Eugene, OR: Cascade, 2010).

664

two major sections. The first section delineates the different factors that shape identity talks in African Christianity. These factors will highlight key issues in African Christians' discussion of identity. The second section focuses on two general self-identifying markers that may be discerned in African Christianity, particularly in sub-Saharan Africa. The self-identifying markers will underscore the similarities and dissimilarities of African Christian communities.

Conceptualizing African Christian Identities

Since the 1950s, sub-Saharan African theologians have been perturbed about the manner in which the Christian faith ought to relate to the primal cultures and religions of Africa. Many of the theologians responded to the threat or what they judged to be the threat that Western versions of Christianity posed to African cultures and the traditional way of life. In 1955, K. A. Busia, a sociologist, asked a question that summed up the anxiety of African Christians who struggled to hold in tension their Christian and African identities. "Can the African be Christian only by giving up his culture," asked Busia, "or is there a way by which Christianity can ennoble it?"[3] This question has shaped the discourse on the identities of Christian communities in Africa. Busia's terse response to this question does not provide much help. According to Busia, "Something . . . must die but only in order that it may bear fruit. To us is entrusted the husbandry."[4] Busia does not tell us the nature of the "something" that he believes must die in order to bear fruit. Was it African culture? Or was it the Christian faith? Or did Busia have in mind some aspects of both African cultures and the Christian faith? It is also not entirely clear if the horticultural and husbandry metaphors of dying and germinating are the most appropriate way of conceptualizing the relationship between the Christian faith and African culture. Busia's question, however, highlights the need to attend to the anxiety of Africans who desire to be truly African and truly Christian. Dealing with this anxiety, as I will show, is an onerous task because it requires the complex process of bringing together two different identities and also pressing them to enjoy a symbiotic relationship.

Context shapes identity discourse. A context may be described as the *Sitz im Leben* of a community that includes history, thought, social location, experience, and culture. C. C. Baeta has noted that the term "African culture"

---

3. K. A. Busia, "The African Worldview," in *Christian and African Culture: The Proceedings of a Conference held at Accra, Gold Coast, May 2–6, under the auspices of the Christian Council* (Accra: Christian Council of the Gold Coast, 1955), 6.

4. Busia, "The African Worldview," 6.

should be understood in the broader context of the "worldview—the beliefs, values, practices, and inhibitions deriving from it—originating entirely from African societies and peculiar to them." Baeta also noted that African culture "represents the African's response to the demands made upon himself by life itself."[5] The context of the discourse on African Christianity is deeply shaped by several historical, cultural, and religious factors such as colonialism, post-colonial agendas, ethnic conflicts, Western missions and theologies, and the relationship between African traditional religions and other religions, especially Christianity and Islam. Discussing how each of these factors has shaped African Christian identity is beyond the scope of this essay. However, I will describe three factors that underscore the complexity of identity relations in African Christianity.

The Taxonomy Factor

Given that the continent of Africa is culturally, ethnically, linguistically, religiously, economically, and politically multifaceted, the extent to which one can meaningfully speak of "African Christianity" will largely depend on how the terms "African" and "Christianity" are construed and also how one understands the relationship of these terms when they are used conjointly.[6] Some use the term "Christian" to describe the communities that worship Jesus Christ or have adopted one of the commonly recognized Christian biblical canons and ecclesiastical traditions. J. N. K. Mugambi, for example, defines a Christian as "a person who has accepted the Christian faith and made a firm decision to become a follower of Jesus Christ."[7] Others use the term "Christian" in a highly selective way to describe the communities that have adopted a particular Christian tradition. They sometimes use adjectives such

5. C. C. Baeta, "The Challenge of African Culture to the Church and the Message of the Church to African Culture," in *Christian and African Culture*, 51.

6. "African religions," writes Jacob K. Olupona, "are as diverse as the African continent itself. Africa is home to more than fifty countries, nearly every form of ecological niche found on Earth, and hundreds of ethnic groups who together speak more than a thousand languages. It is not surprising, then, that this enormous range of peoples, cultures, and modes of living would also be reflected in a diverse range of religious expressions." Olupona, *African Religions: A Very Short Introduction* (New York: Oxford University Press, 2014), 1. Some texts use the terms "African" and "Africa" to refer to the regions south of the Sahara desert. Others use the terms for all the countries in the present-day continent of Africa. For more discussion, see V. Y. Mudimbe, *The Idea of Africa* (Bloomington: Indiana University Press, 1994).

7. J. N. K. Mugambi, "Christianity and the African Heritage," in *African Christianity: An African Story*, ed. Kalu, 451–73, at 451.

as "true" and "real" or qualifiers such as "backsliding" or "born again" as identity markers when describing their understanding of Christian identity or drawing out the boundaries of the Christian faith. For example, many evangelical Christians in Africa do not recognize African Initiated Churches (AICs) as true Christian communities.[8] Many such evangelicals see AICs as mission fields—the arenas that are in need of true Christian doctrines and practices.

When the terms "African" and "Christian" are conjoined, how should one understand the meaning of "African" in this context? Does "African" refer to who and what is physically present in or originated from the continent of Africa? If one adopts a spherical description of "African," would children born outside of the continent of Africa to parents who were born in Africa qualify as "African"? Though there may be no tidy way to approach the question of identity with reference to "African Christianity," I will highlight two broad paths that can be helpful for entering into the complex discourse on African Christian identity. I will refer to these paths as the *origins path* and the *culture path*. Since these two paths intersect, they should not be seen as mutually exclusive. I will say brief words about these two paths.

Origins path: When approached from the perspective of origins, the term "African" refers to a cluster of peoples, some of whom share the same ethnic, regional, or national backgrounds. The shared backgrounds will vary depending on several factors: kinship, method of acquiring citizenship (e.g., through birth, marriage, or adoption), and experience, which is both multilayered and nonstatic. As Nils Bloch-Hoell has noted, "The identity of people, nation or continent is never static or unchangeable. It is historically, geographically and sociologically conditioned. African identity, if it is possible to use the term without a more precise qualification, could not have been the same in 1300 and in 1991."[9] When discussing African identity, it is important to attend to the role that ethnicity plays in identity talks in African communities. Whereas

---

8. African Initiated Churches (also known as African Independent Churches, African Instituted Churches, and AICs) were the churches that sprang up in response to the overtly Western-oriented modes of expression of the mission-founded churches in Africa. Some of the earliest founders of the AICs are William Wade Harris (the Harrist churches), Simon Kimbangu (the Kimbanguist churches), and Garrick Braide (Christ Army Church). For more discussions on the AICs, see Bengt G. M. Sundkler, *Bantu Prophets in South Africa* (Oxford: Oxford University Press, 1961); J. D. Y. Peel, *Aladura: A Religious Movement Among the Yoruba* (Oxford: Oxford University Press, 1968); Allan H. Anderson, *African Reformation: African Initiated Christianity in the 20th Century* (Trenton, NJ: Africa World Press, 2001).

9. Nils E. Bloch-Hoell, "African Identity: European Invention or Genuine African Character?" *Mission Studies* 9, no. 1 (1992): 98–107, at 101.

non-Africans may refer to the peoples of Africa simply as Africans, the peoples of Africa usually prefer to describe themselves with their ethnic identities, especially when speaking to an audience that is aware of Africa's diverse ethnic groups. In some situations, some may choose to identify themselves by mentioning their lineage or village.[10] A person whose ethnic group is Igbo, for instance, would most likely not refer to herself as an Igbo when she is speaking to someone familiar with the many clans, villages, and lineages that make up the Igbo ethnic group. She might say, "*abu mu onye Alor*" (I am from Alor), if she was born in Alor—a town in Anambra state, Nigeria. If she was speaking to someone that knew about Alor, she might say, "*abu mu onye Okebunoye*" (I am from Okebunoye).[11] If she was speaking to someone that knew about Okebunoye, she might say, "*abu mu onye Umudim*" (I am from Umudim).[12] Towns, villages, and clans that make up an ethnic group may have slightly different cultures.

Culture path: Edward Tylor defined culture broadly as "that complex whole which includes knowledge, belief, art, morals, law, custom and any other capabilities and habits acquired by a [person] as a member of a society."[13] Cultures are a community's modes of believing, relating, thinking, and living. Such ways of living, thinking, believing, and relating may be predominant or marginal, may or may not be acceptable by the majority of people that belong to the community, and may or may not be tangible. When approached from the *culture path*, "African" may refer to what and who exhibits or shares the peculiar cultural characteristics of the cluster of communities that constitute the continent of Africa. There is no generic or one-size-fits-all "African culture" but rather diverse, self-imposed, and socially constructed ways in which communities act, live, and form relationships. Therefore, when speaking about "African Christianity," it is helpful to study the communities that identify themselves as such and also to avoid superimposing foreign assumptions on such communities.

It is noteworthy that identity talks have sometimes impelled the ideas of exclusion and inclusion. In this context, it is perhaps more useful to focus on the ethnic identities of the groups that constitute the nations of Africa than to focus on national identities. Identity construction sometimes precipitates conflicts that have devastating consequences for the excluded. Identity talks, with reference to human communities, have sometimes led to ethnic conflicts, genocide, intrareligious conflicts, and interreligious conflicts. In Africa, the quest for identity, like

10. Kwame Anthony Appiah, *In My Father's House: Africa in the Philosophy of Culture* (New York: Oxford University Press, 1992), 177.

11. Okebunoye is one of the villages of Alor.

12. Umudim is one of the clans of Okebunoye.

13. Edward Tylor, *Primitive Culture* (New York: Harper, 1958), 1.

a devastating storm, has left behind the debris of human bodies that have been crushed under the weight of genocide, ethnic cleansing, and competing religions traditions. Ethnicity, rather than religion, has in many cases had the upper hand in the conflicts that stem from identity construction. I will cite a few examples to highlight some of the negative impacts of identity talks on some communities in Africa. The Rwanda genocide is a painful reminder of the danger of ethnic identity talks and prejudices. I cite the Rwanda genocide partly because, at the time of the genocide, it was a predominantly Christian nation. Some of the perpetrators of the genocide and their victims were Christians.[14] On the role of the church in the Rwanda genocide, Timothy Longman has remarked:

> In the aftermath of the Rwandan genocide, many people inside and outside the country have struggled to comprehend the involvement of Rwanda's churches in the violence. Many Christians in particular have wondered how such carnage could have taken place in one of Africa's most Christian countries, how the population could have become so willingly involved in such deplorable acts in a country where more than 90 per cent of the population were members of Catholic or Protestant churches. As critics of Rwanda's churches have pointed out, not only did church buildings become the sites of massacres, but most of the killers were Christians, and even some pastors and priests participated in the slaughter.[15]

To cite another example in which identity talks and political agendas stoked conflicts and violence in Africa, between 1948 and 1994, many South Africans suffered greatly during the apartheid regimes and the anti-apartheid uprisings. South Africa deteriorated immensely under the crushing weight of those policies, with the Blacks, Indians, and Coloreds bearing the brunt of those policies. In his acceptance speech for the 1984 Nobel Peace Prize, Desmond Mpilo Tutu bemoaned the devastating consequences of the apartheid laws, such as "the Population Registration Act, which decrees that all South Africans must be classified ethnically, and duly registered according to [the established] race categories." Such laws meant that in some cases "in the same family, one child [was] classified white while another with a slightly darker hue, [was] classified colored, with all the horrible consequences for the latter of being shut out from the membership of a greatly privileged caste."[16]

14. Timothy Longman, "Church Politics and the Genocide in Rwanda," *Journal of Religion in Africa* 31 (2001): 163–86.

15. Longman, "Church Politics and the Genocide in Rwanda," 164.

16. Desmond Mpilo Tutu, "Nobel Lecture," December 11, 1984, Oslo, Norway, in *Statements:*

Returning to the issue of naming, when discussing the identity of an "African," it may be more useful to attend to the cultures of each African ethnic group. As noted earlier, Africa's diversity extends across the national spheres and also permeates the ethnic spheres. To use Nigeria as an example, the Igbo people differ linguistically and culturally from the Tiv of the middle belt region, the Hausas of the northern region, and the Yorubas of the southwest region. While in the traditional Yoruba culture a younger person is expected to squat or sometimes to lie prostrate on the ground in front of an elder as a sign of respect, such acts are neither expected nor encouraged in Igbo communities. A Nigerian that grew up in a town in northern Nigeria made the following remarks after his first visit to the southeast region of Nigeria: "I felt I was in a new country without a visa."[17] These remarks show that it is unhelpful to speak of Africans or African Christianity without some qualifications.

The Ecclesiastical Factor

Christianity in Africa is punctuated by different ecclesiastical traditions—each distinct, some loosely related, and others closely related. While some of the church traditions share similar beliefs, others have quite different beliefs. Not every community that self-identifies as "Christian" and "African" holds the same beliefs, worldviews, liturgy, modes of dressing, and modes of forming communal relations. Take, for instance, the Coptic Church and the Redeemed Christian Church of God (R.C.C.G). Both of these Christian traditions have their roots in the continent of Africa. However, they differ in their doctrines, liturgy, and ecclesiastical structures. As a Pentecostal church, the R.C.C.G., under the leadership of pastor Enoch A. Adeboye—its general overseer and chairman of the governing council—exhibits the cultures of most Pentecostal and charismatic movements in Africa: prophesying, healing, breaking of curses, emphasis on the empowerment of the Holy Sprit, and exposition of Scripture. Though the R.C.C.G. began in Nigeria, specifically in the Yoruba region, it neither emphasizes a Nigerian culture nor represents a political or ethnic identity. The Coptic Church, unlike the R.C.C.G., in some significant ways, represents the ethnic, religious, and political interests of the Copts in Egypt. One essential feature of the Coptic Church that is nonexistent in the R.C.C.G. is monasticism. The

---

The Nobel Peace Prize Lecture: Desmond M. Tutu (New York: Anson Phelps Stokes Institute for Africa, Afro-American, and American Indian Affairs, 1986), 29–39.

17. Professor Samuel Zalanga, who made these remarks, currently teaches sociology at Bethel University, Saint Paul, Minnesota (USA).

Coptic Church traces their monastic history back to notable Egyptian monks such as St. Anthony (ca. 251–356), St. Pachomius (ca. 292–346), St. Macarius (ca. 300–390), and St. Shenoute (348–466).[18]

To cite another example, Evangelical Churches Winning All (formerly known as Evangelical Churches of West Africa or ECWA) does not allow women to serve as pastors of a local church. Its leaders usually cite the apostle Paul's injunction in 1 Timothy 2:12 and Jesus's selection of twelve male disciples as warrants for their male-only priestly class.[19] Conversely, some churches in Africa, particularly African Initiated Churches (AICs), Pentecostal churches, and charismatic churches, have women pastors and leaders. Though significantly fewer than men, women occupy ordained pastoral positions in many of these ecclesiastical traditions.[20] Damaris Parsitau has observed that a "striking feature of Pentecostalism in Kenya is the proliferation of ordained female church leaders, many of whom are founders, presidents, bishops, evangelists, healers, or prophetesses in these churches."[21] In a continent that is predominantly patriarchal, women holding ecclesiastical offices in Africa, irrespective of their denominations, have continued to struggle to establish themselves as those who can effectively perform their duties without having men as chaperones.

Another example of the diverse ways in which Christian communities in Africa imagine their Christian identities can be discerned in the manner they navigate Christian-Muslim relations. They differ in their approaches and goals depending on the political climate of the country. In Egypt, the Coptic community (the church and the community at large) has had to reimagine the "Coptic question" in a Muslim majority country.[22] The issue of citizenship is one of the factors that shape the Copts' discourse on identity. The full-citizenship of the Copts in Egypt has been employed by different Coptic communities to convey

18. See Otto F. A. Meinardus, *Two Thousand Years of Coptic Christianity* (Cairo: The American University in Cairo Press, 1999), esp. chap. 3; Lois M. Farag, "Monasticism: Living Scripture and Theological Orthodoxy," in *The Coptic Christian Heritage: History, Faith, and Culture*, ed. Lois M. Farag (New York: Routledge, 2014), 116–31.

19. In 1 Timothy 2:12, Paul wrote: "I do not permit a woman to teach or to exercise authority over a man; rather she is to remain quiet" (ESV).

20. Sarojni Nadar, "On Being the Pentecostal Church: Pentecostal Women's Voices and Visions," *The Ecumenical Review* 56, no. 3 (2004): 354–67.

21. Damaris Parsitau, "'Arise, Oh Ye Daughters of Faith': Women, Pentecostalism, and Public Culture in Kenya," in *Christianity and Public Culture in Africa*, ed. Harri Englund (Athens, OH: Ohio University Press, 2011), 131–45, at 131.

22. See Sebastian Elsasser, *The Coptic Question in the Mubarak Era* (Oxford: Oxford University Press, 2014); Marlis J. Saleh, "Government Intervention in the Coptic Church in Egypt during the Fatimid Period," *The Muslim World* 91, no. 3–4 (2001): 381–97.

their agendas both in Egypt and in diaspora.[23] As Yvonne Haddad and Joshua Donovan have pointed out, "For decades, Egypt's Copts have engaged in a debate over their place and role in Egyptian society. This debate hinged on their fundamental identity. Would they continue to see themselves as a persecuted minority—with a history and culture distinct from Muslim Egyptians—or as a part of a united Egypt, placing their Egyptian nationality over their sectarian identity?"[24] In Nigeria, unlike in Egypt, citizenship is not a major factor in Christian-Muslim relations. Many Christians and Muslims in Nigeria share a mutual mistrust: while Christians fear that Muslims seek to Islamize the country, Muslims fear that Christians equally seek to Christianize the country.[25]

The Interreligious Factor: Jesus Christ, Christianity, and African Traditional Religions

Does the term "African Christianity" express what makes an African community "Christian"? Or does the term express what makes a Christian community "African"? Some Christian theologians, for instance, insist that identifiers such as culture and ethnicity should not function as the primary factors when discussing the identity of African Christians. On the contrary, Jesus Christ should be construed as the primary marker or factor that ought to define Christian identity. Charles Nyamiti, who is deeply shaped by the Vatican II's *Lumen Gentium, Ad Gentes, Gaudium et Spes*, has argued for the contextualization of the Christian faith in order that it may purify the primal traditions of Africa. He writes, "One of the means for the building up of African theology is the examination of the African traditional religious teachings in the light of Christian doctrine so as to find out how the African beliefs could be purified, wherever necessary, and be brought into Christian doctrine to form with it a coherent and integrated whole. The foundation for this procedure is the official Church's teaching itself, especially as formulated by Vatican II."[26]

John Mbiti identifies religiosity as a universal distinctive mark of Africans. He writes: "in their traditional life African peoples are deeply religious.

---

23. Paul Sedra, "Class Cleavages and Ethnic Conflict: Coptic Christian Communities in Modern Egyptian Politics," *Islam and Christian-Muslim Relations* 10, no. 2 (1999): 219–35.

24. Yvonne Haddad and Joshua Donovan, "Good Copt, Bad Copt: Competing Narratives on Coptic Identity in Egypt and the United States," *Studies in World Christianity* 19 (2013): 208–32.

25. Frieder Ludwig, "Christian-Muslim Relations in Northern Nigeria since the Introduction of Shari'ah in 1999," *Journal of American Academy of Religion* 76, no. 3 (2008): 602–37.

26. Charles Nyamiti, "The African Sense of God's Motherhood in the Light of Christian Faith," *Ahcan Ecclesiastical Review* 23, no 5 (1981): 269–74, at 269.

It is religion, more than anything else, which colors their understanding of the universe and their empirical participation in that universe, making life a profound phenomenon. To be is to be religious in a religious universe."[27] Writing specifically about Christian identity, he argues that a "Christocentric identity" ought to surpass national, cultural, and denominational identities of African Christians. By christocentric identity, Mbiti means rethinking other identities that African Christians may cling to in light of the life, teaching, and work of Jesus Christ.[28]

Kwame Bediako developed further the centrality of Jesus Christ in the formation of Christian identity. In *Jesus and the Gospel in Africa*, Bediako argues that people's "true human identity as men and women made in the image of God, is not to be understood primarily in terms of racial, cultural, national or lineage categories, but in Jesus Christ himself. The true children of Abraham are those who put their faith in Jesus Christ in the same way that Abraham trusted God (Rom 4:11–12)."[29] When understood in this way, we may pragmatically speak of "Christian Africans" and not "African Christians." Bediako, however, does not diminish the cultures of Africa in his imagination of Christian identity. To speak of Jesus Christ, and not Christianity, as the principal factor in Christian identity, indicates that Bediako's aim is to present Jesus Christ as the one who has pride of place in the formation of Christian community. Bediako writes, "we [Christians] have not merely our natural past; through our faith in Jesus, we have also an 'adoptive' past, the past of God, reaching into biblical history itself, aptly described as the 'Abrahamic link.'"[30] For Bediako, although Jesus Christ was a Jew by birth and culture, his universal significance in Christian identity formation is grounded in his ontology and work: he reflected "the brightness of God's glory and the exact likeness of God's own being (Heb 1:3), took our flesh and blood, shared our human nature, and underwent death for us to set us free from the fear of death (Heb 2:14–15)."[31] Bediako sometimes speaks of the "Gospel of Jesus Christ" as the key factor in determining Christian iden-

---

27. John S. Mbiti, *African Religions and Philosophy* (New York: Praeger, 1969), 262.

28. Mbiti, *African Religions and Philosophy*, 267.

29. Kwame Bediako, *Jesus and the Gospel in Africa: History and Experience* (Maryknoll, NY: Orbis, 2004), 24. Stan Ilo argues that the "search for the foundations of the Christian faith in Africa" should "begin with a deepening of the testimony from Scripture, tradition, and the living faith of the Church in the divine identity of Christ." See Stan Chu Ilo, "Beginning Afresh with Christ in the Search for Abundant Life in Africa," in *The Church as Salt and Light: Path to an African Ecclesiology of Abundant Life*, ed. Stan Chu Ilo, Joseph Ogbonnaya, and Alex Ojacor (Eugene, OR: Pickwick, 2011), 1–33.

30. Bediako, *Jesus and the Gospel in Africa*, 24.

31. Bediako, *Jesus and the Gospel in Africa*, 30.

tity.[32] Although Bediako does not unpack the content of the "Gospel of Jesus Christ," it is clear from his writings that he is referring to the life, experience, and significance of Jesus of Nazareth as described in the Bible.

The "Gospel of Jesus Christ," for Bediako, functions as a hermeneutical frame with which Christian communities can interpret and judge their history, experiences, and cultures. In his discussion on the relationship between the Christian faith and African primal religions and traditions, Bediako remarks:

> [The] Christian Gospel came to constitute an intellectual and historical category in its own right: it not only provided [the early Christian thinkers] with a precious interpretative key for discerning the religious meanings inherent in their heritage, so that they could decide what to accept and what to reject; in the Gospel they also found an all-encompassing reality and an overall integrating principle which enabled them to understand themselves and their past, and face the future, because the Gospel of Jesus Christ became for them the heir to all that was worthy in the past, whilst it held all the potential of the future.[33]

Other African theologians have proposed Africa's primal cultures and traditional religious values as what ought to be the primary factors when imagining African Christian identity. In this sense, we may speak of "African Christianity" and "African Christians." One such theologian is Ka Mana. In *Christians and Churches of Africa*, he wrote: "In accordance with the threefold understanding of salvation as basis, unity, and goal, it should be said that as Africans, we view salvation in Jesus Christ from the following perspectives: we view it especially from the primordial place where our ancestors of old handed down to us a great wisdom, tools of knowledge, customs and lifestyle, through which we may welcome Jesus Christ as one of us, deep within the grove of initiation, in this ancestral hearth, vital energy which determines our identity as a people, civilization and culture."[34] Mana locates Jesus Christ within African heritage, focusing on how his life and teaching can be integrated in Africans' cultural and spiritual yearnings for salvation.[35] Though Mana sees Jesus Christ as one who "comes to us as the absolute otherness of

---

32. Kwame Bediako, *Theology and Identity: The Impact of Culture upon Christian Thought in the Second Century and Modern Africa* (Oxford: Regnum, 1992), 440–41.

33. Bediako, *Theology and Identity*, 439–40.

34. Ka Mana, *Christians and Churches of Africa: Salvation in Christ and Building a New African Society* (Maryknoll, NY: Orbis, 2004), 3.

35. Mana, *Christians and Churches of Africa*, 32.

God" and therefore could not be "reduced to our inner cultural world,"[36] he should be understood by African Christian communities against the backgrounds of Africa's religious ideals and spiritual powers "where Christianity occupies an equally important place alongside Islam and African Traditional religions."[37]

To speak in pragmatic terms of either an "African Christian" or "Christian African" in the context of identity discourse may be misleading. Such characterizations adopt a primary-secondary mindset: they focus on what ought to be the primary and secondary factors in the identity formation of African Christian communities. But we need not approach the relationship between the Christian faith and African cultures in terms of the primary and secondary nexus. Also, there is no need to pit them against each other. Their relationship may be construed as existing on a continuum. Since the religious values of the Christian faith are translatable and also African cultures are not static, we may construe their relationship as a continuum in which both are forged together to produce communities that are simultaneously African and Christian.[38] Such relationship may be construed as a symbiotic relationship: the cultures of both the Christian faith and Africa are forged together in the lives of African Christians. This, of course, implies that "Christianity and African Indigenous [or traditional] Religions can enjoy a symbiotic relationship. The latter provides unique cognitive and religious tools for contextualizing the former in Africa. Christianity provides the knowledge of the Christ-event as a new outlook to imagine and appropriate God's presence from within African indigenous religious and cultural contexts."[39]

36. Mana, *Christians and Churches of Africa*, 34.

37. Mana, *Christians and Churches of Africa*, 3.

38. On the translatability of the Christian faith, Lamin Sanneh argues: "Except in extremist sectarian groups, Christians never made the language of Jesus a prerequisite for faith or membership in the fellowship. It is this linguistic revolution that accounts for the entire New Testament canon being written in a language other than the one in which Jesus preached. Thus it is that translation, and its attendant cross-cultural implications, came to be built into the historical make-up of Christianity." Sanneh notes two implications of the linguistic pluralism and translatable character of Christianity. He writes, "Two major consequences for the religious status of culture may be characterized as, first, the relativization of all cultural arrangements, and, second, the de-stigmatization of all Gentile or taboo cultures." Lamin Sanneh, "The Gospel, Language, and Culture: The Theological Method in Cultural Analysis," *International Review of Mission* 84, no. 332 (1995): 47–54. See also Lamin Sanneh, *Translating the Message: The Missionary Impact on Culture* (Maryknoll, NY: Orbis, 1991).

39. Victor I. Ezigbo, "Religion and Divine Presence: Appropriating Christianity from within African Indigenous Religions' Perspective," in *African Traditions in the Study of Religion in Africa: Emerging Trends, Indigenous Spirituality and the Interface with Other World Religions*, ed. Afe Adogame, Ezra Chitando, and Bolaji Bateye (Surrey, UK: Ashgate, 2012), 187–203.

African Christian communities—both the academic and grassroots communities—have imagined the person, work, and significance of Jesus Christ in different ways.[40] Christians—those who commit to follow Jesus Christ and to identify with the communities (churches) that are grounded in his life and teaching—sometimes see themselves as a community with a "new" identity. What is, however, unclear is the meaning of "new" and how it relates to the "old." For some, to have a new identity, which is grounded in Jesus Christ, is to secede from the "old ways"—the cultures that either oppose or do not promote the teaching of Jesus Christ. A Christian's new identity is largely imagined in light of the ways Christian communities in Africa understand the relationship between the Christian faith and African heritage, particularly the traditional religions and customs. Ben Udoh has argued that where the relationship between Christianity and African heritage or primal cultures is not understood properly, many Africans experience a "religious schizophrenia"—a double mindedness that usually leads to identity crisis.[41] In *Theological Pitfalls in Africa*, Byang Kato described African traditional religions as a cancerous tumor that could only be cured by Christianity, which he called a "divinely revealed religion."[42] For Kato, there is no continuity between Christianity and African traditional religions. Other African Christians, however, do not see Christianity and African traditional religions as mutually exclusive.

An example can help highlight the different ways in which African Christians understand the "new" identity of Africans who become Christians. Most Igbo communities require a retrospective honoring of the dead with animal sacrifices (usually cows). Many of these communities consider the practice as a debt that cannot be revoked. In some cases, the debts of cows (*ugwo ehi* in Igbo) are passed on to later generations. While some Christian communities allow the practice, other churches forbid the practice on the grounds that it promotes ancestor worship or veneration. In such retrospective honoring of the dead, people are not allowed to celebrate the passing of their parents with a cow if their late grandparents or great grandparents (or as far back as they care to remember) were not celebrated with *ehi* (cows). If they choose to honor the passing of their parents, they must pay the debt of cows owed to their late grandparents, their great grandparents, and so on. The traditional belief is that people who know-

40. For more discussions on the ways in which African Christian communities understand and interpret the person, work, and significance of Jesus Christ, see Ezigbo, *Re-Imagining African Christologies*, chaps. 1–4; Diane B. Stinton, *Jesus of Africa, Voices of Contemporary Christian Christology* (Maryknoll, NY: Orbis, 2004).

41. Ben E. Udoh, "Guest Christology: An Interpretative View of the Christological Problem in Africa" (PhD diss., Princeton Theological Seminary, 1983), 263.

42. Byang H. Kato, *Theological Pitfalls in Africa* (Kisumu: Evangel Press, 1975), 93, 114.

ingly or unknowingly violated this custom would be punished by the ancestors, which may come in the form of death, disease, and poverty. Some Christian communities (for example, the Roman Catholics and Anglicans) permit such sacrifices sometimes under the guise of "thanksgiving" or "celebration" of life. Other Christian communities such as evangelical and Pentecostal churches forbid the custom and would excommunicate those who practice it.

In the remainder of this essay, I will focus on two general characteristics that can be discerned in some contemporary Christian communities in the continent of Africa. It should be borne in mind that not every church in Africa exhibits these characteristics.

General Self-Identifying Markers in Contemporary African Christianity

Christian communities have been, from an early period, diverse in terms of beliefs, social locations, cultures, and ethnicity. The first Council of Jerusalem recorded by Luke in Acts 15 highlighted and also affirmed the diversity of Christian communities. The council ruled in favor of those that argued against requiring Christians in Antioch to be "circumcised, according to the custom taught by Moses" in order to be saved (Acts 15:1). The decision of the council, however, to require some Jewish customs shows that the early church struggled to address the issue of Christian identity that arose as Christianity crossed into non-Jewish cultures. As Andrew Walls observes, the Council of Jerusalem concluded "that Gentile believers in Jesus were members of Israel by virtue of their faith in Israel's Messiah (Acts 15:13–41). They did not have to become Jewish proselytes or adopt the Torah and accept circumcision."[43] Though the Council of Jerusalem might not have fully grasped the implications of its decision, it created the path for Christian communities that developed outside of the Jewish culture to appreciate, in the words of Lamin Sanneh, "the idea of God as boundary-free truth, of God as one who is without partiality and who, as such, is open to the genuine moral aspirations of all humanity."[44] To Andrew Walls, the decision of the Council of Jerusalem "built cultural diversity into the church forever. What is more, it gave rise to situations that were open-ended and unpredictable."[45]

43. Andrew Walls, "The Rise of Global Theologies," *Global Theology in Evangelical Perspective: Exploring the Contextual Nature of Theology and Mission*, ed. Jeffrey P. Greenman and Gene L. Green (Downers Grove, IL: InterVarsity Press, 2012), 23.

44. Sanneh, *Disciples of All Nations*, 4.

45. Andrew F. Walls, "Converts or Proselytes? The Crisis Over Conversion in the Early Church," *International Bulletin of Missionary Research* 28, no. 1 (2004): 5.

Approaching the issue of identity from the perspective of a community can be misleading because of the temptation to present a unifying picture and also to minimize the real differences within the community. I have intentionally chosen the expression "general characteristics" and not "common characteristics" as a way of acknowledging the diverse beliefs, traditions, and modes of expression of African Christian communities.[46] The general characteristics described below are neither peculiar to African Christianity nor commonly shared by all Christian communities.

Radical Faith

The term "faith," when understood in theological terms, entails a movement: an act of moving away from self-reliance and toward reliance on God. By "radical faith," I mean a far-reaching attempt to understand human daily experiences in terms of the beliefs in God's existence and God's providential care. Though they do not always carefully or even clearly articulate the identity of God to whom they are devoted, many Christian communities in Africa speak of God as a triune being: God the father who acted in and through the event of Jesus Christ and continues to act now through the power of the Holy Spirit. The emphasis on the three divine persons varies from denomination to denomination. In most Pentecostal churches, the Holy Spirit is sometimes emphasized more than God the father. However, each of these divine persons is invoked during communal worship in the majority of African Christian communities.

Two beliefs in particular nourish the radical faith of African Christian communities. First is the belief in divine providence: the belief that God's sovereign care extends to the daily lives of human beings. Some hold a view of divine providence that borders closely with fatalism: the belief that God has set everything in advance and nothing could change what is already set by God. Others hold a view of divine providence that is robust enough to include human beings' ability to move God to change a course of direction as a result of their faith, petition, prayer, and lament. The lyrics of a popular Igbo gospel song highlight this view of divine providence: *Obi etiwara-etiwa, na nke egwepiara egwepia, Chineke, adighi eleda anya* (God does not despise a broken and distraught heart). The second belief that nourishes African Christianity's radical faith is grounded in the idea of a symbiotic relationship between the

46. For the purpose of this essay, I focus only on the Christian communities situated in the continent of Africa. Therefore, I do not intend to describe the general characteristics of African Christian communities in diaspora.

human or physical world and the spirit world. "The physical and spiritual," writes John Mbiti, "are but two dimensions of one and the same universe. These dimensions dovetail into each other to the extent that at times and in places one is apparently more real than, but not exclusive of, the other. To African peoples this religious universe is not an academic proposition: it is an empirical experience, which reaches its height in acts of worship."[47] Most Africans are religious not merely because of their association with any organized religions but rather because they see the world and construe their role in the world in religious terms: they understand their existence in the light of their beliefs in God, lesser deities, and particularly the belief in the interconnectedness of the physical and spiritual realms.

As Paul Gifford has noted, in the traditional African religion, the "physical realm and the realm of the spirit are not separate from each other. Nothing is purely matter. This world is one of the action and counteraction of potent forces, spirit acting upon spirit. A stronger or higher being can easily destroy or impair the weaker or lower, and since humans are relatively low beings, they can be controlled by the former."[48] Recognizing their lower status in the hierarchy of beings vis-à-vis the spirit-human world continuum, humans are to carefully negotiate their subsistence by aligning with the most potent spirit beings that can protect them from malevolent spirits. Gifford claims that regarding religion as "very largely the means of manipulating" malevolent spirits is misleading.[49] Most Africans do not become religious in order to manipulate or control spirit forces but rather to negotiate and understand the purpose of their existence by appeasing and worshiping spirit beings. This mindset permeates African Christianity. Many African Christians express a radical faith by seeking God's guidance and protection, albeit through the Bible, oracles, and the clergy. Also, Africans do not typically use religion as a means to control spirit beings. On the contrary, they see human beings as potential instruments of the more powerful spirit beings that empower humans and use them as surrogates to accomplish either malevolent or benevolent works in the world.

Conversion is one of the essential components of the radical faith of African Christian communities. While the motives or rationales for conversion vary, what conversion actually is or entails is debatable. For some African Christians, conversion requires abandoning one's previous religious beliefs and practices and replacing them with Christian beliefs and practices. For many such people,

---

47. Mbiti, *African Religions and Philosophy*, 57.
48. Paul Gifford, *Christianity, Development, and Modernity in Africa*, 13.
49. Gifford, *Christianity, Development, and Modernity in Africa*, 13.

conversion is an event that occurs at a point in time: the moment a person makes a conscious decision to follow the ways of Jesus Christ.[50] This idea of conversion is prevalent in evangelical, Pentecostal, and charismatic churches. The evangelical theologian Yusufu Turaki is critical of Africans who see "conversion to Christianity" as a process in which Jesus Christ "shares his lordship" over the convert with "other overlords." To Turaki, "Christ does not share his lordship with any other lord. You cannot 'serve God with mammon' and you cannot serve two masters either (Matthew 6:24). Christ exercises exclusive claim and lordship over a person who comes to him in faith and becomes his purchased property and possession."[51] Abandoning one's previous religion in place of a new religious belief is not restricted to a movement from one major religion to another—for instance, from Islam to Christianity. Sometimes it is also used for a movement from one Christian denomination to another—from Anglicanism to Pentecostalism.[52] Others, however, see conversion as a gradual process in which the African lifestyle and traditional beliefs are turned toward Christ.[53] In this view of salvation, Jesus Christ does not abolish Africa's primal religions and traditions but rather reconstructs them, remaking them in his image.

Praxis in Spiritual Warfare

Confronting the malevolent spirits and persons is one of the ways in which African Christian communities express their radical faith. Expressions such as "die by fire" and "I condemn them" are routinely chanted during church prayer meetings and Sunday worship. The belief in a close relationship between the spirit and physical worlds provides a helpful path into the practice of spiritual warfare in African Christianity. In the words of Allan Anderson, "The African spirit world infiltrates the whole of life. The same essential experience permeates everywhere and is not easily verbalized. All things are saturated with religious meaning."[54]

In the contest between Christianity and African traditional religion, many Christians expect Christianity to "prevail in the contest with the agents of Baal

---

50. For a helpful discussion of the models of conversion, see Alan R. Tippett, *Verdict Theology in Missionary Theory* (Pasadena, CA: William Carey Library, 1973).

51. Yusufu Turaki, *The Unique Christ for Salvation: The Challenge of the Non-Christian Religions and Cultures* (Nairobi: International Bible Society, 2001), 110.

52. Walls, "Converts or Proselytes?" 1.

53. Mana, *Christians and Churches of Africa*, 3, 32.

54. Allan H. Anderson, "Exorcism and Conversion to African Pentecostalism," *Exchange* 31 (2006): 116–33, at 132.

of Africa, just as Elijah did against the prophets of Baal."[55] Yet many Christian theologians have convincingly shown that African traditional religious values permeate the Christian sphere—the life and beliefs of many African Christians. Given this state of affairs, John Mbiti states: "Unless Christianity and Islam fully occupy the whole person as much as, if not more than, [African] traditional religions, most converts to these faiths will continue to revert to their old beliefs and practices for perhaps six days a week, and certainly in times of emergency and crisis."[56]

In the summer of 2016, I interviewed Ogechukwu—a youth leader in Grace of God Mission International, Awka, Anambra State, Nigeria.[57] Grace of God Mission International is one of the major Pentecostal churches in Anambra State. Ogechukwu was responsible for providing spiritual guidance to young adults in the church. About five minutes into the interview, Ogechukwu shared a personal story to illustrate her experience of God's empowerment and miraculous healing. In her words, "God saved me *mgbe ha ghara mu* pins" (God saved me when I was infected with [diabolic] pins)." When I pressed further to find out how she was infected with the pins, she said: "It was a spiritual attack. An evil man sent rust pins into my body; it was a spiritual attack. I became ill as a result of the attack. My parents took me to our pastor. As he prayed for me and anointed me with oil, rusty pins started coming out of my body." I asked other interviewees if they were aware of spiritual pin-attacks and each said it was a well-known form of spiritual attack. Though Ogechukwu's story of a spiritual pin-attack may seem bizarre, her stories and other stories of spiritual attacks show that many African Christians expect to engage in spiritual warfare. Spiritual attacks, such as the one experienced by Ogechukwu, are a major reason many churches in Africa (especially the Pentecostal churches, charismatic churches, and AICs) emphasize the deliverance work of God through the church or through the individuals that are endowed with the spiritual gift of healing.[58]

---

55. Sanneh, *Disciples of All Nations*, 188.

56. Mbiti, *African Religions and Philosophy*, 3.

57. Ogechukwu is a pseudonym. All the interviewees that participated in our research project agreed to the use of pseudonyms for privacy reasons. The term "youth" is used by many Christian churches in Nigeria to describe individuals, typically unmarried, whose ages range from 18 to 45.

58. See J. Kwabena Asamoah-Gyadu, "Mission to 'Set the Captives Free': Healing, Deliverance, and Generational Curses in Ghanaian Pentecostalism," *International Review of Mission* 93, no. 370–71 (2004): 389–406.

VICTOR I. EZIGBO

Upholding Christian Faith, Affirming African Identity

The present study of African Christian identities further confirms the conclusion reached in my earlier work. Christian publics, as communities of Christ's followers, have the responsibility of addressing the issue of *shared Christian identity* containing the essential characteristics of the Christian faith that all Christian communities ought to uphold.[59] However, since Christianity is translatable, it should be expected that the modes of expression of such essential characteristics of the Christian faith will vary from culture to culture. "A Christian community, however, may not successfully construct its 'Christianness' in isolation from other Christian communities."[60]

The issue of Christian identity vis-à-vis the relationship between the Christian faith and African cultures may be likened to the famous christological debates of the fourth and fifth centuries CE that explored the relationship of the two natures of Jesus Christ. At the heart of the christological debates were these questions: Do the two natures—divine and human—constitute one person, namely, Jesus Christ? Or do the two natures reside as two different, albeit not disparate, entities within Jesus Christ? As the early Christian theologians explored these questions and sought to present their answers in precise terms, they faced the difficulty of speaking of the two natures without repressing either the humanity or divinity of Jesus Christ. African Christians, when imagining their Christian identity, should strive to uphold the teachings of the Christian faith without repressing African cultures and thought forms. As I have showed in this essay, discussions on African Christian identities should take cognizance of the taxonomy, ecclesiastical, and interreligious factors that influence identity talks in Africa. They should equally engage the general characteristics of African Christian communities, which include a radical expression of the Christian faith and praxis in spiritual warfare. Also, such discussions should attend to the peculiarities of African cultures and the Christian faith. Since both entities are not closed canons, it should be expected that they would take on new forms of expression when they are brought into a dialogical communication or relationship. In this relationship, the Christian faith, particularly the person and work of Jesus Christ, should be understood and expressed in the languages, religious ideas, and thought forms of African Christian communities. Yet the person and work of Jesus Christ should be allowed to critique and also redirect the cultures of Africa, particularly the ways in which African Christians have appropriated African cultures.

59. Victor Ezigbo, "Imagining Mutual Christian Theological Identity: From Apologia to Dialogic Theologizing," *Journal of Ecumenical Studies* 50, no. 3 (2015): 452–72, at 458.
60. Ezigbo, "Imagining Mutual Christian Theological Identity," 458.

Contributors

Markus Bockmuehl (PhD, Cambridge) is the Dean Ireland's Professor of the Exegesis of Holy Scripture at the University of Oxford and a fellow of Keble College. He previously taught at the University of Cambridge and the University of St. Andrews. He is the author or editor of numerous books, including *Simon Peter in Scripture and Memory* (2012), *The Remembered Peter in Ancient Reception and Modern Debate* (2010), and *Seeing the Word: Refocusing New Testament Studies* (2006).

Keith Bodner (PhD, Aberdeen and Manchester) is professor of religious studies and Stuart E. Murray Chair of Christian Studies at Crandall University. He is the author of *Elisha's Profile in the Book of Kings: The Double Agent* (Oxford University Press, 2013), *The Artistic Dimension: Literary Explorations of the Hebrew Bible* (T&T Clark, 2013), and *Jeroboam's Royal Drama* (Oxford University Press, 2012).

Gerald P. Boersma (PhD, Durham) is associate professor of theology at Ave Maria University. He is the author of *The Origins of Augustine's Early Theology of Image: A Study in the Development of Pro-Nicene Theology* (Oxford University Press, 2016).

Hans Boersma (ThD, Utrecht) is the J. I. Packer Professor of Theology at Regent College. Among his publications are *Sacramental Preaching: Sermons on the Hidden Presence of Christ* (Baker, 2016), *Embodiment and Virtue in Gregory of Nyssa: An Anagogical Approach* (Oxford Early Christian Studies, 2013), *Heavenly Participation: The Weaving of a Sacramental Tapestry* (Eerdmans, 2011), and *Nouvelle Théologie and Sacramental Ontology: A Return to Mystery* (Oxford, 2009).

CONTRIBUTORS

Robert Bork (†) was an American legal scholar who served as a Yale Law School professor, solicitor general, acting attorney general, and a judge of the United States Court of Appeals for the District of Columbia Circuit. He was the author of *Slouching towards Gomorrah* and *The Tempting of America*.

Paul C. Burns (PhD, Toronto) is director of Liberal Arts for Corpus Christi College and professor of church history at St. Mark's College in Vancouver, British Columbia. A specialist in early Christian thought, he is the author of *A Model for the Christian Life: Hilary of Poitiers' Commentary on the Psalms* (Catholic University of America Press, 2012) and editor of *Jesus in Twentieth-Century Literature, Art, and Movies* (Continuum, 2007).

Julie Canlis (PhD, St. Andrews) is an independent researcher in Wenatchee, Washington. She is the author of *Calvin's Ladder: A Spiritual Theology of Ascent and Ascension* (Eerdmans, 2010), which received a Templeton Prize and a *Christianity Today* Award of Merit.

Victor I. Ezigbo (PhD, University of Edinburgh) is professor of contextual and systematic theology and chair of Biblical and Theological Studies at Bethel University in Minnesota. He is the author of *Re-Imagining African Christologies: Conversing with the Interpretations and Appropriations of Jesus Christ in African Christianity* (Pickwick, 2010) and *Introducing Christian Theologies: Voices from Global Christian Communities*, 2 vols. (Cascade, 2013, 2015).

Craig M. Gay (PhD, Boston) is professor of interdisciplinary studies and lectures in the area of Christianity and culture and directs Regent's ThM degree program. He is the author of *Dialogue, Catalogue and Monologue* (Regent College Publishing, 2008), *Cash Values: The Value of Money, the Nature of Worth* (Eerdmans, 2004), *With Liberty and Justice for Whom?* (Eerdmans, 1998), and *The Way of the (Modern) World: Or, Why It's Tempting to Live as If God Doesn't Exist* (Eerdmans, 1998).

Yonghua Ge (PhD, Cambridge) is a Post-doctoral Fellow at Regent College and a senior research fellow in School of Philosophy, Beijing Normal University. He has published articles in *Philosophy East and West, Logos & Pneuma (HK), Crux, Sino-Christian Studies, Tyndale Bulletin, The Heythrop Journal, Chinese Social Studies Today*, and *Regent Review of Christian Thoughts* and has contributed a chapter in *Transcendence, Immanence and Intercultural Philosophy* (Palgrave Macmillan, 2016).

684

Christopher Hall (PhD, Drew University) is president of Renovaré, after previously serving as director of Academic Spiritual Formation and distinguished professor of theology at Eastern University. He is the author of several books, including *The Mystery of God*, with Steven D. Boyer (Baker Academic, 2012), *Worshiping with the Church Fathers* (InterVarsity Press, 2009), *Learning Theology with the Church Fathers* (InterVarsity Press, 2002), *The Trinity*, with Roger Olson (Eerdmans, 2002), and *Reading Scripture with the Church Fathers* (InterVarsity Press, 1998).

Ross Hastings (PhD, St. Andrews) is the Sangwoo Youtong Chee Associate Professor of Theology at Regent College. In addition to a PhD in theology, he also holds a PhD in organometallic chemistry from Queen's University. His published works include *Where Do Broken Hearts Go? A Theology and Psychology of Grief* (Cascade, 2016), *Jonathan Edwards and the Life of God: Toward an Evangelical Theology of Participation* (Fortress Press, 2015), and *Missional God, Missional Church: Hope for Re-evangelizing the West* (InterVarsity Press, 2012).

Bruce Hindmarsh (DPhil, Oxford) is the James M. Houston Professor of Spiritual Theology at Regent College. He is the author of *The Spirit of Early Evangelicalism: True Religion in a Modern World* (Oxford University Press, 2017), *The Evangelical Conversion Narrative* (Oxford University Press, 2005) and *John Newton and the English Evangelical Tradition* (Oxford University Press, 1996). He has been a Mayers Research Fellow at the Huntington Library and a holder of the Henry Luce III Theological Fellowship. A fellow of the Royal Historical Society, he is also a past president of the American Society of Church History.

Richard V. Horner (PhD, Virginia), formerly a fellow of the Institute for Advanced Studies at the University of Virginia, is now the Executive Director of the Christian Study Center of Gainesville, Florida. His research focuses on the intersection of French thought and American Pragmatism.

James M. Houston (DPhil, Oxford) is the Board of Governors Professor of Spiritual Theology and founding principal of Regent College. He is also a co-founder of the C. S. Lewis Institute in Washington, DC, and still acting as a senior fellow. Among his many books are *A Vision for the Aging Church: Renewing Ministry For and By Seniors*, with Dr. Michael Parker (InterVarsity Press, 2011), *The Psalms as Christian Worship: A Historical Commentary*, with Bruce Waltke (Eerdmans, 2010), two volumes of *Letters of Faith through the Seasons* (David C. Cook, 2006, 2007), *Joyful Exiles* (InterVarsity Press, 2006), and *The Mentored Life* (NavPress, 2002).

Robert A. Kitchen (DPhil, Oxford) is the minister of Knox-Metropolitan United Church in Regina, Saskatchewan. He is the translator and editor of *The Discourses of Philoxenos of Mabbug* (Cistercian, 2013), *The Book of Steps: The Syriac Liber Graduum*, with Martien F. G. Parmentier (Cistercian, 2004), and coeditor of *Breaking the Mind: New Studies in the Syriac Book of Steps*, with Kristian S. Heal (Catholic University of America Press, 2014). He was the president of the Canadian Society of Patristic Studies/Association Canadienne des Etudes Patristiques (CSPS/ACEP) for 2014–2016.

Mariam Kamell Kovalishyn (PhD, St. Andrews) is assistant professor of New Testament studies at Regent College. She has coauthored a commentary on James (Zondervan, 2008) and has published several articles in books and journals, primarily focused on the Epistle of James, and is currently working on a biblical theology of social justice (for Zondervan).

Pak-Wah Lai (PhD, Durham) is a professor of church history and patristics at Biblical Graduate School of Theology in Singapore. His doctoral dissertation is entitled "John Chrysostom and the Hermeneutics of Exemplar Portraits."

Jay Langdale (PhD, University of Florida) is an independent researcher who has taught at Troy University, Andrew College, the University of Florida, and Virginia Wesleyan College. At the University of Florida, he studied under Bertram Wyatt-Brown. His dissertation titled "Superfluous Southerners: Cultural Conservatism and the South" was awarded the 2006 M. E. Bradford Prize by the St. George Tucker Society. The revised manuscript was published by the University of Missouri Press in 2012.

Bo Karen Lee (PhD, Princeton) is associate professor of spiritual theology and Christian formation at Princeton Theological Seminary. She is the author of *Sacrifice and Delight in the Mystical Theologies of Anna Maria van Schurman and Madame Jeanne Guyon* (University of Notre Dame Press, 2014). Currently she is working on a volume entitled *The Soul of Higher Education*, which explores contemplative pedagogies and research strategies.

Jonathan Sing-cheung Li is a ThD candidate in systematic theology at the Toronto School of Theology, University of Toronto, where he researches Jonathan Edwards's eschatological construction of theology. He is an adjunct lecturer at the Canadian Chinese School of Theology at Tyndale Seminary (Toronto), a visiting lecturer at the same school at Ambrose Seminary (Cal-gary), and a part-time lecturer at Chinese Online School of Theology of New York Theological Education Center (Toronto). He is also an independent scholar and lecturer of Chinese for the Online School of Theology, New York Theological Center.

V. Phillips Long (PhD, Cambridge) is a professor of Old Testament at Regent College. His book publications include *The Reign and Rejection of King Saul: A Case for Literary and Theological Coherence*; *The Art of Biblical History*; the edited volumes *Israel's Past in Present Research* and *Windows into Old Testament History*; the coauthored work *A Biblical History of Israel*; and *1 and 2 Samuel* in the Zondervan *Illustrated Bible Background Commentary*. He has published a number of scholarly and popular articles and reviews, has served on a variety of translation projects (*NLT*, *ESV*, *Message*), and has contributed commentary notes in the *ESV Study Bible*, the *Spirit of the Reformation Study Bible*, the *Gospel Transformation Bible*, and the *NIV Study Bible*.

Howard Louthan (PhD, Princeton) is Director of the Center for Austrian Studies and Professor of History at the University of Minnesota. He specializes in the history of early modern central Europe with an emphasis on cultural and religious history. His publications include *Sacred History: Uses of the Christian Past in the Renaissance World* (Oxford University Press, 2012), *Converting Bohemia: Force and Persuasion in the Catholic Reformation* (Cambridge University Press, 2009), *John Comenius: The Labyrinth of the World* (Paulist Press, 1998), and *The Quest for Compromise: Peace Makers in Counter Reformation Vienna* (Cambridge University Press, 1997).

Elizabeth Ludlow (PhD, Warwick) is professor of English literature at Anglia Ruskin University. She is the author of *Christina Rossetti and the Bible: Waiting with the Saints* (Bloomsbury Academic, 2014) and is currently working on her second monograph, *Prodigal Daughters: Representations in Mid-Victorian Literature*.

Eleanor McCullough (PhD, University of York) is a post-doctoral fellow and tutor of Spanish at the University of York. Her PhD thesis is titled "Praying the Passion: Laypeople's Participation in Medieval Liturgy and Devotion" (2011).

Stephen Ney (PhD, University of British Columbia) is an assistant professor of English on the Faculty of Arts and Sciences at the University of Gambia. He wrote his doctoral dissertation on the literary history in colonial and postcolonial Nigeria.

Ryan S. Olson (DPhil, Oxford) is a fellow in late antiquity at the Center for Hellenic Studies at Harvard University and an independent researcher working in philanthropy. He is the author of *Tragedy, Authority, and Trickery: The Poetics of Embedded Letters in Josephus* (Center for Hellenic Studies, 2010).

Steven L. Porter (PhD, University of Southern California) is professor of theology, spiritual formation, and philosophy at Talbot School of Theology and at Rosemead School of Psychology (Biola University) and scholar-in-residence at the Center for Christian Thought (Biola University). He is the author of *Restoring the Foundations of Epistemic Justification: A Direct Realist and Conceptualist Theory of Foundationalism* (Lexington Books, 2005) and serves as the managing editor of the *Journal of Spiritual Formation and Soul Care.*

Iain Provan (PhD, Cambridge) is the Marshall Sheppard Professor of Biblical Studies at Regent College. He is the author of *Discovering Genesis: Content, Interpretation, Reception* (Eerdmans, 2016), *A Biblical History of Israel*, with Phil Long and Tremper Longman, 2nd ed. (John Knox Press, 2015), *Seriously Dangerous Religion: What the Old Testament Really Says and Why It Matters* (Baylor University Press, 2014), *Convenient Myths: The Axial Age, Dark Green Religion, and the World that Never Was* (Baylor University Press, 2013), and commentaries on Lamentations, 1 and 2 Kings, Ecclesiastes, and Song of Songs.

Murray Rae (PhD, Kings College) is a professor of theology at the University of Otago, New Zealand. He is the author of *Christian Theology: The Basics* (Routledge, 2015), *Kierkegaard and Theology* (T&T Clark, 2010), and *Kierkegaard's Vision of the Incarnation: By Faith Transformed* (Clarendon Press, 1997).

Jonathan Reimer (PhD, Cambridge) studied early modern British history at the University of Cambridge. His doctoral work explores the life and works of Thomas Becon, a Tudor clergyman and bestselling devotional writer.

Ronald K. Rittgers (PhD, Harvard) is the Erich Markel Chair in German Reformation Studies and professor of history and theology at Valparaiso University. He is the author of *The Reformation of Suffering: Pastoral Theology and Lay Piety in Late Medieval and Early Modern Germany* (Oxford University Press, 2012) and *The Reformation of the Keys: Confession, Conscience, and Authority in Sixteenth-Century Germany* (Harvard University Press, 2004), which was nominated for the American Society of Church History 2005 Philip Schaff Prize and for the 2006 Columbia Council for European Studies Book Award.

Sharon Jebb Smith (PhD, St. Andrews) is a freelance lecturer and speaker on literature, theology, and Christian spirituality. She is the author of *Writing God and the Self: Samuel Beckett and C. S. Lewis* (Wipf & Stock, 2011).

Sven Soderlund (PhD, Glasgow) is professor emeritus of biblical studies at Regent College. He is the author of *The Greek Text of Jeremiah: A Revised Hypothesis* (JSOT, 1985), and coeditor of *Romans and the People of God: Essays in Honour of Gordon D. Fee*, with N. T. Wright (Eerdmans, 1999), and *The Way of Wisdom: Essays in Honour of Bruce K. Waltke* (Zondervan, 2000).

Janet Martin Soskice (PhD, Oxford) is professor of philosophical theology at the University of Cambridge and a fellow of Jesus College. She is the author of *Metaphor and Religious Language* (Oxford University Press, 1984); *The Kindness of God* (Oxford University Press, 2007); has edited, with Grant Gillett and K. W. Fulford, *Medicine and Moral Reasoning* (Cambridge University Press, 1994); with Diana Lipton, *Feminism and Theology*, Oxford Readings in Feminism (Oxford University Press, 2003); and with Carlo Cogliati, David Burrell, and W. Stoeger, *Creation and the God of Abraham* (Cambridge University Press, 2010), a collection that examines the doctrine of creation from nothing in Jewish, Christian, and Muslim thought.

Andrea Sterk (PhD, Princeton Theological Seminary) is Associate Professor of History at the University of Minnesota and co-editor of the journal *Church History: Studies in Christianity and Culture*. She is the author of *Renouncing the World Yet Leading the Church: The Monk-Bishop in Late Antiquity* (Harvard, 2004) and has co-edited the sourcebook *Readings in World Christian History: Earliest Christianity to 1453* (Orbis, 2004) and the volume of essays, *Faithful Narratives: Historians, Religion, and the Challenge of Objectivity* (Cornell, 2014).

Mikael Tellbe (PhD, Lund University, Sweden) is associate professor of New Testament (Lund University) and lecturer at Örebro School of Theology. He is the author of several books in Swedish, as well as in English: *Christ-Believers in Ephesus: A Textual Analysis of Early Christian Identity Formation in a Local Perspective* (2009) and *Paul between Synagogue and State: Christians, Jews, and Civic Authorities in 1 Thessalonians, Romans, and Philippians* (2001).

Colin Thompson (DPhil) is faculty lecturer in Spanish and fellow of St. Catherine's College, Oxford. He works primarily in Golden Age Spanish literature and has a particular interest in the writing of the Spanish mystics St. Teresa of

Avila and St. John of the Cross. He is the author of *St. John of the Cross: Songs in the Night* (SPCK, 2002) and *The Strife of Tongues: Fray Luis de León and the Golden Age of Spain* (1995).

Bruce K. Waltke (PhD, Harvard) is professor emeritus of Old Testament studies at Regent College and distinguished professor of Old Testament at Knox Theological Seminary. He is the author of several scholarly articles and editor or contributor to various editions of the Bible, including the New American Standard Version, the New International Version, the Today's New International Version, and the Spirit of the Reformation Study Bible. He is the author of *An Old Testament Theology: An Exegetical, Canonical, and Thematic Approach* (Zondervan, 2007), *Finding the Will of God: A Pagan Notion?* (2nd ed., Eerdmans, 2016), and commentaries on Genesis, Micah, and Proverbs. He is coauthor of *The Psalms as Christian Worship: A Historical Commentary*, with James Houston (Eerdmans, 2010). He currently serves as an Anglican priest in the state of Washington.

Steven Watts (PhD, St. Andrews) is a post-doctoral fellow at the Pontifical Institute of Mediaeval Studies in Toronto. His doctoral dissertation is entitled "Let us run in love together: Master Jordan of Saxony (d. 1237) and the participation of women in the religious life of the Order of Preachers" (2016). He has lectured on church history at Regent College and Westminster Theological Centre in Cheltenham, UK.

Robyn Wrigley-Carr (PhD, St. Andrews) is a professor of Christian spirituality and theology at Alphacrucis College in Australia. Her doctoral dissertation is entitled "The Baron, His Niece and Friends: Friedrich von Hügel as a Spiritual Director, 1915–1925."

Jens Zimmermann (PhD, Johannes von Gutenberg University, Mainz, and University of British Columbia) is the Canada Research Professor in Interpretation, Religion and Culture at Trinity Western University and research fellow at Trinity Hall, Cambridge University. He is the author or editor of several books, including *Re-Envisioning Christian Humanism: Education and the Restoration of Humanity* (Oxford University Press, 2016), *Hermeneutics: A Very Short Introduction* (Oxford University Press, 2015), *Humanism and Religion: A Call for the Renewal of Western Culture* (Oxford University Press, 2012), *Incarnational Humanism: A Philosophy of Culture for the Church in the World* (InterVarsity Press, 2012), and *Being Human, Becoming Human: Dietrich Bonhoeffer and Social Thought*, coedited with Brian Gregor (Wipf & Stock, 2010).

Index

Abelard, Peter, 305–6

Abraham, 38, 45, 56, 130, 131, 673; character of, 6–7, 19–20; as father of the faithful, 7–9, 17–18; God's engagement with, 4, 5–6, 9–10, 12–13, 14–15, 18–20

Acts of Peter, 81–82

African Christianity: and African traditional religions, 674–76; characteristics of, 678–81; Christocentric nature of, 673–74; and complexity of identity, 666–70, 682; ecclesiastical traditions in, 670–72; identity discourse and, 664–66

Allegorical interpretation, 136–39

Ambrose of Milan: *De Isaac*, 169, 171–72, 174, 184; theological anthropology of, 174–78, 184–91

Anselm, 348, 351; formative influences on, 288–91; integrated identity of, 284–85, 288, 291–93; and intellectual rigor, 278–83; and interpersonal connections, 286–88; theological method of, and devotion to God, 283–86

Anthropology: baptismal, 168–69, 171–72, 178, 184–91; Barth's theological, 585, 587–88, 594, 596–98, 600, 601–2; Chrysostom's, 199, 201; Luther's theological, 380–83, 384–91; theological, 53, 143, 174–78, 308, 345–47, 365–66, 530

Aquinas, Thomas, 290; background of, 328–29; Christian identity of, 329–30, 334, 335, 337, 340; and participation in Christ's poverty, 330, 332–34, 336; and participation in Christ's teaching mission, 336–39

Ascetism, 193, 196, 198–99, 201, 202, 207–8

Atonement, 45, 285–86

Augustine of Hippo, 203, 474, 503–4, 579–80, 606; background of, 209–11; and Christian self in *Expositions of the Psalms*, 214–22; *Confessions* and development of the self, 211–12; influence of, on the *Divine Comedy*, 354, 361, 364; and pastoral use of the *City of God*, 212–14; theology of the soul, 346–47

Baptism, 13, 20, 127, 202, 365; in Ambrose's *De Isaac*, 169, 171–72, 174, 179–84; and Christian identity, 169, 174, 184, 185–86; and theology of ascent, 185–91

Barth, Karl, 110, 292–93; divine freedom and human identity, 588–93; freedom and the humanity of Christ, 594–602; self and freedom in Christ, 585–88

Beatific vision, 146–50

Becon, Thomas: background of, 411–16; and importance of dying well, 420–22; and importance of English Bible, 417–19; and obedience in Christian life, 419–20

Bernard of Clairvaux: and Christian identity, 308; and humanity of Mary, 309–10; identities of, 294–99; and love of Jesus, 299–304, 310–11; and recovery of biblical ideas of freedom and love, 306–8